Human Behavior and the Social Environment

Theory and Practice

2nd edition

Joan Granucci Lesser
Smith College

Donna Saia Pope
New York University

Allyn & Bacon

Boston Columbus Indianapolis New York San Francisco Upper Saddle River
Amsterdam Cape Town Dubai London Madrid Milan Munich Paris Montreal Toronto
Delhi Mexico City Sao Paulo Sydney Hong Kong Seoul Singapore Taipei Tokyo

Executive Editor: Ashley Dodge
Editorial Assistant: Carly Czech
Senior Marketing Manager: Wendy Albert
Marketing Assistant: Kyle VanNatter
Senior Production Project Manager: Roberta Sherman
Manufacturing Buyer: Debbie Rossi
Cover Administrator: Kristina Mose-Libon
Editorial Production Service: Laserwords, Maine
Electronic Composition: Laserwords, India
Photo Researcher: Rachel Lucas

Cataloging-in-Publication data unavailable at press time.

Photo Credits:
p. 1, Library of Congress; **p. 4,** Getty Images Inc.—Hulton Archive Photos; **p. 8,** © Bettman/Corbis; **p. 32,** lom123/Fotolia; **p. 56,** © M. Siluk, The Image Works; **p. 93,** © Savage Productions, Inc.; **p. 123,** Blend Images/ Alamy; **p. 156,** © AP/Wide World Photos; **p. 161,** © AP/Wide World Photos; **p. 182,** © Flying Colors Ltd./ Getty Images; **p. 189,** © Rudi Von Briel/Photo Edit. All rights reserved; **p. 224,** © Donald Uhrbrock/Time Life Pictures/Getty Images; **p. 226,** © Getty Images; **p. 243,** © Nancy Brown/The Image Bank/Getty Images; **p. 263,** © James Shaffer/Photo Edit. All rights reserved; **p. 286,** © Kevin Dodge/Corbis; **p. 308,** © James Shaffer, PhotoEdit, Inc.; **p. 331,** © Image Source/Getty Images; **p. 335,** © Jon Riley/Stone/Getty Images; **p. 353,** © Leland Bobbe/Corbis; **p. 373,** Tom & Dee Ann McCarthy/Corbis Bridge/Alamy; **p. 409,** © bildagentur-online/begsteiger/Alamy; **p. 437,** © Masterfile Royalty-Free (RF); **p. 465,** © Mark Wilson/Getty Images.

Allyn & Bacon
is an imprint of

www.pearsonhighered.com

ISBN 10: 0-205-79274-X
ISBN 13: 978-0-205-79274-0

Dedication

To our clients and our students

Contents

CHAPTER 4 Identity Development | 93

PART III The Sociocultural Context of Human Development

CHAPTER 5 The Family in Society | 123

CHAPTER 7 Communities and Organizations | 189

Preface

We decided to write this book because as practitioners and educators in the field of social work, we saw a need to provide a book that integrates developmental theory and clinical practice. Our book is organized into five parts. Part I includes two chapters on conceptual issues. Chapter 1 provides the integrating framework for human behavior theory and social work practice and illustrates our overall perspective on human behavior and the social environment, especially as it relates to social work practice. This framework rests on ecosystemic concepts, and is informed by a variety of post-modern paradigms that emphasize social justice, multi-cultural competence, strengths and empowerment perspectives, development in context and the spiritual dimension. It assumes the interrelatedness of the personal, interpersonal and wider social spheres, and informs a model for social work practice that integrates skills at the micro, mezzo and macro-levels. The chapter begins with a historical overview of the social work profession as it relates to human behavior theory and practice; it moves on present the fundamental constructs of an ecosystemic approach, as well as an introduction to contemporary perspectives that build on and refine that approach.

Chapter 2—"Neurobiological Underpinnings of Human Development"—begins with psychobiological models of resilience and a description of the neuroanatomy of the brain, the functions of the limbic system, how neurons communicate with each other, and the interface of experience (nurture) and gene expression (nature). This chapter also includes a section on neurobehavioral conditions such as autism spectrum disorders, attention deficit hyperactivity disorder, Asperger's disorder, dyslexia, mental retardation, and mood disorders. Clinical examples are provided to illustrate many of these conditions. A section on stuttering has also been added to this chapter.

Part II includes chapters organized around the individual. Chapter 3—"Theories of Development"—lays the groundwork for conceptual thinking about human behavior and clinical practice across the life span. We begin this chapter with multicultural theory and move to the historical development of psychodynamic theory, including drive theory, ego psychology, object relations theory, self-psychology, relational theory, intersubjectivity, and mindfulness. Next, we discuss cognitive theory and behavior theory and include a section on the third wave of behavior therapy: mindfulness-based cognitive therapy and acceptance and commitment therapy. We also add a section on motivational interviewing, a model initially developed to support change with clients challenged by addictions but now found useful with a wide range of problems. Constructivism is included as a philosophical/behavioral/methodological conceptual framework that can be integrated with theories of human behavior. Narrative therapy is presented as an example of a treatment model grounded in constructivist thought. The next section of this chapter is on feminist practice. Self-in-relation theory which evolved into cultural relational theory is presented as a model of human development and an approach to clinical practice. The final part of this chapter discusses the importance of play at different developmental levels of childhood and provides several theories of play therapy: psychoanalytic, relational, cognitive-behavioral, filial therapy, and theraplay. Chapter 4 of Part II addresses models of identity development. We begin this chapter with Eric Erikson's contributions, include the conceptual paradigm of intersectionality and present Sue and Sue's framework for assessing the multiple and interlocking dimensions of identity and for assessing identity at the individual, the group, and the universal level. We focus on the group level of identity development including racial identity; black identity; biracial identity; ethnic identity; white identity; gender and transgender identity; gay, lesbian and bisexual, identity; and social class identity.

Part III—"The Sociocultural Context of Human Development"—begins with Chapter 5 on the family as a societal subsystem. The concept of family in a postmodern context is defined. Fundamental concepts of family systems theory, including family structure and and interactional processes are discussed. The development and adaptation of the family during various transitional, stressful points in life is traced with an emphasis on sociocultural and socioeconomic variables and a strengths-based perspective. The chapter includes a greater emphasis on connections to practice, with more examples and a new section on practice with multi-stressed families. The chapter on the family concludes with a section on a variety of family contexts in contemporary society, such as divorced and blended or reconstituted families, gay and lesbian families, adoptive families, military families and families affected by migration. Chapter 6 introduces the small group as an influential context for human behavior. It begins with a short history of group practice in the field of social work and offers a definition of a group, attending to the concepts of group norms, group roles, the importance of a theoretical foundation for group practice, and different models of group leadership. Two models that attend to the structure of groups are offered, and the process of group development is described with examples that illustrate each stage. Different types of groups such as task, treatment, and self-help groups are discussed. Chapter 7—"Community and Organizations"—begins with a discussion of social structure and patterns of social interaction, including power and oppression. The concept of community is broadly defined and presented within a conceptual framework that recognizes the fact that communities and their subsystems are embedded in even larger, more complex systems that exert a profound influence on them. The chapter includes a discussion of the societal context for community life, including how economic, demographic and technological changes at the societal level affect local communities and organizations; the significance of structural linkages in organizations and communities is also discussed. We present an expanded discussion of formal organizations as social systems and have added a section on interorganizational collaboration. We have included a new section on contemporary models of organizational management and structure including total quality management, learning organizations, antiracist and multiculturally competent organizational paradigms, and global and international organizations. Additional practice examples are provided in this chapter to illustrate the theoretical constructs. The final section presents contemporary issues in community practice with an expanded section on community-based clinical practice as a means of building bridges between micro and macro social work. Chapter 8 focuses on spiritual development through the life cycle. It includes the definition of spirituality, cultural diversity and spirituality, feminist spirituality, family, and community. This chapter also includes a section on the role of the social worker and spiritual assessment and a new section on the connection between spirituality and mindfulness. The book *The Secret Life of Bees* by Sue Monk Kidd provides a text with examples to explicate the complexity of spiritual identity development.

Part IV begins with the human life cycle. Chapters 9 through 15 are each devoted to one stage of human development (infancy, early childhood, middle childhood, adolescence, early adulthood, middle adulthood, and diversity in older adulthood). Each chapter provides expanded information on biological, cognitive, and psychological development within a sociocultural context. Contemporary topics such as cyberbullying, self-harm during adolescence, and life course theory as a basis for understanding the significance of history on identity development among gay youth have been added to relevant life-cycle chapters. We have also included greater attention to veterans and military families and immigrant and refugee populations, non-English speakers, and illiterate adults. The chapter on diversity in older adulthood includes a report on the pilot findings of a study of Chinese elders and depression conducted in Boston and China. Chapter 16 is devoted to trauma and development, beginning with a definition of trauma, introduction to the various types of trauma, and a description of acute stress disorder and posttraumatic stress disorder. The neurobiology and assessment of trauma is presented with a discussion of traumatic memories, false memory syndrome, dissociation, and the treatment of trauma. The chapter includes a new section on PTSD as a chronic illness and a developmental disorder. There is a section on trauma and children, tables that outline the signs of traumatic stress in children, the types of disorders that can develop in response to different catastrophic events, child maltreatment as a very particular kind of interpersonal trauma, a discussion of play therapy in the treatment of trauma, and a framework of nine traumagenic states that should be addressed when treating traumatized children. A new section on trauma and the military suggests war-related PTSD may be better understood as an identity disorder, than a stress disorder. There are also sections in this chapter on trauma and aging, referencing adults who were child survivors of the Holocaust. Trauma and culture, cultural countertransference, and racial trauma also provide information about the experience of massive trauma and the intergenerational transmission of trauma. We end this chapter with a discussion of vicarious traumatization, compassion fatigue and the importance of self-care for the helpers. Chronic illness and disability are the focus in Chapter 17, beginning with definitions of disability from historical, medical, economic, and sociopolitical perspectives. The concept of a disability culture is also discussed. This chapter provides information on the type and range of disabilities and chronic illnesses, including progressive permanent conditions, constant, permanent conditions, and relapsing, or episodic, conditions with examples in each category. There is a section on chronic pain that describes the sensory physiology of pain, the psychological response to pain, and pain behaviors. This chapter provides an overview of the impact of disability over the life cycle as well as family adjustment to disability. Psychiatric disabilities; the intersectionality between disability and diversity and disability and the abuse of women are addressed. The book concludes with a chapter on social policy through the life cycle and how the context for social work practice is shaped by social welfare policy. This chapter describes the functions and scope of social welfare and gives a description of income support programs such as public assistance, insurance, and health-care programs. Policies that affect infants and children in the early and middle years of childhood, such as the National School Breakfast and Lunch Programs, the Child and Dependent Care Tax Credit, and the Keeping Children and Families Safe Act, are discussed. The section on adolescence includes legislation governing academic failure, substance abuse, delinquent behaviors, sexually transmitted diseases, and teen pregnancy. The Personal Responsibility and Work Opportunity Reconciliation Act, Job Corps, Federal Pell Education Grants, the Fair Labor Standards Act, and the Workforce Investment Act are examples of policies directed toward young adults and individuals in the middle years of life. The Older Americans Act authorizes grants to states for community planning and service programs, research, demonstration, and training projects in the field of aging. Please refer to Figure P.1 for an illustration of the conceptual basis and organization of the chapters presented in our book.

We enjoyed writing this book and pulling together the many facets of human behavior that manifest in social work practice with individuals, families, groups, organizations, and communities. We have tried to be comprehensive in our approach, but recognize that no book can include the multiple nuances involved in working with people, especially those from many different walks of life. We therefore remind our students to be guided in their professional practice by the Code of Ethics for our profession (available from the National Association of Social Workers). We also encourage our readers to remain current with the professional literature and research and to seek supervision and consultation when necessary. We believe it is important to educate those we work with about different models of care. This kind of dialogue empowers clients to make informed decision about their lives. From its roots in the settlement house movement, our field has grown into a respected and complex profession—we hope our book provides our students with the knowledge to take their place in it.

FIGURE P.1

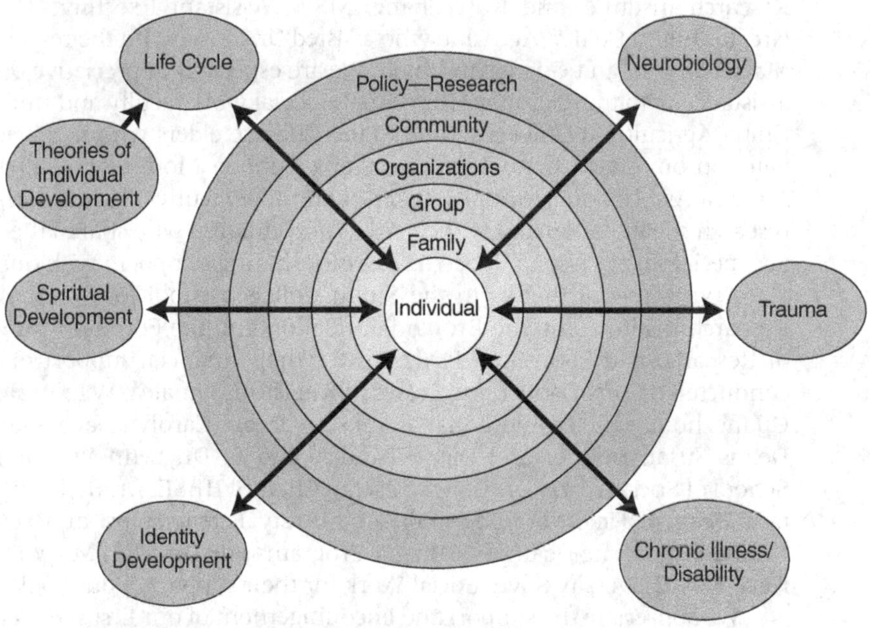

Acknowledgments

We acknowledge with gratitude all those whose contributions have made this book possible: Dean Carolyn Jacobs of the Smith College School for Social Work, Professor Joyce Everett of the Smith College School for Social Work, and Professor Ann Roy of the Springfield College School for Social Work for each contributing a chapter to our book. We appreciate your scholarship and your encouragement. Sincere praise and thanks go to Steve Bogatz, MSW, LCSW, Adjunct Assistant Professor at the Springfield College School for Social Work, and the Smith College School for Social Work, and Clinical Social Worker at Central Connecticut Dialysis for his illustrative reading and for his patient technical support and research assistance; Michele Bala, Administrative Assistant at Smith College School for Social Work, for her administrative support and research assistance; Kate Baquis, Ariel Miller, and Johanna Pope for their research assistance; and April Goss, Crystal Hayes, Mary Triulzi, and Margarita Forbath, LCSW and Annalisa Cusi LCSW, who allowed us to include excerpts from their clinical practice: thank you for your contributions to this book and the social work field. We would also like to thank Dr. Marlene Cooper, PhD, Associate Professor at Fordham University Graduate School of Social Services, coinvestigator with Dr. Lesser on the research conducted in Kingston, Jamaica, and to Dr. Marlene Cooper, Dr. Ann Roy, Professor at Springfield College School for Social Work,

Florence Loh, PhD candidate at Smith College School for Social Work, Dr. Cheng Yu, Executive Director and Han Li from the Guandgzou Community Health Research Institute, and Kun Chang, MSW, Assistant Executive Director of the Greater Boton Golden Age Club who assisted Dr. Lesser with the research in Boston, Massachusetts, and Guangzou China. We are especially appreciative of Mary Fong's assistance with translation in China, to the social work faculty and students at South China Agricultural University, and to the Chinese elders who so graciously participated in our study. In addition, we thank Yunena Morales, past President of the Jamaica Association of Social Workers, and the Executive Board for their generous research collaboration and to the parents and children who shared their stories with us. Special thanks also to Rebecca Lesser for sharing her poem with our readers.

A very special thanks to the Smith College School for Social Work Clinical Research Institute and the Brown Foundation and the Fordham University Office of Research and Sponsored Programs for their financial support of the research conducted by Drs. Cooper and Lesser in Kingston, Jamaica, W.I.; Boston, MA.; and Guangzhou, China. Additional thanks to Dean Carolyn Jacobs and Associate Deans Susan Donner and Diane Tsoulas, and to Dr. Lynn Videka, Dean, Silver School of Social Work; Dr. Theresa Aiello, Chair of HBSE; Dr. Helle Thorning, Assistant Dean of Field Learning and Community Partnerships; and Dr. Mary Ellen Noonan, Associate Dean of Academic Programs and Director, MSW Program at the New York University Silver Social Work for their support of our book.

We appreciate the support and encouragement of our first series editor, Patricia Quinlin, our current series editor, Ashley Dodge, Editorial Assistant, Carly Czech, Project Manager, Patty Donovan, and Senior Production Project Manager Roberta Sherman for their assistance and patience with the completion of this book. We would like to thank the following reviewers of the text, whose comments contributed to the book's development: Stephen Anderson, New Mexico State University; Sarah Ferguson, St. Catherine University/St. Thomas University; Roger Nooe; University of Tennessee, Knoxville; Julia Rembert, University of Iowa; and Matthew Theriot, University of Tennessee, Knoxville. Also, we would like to again thank the following reviewers of the first edition: Carrie Elliott, Benedict College; Ski Hunter, University of Texas at Arlington; Dezette Johnson, Johnson C. Smith University; Theresa C. Jones, Michigan State University; Denise Krause, University at Buffalo, State University of New York; John Allen Lemmon, San Francisco State University; Mary Beth Montgomery, California State University, Sacramento; Margaret Waller, Arizona State University; Joseph Walsh, Virginia Commonwealth University; and Lindee Peterson Wilson, Avila University.

Joan gives special thanks to her husband Martin, her children, Eric, Rebecca, and Julia, and her entire extended family, where she first learned all about "human behavior and the social environment." She also recognizes and appreciates her colleagues at Smith College School for Social Work for their inspiration as scholars, and her co-author Donna who shared the writing journey with grace and humor. Donna gives special thanks to Geoff, Johanna, and Eliza for their love, support, patience, and inspiration, and to Joan, a true friend. Thanks also to Dr. Peggy Morton, Coordinator of Undergraduate Field and Service Learning at the Silver School of Social Work, Dr. Hansell Patterson, Nancy Tricamo LCSW, Susan Ziskin LCSW, and Jennifer Filos for their unyielding positive regard and expressions of support whenever needed.

About the Authors

Joan Granucci Lesser, PhD, is currently a Resident Adjunct Associate Professor and Chair of Social Work Practice at the Smith College School for Social Work. She was previously Associate Professor at the Springfield College School of Social Work, where she served as chair of Human Behavior and the Social Environment and Social Work Practice sequences. Dr. Lesser received her PhD from New York University and her MSW from Columbia University, where she was the recipient of a National Institute in Mental Health Training Grant. Dr. Lesser has also served on the adjunct faculties of New York University School of Social Work and Fordham University Graduate School of Social Services in New York City. She has held various clinical, supervisory, and administrative positions, including Director of Social Work at Flower Hospital in New York City. She is the author, with Dr. Marlene Cooper, of *Clinical Social Work Practice: An Integrated Approach* (Allyn & Bacon). Dr. Lesser is also the founder of the Pioneer Valley Professionals, a multidisciplinary community-based practice in Holyoke, Massachusetts, which provides services to children, adolescents, adults, and families. Dr. Lesser has presented locally, nationally, and internationally, most recently in Guangzhou China, on the "treatment of elders with trauma histories" and in Athens, Greece, and Barcelona, Spain, on "Cross Cultural Research, Training, and Practice: A Relational Framework."

Donna Saia Pope, LCSW is currently an Adjunct Lecturer at New York University's Silver School of Social Work. She was previously a member of the faculty of the Mercy College Social Work Program, where she developed and taught the Human Behavior and the Social Environment course sequence and served as coordinator of field education. She received her MSW from Hunter College of the City University of New York. Ms. Pope's varied background in social work practice includes having served as director of the social work department at an urban health-care setting in New York City and as a private clinical practitioner and consultant. Her experience in clinical practice, social work administration, and program development spans several fields of practice, including substance abuse, eating disorders, developmental disabilities, medical social work, and aging.

About the Authors

1 An Integrating Framework for Human Behavior Theory and Social Work Practice

Introduction

The *person-in-environment* (or person-in-situation, biopsychosocial, psychosocial) perspective has historically been the central organizing focus of the social work profession's approach to the helping process. This perspective underscores "the interdependence of individuals within their families, other social networks, communities and larger environments" (Northern & Kurland, 2001, p. 49). From its inception, the profession has drawn from a variety of disciplines (for example, psychology, sociology, biology, anthropology, economics, and political science) to inform its theoretical base for practice. Over time, it has attempted (with greater or lesser degrees of success) to synthesize data from these disparate fields to develop a theory base and practice models that reflect its traditional dual focus: to enhance the biopsychosocial functioning of individuals and families and to improve societal conditions (Greene, 1991).

This chapter will set the stage for the chapters that follow by providing a framework for integrating the wide range of theories and information presented throughout this text. This framework rests on ecosystemic concepts and is informed by a variety of postmodern paradigms that emphasize social justice, multicultural competence, strengths and empowerment perspectives, and principles of developmental contextualism. It assumes the interrelatedness of the personal, interpersonal, and wider social spheres and informs a model for social work practice that integrates skills at the micro, mezzo, and macro levels. We begin by providing a historical overview of the social work profession as it relates to human behavior theory and practice. We will present fundamental assumptions of an ecosystemic approach, as well as an introduction to contemporary perspectives that build on and refine that approach.

Human Behavior Theory and Social Work Practice: A Historical Perspective

The Roots of Modern Social Work Practice: A Person-in-Environment Focus

Modern social work practice can trace its roots to several social movements of the 19th century, and to two, relatively distinct, perspectives on the origin of human problems: those perspectives that viewed the *person* as the focus for change, and those that saw problems in the *environment* as contributing most significantly to human distress. Three movements that illustrate these perspectives are described in the following sections.

The Person The first of these movements had its roots in the development of the relief aid and charity organization societies in the United States during the 1880s. Here, early social workers, or *friendly visitors,* visited homes to help families resolve social and emotional problems (Richmond, 1917). This movement focused on the need for change within individuals and families and "one might say the *person* part of the person-in-environment was emphasized" (Greene, 1991, p. 10). Inspired by scientific advances in such fields as medicine and engineering, the Charity Organization Societies began to develop a scientifically based theoretical foundation for practice—one that emphasized diagnosis and cure and called for more education and training for practitioners (Kirst-Ashman & Hull, 2009). This person-based perspective underlies traditional approaches to social casework.

The Environment In the late 19th and early 20th centuries, both the settlement house movement and the emergent social welfare system in the African-American community tended to emphasize the "*in-environment* part of the formulation" (Greene, 1991, p. 10).

The Settlement House Movement The settlement house movement developed in response to the social effects of the Industrial Revolution. As America became increasingly industrialized, people from rural areas in the United States (as well as immigrants from other countries) moved to American cities in search of economic opportunities. They were frequently forced to live in the poor, overcrowded parts of these cities and to contend with such adverse conditions as deteriorating housing, inadequate sanitation, and lack of worker protections. In the case of foreign immigrants, issues related to the need for adaptation to the new culture added to their stress. The first settlement house was developed in New York City in 1886, and by the turn of the century, there were many such programs across the country. These programs provided educational, medical, and social services designed to help poor Americans and recent immigrants better understand and cope with their new, complex environments. Settlement house workers such as Jane Addams "accepted the role of applied sociologist" (DeHoyos & Jensen, 1985) and used social action as a means of creating a better society. They lived and worked with poor people, challenging the status quo by advocating for such programs as public housing and public health, supporting legislation designed to improve people's lives, such as child labor laws and the granting of women's suffrage, and mobilizing people in poor communities to help improve their own lives (Popple, 1995; Smith, 1995).

Social Welfare Systems in the African-American Community During the time that Jane Addams and other settlement house workers were trying to address the needs of poor European Americans, the African-American community was establishing several major social welfare organizations of its own (Carlton-LaNey, 2001). Within a societal context that advocated segregation between African and European Americans and a social science community context that largely viewed African Americans as an inferior race (Newby, 1965), organizations such as the National Association of Colored Women (NACW), the National League on Urban Conditions Among Negroes (NLUCAN), and the American branch of the Universal Negro Improvement Association (UNIA) eventually grew to form "the foundation and framework for social welfare service delivery in the African American community" (Carlton-LaNey, 2001, p. xiii) and were founded on what was later termed an empowerment perspective. This perspective, which focuses on reducing the sense of powerlessness engendered in oppressed people by their social status, will be discussed later in this chapter (see also Chapter 5, "The Family in Society," and Chapter 7, "Communities and Organizations," for further discussion of this perspective). For the moment, it is important to understand the context in which African-American citizens found themselves during the so-called Progressive Era (1898–1918), as social work became professionalized and increasing numbers of private social welfare agencies were developing. With institutionalized racism permeating American life, African Americans were denied access to resources and opportunities; discrimination in housing, employment, education, health care and so forth made the road to overcoming poverty plagued with obstacles.

> The problems to which these groups responded included an array of life-threatening social ills. Clearly, racism and its attenuating grasp made life harsh and oppressive for African Americans. This institutionalized racism permeated American life, denying access for African Americans to opportunities and resources. The race lens through which nearly all of life's circumstances were viewed, and significant decisions addressed, was always in place. Furthermore, among African American social

With institutionalized racism permeating American life, African Americans were denied access to resources and opportunities: discrimination in housing, employment, education, health care and so forth, made the road to overcoming poverty plagued with obstacles.

> welfare leaders, life circumstances had produced a "profound distrust of white people" in spite of the fact that some were valued benefactors and others even carried the label "friend" (Carlton-LaNey, 2000; White, 1999, p. 98). . . . many other social problems existed among African Americans. . . . Because of poverty, the quality of life for African Americans in both the South and nationwide was miserable. Hemingway (1980) noted that the typical African-American Carolinian, for example, "lived in a weather-beaten, unpainted, poorly ventilated shack, subsisted on a thoroughly inadequate diet and was disease ridden. Hook worms, pellagra and a variety of exposure-induced ailments consistently plagued him, limiting his life expectancy rate" (p. 213). Their northern, urban counterparts did not fare much better. They, too, found life harsh and difficult; however, circumstances in the North offered some room for self-respect and the hope for a better future. Nonetheless, the road to overcoming poverty was plagued with discrimination in housing and employment; inadequate education, health care and diet, and disproportionate rates of delinquency, crime and death. (Carlton-LaNey, 2001, p. xiv)

The Emergence of the Medical Model

The movements described served as precursors to modern professional social work practice. In addition to their differences in approach and emphasis, each of these movements drew, over time, from different bodies of theory to inform their practices. Mary Richmond, an early social caseworker, wrote the first formal social work practice text, *Social Diagnosis,* in 1917. Although Richmond's work relied heavily on sociological research that emphasized the effects of the environment on personality development (Cooper & Lesser, 2005), this strong connection between sociology and social casework weakened considerably after World War I and during the Great Depression, when societal problems often seemed too overwhelming for *sociological fixes.* Searching for a scientific base for practice, *person*-oriented social caseworkers were increasingly drawn to the nascent discipline of developmental psychology and the medical model of psychoanalytic theory as conceived by Sigmund Freud (see Chapter 3, "Theories of Development"). This growing interest in psychological processes shifted the focus of social work practice away from environmental concerns toward a view of human problems as primarily intrapsychic in nature. Soon, the *person's* internal psychological problems were seen as the root cause of all forms of human difficulties, poverty included.

This *medical model* approach gained dominance in the profession during the 1920s and 1930s. With the enormous economic upheavals of the Great Depression, social caseworkers found themselves working more and more frequently with middle-class clients whose adjustment issues were responsive to this focus. The profound, reality-based issues affecting America's poor required a sociologically based approach and wider societal changes that were beyond the rather narrow scope of social casework as it was being practiced at that time. Ultimately, many of these structural problems were addressed with relative success by broad social reforms instituted by the federal government over time.

Empowerment Perspectives: Integrating Group Work and Emphasizing Racial Justice and Social Change

A pioneer in the area of helping to move social work toward a more even balance between the *person* and *environment* perspectives was E. Franklin Frazier, the director of the Atlanta School of Social Work from 1922–1927. Frazier, an African-American sociologist, had a somewhat conflicted relationship with the social work profession, despite the fact that he was instrumental in helping to establish and accredit the first African-American school of social work (the Atlanta School of Social Work).

> Three of Frazier's intellectual and social commitments united him in part with social work and at the same time led to significant disjunctures with the profession. These are (1) a worldview that included socialism and the empowerment of the African American community through economic cooperation; (2) a radical commitment to racial justice, including an intense dedication to the kind of rigorous and scientific education that would "(fill) the Negro's mind with knowledge and (train) him in the fundamental habits of civilization" (Frazier, 1924d, p. 144); and (3) a controversial effort to use the combined tools of psychoanalysis and social inquiry to probe the internal operation of race prejudice and racial oppression in both Whites and Blacks. (Kerr-Chandler, 2001, p. 190)

Frazier's attraction to social work came from its integration of three fields that interested him: psychology, social study, and interest in working people. He was particularly interested in using Freud's work to understand the psychology of racism (Frazier, 1924a, 1924b, 1924c, 1924d, 1925, 1926, 1927), as well as the internal constraints that prevented African Americans from moving forward. However, Frazier's interest in using Freud's work to explore the "characteristics ascribed to insanity" (Frazier, 1927, p. 856) as they related to Southern racism was rejected by the relatively conservative social work community, which was reluctant to threaten the segregationists within its midst (Carlton-LaNey, 2001).

Despite the dominance of the medical model and the high status granted to the psychiatric social work practice, descendants of the early settlement house movement gradually began to establish themselves within the social work profession during the 1930s. These workers, with their emphasis on *social change, advocacy,* and *community-oriented* group-work programs, had drawn on theories of practical democracy and group dynamics to inform the theoretical base for their practice. Of particular significance was the work of Grace Coyle (1930), a social worker whose dissertation, *Social Process in Organized Groups,* drew on her work in settlement houses, YWCAs, and industrial settings and helped to establish group work as a method of social work practice that could be effective in a wide variety of agency settings (see Chapter 6, "Group Work"; Northern & Kurland, 2001; Toseland & Rivas, 2004).

The Diagnostic School and the Family Therapy Movement

Further challenges to the professional dominance of the medical model and its narrow focus on the client's internal conflicts came in the 1940s, when the *diagnostic school* of social work theory and practice began to exert its influence.

This school of thought held that all human problems had both psychological and social aspects (Cooper & Lesser, 2005) and proponents of this approach originated the term *psychosocial* to reflect their more balanced, dual-focused view of the human condition. During World War II and the years that followed, disciples of the diagnostic, psychosocial school drew on concepts from ego psychology to develop their theoretical base for practice. Ego psychology, an offshoot of Freudian theory, focused less on intrapsychic motivation and more on how individuals learn to cope with their environments and how interactions between the person and environment may affect personality development (see Chapter 3, "Theories of Development"). During the 1950s, the gap between psychological and sociological perspectives was further bridged, as social workers became increasingly interested in the developing family therapy movement, with its emphasis on how families change and develop over time, how the behavior of one family member influences another, and how to help families to function more effectively.

Historical Division by Professional Fields and Methods of Practice

Due in large part to the profession's two-pronged philosophical evolution, social workers in direct practice tended, for many years, to be identified by a particular method (for example, casework, group work, community organization, and administration), or field of practice (for example, medical, psychiatric, industrial, child welfare, education). Social caseworkers, with their emphasis on locating problems with the individual (*the person*), and the more socially oriented group and community workers, maintained fairly separate professional identities and in fact did not even merge into a single professional organization until the formation of the National Association of Social Workers (NASW) in 1955. Despite the professional merger, the practical divisions by method and field of practice persisted for many years.

Reform Approaches

With the advent of the 1960s came a renewed interest in social issues and social action—the War on Poverty, Civil Rights movement, Women's and Gay Liberation movements—all had a profound effect on the practice of social work (DeHoyos & Jensen, 1985). Although the dominance of the medical model had been attenuated somewhat during the 1940s and 1950s, with renewed interest in environmental influences on human behavior, the profession had remained grounded in a primarily psychological approach to human behavior. It gave a nod to the environment as an important influence on personality development, but the literature reflected little real attention to sociological research.

As the 1960s unfolded, a reform approach began to take hold as calls for more outreach programs and more serious study of specific social forces and the nature of their influence became louder. Sociological models, particularly those related to ethnicity, social class, and social roles were increasingly introduced into the social work literature (DeHoyos & Jensen, 1985).

With the advent of the 1960's came renewed interest in social issues and social action: the War on Poverty, the Civil Rights Movement, and the Women's and Gay Liberation movements all had significant impact on social work practice.

An Integrating Framework for Human Behavior Theory: The Foundation for Multilevel Practice

It became increasingly clear that none of the traditionally dominant theories that viewed human behavior as fixed in place (either by genetic programming, past intrapsychic phenomena, or environmental stimuli) were adequate, in isolation, to explain the complexities of human growth and development throughout the life cycle. With the developments associated with the reform approach came increased pressure for theoretical models that could challenge the dominant, deterministic perspectives, help integrate practice methods (Middleman & Goldberg, 1987), and support the expansion of social work services from the psychological to the interpersonal, to the broader sociocultural arena (De Hoyos & Jensen, 1985).

In this section, we will describe the social systems model and the ecological perspective, both of which provide the foundation for contemporary, multilevel social work practice and for thinking about human behavior and development in the postmodern era.

The Social Systems Model

It was also during the 1960s that general systems theory began to gain stature in the scientific community through the work of a biologist, L. Bertalanffy (1962). A *system* is a complex whole comprised of component parts that work together in an orderly way, over an extended period of time, toward the achievement of a common goal. *General systems theory* is a set of rules for analyzing how systems operate and relate to one another, a concept that can be applied to many fields of study. It was embraced by the social work community and applied to social systems. A *social system* is a person or group of persons who function interdependently to accomplish common goals over an extended period of time.

Social workers felt this conceptual framework provided a way to bridge the profession's historical interest in both the person and the environment. In other words, the *systems model*, as it applied to social systems, seemed to provide the social work practitioner with a means to view human behavior through a wide lens that allowed for assessment of the client across a broad spectrum of human conditions—as a person, as a member of a family, and as a participant in the community and the wider society (DeHoyos & Jensen, 1985). The *person-in-environment system* becomes the unit of analysis (for example, the child in the context of family, school, or peers).

Psychosocial Assessment and the Social Systems Model Social Work practitioners use an assessment process to understand the nature of the presenting situation; the social worker gathers information about the many systems involved (including the individual's past and present biological, cognitive, and emotional functioning and family and wider social networks, such as employment, education, religious, and other relevant sociocultural systems). In collaboration with the client, the social worker forms an opinion of which system(s) appears to be most in need of intervention to most effectively resolve the problem for which the client is requesting assistance (Hollis, 1972). This system is referred to as the focal or target system.

For example, if a young boy is referred to a social worker because of problem behaviors he exhibits at school, the assessment process may reveal that the child's behavior is a symptom of frustration due to an undiagnosed learning disability (neurobiological and psychological systems); anxiety over strife at home (psychological and family systems); reaction to an overwhelmed teacher in an overcrowded classroom (school and/or community system); and/or any combination of these or other issues. Decisions about intervention follow accordingly, with the social worker focusing attention on the system(s) most in need of change and most likely to effect a positive change in the overall situation (a focal system).

The social systems model allowed for the easy integration of knowledge from a wide variety of biological, psychological, and sociological sources and treated the person–environment as a single system, with the person and environment being inseparable and continually shaping one another. Here, biological functioning, psychological functioning, and sociocultural functioning are related in a contingency fashion. A disturbance of any part of this system affects the system as a whole (Wapner & Demick, 1999).

Transaction and Reciprocal Causality Central to this model are the concepts of transaction and reciprocal causality. The term *transaction* refers to a process of acting and reacting between systems and is defined as a constant exchange between systems, in which each shapes and influences the other over time. This process of mutual influence is referred to as *reciprocal causality*. It must be understood that there is no simple cause-and-effect relationship between any two systems, including the person and his/her environment. Rather, there is a reciprocal or circular relationship in which, in the case of the person–environment unit, environmental forces affect the individual's behavior, whereas at the same time, the individual brings forth behaviors and other personal characteristics that help to create conditions in the environment with which he/she must then deal. For example:

> An 18-month-old boy is hungry and tired and begins to whine and cling to his mother. His mother is busy cooking dinner, helping her elder children with their homework, and dealing, by telephone, with her own elderly mother's latest medical crisis. Needless to say, this mother is feeling frustrated and overwhelmed, and she begins to yell in response to the toddler's whiny demands. The toddler reacts to his mother by losing what little control he has left, falling to the ground, kicking and sobbing. The mother now feels more overwhelmed, frustrated, and guilty and begins to lose patience with her two elder children. In response to their mother's sharpness, these children protest loudly, slamming their notebooks shut as their mother storms out of the room.

This example illustrates the circular nature of the transactions among members of this family system, with the toddler's demands triggering the mother's anger, the mother's angry reaction triggering the toddler's tantrum, which leads the mother to lose patience with her elder children, who respond emotionally, disrupting their homework and provoking more anger from their mother.

The concept of reciprocal causality also gives rise to the premise that a change in one part of a system or in the relationship between parts will create change in the whole system. (See Table 1.1.) This same example may be extended to illustrate that premise. Imagine the same situation, except that when the toddler begins to whine and cling, the mother is instead able to collect her thoughts enough to realize that the child is hungry and needs soothing. Instead of yelling, she musters up her last bit of self-control, picks the toddler up, offers him a glass of milk, and is then able to put him in his high chair. The toddler's needs are met, the situation de-escalates, the mother retains a sense of control and competence, and the elder children complete their homework. Here, by altering one small part of the person–environment configuration (the mother's initial response to the toddler), the outcome of the entire transaction is altered.

The social systems model is based on several fundamental assumptions that are important to understand if one is to fully appreciate the nature of the person-in-environment gestalt. These are described in Table 1.1.

TABLE 1.1

The Social Systems Model: Fundamental Assumptions

All forms of matter "from sub-atomic particles to the entire universe" can be viewed as systems, and all systems have certain common properties that cause them to behave according to a common set of "rules" (Anderson & Carter, 1990).	This is a basic assumption of a social systems approach. It is this assumption that makes generalist practice possible. That is, this is the principle that allows us to view a school system as a client as easily as we see an individual person as such. If both function as systems, then both share common characteristics, both will behave in certain predictable ways, and both will potentially be responsive to social work intervention. This statement, of course, oversimplifies the issues for the sake of explanation, but we believe it is nonetheless true at its core. As noted by Berger and Federico: The physical and social sciences share the belief that the universe has some underlying order and that behavior, be it the behavior of atomic particles or interacting individuals, is a patterned, regulated activity than can be understood and in many instances, predicted and controlled (Berger & Federico, 1982).
Every system is at the same time a unit unto itself, made up of interacting parts, and a part of a larger whole.	Anderson and Carter (1990) borrow the term *holon* (Arthur Koestler, 1967) to describe this phenomenon: Each entity is simultaneously a part and a whole. The unit is made up of parts to which it is the whole, the suprasystem, and at the same time, is a part of some larger whole of which it is a component or subsystem. The individual human being is on one hand, a whole system composed essentially of three subsystems that interact to promote the individual's development through life: the biological system (the physical body), the psychological system (thoughts, feelings, and behaviors) and the sociocultural environmental system (the social and physical environments). On the other hand the individual human being is itself a subsystem (i.e., component part) of a supra system (a larger system); that is, the family. As a family member (subsystem of the family), the individual works with other family members (other subsystems) to maintain family functioning. These examples, which are again simplified for the sake of understanding, can be extended, ad infinitum, with the family seen as a subsystem of a community, the community as a subsystem of a nation or larger culture, and a nation as a subsystem of a global community.

(Continued)

TABLE 1.1

The Social Systems Model: Fundamental Assumptions (Continued)

The whole system is different from the sum of its parts: it has definite properties of its own (Anderson & Carter, 1990).	Each social system has an identity of its own that is different from the identities of its individual members. It is the way in which the individual members relate to one another, how they organize themselves to work together toward their common purpose, which gives the social system its unique identity. For example, two hospitals may serve the same patient population, employ the same type and number of staff, and share the same mission. Despite these similarities in composition, each may have distinctly different reputations with regard to quality and medical outcomes of care. Many factors, including distribution of power, patterns of organization and communication, degree of involvement with the community etc. may, in effect, form two distinct institutional cultures. Simply put, when the component parts of systems are combined, they take on characteristics that they did not possess in isolation. The social worker must acknowledge and respect this wholeness whether he/she is examining an individual, a family, an organization or the broader society if social work intervention is to be effective.
A change in one part of a system or in the relationship between parts will create change in the system as a whole.	Because systems are composed of interrelated parts that operate in transaction with one another, "whatever affects one part of the system affects all parts to some degree" (Hollis, 1972, p. 11).
Every system must be able to adapt to changing internal and external demands and challenges while continuing to maintain its identity and its unique sense of wholeness. Some degree of stress and tension is therefore a natural and, indeed, necessary part of any adaptive system's existence as it interacts with its environment and develops over time.	As noted previously, all systems are goal oriented or purpose driven. That is, the system's components, or subsystems, work together to achieve common goals. When the system's components are able to work together effectively, the system is said to be "functional" or "adaptive." In other words, a functional system is one in which: • The system is flexible enough to change as necessary in response to constantly changing conditions and demands from within and from the environment. • While remaining flexible, the system is cohesive enough to maintain its sense of "wholeness." The subsystems are able to fulfill their individual needs and purposes while working together successfully fulfill the overall system's goals over time. • The system works to maintain a "good fit" with its environment, and as the system develops, it becomes increasingly capable of responding to change and improving its system–environment "fit."

Obviously, the reverse will be true for dysfunctional or maladaptive systems. Here, the system's components are less successful in working together to achieve the system's goals. Such a system may be so internally disorganized that its components are unable to work together effectively. On the other hand, the system may be rigid and inflexible, and therefore less able to adjust to changing circumstances and demands. Over time, such a system will be less and less likely to develop the capacities required to respond to changing circumstances while maintaining effective functioning.

Characteristics of Living Systems As noted in Table 1.1, all systems, smaller than the smallest cell, to the global community and beyond, share certain common properties. The following section will first introduce and define some of these properties and will clarify how each affects a system's overall ability to function effectively. We have selected, for discussion, six characteristics that are basic to the workings of all living systems. These are boundaries, adaptation, steady state, energy, communication, and organization; each is described in Table 1.2.

TABLE 1.2

Characteristics of Living Systems

Boundaries	Every system has boundaries. Boundaries can be defined as the borders or lines of separation that distinguish the system from the rest of its environment. Boundaries also regulate the flow of energy into and out of the system (Greene, 1991; Zastrow & Kirst-Ashman, 1997). Boundaries may be physical (e.g., a person's skin physically distinguishes the person from the environment) or conceptual (e.g., who is a member of a particular family system and who is not). As the regulators of energy flow, a system's boundaries may be relatively open or relatively closed (Anderson & Carter, 1990; Greene, 1991). Systems with relatively open boundaries are more receptive to interchanges of energy (e.g. information, resources) among the various parts of the system and between the system and its environment. Functional systems have relatively open boundaries that permit energy to flow in and out of the system, enabling them to maintain a steady state as they grow and develop. Systems whose boundaries are relatively closed are less receptive to such interchanges of energy. In these systems, energy reserves tend to run down. Here, the system may find itself increasingly hard-pressed to maintain a steady state and to continue to develop and function effectively over time.

(Continued)

TABLE 1.2

Characteristics of Living Systems (Continued)

Adaptation	As any system interacts with its environment over time, it experiences pressure or tension as the environment makes demands on it, presenting it with challenges to its ability to function. Adaptation refers to a system's capacity to adjust to changing environmental conditions and demands. Functional systems respond to the environmental pressure by making changes to adjust to new demands. These changes or adjustments serve to reduce the tension and to cause the system to grow and develop. Over time, adaptive systems tend to achieve a better *fit* with their environment, growing more complex (or *differentiated*), increasingly able to effectively handle challenges and demands. The ability to change and grow in response to new circumstances is crucial to a system's continued viability and effectiveness (Zastrow & Kirst-Ashman, 1997). Adaptation however, is not a passive process whereby the system simply adjusts to whatever environmental circumstances present themselves. It is an active process in which human beings strive to achieve the most congruent person-in-environment system state or *fit* possible between their own needs and abilities and the characteristics of their environment. There are critical person-in-environment transitions at every stage of the life cycle. If the fit is not good, they may choose to make changes within themselves, in their environment, or in both. These changes are known as adaptations (Germain, 1991).
Steady State (also referred to as "equilibrium"	Every system constantly strives to maintain a balance between changing in response to internal and external demands, while at the same time preserving its unique identity and sense of wholeness. We will refer to this dynamic balance as a steady state (although it is sometimes referred to as equilibrium; see Anderson & Carter, 1991 for distinctions). The maintenance of this balance is essential for a system's viability over time. If some internal or external stressor disturbs the steady state, the system must work to restore the balance by making adjustments in its functioning. A functional system can maintain and restore a steady state by remaining flexible, alert and responsive to continuously changing internal and external circumstances while it grows and develops, maintains its sense of wholeness, and actively pursues its goals. A dysfunctional system has difficulty maintaining and restoring a steady state. If the system is unable to recover successfully from a disruption to its steady state, its overall effectiveness and, indeed, its very existence may be seriously threatened. According to Anderson and Carter (1990): Systems never exist in a condition of complete change or complete maintenance of the status quo. Systems are always both changing and maintaining themselves at any given time. The balance between change and maintenance may shift drastically toward one pose or another but if either extreme is reached, the system would cease to exist. (p. 26)

Energy	Energy is basic to the functioning of all systems. According to Zastrow and Kirst-Ashman energy is the "natural power of involvement between people and their environments" (Zastrow & Kirst-Ashman, 1997). Energy can take many forms, for example, financial resources, information, emotional support, physical assistance, etc. Energy is essential to a system's ability to cope with change and to develop and grow while continuing to preserve its identity and to maintain its steady state. For a system to be functional, energy must be able to flow into the system from the environment (input), out from the system into the environment (output), as well as internally among the system's components. When a system is functioning effectively, maintaining a steady state, taking in and generating energy, a synergistic effect occurs, whereby energy increases. This causes the system to develop and grow in complexity, acquiring characteristics that increase its overall viability. Dysfunctional systems tend to restrict the internal and external flow of energy, isolating themselves from the environment. Here, energy reserves eventually become depleted, making it increasingly difficult for the system to maintain a steady state and to function effectively.
Communication	Communication is a process in which information, a specific type of energy, is transferred between the parts of a system and between the system and its environment. Functional communication serves to transmit information clearly and directly. A functional communicator demonstrates the flexibility to clarify messages as necessary, asking and responding to questions, restating messages, and maintaining focus on the issue(s) at hand. Feedback is one form of communication in which a system receives information about how it is performing, from the environment or from within, and then reacts to this information as appropriate. If the system receives negative information or negative feedback about its performance, it may choose to modify or adapt its behavior or to make a change in its environment. Positive feedback lets the system know that it is functioning effectively. A system's ability to establish effective patterns of communication and feedback mechanisms is crucial to its ability to adapt and function effectively (Anderson & Carter, 1990; Greene, 1991).
Organization	Over time, systems organize themselves to facilitate the exchange of energy and the system's ability to function effectively and achieve its goals. The system becomes increasingly differentiated and complex; subsytems develop and relationships among parts of the system are structured in various ways to facilitate the exchange of energy; roles are differentiated to divide the labor and put the system into working order. Vertical hierarchies are established that regulate the distribution of power, control, and authority.

Practice Example 1.1 illustrates fundamental concepts of the social systems model.

PRACTICE EXAMPLE 1.1

A Hospital in Crisis

In the mid 1980's, I accepted a position as a social work administrator in an urban medical setting that provided services to persons with developmental disabilities. One such service was an inpatient hospital unit. As originally conceived, this specialized hospital unit was to provide medical and habilitative care to patients with severe developmental disabilities and extraordinary medical needs. It was expected that these patients would be discharged back to the community, once their medical conditions were stabilized. Many of these patients had previously lived in state institutions, and few, if any, had families who could provide care. The plans for discharge therefore, presupposed the development of a continuum of community-based residential and habilitation programs that would provide necessary services, in accordance with federal law, in a less restrictive (and less costly) community environment.

Although the hospital's patient population had previously been severely underserved, the hospital unit had been developed at a time when government policies toward people with developmental disabilities were quite progressive. It was fully expected that the future would bring our patients an array of appropriate community-based services. In reality however, the development of such community-based services had proceeded more slowly than had been anticipated. This was due in part, to changes in the national political climate that led to significant reductions in federal funding for social programs during the 1980's. This paucity of appropriate community services left many of our inpatients languishing in the hospital far past the time that their medical conditions warranted such an intensive level of care.

By the mid-1980's, our difficulties with regard to timely patient discharge were compounded by three new and largely unanticipated challenges which faced many urban healthcare systems at that time. First, it was just becoming apparent that the problem of HIV/AIDS, initially thought to be a health crisis limited to gay men, was far more widespread than had been previously imagined. As knowledge increased about the virus, its modes of transmission and its detection, the number of people characterized as "at-risk" for infection seemed to grow exponentially to include such diverse populations as recipients of blood transfusions, drug addicted individuals, and the heterosexual partners of infected individuals as well as babies born to infected mothers.

The second major healthcare challenge arose out of the growing abuse of crack cocaine, a form of the drug that was widely accessible due to its low cost. A side effect of this "epidemic" was the rising number of infants born with serious medical and developmental problems associated with prenatal drug exposure.

Third, and on a more positive note, major technological advances in medicine had recently made it possible for extremely premature, low birth-weight newborns to survive at rates never before possible. Although many of these children went on to enjoy good health and normal development, many others suffered serious medical and developmental complications. This group included, but was not limited to, babies who had experienced prenatal exposure to crack-cocaine and/or HIV.

These three developments threatened to overwhelm the healthcare community. Fear over HIV/AIDS was fueled by ignorance. In fact, little was known for certain about the disease, newly developed diagnostic tests were often unreliable, and effective forms of treatment were years away. Premature infants with extremely low birth-weights and those exposed to crack-cocaine *in utero* presented unusual and extraordinary medical and developmental issues. Health care professionals, who were hard-pressed to diagnose and treat these new patient populations, found it almost impossible to predict what their future needs would be.

As the social work administrator, I was ultimately responsible for the success of the hospital's discharge planning program. Again, this meant that once a patient's medical condition improved enough that hospitalization was no longer necessary, the social work department was mandated by Federal and State regulations to see to it that each patient received all necessary health and habilitative services in the "least restrictive" community environment possible. As noted previously, this was problematic at best. Although some community resources did exist for our older, less fragile patients, these were relatively scarce and difficult to access. On the other hand, the community seemed totally unprepared to provide for our youngest, most complex patients. This left the hospital (along with many other urban hospital centers), in the position of housing a patient population that soon came to be known in the popular press as "boarder babies". These "boarder babies" had extraordinary developmental and health needs, and remained in hospitals essentially because they had nowhere else to go. Many had highly unstable family situations with parents who were struggling with drug addiction, AIDS and/or poverty and who were in no position to assume the care of a seriously ill child. Other patients came from more stable homes, but their parents' realistic fears and uncertainties about providing such a high level of care, combined with a real dearth of community services, had prevented them from returning home.

Soon after assuming my position as social work administrator, I realized that the hospital's problems with discharge planning were far more complex than I'd anticipated. In addition to the very real problem of a shortage of appropriate community resources for our patients, the social work staff seemed to have succumbed to frustration and to have given up on trying to find homes for our patients, believing that any effort toward that aim would be futile at best. This belief seemed also to permeate all parts of the hospital system. Many of the medical and habilitative staff seemed convinced that a large portion of the patients would be better off remaining in the care of hospital personnel despite the fact that their medical conditions no longer warranted hospital care. Patients' families had grown comfortable with the care their very fragile children had been receiving and were not at all anxious to have them leave the safety of the hospital setting. The hospital administration also seemed reasonably comfortable with the situation, despite the fact that the State Health Department had cited the facility for inadequate discharge planning services. Although the State had threatened to apply sanctions, for the moment the hospital continued to receive its relatively high rate of payment per patient, and so, felt little pressure to exert a great deal of effort to comply with the health department's demand for more active planning. I however, felt enormous pressure to create a successful discharge planning program. As the administrator responsible for these services, I knew I would be held accountable for any lack of compliance with State regulations. I was also aware, from previous work experience in community based programs for people with developmental disabilities, of the improved quality of life our patients would experience living in the community. Having successfully "deinstitutionalized" many clients in the past, I knew we could create a successful program despite the scarce resources.

After carefully assessing the situation, I realized that my first intervention needed to be to facilitate a change in attitude among the social work staff. I felt this would set in motion a string of changes inside and outside the hospital system which would, I hoped, eventually lead to appropriate community placements for our patients.

I began my intervention by raising the issue of discharge planning at our weekly social work staff meetings, initially exploring the staff's past efforts toward discharge planning and the obstacles they encountered. Discussions about patients' needs and the benefits of community living quickly gave way to a venting of their feelings of frustration and hopelessness around this issue. Realizing that they needed to experience some success, I suggested two or three community based programs which I knew could provide appropriate services for some of our older, less fragile patients. I assisted the staff in preparing referral materials and in arranging

(Continued)

appointments for our social workers to visit those agencies, evaluate their programs, forge relationships with them and discuss referrals of specific patients. The staff began to feel excited as a handful of our patients left the hospital for the community. Admittedly, those patients were among our least needy, most stable group, but their successful discharges served to motivate and energize the social workers into further action.

In an effort to locate community based programs for even our most "hard-to-place" patients, we decided to broaden our search to cover a wider geographic area. The staff developed a questionnaire, which they mailed to community agencies across the state. This questionnaire was designed to fully acquaint us with statewide community-based services. Focusing their attention on those agencies whose responses described the kinds of services we were looking for, social work staff enlisted the cooperation of some of our medical and habilitative personnel and arrange group site visits to programs around the state. As the process unfolded, we were able to locate several agencies willing to accept even some of our "harder to place", more fragile patients.

Our "boarder babies" however, presented more difficulties. As noted, most of these babies needed to live in stable homes with a full range of community support services in place. Family instability, lack of appropriate support services and/or parental anxiety and ambivalence presented major obstacles to such a plan. The social work staff, now energized by success, began to aggressively pursue planning for these children. As some of the babies had been abandoned by their parents, staff began to exert pressure on the city's Department of Children's Services to pursue the legal processes necessary to free them for adoption. Realizing that they could not depend on the over-extended city agency to expeditiously locate foster and adoptive families, social work staff began to reach out and form relationships with private agencies who were just beginning to develop foster and adoption programs for children with special medical and developmental needs. For those children who were fortunate enough to have more stable family situations, the social workers provided intensive counseling to parents to help them resolve their conflicted feelings about assuming full-time responsibility for children with multiple problems and uncertain prognoses.

Although locating stable homes was an important first step, many obstacles to discharge remained ahead. Parents (whether they were adoptive, foster or by birth) all required highly specialized training to deal with the children's varying medical and nursing needs, appropriate educational and therapeutic services had to be located, medical equipment and support services had to be approved and funded and in some cases, issues of inadequate housing and family financial resources had to be resolved before the children could safely go home.

In addition to the many external obstacles, the social workers were surprised to meet with quite a bit of resistance from our own in-hospital medical and nursing staff who were not convinced that the babies could receive adequate care by non-professionals (i.e. parents) outside the relative shelter of the hospital environment. Needless to say, support and cooperation from the medical and nursing staff was critical for many reasons. In addition to needing their advice and guidance regarding the types of community health care services we needed to obtain, we needed them to train the families in patient care techniques before the children could go home.

On an administrative level, I applied continuous pressure on the hospital administration by keeping them apprised of our progress, needs and problems. Despite the tension, the social work staff worked hard to directly collaborate with the doctors and nurses, soliciting their opinions and expertise, addressing any and all concerns promptly and maintaining close communication throughout the process.

Although the process of change often seemed endlessly fraught with obstacles, within a three year period we had developed a thriving, successful discharge program which essentially transformed the hospital back to the short-term medical facility it was originally meant to be, and provided a vehicle for our patients to lead their lives in the "least restrictive" environment (i.e. outside the institution, in the community with medical and educational services to support their development) possible.

Analysis of Practice Example 1.1 from a Social Systems Perspective

In Practice Example 1.1, the hospital itself may be viewed as a system. The hospital system is composed of transacting subsystems that mutually influence one another. These subsystems include the patients and their families, the hospital administration, and the medical, nursing, habilitative, and social work departments. The hospital system may be seen as a holon, as it operates in transaction with its environment. This environment includes its geographic location, a low-income section of a large metropolitan area, as well as the wider health-care community of which the hospital is a part. Other subsystems of the health-care community are all agencies that oversee the hospital's functioning and/or provide funding for its services (for example, the Office of Developmental Disabilities, the Department of Health, the Department of Children's Services), as well as various community-based agencies serving similar patient populations across the city and state. The hospital system and its community also transact with the wider society within which they are embedded. From this perspective, broad social forces such as the culture and its values, the political and economic climate, and any variety of social developments may be seen as important influences. In this case, environmental forces influencing the functioning of the hospital system include the relatively progressive political and economic climate at the time during which the hospital was originally conceived, as well as the eventual changes in the political and economic climate, which restricted funding for social programs and delayed development of anticipated community services for the hospital's original patient population. Additional influential environmental forces include the rising epidemics of HIV/AIDS and crack cocaine abuse, as well as advances in medical technology, which increased survival rates for the epidemics' youngest victims.

Reciprocal Causality: Systems in Transaction The concepts of reciprocal causality and transactional functioning between systems is clearly illustrated in this example, as changes in the political and economic climate began to create changes in the functioning of the hospital system. As the hospital found itself dealing with catastrophic social problems in an increasingly resource-poor environment, it began to invest less and less effort toward discharging its "medically ready" patients. The environmental response to this change in the hospital system's internal system of controls is the Department of Health's threat to apply sanctions. This led to a further series of internal changes, beginning with the hospital's designation of a social work administrator to be responsible for discharge planning. The social work administrator's decision to focus her initial intervention on the functioning of the social work department illustrates the concept of the focal system (that is, the system most in need of change to most effectively resolve the problem at hand). As the administrator's interventions gradually led to changes in the focal system and the social work staff began to actively pursue community resources, the community responded with changes of its own. Programs began to accept referrals of the hospital's patients, and gradually these patients began to move out into the community. Further change occurred when the Department of Health lifted the threat of sanctions. This served to energize the hospital system, with the social work staff initiating aggressive partnerships with community-based agencies to develop new services for the "boarder babies." As these efforts began to bear fruit, further changes in the hospital's internal functioning occurred, with the hospital's discharge process eventually making it possible for the boarder babies to return to the community.

Adaptation The hospital system faced many environmental obstacles and challenges to its ability to fulfill its goal of discharging patients to the community once they no longer needed hospitalization. The hospital system initially had difficulty adapting to these challenges, and eventually its very existence was threatened by the possibility of sanctions from the Department of Health. The hospital system was eventually successful in adapting to these challenges by making internal changes (for example, hiring a new administrator to develop an active discharge planning program) and external changes (for example, working with other agencies to develop appropriate community resources). These adaptations resulted in a better "fit" with its environment (for example, the Department of Health removed the threat of sanctions, and the community ultimately provided the hospital's patients with appropriate services) and caused the hospital system to develop and grow into a more complex, viable system (e.g., it now had an active discharge planning program with a strong network of community relationships in place and could therefore better function to fulfill its intended purpose).

Energy Flow and Steady State The example clearly demonstrates the importance of energy flow to a system's functioning. As the hospital system became overwhelmed by the many environmental obstacles it faced with regard to discharge planning, it began to close off the flow of energy coming in (input) and going out (output) of the system. The social workers limited their efforts to reach out to the community (output), and as a result, less and less information about resources came in (input). Eventually, the hospital system began to lose its sense of identity, gradually coming to more closely resemble a nursing home than a hospital. Its supply of energy gradually ran down, resulting in a sense of inertia, especially in the area of discharge planning. Ultimately, the hospital system's very existence was threatened as the Department of Health prepared to institute sanctions against it. A viable steady state was gradually restored as the hospital system began to export energy via the social workers' increased efforts to explore community resources and establish connections with other agencies. Energy then flowed in from the community in the form of resources, information, and working alliances. The resultant synergy allowed for an increased flow of energy within the system, with the various subsystems (such as medical, nursing, habilitation, and administrative departments) eventually working together effectively toward their common goal.

Communication and Feedback Mechanisms The hospital system received negative feedback about its discharge planning efforts from the Department of Health, and it responded by beginning a process of, first, internal (increasing its efforts toward discharge planning) and then external (working to develop new community resources) change. In Practice Example 1.1, when the hospital initially tightened its boundaries, it limited its access to resources, however scarce, in the community. As noted, this led to a sense of inertia that eventually threatened its continued existence. As it opened its boundaries, forming alliances with resources in the community, it became increasingly energized, gradually regaining its ability to function effectively and to better its fit with its environment.

The Ecological Perspective

The social systems model, as it related to social work, evolved as the profession struggled to integrate its often abstract and complex terminology and concepts into its theory base. By the 1970s and 80s it had expanded to include the ecological perspective (Germain, 1979a, 1979b, 1979c, 1981, 1987, 1991). Although rooted in systems theory and using systems concepts to integrate information, the ecological perspective provides a broader base from which to integrate theories from several disciplines and to more fully explore the nature of the relationship between the individual and the environment. For example, this perspective incorporates concepts from role theory (among many others) to explain how behavior and relationships are affected by sociocultural factors. From an ecological perspective, social roles determine not only how a person in a particular position behaves, but also how others behave toward that person. "In short, roles serve as a bridge between internal processes and social participation" (Greene, 1991, p. 276). In addition to social roles, patterns of communication, individual coping behaviors, interpersonal networks, and characteristics of the physical and social environment that either support, or impede, human development are examined in the context of the complex, reciprocal interactions between the person and environment. Here, the concept of the environment includes the physical (natural and constructed), the interpersonal (all levels of social relationships), and the sociocultural (social norms and rules and other cultural contexts; Harkness & Super, 1990). As is the case in the social systems model, the individual is understood in the context of his or her environment—the person and environment are viewed as parts of the same system operating in continuous transaction—mutually influencing, shaping, and changing one another.

Goodness of Fit: An Evolutionary Perspective The overarching view of human development from an ecological perspective is an evolutionary one: people are born with genetically based potentials that are either nurtured or impeded by transactions with the environment throughout the life course. A central tenet of this perspective is the notion of "goodness of fit" between the person and the environment. This refers to a reciprocal process in which a good fit results when the physical and social environment provides the resources, nurturance, and support the individual needs to grow and develop in an adaptive manner. Notably, this perspective recognizes that diverse environments are necessary to support the needs, goals, and life experiences of diverse human beings, acknowledging that no one type of social or physical environment can be considered optimal for all people. Of particular interest are complex social networks such as family members, coworkers, community groups, and so forth that have the potential to provide mutual aid and contribute to growth, development, and emotional and physical well-being. Likewise, such social toxins as oppression, racism, and classism that devalue and disempower certain individuals and groups may serve to impede growth and well-being.

The ecological perspective builds on the traditional view that the central task of the social work profession is to maintain a focus on both the environment and the individual person's coping capacities, and that depending on the situation at hand, the goal of the social worker is to work to change again. The view is transactional in nature—improvement in an individual's coping and problem-solving skills, and an increase in an individual's self-esteem and sense of competence, will "facilitate primary group functioning . . . and (positively) influence organizational structure's social networks and physical settings" (Germain & Gitterman, 1979, p. 20).

Fundamental Concepts of the Ecological Perspective Several specific concepts are fundamental to the ecological perspective and are viewed as expressions of person–environment transactions. These are human relatedness, competence, self-direction and self-esteem, adaptiveness, coping, life stress, and power and oppression. These are described in Table 1.3.

TABLE 1.3

The Ecological Perspective: Fundamental Concepts

Human relatedness, competence, self-direction and self-esteem	Human relatedness, competence, self-direction, and self-esteem are seen as interdependent, innate processes that first emerge through the earliest attachment relationships and continue to develop as life progresses and the individual's social networks expand. It is important to note that each of these qualities is seen as an expression of person–environment transactions—that is, each depends on attributes of both the person and the environment for its development. Each of these qualities first emerges during early childhood, as the individual first interacts with his/her primary caretakers and each continues to develop as the individual continues to interact with an ever-widening social and physical environment. Depending on the nature of these person–environment transactions the qualities of relatedness, competence, self-direction, and self-esteem may be supported and nurtured or inhibited in their development. **Relatedness** refers to the human being's inborn capacity to form attachments to other people; the ability to connect to others through attachments and other social affiliations is seen as a central component of optimal functioning throughout the life span. **Competence** is the ability to feel "effective" within one's environment; that is, it is the ability to feel self-confident, trust one's judgment, achieve one's goals and engage in positive relationships with others (Germain, 1991). **Self-direction** refers to the capacity to maintain a sense of control and purpose in the face of internal strivings and impulses as well as environmental pressures; that is, it is the feeling of personal power that enables one to make choices and decisions and to take effective action on behalf of oneself and one's primary groups. The ecological perspective also recognizes that the ability to be self-directing is highly influenced by one's social position and it recognizes the social worker's responsibility to help disempowered people restore their personal power. **Self-esteem** refers to the person's positive feelings about him/herself; these develop as the individual experiences feelings of relatedness, competence, and self-direction over time. Self-esteem incorporates the concept of self-efficacy, or a belief in one's effectiveness. One's self-identity or self-concept continues to develop throughout the life span, and these "are subject to greater opportunities and greater threats as the child moves into larger circles of relatedness where her or his personal and cultural characteristics will be appreciated or rejected by others" (Germain, 1991, pp. 26–27).

Adaptiveness	Basic to the ecological approach is the idea that human beings and their environments continually exert mutual influence to achieve maximum "goodness of fit"—one in which social networks and organizations, physical, cultural, political, and economic forces support peoples' inborn desire to grow and to achieve their goals. If the fit is not good, people may seek to make changes within themselves, in their environment or, in both. These changes are known as adaptations (Germain, 1991).
Coping capacity	Coping capacity is viewed as a transactional process that reflects the person-in-environment relationship. According to Germain (1991): Two major functions of coping are problem solving (what needs to be done to reduce, eliminate or manage the stressor) and regulating the negative feelings aroused by the stressor (Coyle and Lazarus 1980). They are interdependent functions inasmuch as each is a requirement of the other, and each supports the other. Progress in problem-solving leads to the restoration of self-esteem and to the more effective regulation of the negative feelings generated by the stressful demands. Progress in managing feelings and restoring self-esteem frees the person to work more effectively on problem solving . . . problem solving skills, although they are personal resources, require training by environmental institutions such as the family, the school, the church or temple, or the hospital. Similarly, the person's ability to manage negative feelings and to regulate self-esteem depends, in part, on social and emotional supports in the environment. Successful coping also requires additional personality attributes such as motivation, self-direction, which depends on the availability of choices and opportunities for decision making and action as well as access to material resources. (Mechanic, 1974a; White, 1974). (Germain, 1991, pp. 21–22)
Life stress	The ecological perspective emphasizes the idea that stress is not just a function of individual or environmental characteristics. It is, rather, a biospsychosocial phenomenon that emerges as a result of person–environment transactions. Attention is given to both the external and internal aspects of the stressful experience, including the environmental stressor (external), the physiological response (internal), and the resultant emotional and cognitive response. Additionally, the subjective aspects of the stress experience are highlighted; that is, depending on such factors as culture, age, gender, mental and emotional condition, and so on, the same situation may be viewed as stressful by some, exciting by others, and barely noticeable by still others Although some degree of stress is positive and necessary to challenge the individual to grow and develop, "problems in living" (Germain & Gitterman 1980) occur when the person's ability to deal with stressful events or situations is severely strained. According to Germain and Gitterman (1980), problems in living may arise from any of three interconnected aspects of life: (a) life transitions and/or new demands and roles that come with advancing development, (b) dysfunctional interpersonal processes in one's family or other personal social networks, or (c) demands of the physical and/or social environment, including problems related to organizational and community resources.

(Continued)

TABLE 1.3

The Ecological Perspective: Fundamental Concepts (Continued)

Power and oppression	The ecological perspective underscores the need for social workers to be mindful of value conflicts and culturally based assumptions "masquerading as knowledge" (Germain, 1991, p. 12). This implies the need for awareness of the impact of culture, ethnicity, racism, and oppression on human development and behavior. It calls for acknowledgment on the part of the practitioner of his/her own cultural biases and of the impact of issues related to social power and oppression on the human condition. For example, social power may be withheld from some groups on the basis of such characteristics as age, race, ethnicity, gender, religion, sexual orientation, social class, and/or a variety of physical traits and conditions. The abuse of power by dominant groups is related to such societal ills as poverty, unemployment, and inadequate social supports in education, health care, and housing. Inequities in the distribution of power define the contexts in which members of vulnerable groups develop and function—these contexts impose enormous stress on affected individuals and threaten their mental, physical, and social well-being.

Contemporary Perspectives: An Ecosystems Approach for the Postmodern Era

Despite some difference in origin, language, scope, focus, and applicability, the terms *social systems model* and *ecological perspective* are frequently used interchangeably. As previously noted, contemporary social work's perspective on human behavior and its relationship to practice integrates concepts from both social systems and ecological models to create what we will, for the sake of practicality, referred to as an ecosystems approach; this creates an overarching framework that provides a "systemic, contextual and transactional focus for defining problems and solutions" (Lightburn & Sessions 2006, p. 23). The approach has continued to evolve and has been increasingly influenced by a postmodern perspective that reflects an appreciation of the existence of multiple truths and multiple ways of knowing, based on context, culture, power differentials, and so forth. The contemporary ecosystemic view that human behavior and development can only be understood in the context of social relationships and broader social forces has transformed not only our thinking, but also our practice. Table 1.4 shows a multicontextual framework (Carter, 1993 in Carter & McGoldrick, 2005) for assessment that allows the clinician to "consider relevant issues in every system that may impact a client's situation" (Carter & McGoldrick, 1998, p. 16). The constructs described next represent some of the

TABLE 1.4

Social Work Assessment: Multiple Dimensions

The Individual	Immediate Household	Extended Family	Community and Social Connections	Larger Society
• Age • Gender roles and sexual orientation • Temperament • Developmental or physical disabilities • Culture, race, ethnicity • Class • Religious, philosophical, spiritual values • Finances • Autonomy skills • Affiliative skills • Power/privilege or powerless-ness/abuse • Education and work • Physical or psychological symptoms • Addiction and behavioral disturbances • Allocation of time • Social participation • Personal dreams	• Type of family structure • Stage of family life cycle • Emotional climate • Boundaries, patterns, and triangles • Communication patterns • Negotiating skills • Decision-making process	• Relationship patterns • Emotional legacies, themes, secrets, family myths, taboos • Loss • Socioeconomic level and issues • Work patterns • Dysfunctions: addictions, violence, illness, disabilities • Social and community involvement • Ethnicity • Values and/or religion	• Face-to-face links between individual, family, and society • Friends and neighbors • Involvement with governmental institutions • Self-help, psychotherapy • Volunteer work • Church or temple • Involvement in children's school and activities • Political action • Recreation or cultural groups	• Social, political, economic issues • Bias based on race, ethnicity • Bias based on class • Bias based on gender • Bias based on sexual orientation • Bias based on religion • Bias based on age • Bias based on family status (e.g., single parent) • Bias based on disability • Power and privilege of some groups because of hierarchical rules and norms held by religions, social, business or governmental institutions • How does a family's place in hierarchy affect relationships and ability to change?

Source: B. Carter & M. McGoldrick (Eds.). (2005). *The Expanded Family Life Cycle: Individual, Family, and Social Perspectives* (3rd ed.). Boston: Allyn & Bacon/Pearson Education. Reprinted by permission of the publisher.

most salient components of contemporary thinking; these will provide a frame for the chapters that follow.

A Social Justice Orientation

The value of social justice has become increasingly prominent as an organizing principle of ecosystemic practice (Swenson, 1998). Several contemporary perspectives embody and support the relevance of a social justice orientation to the clinical process. As noted earlier, most postmodern perspectives on human behavior acknowledge the existence of multiple truths, and at some level they challenge our most fundamental notions about the meaning and construction of knowledge and reality. For example, social constructionist thought emphasizes that knowledge is socially created—that is, people create meaning by filtering information through the lens of their personal experiences, values, and previous understanding. Postmodernism emphasizes that "ideas that become privileged as knowledge are those that support powerful interests (and which powerful interests support)" (Swenson, 1998, p. 530). In other words, traditional mental health theories (having emerged from a white, heterosexual, Western European perspective) use the norms of the dominant majority groups as the standard against which other groups are to be understood. From this perspective, the experiences of minority group members seem "not quite normal" and require some form of explanation, whereas the majority group experience is perceived simply as normal and therefore not requiring any explanation at all (Green, 2007). Contemporary ecosystemic practice utilizes principles of feminist, profeminist, multicultural, and narrative family systems, gay affirmative and disability affirmative therapies that view differences in ethnicity, race, gender, sexual orientation and ability as normal variations and emphasize that it is often societal discrimination and prejudice based on those variations that leads to a host of pathological symptoms (Green, 2007).

> This is the crux of the minority model, the shift in focus from personal, individual and problem in isolation, to group, environment, attitudes, discrimination—from individual pathology to social oppression. (Olkin, 1999, p. 28, as quoted in Green, 2007)

Worldview

The construct of worldview is central to postmodern, ecosystemic practice. Worldview has traditionally referred to beliefs, assumptions, and values that emerge from a specific cultural context (Ibrahim, 1984) and how these influence a client's cognitive structures, affects, and behaviors. Again, more recently, attention has been paid to variables, in addition to culture, that interface with worldview, including societal norms, educational level, social class, gender, religion, life stage, sexual orientation, and disability/ability status (Ibrahim, 1991, 1999). The ability to provide high-quality, effective services to diverse groups, rests on the understanding that they may each have diverse worldviews that affect their priorities, interpretations of reality, perspectives on human nature, standards of normalcy, and ideas about what constitutes effective forms of help. An understanding of the client's worldview greatly increases the clinician's ability to provide useful (and ethical) assistance throughout all phases of treatment, including diagnosis, treatment planning, and implementation and evaluation of the effectiveness of services (Ibrahim, Roysircar-Sodowwsky, & Ohnishi, 2001).

Contemporary thinking also emphasizes the need for clinicians to recognize the relativity of their own worldviews and to examine their contextually based assumptions and values; this level of self-awareness is necessary for the clinician to provide effective services to diverse populations (Lightburn & Sessions, 2006; Sue, 2001).

Globalization and Multicultural Competence

As the population of the United States has become increasingly diverse, and as technology shrinks and rapidly transforms our world, the concept of multicultural competence has become a central consideration of social work practice from an ecosystemic perspective. The notion of multiculturally competent practice emerged from the recognition, noted earlier, that because our traditional theories of human behavior and approaches to practice grew from Western European (the psychodynamic movement) and American (reinforcement theories of American behaviorism) contexts, "the worldview they espouse as reality may not be that shared by racial/ethnic minority groups in the United States nor by those who reside in different countries" (Parham, White, & Ajamu, 1999, in Sue 2001, p. 796). The effects of this history have given rise to the recognition that, in comparison to the help given to majority populations, services to ethnic and racial minority communities have often been of significantly lower quality and that problems of accessibility, discrimination, and culturally inappropriate intervention have persisted. For example, formulating an accurate diagnosis is difficult within cultures; these difficulties are magnified when the clinician and client are from different social–cultural contexts and the clinician is unfamiliar with the contextual assumptions that the client has internalized. These assumptions may be particularly salient when they apply to the meaning and implications of a presenting problem, as well as what processes might be most effective in helping to resolve that problem (Castillo 1997; Lonner & Ibrahim, 1996). In addition, given the global influence of Western cultures, many countries rely on Western models as they develop systems of health care; for maximum effectiveness, these models must be adapted to provide care within the context of appropriate cultural norms.

In recent years, our understanding of the meaning of culture, identity, and minority group status has broadened. For example, Greene (1997) defined culture as "the behaviors, values and beliefs that characterize a particular social group and perhaps distinguish it from others" (p. xi). As a result, our concept of multicultural counseling has expanded beyond considerations related to race and ethnicity to include the ways that other components of identity such as age, socioeconomic class, religion, skin color, gender, regional affiliation, and sexual orientation affect worldview and the degree of privilege or discrimination one experiences. Robinson (1999) discussed the idea of multiple identities that exist within the self and how these are affected by their position "in a society that differentially allocates privilege".

Empowerment and Strengths-Based Perspectives

Empowerment Perspectives These were discussed from a historical perspective earlier in this chapter, and the effects of powerlessness and oppression are briefly outlined in Table 1.3. (also see Chapter 7, "Communities and Organizations"). Because one's social position has a profound effect on one's access to resources, opportunities, and the ability to make proactive choices that affect one's life, family, and cultural group, and because certain vulnerable groups occupy social positions that block such access, disempowerment in the form of discrimination, racism, and oppression is a major contributing factor to emotional distress in minority populations (Germain, 1991; Schriver, 2005; Sue, 2001). Empowerment practice focuses on changing the distribution of power; it seeks to increase the ability of vulnerable individuals/groups to be self-directing, make choices, and act effectively to advance their own interests (Germain, 1991).

A Strengths-Based Perspective The concepts described earlier also underlie what has been termed the strengths-based perspective—in the words of Gibelman and Furman (2008, p. 199), "the strengths perspective looks to the power of people to overcome and surmount adversity (Rapp, 1998; Saleebey, 1999)." Once again, because traditional theories of human behavior and development were grounded in a White, European worldview, racial/ethnic differences were often interpreted as deficits, or abnormalities (Guthrie, 1997; Lee, 1993; White & Parham, 1990). A strengths-based perspective is one that seeks to identify the factors that support the resilience of people and groups across the life span and to build on these personal and social assets to promote growth and change (Hill, 1998). Intervention from a strengths-based perspective "is about more than managing symptoms and coping; it is about liberation, hope, resilience and transformation" (Lightburn & Sessions, 2006, p. 10)

Developmental Contextualism

Contemporary developmental theories use an ecosystemic framework and incorporate concepts from attachment, family systems, and other sociocultural theories to explain development across the life cycle (Carter & McGoldrick, 2005, p. 5). Building on the ecosystemic premise that the person and environment operate as a unified whole, current developmental thinking postulates that understanding human development requires understanding of "the endless interaction of internal and external and how the one is constantly influencing the other" (Bowlby, 1988). A related and equally important proposition is that individual development can only be understood in the context of significant emotional relationships—that human identity is inseparable from one's relationships with others. Here, healthy, human development necessitates finding a satisfactory "balance between connectedness and separateness, belonging and individuation, accommodation and autonomy" (Carter & McGoldrick, 2005, p. 9). Current thinking also posits that historical and social processes have a profound effect on development; for example, people who grew up in the era of the Great Depression were socially and emotionally shaped by historical forces and life experiences different from those experienced by the group known as the baby boomers.

Central to a developmental contextual approach is its consideration of positive development, adaptive behavior, and human resilience, as well as the belief that one must understand successful development before one can understand disordered development. This approach focuses attention on maturational milestones, life transitions, psychosocial factors, and the plasticity and reciprocity of the individual's relationship with his or her environment. Here, intervention aims to help move the individual from a maladaptive developmental pathway to a more adaptive one by strengthening positive, protective influences and reducing environmental risk. Key concepts of this approach are described next. Part II of this text examines human behavior across the life span from a developmental contextual perspective.

Attachment The concept of attachment is considered to be particularly significant in many developmental theories. The predisposition to develop affectional bonds is viewed as an innate need and capability that evolved for reasons of protection and survival and is now built into the human genome. Patterns of emotional regulation, strategies for behavioral control, the development of a sense of self-esteem, and self-reliance are developed within the context of the early attachment relationship(s) (Blatt, 1995 in Ollendick, p. 93; Cassidy, 1994). The child develops an internal working model of his/her primary attachment relationship that contains information about the self and the primary caregiver(s); the quality of these models then becomes predictive of later behavior in other relationship contexts (Elicker, Englund, & Sroufe, 1992 in Ollendick, p. 95) and, to some extent, the person's overall resilience or vulnerability to life stress.

Developmental Pathways In this view, the course of development is not fixed in a series of stages; rather, development is seen as occurring within a complicated system of social contexts. The nature of an individual's transactions with his or her environment shapes the developmental process, creating pathways along which development proceeds. Throughout the life span, the person experiences critical person–environment transitions, prompted by internal or external changes (for example, some form of trauma or the onset of a chronic medical condition). As long as environmental (especially relational) factors remain favorable, or improve, the person will continue along an adaptive pathway, one that supports resilience and healthy development. However, if the nature of the particular person–environment transaction is negative, thereby lessening the "goodness of fit" between the person and the environment, the person may move onto a more maladaptive pathway. This may lead, to a greater or lesser extent, to some form of vulnerability in development. Although the direction of development can change at any point as one proceed through the life cycle, change becomes, to some degree, limited by the pathways one has already taken.

Risk and Resilience Central to current developmental thinking is the consideration of positive development, adaptive behavior, and human resilience, as well as the belief that one must understand successful development before one can understand disordered development. Contemporary developmental theories pay particular attention to the concept of resilience. This concept gained prominence as researchers, studying the effects of psychosocial risk, noticed that people who were exposed to the same risk factors were often affected differently by them. In other words, some people developed serious problems, others were only minimally affected, and still others seemed to become stronger as a result of the experience of adversity. "Resilience is not a trait or an endpoint. Rather, it is the cumulative acquisition and expression of emotions, ideas, capacities, behaviors, motivations, understanding and resources that lead a person to be more capable of overcoming or withstanding life's adversities and ordeals" (Saleebey, in Lightburn & Sessions, 2006 p. 48). Research has identified three basic types of resilience; these include the ability to recover from trauma, demonstration of competent behavior under prolonged stress, and the achievement of positive developmental outcomes under high-risk conditions (Kirby & Fraser, 1997, p. 13).

A cornerstone of the literature on resilience is the attention paid to risk and protective factors that exist within the individual, family, community, and wider culture. Risk factors are any influences that "undermine adaptation or amplify the vulnerability of the individual" (Saleebey, 2006, p. 48). These may include inherent vulnerabilities in the individual (for example, having a developmental disability), impairments in primary group functioning (for example, being raised by an alcoholic parent), or socioeconomic and institutional factors such as chronic poverty, lack of access to health care, or quality education (Davies, 2004). The term "risk accumulation" is used to describe the effects of multiple risks—that is, risk factors become increasingly pernicious as their number increases because they operate in transaction with one another, facilitating one another's negative effects, and increasing stress and vulnerability. Situations in which risk processes operate over time and in which few protective factors exist are predictive of the most negative outcomes (Davies, 2004, p. 66).

Protective factors are those elements, whether internal or environmental, that enhance coping capacity and the ability to adapt to life stress, and that generate opportunities for growth. (Davies, 2004; Saleebey in Lightburn & Sessions, 2006). Protective factors may include such individual qualities as self-efficacy, empathy, social problem-solving skills, reality testing, temperament, intelligence, sense of humor, and so forth and/or qualities of the environment such as a cohesive, supportive, and harmonious family and access to social resources such as quality education and comprehensive health care (Garmezy, 1993 in Lightburn & Sessions, 2006, p. 48; Kirby & Fraser, 1997 in Davies, 2004). As is the case with risk factors, protective factors appear to be most effective as their number and duration increase.

Summary

We began this chapter by providing a historical overview of the social work profession and the evolution of its theory base. We have explicated a framework that can be used to integrate the material presented throughout this text. This framework rests on ecosystemic principles and is informed by postmodern paradigms that emphasize social justice, multiculturalism, world-view, strengths-based and empowerment perspectives as well as principles of developmental contextualism. It provides the foundation for a model of social work practice that allows for multilevel assessment and intervention. "It is the social work practitioner's ability to see meaningful consistencies in the data derived from multiple sources and methods, to integrate and accurately explain contradictory assessment findings in a way that allows for a meaningful description of the client that separates the clinician from the technician" (Johnson & Sheeber, 1999, p. 45). Our description of this framework sets the stage for the chapters that follow. The ideas presented in this chapter will form a thread; they will reappear in a variety of forms throughout the remainder of this book, and will serve to connect seemingly disparate issues. It will therefore be of great value to the student to periodically revisit this section for reference and clarification.

2

Neurobiological Underpinnings of Human Development

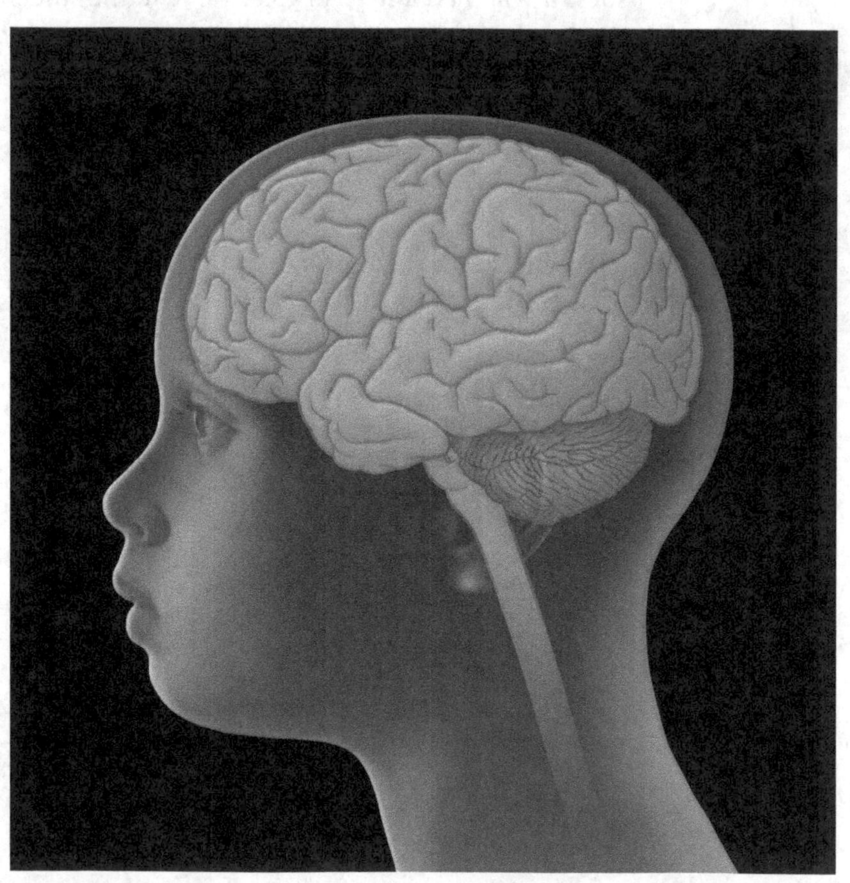

Introduction

This chapter introduces recent findings from the study of neurobiology that contribute to understanding human development and human behavior. In 1895, in *The Project for a Scientific Psychology,* Freud, who began his career as a neurologist, speculated that conscious and unconscious thought processes are reflected in the neural anatomy of the brain and nervous system. He attempted to construct a model of the mind and its neurological mechanisms by drawing interconnecting neurons to represent human emotions, behaviors, and psychological defenses. Because of the constraints of the medical climate in which he practiced, Freud shifted his focus from a neurobiological understanding of the brain to a psychological understanding of the mind (Cozolino, 2002, pp. 6–7), developing the controversial study of psychoanalysis. The field of mental health seems to have come full circle at this time, with attention being paid once again to the neurobiological origin of many disorders. The rapid advances in neurobiological knowledge since the 1980s are due to a number of reasons. The first is the technological revolution, including the evolution of brain imaging techniques that allow us to see the functions, as well as the structures, in the living brain; the development of light and electron microscopes that photograph minute structures in the brain such as neurons, synapses, and molecules; and microelectrodes that permit wiring and measuring the activity of a single neuron. These technological advances have contributed to the accumulation of evidence about neurobiological structures and functions underlying psychiatric and learning disorders. Advances in *psychopharmacology* have been able to show that specific symptoms (such as panic attacks, delusions, and compulsive rituals) respond to specific medication. Finally, mental health consumer advocacy groups are educating the public about the role of neurobiology in mental illness and mental health (Johnson, 1999). Social workers and other mental health professionals face the challenge of now weaving this information together with the influence of genetic, developmental, environmental, and cultural factors (Hyman, 1999). Social workers conduct assessments on people across the life cycle and in many different settings. It is important that we be aware of the complexity involved in accurate diagnosis and intervention. It is our belief that the neurobiological basis of the disorders described in this chapter often necessitate assessment by a number of other disciplines—psychiatry, psychology, and special education, among others—to provide appropriate diagnosis and collaborative, multidisciplinary interventions.

The Neuroanatomy of the Brain

The brain is composed of interrelated structures, each with its own function and each contributing to the whole. A brief overview of the parts and location of the brain will enable the reader to understand the relevance of the brain's anatomy for

FIGURE 2.1

Anatomy of the Brain

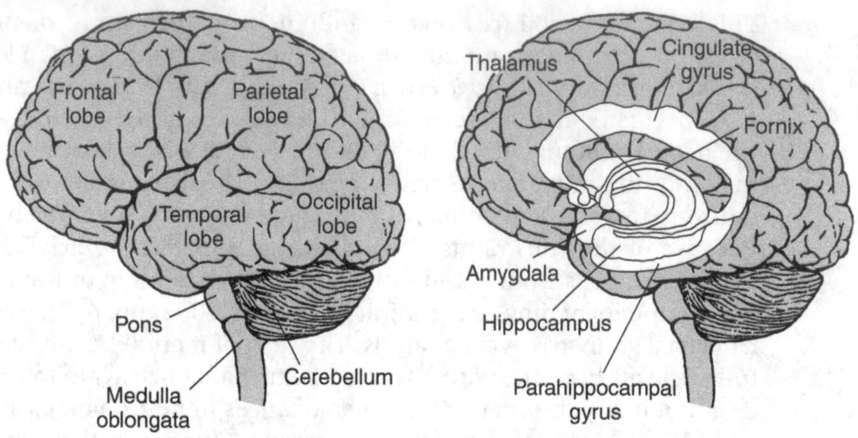

Source: Illustration provided courtesy of the American Health Assistance Foundation.

coordinated functioning. An illustration of the anatomy of the brain is depicted in Figure 2.1.

Functions of the Limbic System

The *thalamus* (a part of which is included in the limbic system) is located at the top of the brain stem and is the gateway for incoming sensory information (a relay station between the senses and the *cortex*—the outer layer of the brain consisting of the parietal, occipital, frontal, and temporal lobes). The thalamus connects to the *neocortex,* located just above the brain stem. The neocortex mediates conscious experiences such as perception, thinking, and reasoning. These, in turn, mediate the representations that constitute thought processes. The *limbic system* is a group of interrelated structures that mediates emotions, learning, and memory. The limbic system (which includes the orbitofrontal cortex, anterior cingulate, and *amygdala*) houses the *medial temporal lobe*. It is here that the *hippocampus,* considered to play a central role in consciously accessible forms of memory, is located. The *hypothalamus* and the *pituitary* are the two organs of the brain responsible for physiological homeostasis. This homeostasis is established through *neuroendocrine activity—neuronal firing* and *hormonal release*. The *hypothalamic-pituitary-adrenocortical* (*HPA neuroendocrine axis*) along with the *autonomic nervous system* and the *neuroimmune system,* link the functions of the brain and the body (Goldberg, 2001). Some of the core symptoms of depression, such as changes in appetite and sleep patterns, are related to the functions of the hypothalamus—in turn, tied to the function of the pituitary gland. Abnormalities of pituitary function, such as increased rates of circulating cortisol and *hypo-* or *hyperthyroidism* are well-established features of depression in adults.

Emotions are regulated by the limbic system in communication structures such as the *basal ganglia* and the *frontal cortex,* the thinking part of the brain. Changes in metabolic activity during development are most marked for the cortex, somewhat less so for the basal ganglia, and least evident in the limbic system (Johnson, 1999, p. 58).

A major portion of the brain is split into the left and right hemispheres. The *left hemisphere* handles verbal, conscious functions, and sequential analysis such as logical interpretation of information; interpretation and production of symbolic information; language, mathematics, abstraction, and reasoning; and memory stored in language format. The *right hemisphere* modulates emotions and is dominant for nonverbal functioning such as the processing of multisensory input, visual–spatial functions, and memory, stored in auditory, visual, and spatial modalities. These two hemispheres are connected by a band of tissue called the *corpus callosum* and the *anterior commissures,* which together transfer information between the two sides of the brain. The *cerebellum* also carries out various informational and integrating processes between the two sides of the brain (Johnson, 1999, 2002; Carter, 1999).

Functions of the Parts of the Brain

The *frontal lobes* of the brain (see Figure 2.2; Dawson & Guare, 2004, p. 3) are considered "executive functions" (Goldberg, 2001, p. 26) because they are metacognitive—they provide an organizational structure for the cognitive functions of the brain. These include memory, the ability to concentrate and attend, elaboration of thought, judgment, inhibition, personality, and emotional traits. The *orbitofrontal* region is thought to play a large role in the integrating processes of memory, emotion, and attachment. The *lateral prefrontal cortex* plays a major role in working memory and the focusing of attention (Pliszka, 2003). The executive functions of the brain will be discussed further in the section on attention deficit hyperactivity disorder in this chapter and in Chapter 11 on middle childhood, which is the time of life when executive functions develop.

How Neurons Communicate with Each Other

The brain is made up of two types of cells—neurons and neuroglia. *Neuroglia* provide the neurons with nourishment, protection, and structural support. *Neurons* are tiny cells in the brain, spinal cord, and throughout the body. They are the building blocks that carry out the brain's functions of sending and receiving nerve impulses or signals (messages), making decisions, and sending out commands. The brain has an estimated one hundred billion neurons, and they come in different sizes and shapes. Each neuron sends an electrical impulse down its axons, releasing a neurotransmitter at the space—called a *synapse*—at the end. This synapse excites or inhibits the neuron and links neurons to one another. The activity of one

FIGURE 2.2

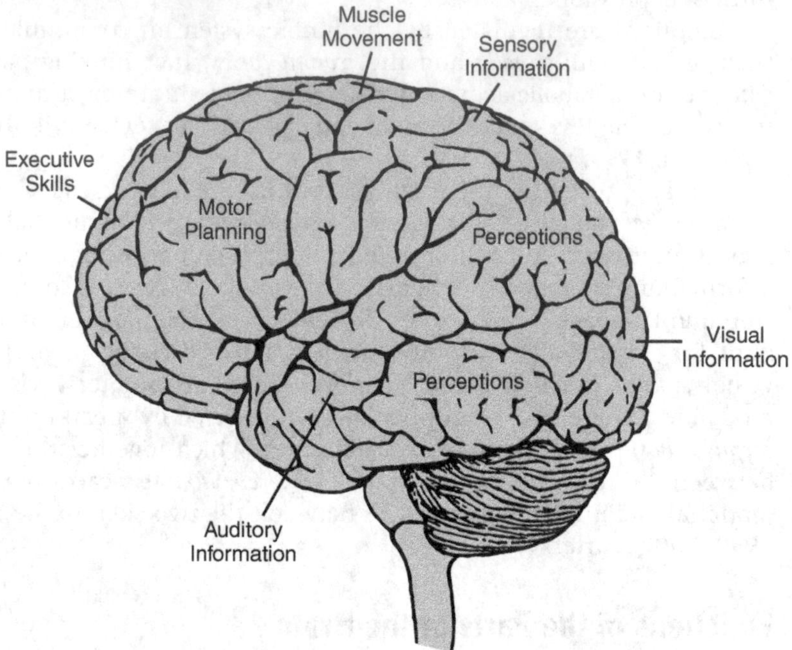

Source: P. Dawson and R. Guare, 2004, *Executive Skills in Children and Adolescents*. New York: Guilford Press. Copyright © 2004. Reprinted with permission.

neuron, therefore, can influence thousands of neurons at the receiving end, resulting in a huge variety of neuronal firing activity. *Neurotransmitters* (molecules that act as chemical messages) travel from neuron to neuron in an orderly fashion and are specifically shaped so that after they pass from a neuron into the synapse, they can be received onto certain sites, called *receptors.* Receptor sites can only receive specific types of neurotransmitters (for example, *serotonin, adrenalin,* and *noradrenaline*). These neurotransmitters communicate thoughts, feelings, and memories and can be excitatory or inhibitory. The chemical message of the neurotransmitter can be changed into an *electrical impulse* and continue on its way through the next neuron, or it may stop. In either case, the neurotransmitter releases from the receptor site and floats back into the synapse and is then removed from the synapse in one of two ways. The neurotransmitter may be broken down by a chemical called *monoamine oxidase,* or it may be taken back in by the neuron that originally released it. The latter case is called *reuptake* (Price, 2004). The speed and efficiency of brain neural processing increases gradually until midadolescence. Those synapses that are not stimulated and/or used are gradually "pruned away" throughout childhood and into adolescence. Either the depletion or excess of neurotransmitters can result in neurological or psychiatric disorders (Huttenlocker & Dabholkar, 1997, cited in Davies, 2004, p. 42; Carter, 1999, p. 21).

The Mindful Brain

"Experience" for the nervous system involves the activation of neural firing in response to a stimulus. Neurons fire when we have an experience, and experience can create structural changes in the brain, a process called neuroplasticity. Mindful awareness is a form of experience that seems to promote neural plasticity. Focusing attention in specific ways activates the brain's circuitry, which in turn strengthens the synaptic linkages in those areas (Siegel, 2007, pp. 30–31). By introducing thc notion that "mindfulness, as a form of relationship with yourself, may involve not just attentional circuits but also social circuitry, we can then explore new dimensions of the brain aspect of our mindful experience"(Siegel, 2007, p. 31). The neural structures of the social brain include the amygdala, the anterior cingulate, the orbitofrontal areas of the prefrontal cortex (Ofc), and the frontal portion of the temporal lobes. The Ofc, considered to be the apex of the limbic system, is positioned as a convergence zone for polysensory and emotional information, mediating information concerning our internal and external worlds. It also has an inhibitory role in autonomic functioning, contributing to the organization of higher-order behavior and affect regulation (Siegel, 2006, p. 31; Cozolino, 2002, p. 182). The amygdala working in concert with the Ofc is also a core component of the social brain in humans. Damage to the amygdala creates problems in many areas of social functioning, for example, reading emotional expressions and estimating the trustworthiness of other people. The amygdala has a direct connection with the autonomic nervous system and is able to communicate messages related to fight and flight (Cozolino, 2002, p. 181) The Ofc and the amygdala are key components of the neurology of attachment and fear.

Cozolino writes:

> The architecture of the social brain contains our implicit and procedural memories of our early interpersonal learning history. It is within this neural system that early interpersonal experiences are organized into schemas for attachment. Attachment schemas are implicit procedure memories reflecting sensory, motor, affective, and cognitive memories of caretaking experiences. These memory networks become evoked in subsequent interpersonal experiences throughout life. (p. 183)

The organization of attachment patterns and the regulation of emotions are behaviorally associated because they are two ways of understanding the same process. Attachment is at its primitive, biological core, a means of survival and hence a means of controlling anxiety (Cozolino, 2002, p. 182).

For further discussion of neurobiological development, see Chapter 9, "Infancy," and Chapter 10, "Early Childhood."

Experiences and Gene Expression

Experiences activate specific neural pathways. A pathway is a bundle of interconnecting neurons that performs specific tasks. Transmission paths for different neurotransmitters extend throughout the brain. Examples are *dopamine* and *neurotonin* pathways. Experiences also directly shape *gene expression* and lead to the creation and maintenance of the connections that form the *neural substrate* of the mind—the specialized circuits that give rise to *mental processes. The development of the brain is therefore dependent on experiences.* "The brain is both 'experience-dependent' and 'use-dependent'" (Davies, 2004, p. 39). Consider, for example, that an infant is born with a genetically programmed number of neurons. *Genes* contain the information for the organization of the brain's structure; however, *experience* determines which genes become expressed, how they become expressed, and when they become expressed. Repeated experiences become encoded in implicit memory as mental models of attachment. The infant thus plays a part in shaping the experiences to which the child's brain adapts, leaving the mark of experience in its structure. Siegel (1999) calls this process "interpersonal neurobiology," proposing that the mind develops "at the interface of neurophysiologic processes and interpersonal relationships" (p. 21). He proposed that relationship experiences have a dominant influence on the brain because the circuits responsible for social perception are tightly linked to those that integrate the important functions controlling the creation of meaning, the regulation of body states, the modulation of emotion, the organization of memory, and the capacity for interpersonal communication. This expression of genes (in combination with the infant's interpersonal and environmental experiences) leads to the production of proteins that activate certain pathways in the brain, strengthening existing connections and creating new ones. The infant is consequently both a participant in and an activator of the dialogue with the caretaker, not simply a recipient. *Experience, gene expression, mental activity, behavior,* and *continued interactions with the environment* are linked, making *nature and nurture* inextricably bound. For further discussion of the roles of gene expression and experience, see Chapter 9, "Infancy."

Neurobehavioral Disorders

The following section discusses a number of disorders that suggest a linkage between brain dysfunction and the particular behavioral manifestations of each of the conditions. The assessment and developmental mapping of these disorders is complex and does not proceed in a linear fashion. Werner (1957) proposed a developmental perspective known as "developmental multi uniformity," suggesting that similar developmental achievements can actually be reached through different developmental paths, and different paths can also lead to similar maladaptive outcomes. The "developmental-pathways" model posits that (a) the earlier a change is seen in environmental circumstances, the shorter the time a particular pathway remains established; and (b) the more sustained the forces of change, the more permanent the change will be (Stroufe, 1997). This model of developmental uniformity stands in contrast to the classification system in the *Diagnostic and Statistical Manual of Mental Disorders* (*DSM-IV;* American Psychiatric Association [APA], 2000), which classifies disorders on the basis of symptoms. The *DSM-IV,* although of enormous importance, does not allow for the fact that,

TABLE 2.1

Neurobehavioral Disorders

1. Learning Disorders
   a. Learning Disabilities
      1. Language-based learning disabilities
      2. Problems in language reception
         a. Dyslexia
         b. Central auditory processing problem
         c. Expressive language problems
   b. ADHD
   c. Executive function disorders
   d. Nonverbal learning disabilities
   e. Asperger's disorder
   f. Motor problems
2. Brain-based disorders
   a. Autism
   b. Mental retardation
   c. Tourette's syndrome
   d. Genetic disorders
   e. Diorders from head injuries

Source: From *Learning Disorders and Disorders of the Self in Children and Adolescents* by Joseph Palombo. Copyright © 2001 by Joseph Palombo. Used by permission of W.W. Norton & Company, Inc.

as Werner suggested, different underlying developmental processes may have contributed to similar emotional or behavioral problems. Neurobehavioral disorders (adapted from Palombo's 2001 [pp. 13–14] model of classification) are listed in Table 2.1.

Briefly summarized, the neurobehavioral disorders constitute the largest category. These disorders include learning disorders, learning disabilities, and disorders such as autism, mental retardation, Tourette's syndrome, and conditions resulting from acquired brain changes due to strokes, lesions, and closed head injuries. *Learning disorders,* a subset of neurobehavioral disorders, include language-based learning disabilities, ADHD/attention deficit disorder (ADD), executive function disorders, nonverbal learning disabilities, Asperger's disorder, and motor problems that involve difficulties with large and small muscle coordination. *Learning disabilities,* a subset of learning disorders, would include language-based learning disabilities, language-reception problems such as *dyslexia* and central auditory processing difficulties, and expressive language problems (verbal or written expression). Table 2.1 is not intended to be a comprehensive account of all such disorders. We refer the reader to *DSM-IV* (APA, 2000) for subcategories and specific criteria for each of the disorders.

The following section offers a description of a select number of the neurobehavioral disorders and case examples that illustrate the complexity of diagnosing and treating these conditions in clinical practice.

Autism Spectrum Disorders

Autism spectrum disorders are also known as pervasive developmental disorders (PDD), a category designated by the APA (2000) to indicate children with delay or deviance in their social, language, motor, and/or cognitive development (Volkmar, 2007). Pervasive developmental disorder encompasses a wide range of delays of different magnitude in different domains. Autism is the most severe; other pervasive developmental disorders include Rett syndrome and childhood disintegrative disorder, also known as Heller's syndrome. Autism involves major deficits in language and social communication skills. These include difficulty imitating the behavior of others, a limited range of emotional expressions, difficulties in social bonding and social communication, unusual speech patterns, repetitive body movements, difficulty with changes in routine, and unusual responses to auditory and tactile sensations (Carter, 1999). Contemporary theories on the etiology of autism posit that this is primarily a genetic disorder associated with organic or brain damage and genetic predispositions. There is, for example, a much greater concordance in identical than in fraternal twins. The search for genes that predispose to autism is actually a high research priority for the National Institute of Mental Health. There is also evidence that several different causes of toxic or infectious damage to the central nervous system during early development may also contribute to autism, such as congenital rubella or German measles. There is a wide range of variability in children diagnosed with autism. For example, between 40% to 50% of children diagnosed with autism do not speak; others have limited language that includes repetitive phrases, and other children may have a small, restricted range of conversation topics. The challenging behaviors associated with autism, such as head banging and aggression, are now thought to be adaptations for the lack of verbal communication skills.

Although some children may show autistic patterns of social interaction almost from birth, it is difficult to make a definitive diagnosis of autism before age 3. This is due to the variable rates of development in infants and young children. For example, many young children are late to begin speaking.

Ten to 15% of otherwise normal children do not reach language milestones at the expected time; therefore, not talking at the developmentally "normal" time does not necessarily mean that a child has autism. Other signs that may indicate autism would include the child's continual failure to respond to his or her own name, difficulty making eye contact with others at appropriate times, and an obsessive interest in unusual objects or activities. Although autism has no cure, early diagnosis and intensive early intervention are necessary to prevent autism from becoming more severe as the child develops. Children with autism

PRACTICE EXAMPLE 2.1

Jenny

Jenny is an 8-year-old girl diagnosed with autism, who was referred for counseling by the school nurse following numerous incidents in which she became ill in school and vomited. After each of these episodes, the nurse contacted the child's parents, who were then expected to take the child home from school. At the time of referral, the nurse, school officials, and parents were all experiencing a sense of frustration and despair—the parents felt that the child should not leave the school every time this occurred, and the school (personnel) felt that the child was ill and the parents might even be considered neglectful. Visits to the child's pediatrician did not show any evidence of physical illness. The social worker assigned to this case recognized that the child's throwing up could be a reaction to the school environment. After several meetings with the child, the child's parents, and the teachers, it became apparent that this child was being overstimulated in the school environment—she was primarily educated in a contained classroom but was mainstreamed for certain activities such as gym, music, and art. The child did not have the verbal means to express her feelings of insecurity and fear around these changes but instead became ill. A decision was made that the current schedule was not benefiting Jenny, and it was revised so that she did not have to attend activities outside the contained classroom. Jenny was eventually transferred to a special school for children with autism.

are eligible for special education services under the Individuals with Disabilities and Education Act (IDEA; see Chapter 18 for further discussion of this federal legislation). An intervention program must be individualized, and have a strong communication component, systematic structured teaching, some contact with typical peers, intensity of engagement (a minimum of 20 hours per week), some naturalistic activities ("downtime"), and family involvement (Asperger, 1991; Bondy & Frost, 2002; Cohen & Volkmar, 1997; Durand & Mapstone, 1999; Green & Luce, 1996; Mesibov, Shea, & Adams, 2001; Powers, 2000; Yale Developmental Disabilities Clinic, 2005; see also, Chapter 10, "Early Childhood"). See Practice Example 2.1: Jenny.

Attention Deficit Hyperactivity Disorder

ADHD and ADD are spectrum disorders. This means that it often includes comorbidity with other conditions (more than one disorder occurring simultaneously), such as mood disorders, anxiety disorders, oppositional disorders, learning disorders, and executive function disorders (Barkley, 1998, 2000; Brown et al., 2001; Brown, 2000a, 2000b; Ellenberg, 1999; Palombo, 2001). As a spectrum disorder, the symptoms of ADHD/ADD can also show considerable variation. The *DSM-IV* (2000) breaks ADHD into three subtypes: ADHD combined type, ADHD predominantly inattentive type, and ADHD predominantly hyperactive-impulsive type. Inattention or attention deficit may not become apparent until a child enters the challenging environment of elementary school. Hyperactive children often behave in an inappropriate and uninhibited way, such as not waiting their turn, blurting out answers, and interrupting or intruding on others' conversations (Waslick & Greenhill, 2003).

Imaging studies show that the brains of children with this condition have a marked lack of activity in several right hemisphere regions. These include the *anterior cingulate*—the area associated with fixing attention on a given stimulus—and the *prefrontal cortex,* the area concerned with controlling impulses and planning actions. An area in the *upper auditory cortex*—the region of the brain thought to be concerned with integrating stimuli from several sources—was found to be hypoactive as well. All these factors may contribute to fragmentation, with different stimuli catching the individual's attention and resulting in an inability to grasp the whole picture (Carter, 1999, p. 185).

Russell Barkley (1998, 2000) has made perhaps the most significant contributions to the study of ADHD/ADD. His research shows that ADHD/ADD involves deficits in *disinhibition* and executive functions. Put another way, the delay in inhibition contributes to secondary deficits in the executive functions of working memory, internalization of speech, self-regulation of affect, motivation and arousal, and reconstitution. *Working memory* is the ability to keep events in mind while attending to a particular task (for example, copying instructions from the blackboard to the page). *Internalization of speech* involves reflection, reading comprehension, and moral reasoning (for example, thinking before speaking). *Self-regulation* involves the regulation of affect stages and motivation in completing a task (for example, doing homework without frustration); *reconstitution* involves the kind of analysis and synthesis related to the task at hand (understanding and organizing to make sense of what one is doing; Palombo, 2001, p. 148). Please refer to Figure 2.3 for Barkley's model of executive functions. It is important to note that the symptoms of inattention and overactivity associated with ADHD may also be caused by early trauma and deprivation (Barkley, 2003; Kreppner, O'Connor, & Rutter, 2001).

Levy (2008) revisits the original theory of motivational deficit with an intervention he terms "Acknowledgments." He suggests that if the child with ADHD has a decreased sensitivity to rewards and negative consequences, they need to be increased to have an impact on the child's behavior. The idea is to give the child positive acknowledgement for even low-level positive behaviors, reinforcing the ADHD child's "connection to the adult, not their connection to a specific reward" (p 16). The aim is to improve the child's behavior based on improving their relationship with the important adult(s) in their lives. Once the child's relationship and behavior have improved, negative consequences can be used to increase motivation. Finally, this approach has a skill-building phase with exercises that help the child, for example, do their homework when they would rather play a video game. The child is taught to talk herself through misperceptions she may have about how long it will actually take to do the homework.

ADHD/ADD runs in families, and possibly 80% of traits such as inattentiveness, impulsivity, and hyperactivity are the result of genetic factors. For example, if a parent has ADHD/ADD, a child has more than a 50% chance of also having this condition. Siblings have a 32% risk, and identical twins are both more likely to have the disorder than fraternal twins. ADHD/ADD occurs more frequently in

FIGURE 2.3

Model of Executive Functions

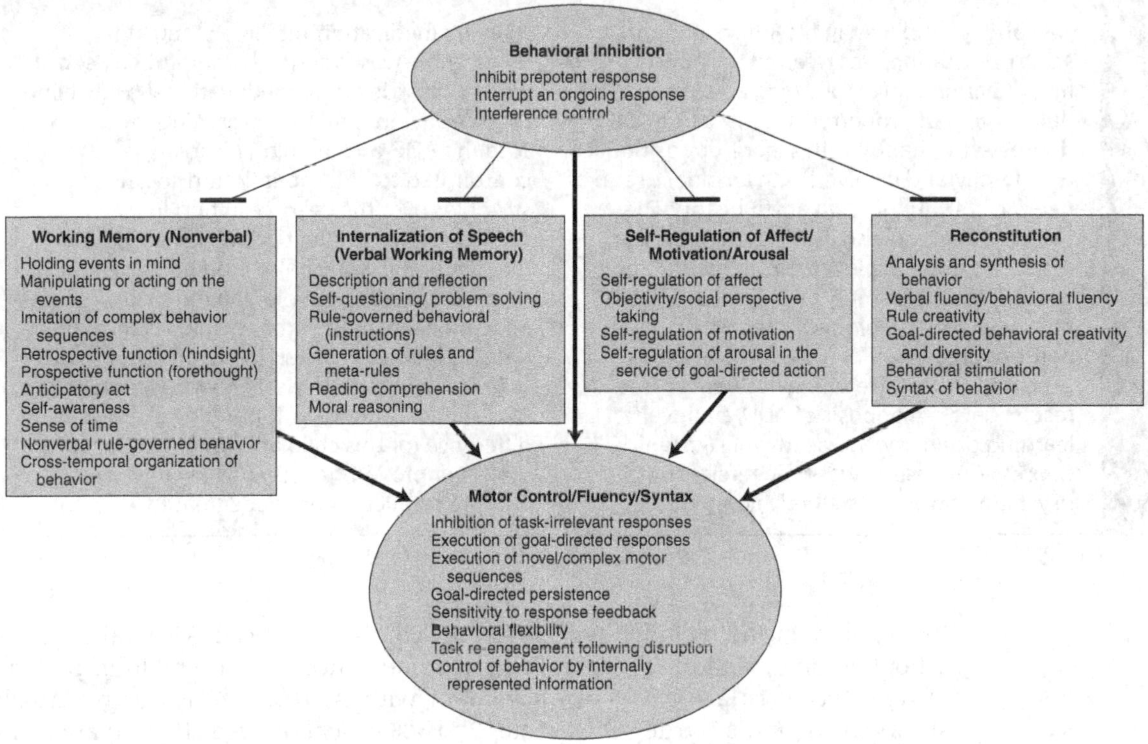

Source: Adapted from R. A. Barkley, 1997, *ADHD and the Nature of Self-Control* (p. 191), New York: Guilford Press.

males than females and occurs in various cultures. ADHD/ADD affects approximately 35% of school-age children who are often incorrectly diagnosed with conditions such as oppositional defiant disorder and conduct disorder. These secondary disorders (as well as substance-abuse-related disorders and antisocial personality disorders) can develop in adolescents with incorrectly diagnosed or untreated ADHD. See Practice Example 2.2: Joseph (Brown 2000a; 2000b; Tannock & Brown, 2000).

Children like Joseph have difficulty with siblings and with peers and often appear unhappy or discontent. The latter may be due in part to the child's feeling that he or she is misunderstood as well as difficulty understanding the motives of others. This may include experiencing parents as punitive or controlling when limits are set. Children with ADD/ADHD are at risk for problems with self-esteem and depression because they are often not introspective about how their behaviors may lead to negative consequences from interactions with others. A comprehensive assessment is essential to determine the range of interventions that may

PRACTICE EXAMPLE 2.2

Joseph

Joseph, a young man in his 8th year of public school education, was referred to counseling by his probation officer following an arrest for defacement of property. Joseph was clinically depressed, unhappy with school, oppositional with family, and involved with an older group of peers, each with his own arrest history. The clinical screening also indicated a history of academic underachievement. In consultation with the child's primary care physician (PCP), the social worker referred Joseph to a neuropsychologist for a comprehensive psychological and learning evaluation. Test results gave a diagnosis of ADD, a nonverbal learning disability, and dysthymia (chronic depression). Joseph was then referred to a psychiatrist who prescribed and monitored Joseph's medication. Ritalin, a stimulant medication, was found to be helpful. The social worker provided psychoeducational counseling for Joseph and his family regarding how Joseph's ADD and learning disability contributed to his academic and social struggles over the years, resulting in depression. In conjunction with the psychologist, the social worker also worked closely with Joseph's school to develop an individual educational plan (IEP) that would accommodate his learning needs. Finally, ongoing social skills training and counseling were provided for Joseph. These interventions made an enormous difference for this child and his family. Joseph's grades improved, he found a new peer group, and the conflicts at home decreased.

be required, including individual and family counseling, social skills training, and school accommodation. There have been some concerns that children, particularly active boys, are being overdiagnosed with ADHD. The research actually shows the opposite is true—fewer than 2 to 3% of school-aged children are being treated for ADHD than actually suffer from it. Treatment rates are much lower for selected groups such as girls, minorities, and children receiving care through the public school systems (Brown, 2000a; 2000b; Tannock & Brown, 2000). For a further discussion of this disorder, see Chapter 10, "Early Childhood."

ADHD in Adults Barkley, Murphy, and Fischer (2008, p 25) wrote, "Clinicians should appreciate that ADHD is now a recognized and scientifically validated disorder in adults and has been so for at least 15 to 30 years . . ." The current diagnostic criteria for ADHD is included in the *DSM–IV-TR* (American Psychiatric Association, 2000), making an accurate diagnosis difficult for a number of reasons. Many adults have adopted lifestyles that minimize self-reported dysfunction across the multiple domains listed in the criteria for diagnosis. For example, adults may no longer attend school or may be working in jobs that minimize the challenges ADHD presents in the workplace. The subtyping approach recommended for children does not account for the developmental trajectory of the two different lists of symptoms; for example hyperactive symptoms decline earlier than the inattentive symptoms (pp. 38–39) The major difficulties faced by adults with ADHD include impulsive decision making, stopping, starting, and organizing activities, persistence toward goals, and planning for future events (p. 204).

Asperger's Disorder

Asperger's disorder is marked by restricted repetitive and stereotyped patterns of behavior and activities, persistent preoccupation with parts of objects, and social impairment in the areas of social communication and social reciprocity. These behaviors may translate as self-interest and inability to appreciate the interests of others. Children with Asperger's disorder often lack the capacity for nonverbal communication and are deficient in pragmatic language communication, although there is generally less impairment in cognitive functioning. They often do not follow rules; however, this "noncompliant behavior" is due to a lack of understanding of social conformity, rather than trying to be oppositional. The children who suffer from this condition are often ostracized by other children, but may lack the ability to understand that their behavior is problematic. Children with Asperger's disorder are often overstimulated, have exaggerated expressions of feelings, and may have tantrums beyond the age when these should cease. Attempts to cope with these deficits may result in regressed behaviors and excessive dependency in order to alleviate anxiety. Recommended interventions include occupational therapy, speech therapy, social skills training, and academic supports, particularly if a child has both Asperger's disorder and a learning disability (Durand & Mapstone, 1999; Klin, Folkmar, & Sparrow, 2000; Klin & Volkmar, 1997; Schopler & Mesibov, 2001). See Practice Example 2.3: Susan.

Dyslexia

Dyslexia is a phonological processing disorder that involves a specific neuropsychological deficit or brain dysfunction (Shaywitz, 1998, 2003). Dyslexia is not caused by impoverished educational conditions or parental or social neglect,

PRACTICE EXAMPLE 2.3

Susan

Susan is a 9-year-old girl in fourth grade. She began counseling because she was not "making friends." Susan, a kind-hearted child, had difficulty interacting with other children, but instead tried to get them to "do things the way I like to do them." She was also ostracized by the children in her class because they felt that she "was bad" because she didn't listen to the teacher. Susan also repeated herself quite frequently, appeared to be unaware that she was doing this, and became angry when anyone pointed it out to her. She also engaged in repetitive behaviors such as picking lint off the carpet and became very anxious and upset, even to the point of throwing tantrums, when things were not going her way. Neuropsychological testing indicated a diagnosis of Asperger's disorder, and recommended interventions included individual counseling (play therapy) and a social skills group for Susan; psychoeducational counseling for Susan's parents along with the development of a behavior management plan at home; implementation of a behavior management plan for the school classroom; and referral to a speech therapist to enable Susan to develop greater verbal fluency.

although remediation may be seriously compromised by these factors. This disorder is first noticed when children begin to read, and it is marked by difficulty identifying letters and recognizing and sounding out words (decoding), as well as writing and spelling (encoding). The incidence of dyslexia is the same in males and females. Although studies have found the brain mechanism involved in dyslexia to be universal, an irregular language—such as English—may more adversely affect dyslexia (Shaywitz, 1998, p. 254). Although learning to read in English may be a challenge to all children diagnosed with dyslexia, particular consideration may need to be extended to bilingual children, whose primary language may not be English and where English language skills may not be reinforced in the home. Certain medications can be helpful in treating dyslexia if a child also has ADHD/ADD, but otherwise treatment focuses on direct remediation of the deficits in phonological processing through school-based academic interventions (National Center for Learning Disabilities, 1994).

Children with dyslexia are at risk for self-esteem problems, particularly if they do not have an understanding of the learning problems they are struggling with in the school environment. Improvements in feelings of self-esteem generally occur when these children "can function adequately academically, have experienced real-life successes, and have developed a good understanding of the reading disability" (Palombo, 2001, p. 134). Social workers, school adjustment counselors, and other specialists working with this population need to ensure that psychoeducation regarding the learning disability occurs at different stages of the child's academic and social development (Elbaum & Vaughn, 2003). Dudley-Marling (2004) lends a social constructivist perspective to learning disabilities such as dyslexia. Educators and counselors working from this orientation would "begin by assessing the various factors that makes up the social context in which students' learning identities are constructed so they might contemplate moves that might disrupt the performance of a learning problem" (pp. 488–489). This approach is not intended to replace appropriate instructional support, but underscores the fact that students identified as learning disabled are constructed as part of the interactional mix in which learning disabilities are performed—"on the stage we call school" (p. 489). (For further information on dyslexia and other learning disabilities, please see Swanson, Harris, & Graham, 2003.)

Mental Retardation

The diagnosis of mental retardation is based on *intelligence quotient (IQ) tests* and a child's learning problems. The current definition of mental retardation in the *DSM-IV* (APA, 2000) includes the following criteria: the individual must have significant subaverage intellectual functioning as defined by an intelligence score of 70 or below; the individual must also have significant deficits in adaptive functioning that are present before the age of 18. Mental retardation can be further categorized in the following way: mild retardation (IQs range from 50–55 to 70–75), moderate retardation (IQs range from 35–40 to 50–55), severe retardation (IQs range from 20–25 to 35–40), and profound retardation (IQs are below 20–25). The American Association on Mental Retardation (AAMR, 2002) has made some changes to this definition, raising the intelligence cutoff from 70 to 75. The AAMR process for the diagnosis of mental retardation includes three steps: (a) a standardized intelligence test and a standardized adaptive skills test; (b) a description of the individual's strengths and weaknesses in the areas of intellectual and adaptive skills, physical health, psychological well-being, and environmental considerations; and (c) the determination of needed supports across four levels of intensity (intermittent, limited, extensive, and pervasive). The diagnosis of mental retardation, therefore, rests on IQ tests and a child's learning problems.

Mental retardation can be caused by genetics, problems during pregnancy (for example, malnutrition or use of drugs or alcohol by mother), problems at birth (such as prematurity), or problems after birth (head injury, childhood diseases). Environmental conditions such as poverty and racial discrimination, which can result in inadequate medical attention, educational and sociocultural deprivation, and disease-producing conditions (exposure to lead paint, for example) can also contribute to mental retardation. Individuals with mental retardation frequently, if not always, have deficits in motor, speech, and developmental milestones. There is a high incidence of behavior problems in this population, possibly attributable to deficits in memory, impulse control, speech, self-help skills, and social skills (Alexander, 1998; Baker et al., 2004; Borthwick-Duffy, 1994; Matson & Smiroldo, 1999).

The majority of persons with mental retardation are in the mild range of intellectual impairment and may only be a little slower than average in learning new information and skills. Although they struggle academically, as adults these individuals are often able to lead fairly independent lives. Nonetheless, they may need additional family and community supports. See Practice Example 2.4: Jamie.

This brief case study illustrates that with appropriate intervention, individuals such as Jamie can lead productive and fulfilling lives in the community. (For

PRACTICE EXAMPLE 2.4

Jamie

Jamie, a young woman in her early 30s *is one such individual.* Jamie lives alone and works on an assembly line in a small factory. She entered therapy with mild clinical depression, reactive to what she described as problems with her current boyfriend. A clinical interview indicated history of academic and social problems. Jamie referred to herself as being "slow to learn" and was in special education classes, which she still felt ashamed of. Testing revealed an IQ of 70. Jamie was clearly being taken advantage of in her relationship by a boyfriend, who often called her "stupid." The situation became more complicated and problematic when Jamie became pregnant and gave birth to a baby boy. She was a wonderful, loving mother, but she clearly needed assistance with understanding the developmental needs of her child. With supportive and psychoeducational counseling and the assistance of her family, Jamie was able to understand some of her limitations and to appreciate her strengths (motivation to do well, perseverance, attachment to her son, etc.). She began to set limits with her son's father and took him to court for child support (something she had been afraid to do, based on her lack of understanding and fear that he would "take her son away").

further information on mental retardation, contact the American Association on Mental Retardation at www.aamr.org.)

The Mood Disorders

Another group of neurobiologically based disorders—the mood disorders—are presented in Table 2.2. We again present an overview of a select number of these conditions and illustrate with case examples. We refer our readers to the *DSM-IV* (APA, 2000) for a complete description of each of these conditions.

Depression

Depression can range from mild to severe and may result from a combination of factors. Some of these include, but may not be limited to, family history, trauma, serious medical conditions (for example, cancer, HIV, and heart disease), medications

TABLE 2.2

Mood Disorders

1. Mood Disorders
    a. Depressive disorders
        1. Major depressive disorder, single episode
        2. Major depressive disorder, recurrent
        3. Dysthymic disorder
    b. Bipolar disorders
        1. Bipolar I disorder
        2. Bipolar II disorder
        3. Cyclothymic disorder
    c. Anxiety Disorders
        1. Panic disorder without agoraphobia
        2. Panic disorder with agoraphobia
        3. Specific phobia
        4. Social anxiety disorder
        5. Obsessive compulsive disorder
        6. Generalized anxiety disorder
        7. Acute stress disorder
        8. Posttraumatic stress disorder

Source: Adapted from *Diagnostic and Statistical Manual of Mental Disorders*, 2000. Arlington, VA: American Psychiatric Association.

used to treat these diseases, discrimination and oppression, poverty, childbirth, and the death of a close relative or friend (Moore & Garland, 2000; Persons, Davidson, & Tomkins, 2001). Severe depression appears to be a universal cultural phenomenon, found among all societies all over the world (Kleinman & Good, 1985). Mild depression, however, may be seen differently within distinct cultural contexts. For example, in Japan, where Buddhism is the majority religion, acceptance of sadness is valued over the pursuit of happiness. Mild depression, therefore, has not historically been viewed as a disease in Japanese society (Schulz, 2004). Many individuals with major depressive disorder may also have another mental disorder. The most commonly associated disorders are dysthymia (chronic, milder form of depression), an anxiety disorder, a disruptive or antisocial disorder (especially in adolescents), or a substance abuse disorder. When more than one diagnosis is present, depression is more likely to begin after the onset of the accompanying disorder, except when the disorder is substance abuse. In other words, depression may arise in response to an associated disorder. Before puberty, major depressive disorder and dysthymic disorder are equally common in boys and girls; however, after age 15, depression is twice as common in girls and women as in boys and men and remains that way throughout adulthood (Linehan, 1993). Children who become depressed before puberty are at risk for another episode of depression during adolescence and for some form of mental disorder in adulthood.

Depression is more than a mood. Some of the symptoms of depression (depending on its severity) are feelings of sadness; irritability and tension; fatigue; significant and often rapid weight loss or weight gain; sleep disturbance, such as difficulty sleeping, staying asleep, or sleeping too much; decreased ability to concentrate and make decisions; compromised judgment; decreased interest in activities or special interests; feelings of worthless, helplessness, and guilt; and thoughts of suicide or death (Carter, 1999; Clark, Beck, & Alford, 1999; National Foundation for Depressive Illness, n.d. ; Papageorgiou & Wells, 2003; Smith Reine, 2004).

Suicide can be a serious by-product of depression, and threats of suicide, especially by adolescents, should always be taken seriously. It is important to note that although depression is higher among adolescent girls than boys, boys between the ages of 15 to 19 are twice as likely to *commit* suicide as girls. Adolescent girls in this same age group are twice as likely to *attempt* suicide as boys. Other high-risk groups are people above the age of 75, psychiatric patients, and individuals with serious and/or chronic physical illness. There is currently a debate over the risk of suicide following the use of certain antidepressant medications for children and adolescents. (See Cooper & Lesser, 2005; Rudd, Joiner, & Rajab, 2001; and Shea, 1998 for further discussion of suicide, including guidelines for assessing suicide, providing safety, and coping strategies for practitioners.)

Depression is related to physical changes in the brain and connected to an imbalance of a type of chemical—*neurotransmitters*—that carries signals in the brain and nerves. The three neurotransmitters found to be important in depression are *norepinephrine, dopamine,* and *serotonin,* with dopamine increasingly seen as the major neurotransmitter related to depression. The pathways for these different neurotransmitters are called the catecholamines. These *catecholamines* go into the many parts of the brain (such as the limbic system and the hypothalamus), which control functions such as mood. In depression, these areas of the brain do not work effectively.

One catecholamine starts in the midbrain (ventral tegmental nucleus) that is packed with dopamine-producing cells. Another catecholamine goes to an area in the brain stem called the *locus noradrenaline.* And still another catecholamine goes into the limbic system and then on through to the olfactory bulb. A branch of this path travels up the frontal lobes, which is the cortical area concerned with emotion. The various pathways meet, intersect, and merge; therefore, overactivity in one path is likely to affect another. Too little dopamine in this region of the brain is thought to be one cause of depression. Too much dopamine is thought to be a factor in mania (see next section on bipolar disorder). *Dopaminergic cells* travel along another pathway from a nucleus in the brain stem called the *substantia nigra* to the basal ganglia. This is a cluster of nuclei that includes the *putamen* and the *caudate nucleur* (the *striatum*) that control tic movement. The basal ganglia are connected by dopamine pathways to various cortical areas. The putamen is mainly connected to the *premotor* and *motor cortex.* Overactivity in this pathway is thought to account for the tics in Tourette's syndrome (Carter, 1999, p. 67; Johnson & Leahy, 2004).

It is believed that antidepressant medications are helpful in relieving depression in some people because they regulate the amount of specific neurotransmitters in the brain. For example, many people who are depressed have low levels of the neurotransmitter norepinephrine. Some antidepressants can increase the level of norepinephrine in the brain and relieve depressive symptoms. However, there is not necessarily a direct causal link between the level of a neurotransmitter in the brain and depression because antidepressant medications do not work for everyone and also because it generally takes awhile (about 2 to 3 weeks in most cases) for the effects of the antidepressant to manifest a behavioral change (Price, 2004).

Communication in the brain slows down when messages cannot easily get across synaptic gaps (which can happen when neurotransmitters are at abnormally low levels). Antidepressant medications are often effective because they regulate the amount of specific neurotransmitters in the brain. What remains unclear, however, is the exact nature of the link between the level of a neurotransmitter in the brain and depression (again, because antidepressant medications do not work for everyone).

Hormonal irregularities may also contribute to the development of depression. A second area of depression research focuses on the *endocrine system,* which creates *hormones* and releases them into the blood. It is believed that problems with hormone levels may be intertwined with the changes in brain chemistry through the hypothalamus. The *hypothalamus* manages the endocrine system and therefore uses some of the neurotransmitters associated with depression. The hypothalamus not only controls bodily activities such as sleep, appetite, and sexual drive, but it also regulates the *pituitary gland,* which in turn controls the hormonal secretion of other glands. Serotonin, norepinephrine, and dopamine all have roles in the management of hormone function.

There are environmental causes of depression that are not related to brain function or inherited traits. There is a complex relationship among stressful situations, the mind and body's reaction to stress and the onset of clinical depression. For those who struggle with chronic stress, a single difficult event is more likely to trigger a depressive episode. For those who struggle with chronic depression, the effects of stress may be more complicated. Researchers have presented an explanation called the "kindling effect" or "kindling-sensitization hypothesis." This theory supposes that initial depressive episodes spark changes in the brain's chemistry or limbic system that make it more prone to developing future episodes of depression (All About Depression, 2008).

Treatment of depression can include a range and combination of interventions, including medication, talk therapy, exercise, and prayer. The types of talk therapy or psychotherapy include psychodynamic, interpersonal, cognitive behavioral, and group therapy. Beck (1963) developed a highly researched and evidence-based model of treatment for depression called *cognitive therapy.* He hypothesized that a depressed person has a cognitive triad of negative thinking about the self, the world, and the future. Beck felt that motivational, behavioral, and physical symptoms of depression stem from these cognitive patterns—a mind-set or approach to perceiving external situations that readily assumes personal blame for events. Treatment focused on challenging the negative thinking and initiating activity that reduces inertia and fatigue contributes to recovery (see Chapter 3 for a fuller discussion of cognitive therapy). Community-based self-help groups (see Chapter 6 on group work) also benefit many individuals who suffer from depression.

Bipolar Disorder

Bipolar disorder (also referred to as *manic-depressive disorder*) is a complex mood disorder distinguished by episodes that range from extreme highs (manic episodes) to serious lows (depressive episodes) with periods of mood stability in between. Manic episodes may include feelings of restlessness, racing thoughts, rapid speech, decreased need for sleep, euphoria, agitation, grandiosity, pursuit of reckless or pleasurable activities, and distractibility. There may also be episodes of *hypomania,* which involve almost all the characteristics of mania but without the intensity. Hypomania is often the first indication of a manic episode and should be monitored carefully. Depressive episodes involve insomnia or hypersomnia, irritability and agitation, loss of appetite and weight loss or weight gain, chronic pain, fatigue, hopelessness, and recurrent thoughts of death or suicide. There are several types of bipolar disorder. Bipolar I is the most severe and involves long bouts of depression and mania or mixed episodes. Bipolar II disorder is characterized by hypomanic and depressive episodes. *Cyclothymia* includes irregular, short cycles of depression and hypomania. (Refer to the *DSM-IV* for further elaboration on bipolar disorder and its various subcategories and symptoms.) Bipolar disorder is most likely inherited, and although the precise cause is not known, there may be an inborn vulnerability to the disorder, probably caused by biochemical instability in the transmission of nerve impulses in the brain interacting with an environmental trigger (in other words, trauma, substance abuse, etc.). Psychological explanations alone clearly do not provide the rationale for the behavioral manifestations of bipolar disorder. Although previously thought to begin in late adolescence or early adulthood, it is now understood that bipolar disorder can be early onset (prior to 18 years of age) or very early onset (prior to 13 years of age). This condition overlaps with other disorders of childhood, including, but not limited to, generalized anxiety disorder, depression, Tourette's syndrome, and most notably, ADHD, making accurate diagnosis difficult (Biederman et al., 2000; Carlson, 2002; McClellan & Werry, 1997).

Some of the symptoms of early onset bipolar disorder include separation anxiety, rages and temper tantrums, oppositional behavior, distractibility or hyperactivity, rapid cycling, mood lability, aggressive behavior, risk-taking behaviors, carbohydrate cravings, depressed mood, low self-esteem, social anxiety, oversensitivity to emotional or environmental triggers, grandiosity, lack of organization, bed wetting, rapid or pressured speech, hypersexuality, lying, paranoia, destruction of property, migraine headaches, and suicidal thoughts (several times during one day; Biederman et al., 2000; Carlson, 2002; Papolos & Papolos, 1999). Wozniak and Biederman (1996) and Wozniak and colleagues (1995) caution that these symptoms of early onset bipolar disorder differ from the episodic course listed in the adult criteria in the *DSM-IV* and may actually represent the child's baseline state, rather than a change in functioning (Youngstrom, Findling, & Feeny, 2004).

Treatment for bipolar disorder involves a combination of medication, counseling, and behavior-management skills training. Acupuncture treatments and herbal and nutritional supplements may also be helpful. Antidepressant medication is generally not indicated for bipolar disorder as it can encourage episodes of mania, moving from too little dopamine to too much dopamine. Certain exceptions include selective *serotonin reuptake inhibitors* (such as Zoloft, Paxil, and Prozac) and *monocyclic aminoketeones* (such as Wellbutrin). Generally, mood stabilizers such as lithium in combination with an antipsychotic medication (such as Zyprexa) or an anticonvulsant medication (such as Depakote) are most effective in treating this disorder. *Electroconvulsive therapy* (ECT) is also helpful in relieving the symptoms of bipolar disorder (Eli Lilly and Company, 2004).

Generalized Anxiety Disorder

One theory of anxiety disorders (Barlow, 2002) suggests that generalized anxiety disorder (GAD) is a major feature of all anxiety disorders. This "anxious apprehension" (Rygh & Sanderson, 2004) is described as "a state of high negative affect that is part of a diffuse cognitive-affective structure" caused by "the perception that one is unable to predict, control, or obtain vital results with a strong physiological substrate of arousal or readiness for counteracting this state of helplessness" (p. 13). This sets off a vicious cycle in which the sense of unpredictability triggers physiological arousal that in turn compels the individual's attention inward, thus increasing arousal. The increased physiological arousal causes attention to narrow further, with more self-reflection and evaluation, again leading to increases in physiological arousal, and so forth. Anxiety then can be divided into three components: cognitive, physiological, and behavioral. The *cognitive* component of GAD includes perceptions of threat and the cognitive responses to these perceptions. These cognitions lead to responses such as excessive worry or avoidance. The *physiological* component of GAD is evidenced in increased activity in the sympathetic division of the autonomic nervous system and reduced flexibility in the parasympathetic division of the autonomic nervous system. Symptoms include muscle tension, shaking, trembling, heart palpitations, shallow breathing, dry mouth, hot flashes or chills, clammy hands, and frequent urination. These symptoms will often result in flight and fight behaviors such as avoidance, evasion, and procrastination, overpreparation, checking, and repeated requests for support and advice (Rygh & Sanderson, 2004). Hooper and March (1995) postulated that the relationship between neuropsychology and manifest anxiety is bidirectional. They state: "Clearly there can be situations in which specific anxiety disorders and symptoms can influence neurocognitive functioning and, conversely, in which impaired neurocognitive functioning can create increased anxiety" (p. 52).

The diagnosis of GAD can be complicated and may include other anxiety disorders as well, such as *social phobia* and *obsessive compulsive disorder*. Due to the somatic nature of many of the complaints, it is also advisable to rule out the possibility of a medical condition; therefore, referral to a primary-care physician is important. Treatment of anxiety disorders generally includes a combination of psychotherapy and pharmacotherapy. Cognitive behavioral models of therapy (see Chapter 3), which include gradual exposure to the fearful/anxious stimuli (for example, in treating a phobia), contingency management, modeling, and self-control procedures, have proven promising in the briefest amount of time (Barlow, 2002; Kagan, Reznick, & Snidman, 1988; Silverman & Ginsburg, 1995).

Stuttering

Stuttering is a fluency disorder or communication disability with physical, psychological, and social causal factors that can lead to psychosocial issues (Athol & Golensky, 2004, p. 197). It is not an indicator of intelligence nor is it a language disorder, although the person's use of language can be affected or limited by a stutter. Stuttering affects the fluency of speech. It begins during childhood and can last throughout childhood. It is characterized by disfluencies or disruptions in the production of speech sounds. Stuttering includes repetition of words or parts of words as well as prolongations of speech sounds. Speech may also become blocked; for example, the mouth is positioned to say a word sometimes for several seconds but no sound is forthcoming. With effort, the individual may complete the word, often interjecting sounds such as "um" or "like." Core stuttering behaviors include disordered breathing, phonation (vocal fold vibration), and articulation (lips, jaw, and tongue). Secondary stuttering behaviors are not related to speech production and include physical movements such as eye blinking or head jerks; avoidance of feared words and substitution of less-suitable words that are easier to pronounce; interjected "starter" sounds such as "um," "ah," and "you know"; and vocal abnormalities to prevent stuttering (Answers.com, 2008).

The diagnosis of stuttering requires the skills of a certified speech language pathologist. In the case of bilingual children (those who speak or have been spoken to in two languages at school), it is important to speak one language at a time to the child and monitor the stuttering in the child's strongest language, which is generally where the most frequent stuttering would be noticed (Athol & Golensky, 2004). The risk factors for stuttering include family history, stuttering for 6 months or longer, the presence of other speech and language disorders, and strong fears or concerns about stuttering on the part of the child or the family.

Neurogenic Stuttering

Neurogenic stuttering is a fluency disorder in which a person has difficulty producing speech in a normal, smooth fashion. It generally occurs following an injury or disease to the central nervous system such as head trauma, tumors, strokes, drug-related causes, and degenerative diseases such as Parkinson's. The highest incidence of neurogenic stuttering are repetitions of phrases or words, excessive interjections or revisions, cessation of speech without finishing a word, hesitation and pauses in unexpected or inappropriate locations when speaking, and intrusive sounds during speech production. Neurogenic stuttering can often look like and coexist with other types of neurological disease or illness such as dysarthria (errors in production and speech sound such as slurring of words); apraxia of speech (irregularities of the timing and inaccuracies in movement of the muscles used in speech production), palilalia (a word, phrase, or sentence may be repeated several times), and aphasias (complete or partial impairment in language comprehension, formulation, and use; The Stuttering Foundation, 2008).

Summary

This chapter has condensed a vast amount of information related to the neurobiological underpinnings of human development. A comprehensive discussion of such a complex topic, involving neuropsychological testing, psychopharmacology, learning specialists, educators, and a host of other professionals, is clearly beyond the scope of the chapter or the expertise of the authors. What we hoped to convey, however, is that clinicians and other service providers must appreciate that some thoughts and behaviors "are neurologically driven rather than motivated by psychological factors" (Palombo, 2001, p. 7). It is extremely important to educate clients, including children (as developmentally appropriate) and their parents, and other family members to ensure that the environment does not continue to make demands that the individual cannot meet. When this occurs, the individual is exposed to additional risk (beyond the initial disorder).

Risk is probabilistic; individuals exposed to risk factors are more likely to experience negative outcomes. School failure, for example, which many children with the disorders described in this chapter are at risk for, may become associated with behavior problems over time (Loeber & Farrington, 2000). We must remember, however, that human resilience is an important variable. Resilience is defined "as observing a normal or even exceptionally positive developmental outcome in spite of exposure to major risk for the development of serious social or health problems" (Fraser, Kirby, & Smokowski, 2004, p. 22). Individual characteristics connected with resilience develop within the context of encouraging relationships. A resilience perspective ensures that the strengths of individuals, families, and communities are assessed to ameliorate problems. This strategy explores assets or resources in the environment that can be drawn on to reduce the risk factors faced by individuals with neurobiological disorders (see Chapter 16 on trauma and development for discussion of resilience to extreme stress). It helps to move people beyond a diagnosis and empower them with the personal control necessary to change their own behaviors well as effect the behavior of others. Fraser and Galinsky (2004) wrote: "Empowerment denotes a partnership between the practitioner and the client or consumer. It involves the development and use of the capacities of the individual, family, organization, and community. Drawing on these capacities helps the consumer of services fully realize his or her own abilities and goals" (p. 395). To be considered resilient, individuals must manifest competence even though they may have experienced challenges on the path to adaptation. "Without risk there is no possibility or need for resilience, but competence, regardless of risk, is always possible and usually necessary for positive adaptation" (Fraser, Kirby, & Smokowski, 2004, p. 24).

3 Theories of Development

Introduction

This chapter presents a number of the major theoretical models represented in the literature. We chose these particular theories because they present a range of conceptual thinking about human behavior and clinical practice and have had enduring value in educating clinicians and helping clients. The language used to describe the practitioner and the client differs in each of the models in this chapter. As Cooper and Lesser (2005) wrote, "Different theories use different language, and there is room for all of these terms" (p. xv). These models serve as guides to assessment, case conceptualization, and the process of ordering facts in a meaningful way in practice. Individuals must also be understood within their developmental, sociohistorical, organizational, political, and cultural contexts. Harry Guntrip (1969), a noted object relations therapist, considers all theories, especially those about human nature, to be conditioned by the cultural era, the prevailing intellectual climate, and the dominant ideas of the time in which they were developed. It is important to consider theories in terms of what is universal and what is not; what is specific to Western civilization and not cross ethnic. Each culture has its own ideas about what is required for individuals to emerge from infancy with an integrated sense of self. Indigenous cultural values are not homogeneous or static but pose problems with which the individual and family must cope (Wing, 2001, p. 56). Pamela Hayes (2007) suggests that we need to know the history of cultures and societies and not just of individuals. She wrote, "Understanding that social locations, the places in the social network where people are interpersonally situated, develop within a particular historical period and are also the inheritors of other historical periods, allows for careful, critical examination of psychotherapist's assumptions about each of these potential components of identity" (pp. 24–25). Therefore, as practitioners, we use theories with caution, sensitivity, and inquiry regarding whether and with whom they are most applicable. Theories of behavior may be useful in guiding clinical work, but practice experience, empirical research, and intellectual debate are what motivate changes in theory (Payne, 1996). This is evident in the evolution of psychodynamic thinking as it moved from classical drive theory to the more contemporary relational models as the following discussion will illustrate.

Most of the theories presented in this chapter have arisen from a Western cultural milieu. Therefore, we begin our chapter with a brief description of a "metatheoretical framework," or "theory of theories" (Sue, Ivey, & Pedersen, 1996) that would "apply not only to Euro-American culture, but also Asian, African, Latin American, and other world cultures" (pp. 11–12). We agree with these authors that although this framework provides a conceptual tool, you will also need to acquaint yourselves with the study of the indigenous systems of healing unique to each client (culture) you work with. As you read the theories we are presenting in this chapter, you face the challenge of weaving them with the material presented in other chapters of this book: genetic predispositions, neurobiological factors, identity development, family context, group and community membership, and the powerful influence of oppression. Finally, we remind you to have respect and appreciation for the human resilience that our clients show.

Multicultural Theory

Multicultural theory is actually a conceptual framework that guides the practitioner in selecting and using the theoretical approach most consistent with the life experiences and cultural perspective of the client. It emphasizes the importance of viewing the individual "in context" and including relevant family or community members in treatment whenever possible and appropriate. Formal methods of counseling, in office settings, may be supplemented by informal methods and/or settings—such as community-based services—when appropriate (Lightburn & Sessions, 2006). *Multicultural counseling* emphasizes working "with" the client, rather than "on" the client, minimizing the use of technical or unfamiliar language. This model is concerned with helping clients "living with intentionality"—within their own cultural frameworks and with respect for other's (Sue et al., 1996, p. 15). It cautions against either over- or underemphasizing cultural differences, respecting each person's individual and group identity. For example, consideration of cultural similarity must come second to client preferences, which may either be for a culturally different—or a culturally similar—counselor. The practitioner working with people from different cultures should be engaged in a process of cultural identity development (see Chapter 4 on identity development) and recognize the inherent power imbalance in the practitioner/client relationship. This approach considers the helping relationship as the interpersonal context in which culture must be negotiated. The dialogical process within the helping relationship is the foundation of the "third space" postmodern cultural competence: eliciting, reflecting, reframing and contextualizing problematic narrative affecting the client (Kaplan, 2004).

Practitioners must also be committed to learning multicultural skills to be effective with diverse people. These include the ability to engage in a variety of verbal and nonverbal counseling methods; understanding whether a problem stems from racism or bias in others so that clients do not inappropriately personalize problems; seeking consultation with others, including traditional and spiritual healers; being able to interact in the language requested by the client or making an appropriate referral when this is not possible; awareness of limitations of diagnostic tests and instruments that may be culture-bound; showing sensitivity to issues of sexism, elitism, and racism when conducting evaluations; and assuming responsibility in educating clients about counseling, including expectations, goals, legal rights, the counselor's theoretical orientation, and alternative methods of counseling that may be available in the community (Sue et al., 1996, pp. 48–49).

Psychodynamic Theory

The basic conceptual underlying principle of *psychodynamic theory* is that of *psychic determinism,* meaning that in mental functioning, nothing happens by chance, but everything has a psychological motive. Events in people's lives are shaped not only by external forces but also by unconscious, or internal, forces as well (Freud,

1939). Several major psychological theories form the conceptual foundation for psychodynamic psychotherapy. These include *drive theory, ego psychology, object relations theory, self-psychology,* and *relational theory.* Each of these theoretical models, although rooted in long-term treatment, can provide a framework for brief treatment as well as for longer-term treatment. The difference is a function of the goal and focus of the treatment. We include a discussion of each of these theories both from a long-term and a brief-treatment focus. Relational theory is also discussed in the section on feminist theory.

Drive Theory

The historical roots of psychodynamic psychotherapy can be found in Freud's original drive—or conflict—theory. Freud saw personality from several intermeshing, but distinct, points of view, referred to as the metapsychological approach to psychotherapy: dynamic, economic, topographical, structural, interpersonal, and cultural. Even today, the metapsychological model is the most complete system of psychology available. It considers both the inner experiences and the outer behaviors of individuals in their present and in their past. We will look at each of these components separately.

Dynamic This concept refers to Freud's instinct theory (1905) and concerns the innate biological aggressive and libidinal (sexual) drives. An instinct has four characteristics: source, aim, object, and impetus. The source of an instinct is always a bodily condition or need. The aim is gratification. The object includes both that on which the need is focused and the activities necessary to secure it. Finally, the impetus of an instinct is its strength that is determined by the force of the underlying need.

Economic The economic perspective postulates that all behavior is regulated by the need to dispose of psychological energy. This energy is discharged by forming cathexes to a person or an object. Something or somebody is cathected if the object or person is emotionally significant to the person (Freud, 1905, 1911, 1915).

Topographical This refers to the *unconscious, preconscious,* and *conscious.* The conscious part of our mind is that of which we are fully aware at all times. The preconscious refers to thoughts and feelings that can be brought into conscious awareness. The unconscious refers to thoughts, feelings, and desires that we are not aware of but that nonetheless exert a powerful influence on behavior. The chief characteristic of the unconscious is *primary process thinking.* Freud considered primary process to be the original (or primary) way in which the psychic apparatus functioned. The *id* functions in conformity with primary process thinking throughout life; the *ego* does so during the first years of life when its organization is immature. Contrasted to primary process thinking is *secondary process thinking,* which governs conscious thinking. Secondary process thinking develops gradually and progressively during the first years of life, is based on realistic approaches to problem solving, and is characteristic of the operations of the relatively mature ego (Brenner, 1974, p. 45).

Genetic According to the genetic point of view, all individuals are recapitulating their pasts in the present. This includes an understanding of the person's *psychosexual development.* People move through different stages throughout the course of their development. Each stage of psychosexual development represents a different area of sexual focus. Infants, for example, are invested in biologically predetermined areas of the body, and their sexual energy (id, libido, drive) is directed toward physical pleasure. Toddlers move through an anal focus, and so forth. The stages of psychosexual development are listed in Table 3.1. The development of personality, according to psychoanalytic drive theory, depends on how the child handles each of these successive stages. If either excessive gratification or excessive frustration is experienced during any one of the stages, *fixation* occurs, and the child will not be able to proceed to the next stage of development. Early childhood development, therefore, is critical in the development of personality and is essentially formed by the age of 5 or 6—the completion of the primary psychosexual stages. The child's sexual energy decreases during the *latency period* and is revived during adolescence (Ashford, LeCroy, & Lortie, 2006, pp. 77–78). Freud based his stages of psychosexual development on heterosexual identity. He felt that homosexuality was the result of unresolved conflicts of early childhood (see Chapter 4 on identity development for contemporary thinking on gay and lesbian identity development).

Structural Freud laid the foundation for the contemporary study of the ego in 1923 with the creation of *structural theory* on which later psychoanalytic theory is built. The human psyche is composed of the *id,* the *ego,* and the *superego.* The *id* is the repository of the drives (libido), and these must be released to reduce tension. The id is concerned with gratification of those drives. The *ego* is the executive arm

TABLE 3.1

Stages of Psychosexual Development

Oral stage	Birth to 18 months	The mouth is the focus of pleasurable sensation as the baby sucks and bites.
Anal stage	18 months to 3 years	The anus is the focus of pleasurable sensation as the baby learns to control elimination.
Phallic stage	3 to 6 years	Children develop sexual curiosity and obtain gratification when they masturbate. They have sexual fantasies about the parent of the opposite sex and feel guilt.
Latency	7 to puberty	Sexual urges are submerged. Focus is on mastery of skills.
Genital	Adolescence	Adolescents have adult desires, and they seek to satisfy them.

Source: Adapted from M. Cole and S. R. Cole, 1996, *The Development of Children* (3rd ed.). New York: W. H. Freeman.

of the personality that mediates between the inner world of id drives and of superego commands and the demands of the external world. The *superego* is the censor of the mind and is essentially the product of interpersonal experiences. It helps balance the drives associated with the id (that are oriented toward pleasure). The superego is divided into the *conscience* (that forbids) and the *ego ideal* (the storehouse of ethics and values). Freud considered the process of identification to be the most important determinant of moral conduct (Ashford et al., 2006, p. 77).

Theories of Development

Interpersonal Freud introduced the concept of transference as a universal characteristic of human beings. Freud defined *transference* as the experience of feelings, drives, attitudes, fantasies, and defenses toward a person in the present that are a repetition of reactions originating in regard to significant persons of early childhood, unconsciously displaced onto figures in the present. Freud defined *countertransference* as the therapist's unrealistic and inappropriate reactions to the client as a result of his or her own unconscious conflicts or developmental arrests. *Transference* and *countertransference* were based on relationships from the past and not the actual relationship between the client and the therapist. These original definitions of transference and countertransference form the framework for the neutral role of the therapist in classical models of psychoanalytic psychotherapy. The intent was to ensure that the therapist did not contaminate the developing transference or interfere in any way with what the patient had to say. Freud referred to the actual relationship (in the present) between the therapist and the patient as the "real relationship." The concept of the real relationship as originally defined by Freud is the precursor, in many ways, to the concept of the working alliance, which is the rapport between the therapist and the patient that makes collaboration possible.

Cultural Freud (1912–1913, 1930) felt that the same psychological mechanisms were to be found in all cultures (sexual and aggressive drives), but they are molded in different ways by different societies.

Treatment from a Drive Model Perspective The technique of psychoanalytic psychotherapy derives from its metapsychological framework. The fundamental rule or technique is that of *free association,* meaning that the client should say everything that comes to mind without censorship. Because the client has the opportunity to verbalize without interruption, she begins to recover memories that influence her functioning in the present.

Resistance Resistance is the term used to describe any behavior on the client's part that impedes the course of free association and the therapeutic work—"a counterforce in the patient operating against the progress of the analysis, the analysand, and the analytic procedures and processes" (Freud, 1912, cited in Cooper & Lesser, 2005, p. 67). Psychoanalytic theory is characterized by a thorough examination of the resistances—the cause, purpose, mode (function), and history of them. Strean (1996) noted that "interpretation of the psychodynamic meaning of the patient's thoughts, feelings and fantasies, especially in terms of the psychogenetic origin, is the hallmark of psychoanalytic therapy" (p. 544). *Interpretation* means helping something unconscious to become conscious by naming it. A valid interpretation on the part of the therapist brings a dynamic change in the patient, which is manifested in the patient's behavior. "Working through" is the term used to describe this process of integrating an interpretation cognitively, affectively, and behaviorally. The final outcome is synthesis of the insights into a way of life in which the patient's past anxieties no longer interfere with a mentally healthy life, defined by Freud as the ability to "love and work."

The following model of brief treatment is based on Freud's drive/structural theory.

Brief Intensive Psychotherapy (BIP)

This is a 20-session model of brief therapy in which the focus of the treatment is to resolve (as much as possible) conflicts that are determined at the initial session, at which time the therapist does a full assessment and tests the patient's responses to trial interpretations. Malan (1978a) proposed two essential areas of conflict that need to be resolved. He referred to them as the triangle of conflict and the triangle of person. The *triangle of conflict* includes the impulse or feelings, the defense erected against it, and the anxiety or symptom that results when the defense fails. This triangle represents the classical psychoanalytic theory of symptom formation; that is, an unacceptable impulse generates anxiety, which is in turn defended against. Defenses, generally erected to avoid fear of psychic pain, can result in depression, phobias, or other symptoms. Thus, the presence of anxiety signals that there is some unacceptable impulse that is being denied expression. Psychotherapy, aimed at helping patients cope with their fears, can result in fewer defenses and thus a reduction in symptoms and an increase in psychic energy (Bloom, 1997, p. 37). The *triangle of person* includes the objects toward whom the impulse is felt: the therapist, the significant people in the patient's current life, and significant people in the past, usually caretakers and siblings (Messer & Warren, 1995). The triangle of person is evident when the patient's feelings toward the therapist are similar to those experienced with significant others in the patient's past (Bloom, 1997, p. 37). Therapy focuses on the three component sets of each triangle (see Figure 3.1). For example in the triangle of person, connections can be made between the people from the patient's past, significant persons in the present, or between the patient's past and his transference with the therapist. In the triangle of conflict, connections can be drawn between impulse and defense, impulse and anxiety, or defense and anxiety.

The focus of this brief model is to work through a particular conflict(s) partially and then see what results follow. Interpretations are kept focal and made within the therapist's overall formulation of the client's problems within the dual-triangle framework. (See Malan, 1978a, 1978b, 1979, for further understanding of this treatment model.)

FIGURE 3.1

Triangle of Conflict (left) and Triangle of Person (right)

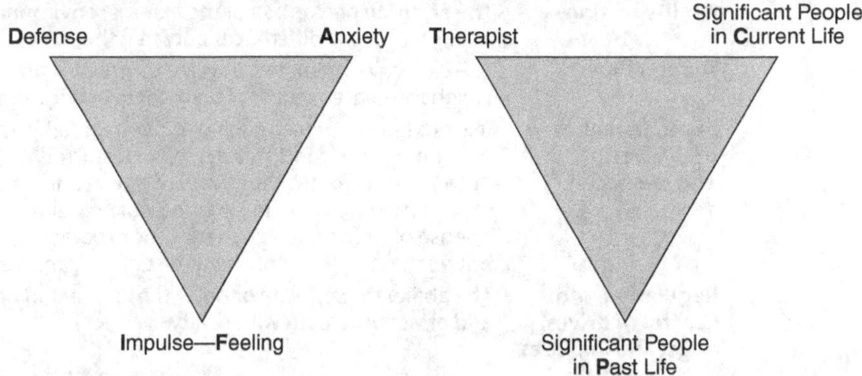

Source: S. Messer and C. S. Warren, 1995, *Models of Brief Psychodynamic Therapy: A Comparative Approach* (p. 82). New York: Guilford Press. Reprinted with permission.

Ego Psychology

Ego psychology shifted psychoanalytic thinking from its focus on the drives (in other words, the id) to a focus on the ego. *Ego psychology* comprises a set of theoretical concepts about human behavior that focus on the origins, development, structure, and functioning of the executive arm of the personality—the ego—and its relationship to other aspects of the personality and the external environment. The four major theoretical constructs of ego psychology are (a) *ego functions,* (b) *defense mechanisms,* (c) *ego mastery and adaptation,* and (d) *object relations.*

Ego Functions The terms *ego strength* and *ego weakness* are used to describe the ego functions. Ego strength refers to the "internal psychological equipment that an individual brings to his interactions with others and with the social environment." Ego weakness "reflects deficiencies in an individual's internal equipment that may lead to maladaptive transactions with the social environment" (Goldstein, 1996, p. 199). The situational context is an important variable in evaluating ego. The major ego functions (Bellak, Hurvich, & Gediman, 1973) are listed in Table 3.2.

Defense Mechanisms A pivotal contributor to ego psychology was Anna Freud (1936) with her expanded work on Freud's earlier presentation of ego defenses. Anna Freud viewed many of the behavioral manifestations previously considered by Freud to be direct expressions of instincts as serving defensive functions; for example, anger could now be seen as a defense against anxiety. Defenses are unconscious and thought to originate in certain psychosexual developmental phases. Efforts directed at modifying defenses create anxiety and are often "resisted" by the individual. Resistance operates unconsciously. Defenses can be adaptive when they serve protective functions or maximize coping; however, they can be maladaptive when they minimize coping. A list of defenses (Goldstein 1995) is presented in Table 3.3.

TABLE 3.2

Ego Functions

Reality testing	The accurate perception of the external environment, of one's internal world and of the differences between them.
Judgment	The capacity to identity a possible course of action and to anticipate and weigh the consequences of behavior to engage in appropriate action.
Sense of reality of the world and of oneself	It is possible to perceive inner and outer reality accurately but to experience the world and the self in distorted ways. The need to feel or to be aware of the world and of one's connection to it as real, to experience one's own body as intact and belonging to oneself, to feel a sense of self and to experience the separation or boundaries between oneself and others as distinct organisms.
Regulation and control of drives, affect and impulses	The ability to modulate or delay the expression of impulses and affects in accord with reality.
Object relations	The quality and patterning of an individual's interpersonal relationships and internalized sense of self and others.
Thought processes	An important development is the shift from primary process to secondary process thinking, which follows the reality principle and is characterized by the ability to postpone instinctual gratification or discharge until reality conditions are appropriate.
Adaptive regression in the service of the ego	The individual returns to an earlier stage of psychosexual development to avoid anxiety or conflict. This regression can serve adaptive ends.
Defensive functioning	Unconscious, internal mechanisms used to ward off anxiety or fear inducing situation. Defenses can be adaptive or maladaptive.
Stimulus barrier	The degree to which an individual is able to maintain his level of functioning or comfort amid increases or decreases in the level of stimulation to which he or she is exposed.
Autonomous functions	Attention, concentration, memory, learning, perception, motor functions, and intention have a primary autonomy from the drives and are conflict free (meaning they do not arise in response to conflict). These functions can lose their autonomy and become associated with conflict during early childhood development.
Mastery-competence	The degree to which one feels competent originates early in childhood as a function of one's innate abilities, the mastery of developmental tasks and the appropriate feedback of significant others in the environment. The gradual accrual of a sense of mastery or competence becomes a crucial part of self-confidence with the world and thus becomes an important aspect of identity of sense of self. Coping is related to mastery but implies the individual's capacity to use basic internal resources and available external resources to develop novel solutions.
Synthetic–integrative function	This function is responsible for binding or fitting all the disparate aspects of the personality into a unified structure that acts on the external world. The synthetic function is responsible for personality integration, resolution of splits, fragmentations, and conflicting tendencies within the personality.

Source: L. Bellak, M. Hurvick, and H. Gediman, 1973, *Ego Functions in Schizophrenics, Neurotics, and Normals.* Hoboken, NJ: John Wiley & Sons, Inc.

TABLE 3.3

Ego Defenses

Repression	The active pushing out of painful memories or feelings.
Denial	Ignoring painful realities and treating them as if they do not exist.
Reaction formation	Exaggerating an emotion tends to help repress the opposite emotion.
Displacement	Changing the object of one's feelings from the real object to a safer one.
Reversal	Changing an impulse from active to passive (and vice versa) or directing an impulse toward the self instead of toward another person (or vice versa).
Inhibition	Constriction of thought or activity to avoid thoughts or activities that stir anxiety.
Identification with the aggressor	The tendency to imitate what is perceived as the aggressive or intimidating manner of an external authority.
Asceticism	Denial of pleasures to oneself (may involve food, sleep, exercise, or sexual gratification). This defense is often used by adolescents to control the pressures of the intense sexual feelings after puberty.
Intellectualization	Factual and excessively cognitive way of experiencing and talking about conflicted topics.
Isolation of affect	Related to intellectualization, repression of feelings connected with a particular thought.
Regression	Return to earlier modes of psychosexual functioning to avoid the conflicts experienced at a later developmental stage.
Sublimation	Mature mechanism of defense; the hoped for healthy, nonconflicted evolution of a primitive childhood impulse into a mature level of expression.
Projection	Attributing one's own conflicted impulses to another person.
Projective identification	A projection onto someone whom the patient then attempts to control.
Omnipotence	Exaggerating one's own power.
Devaluing	Minimizing and dismissing with contempt.
Primitive idealization	Exaggerating the power and prestige of another person.
Internalization	"Taking in" (not just modeling, as in identification).
Introjection	Turning unacceptable impulses one has toward others toward the self (turning against the self). Does not take in the object but the feelings associated with the object.
Compensation	Trying to make up for what an individual perceives as a deficit or deficiency.
Splitting	Keeping apart two contradictory ego states such as love and hate. Does not allow the individual to integrate in consciousness. Contradictory aspects of their own feelings or identity or the contradictory characteristics of others.

Source: E. Goldstein, 1995, *Ego Psychology and Social Work Practice.* New York: The Free Press, a Division of Macmillan, Inc.

Ego psychologists feel that after latency, if development has progressed reasonably well, the superego will be less punitive in responding both to forbidden wishes and to situations that threaten its moral standards. The mature superego's flexibility reduces pressures on the ego, thereby making it possible for the ego to consider a greater range of options in attempting to resolve intrapsychic and interpersonal conflict. People who have mastered the developmental tasks intrinsic to the *oral, anal, phallic,* and *genital* stages of development tend to experience anxiety in more transient ways, to employ healthier ego defenses, and to become less dysfunctional in the face of perceived psychological danger. Certain anxieties are linked to the different psychosexual stages of development: oral (*autonomic anxiety*); anal (*fear of loss of object*); phallic (*fear of loss of the love object*); genital (*castration anxiety*); and latency (*during latency children may selectively experience anxiety associated with any or all of the earlier stages of psychosexual development*) (A. Freud, 1936).

Ego Mastery and Adaptation Another major contributor to ego psychology was Heinz Hartman (1939), who introduced two important concepts: ego autonomy and ego adaptation. Hartman proposed that certain ego functions are innate and autonomous and independent of instinctual drives. Some of these ego functions include memory, reality testing, motor activity, and intelligence. Ego functions can arise or lose their autonomy by their connection to conflict; for example, learning can be compromised by anxiety. The goal of treatment is to neutralize and divest the ego of such conflict. The ego then develops secondary autonomy and serves adaptive purposes. Hartman felt that an individual is born "preadapted" to an "average expectable environment" and matures independent of conflict. Hartman proposed that (a) an individual could change outside reality to suit himself; (b) an individual could change himself to comply with the demands of reality; and (c) an individual could search for an environment that might best suit his psychological potential.

Psychosocial Development Erik Erikson (1950, 1959) focused on *ego mastery* and described ego development as psychosocial, involving mastery of developmental tasks in each of eight successive stages of the human life cycle. The beginning of each stage brings a normal, developmental crisis or disequilibrium resulting from new coping demands. Successful crisis resolution is contingent on mastery of biopsychosocial tasks inherent in each stage and contributes to identity formation. Erikson was one of the first theorists to view adulthood as a time for continued growth and change (Goldstein, 1996, p. 192). Erikson's psychosocial stages of development are described in Table 3.4.

Another important ego psychologist who emphasized the ego's drive toward mastery and competence was Robert White (1959, 1963), who felt that the ego actually seeks opportunities in the environment that contribute to feeling and being effective. The more effective experiences an individual has, the more the ego is strengthened.

TABLE 3.4

Erikson's Psychosocial Stages of Development

Stage	Description
1. Trust vs. Mistrust	Infants learn to trust others to care for their basic needs or to mistrust them.
2. Autonomy vs. Shame and Doubt	Children learn to exercise their will and to control themselves, or they become uncertain and doubt that they can do things by themselves.
3. Initiative vs. Guilt	Children learn to initiate their own activities, enjoy their accomplishments, and become purposeful. If they are not allowed to follow their own initiative, they feel guilty for their attempts to become independent.
4. Industry vs. Inferiority	Children learn to be competent and effective at activities valued by adults and peers or they feel inferior.
5. Identity vs. Role Diffusion	Adolescents establish a sense of personal identity as part of their social group, or they become confused about who they are and what they want to do in life.
6. Intimacy vs. Isolation	Young adults find an intimate life companion, or they risk loneliness and isolation.
7. Generativity vs. Stagnation	Adults must be productive in their work and willing to raise a next generation, or they risk stagnation.
8. Integrity vs. Despair	People try to make sense of their prior experience and to assure themselves that their lives have been meaningful, or they despair over their unachieved goals and ill-spent lives.

Source: Adapted from M. Cole and S. R. Cole, 1996, *The Development of Children* (3rd ed.). New York: W. H. Freeman.

Object Relations Margaret Mahler (1968; Mahler, Pine, & Bergman, 1975), Mary Ainsworth (1973), John Bowlby (1958), and Renee Spitz (1965) are considered ego psychologists who provided a bridge to the third wave of psychoanalytic thought-object relations (see next section). At this time, however, object relations were still considered one of the major tenets of ego psychology and one of the important functions of the ego. *Object* refers to the significant person or thing that is the target or "object" of another's feelings or drives. As a construct of ego psychology, object refers to interpersonal relations and suggests an inner residue of past relationships that shape an individual's current interactions with people. Individuals therefore interact not only with an actual other, but also with an internal "other," a psychic representation that might be a distorted version of some actual personal experience. Mahler described a *separation-individuation process* of internalized object relations (Maher et al., 1975, p. 110), and this process is depicted in Table 3.5. At the end of this developmental sequence, the child has achieved "object constancy" (the ability to internalize the primary caregiver and hold that figure in memory).

TABLE 3.5

Stages of Mahler's Separation–Individuation Process

Autistic Phase	Infant is dominated by physiological needs/primary autonomous ego apparatuses are undifferentiated; this is the preattachment phase of object relations.
Symbiotic Phase	Infant begins to experience the need-satisfying object, but the object is experienced within the infant's ego boundary and lacks a separate identity. The mother's ego functions for the infant, and the mother mediates between the infant and the external world. This period marks the beginning of the infant's capacity to invest in another person.
Separation–Individuation Phase The Differentiating Subphase	This phase begins at roughly 4 or 5 months when the infant begins to separate itself from the representation of the mother (first with respect to body image). Transitional objects become important during this time.
Separation–Individuation The Practicing Subphase	The infant continues the process of separation of self and object representation, and the infant's own autonomous ego functions become more important. The term "practicing" implies a testing of one's individual capacities (such as crawling) and of being on one's own in a limited sense (maturation of motor functions but within close proximity to mother). Separation anxiety may ensue until the child becomes reassured that mother is still there despite the child moving away from her. The child attempts to keep track of the mother as he or she moves away. The mother's ability to support the child's growing individuation while maintaining a continued supportive presence when the child needs her is a critical factor in fostering optimal individuation.
Separation–Individuation The Rapprochement Subphase	The child becomes more needful of mother's presence. The child's capacity for attachment to others expands beyond an exclusive relationship with the mother; emotional range becomes greater. The development of language is important—positive resolution of this phase begins to enable the child to overcome the splitting of the self and the object world into all good and all bad and to develop integrated self and object representations. This process is essential to object constancy and development of empathic capacities essential to mature love.
Separation–Individuation On the Road to Object Constancy	The two major tasks of this phase are the attainment of individuality and the attainment of object constancy. Gender identity and ego functioning also advance during this time.

Source: M. S Mahler, F. Pine, and A. Bergman, 1975, *The Psychological Birth of the Human Infant* (p.110). New York: Basic Books.

Treatment from an Ego Psychological Perspective Treatment conducted within an ego psychological framework includes an assessment of the patient's ego functions, including their strengths and weaknesses. Ego psychological treatment can be ego-supportive or ego-modifying or a combination of both. The goal of ego-supportive intervention is to restore, maintain, or enhance the individual's adaptive functioning and to build or strengthen the ego where there are deficits or impairments. The therapist is active when using this approach and uses directive, educative, and structured techniques that may include environmental modification and mobilization of resources. Ego-supportive interventions can be either short term or long term. Ego-modifying interventions focus on changing basic personality structures or patterns. They focus on insight and conflict resolution and are nondirective, reflective, and interpretative in nature. Ego-modifying interventions are generally long term, "although ego modification may result from crisis work or short term interventions as well as from the impact of life events themselves" (Goldstein, 1984, p. 154).

Object Relations Theory

According to object relations theory, human development takes place within the context of relationships. Therefore, rather than being an ego function, object relational theorists conceptualized "object relations" as the context within which all other ego functions develop. The most significant tension in psychoanalytic theory has been between the Freudian model of drive theory and the object relations school of Sullivan (1953) and Fairbairn (1952), which explains psychic structure as evolving from the individual's relations with other people (Greenberg & Mitchell, 1983). Object relational theorists challenge the Freudian understanding of the personality structure (id, ego, superego) and look to the influence of external objects (parents, caretakers, and transitional objects such as stuffed toys and blankets) to build internal psychic organization. Melanie Klein (1948) was the first theorist to revise Freud's notion of object by giving greater weight to the interpersonal environment as a determining influence over developing personality. She—and other object relational theorists who followed—now defined object as the target of relational needs: *relationship seeking.* It is through our relationships with the significant people around us that we take in parts of others (objects) and slowly build a self-structure that we eventually call a personality (Klee, 2005). The mental process by which an individual transforms the regulatory characteristics of her environment into internal regulations and characteristics is called *internalization* (Greenberg & Cheselka, 1995). Klein (1948) also introduced the defenses of splitting and projective identification. Projective identification involves the patient's splitting off a part of the self and fantasizing it as being part of the other person in an attempt to control that person and keep him from doing psychic harm. Splitting involves keeping two contradictory feeling states (such as love and hate) apart, which then leads to an identification by projection (the object or person becomes an extension of the self).

Interpersonal trauma, such as abuse by caretakers, can lead to a pathological delay in the developmental sequence. The child then lacks the ego strength necessary to form and maintain healthy relationships. The adult with a weakened sense of self repeats the traumatic pattern through relationships with others in the hope of reaching a resolution. However, these attempts are futile because the immature self never develops sufficient ego strength to overcome the traumatic pattern. Those selected as partners are themselves often immature and bound in their own destructive relational patterns. The goal of treatment from an object relational perspective can either be the modification of certain defenses (such as denial, splitting, idealization, devaluation, and projective identification) and internalized self and object representations (such as the bad object; Klein, 1948; Masterson, 1972, 1976) or facilitation of developmental progression and building of new internal structures (Fairbairn, 1952; Guntrip, 1969; Winnicott, 1965).

Object Relations and Brief Treatment A number of brief treatments are based on object relations theory. Generally referred to as "relational models," they include (a) the supportive–expressive psychotherapy of Luborsky and the Penn Psychotherapy Project (Luborksky et al., 1980); (b) the short-term dynamic therapy model of Horowitz and the Center for the Study of Neuroses (Horowitz, 1991); (c) the control-mastery therapy of Weiss, Sampson, and the Mount Zion group (1986); and (d) the time-limited dynamic psychotherapy of Strupp, Binder, and the Vanderbilt group (Messer & Warren, 1995, p. 116). We discuss one of these models next.

Time-Limited Dynamic Psychotherapy (TLDP) The focus of treatment in this model of psychotherapy, which lasts between 20 to 25 sessions, is on the maladaptive relational problems that a person learned in the past, maintains in the present, and could potentially reenact in the therapeutic relationship. The cyclical maladaptive pattern (CMP) is the organizing framework the therapist uses to understand the patient's problem(s), determine the treatment goals, and guide clinical interventions. The CMP is comprised of four categories. The first category, *acts of the self*, includes the interpersonal thoughts, feelings, motives, perception, and behavior of the patient. The second category, *expectations of others'* reactions, focuses on how the patient imagines others will react in response to his interpersonal behavior. The third category is *acts of others toward the self.* Here the focus is on the actual behaviors of the other people as observed and interpreted by the patient. Fourth, is the category of *acts of the self toward the self,* which includes all the patient's behaviors or attitudes toward her- or himself. The therapist also considers his or her own reactions to the patient as they work together, as TLDP uses the relationship between the therapist and the patient to discuss and change the ways in which the patient interacts (see Cooper & Lesser, 2005, p. 87, for a case example using this model).

Self-Psychology

Self-psychology was developed by Heinz Kohut (1971), who was originally trained in Freudian theory and technique. Although Kohut felt that self-psychology was a distinct psychoanalytic theory of development, other self-psychologists (Bacal & Newman, 1990) feel it rests on an object relations foundation. Self-psychologists explore how early relationships form the self and the structures of the self. Kohut did not focus on object relationships between two separate and distinct persons. He felt that healthy self-development proceeds from the adequate responsiveness of caregivers to the child's emotional needs. Kohut introduced the term *selfobject* to describe three distinct relationships (experiences) he felt took place between the self and its objects: the *mirroring, idealizing,* and *alter ego selfobject relationships.* The *mirroring selfobject* recognizes the child's unique capabilities and talents (children need to feel understood and appreciated). The *idealizing selfobject* links the child with the admired caretakers (children need to feel attached to an emotionally stable caregiver who can soothe and calm them). The *alter ego* (also called *twinship* or *partnering selfobject*) provides a sense of sameness with the selfobject that is essential to psychic growth and a developing sense of competence children need to have involvement with other beings like themselves (Cooper & Lesser, 2005; Wolf, 1988). Through a process called *transmuting internalization,* Kohut felt that the child (individual) will gradually be able to perform the psychological functions of soothing and tension regulation on their own. In the absence of these selfobject experiences, internalization of psychic structures cannot occur. In addition, the child, anxious for the support of the caretaking selfobject(s), may falsely comply with the caretakers' needs, interfering with the development of a true self and resulting in feelings of shame, humiliation, and early narcissistic needs. The child (and later, the adult) is on a continual search for selfobject experiences that will provide what is lacking, often making choices based on these early, unmet needs.

Treatment from a Self-Psychological Perspective Kohut (1959/1978) developed an *empathic–introspective* model of psychological investigation that he considered essential to the psychotherapeutic process. He referred to empathy as "vicarious introspection" and considered it the tool with which the therapist gathered psychological information, made interpretations, and evaluated the outcome of treatment interventions (Siegel, 1996). The therapist is needed to fulfill those selfobject functions that the patient had earlier sought and failed to find—admiration, guidance, and the opportunity to merge with the calmness and competence of an idealized figure through whom their own worth and capability can take reliable form. Through transmuting internalization (previously discussed), these functions, now provided by the therapist, become the patient's own.

The patient thus internalizes mature empathy as a self-function and is able to seek out relationships with others who have achieved the same. Kohut felt that we never outgrow our need for selfobjects, but we do outgrow their exploitation by achieving mature empathy as a self-function. According to self-psychological theory, the hallmark of mental health is the capacity of the individual to seek and find appropriate self-objects (Cooper & Lesser, 2005; St. Clair, 2000; Siegel, 1996) based on adult developmental levels and not unmet childhood needs.

Self-Psychology and Brief Treatment Several authors have applied Kohut's model of self-psychology to brief treatment (Balint, Orenstein, & Balint, 1972; Elson, 1986; Gardner, 1999; Goldberg, 1973; Lesser, 2000; Seruya, 1997). The goal is to enhance the patient's self-esteem and restore him or her to the level of functioning (premorbid level) prior to the loss of a selfobject (such as the death of a spouse). The therapist, through focused empathy, validates the patient's needs and feelings, promoting awareness, understanding, and acceptance. The therapist becomes the responsive selfobject for the patient, helping to reestablish a supportive selfobject environment outside the treatment (Cooper & Lesser, 2005;

Gardner, 1999; Lazarus, 1982; Lesser, 2000). Whenever possible, the therapist should encourage and assist the patient in finding supportive selfobjects that can provide additional supports to the therapy. Lesser (2000) wrote about establishing a short-term group (from a self-psychological perspective) for women with abuse histories who didn't have any supportive selfobjects in their lives but found them in the group.

Relational Theory

Relational theory evolved from the several psychoanalytic theories that preceded it: interpersonal, object relations, and self-psychology (Greenberg & Mitchell, 1983). Psychic reality was now viewed as a relational matrix, encompassing both the intrapsychic and the interpersonal worlds. Intrapsychic representations contain the imprint of interpersonal relationships as they are experienced by the individual. These include a representation of the self, the other, and the interaction between them. These "intrapsychic relational processes" reshape interpersonal relationships, and they in turn alter intrapsychic processes in a continuous cycle (Cooper & Lesser, 2008, p. 124; Fonagy & Target, 2003). Within this new theoretical paradigm, the therapist is "an engaged participant whose subjectivity and emotional responsiveness interact with that of the patient, creating an interactional dynamic that constitutes the therapeutic relationship" (Safran & Reading, 2008, p. 124 citing Aron, 1996; Benjamin, 1988; Mitchell, 1988, 2000; Safran & Muran, 2000). The relational patterns that unfold in the therapeutic relationship are viewed as expressions of the patient's and the therapist's personal histories and ways of relating to the world. They involve unconscious contributions by both therapist and patient and are termed "enactments." These enactments reflect the unique personal histories of both the patient and the therapist and reflect patterns that also emerge for the patient in interpersonal relationships outside therapy. By working through these enactments, therapists and patients can discover internal processes and relational patterns that are problematic for patients and provide them with new, constructive relational experiences that modify their maladaptive relational schemas (generalized expectations about self–other interactions; Safran & Reading, 2008, pp. 123–124).

Multicultural Relational Theory

McClure and Teyber (1996) applied relational theory to multicultural counseling with attention to the "process" dimension of multicultural counseling. This includes attention to all the factors that contribute to identity development and subjective worldview and stresses the importance of the therapist's attunement to the subjectivity of the therapists perceptions in the counseling process. They wrote, "This awareness of the subjective nature of their own worldview seems to make effective counselors willing to suspend their worldview more readily and to enter more fully into the subjective experience of others" (p. 12). This focus on the process of therapy allows multicultural relational counselors the flexibility to draw from a range of theoretical models and serve as an "integrating focus for treatment" (p. 19). Multicultural "relational" theory offers a contemporary, expanded view of multicultural theory as a metatheoretical framework, which we described at the start of this chapter.

Intersubjectivity

Atwood and Stolorow (1984) expanded the relational framework by introducing the intersubjectivity perspective with a focus on the "interface of reciprocally interacting subjectivities" of the therapist and the client. The intersubjectivitists feel that countertransference includes the ways in which the therapist's subjectivity shapes experience of the therapeutic relationship and of the patient's transference. Transference and countertransference now form an intersubjective system of mutual influence. The success of the therapy is dependent on the "goodness of fit" between what the patient most needs to have understood and what the analyst is capable of understanding (Stolorow, 1991, p. 24 cited in Spencer, 2000, p. 11). The goal of a relationally informed psychodynamic psychotherapist is the "reflexive ability to consider different forms of actions based on a variety of theoretical perspectives, to consider how these different options complement the analyst's own personal style can character, and to consider the impact of these options within the individual psychoanalytic relationship" (Spencer, 2000, p. 10).

Relational Mindfulness

Mindfulness can be conceptualized as "the process of locating and directing one's awareness to the present moment as it unfolds" (Safran & Reading, 2008, p. 122). Hicks (2008, p. 5) referenced Kabat-Zinn (1990) and Segal, Williams, and Teasdale (2002), who describe mindfulness as a "nonelaborative, nonjudgmental, present-centered awareness in which each thought, feeling or sensation that arises in the attentional field is acknowledged and accepted as it is."

Within the context of the therapeutic relationship, these authors described mindfulness as a way of paying attention "with empathy, presence and deep listening that can be cultivated, sustained and integrated into our work as therapists through the ongoing discipline of meditation practice" (Hicks, 2008, p. 5).

Safran and Reading (2008, p. 126) make a connection between mindfulness and metacommunication: "a key tool for applying mindfulness practice to the collaborative exploration of enactments consists of therapeutic metacommunication—communicating about the implicit communication that is being enacted in the therapeutic relationship." Essential to metacommunication is the therapist's careful understanding of his or her reactions and experiences in the therapeutic encounter, combined with an attunement to the client's early attachment experiences (Sterlin, 2006, p. 165).

Surrey (2005) extends mindfulness practice to the feminist version of relational psychotherapy (originally referred to as self-in-relation and more contemporarily called cultural relational theory (Jordan, Kaplan, Miller, Stiver, & Surrey, 1991; Miller, 2002, 2003) by focusing on how the therapist and patient are working "with the intention to deepen awareness of the present relational experience, with acceptance" (Jordan et al., 1991, p. 92). In mindfulness-informed relational therapy, therapists remain attentive to their own feelings, thoughts, memories, and sensations. The therapist is also paying attention to the experiences of the patient as the object of awareness, using these perceptions to facilitate the movement of the relationship. The therapist is attending to the "flow of the relationship" and the shifting qualities of connection and disconnection. Surrey refers to this as a "tripartite awareness" (self, other, and the movement or flow of the relationship; p. 94). She further describes the therapeutic relationship as a "co-meditation" wherein the therapist's empathic attunement and acceptance offers the patient the possibility of staying emotionally present with difficult feelings. This extends the patient's capacity for mindful awareness of "self-in-connection" and "mindfulness becomes a collaborative process . . . mindfulness and the attuned relationship seem to support each other" (pp. 94–95). This concept is illustrated in the clinical example of Carla, who shares a profoundly traumatic story about her experience of just missing death at the hands of her violent former boyfriend. Following her story, she and the therapist sit together in what mindfulness practice suggests is a "conscious silence that envelopes an inexpressible, direct perception of the intangible, all-encompassing relational world in which we are all connected" (p. 101).

Surrey (2005, p. 96), like Safran and Reading (2008), relates the experience of connection in mindfulness-based relational therapy to the psychoanalytic concept of intersubjectivity, the interplay between subjects and how we draw conclusions from within the "intersubjective field." She cites the work of Evan Thompson (2001), suggesting we move from "intersubjectivity to "interbeing," a term that describes the interconnectedness of all beings.

Cognitive Theory

The rationale behind cognitive theory is that the affects and behaviors of human beings are largely determined by the way in which they structure their world (Beck, 1963; Beck, Emery, & Greenberg, 1985). Several unifying principles that guide this school of thought are as follows.

- Human emotion is the result of what people think, tell themselves, assume, or believe about themselves.
- Many misconceptions, irrational thinking, and erroneous beliefs are outside a person's conscious awareness.

- Some dysfunctional thoughts may be the result of organic, physiological, neurological, or chemical problems.
- Not all unpleasant emotions are dysfunctional, and not all pleasant emotions are functional.

Change occurs when the cognitive therapist is able to facilitate a cognitive reflection process in which the client identifies, challenges, and changes misconceptions, faulty beliefs, distorted cognitions, and irrational self-talk that have contributed to dysfunctional emotions and behavior. Three of the fundamental constructs of cognitive theory are *collaborative empiricism* (the therapist and the patient are coinvestigators who examine the evidence to support or refute the patient's cognitions); *Socratic dialogue* (the therapist poses a number of questions designed to help the patient arrive at logical conclusions); and *guided discovery* (the therapist encourages the patient to use facts, probabilities, and behavioral experiments to modify maladaptive cognitive beliefs; Beck & Weishaar, 1989). Other important theoretical constructs of cognitive theory explicated by Freeman and Reinecke (1995) are discussed next.

Cognitive Specificity Hypothesis

This presumes that emotional states can be distinguished by their specific cognitive contents and processes. For example, anxiety disorders are generally based on a perception of threat and a belief that the person is not able to cope with that threat. Each of the anxiety disorders (such as obsessive compulsive disorder or social anxiety disorder) can be distinguished by the specific focus of the threat. The cognitive specificity hypothesis, therefore, directs therapeutic focus to specific beliefs and information processing styles found among patients with these specific disorders. Beck (1995) identified what he called the "cognitive profile of neurotic disorders" (p. 240), each of which has a systematic bias in processing information. For example, depressed individuals tend to have a negative view of self, experience, and the future. Persons suffering from anxiety disorders have a sense of physical or psychological danger. In phobias, there is anticipation of physical or psychological harm in specific situations. There are also behavioral interventions that are specific to clinical syndromes and protocols that include step-by-step instructions on working with individuals who suffer from conditions such as social anxiety, panic disorder, and other psychosocial disorders (Barlow, 2001).

Schemata

These are generalizations that are stored in memory and influence the cognitive processes of attention, encoding, retrieval, and inference. Individuals have a tendency to accommodate their experiences to preexisting schemata that originate in childhood experiences. Bricker, Young, and Flanagan (1993) identified 15 schemata that the therapist and the client work to uncover (see Table 3.6).

TABLE 3.6

Schema

1. **Emotional Deprivation (ED)**
   Expectation that one's desire for a normal degree of emotional support will not be adequately met by others.
   A. *Deprivation of Nurturance:* Absence of attention, affection (physical or emotional), or warmth from others.
   B. *Deprivation of Protection:* Absence of strength, direction, or guidance from others.
   C. *Deprivation of Empathy:* Absence of understanding, listening, self-disclosure, or mutual sharing of feelings of others.
2. **Abandonment/Instability (AB)**
   The perceived instability or unreliability of those available for support and connection. Involves the sense that significant others will not be able to continue providing emotional support, connection, strength, or practical protection because they are emotionally unstable, unpredictable, unreliable, and erratically present; because they will die imminently; or because they will abandon the patient in favor of someone else.
3. **Mistrust/Abuse (MA)**
   One's expectation that others will hurt, abuse, humiliate, cheat, lie, manipulate, or take advantage of him or her. Usually involves the perception that harm is intentional or the result of unjustified and extreme negligence.
4. **Social Isolation/Alienation (SI)**
   The feeling that one is isolated from the rest of the world, different from other people, and/or not part of any group or community.
5. **Defectiveness/Shame (DS)**
   The feeling that one is inwardly defective, flawed, or invalid; that one would be fundamentally unlovable to significant others if exposed, or a sense of shame, regarding one's perceived internal inadequacies.
6. **Social Isolation/Alienation (SI)**
   The feeling that one will inevitably fail, or is fundamentally inadequate relative to one's peers, in areas of achievement (school, career, sports, etc.). Often involves the belief that one is stupid, inept, untalented, and ignorant.
7. **Functional Dependence/Incompetence (DI)**
   Belief that one is unable to handle one's everyday responsibilities in a competent manner, without considerable help from others (e.g., take care of oneself, solve daily problems, exercise good judgment, tackle new tasks, make good decisions).
8. **Vulnerability to Harm and Illness (VH)**
   Exaggerated fear that disaster is about to strike at any time (natural, criminal, medical, or financial) and that one is unable to protect oneself. May include unrealistic fears that one will have a heart attack, get AIDS, go crazy, go broke, be mugged, crash, etc.
9. **Enmeshment/Undeveloped Self (EM)**
   Excessive emotional involvement and closeness with one or more significant others (often parents) at the expense of the full individuation or normal social development. Usually leads to insufficient individual identity or inner direction. May include feelings of being smothered or fused with others.

10. **Subjugation (SB)**
Excessive surrendering of control over one's own decisions and preferences—usually to avoid anger, retaliation, or abandonment. Involves the perception that one's own desires are not valid or important to others. Frequently presents an excessive compliance and eagerness to please.
11. **Self-Sacrifice (SS)**
Excessive voluntary focus on meeting the needs of others at the expense of one's own needs and preferences. The most common reasons are to avoid guilt, to prevent causing pain to others, to gain in esteem, or to maintain the connection with others perceived as needy.
12. **Emotional Inhibition (EI)**
Excessive inhibition of emotions or impulses because one expects their expression to result in loss of esteem, harm to others, embarrassment, retaliation, or abandonment. May result in loss of spontaneity and warmth, flatness of affect, mishandling of anger, obsessive-compulsive, symptoms, etc.
13. **Unrelenting/Unbalanced Standards (US)**
The relenting striving to meet high expectations of oneself, at the expense of happiness, pleasure, health, sense of accomplishment, or satisfying relationships.
14. **Entitlement/Self-Centeredness (ET)**
Insistence that one should be able to have whatever one wants, regardless of what others consider reasonable or regardless of the cost to others. Often involves excessive control over others, demandingness, and lack of empathy for others' needs.
15. **Insufficient Self-Control/Self-Discipline (IS)**
Pervasive difficulty exercising sufficient self-control and frustration tolerance to achieve one's personal goals to restrain the excessive expression of one's emotions and impulses.

Source: D. Bricker, J. Young, and C. Hanagan, 1993, "Schema-Focused Cognitive Therapy: A Comprehensive Framework for Characterological Problems." In K. T. Kuehlwein and N. Rosen (Eds.), *Cognitive Therapies in Action: Evolving Innovative Practice* (pp. 88–125). San Francisco, CA: Jossey-Bass.

Cognitive Distortions

A number of negative cognitive biases in individuals may contribute to feelings of depression, anxiety, and so forth. Some of these are listed in Table 3.7 (Beck, 1995, pp. 238–239).

Treatment Agenda

Sessions are structured through the establishment of an agenda that includes items such as discussions of events during the past week, a review of self-report scales completed by the patient during the past week, and a review of the patient's homework. Other items might include focus on skill attainment or the examination of dysfunctional thoughts.

Rating Scales

Several empirically tested rating scales are used in cognitive therapy, and these are symptom focused. Examples of these tools would be the Beck Depression Inventory (BDI; Beck et al., 1961) and the Beck Anxiety Inventory (BAI; Beck et al., 1988).

TABLE 3.7

Cognitive Distortions

Although some automatic thoughts are true, many are either untrue or have just a grain of truth. Typical mistakes in thinking include the following:

1. *All-or-nothing thinking* (also called black-or-white, polarized, dichotomous thinking): You view a situation in only two categories instead of on a continuum.
   Example: "If I'm not a total success, I'm a failure."
2. *Catastrophizing* (also called fortune telling): You predict the future negatively without considering other, more likely outcomes.
   Example: "I'll be so upset, I won't be able to function at all."
3. *Disqualifying or discounting the positive:* You unreasonably tell yourself that positive experiences, deeds, or qualities do not count.
   Example: "I did that project well, but that doesn't mean I am competent; I just got lucky."
4. *Emotional reasoning:* You think something must be true because you "feel" (actually believe) it so strongly; ignoring or discounting evidence to the contrary.
   Example: "I know I do a lot of things OK at work, but I still feel like I'm a failure."
5. *Labeling:* You put a fixed, global label on yourself or others without considering that the evidence might more reasonably lead to a less disastrous conclusion.
   Example: "I'm a loser. He's no good."
6. *Magnification/minimization:* When you evaluate yourself, another person, or a situation, you unreasonably magnify the negative and/or minimize the positive.
   Example: "Getting a mediocre evaluation proves how inadequate I am. Getting high marks doesn't mean I am smart."
7. *Mental filter:* (also called selective abstraction): You pay undue attention to negative detail instead of seeing the whole picture.
   Example: "Because I got one low rating on my evaluation [which also contained several high ratings] it means I am doing a lousy job."
8. *Mind reading:* You believe you know what others are thinking, failing to consider other more likely possibilities
   Example: "He's thinking that I don't know the first thing about the project."
9. *Overgeneralization:* You make a sweeping negative conclusion that goes far beyond the current situation.
   Example: "[Because I felt uncomfortable at the meeting] I don't have what it takes to make friends."
10. *Personalization:* You believe others are behaving negatively toward you without considering more plausible explanations for their behavior.
    Example: "The repairman was curt to me because I did something wrong."
11. "Should" and "must" statements (also called imperatives): You have a precise fixed idea of how you or others should behave and you overestimate how bad it is these expectations are not met.
    Example: "It's terrible that I made a mistake. I should always do my best."
12. *Tunnel Vision:* You only see the negative aspects of a situation.
    Example: "My son's teacher can't do anything right. He's critical and insensitive and lousy at teaching."

Source: Judith Beck, 1995, *Cognitive Therapy: Basics and Beyond*. New York: Guilford Press. Reprinted with permission.

Although advocacy and environmental modifications can be a part of treatment, the central focus is on helping the client to change cognitive misconceptions. The past is not given a lot of importance in cognitive behavioral theory; what matters most is the present and how healthier ideas and beliefs could be used in the present to improve mood and behavior. Cognitive theory addresses the fact that race, class, gender, and other collective identity experiences can affect one's beliefs and cognitions (Lantz, 1996, pp. 69–94).

Behavioral Therapy

Behavioral theory emphasizes positive learning experiences with a focus on helping clients acquire new skills, improve communication, or learn to break maladaptive habits. This involves "broad changes in cognitive, affective, and behavioral functioning" (Wilson, 1995, p. 208). The treatment principles of behavioral theory are based on three specific learning modes: classical (or respondent), operant, and social learning. *Classical conditioning* makes the direct link between stimulus and response. Behavior is produced by a stimulus (a person, situation, or thing). Conditioning is the process by which behavior is learned (or connected with the stimulus). When a particular response to a stimulus is learned, behaviors are *conditioned* or associated with a stimulus that does not naturally produce the response (for example, an unconditioned behavior might be the natural blinking of our eyes; Payne, 1996). This theoretical formulation is the basis of behavioral interventions such as relaxation training and desensitization (see further discussion of these techniques later in the chapter). *Operant conditioning* focuses on the individual's ability to change or modify a behavior by changing the consequences of that behavior. *Social learning theory* (Bandura, 1977, 1980)—currently referred to as *social cognitive theory* (Bandura, 1986)—demonstrates that behaviors are learned through imitation, modeling, and observation. An antecedent event (A) occurs, which produces a behavior (B), and as a result of that behavior, consequences (C) arise. *Contingencies* are used to affect the relationship between behavior (B) and consequences (C). These contingencies include techniques such as positive and negative reinforcement, token economies, and exposure techniques (also discussed further later) that are used to *reinforce* or *extinguish* the *target behaviors* that become the focus for change (Payne, 1996).

Reinforcement

The use of positive behavioral consequences is one of the main techniques used in behavioral therapy to change maladaptive or undesirable behaviors. This is often done through "token economies"—a work payment incentive system in which the participants receive tokens when they display the desired behaviors. These tokens can then be used in exchange for a desired item or activity. Barkley (1997a) has presented a detailed token economy program to help children with ADD/ADHD that focuses on curbing impulses as well as oppositional behaviors.

Social Skills Training

This technique is generally used to coach children (such as those who have learning disorders) in a variety of socially acceptable behaviors. It can also be used with adults who have difficulty with socially acceptable skills, such as those who suffer from developmental delays or schizophrenia. The social skills addressed generally include listening, speaking, body posture, voice training, and eye contact (Cooper & Lesser, 2005).

Assertiveness Training

Clients are taught to discriminate between behaviors that are aggressive, overly compliant, and appropriately assertive. The focus is on teaching them to accurately and directly state their point of view to others. The therapist encourages clients to practice these new skills both during treatment and outside in the real world to ensure generalization.

Imagery-Based Techniques

Systematic desensitization and relaxation training techniques involve helping clients to construct a stimulus hierarchy in which different situations that the client fears are ordered along a continuum from mildly stressful to very threatening. The client is instructed to imagine each event while deeply relaxed. The client is asked to concentrate on systematically relaxing different muscle groups. When a particular situation produces excessive anxiety, the client is instructed to cease visualizing the particular item and to restore feelings of relaxation. The item is repeated until the client can visualize it without experiencing undue anxiety. The therapist then chooses another item from the constructed hierarchy and works with the client in a similar fashion. When possible, real-life exposure is used instead of imagery-based techniques that take place in the therapist's office (Wilson, 1995).

The Third Wave of Cognitive Behavior Therapy

These therapies are empirically, principle-focused approaches that emphasize contextual and experiential change strategies in addition to the more traditional direct and didactic ones. The "third wave" reformulates and synthesizes traditional cognitive and behavioral therapy with a postmodern flavor in the hope of improving understanding and outcomes. Three of the third-wave therapies are described next.

Mindfulness-Based Cognitive Therapy

Segal, Williams, and Teasdale (2002) wrote about mindfulness-based cognitive therapy (MBCT) for depression. The core skill of this model is to teach patients, at times of potential relapse into depression, to recognize and disengage from mind states characterized by self-perpetuating patterns of ruminative, negative thought that can produce a downward spiraling of mood. Patients are taught to disengage from one mode of mind and enter another, incompatible, model of mind that will allow them to process depression-related information in ways that are less likely to provoke relapse. This involves moving from a focus on content to a focus on process. This is a departure from cognitive therapy's emphasis on changing the content of negative thinking, toward attending to the way all experience is processed.

The basic techniques of this theoretical model are the intentional use of attention and awareness in particular ways—being mindful. Awareness of the patterns of thoughts, feeling, and bodily sensations that characterize relapse-related mind states is the first step in recognizing the need for corrective action. Intentionally changing the focus and style of attention is the mental lever by which processing can be switched from one cognitive model to another. The nonjudgmental, present moment focus of mindfulness provides "both the means to change mental gears when disengaging from dysfunctional 'doing-related' mind states, and an alternative mental gear, or incompatible mode of mind, into which to switch" (Segal et al., 2002, pp. 76–77). These authors describe an eight-session MBCT program aimed at helping patients recognize "doing mode" in its many forms and to begin "being model" by intensive, formal mindfulness practice. As mindfulness skills develop, patients are taught to recognize when negative emotions and reactions trigger "doing mode" and learn how to disengage from that mode, enter "being mode," and if necessary to simply "be with" difficult emotions.

Finally, the skills of disengaging from emotional-related modes of mind is supplemented by coping strategies that provide patients with a range of options for responding more skillfully to negative emotion (Segal et al., 2002, p. 78). (See Segal, Williams & Teasdale, 2002, for further information on this theoretical model.)

Dialectical Behavioral Therapy

Dialectical behavioral therapy (DBT) begins with the therapist creating a context of validation for the patient. Within that context, the goal is to extinguish problematic behaviors and figure out a way to make nonproblematic behaviors reinforcing so that the patient continues the "good ones" and stops the "bad ones" (Linehan, 1993, pp. 97–101). The steps involved include the following:

1. Agreeing on goals and orienting the patient to treatment.
2. Establishing a relationship.
3. Applying core strategies: Validation and Problem Solving.
    - Validation includes finding the correctness or wisdom in the individuals' emotional, cognitive, and behavioral responses in the context of their experiences. The second type of validation involves the therapist's observing and believing in the patient's ability to make changes.
    - Problem solving includes (a) performing a behavioral analysis—a "moment-to-moment" chain analysis to determine the events that prompt targeted maladaptive behaviors; (b) performing a solution analysis in

which alternate behavioral solutions are developed; (c) orienting the patient to the proposed treatment solution; (d) eliciting a commitment from the patient to engage in the recommended treatment procedures; and (e) applying the treatment.

4. Balancing interpersonal communication styles: DBT balances "irreverent" and "reciprocal" communication. In irreverent communication, the therapist frames the problem or issue under consideration in a context different from the patient's, pushing the patient "off balance" so that rebalancing can occur. Reciprocal communications are warm, empathetic, and directly responsive to the patient. It can also include appropriate therapist self-disclosure to provide a model of normative responses in coping with life's problems.
5. Combining consultation to the patient strategies with interventions to the environment. The DBT therapist "coaches" the patient in how to solve problems and/or coordinate treatment with other professionals. Interventions in the environment take place when the patient does not have the capacity to produce the desired outcome.
6. Treating the therapist: An important part of DBT is the treatment of the therapist by supervision, case consultation group, or treatment team.

Acceptance and Commitment Therapy (ACT)

This model is a branch of cognitive behavioral therapy that integrates acceptance and mindfulness strategies in combination with commitment and behavior change strategies to increase psychology flexibility. Rather than trying to teach clients to better control their thoughts and feelings, ACT teaches them to notice, accept, and embrace them. The core conception of ACT is that psychological suffering is caused by experiential avoidance, which leads to cognitive distortions and entanglements and ultimately to a psychological rigidity that keeps people from taking actions that would improve their lives. The focus is therefore on helping clients "accept themselves and others with compassion, choose valued direction for their lives and commit to action that leads them in those directions" (Eifert & Forsyth, 2005, pp. 6–7).

The ACT acronym also stands for the three core steps of this approach (Eifert & Forsyth, 2005, p. 7).

1. Accept thoughts and feelings: Through various mindfulness exercises, clients learn to live with their unwanted thoughts and feelings by not attempting to eliminate or change them.
2. Choose directions: Help clients to choose directions for their lives by focusing on what they value in life and going forward in directions that are uniquely theirs.
3. Take action: This step involves committed action toward the client's life goals, in other words changing what they can change. There is a difference between the client as a person, the thoughts and feelings they have about themselves, and what they do with their lives.

Constructivism

Constructivism is a philosophical–behavioral–methodological system of conceptual thought that is concerned with the nature of reality and the acquisition of human knowledge. From a philosophical perspective, constructivism holds the position that nothing is universally true because there can always be different interpretations of the same phenomena. Common human experiences, therefore, are based on a consensual world of language, thought, and experience, not objective facts. This is a *postmodern perspective,* meaning that, contrary to previous thinking, *knowledge is not imparted to the human mind from an external objective world* but is a function of the interaction of the world of experience (empirical) and the basic nature (a priori state) of the human mind. Constructivism introduces nontraditional views of human nature, human development, and human functioning and can inform practice theories and approaches. It is rooted in neurobiology, as opposed to the social and behavioral sciences, and influenced by the work of Maturana and Varila (1987). The principles of constructivism (Carpenter, 1996) follow.

- Structural Determinism. The elements comprising a human experience are characterized primarily by an "inside-in process"—or the forming of information from within.
- Autopoeisis. These living systems are structure determined and organizationally closed and therefore engaged in the process of producing more of themselves.
- Structural Coupling. This principle of constructivism allows *autopoietic* individuals to interact with entities other than themselves and their own nervous systems. Interactions between individuals and their environments are triggered through mutual *perturbations* that form the basis for change in the person and in the environment. However, these *perturbations* do not determine those changes that are brought about independently by the nature of their respective structures. Interaction is seen as interactional, and not internal. In addition, it is each person's structure, or internal dynamics, that determines what environmental stimulus can trigger changes (*perturbations*) in each.

Cognitive Behavioral Constructivist Theory

In the last decade, cognitive behavioral theory has joined with constructivist theory and evolved into cognitive-behavioral-constructivist theory (Mahoney, 1999; Nagae & Nedate, 2001; Ronen, 2004). A constructivist perspective focuses on "stories" that clients have about the important events in their lives. Constructivists do not believe that clients, for example, are depressed because they "distort reality" because there may be a number of different realities. One of the goals of therapy is to help the client understand *how* and *why* she constructed her particular reality (story) and the consequences that have resulted from that construction. Meichenbaum (1996) feels that this is more empowering for clients than challenging the "irrationality" of the clients' thoughts and beliefs. There is a focus on strengths and resilience or "the rest of the story" (in addition to the problem story). Another goal of therapy would be to help the clients change the stories (or narratives) they have constructed about themselves. Assessment and treatment within this theoretical framework are interdependent processes. For example, as Meichenbaum (1996) wrote: "The types of questions the therapist asks, the specific tests that are administered, the self-monitoring exercises clients are asked to do, and the feedback provided to clients and significant others are all means of assessment as well as ways to treat clients through education and the instillation of hope" (p. 19). Assessment tools may include clinical interviews, self-report measures, self-monitoring data (such as keeping a diary of when panic attacks occur), and behavioral indicators. The therapist designs each session in collaboration with the client. Together, they collect baseline information about the client's functioning and areas of difficulty. They evaluate whether the client has improved in these specific areas after treatment interventions. The combination of cognitive, behavioral, and constructivist treatment approaches offers a flexible, dynamic model for change that can be used with diverse clients and with a wide range of problems (Ronen, 2004).

Narrative Therapy

The principle guiding narrative therapy is that psychotherapy is a "process in which therapists create the conditions and facilitate the process through which their clients can construct new meanings and transform old meanings" (Rosen, 1998). Individuals make meaning of their lives within the contexts of their family, culture, and community, and these meanings are considered to be socially constructed. The use of language plays a central role in the postmodern paradigmatic shift from objective to subjective reality because reality is constructed through social discourse. Consequently, the therapist listens to clients' stories—or narratives—about their lives.

Narrative therapy posits that people's lives have been both authored by themselves and coauthored by others. The person's story line may contain problems and story lines that do not feel authentic to the person's true life experiences. The basic goal, then, is to "deconstruct" these old and inauthentic story lines and to help individuals become the author of their own life stories. This means revising, or "reconstructing," the story in a way that has value and meaning to the person but is ethical and fair to others. The process of giving new meaning to one's life story is called "reauthoring." The therapist helps clients find alternate ways of viewing the "problem-saturated" story they are telling about their life. This is achieved through tellings and retellings of life stories through which people's lives are "thickened" and alternatives are generated. The therapist and the client may decide to invite other people in the client's life to participate in the therapeutic reconstruction of the story, as witnesses to the client's *preferred claims,* in a "definitional ceremony." These invited guests, the client, or the therapist may also write a letter or letters—called "therapeutic documents"—affirming the new story about the client. This is an empowering and depathologizing approach to working with clients, in which discussion of social justice, poverty, gender, and power are encouraged (Kelley, 1996; Rosen, 1998).

Feminist Theory

Land (1998) noted that feminist practitioners utilize a range of theoretical orientations, including cognitive-behavioral, psychodynamic, psychosocial, problem-solving, family systems, constructivist, and relational approaches (pp. 3–19). What these practitioners have in common, more than a specific theoretical model, is a philosophy of practice that includes validating the social context, recognizing differences in male and female experience, rebalancing perceptions of normality and deviance, an inclusive stance, attention to power dynamics in the therapeutic relationship, recognizing how the personal is the political, a deconstructive approach, and a partnering stance (Land, 1998; Worell & Remer, 1992). Gilligan (1982, 1991) stressed the importance of girls and women expressing the full range of their feelings and experiences and providing the conditions necessary for healthy psychological development to occur. Gilligan felt that *voice* was the essential ingredient in female development and that the expression of one's voice becomes a barometer of relationships, signifying either psychological health or distress. Gilligan suggests that attending to *voice* includes four basic questions:

1. Who is speaking?
2. In what body?
3. From whose perspective is the story about what relationship being told?
4. In what societal and cultural frameworks is the story being told? (Brown & Gilligan, 1992, p. 21)

Gilligan introduced the concepts of "political resistance" and "psychological resistance" to define the ways in which girls and women handle their resistance. Political resistance is an insistence to know what one knows and a willingness to be outspoken. Psychological resistance involves a reluctance to know what one knows and a fear that such knowledge, if spoken, will endanger the relationship(s). In fact, Gilligan (1982, 1990, 1996) felt that females make decisions, moral and otherwise, based on a principle of care, in contrast to men, who base their moral decisions on a principle of justice. Gilligan's (1982) work on moral development challenged the classical (drive) psychoanalytic theory that the superegos of females are less developed than those of males (see Chapter 11 on middle childhood for further discussion of Gilligan's work on moral development in females). A model of feminist relational psychotherapy—offering a psychology of women—expands on Gilligan's work and is presented next (also see Jordan et al., 1991, 1998; Miller, 2002, 2003).

Cultural Relational Theory

The general assumption of this feminist theory initially known as self in relation and relabeled cultural relational theory is that a woman's self develops not as a result of movement away from infant symbiosis toward adult autonomy and individuation, but as a part of relationships and in interpersonal connection and interaction. The goal of development is not an increasing sense of separation, but one of enhanced connection. It is the process of mutual engagement, mutual empathy, and mutual empowerment that lead to personal growth through connection. Negative development sequelae emerge when the need for engagement and mutual empathy are not met. Disconnection occurs when a child or adult is prevented from participating in mutually responsive and mutually enhancing relationships—when the surrounding relational context is unresponsive to the child. This context includes not only the child's primary caretakers but also the importance of the larger context within which these relationships occur. When particular groups of people are privileged based on gender, ethnicity, class, sexual preference, and religion, it creates a context in which whole groups of people exercise power over others (Coll, 1992; Coll, Cook-Nobles, & Surrey, 1995; Spencer, 2000). This may result in diminished self-esteem and efforts to make oneself into what one believes is necessary to be accepted in a nonaccepting relationship. A woman's developmental problems are seen not from failure to separate, but from difficulties in trying to maintain a relationship and a connection while asserting her own needs or desires. The development of the capacity for empathy must grow in the context of mutually empathic and empowering relationships. Most women do not develop self-empathy because the pull of empathy for the other is so strong and because females are conditioned to attend to the needs of others first and because women often experience so much guilt about claiming attention for themselves, even from the self. According to cultural relational theory, women feel the need not only to be understood but also to understand others (Chodorow, 1978; Dinnerstein, 1977; Jordan, 1994; Surrey, Kaplan, & Jordan, 1990). Several constructs of this theoretical model are defined later (see also Cooper & Lesser, 2005, p. 115).

Mutual Empathy

Empathy is a mutual, interactive process and is the basis for creating and being in a growth-enhancing relationship. For example, although it is important to be understood, it is also important to understand others.

Relationship Authenticity

This is the ongoing challenge to feel emotionally real, connected, vital, clear, and purposeful in a relationship (Cooper & Lesser, 2005, p. 116). Dialogue between two individuals relies on both initiative and responsiveness.

Relationship Differentiation

This is a process of increasing levels of complexity in a relationship within which individual development occurs. Relationship is defined intersubjectively as the ongoing, intrinsic inner awareness and responsiveness to the continuous existence of the other(s) and the expectation of mutuality in this regard (Jordan, 1997, p. 61).

Self-Empathy

This means that one's internalized self-representations must undergo a change so that women can direct the empathy they bring to their relationships with others toward themselves. Empowering the empathy of another person is one way to facilitate this process because the individual is joined with another in a process of "empathic witnessing and acceptance with a resulting decrease of harsh self judgments" (Surrey, Kaplan, & Jordan, 1990, p. 13).

Van den Bergh (1995), a postmodern feminist, challenged the practice of gender-associated thinking that she feels promotes binary gender categories and stereotypes. She feels that when gender possibilities are dichotomized, we privilege some arrangements (for example, in cultural relational theory, women tend to be idealized somewhat) and marginalize others. Comas-Diaz (1994) cautioned that the theory may emphasize the mother–daughter relationship to the exclusion of others. She also discussed the variance of child-rearing practices among different racial and cultural groups. Race, class, age, health, and ethnicity always mediate the meaning of being female, and the postmodern feminists favor psychologies of women that are pluralistic, multicultural, contextual, and egalitarian.

Theories of Play Therapy

Erikson (1950) defined play as a "function of the ego, an attempt to synchronize the bodily and social processes within the self" (p. 214). Play therapy consists of a cluster of treatment modalities. It is "the systematic use of a theoretical model to establish an interpersonal process wherein trained play therapists use the therapeutic powers of play to help clients prevent or resolve psychosocial difficulties and achieve optimal growth and development (Association for Play Therapy, 1997, p. 7). Gil and Drewes (2005) remind us of the importance of maintaining "a competent cross-cultural focus" when providing play therapy services. This includes the availability of toys and play materials that are representative of cultural diversity. The following section describes three major theoretical perspectives of play therapy: *Relational, cognitive-behavioral,* and *developmental.* Each of these theoretical frameworks encompasses different models and techniques (see O'Connor & Braverman, 1997, for further discussion).

Relational Play Therapy

The therapist uses play in relational play therapy to interact with the child. One of the clinical challenges for the therapist is to determine and create a therapeutic interaction, including a role in the play process. Through the medium of play and the mutual creativity of the child and the therapist, the child experiences a newly developed self or self-and-other experience. The child discovers a new way of interacting with another person (for example, the therapist), which allows the child to bring forth a new sense of himself or herself and others. This can lead to the development of new possibilities for interactions with others outside the play therapy sessions. The relational approach to play therapy places less emphasis on the role of interpretation than more traditional forms of psychoanalytic play therapy that may use the play to help the child "work through" unconscious conflicts (Lee, 1997; O'Connor, Ewart, & Wolheim, 2001). As Altman and colleagues (2002) wrote: "The shape of the interaction itself—the particular negotiations between therapist and child, and what the two participants in the play process create—is the essential element in the therapeutic action of child treatment" (p. 209).

The specific meaning of any play sequence is less meaningful than the quality of the child's playful participation, how that participation engages the therapist, and what the structure of the plays tells us about the dilemmas of the child. A clinical challenge for the relational child therapist is to determine when, and if, interpretations to the child about the child's play can be useful at all. It may be facilitative for some children, but inhibitory for others. The therapist's role can be either directive or nondirective with regard to the child's play. Therapists are guided in these instances by their own experience of being with the child; a therapist is in a sense learning what the child needs from the experience of being with the child. The therapist must consider whether this direction is coming from the child or from the therapist's own issues. Relational play therapists also use themselves to facilitate the process of play between the children they work with and, when appropriate, their parents. This can be done through suggestion, encouragement, or modeling in parent–child or family sessions (Altman et al., 2002, p. 213).

Cognitive Behavioral Play Therapy

The goal of this type of therapy is to "correct the child's interpersonal schema as well as to facilitate the child's use of more cognitive/verbal mediation strategies" (O'Connor, 2000, p. 36). The focus is on identifying and changing the patterns of reinforcements, consequences, and cognitions that contribute to the child's developmentally inappropriate behavior. Play is the medium the therapist uses to establish a relationship with the child and to introduce reinforcement schedules that expose the child to positive and negative consequences for his or her behavior. Altering the child's thoughts and beliefs is also considered important in effecting behavioral change. The therapist works closely with others in the child's environment, such as parents and teachers, to obtain behavioral records and dispense reinforcements (which are suggested by the therapist). Various techniques are employed with this theoretical framework, and they vary depending on the specific focus. A good example of this type of a reinforcement strategy (based on the concept of operant conditioning previously discussed) is Dr. Russell Barkley's (1997b) token economy used with children with oppositional or defiant behaviors. Children are rewarded with a designated number of tokens for desired behaviors that they, in turn, may use to purchase specific rewards (an hour of television might be given in exchange for three tokens). Tokens can also be taken away for certain behaviors that have been identified in advance as being unacceptable (throwing a tantrum, hitting a sibling). Interpersonal problem-solving training programs, such as social skills training groups used with children with ADD/ADHD, focus on increasing cognitive awareness as well as behavioral change through the use of modeling and changing thought processes.

Developmental Play Therapy

This school of thought emphasizes the role of the child's interactions with caretakers as being essential to healthy development. Two types of developmental play therapy are discussed next.

Theraplay This model, developed by Ann Jernberg (1979), focuses on problems of attachment in young children, including problems relating to people, problems in accepting care, problems with transitions, lack of a conscience, emotional immaturity, and problems with trust and self-esteem (Jernberg & Booth, 1999). Jernberg felt that if these fundamental caretaking interactions are disturbed early in children's lives, there will be severe consequences in their ability to engage in functional interpersonal interactions.

The goal of theraplay is to overcome the behaviors that prevent the child from having the kind of interpersonal relationships necessary to function optimally. The therapist establishes a caretaker relationship with the child and implements activities that promote the experience of positive interpersonal interactions. These experiences are then generalized to the child's world outside the therapy. Theraplay focuses on four specific early child/caretaker interactions, which are summarized in Table 3.8 (Hill, 1995).

Filial Therapy Filial therapy is a method for treating children that focuses on training the parent or caregiver to become the child's primary therapeutic agent. This model was developed by Bernard Guerney (1969), who felt that many problems of maladjustment with children either were caused by or resulted in strained interpersonal relationships within the family. Originally developed as a long-term group approach for children under the age of 10, it has been adapted for brief

TABLE 3.8

Theraplay Interactions

I. Structuring activities	These are behaviors that create boundaries for the child with the aim of reducing arousal (stimulation). These activities promote trust in the caretaker and a sense of predictability and safety for the child. Structuring activities decrease as the child is able to assume more of these functions for herself.
2. Challenging activities	The caretaker encourages the child to perform at the upper end of his present capacities to increase the level of arousal, pushing the child toward appropriate independence.
3. Engaging activities	Behaviors that the caretaker engages in to initiate or maintain interaction with the child to provide developmentally appropriate stimulation and alertness.
4. Nurturing activities	The caretaker provides for the child's physical and emotional needs.

Source: S.W. Hill, 1995, *Theraplay: An Overview*. www.angelfire.com/oh/avalanchDiode/THERAPLY.html

treatment with diverse ages and populations and is now considered potentially useful for most parent–child dyads irrespective of the child's developmental level (Guerney, 1990; Landreth, 1991; Rennie & Landreth, 2000). The full course of filial therapy is usually 6 to 12 sessions. Filial therapy teaches the parent a new way of interacting with their child through the use of therapeutic play. By engaging in this type of play, the parents are able to break previous unrewarding and/or difficult patterns of parent–child interaction. Parents are taught basic child-centered play therapy principles and skills, including reflective listening, recognizing and responding to children's feelings, therapeutic limit setting, building children's self-esteem, and structuring weekly play sessions with their children using selected toys (Landreth, 2002). Therapeutic techniques utilized by the play therapists in the training include didactic instruction, demonstration play sessions, role playing, group discussion, required at-home laboratory play sessions, and psychoeducation (Guerney, Guerney, & Andronico, 1999). In addition to the play therapy sessions with their child and the play therapist, the parents attend group meetings with other parents that focus on different techniques, the meaning of their child's play, and the parents' emotional responses to the play therapy sessions. The consistency of the special playtime, the toys used, and the relationship between the parent and the child results in a change in perception of the parent by the child. The types of toys utilized during the play therapy sessions include baby bottles, dolls, kitchen food and kitchenware, paints, crayons, markers, clay, puppets, small plastic soldiers, animals and dinosaurs, blocks, and play money. The toys are used to facilitate expression of feelings such as nurturance, anger and aggression, and competition, as well as to focus on mastery and competence. The parent learns to set limits on the child's behavior with empathy and firmness. The parent learns to both accept the child's feelings and to facilitate their expression in a socially appropriate manner (Guerney et al., 1999; VanFleet, 1994, 2000). During the initial phase of treatment, the parents are trained and closely supervised by the therapist during play sessions with their child. During the middle phase, the parent practices with the child at home, and the therapist reviews the parents' report of the sessions. During the final sessions of the training/play therapy sessions, the parent continues the play sessions with the child and is slowly weaned from supervision by the therapist (O'Connor, 2000, p. 51).

Motivational Interviewing

The conceptual basis for this model is preparing people for change. It can be used with a wide range of client populations, including those challenged by substance abuse, eating disorders, gambling, and other addictions. It is helpful with adolescents and young adults (Baer Peterson, 2002), criminal justice populations (Ginsburg, Mann, Rotgers, & Weeks, 2002), patients with dual mental and substance abuse disorders (Handmaker, Packard, & Conforti, 2007). Other authors have also used it with couples and groups (Burke, Vassilev, Kantchelov, & Zweben, 2007; Walters, Ogle, & Martin, 2007).

The four conceptual principles behind motivational interviewing are (Miller & Rollnick, 2002, pp. 36–41) the expression of empathy; developing discrepancy between the client's present behavior and personal goals; rolling with the resistance and avoiding arguments about change; and supporting self-efficacy, recognizing that the client remains the primary resource in finding answers and solutions. Finally, remember that the therapist's belief in the person's ability to change, as well as the client's belief in the possibility of change, are important motivators. The basic skills of Motivational Interviewing are described below (Arkowitz & Miller, 2008, pp. 7–8)

1. Ask open ended questions: The therapist uses selective, open ended questions to engage the client and focus on areas of importance to the client.
2. Listen reflectively: Reflective listening is used to help the client verbalize the true meanings behind what they say which may not always be expressed explicitly due to fears, lack of awareness of what they mean, or not being able to find the right words to convey their experience. This may include repeating, rephrasing, or paraphrasing what the client has said as well as reflecting emotional feelings the client may be experiencing.
3. Affirm: The therapist uses statements of appreciation or understanding that encourage and support the client during the change process.
4. Summarize: At the end of each session the therapist summarizes what has taken place and emphasizes certain points, using the client's own statements of motivation for change whenever possible.
5. Elicit change talk: The therapist intentionally elicits change talk without becoming an advocate for change. Change talk consists of "statements reflecting desire, perceived ability, need, readiness, reason, or commitment to change."(p. 8)

Summary

We did not intend this chapter to be inclusive of all theories but to provide a selection that encourages critical thinking about human development and that can be used with individuals at different points in the life cycle. We feel strongly that theory should not be applied uniformly or chosen because it is preferred by the practitioner. We must remain current with the literature and with the research. There are different methods that can be used to evaluate practice. For example, evidenced-based practice has gained popularity in recent years. This model of evaluation is based on quantitative research and has been used to demonstrate the effectiveness of cognitive and behavioral therapies. Other types of treatment models, such as the brief psychodynamic models, have withstood empirical testing (Messer & Warren, 1995). Kohut felt that empathy was the evaluative tool in determining the efficacy of self-psychology (Kohut, 1959/1978; Siegel, 1996). Regardless of the method, practitioners should have some way of determining whether their practice is effective. Two methods of research that we consider particularly appropriate for social workers are the quantitative single-system design and qualitative inquiry (see Cooper & Lesser, 2005 for further discussion and examples of these research methods). We must also be cognizant of the value base of our profession, which espouses respect for client self-determination, attention to strengths, the impact of culture and other forms of diversity, and social justice. This is a challenge in today's managed mental health environment, where the emphasis is on diagnosis, medication management, and symptom reduction. Social workers need to meet this challenge by remaining loyal to the profession's enduring legacy of grounding our practice in a *biopsychosocial framework*.

4 Identity Development

Introduction

This chapter addresses models of human development that help us understand the multiple dimensions of identity. One of the most proficient contributors to the study of identity was Erik Erikson (1956, 1963, 1968a, 1968b), who felt that the search for identity was the main thrust of life. Erikson (1963) described identity as providing "the ability to experience one's self as something that has continuity and sameness and to act accordingly" (p. 42). He felt that identity included biological maturation, unconscious psychological development, and a conscious process that involved interaction between an individual and the sociohistorical and cultural milieu. According to Erikson, individuals pass through eight psychosocial stages of development over the course of life. In each stage, the individual faces a main task of development that must be accomplished to move to the next stage. These stages are referred to as "crises" because they provide conflicts that require some resolution. It is in the process of resolving these crises that maturation opens up both new possibilities and new social demands. The eight psychosocial stages of development identified by Erikson (1963, 1968b) are shown in Table 4.1.

Erikson felt that individual life cycles develop in the context of a specific culture. Therefore, each developmental stage provides new ways of experiencing and interacting with cultural practices. Desai (1999), for example, talks about the influence of the South Asian culture, where family and relationships with gods are part of the individual's "collective identity." Erikson (1975) felt that appreciating

TABLE 4.1

Psychosocial Stages of Identity Development

1. *Trust vs. Mistrust:* Infants learn to trust others to care for their basic needs or to mistrust them.
2. *Autonomy vs. Shame and Doubt:* Children learn to exercise their will and to control themselves or they become uncertain and doubt that they can do things by themselves.
3. *Initiative vs. Guilt:* Children learn to initiate their own activities, enjoy their accomplishments, and become purposeful. If they are not allowed to follow their own initiative, they feel guilty for their attempt to become independent.
4. *Industry vs. Inferiority:* Children learn to be competent and effective at activities valued by adults and peers or they feel inferior.
5. *Identity vs. Role Confusion:* Adolescents establish a sense of personal identity as part of their social group or they become confused about who they are and what they want to do in life.
6. *Intimacy vs. Isolation:* Young adults find an intimate life companion or they risk loneliness and isolation.
7. *Generativity vs. Stagnation:* Adults must be productive in their work and willing to raise a next generation or they risk stagnation.
8. *Integrity vs. Despair:* People try to make sense of their prior experience and to assure themselves that their lives have been meaningful or they despair over their unachieved goals and ill spent lives.

Source: M.Cole and S.R.Cole, 1996, *The Development in Children* (3rd ed.). New York: W.H. Freeman. Adapted with permission.

the intersections of an individual's intrapsychic world and sociohistorical context is important in understanding identity development. More recent authors (Ganzer & Ornstein, 2002; Kroger, 2000; Liu, Soleck, Hopps, Dunston, & Pickett, 2004; Sue & Sue, 2003) expand on this concept, emphasizing how social context and social discourse contribute to identity over time. Milville and colleagues (2000, p. 1) also talked about "collective identities," such as race, class, and gender, which affect an individual's self-concept. Other authors refer to race, class, and gender "as a constellation of positionalities (e.g., social locations) that classify, categorize, and construct the social value that is assigned to individuals according to various components (e.g., beliefs, concepts and structures that define social practice)" (Harley, Jolivette, McCormick, & Tice, 2002, p. 216). These authors label the intersections between and among these constructs as "multiplicities of oppression" (p. 217). Several authors add to this discussion with the introduction of the paradigm of "intersectionality." They argue that different identities include relative amounts of oppression and privilege and that these simultaneously interact to create unique life experiences (Mccall, 2003; Murphy, Hunt, Zajicek, Norris & Hamilton, 2009; Hulko, 2009). Despite their intersectionality Anderson (2005) argues that not all social identity categories should be considered equal, citing for example, racial identity, which has been used to define legal person hood.

Sue and Sue (2003, pp. 10–13) offer a tripartite model (see Figure 4.1), which we feel provides an integrated conceptual framework for appreciating the multiple and interlocking dimensions of identity. Their model assesses identity at the individual, group, and universal level. The *individual level* includes the uniqueness of each person by nature of their genetic endowment and nonshared experiences. The *group level* includes both the similarities and differences individuals share by gender, socioeconomic status, geographic location, marital status, race, sexual orientation, ethnicity, disability/ability, and culture. On the *universal level* are the shared experiences of humanity. These include universal life events such as birth and death and the ability to use symbols such as language.

This chapter focuses on the group level described by Sue and Sue, specifically the group constructs of race, ethnicity, gender, sexual orientation, and social class. (We will discuss the equally important constructs of spirituality and disability in Chapters 8 and 17, respectively.) Each of the constructs that follow is discussed as a separate entity; however, it is important to appreciate that they are "co-constructed, interdependent constructs that should be, and need to be, understood together" (Liu, Soleck, et al., 2004, p. 96).

Racial Identity Development

Race is a system of social identity constructed over years through cultural, social, economic, and political relations. Several research studies have found that persons of color self-rated "race and ethnicity" as an important or very important identity areas (Canabal, 1995; Casas, Wagenheim, Banchero, & Mendoza-Romero, 1994;

FIGURE 4.1

Tripartite Model of Personality Identity Development

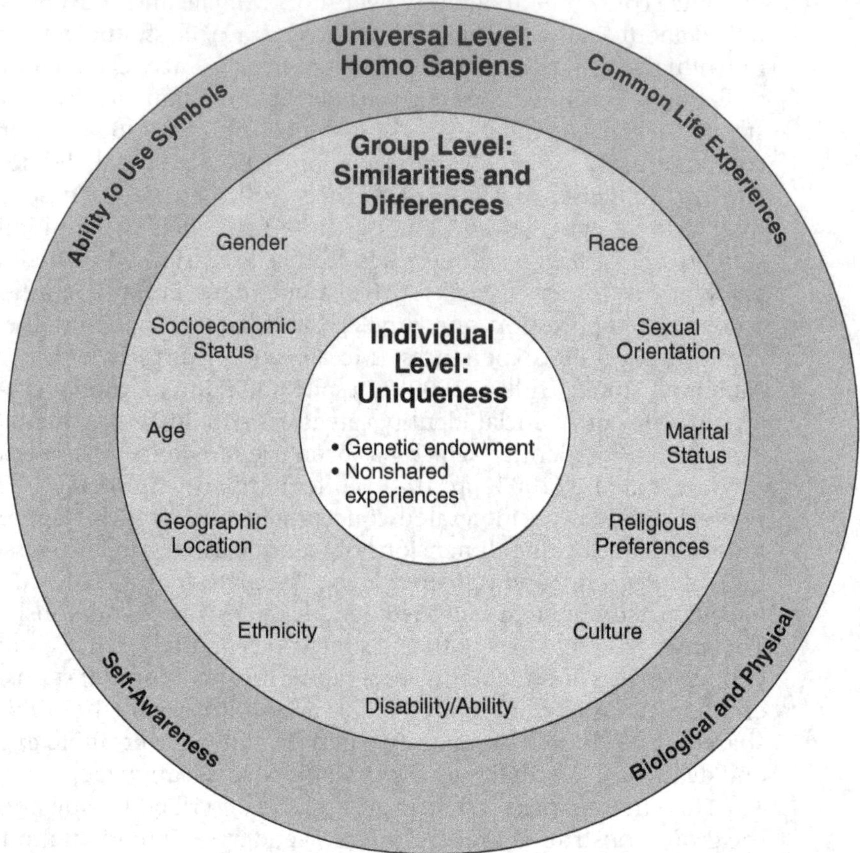

Source: D.W Sue and D. Sue, *Counseling the Culturally Different: Theory and Practice* (4th ed.), (p.12). Hoboken, NJ: John Wiley & Sons, Inc. Copyright © 2003 by D.W. Sue and D. Sue. Reprinted with permission of John Wiley & Sons, Inc.

Hurtado, Gurin, & Peng, 1994; Milville & Helms, 1996; Phinney & Alipuria, 1990). Most therapeutic approaches, including many of those described in Chapter 3, neglect the sociopolitical context of individual development. Racial identity theories, however, evolve from a tradition of treating race as a sociopolitical and/or cultural construction as opposed to a biological one (Helms, 1995; Sue & Sue, 2003). "Race is also a social construction necessary to racism" (Miller & Garan, 2007 p. 25). Critical race theory addresses the experiences of different racial groups in the United States, including those who are socially targeted as well as those who are socially privileged (p. 28).

Sue and Sue (2003) considered the work on racial and cultural identity development "to be one of the most promising approaches to the field of multicultural counseling" (p. 207). We need to understand the effects of racism and oppression on identity formation for many reasons. For example, clients may present with issues of internalized racism. A dark-skinned Latina woman described her daughter to me in the following way: "She's a real beauty . . . she has blue eyes and she's light skinned like her father . . . not dark like me." A client may have a preference for a racially similar therapist or even in some cases for a therapist of another race. An excerpt from a counseling session between an African-American client and a white counselor illustrates this point (Cooper & Lesser, 2005, p. 77; see Practice Example 4.1).

An individual's reaction to counseling, the counseling process, and the counselor may be influenced by cultural and racial identity, not simply membership in a minority group (Sue & Sue, 2003). This awareness was further illustrated recently in an article by an African-American male reporter in his middle years. He was commenting on what he said were complaints by some university students as well as others in the minority community who feel burdened when white students, and instructors in some cases, expect the person of color to teach them about racism. He was perplexed by this and in his article asked the question, "If not us [meaning other African Americans or members of other minority groups as the case may be], then who?" His perspective, perhaps a function of his own racial identity development and life experience, was that he felt that other African Americans, like himself, were best suited to educate peers, colleagues, and members of the white majority.

We begin our discussion of racial identity with black identity development, followed by biracial identity development and ethnic identity development. It is also important for white people to consider their identity development as members of a society where being white has, in at least one of the many aspects of a person's collective identities—racial identity—been a privileged status. Therefore, we conclude the section on racial identity development with a discussion of white identity development. It is important as we review the following unidimensional identity models to also appreciate that individuals have many identifiers. It is also noteworthy that "with multiple memberships come multiple processes of understanding both one's self-identity and identity in relation to others. Identity is influenced by individual and social perceptions, and these perceptions gain credence, whether accurate or not, through one's interaction with others" (Stanley, 2004, p. 163).

PRACTICE EXAMPLE 4.1

Cross-Racial Counseling Session

The worker asks: "I'm wondering if you're concerned about whether a White woman can understand your feelings? Do you think you might receive more understanding from a Black therapist? The client reponds: "In some ways it is difficult to talk to you but I would like to tell you about my experiences. In all the time I have spent with White people I feel I have never really been honest about who I am. Sometimes, I don't even know who I am. It's important for me to be honest with you and for you to be able to hear what I have to say. Working with you gives me a chance to practice being a Black woman in a White world—but in a real way."

Black Identity Development

One of the most influential models of black identity development was proposed by Cross (1971, 1991, 1995). This model has been used as a template for the development of other minority identity development models, including those for Latinos, Native Americans, and Asians. Each of these groups has experienced sociopolitical identity transformations around the unifying theme of oppression, referred to as a "Third World consciousness." (See Sue & Sue, 2003, for further discussion of these specific models.) The Cross model includes five stages through which an individual moves to reach positive race identity. These stages are presented in Table 4.2.

TABLE 4.2

Black Identity Development Model

Stage #—Name	Description
1. Pre-Encounter	This is a stage in which the individual has a "pre-encounter" assimilation Euro-American frame of reference and either a natural valence toward being Black, a devaluing of Blackness or a valuing of Whiteness.
2. Encounter	Marked by an experience or an "encounter" that shocks the individuals into a new awareness of being Black and makes the individual aware of a certain level of inappropriateness of previously held beliefs. The person becomes motivated to search for a Black identity at this time.
3. Immersion-Emersion:	In this stage, the person withdraws from the dominant White culture and becomes immersed in Black/African-American culture; development of Black pride and anti-white attitudes. This is followed by a leveling off of the anti-white feelings and an ability to be more flexible in interacting with members of the white culture/community.
4. Internalization	Characterized by inner security and positive sense of Black identity is integrated into overall personality.
5. Internalization-Commitment:	Marked by individuals who have increased their commitment to social justice, social change and activities supporting the civil rights and welfare of Black communities.

Source: W. Cross, 1995, "The Psychology of Niegrscence: Revising the Cross Model." In J. Ponterotto, J.M. Casas, L.A. Suzuki, and C.M. Alexander (Eds.), *Handbook of Multicultural Counseling* (pp. 93–122). Thousand Oaks, CA: Sage Publications, Inc.

TABLE 4.3

The Racial Cultural Identity Model

Stages of Minority Development Model	Attitude Towards Self	Attitude Toward Others of the Same Minority	Attitude Toward Others of a Different Minority	Attitude Toward Dominant Group
Stage 1. Conformity	Self-depreciating or neutral due to low race salience	Group-depreciating or neutral due to low race salience	Discriminatory or neutral	Group-appreciating
Stage 2. Dissonance and appreciating	Conflict between self-depreciating and group-appreciating	Conflict between group-depreciating views of minority hierarchy and feelings of shared experience	Conflict between dominant-field and group depreciating	Conflict between group-appreciating
Stage 3. Resistance and immersion	Self-appreciating	Group-appreciating experience and feelings of culturocentrism	Conflict between feelings of empathy For other minority	Group-depreciating
Stage 4. Introspection	Concern with basis of self-appreciation	Concern with nature of unequivocal appreciation	Concern with ethnocentric basis for judging others	Concern with the basis of group-depreciation
Stage 5. Integrative Awareness	Self-appreciating	Group-appreciating	Group-appreciating	Selective appreciation

Source: D. R. Atkinson, G. Morten, and D. Sue, 1998, *Counseling American Minorities: A Cross Cultural Perspective* (5th ed.). Dubuque, IA: Wm. C. Brown Publishers. In D. W. Sue and D. Sue, 2003, *Counseling the Culturally Diverse: Theory and Practice* (4th ed.), (p. 215). Hoboken, NJ: John Wiley & Sons, Inc. This material is reproduced with permission of The McGraw-Hill Companies.

Sue and Sue (2003) refined the minority identity development model (MID) developed by Atkinson, Morten, and Sue (1989), which integrates the experiences of the minority groups mentioned earlier. They call their model the racial/cultural identity development model (R/CID) and present it as a conceptual framework that helps to understand the culturally different attitudes and behaviors of their clients. This model is presented in Table 4.3.

Biracial Identity Development

The term *biracial* is generally used to refer to a person whose parents are from two different racial backgrounds. It is sometimes used interchangeably with the term *bicultural.* Although historically used to identify children of black and white racial heritage, it is not limited to this combination (Aldarondo, 2001; Poston, 1990; Root, 1990, 1994, 1999). Monoracial identity development models do not adequately describe the experiences of biracial individuals because (a) the biracial individual may choose one group over the other at different stages of life; (b) biracial individuals may have a stake in both the majority and the minority cultures; (c) monoracial identity development models do not include the possibility of integrating more than one racial group identity; and (d) monoracial models assume the minority community will be completely accepting as the individual immerses herself into the culture at a given stage (Kerwin & Ponterotto, 1995, p. 205).

Kerwin and Ponterotto (1995) developed a model of biracial identity development based on the developmental stages of preschool, entry to school, preadolescence, adolescence, college/young adulthood, and adulthood. Although not as fully conceptualized as some of the other stage models, it is one of the few models that actually addresses racial identity from a child's perspective. During the preschool phase (up to 5 years of age) racial awareness emerges, and children notice the difference in their parents' appearances. Children enter school with an awareness of their racial heritages and generally have been given some descriptive way to self-identify. During preadolescence, environmental factors appear to trigger increased racial awareness. Children tend to use labels that represent membership in groups by race, culture, and ethnicity during this stage. Adolescence (see Chapter 12) may be the most challenging stage for biracial children, when issues of wanting to be like one's peers emerge more strongly. The development of a biracial identity continues throughout adulthood, and a person who has an integrated sense of both (or all) of his or her cultures may be able to function comfortably in a variety of settings (Poston, 1990; Root, 1994, 1999).

A second biracial identity development model based on black/white racial heritages, but which can be applied to other biracial and bicultural combinations, has been proposed by Henriksen and Trusty (2004, pp. 72–73). This model includes six periods that identify an individual's movement toward the development of a biracial identity and is depicted in Table 4.4.

TABLE 4.4

Biracial Identity Development Model

Stage #—Name	Description
1. Neutrality	Awareness or acceptance of the fact that racial differences exist. She might still be unaware of how race will affect her social interactions with individuals of other races.
2. Acceptance	Recognition and acceptance of a racial heritage based on statements from family and peers; recognition of not having a single racial reference group; impact of family on racial identity development

3. Awareness:	Understanding of what it means to be racially different from others accompanied by feelings of isolation due to lack of an identified racial reference group. Unlike the acceptance phase, now able to provide meaning to the experience. Acceptance and awareness were sometimes experienced simultaneously (or separately).
4. Experimentation	Attempt to identify more with one racial group or the other, or trying to determine their own racial identity. Having the acceptance of a peer group is important during this time.
5. Transition:	Movement toward a sense of racial self-recognition fueled by inner turmoil and a search for racial identity or a racial group with whom to identify. Awareness that it was not possible to choose without denying a part of their own identity.
6. Recognition	Individual accepts their biracial heritage and understands and appreciates who they are. The recognition phase can include many forms of identification; for example, identification with a single race group, with both racial groups, as a new racial group;

Source: R.C. Henriksen and J. Trusty, 2004. "Understanding and Assisting Black/White Biracial Women in Their Identity Development." In A. Gillem and C. Thompson (Eds.), *Biracial Women in Therapy: Between the Rock of Gender and the Hard Place of Race* (pp. 65–84). Binghamton, NY: The Haworth Press, Inc.

Ethnic Identity Development

Ethnicity or ethnic identity refers to how ethnic groups define themselves and maintain meaning for living individually and as a group (Cousins, 2003). Ethnic identity is an important self-concept for many diverse groups including Latino/as, Asians, and white ethnic groups (such as Italians, Irish, or Polish). Models of ethnic identity focus on the shared culture, religion, geography, and language of individuals who are connected by strong loyalty and kinship as well as proximity. Aspects of a culture may include rituals, symbols, values, beliefs, assumptions, and behaviors. The process of ethnic identity formation "involves an exploration of the meaning of one's ethnicity that leads to a secure sense of oneself as a member of a minority group" (p. 345). Phinney (1992, p. 160) described a model of ethnic identity development that she considered applicable to all ethnic groups in the United States. The components of ethnic identity described by Phinney include (a) self-identification or the ethnic label one uses for oneself; (b) ethnic behaviors and practices; and (c) feelings of affirmation by, and belonging to, an ethnic group. Phinney did not feel that attitudes toward other groups were a part of ethnic identity; however, she did feel that nondominant groups must resolve the stereotyping and prejudicial treatment by dominant white populations as they negotiate an ethnic identity.

The history of immigration to the United States at the turn of the 19th century, when vast waves of immigrants were arriving from different countries, offers some insight into the stereotyping and prejudice that each of these nondominant groups faced. The countries from which people are immigrating have shifted since that period in U.S. history; newer immigrants include greater numbers of persons from Central America, South America, the Caribbean, Africa, and Asia (U.S. Census Bureau, 2000).

Many newer immigrants maintain social connections with extended family in their countries of origin. Others have financial obligations to support children left behind with relatives. Falicov (2007) refers to this group of individuals as "transnational immigrants." We see a similar pattern of stereotyping and prejudice directed against newer, nondominant ethnic immigrants, particularly those who are persons of color. Most ethnic minorities must resolve the clash of value systems between nondominant and dominant groups and the manner in which minority members negotiate a bicultural value system. These groups arrive in the United States with different cultures that undergo transformation or "cultural change" that involves assimilation, accommodation, acculturation, and bicultural socialization, each of which is defined in Figure 4.2 (Cousins, 2003, p. 343).

Strong cultural ties can provide a solid foundation of support in a new land where customs are different and challenging to families. On the other hand, it

FIGURE 4.2

Culture Transformation

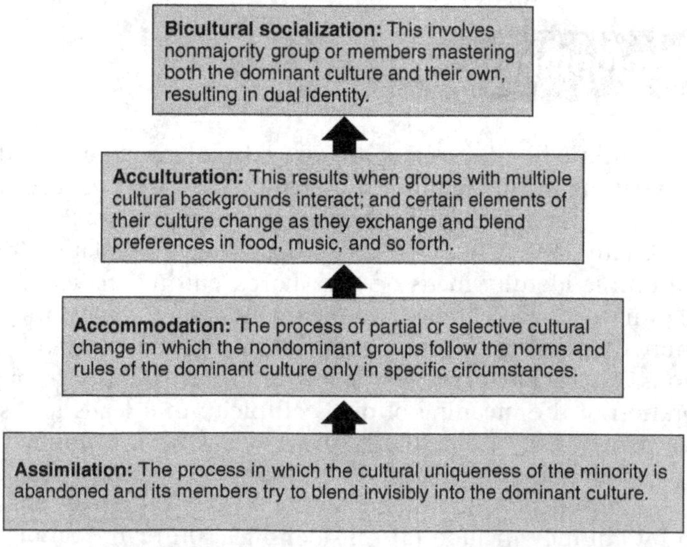

Bicultural socialization: This involves nonmajority group or members mastering both the dominant culture and their own, resulting in dual identity.

Acculturation: This results when groups with multiple cultural backgrounds interact; and certain elements of their culture change as they exchange and blend preferences in food, music, and so forth.

Accommodation: The process of partial or selective cultural change in which the nondominant groups follow the norms and rules of the dominant culture only in specific circumstances.

Assimilation: The process in which the cultural uniqueness of the minority is abandoned and its members try to blend invisibly into the dominant culture.

Source: L. Cousins, 2003, "Culture." In E. D. Hutchinson (Ed.), *Dimensions of Human Behavior: Person and Environment* (2nd ed.), Thousand Oaks, CA: Sage Publications, Inc.

can be difficult for adolescents and young adults to navigate the world of their peers and the world of their parents without confusion and stress if families are not willing to appreciate that their children are now growing up in a different sociocultural context than they had. These are important challenges for families to face together. The strength of the individual's cultural experience may be what makes the difference (Chavez & Guido-DiBrito, 1999; Falicov, 2007; Gonzalez, 2002; Portes & Rumbaut (2001).

White Identity Development

Sue and Sue (2003), Sue (2004) discuss some compelling reasons why it is important for white people to think about what being white means in the United States. First and foremost, it is the "ethnocentric monoculturalism" manifested in the historical legacy of the United States. Through a process of cultural conditioning, most, if not all, white people have inherited certain racial biases and stereotypes that inform their views of those from other racial groups.

As members of a multicultural and multiracial society, it is important for white people to understand and take action to overcome their prejudices. It is imperative that they do so if they are to become effective multicultural counselors (Sue & Sue, 2003, p. 240). Helms (1995) explains the process whereby European Americans come to understand the sociopolitical implications of race (Watt, Robinson, & Lupton-Smith, 2002, p. 95). She divided her model into two phases: Phase one, the "abandonment of racism," consists of four components. Phase two, called "non-racist white identity" consists of two components. Helms defined each component of these two phases as a "status." The term *status* denotes an aspect of racial identity that incorporates the attitudes, behaviors, and feelings an individual uses to handle experiences related to race. Helms refers to these attitudes, behaviors, and feelings as an information processing strategy (IPS). The first status described by Helms is *contact.* This status involves a lack of awareness of one's racism, and the IPS is obliviousness. *Disintegration* is the second status and occurs when the individuals recognize their whiteness and may feel confused or guilty when they realize there are differences in the way white people and persons of color have been and continue to be treated in our society. The IPS would be ambivalence. Status three is *reintegration,* an idealization of whiteness and intolerance of people of color. The IPS may be lack of empathy for persons of color and their history of struggle. In the fourth ego status, *pseudo-independence,* there is an intellectual aspect that includes limited tolerance for other racial groups. The IPS is selective perception, or paternalistic overtures to some persons of color. During the fifth ego status of *immersion/emersion,* there is an understanding of racism and of one's participation in it as a member of the white dominant group. The IPS is generally hypervigilance to racism. Finally, there is *autonomy,* the sixth ego status, which is characterized by the individual's commitment to a just society. The IPS is flexibility (Daniels, 2001; Helms, 1995). This model is depicted in Table 4.5.

Rowe, Bennett, and Atkinson (1994) developed a model of white identity development based on white racial consciousness. They classified racial consciousness into two components: unachieved white racial consciousness and achieved white racial consciousness. The *unachieved* group includes three subtypes: (a) *avoidant* individuals

TABLE 4.5

White Identity Development

Phase	Status	Information Processing Strategy (IPS)
1. The Abandonment of Racism	1. Contact	**Obliviousness**
	2. Disintegration	**Ambivalence**
	3. Re-integration	**Lack of empathy for People of Color**
	4. Pseudo-Independence	**Selective perception**
2. Non-racist White Identity	1. Immersion-emersion	**Hyper-vigilance to racism**
	2. Autonomy	**Flexibility**

Source: J.E. Helms, 1995. An update of Helms's "White and People of Color Racial Identity Models." In J. Ponterotto, J.M. Casas, L.A. Suzuki, and C.M. Alexander (Eds.), *Handbook of Multicultural Counseling* (pp. 181–198). Thousand Oaks, CA: Sage Publications, Inc. Copyright © 1995. Reprinted by permission of Sage Publications, Inc.

are those who simply fail to acknowledge the existence of racial problems in the United States; (b) *dependent* people tend to adopt the attitudes and beliefs of those around them; and (c) the *dissonant* type is someone who may be experiencing confusion about racial issues. The second subgroup—*achieved* white racial consciousness—includes four subgroups: (a) The *dominant* people believe that white people are better than people of color; (b) the *conflictive* type is opposed to overt racism, but not to anything that must be done to make things better; (c) the *reactive* individuals are aware of racial discrimination and may react with anger toward white people and try to identify with persons of color; and (d) the *integrative* person appreciates the complexity of race relations and values a pluralistic society.

Sue and Sue (2003) proposed a five-stage model of white identity development that integrates many of the characteristics of the previous models. The first phase is *conformity.* During this time, the white person's attitudes are ethnocentric. The next phase is *dissonance,* when the white individual encounters personal experiences that put the person more directly in touch with his or her racism. In phase three, *resistance* and *immersion,* the white person will begin to question his or her own racism and that of others in society. During the fourth phase, *introspection,* there is a searching and questioning attitude about one's place as a white person in the world as well as the experiences of persons of color. The fifth phase is the *integrative awareness* phase when one's identity as a nonracist white person emerges and is internalized. This individual values multiculturalism and is comfortable around different racial groups.

Integration Identity Development Model

Phan, Rivera, and Roberts-Wilbur (2005, p. 310) introduced the Integration Identity Development Model to describe the multifaceted reality of ethnic refugee groups such as Vietnamese refugee women. These authors described how a Vietnamese woman moves from understanding her identity as a Vietnamese individual to her identity as a woman and then her identity as a Vietnamese refugee woman without the restrictions imposed either by the Vietnamese culture or the U.S. dominant culture. This is an evolution of identity that suggests identity development models must include both gender and identity and accommodate continual change, the integration of culture and ancestral tradition (p. 310).

A study by Friedman, Friedlander, and Blustein (2005) of Jewish identity development describes Jewish identity as somewhat unique because it integrates both a cultural and a religious or spiritual meaning on identity formation (Kiselica, 2003). These authors found that an American Jew's identity is complex, multidimensional, and highly personal, depending on the individual's identification with the cultural heritage.

Gender Identity Development

Gender identity refers to an individual's perception of the self as masculine or feminine. Sigmund Freud's (1921/1949; 1933/1964) psychosexual model of identity is described in Chapter 3. With specific regard to gender identity development, Freud felt that the key development of a girl's sexual identity is her discovery that she does not have a penis. According to his theory, the girl blames her mother and transfers her love to her father. She competes with her mother for her father's attention, begins to feel guilty about this competition, and becomes afraid of punishment by her mother. As a result of her fear and her guilt, the young girl represses her feelings for her father and identifies with her mother. Unlike boys, whose primary identification is with mother and whose secondary identification is with father, the mother is the object both of a girl's primary and secondary identifications. Freud felt that this developmental process left women less developed in their attempts to differentiate from their mothers (Freud, 1925/1961, pp. 257–258).

Horney (1924, 1926) questioned the conceptual basis for penis envy and believed there was a biological drive of heterosexuality that led girls to turn naturally to their fathers as the object of their erotic feelings. She attempted to distinguish between primary penis envy (early narcissistic shame that girls possessed less anatomically than boys) and secondary penis envy (a defensive formation against the girl's hostility to men). Horney also raised the concept of male envy of motherhood, pregnancy, childbirth, and the breast, which she felt carried forth into adulthood for men and was consequently more enduring than penis envy was for females (Stiver, 1991). Moulton (1971) speculated that penis envy reflected one aspect of childhood curiosity and was not to be taken literally. She felt it needed to be understood in terms of how little girls are valued as well as how they experience their mothers being treated by their fathers. Bettleheim (1954) noted that boys were obsessed with the wish to possess their own (male) as well as female genitalia and had corresponding wishes to become a girl.

Identity Development

Later feminist writers, such as Chodorow (1973) and Gilligan (1982), also challenged Freud's views of female identity development. Chodorow proposed that identification is a two-way process involving both the child and the parent. Daughters identify with their mothers, but mothers also identify with their daughters, fusing the process of attachment with the experience of "sex-role identity" (Cole & Cole, 1996, p. 388). Mothers experience their sons as different from themselves. Boys also define themselves as different from their mothers. This difference is what facilitates the differentiation process. Gilligan (1982) builds on Chodorow's explanation and emphasizes that there are two paths to sexual identity development—male and female—each with its own strengths and weaknesses. Males achieve identity through separation, and females achieve identity through attachment.

Queer Theory and Gender Development

Judith Butler (2006) describes gender as what you do at a point in time, not a universal of who you are. This idea of gender identity as "free floating" is one of the key constructs in Queer Theory. This perspective is at odds with the dominant discourse and binary understanding of masculine and feminine. An important point in Queer Theory is that most gay, lesbian, bisexual, and transgender youth are not necessarily raised in a community of similar others from whom they learn about their identity and who reinforce and support that identity. The process of identity is therefore characterized by inconsistency and incongruence among its affective, cognitive, and behavioral components, meaning behavior may not always coincide with identity (Rosari, Schrimshaw, Hunter, & Braun, year, p. 46). This point of view is reinforced by Poggio (2006) as a social practice that is redefined in everyday life and interactions. "Performing gender" is a type of performance that determines the gender order; for example, masculine and feminine. "Positioning gender" is the identity of gender or the concept of a position in society. Persons find their gender identity or position in society by comparing themselves to the positioning of others around them. "Practicing gender" is the way in which masculinity and femininity are represented.

Cognitive Development Theorists

Kohlberg (1966), Slaby and Frey (1975) and Frey and Ruble (1992) have proposed that one's self-perceptions or gender-linked ideas will result in certain types of behavior. Social learning theorists (Bandura, 1969, 1986; Fagot, 1986, Fagot & Leinbach, 1986, 1989; Frable, 1989; Mischell, 1996) feel that individuals acquire gender-typed behaviors through modeling and reinforcement, resulting in gender-linked ideas or self-perceptions. *Gender schema theory* (Levy & Fivush, 1993; Martin & Halverson, 1987; Martin, Ruble, & Szkrybalo, 2002) is an information-processing approach to gender typing that combines social learning and cognitive development components. Gender schema theory begins with the concept of gender schemas. These are masculine or feminine categories that young children use to organize their experiences, generally based on instruction and modeling from caregivers and other adults. It also integrates elements of gender typing such as stereotyping, gender identity, and gender-role adoption to determine how masculine and feminine orientations emerge and are maintained. For example, nurseries are often decorated differently for boys and girls. Once young children are able to label their own sex, they select gender schemas that are consistent with that sex. Consequently, self-perceptions become gender typed and become additional gender schemas that children use to process information and guide their behavior. Such gender stereotyping and gender role preferences are self-perpetuating and often restrict children's alternatives. Parents and caregivers may provide different types of experiences through play materials and social interactions for boys and girls. Culture also plays a significant role in gender development, as many cultures restrict girls more than boys and limit the range of opportunities and experiences available to girls from a very young age. On the other hand, boys are generally more gender typed than girls. Many fathers, in particular, continue to encourage "gender-appropriate" behavior in their sons. Children are exposed to gender typing every day in cartoons, music, television, video and computer games, and children's programs (Berk, 2003, p. 384).

Helms (1990) developed a model of female gender identity that she defined as "womanist" identity development (see Table 4.6). The term *womanist* is widely used among black feminist theologians and was adopted by black feminist writers

TABLE 4.6

Womanist Identity Development

Stage #—Name	Description
1. Pre-Encounter	The woman holds a constricted view about her role which conforms to society's beliefs about gender and gender roles. She supports attitudes and behaviors which value men over women.
2. Encounter	In this stage the woman questions the beliefs she held in the Pre-encounter stage as a result of new information or experiences. This puts her in conflict with her previous values and broadens her view of womanhood suggesting alternative views.
3. Immersion-Emersion:	The woman may actively reject societal definitions of womanhood and actively search for attachments with other women in a search for a positive definition of womanhood.
4. Internalization	The woman incorporates a positive definition of womanhood based on personal attributes and experiences but is not bound by other's definitions. The marker for healthy development in this model is "self valuation."

Source: S. Chiao, 2001, "Woman of Color Bridging the Gap: Conversation with Pioneering Woman Working in the Overlap between Feminist and Multicultural Psychology." Unpublished doctoral dissertation. California School of Professional Psychology. Ann Arbor, MI: ProQuest.

because it highlights the unique contributions of black theorists and activists. It derives from the word "womanish"—a black folk expression of mother to female children—"you acting womanish" (like a woman)—and usually referring to outrageous, courageous, or willful behavior (Walker, 1983, p. xi). Womanism is a philosophy and a consciousness that attends to both racism and sexism in the black community and in the culture at large. Womanist and black feminists' most profound contribution to the feminist movement has been the insistence that all systems of oppression be attacked with equal force at the same time (Chiao, 2001; Saulnier, 1996).

Gay, Lesbian, Bisexual, and Transgender Identity Development

Transgender Identity Development

Many transgender and intersex individuals (persons born with ambiguous genitals) are also challenging society's binary gender system, offering themselves as an example of a third sex (Hunter & Hickerson, 2003). The term *transgender* refers to individuals whose gender identity and gender expression contrast with their biological sex (Nemoto, Operario, Keatley, Nguyen, & Sugano, 2005) This may be due to the fact that there are greater options for and among transgender and intersex individuals. Sex reassignment surgery (SRS) is not the only option, and many individuals live as transgender men and women without altering their genitals. The goal may no longer be biological but the ability to pass as the other sex-gender and publicly present themselves as such (Gagne & Tewksbury, 1996). For transgenderists, coming out means crossing over, either temporarily or permanently, from one gender category to the only acceptable alternative. Sexually active transgenderists must recognize, tolerate, and learn to accept an alternative gender identity. This includes the development of coping strategies to manage public presentations of gender as well as the actual transformation of permanent identity and anatomy. This is a complex process that also involves reexamination of sexual identity; therefore those transgenderists who have SRS must come out to themselves and others by considering their sexual orientations and preferences (see The Harry Benjamin International Gender Dysphoria Association's Standards of Care for Gender Identity Disorders, sixth version, February 2001; www.wpath.org/Documents2/socv6.pdf). Lesser (1999) wrote about the importance of family support for transgendered individuals. This author described the adjustment process that one mother experienced when her son had a sex change operation and became her daughter. This parent moved from a place of shame, self-blame, and secrecy to one of acceptance that "although her son's outward appearance had changed, Leslie remained her child" (p. 188).

Within the transgenderist community, the declassification of transsexualism as a psychiatric diagnosis (removing it from the *Diagnostic and Statistical Manual of*

Mental Disorders (*DSM-IV*, 2000) has been debated between those who challenge medical definitions and those who seek access to hormones and SRS. This latter group feels that being diagnosed transsexual is the only way they can become the gender they truly are (Denny, 1998; Gagne, Tewksbury, & McGaughey, 1997). The theoretical framework of relational dialectics that view relationships as a never-ending process of co-creation was adapted by Meyer (2003) to explain the process of transgender identity formation (Baxter & Montgomery, 1996). The four concepts included in the model are contradiction, change, praxis, and totality, shown in Table 4.9. (See Istar, 2006, for further information on "transgender emergence.")

Gay and Lesbian Identity Development

Homosexuality has existed throughout history and in virtually all societies. Many theories have been put forth to identify the cause of homosexuality. These have included social learning theories, parent–child-oriented theories, sexual-interaction-oriented theories, sex-role-oriented theories, and biologically based theories (Ellis, 2000). This group of individuals is a minority within the larger heterosexual society that defines the dimensions of social power and privilege. Gay, lesbian, bisexual, and transgender individuals often face stigmatization and prejudice that form the backdrop against which they develop their sexual identity. In addition to the complex personal issues involved in acknowledging a nonheterosexual sexual identity, a lesbian, gay, bisexual, or transgender individual faces many interpersonal challenges from family, friends, and the wider social community (Evans & D'Augelli, 1996).

TABLE 4.7

Homosexual Identity Development

Stage One: Sensitization; feeling different. Adults retrospectively recalling their middle childhood years, report they had social experiences that made them feel different from other children.

Stage Two: Self-recognition; identity confusion. During puberty these same children realize they are sexually attracted to members of the same sex and begin to label these feelings as "homosexual." This becomes a source of inner turmoil and identity confusion particularly because they know that homosexuals are stigmatized in our society.

Stage Three: Identity assumption: Some adolescents begin to act on their sexual preference for the opposite sex and others do not even though they may acknowledge these feelings privately. Other youngsters begin to acknowledge their same sex attractions, at least to others like themselves. Homosexual identity is not fully assumed during these early stages.

Stage Four: Commitment, identity integration. This stage is reached by those who adopt homosexuality as a way of life. Sexuality and emotional commitment, expression of satisfaction with oneself and public disclosure of one's homosexual identity are markers of this stage of identity integration.

Source: Adapted from M. Cole and S. R. Cole, 1996, *The Development of Children* (3rd ed.), (p. 700). New York: W. H. Freeman.

The term *sexual identity* is sometimes used interchangeably with the term sexual *orientation*, although the two are distinct concepts. *Sexual identity* refers to how an individual identifies oneself from the larger group of culturally created sexual identities (for example, heterosexual, bisexual, gay, lesbian). *Sexual orientation* concerns itself with sexual behavior but can include self-identification, gender identity, gender role, fantasies, emotional attachments, social preference, sexual attraction, and lifestyle (Cox & Gallois, 1996; Eliason, 1996). Sexual orientation, sexual desires, and sexual behavior are typically congruent with a person's sexual identity, although these can be incongruent as well, for example, men who are incarcerated in prison and have sex with other men and do not self-identify as gay (Hunter & Hickerson, 2003). Cultural issues are also a consideration in sexual identity and self-labeling among gay, lesbian, bisexual, and transgender individuals. In some Latino cultures, for example, bisexual sexual practices are partly extensions of machismo heterosexuality. For others, they hide a same-sex gender sexual orientation. Still other men do not identify with the label "gay" because it is associated with the white gay political movement (Manalansan, 1996). Sex gender identity is one's psychological sense of what one's sex gender is; it is independent of one's sexual orientation. Meyer (2003) suggests: "Sexuality and gender are dialectical constructions that develop when individuals define themselves in terms of dichotomies (heterosexual/homosexual, and/or male/female) that do not allow for framing these identities outside polar endpoints" (p. 161).

Since the mid- to late-1980s the term *queer* has reemerged in the lesbian, gay, and bisexual community. Queer is a political term that symbolizes not only the individual's sexuality but also challenges the traditional heterosexual categories of gendered sexuality. However, for others the term retains pejorative connotations and is not affirming. Nonetheless, the growth of the queer political movement has contributed to an expansive number of identities—many of which are still only socially available within the queer community. The terminology for these identities is also in a state of flux. Some examples of sexual identities among women include *bisexual, queer, lesbian-identified bisexual, bisexual lesbian,* and the *lesbian who has sex with men* identity. Some of these identities may reflect the attraction many women who use them have for both men and women but, for political reasons, choose to express their feelings only toward women. Among men, identities include *gay bisexual; bisensual* (for both men and women who feel that sensuality better describes their range of feelings); *polysexual* and *polyamorous* (used by those who want to define their sexuality independent of gender and sexual dichotomies, and heterosexual norms). Finally, *polyfidelity* is the practice of fidelity within a group of three or more people, in contrast to *monogamy,* which involves fidelity between two people (Rust, 1996, pp. 103–104).

Models of gay, lesbian, and bisexual development center around two theories. The first is the developmental perspective. This theory proposes that identity tasks are about personal adjustment in a hostile societal environment. The second theory is the social psychological perspective, which explains the psychological processes of the individual with explicit reference to the broader social context.

As Cox and Gallois (1996) wrote: "From this perspective, the effects of the wider society on individual development are explored in terms of social groups and membership within them, as well as how individuals (primarily in terms of group membership) affect the wider society" (p. 2).

Cass has suggested that a theory of homosexual identity development should propose a clear definition of identity, the relationship of identity to self-concept, the structure of identity, changes that occur as identity develops, and the internal and external factors affecting such changes (Cass, 1984, cited in Cox & Gallois, 1996, p. 3). Social identity theory, the conceptual framework for the *homosexual identity development* model, provides this type of integrated approach. It examines the processes that occur within an individual as well as the effect that larger societal forces have on these processes and how the processes themselves affect the broader social structure.

Homosexual Identity Development Model

This Homosexual Identity Development Model includes, according to Troiden (1988), two underlying processes. The first process is referred to as "self-categorization." This process involves self-labeling as homosexual and the adoption over time of the behaviors and values associated with the particular group membership. An unfortunate result of self-categorization is that it often contributes to "them/us" social dichotomies that can become stereotypic. A person may apply more than one label to himself, and people generally have multiple identities. In this way, social identities begin to develop that may either be compatible or in conflict with one another (for example, being an Orthodox, religiously observant Jew may conflict with being gay). Therefore, the process of self-categorization and self-labeling incorporates both a personal as well as a social identity. *Personal identity* includes those characteristics that are unique to the individual; *social identities* include those that are based on membership in a particular group. The second process underlying social identity concerns the evaluation made of the social categories to which one belongs. *Personal self-esteem* is derived from comparing oneself to other individuals, whereas *social self-esteem* generally relies on a favorable comparison of the group one belongs to with other groups in society. This view of gay and lesbian development is more concerned with how the process occurs for individuals rather than the specific content of identity that is the focal point of stage models.

The following homosexual identity development model (Troiden, 1988) is based on a developmental perspective and includes a coming-out process. This is a complex process whereby individuals recognize and accept their sexual preference, adopt a sexual identity, inform others of their sexual orientation, and become involved with people of similar sexual identity (Cass, 1979; Gagne et al., 1997). Although many researchers maintain that a public declaration of one's homosexuality is not a necessary part of reaching a homosexual identity, Troiden's model includes such acknowledgement as an important step in identity development (Savin-Williams, 1998; see Table 4.7).

TABLE 4.8

Cass Sexual Identity Formation Model

Stage #—Name	Description
1. Identity Confusion ("Who am I")	One begins to wonder if the information one hears abut gay or lesbian identity pertains to oneself. One of three alternative pathways is taken: (a) accept the relevance and desirability of the meaning of lesbian or gay. (b) accept the relevance but not the desirability of the meaning, try to remove all undesirable elements from one's life (identity foreclosure or no advancement to a new stage); or (c) refuse to accept one's behavior as relevant or desirable, stop behaviors viewed as lesbian or gay, halt access to information about being gay or lesbian, and avoid any provocative situations (identity foreclosure). If one cannot suppress the applicability of the meaning of lesbian or gay to oneself, or if one accepts it, Stage 2 occurs.
2. Identity Comparison ("I am different.")	In this stage, a person experiences attraction to others of the same sex-gender. One of four pathways is taken: (a) develop a positive evaluation of self and anticipate high rewards vs. costs; (b) develop a positive evaluation of self but perceive low rewards which can lead to rejection of the relevance of the meaning of lesbian or gay (identity foreclosure) or, if these actions fail, a conclusion that one is probably lesbian or gay: (c) develop a negative evaluation of self but perceive high rewards which can lead to the desire to assess oneself as heterosexual, not lesbian or gay; or (d) develop a negative evaluation of self and perceive low rewards which can lead to devaluation of a lesbian or gay self-identification and a positive evaluation of a heterosexual self-identification (identity foreclosure). If one acknowledges a lesbian or gay identity at this stage but it is accompanied by a negative self-evaluation, it can result for some persons in self-hatred and possibly self-destructive behaviors such as self-mutilation or suicide attempts.

3. Identity Tolerance ("I am probably lesbian or gay")	In this stage, a person moves in the direction of greater commitment to a lesbian or gay identity and is likely to seek out lesbian or gay community. One of six pathways is taken: (a) develop a positive view of self as probably lesbian or gay and experience positive contacts with lesbian and gay persons; (b) develop a positive view of self but experience negative contact with other lesbian and gay persons; these persons are devalued and contact with them reduced (identity foreclosure); the conception of oneself as lesbian or gay is reevaluated as less positive; (c) develop a negative view of self, but experience positive contacts with lesbian and gay persons that can lessen one's negative evaluation of self as lesbian or gay; (d) develop a negative evaluation of self and experience negative contacts with lesbian and gay persons that can lead to avoidance of contacts (identity foreclosure); a negative evaluation of self is modified if future positive contacts occur; (e) develop a positive evaluation of self and experience positive contacts with lesbian and gay persons that can lead to greater commitment as lesbian or gay with no qualifiers; or (f) develop a positive evaluation of self as partly lesbian or gay and experience negative contacts with lesbian and gay persons that can lead to a devaluation of lesbian and gay persons (identity foreclosure) or the adoption of a somewhat negative evaluation of self as lesbian or gay.
4. Identity Acceptance ("I am lesbian or gay")	In this stage, a person begins to feel being gay or lesbian is a valid self-identity and may prefer being around other gay and lesbian persons. The new identity is disclosed to more persons, decreasing the incongruence between one's self-perceptions and the perceptions of others or between one's positive evaluation of self and the negative evaluations of others. Continued "passing" as heterosexual at this stage is seen as identity foreclosure.

(Continued)

TABLE 4.8

Cass Sexual Identity Formation Model (Continued)

5. Identity Pride ("My sexual orientation is part of me")	At this stage, disclosure of one's sexual orientation are made in all, or most cases of one's life. One may also further resolve the incongruence between self-acceptance and the devaluation by others through disregarding negative opinions. In this stage, everything that is heterosexual is devalued, and everything that is lesbian or gay is valued.
6. Identity Synthesis ("I am lesbian or gay")	The ultimate goal of a person at this stage is to experience psychological integration or congruence between perceptions of one's self and one's behavior and between one's private and public identities. One gradually modifies the "us vs. them" stance of the previous stage and increases contact with supportive heterosexual persons.

Source: S. Hunter, and J.C. Hickerson, 2003, *Affirmative Practice: Understanding and Working with Lesbian, Gay, Bisexual, and Transgender Persons.*

Sexual Identity Formation Model

One of the most popular models of lesbian and gay identity development, the *sexual identity formation* model, was developed by Cass (1979, 1984, 1990). This model is based on *interpersonal congruency theory* and focuses on intrapsychic changes in which "motivation for development is viewed as the need to ameliorate the incongruence that each stage creates interpersonally and in reference to society" (Cox & Gallois, 1996, cited in Degges-White, Rice, & Meyers, 2000, p. 318). Individuals emotionally and interpersonally work through each stage, remain at a particular stage, or undergo identity foreclosure in the movement toward establishment of a homosexual identity. Degges-White and colleagues caution that *synthesis*, the final stage, "may need to be redefined in light of the increasing prevalence of hate crimes and the realistic, even life-preserving, response of fear related to indiscriminate coming out among sexual minorities" (p. 331). The stages of the Cass model are outlined in Table 4.8.

A second model of gay and lesbian identity was put forth by Coleman (1982) and focuses on the process of coming out to other people. This author feels that external validation is important in achieving self-acceptance. The reactions of others—depending on their importance in the person's life—influence the form that the lesbian, gay, or bisexual identity takes.

TABLE 4.9

Relational Dialectics

Stage #—Name	Description
1. Contradiction	An individual struggles to maintain the privacy or secrecy of one's sexual differences, while at the same time longs to be open and honest with those s/he cares for about her/his sexual orientation. As a result, individuals questioning and exploring their sexual or gender identity must constantly manage this tension in formulating that identity. This is especially true for bisexual and transgender individuals who are having to come out to both the heterosexual and the gay/lesbian communities.
2. Change	Bisexual and transgender individuals must frequently adapt to changes in identity formation. For example, bisexual individuals must mediate their identity based on the sex of their significant other. For transgender individuals issues of sexuality are mediated through gender choices rather than sex choices although both could occur simultaneously
3. Praxis	Praxis means that individuals have the ability to make communicative choices based on past experiences that will drive future interactions. Bisexual identity formation is based on prior experiences and the future option of various gendered partners. For transgender individuals the tension is predominantly in terms of gender performance.
4. Totality	Totality in bisexual and transgender identity formation can manifest in several ways. Bisexual and transgender individuals must balance their gender and/or sexual identity with other marginalizing factors that contribute to identity formation such as race, class, ethnicity, education and socioeconomic status. Tensions concerning identity formation can come both from within the LGBT community and from within the heterosexual community.

Source: M. D. Meyer, (2003), "Looking toward the InterSEXions: Examining Bisexual and Transgender Identity Formation from a Dialectical Theoretical Perspective," *Journal of Bisexuality*, 3(3), pp. 151–170.

The steps in Coleman's coming-out model are (1) *exploration*, the stage in which lesbian, gay, and bisexual individuals begin social and sexual activities with others. This is the individual's introduction to gay subculture and includes the development of interpersonal skills; and (2) *first relationship*, when the person is engaging for the first time in a same-gender relationship. Coleman makes the significant points that each of these phases is generally a developmental milestone during adolescence and/or young adulthood; however, the gay, lesbian, or bisexual individual may be experiencing them at a later point in the life span. They also face (at any developmental stage) fewer role models and a lack of social and legal support. These societal pressures can make it very difficult for gay, lesbian, and bisexual individuals to build positive same-gender relationships (Rust, 1996).

The coming-out process is different for gay men and lesbians. The process appears to be more abrupt for men; for women the process seems to be characterized by greater ambiguity. These differences may be influenced by sex-role socialization and filtered through aspects of personality and family structure. For example, lesbians may experience their emerging sexual and emotional intimacy as friendship. A similar longing for emotional and physical closeness for gay men with other males is often immediately perceived as homosexual behavior.

Linear models of coming out also do not allow for the possibility of multiple changes in sexual orientation. Many people experience changes in their sexual feelings and behaviors over the life span. If one has engaged in a coming-out process that they felt had finality, these changes can be confusing and invalidating rather than providing further evolution of their sexual identities (Cohen & Savin-Williams, 1996; Rust, 1996). Finally, politicized public identity may signify developmental maturity to those who developed coming-out models, and a lack of disclosure can signify developmental arrest. This can be short sighted and not sufficiently cognizant of the social realities of geographic locations, membership in diverse ethnic and religious groups, chronic illness and disability, and other factors that may limit access to like-minded persons and influence the coming-out process.

Queer Theory and Gay and Lesbian Identity Development

Queer theory (Langdridge, 2008) provides a perspective that challenges any fixed categories of "homosexual" identity development, in an attempt to undermine the "heterosexual–homosexual binary by actively refusing to engage with identity categories and actively affirming ambiguity. This is a political stance highlighting that with a fixed "homosexual" identity category, there is an "othering" by heterosexuality, as the dominant, privileged center (p. 28). In a major criticism of this postmodern approach, McPhail (2003, p. 15) makes the excellent point that gay activists have "achieved increased power through their tireless work to make their members visible by collective action and identification. . . . Taking away that collectivity engenders fears that it will lead back to invisibility, lack of recognition, and powerlessness." Although heterosexuality/homosexuality may be social constructs, heterosexism and homophobia are not (p. 15). Nonetheless, it may be helpful for social workers to consider some deconstruction of gender and sexuality binaries when working with clients. Among the suggestions offered by McPhail (p. 17) is the challenge of the categories Gender Identity Disorder and Transvestic Festishim in the *Diagnostic and Statistical Manual of Mental Disorders.* She also encourages asking questions that allow the creation of individual narratives when working with persons around issues of gender and sexuality.

Bisexual Identity Development

Bisexual identity formation may not conform to gay and lesbian identity. Cass (1990) described bisexual identity development as a viable sexual identity with a separate developmental pathway distinct from that of a homosexual identity. Meyer (2003) proposed that bisexual and transgender identity are "dialectical constructs that rest largely on tensions and interplays between '*both/and*' ness of bisexuality and transgender. Bisexuals are *both* heterosexual *and* homosexual, and adopt discursive patterns *and* actions of *both* the heterosexual *and* lesbian/gay communities" (p. 154). Bisexual identities do not fit into binary social constructs and are therefore continually challenged both by the heterosexual and the gay/lesbian communities (Calhoun, 2000; Fox, 1995). The term *biphobia* has been used to "describe the parallel set of negative beliefs about and stigmatization of bisexuality and those identified as bisexual" (Paul, 1996, p. 449). Bisexual support networks and social structures are relatively new phenomena, and their numbers are small; therefore, bisexual individuals continue to rely on the more extensive resources of the gay and lesbian communities. It is important to appreciate that bisexual behavior and a bisexual identity may not be a developmental point to a commitment to a gay or lesbian identity. The lack of social recognition given to bisexual identity makes it difficult to develop and sustain a bisexual identity. These individuals are often told they "must overcome their internalized homophobia and finish coming out" (Rust, 1996, p. 112). The growth of the bisexual political movement has caused greater visibility for bisexual individuals and new awareness of its standing as a separate sexual identity.

Social Class Identity

Kerbo (1996) offered the following definition of class: "a grouping of individuals with similar positions and similar political and economic interests within the stratification system" (p. 13). The concept of class is multidimensional and includes issues relating to money, power, prestige, self-concept, lifestyle, and mobility, in addition to economics. Each of these social constructs has a subjective meaning attached to it. Another important class-related concept is that of class location. Class location is determined by ascription (factors such as race, ethnicity, gender, or birth) or by achievement (merit or talent). A number of terms are used to categorize class in our society. Sernau (2001, p. 86) refers to these groups as "class structure" and groups them as capitalist class, upper middle class, working class, working poor, and underclass (p. 86; see Table 4.10).

As the model of class structure depicts, there is a hierarchical element to class in our society that, along with class categorization, becomes a part of identity. This contributes to *classism,* or a message that to be a member of classes with greater socioeconomic resources is better. Those at the lower end of the class structure may therefore have had shaming experiences that undermine self-esteem (Greene, 2001).

Mobility contributes to the elusive quality of class, which makes it somewhat different from the other "collective identities" that have been discussed in this chapter. Russell (1996) talks about the phenomena of class mobility related to class development when he writes: "Any person's current class situation may or may not be consistent with her class status at any other time in her life" (p. 63). Palmer (1996) raises the important issue of class-related losses that women (but we think this is true for men also) experience as they pursue goals that move them beyond their class of birth. This may include grieving for relatives and friends who have suffered from financial hardship and lack of opportunity, as well as those who have suffered illness related to difficult working conditions

TABLE 4.10

A Model of Class Structure

Capitalist class: investors, heirs, and executives; typically with a prestigious university education; annual family incomes (1990) over $750,000, mostly from assets.

Upper middle class: upper-level managers, professionals, and mid-sized businesss owners; with a college education, most often with an advanced degree; family incomes of $70,000 or more.

Middle class: lower-level managers, professionals, semiprofessionals, some sales and skilled craft workers, and foreman and supervisors, with at least a high school education and usually some college, technical training, or apprenticeship, family incomes of about $40,000.

Working class: operatives, clerical workers, most retail sales clerks, routinized assembly and factory workers, and related blue collar employees, high school educated; family incomes of about $25,000.

Working poor: poorly paid service workers and laborers, operatives, and clerical workers in low wage sectors, usually with some high school, family incomes below $20,000.

Underclass: persons with erratic job histories and weak attachment to the formal labor force, unemployed, or only able to find seasonal or part-time work; dependent on temporary or informal employment or some form of social assistance.

Source: S. Sernau, *Worlds Apart: Social Inequalities in a New Century.* Copyright 2001. Reprinted by permission of Pine Forge Press.

(such as the black lung disease suffered by many coal miners). There is also loss involved with moving beyond the experiences of those who are not sharing in upwardly mobile class experiences. Cooper and Lesser (2005) wrote about the experiences of an African-American professional woman from a small Southern town who moved to a large Northeastern city: "The more I continue to advance, the wider the racial gap becomes. I go to this upscale university, and my 16-year-old cousin back home has three kids and is still not married" (p. 75).

Zandy (1996) identified several relational aspects that determine class orientation and socioeconomic mobility in addition to material difference: dislocation; expectations of family; encouragement to obtain security or to experiment (self-discovery); language difference between home and other settings (for example, other languages and dialects of spoken English); and the relationship one has to community (for example, isolation versus network). As one makes the transition from the working class to the middle class, these relational aspects also undergo a transition with the individual. The individual may be required to redefine the relationship with his or her family and community of origin or to shift from a collective worldview to an individualistic philosophy. Lubrano (2004), in his autobiography about moving from "blue collar roots to white collar dreams," is referring to this duality when he describes having dinner with his family in "working class Brooklyn" after spending a day attending classes at Columbia University: "We talked about general stuff and I learned to self censor—no one wanted to hear how the world worked from some kid who was first learning to use his brain" (pp. 48–49). Hart (1994) describes both the external and the internal aspects of social mobility: "Class mobility is living in different worlds with different languages . . . class mobility is different worlds living in you with different values, different wants, different demands" (p. 175).

The following excerpt from a poem, written by a 16-year-old girl born to bicultural, professional parents who were both raised in working-class families, illustrates her appreciation of class and its intersection with culture.

I am from

I am from New York accents and Italian food
I am from my mother's arms, sitting on the stoop, dancing in the park
Rosaries, ricotta cheese, cannolis, photo albums, pots and pans, the smell of garlic.
I am from olive oil aluminum foil and Christmas cakes.
Crowded by cousins, tugging at my mother's leg—my mother who stirs the gravy with one hand and writes a book with the other.

I am from a project in Brooklyn,
I am from the dirty, concrete tubes, the World War II trenches
I am from long black coats, tsit-tsit, politics, crayon colored cards
I am from a taxicab, City College, Coney Island Hospital, I am from Queens
I am the baby in the stroller on the subway, My brother. The park.

I am from two worlds.
I am from satin ballet shoes, bleeding feet, rosin, curtains, scratch tights and tutus

I am from photo albums, shoeboxes, post it notes, song lyrics, pressed flowers and bronzed baby shoes.

I am from the streets, a tiny apartment, a big brick house
I am from catholic school, yeshiva, little Italy and Marine Park.
I am from an Italian Thanksgiving where turkey is eaten after lasagna
I am from latkes under the Christmas tree.
I am from weekends 1:00 o'clock Sunday pasta dinners, then home to prep school, dance classes, bagged bread, take-out.
I am from two worlds.

What this young author is describing are the ways in which class and classism affect individuals intrapsychically from childhood. These "internalized messages and unexamined values . . . whether conscious or unconscious" affect current identity (Palmer, 1996, p. 457). People's assessment of their own social standing and the standing of others influence their behavior toward others and others toward them. Differential status identity (DSI) is a construct offered by Fouad and Brown (2000) to predict the psychological effects of social class. Interestingly, social class may be a more powerful indicator of worldview than family structure, race, religion, national origin, income, or subjective class identification. Persons higher in social class evidenced greater individualism, and those in lower social class reported greater collectivistic orientations.

The stratification paradigm has its limitations in understanding the nature of social class in society. Grouping according to rigid indices such as income, education, and occupation do not allow for a fuller explanation of affect associated with social class, social class relationships, and those individuals who choose to move downward in social class. In an attempt to introduce a more phenomenological approach, Liu, Soleck, et al. (2004) identified five interrelated domains, which they developed into what they call a social class worldview model (SCWM). They are

- *Consciousness, Attitudes, and Salience.* This domain is defined as an individual's capacity to articulate and understand the meaning and relevance of social class in his environment.
- *Referent Groups.* Refers to the people (past, present, and future) in a person's life who help guide the development of worldview and mediate social class behaviors. Such people may include the family of origin, peer or community group, and the group to which one aspires.
- *Property Relationships.* This domain includes materials that people value, use to define themselves, expect as a part of their worldview, and use to exclude others. Property is the perception a person has about his actual material conditions and not solely the objective materials.
- *Lifestyle.* The way individuals choose to organize their time and resources, within their economic and social context.
- *Behaviors.* Learned and socialized actions that reinforce a person's social class worldview.

The capital accumulation paradigm (CAP) was developed by Liu, Soleck, et al. (2004) as a framework for understanding the intrapsychic dimensions of internalized classism. The conceptual basis for this paradigm is that accumulation of capital is the goal. Capital, in this regard is not limited to money but includes social capital, human capital, and cultural capital. *Social capital* is "those relationships and affiliations that can be translated into social class benefits such as perception of, access to and use of specific relationships to define a person's social class." *Human capital* is "the perceived value one gets from education, occupations, or interpersonal skills that are valued in a community." *Cultural capital* includes "the tastes or styles that individuals develop from socialization experiences among family, friends and in school and community activities" (p. 98). People develop behavioral and attitudinal strategies to gain and maintain the capital valued within particular contexts. They also develop worldviews or schemas to help them make sense of their social class in society based on their accumulation of these various forms of capital. Figure 4.3 depicts the intersection between *levels of classism, social class worldview,* and *internalized classism* (Bubolz, 2001; Deaux, Reid, Mizrahi, & Cotting, 1999; Diwan, 2000; Liu & Pope-Davis, 2003; Liu, Soleck, et al., 2004).

FIGURE 4.3

Social Class Worldview Model, Levels of Classism, and Internalized Classism

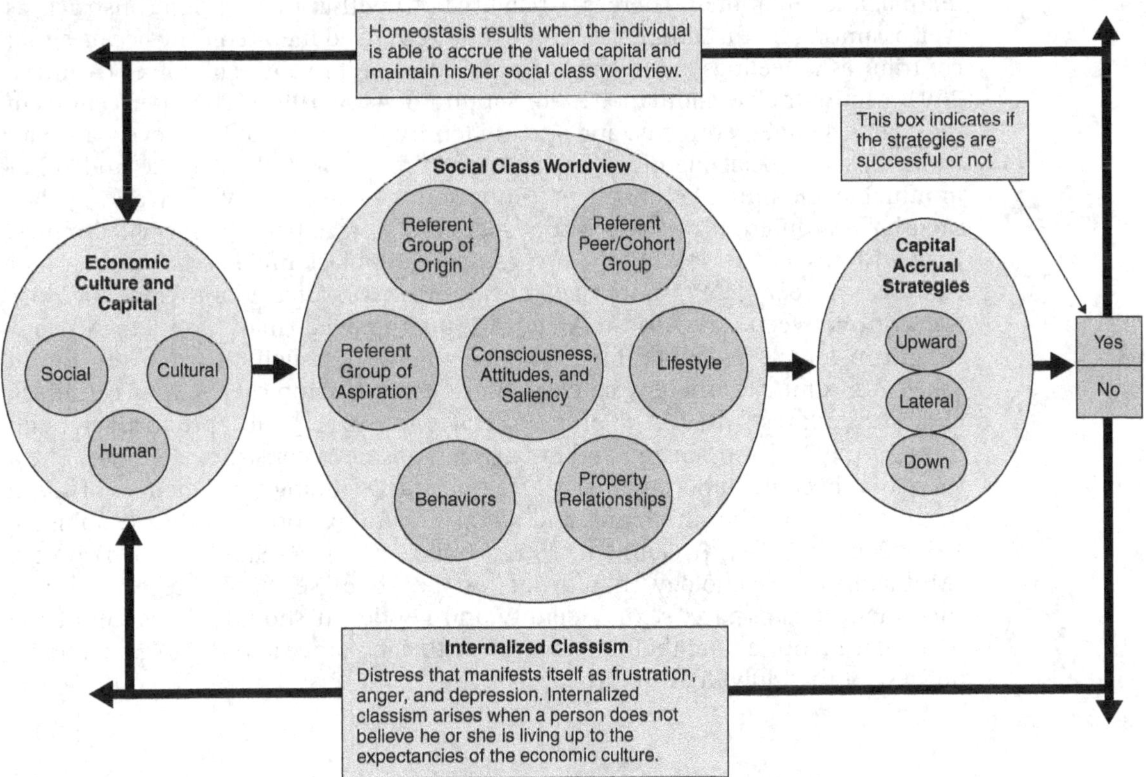

Source: W. Liu, G. Soleck et.al., (2004), "A New Framework to Understand Social Class in Counseling: The Social Class Worldview Model and Modern Classism Theory," *Journal of Multicultural Counseling and Development,* vol. 32 (April), p. 100. ACA. Reprinted with permission. No further reproduction authorized without written permission from the American Counseling Association.

Summary

This chapter addressed the importance of recognizing that most individuals have multiple identities—both personal and social – and that these identities "intersect" in complicated patterns of oppression and privilege. There were many stage models presented in this chapter. These models have provided some rich contributions to the literature and to the understanding of identity development. There are problems with stage models that we must also address. Most are theoretical, and they cast identity linearly rather than with the fluidity often more applicable to people's lives. Some individuals experience stages in different orders, skip stages, or remain in a stage indefinitely (Degges-White, Rice, & Myers 2000; Savin-Williams, 1998). Many of the gender identity models are based on research that excludes individuals who are not middle class. The *racial and ethnic identity development* models exclude the constructs of gender and sexuality. The *sexual identity* research focuses primarily on white, middle-class, gay men, and lesbians. *Class identity* attends to the white middle class or persons of color who are poor (Frable, 1997). We do want to state, however, that the connection between race and class is very powerful because the vast majority of working poor and unemployed are persons of color. We again emphasize that identities are complex, contextual, and situational. There is variability both within these group constructs as well as among them. Differences should not be viewed hierarchically because that contributes to feelings of intolerance and disdain and to abuse of power (Anthias, 2001; McGoldrick & Giordano, 1996; Sandhu & Aspy, 1997). The intersections of race, class, gender, ethnicity, and sexual identity demonstrate that "every human being's psychosocial identities are an embodiment of each of these and other immutable and mutable constructs" (Robinson, 1993, p. 50). White working-class men have a different position with respect to the racial and gender hierarchies, than with respect to class ones, when compared to black middle-class women, for example. An example of how class, rather that race, affected a therapeutic relationship between an African-American unemployed man and an African-American female graduate intern was poignantly highlighted when the intern asked, "In same race therapy between Black clinicians and clients, how can Black clinicians address the issue of class and 'survivor's guilt' productively and thoughtfully?" Contradictory and in-between positions construct identities. They, therefore, become important departures for understanding the dynamics of social stratification, on the one hand, and social integration on the other (Robinson, 1993; Hanna, Talley, & Guindon, 2000; Hulko, 2009). As Stanley (2004) noted, "Multicultural psychology should not just be about separate categorization of such identifiers as race, sexual identity and gender. It should address all of the particular identities and their interactions with each other in order to gain a holistic view of the individual" (p 169).

5 The Family in Society

Introduction: The Family as a Societal Subsystem

"Man survives in groups; this is inherent in the human condition" (Minuchin, 1974, p. 46). These social groups vary by culture in terms of how they are organized and structured, as well as what specific functions they perform. In primitive societies, people are organized in large groups that perform a variety of relatively stable functions. For example, such social functions as economic survival, security, education of the young, and health care may be performed within the context of a single tribe. As societies become more complex and require that people develop new skills, they tend to develop more specialized social structures or systems to perform those necessary social functions.

The family, as society's smallest social structure or system, changes in form (for example, who is included in family membership and what are the relationships among the members?) and function (for example, what purposes or tasks does the family perform for its members and/or for the wider society?) as society's needs and demands change. For example, in Western, postindustrial societies, many of the functions that were once considered the domain of families (for example, physical safety, health care, education of the young, care and support of the elderly) are now provided to one extent or another by other social systems.

The Contemporary Family

As we proceed into the 21st century, we find that a number of social trends have come together, changing how we define the term *family* and contributing to a tremendous diversity in family forms, functions, and contexts. These trends include rising rates of divorce, remarriage, and unmarried cohabitation and increasing numbers of single-parent families, as well as two-wage-earner families. The face of adoptive families is also changing, with increasing numbers of transracial, international, and special-needs adoptions by couples and single parents. Some of these families are choosing to include, to one extent or another, birth family members as part of the adoptive family system. This diversity of family forms is further enhanced, as gay and lesbian families continue to demand recognition of equal rights for their families, and by the increasing levels of racial and ethnic diversity among the U.S. population in general.

The Family Defined

Given the wide variation among cultures and subcultures as well as the rapidity of social change at the beginning of the 21st century, it has become increasingly difficult to define what is meant by the term *family* and to specify the functions performed by *all* families. In the past, the family tended to be seen as "a group of persons related by blood or legal marriage, living together, and cooperating economically and in child rearing" (Germain, 1991, p. 92); this assumed the existence of a heterosexual, legally married couple with children. More recently, family researchers and practitioners have attempted to update the definition of family in terms of forms and functions that more accurately reflect current social mores and structures (for example, the changing role of women; high rates of divorce, remarriage, and unmarried cohabitation in both heterosexual and GLBT communities; higher rates of single-parent households; and families that are child-free by choice, increasing dependence on formal, specialized social systems such as school day-care centers and elder care services to perform many of the family functions of earlier times). Acknowledging the inherent difficulties in conceptualizing a universal definition, Terkelsen (1980) proposed that virtually all families function to provide intense attachment relationships that continue over lifetimes and that form the context for "primary need attainment" (physical survival and security, and cognitive, emotional, and spiritual needs) for family members. Regarding family structure, Terkelsen described the family as "a small social system whose members are related through birth, adoption, or marriage, have strong reciprocal affections, and who comprise a permanent household (or cluster of households)" (Terkelsen, 1980, p. 24). He acknowledged that family systems may take on a variety of forms (for example, a married couple with or without children, a single parent and children, and three-generation units, as well as "units evolved by remarriage from parts of previously existing units" (Terkelsen, 1980, p. 24). However, even Terkelsen's "updated" definition now serves to highlight the enormous changes in the notions of what constitutes a family in the past quarter-century alone in that it excludes unmarried, cohabiting couples (with or without children); unmarried parents living in separate households but sharing parenting functions; same-sex couples (with or without children); extended families that include nonblood relations, and other people who consider themselves to be families but who are not legally recognized.

Hartman and Laird (1983) noted that the way in which family is defined has enormous practical importance for social workers. In addition to influencing the practice models social workers use in dealing with family issues, the legal definition of family has a significant impact on local, state, and federal family policies. Those families who are not legally recognized (for example, gay and lesbian families, unmarried, cohabiting partners) will be ineligible for those benefits typically available to families, such as health and life insurance coverage, medical decision making, or hospital visitation (Hartman & Laird, 1983; Shriver, 2004). Hartman and Laird attempt to combine traditional notions of family with modern social organization, suggesting that most people are members of at least two types of families:

- The ***family of origin:*** "That family of blood ties, both vertical (multigenerational) and horizontal (kinship), living or dead, geographically close or distant, known or unknown, accessible or inaccessible, but always in some way psychologically relevant. Also included in the family of origin are adopted members and fictive kin, people who, although not related by blood, are considered and have functioned as part of a family" (Hartman & Laird, 1983, pp. 29–30).
- The ***family as intimate environment*** (or, ***family of choice***): "That current family constellation in which people have chosen to live. Such a family group in our context consists of two or more people who have made a commitment to share living space, have developed close emotional ties, and share a variety of family roles and functions" (Hartman & Laird, 1983, pp. 29–30).

Family Systems Theory and Practice: A Postmodern Perspective

Given the wide cultural and historical variation in family form and function, the rapid pace of social change, and the ever-growing body of knowledge about the family, it is unlikely that any one definition of family will attain widespread acceptance (Germain, 1991). However, as society's smallest social system, it can be presumed that all families, regardless of form and function, share certain basic systemic elements and that these are then shaped by a variety of biological, psychological, and sociocultural forces. The following sections will examine the inner life of the family using salient concepts from family systems theory as a frame of reference. Family systems theory is founded on the principle that human beings are inherently social, and it views human behavior as organized by the relationship patterns that connect people to one another. It draws from a number of theoretical models including systems theory, cybernetics, social constructivism, attachment theory, and theories of small group dynamics (Nichols, 2008).

Nichols (2008) pointed out that during the early years of the family therapy movement, the field was a "diverse enterprise with competing schools and a multitude of theories" (Nichols, 2008, p. 299). Although each of these "schools" of family therapy (for example, structural, strategic, communicative–interactive, Bowenian) shared the fundamental belief that "problems run in families" (p. 299), they each evolved from different theory bases, and they each had their own, rather orthodox, methods of practice. A common thread among them, however, was that they each grew from a pathology-based perspective in which the family therapist assumed the role of an "expert" charged with *fixing* or *curing* family dysfunction.

By the 1980s, as postmodernist thinking became a major force across every field of human endeavor, and as traditional notions about the meaning of reality were being challenged at every level, the boundaries among the various schools of family therapy began to erode. Family therapists began to accept the need to tailor their thinking and techniques to fit each individual family's needs. The notion of "therapist as expert" was gradually replaced with one of "therapist as partner," or in Madsen's (2007) words, that of "appreciative ally"—one who attempts to build a "compassionate connection" (Madsen, 2007, p. 47) with clients.

- Drawing on social constructionist approaches that view identity as something that one constructs through interaction with others (the *self-in-relation*), postmodern family therapists are encouraged to assume a relational stance with clients that seeks to support their strengths, understand their perceptions of their situations (that is, their *narratives*), and focus on collaborating with them to find solutions. Underlying this relational stance is the understanding that clients bring with them a host of resources—resources that may be constrained, not only by the family's internal structure and interactional patterns, but also by political and economic forces that are largely beyond their control.

The Inner Life of the Family System: Fundamental Concepts

Family systems theory views the family as a social system that adheres to most of the behavioral rules and assumptions that apply to all social systems (such as the whole is greater that the sum of its parts, every system is a subsystem of larger systems, a change in one part changes the reality of the whole system, and the reciprocal nature of transactions between and among systems; see Chapter 1 for more detailed discussion of these assumptions) and that shares properties similar to those of other social systems. Although families share most of the properties of other social systems, Carter and McGoldrick (2005) have pointed out that families differ from other social systems in several ways. These differences emanate from one central issue—"the main value in families is in the relationships, which are irreplaceable" (p. 3). In other social systems, members can leave for whatever reason and be replaced; if a family loses a member for whatever reason, someone may be brought in to fill their function, but the new member can never replace the first in terms of her or his emotional relationship to the other members.

With this in mind, the following section will review systemic rules and properties specifically as they apply to families. Although much of the research in this area has been based on examination of two-parent families with children, we have been careful to extrapolate concepts that seem relevant to all families, regardless of form, function, and sociocultural context, and to specify how and when particular properties may be affected by such variables. It is our view that families, as social systems, cannot be separated from their cultural, economic, political, and historical contexts, and that practitioners must always be cognizant of the connections between the struggles of individual families and the social context within which they exist. We begin our examination of the family as a social system from this perspective. As discussed earlier, the historical divisions among the traditional schools of family therapy have eased in the postmodern era; with this in mind, we will draw from a variety of schools of thought as we present salient concepts of family theory. We base our discussion on the assumption that the internal properties of families generally fall into one of two overriding categories: structure or process (Nichols & Schwartz, 2005).

Family Structure

We base much of our discussion of family structure on the work of Salvador Minuchin (1974). *Family structure* refers to the ways in which the system's tasks are divided and coordinated, its patterns of authority, communication and interactions—essentially, structure is concerned with the predictable, established patterns of relationships and interactions within the family that occur over time. As the family goes about its business, its members begin to assume roles and styles of interacting with each other. These are repeated over time, become ingrained, and "once the patterns are established, family members use only a fraction of the full-range of behavior available to them" (Nichols, 2008, p.185) The family system then begins to operate with a fair degree of predictability. Some aspects of family structure are common to all families; others are peculiar to individual families. For now, we will limit our discussion to what we consider to be universal structural properties of family systems. These include *subsystems, triangulation, hierarchies,* and *boundaries*.

Subsystems Families carry out their various functions by dividing themselves into subsystems. Individuals, dyads (for example, husband and wife, adult same-sex partners, father and son), and/or larger groups within the family (for example, mother and three young children) are all subsystems. Subsystems form on the basis of characteristics such as age, gender, and function. Each family member belongs to more than one subsystem, and each subsystem has its own function(s) to perform. Within each subsystem, individuals learn different skills and have different levels of power. For example, a girl is a daughter to her parents and a sibling to her younger brother. As the elder child in the sibling subsystem, she may assume a degree of authority over the younger brother; as the daughter in the parent–child subsystem, that power is wielded by the parents. In the parent–child subsystem the girl learns who she is in relation to authority figures; as part of the sibling subsystem, she learns about herself in relation to equals (or, as in this case, to *subordinates*) and has the opportunity to learn skills for dealing with peers (and in this case, a peer of the opposite sex). Within the sibling subsystem, children learn how to cooperate, negotiate, develop alliances, compete, submit, and gain recognition.

In families that contain an adult couple (with or without children, legally married or not, same or opposite sex) the *couple subsystem's* functions include providing haven from the external demands and stressors of life and serving as a source of contact with other social systems. For the couple to carry out its functions adequately, the members must learn to develop relationship patterns of complementarity and mutual accommodation (Minuchin, 1974). Each member of the couple must be able to accept and tolerate a state of mutual interdependence in which some degree of individual separateness is relinquished in favor of a sense of belonging. Through mutual accommodation, each partner may support the other's growth and development, and the couple subsystem may serve as a source of support for the development of each partner's best characteristics. On the other hand, the couple may develop more negative transactional patterns that constrain individual growth, and that interfere with the system's protective functions.

If the parental subsystem comprises a couple, the couple subsystem must differentiate itself to continue to perform the function of mutual support while also performing the parental functions. If the parental subsystem comprises a single adult, that adult will do well to maintain a personal boundary outside the parenting role.

Hierarchy If a child is added to the family, the system must form a parental subsystem and a power structure in which parents and children have different levels of authority. This subsystem may take any number of forms, including a married couple, a single parent, an unmarried couple, a grandmother, or a foster parent(s). The existence of a clearly differentiated parental subsystem, with clearly defined authority, is much more important for satisfactory family functioning than is the content of that subsystem.

To perform the parenting function of socializing a child, parents must have the ability to nurture, guide, and exert authority and to do so in relation to the child's developmental needs. In dysfunctional family systems, parents may exert too little or too much control, thereby inhibiting the child's ability to develop self-direction. However, levels of authority do vary by culture. For example, across Asia, an especially high value is given to the hierarchical structure of authority and responsibility; to a great extent, behavioral expectations are based on one's status and role in the extended family system.

Triangulation The term *triangle* refers to the formation of a three-person subsystem in which one member is emotionally excluded. In Murray Bowen's (1966) view, it is difficult for two-person systems to maintain their equilibrium under the pressure of anxiety and tension. When that system experiences intolerable tension or conflict, it includes or "triangulates" a third person or an issue in an attempt to reduce tension (Jantzen & Harris, 1980). In families, triangles sometimes appear briefly and then dissolve; these may be relatively benign or even helpful. At other times, such triangles persist and become habitual, and these create dysfunctional processes that may undermine the family system. For example, a husband and wife may be experiencing some kind of interpersonal conflict that is not readily resolved. At some point, one or the other partner may turn to a third person for support and sympathy. The involvement of the third party may serve to decrease anxiety, and the added support may even provide valuable input for resolving the marital conflict. In this case, the triangle would dissolve once the husband and wife had resolved their differences. A friend, relative, or professional might serve this function.

At other times, such triangles persist and become habitual, and these create dysfunctional processes that may undermine the family system. Persistent triangles serve to decrease anxiety but also divert energy away from resolving the conflict between members of the core subsystem. In this way, they serve to maintain the conflict and undermine the ability of the subsystem to function successfully. For example, a grandmother living with her son-in-law and the children born of his marriage to her deceased daughter may form an alliance with one of the children against the father when he becomes angry about the child's poor grades. Should this triangle prove to be a momentary alliance that shifts, depending on circumstances (for example, becomes an alliance between the son-in-law and grandmother against the child when the child behaves inappropriately or between the son-in-law and child against the grandmother in still another circumstance), it may be seen as a relatively benign, or even functional, family process. However, if the original triangle between the grandmother and child should prove to be stable over time, and to persist regardless of circumstances, it would eventually be seen as a maladaptive process that undermines the son-in-law's authority as parent, erodes his relationship with his child, and creates a dysfunctional environment for the growing child. "Benign or neutral triangles shift depending on the situation, while maladaptive triangles are rigid and unchanging regardless of the situation" (Germain, 1991, p. 128).

Boundaries All families must form a boundary that distinguishes it from the outside, demarcates who is included as a family member, and regulates the level of interpersonal contact between family members and outsiders. The lines of this boundary may vary in relation to sociocultural context. For example, the so-called traditional American family with children and two married heterosexual parents may set a clear boundary that includes the two parents and their children. Some ethnic minority groups might include both sets of grandparents, parental siblings and their children, and/or nonblood relations within the family boundary; some gay/lesbian families form social networks of nonrelated community members who serve a variety of family functions. Two parents, living apart, but sharing child-care responsibilities, also constitute a family system with its own external boundary.

The family's subsystems are also demarcated by interpersonal boundaries. For example, in families that include a couple with or without children, the couple subsystem must form a boundary that separates it from the couple's original families, from the children (when applicable), and from other outsiders. As noted in the previous section, every subsystem in the family has its own functions and makes its own unique demands on its members.

The family and its subsystems must be free from interference from outside systems to perform their functions (and for the members to develop the interpersonal skills these systems are designed to foster), and boundaries function to protect the system from such interference. For the system to function properly, its boundaries must be clear and well defined enough to allow it to carry out its functions, but it must be open enough to allow members of the subsystem to communicate with the outside. The content of the (sub)system (in other words, who is a member) is less important than the existence of a clear boundary around it. For example, the parental subsystem may include a mother, a father, a single parent, a grandparent, two parents and a grandparent, or two same-sex adults. Any of these combinations may function quite well, as long as its lines of authority, power, and responsibility are clearly delineated.

The clarity of boundaries is an important indicator of family functioning. In Minuchin's (1974) view, all families are thought to fall along a continuum of boundary functioning, with most families functioning in the relatively wide, adequate range, even after accounting for cultural differences. At the extremes of this continuum are families with overly rigid boundaries (*disengaged families*) and overly diffuse boundaries (*enmeshed families*). Although most families contain both enmeshed and disengaged subsystems (and these may vary over time according to cultural or developmental factors), it may indicate areas of pathology when a family functions predominantly at either extreme. In highly enmeshed families, the increased communication and concern among family members give them a strong sense of belonging; however, this is at the expense of their sense of individual autonomy. The lack of differentiation in such a system tends to discourage independent exploration and mastery of challenges; when one member experiences a stressful situation, the diffuse boundaries allow that stress to spread to the other family members, causing them to react quickly and intensely. This is potentially overwhelming to the family system and may make it difficult for it to make the changes necessary for a successful adaptation to the stressful circumstance. For example, parents in a very enmeshed family may themselves become excessively upset when their adolescent daughter's boyfriend breaks off their relationship, inhibiting their ability to provide their daughter with emotional support. On the other hand, although families on the disengaged extreme of functioning tend to tolerate a high degree of individuality in their members, communication among members is difficult because of the rigidity of the individual's boundaries. When one member experiences a stressful situation, the family's ability to assist and protect that member is greatly hampered because the stress does not easily cross the rigid boundaries to affect the other members and cause them to react. Such a family tends not to react at all even when some response is clearly called for. For example, parents in such a family may be constrained from responding to reports of their child's truancy or drug abuse.

Interactional Processes in Families

The central concept among the various processes that describe family interaction is *circularity* or *reciprocal causality* (see Chapter 1 for a detailed discussion). Essentially, this refers to the idea that all behavior is sustained by a series of actions and reactions—in other words, by cycles of interaction between and among people (Nichols & Schwarz, 2005). In this view, the defining feature of any relationship is that of *complementarity*—that is, people in relationships engage in interactional patterns over time that are mutually sustaining. In other words, each person in a relationship contributes to what goes on between and among them. If one person changes their behavior, the other person is affected, and the relationship automatically changes. It should be noted, however, that traditionally unequal power relationships between men and women in families make it imperative for practitioners to consider social context and issues of dominance and oppression when evaluating complementary in relationships. The concept of reciprocal causality, when applied to such problems as domestic violence, sexual abuse, or alcoholism, may lead a practitioner to mistakenly ignore issues of responsibility and of external influences such as cultural expectations for appropriate gender role behavior (Nichols & Schwartz, 2005).

Emotional Processes and Self-Differentiation Pioneering family theorists from various schools of family treatment (Bowen, 1966; Kempler, 1973; Minuchin 1974; Satir, 1967) generally agree that it is important that members of families have the ability "to act both in concert with others and individually" (Janzen & Harris, 1980, p. 12). Two strong, opposing emotional forces underlie all human relationships: the need for emotional closeness and the need for individuality and autonomy. The first need brings people together; the second, moves them away from the control of others (Janzen & Harris, 1980).

All human beings must reconcile these two counterbalancing forces within themselves. Friedman (1971) viewed *fusion* and *differentiation* behavior among the members of the family as the fundamental underpinnings of their ability to come together and to separate. He saw fusion behavior as involving actions, thoughts, and language that conform to the family's preferred behavioral patterns. These behaviors encourage closeness as they emphasize similarity. He defined differentiation behavior as the direct opposite; it involves actions that are designed to enable the person to resist the urge to automatically comply with the family preferences. In this way, she or he is released from control by others and is permitted the freedom to be different and to separate from other family members.

Murray Bowen (1974) believed the successful reconciliation of these two polarities of human nature to be critical for mental health in that it allows the person to develop a healthy self-identity that balances autonomy with a sense of belonging. He believed that a person's ability to balance these forces depended on her or his level of *differentiation of self.* This refers to one's ability to maintain a clear sense of self while dealing with the pressure of group (and especially, family) influences (Nichols & Schwartz, 2005). A healthy self-identity is articulated within the context of relationships that affirm one's individuality, self-worth, and sense of interpersonal connection. Well-differentiated people demonstrate the ability to think and reflect before reacting to internal or external emotional pressures (Kerr & Bowen, 1988). In other words, they are able to respond to interpersonal situations with self-directedness, good judgment, and flexibility, despite feelings of anxiety. Although they have the ability to be spontaneous and to feel strong emotions, they are also able to restrain emotional impulses when necessary (Nichols, 2008).

On the other hand, undifferentiated people, in Bowen's view, have a poor sense of autonomy and tend toward a blurring of boundaries with others. Inadequate self-differentiation is related to anxious attachment. (See Chapter 9, "Infancy," and Chapter 10, "Early Childhood," for a more complete discussion of attachment issues.) Undifferentiated people tend to function in reaction to others—responding emotionally with either submissiveness/conformity or defiance/rebellion. Behaviorally, the lack of differentiation manifests itself either as dependence or isolation. Both of these undifferentiated personality types are highly reactive to stress and vulnerable to the emotionality of others (Nichols & Schwarz, 2005).

Carter and McGoldrick (2005) noted that Bowen's concept of self-differentiation has been widely misunderstood to equate maturity with separateness and autonomy (viewed as "male" attributes). Rather, they argue (and we agree) that Bowen placed equal value on both autonomy and emotional connectedness as necessary for mature self-differentiation.

For adequate self-differentiation of family members to take place, the family must come to terms with how it will handle sameness and difference in family relations and find a functional balance in "how its members will come together and support each other and how they will be different and able to be apart from each other" (Jantzen & Harris, 1980, p. 15). Such a balance creates a situation in which members' needs for both closeness/sameness and separateness/difference are satisfied. Families establish behavior patterns that reflect their needs for closeness and individuality. Most families function in a reasonably balanced way; however, some families may favor one extreme or another, emphasizing closeness at the expense of autonomy, or autonomy and self-determination at the expense of members' ability to feel close and to support each other when necessary. Functioning at either extreme may lead to dysfunctional interactional patterns and inadequate differentiation among family members. These stereotypic emotional patterns are related to Minuchin's structural concepts of boundary enmeshment and disengagement.

It is important to note that the value placed on self-differentiation may vary according to such factors as age of members, culture, gender, and circumstance. For example, there is ever-increasing understanding of the fact that Eastern and Western cultures differ fundamentally in their view of human nature (and in fact, of the nature of the world itself; Nisbett, 2003), with Easterners defining development as growth in the capacity for connection to others and Westerners, as growth in the capacity for individuation. In fact, throughout Asia, the family takes precedence over the individual, with one's position in the family defining one's behavior, responsibilities, and roles and with mutuality more highly valued than independence (Germain, 1991; Sue & Sue, 2003).

Emotional Expression Virginia Satir and other "experiential" family therapists believed that most family problems are related to *emotional suppression* (Nichols, 2008). Satir believed that when parents try to regulate children's behavior by controlling their (the children's) feelings, (for example, "Don't be angry!" versus "I know you feel angry but it's not OK to hit when you feel that way"), the children learn that particular emotions are unacceptable, and eventually, these feelings are suppressed altogether. Without access to the full range of human emotions, these individuals experience anxiety and other behavioral and emotional difficulties.

Attachment Issues and Emotionally Focused Family Therapy Johnson and Denton (2002) view emotional accessibility and responsiveness as core characteristics of healthy relationships and relate this to security of attachment. They speak of *attachment injuries* between partners—these are events that threaten their bond and, if unresolved, serve to perpetuate negative patterns and insecure attachment.

Bowlby (1988) believes that although attachment issues are founded in childhood, our relationships and interactions throughout life continue to affect our beliefs about other people's ability to be there and support us when we feel vulnerable. In relationships, this process is, of course, circular—those who feel secure in expressing attachment needs tend to become involved in relationships that affirm their belief that their needs will be met. People who feel less secure about the availability of others may be reluctant to express vulnerability and need, thereby precluding others from knowing how to respond appropriately to their needs; the resulting sense of deprivation may lead to anger, clinging, and/or detachment and negative relational patterns.

In Emotionally Focused Family Therapy, the therapist works to uncover the partners' feelings of hurt, deprivation, and insecurity that lie beneath their expressions of defensive anger and withdrawal. Couples are helped to recognize how these "attachment injuries" play out in their relationship and to use this recognition to reorganize their interactional patterns (Nichols, 2008).

Conflicting Emotions and Internal Family Systems Therapy In general, it is safe to say that people in intimate relationships (such as family members) feel a complex mix of emotions for one another. When they find themselves in conflict with each other, they typically feel multiple conflicting internal emotions; however, they tend to express only one aspect of what they are experiencing internally.

In the Internal Family Systems model, the therapist identifies these conflicting inner feelings as "parts" of the person (for example, "a part of you feels worried and concerned, and another part feels angry and frustrated").

> Thus, by personifying people's polarizing emotional reactions as parts, and then helping them visualize and reassure these reactive parts, Internal Family Systems therapy releases people from the domination of fear and anger, which in turn allows them to work together more effectively to solve personal and family problems. (Nichols, 2008, p. 231)

Family Roles In families, as in all other social groups, individuals take on "roles" that enable the system to function and carry out its various tasks. The family's system of roles has both process and structural functions. Two types of role systems operate in all families (Greene, 1991). *Instrumental roles* deal with socioeconomic tasks such as caretaking, wage earning, and household management. *Expressive roles* deal with emotional tasks. Virginia Satir (1972) described a variety of expressive roles such as the "placator," rebel," or the "good child." Family members assume their specific roles based on their status in the family, their personal characteristics and needs, the family's needs, and cultural expectations. Family members may take on different roles at different times and in different situations. For example, a single mother may be the family wage earner providing economic support for herself and her two adolescent children. When she loses her job, her teenage children may get part-time jobs, each assuming the role of wage earner temporarily until the mother finds new employment. As the mother reassumes the wage-earner role, the children may stop working (or reduce their work hours) to once again devote themselves to their (developmentally appropriate) roles as students.

Family roles tend to be reciprocal and complementary; that is, members take on roles that provide something that the family needs to perform its various functions. In addition to complementarity, the role structure must be flexible enough to accommodate the needs of individual family members (for example, an adolescent's growing need for greater independence), changes in external circumstances (as in the preceding example) and/or changes within the family system (for example, a member's death). This contributes to the growth and development of individual members as well as the family's ability to function and grow when stressed.

Problems may arise if the family role structure becomes too rigid and inflexible. Because of the reciprocal nature of family role structure, members may become trapped in narrow roles that serve to preserve a kind of homeostasis in the system, but which inhibit the family's ability to adapt to change and to meet the individual needs of the members. What begins as a healthy reciprocity of roles may become a maladaptive, polarized complementarity that constrains relationships between members and inhibits individual and family growth and adaptation. For example, one partner in a couple may tend to be somewhat anxious, goal-focused, and ambitious, whereas the other is more relaxed. Initially each may complement the other and contribute to the other's growth and sense of well-being by supporting and encouraging the other's best traits. Over time, however, as the couple experiences the ordinary (or extraordinary) stresses of life, they may find themselves trapped in rigid, mutually reinforcing role patterns in which one "overfunctions" and the other "underfunctions." Examples of other such negative interactional role patterns include pursuing–distancing, controlling–rebelling, strict parenting–lenient parenting, minimizing–maximizing, and demanding disclosure–secrecy and withholding (Madsen, 2007; Nichols & Schwartz, 2005). These may undermine adaptation of individual family members as well as of the system as a whole. Rigid expressive roles prevent individuals from experiencing the full range of human emotions and result in loss of a sense of competence and self-esteem. In the example given earlier, the underfunctioning partner may relinquish self-assertion and self-will, as the overfunctioning partner experiences those at the expense of vulnerability and the need for nurturing. Inflexible instrumental roles may be equally disabling. For example, if a parent is unable to relax her or his caretaking behaviors as his or her child grows into adulthood, maladaptive parent–child interactions such as control–rebel may take hold, potentially resulting in both individual and relational dysfunction.

Again, the role of social context must not be ignored when assessing family role structure, as role expectations, assignments, and level of flexibility will vary widely among various subgroups. For example, as noted previously, women have traditionally been expected to assume oppressive, gender-typed roles, and these role expectations underlie certain types of family dysfunction. Gay/lesbian families are often distinguished by a high degree of gender-role flexibility. African-American families have traditionally exhibited a greater flexibility of role structure than European-American families; this allows for the sharing of wage earning, parenting, and household chores among various members of the extended family and kinship systems and serves as a source of resilience especially in the face of socioeconomic and sociocultural obstacles (Denby, 1996; Hill et al., 1993). Asian cultures tend to prescribe role-based expectations for behavior to a greater extent than most other cultures; in many ways these traditions support a strong social structure and set of moral values. On the other hand, they tend to relegate women to a socially prescribed, lower status that may persist for generations after immigration to the United States (Germain, 1991).

Patterns of Communication Virtually from its inception, family theory has emphasized the importance of communication to family functioning. As early as the 1950s, pioneering family therapists such as Bateson, Haley, Weakland, Jackson, and Fry (Bateson, 1951; Bateson et al., 1956) began to study communication patterns in families. Their work, and the work of other early family theorists such as Virginia Satir, laid the groundwork for the *communicative–interactive approach* to family therapy. A basic tenet of this approach is that all behavior, verbal and nonverbal (for example, language, gestures, style of dress, tone of voice, facial expression, or posture), has communication value and conveys multilayered messages between people. The relationships between and among family members and between the family and its environment are maintained through patterns of communication—that is, the sending and receiving of messages as well as a feedback process. *Feedback* refers to the process by which a system gets information about its performance; that is, it signals to the system whether it needs to work to maintain the status quo (negative feedback) or to modify itself in some way to adapt to changing circumstances and demands (positive feedback). (Again, see Chapter 1 for a more comprehensive discussion of communication and feedback in social systems.) For purposes of this discussion, it is important to note that communication that is unclear or otherwise defective causes problems in the accuracy of feedback. As a result, the family will find it difficult to adapt to changing circumstances, often overreacting or underreacting to change (Nichols & Schwartz, 2005). It is also important to note that communication styles reflect basic assumptions about human behavior and vary considerably across cultures. For example, Westerners teach their children to communicate their ideas clearly and to adopt a "transmitter" orientation, that is, the speaker is responsible for uttering sentences that can be clearly understood by the hearer—and understood, in fact, more or less independently of the context. It's the speaker's fault if there is a miscommunication. Asians, in contrast, teach their children a "receiver" orientation, meaning, that it is the hearer's responsibility to understand what is being said. Westerners—and perhaps especially Americans—are apt to find Asians hard to read because Asians are likely to assume that their point has been made indirectly and with finesse. Meanwhile, the Westerner is in fact very much in the dark. Asians, in turn, are apt to find Westerners—perhaps especially Americans—direct to the point of condescension or even rudeness (Nisbett, 2003, pp. 60–61).

In the West, functional communication is thought to flow from good self-differentiation and self-awareness. Functional communicators are open to feedback and use active listening techniques (asking questions, checking their perceptions, asking for examples) to clarify their understanding. They make good use of concrete behavioral detail to produce messages that are clear and direct, and they assume responsibility for their own feelings, wishes, and interpretations. Dysfunctional communicators may rely on generalizations (for example, "you always disappoint me"), distortions (for example, "you make me treat you badly"), and/or lack of specificity (for example, "I'm just not cut out for college").

Family Rules Family members establish rules that guide their behavior and regulate their interactions with each other and with the outside world. Some rules are explicit and open to discussion and negotiation. Others, however, are implicit and unspoken, and they are established through repeated transactions among family members over time. They exert a strong influence on individual members' behavior, feelings, and reactions to one another. These rules derive their power from the fact that the lack of discussion prevents relevant information from being processed. Many family rules (both explicit and implicit) serve an adaptive function by providing routines that strengthen the family's sense of identity and stability (for example, "we always open one Chanukah present on each night of the holiday"). However, they can also "result in self-perpetuating interactional patterns that limit variety and increase the chances that a particular problem-behavior sequence will occur" (Germain, 1991, p. 132). Practice Example illustrates the power of implicit family rules.

Family Narratives Families, like individuals, organize and make sense of their experience by developing narratives (or stories); these are explanations that families (as well as individuals) construct to organize and make sense of their experiences. The family's narrative exerts powerful influence on the family's expectations, behaviors, attitudes, relationships, and how they view their problems. Narrative therapists work to understand how the world looks to families based on their unique narratives, and then, to help them change their experiences by helping them view things differently. They use the technique of *externalization*, which views problems as external forces that oppress people, rather than as characteristics of a person (Nichols, 2008).

PRACTICE EXAMPLE 5.1

Mrs. A

Mrs. A lives with her husband, her mother, and her two children. Over the past 15 years, Mrs. A has shown symptoms of serious degenerative neuromuscular disease. She has become increasingly debilitated over time and has presently been hospitalized because she is now unable to walk at all or even to get out of bed. In addition to the neuromuscular disease, Mrs. A. presents with severe symptoms of late-stage alcohol dependency. Despite the fact that the symptoms of both illnesses have been apparent to both Mrs. A and all other family members for years, she has never received medical advice or attention for either disorder. Over the years, Mrs. A's medical issues have generated all manner of difficulties to which the family has tried to adapt (for example, the need to move to a house without stairs; serious financial strain resulting from Mrs. A's limited ability to contribute to the household, neglect of many of the children's developmental needs), yet the adults have never openly discussed the medical issues among themselves, nor have they entertained any such discussion by the children. In fact, the children (now young adults) recall being severely admonished for attempting to voice their concerns early on. As such scenarios repeated themselves over time, the family established an unspoken rule that they would not talk about Mrs. A's disabilities.

The Family System Over Time: Family Development, Stress, and Adaptation

Inevitably, all families face a variety of changing circumstances or life issues to which the family system must adapt. These demands may be *normative* (expected life-cycle transitions, such as the birth of a child) or *nonnormative* (unexpected stressors such as unemployment, substance abuse, or illness; McCubbin & Figley, 1983). These life issues create pressure on the family to accommodate to new situations and may emanate from within the family itself or from its environment. To adequately respond to these demands, the family may need to make changes in its usual patterns of behavior, communication, interaction, structure, and/or beliefs and rules so that the family can adapt as necessary while maintaining a sense of continuity and stability. At first, the family may attempt to rely on their usual patterns to cope with the new demand. If this is unsuccessful, the family may experience anxiety, confusion, relationship conflict, and/or difficulties in communication (Reiss, 1981). Minuchin (1974) cautions that although such reactions may appear to be pathological, they may actually represent nothing more than expectable, normal transitional processes that result from the family's attempts to make adaptive efforts to cope with novel challenges. Most families are eventually able to restructure themselves as necessary to meet the new demands. "The label of pathology would be reserved for families who, in the face of stress, increase the rigidity of their transactional patterns and boundaries" (Minuchin, 1974 p. 60). Minuchin further proposed that families are subject to stress from the following four general sources.

- ***Stressful contact of one family member with the outside world.*** Because a primary function of the family is to support its members, when one member experiences stress, the other family members will also be affected and will feel the need to respond to the changed circumstances. For example, if a mother comes home stressed from her job, she may overreact to seeing her teenage daughter's coat and books lying on the floor by the front door and immediately begin to yell at the daughter. An argument between mother and daughter might ensue; this would serve to dispel some of the stress that had built up in the mother. If the argument is later resolved, with an airing of the issues (mother's job stress and dismay about the state of the home; daughter's distress about her mother's overreaction), the interaction will have served to reduce the mother's stress and, possibly, increase mother–daughter sensitivity to each other's needs in the future; this would be considered an adaptive response. If, on the other hand, the argument is not resolved, and the anger between mother and daughter persists and escalates, the same transaction may repeat itself each day, with the mother and daughter arguing over the same issue over and over. In this case, the interaction between family members would be considered maladaptive, in that it serves to increase, rather than reduce, members' stress.

- ***Stressful contact of the whole family with outside forces.*** The family may become overloaded by stress generated from such extrafamilial forces as economic downturn, racism and oppression, chronic poverty, disruptive social policies, inadequate social supports, the need to adapt to a new culture (in the case of immigration), war, natural disasters, and other such forces that may threaten and tax a family's coping capacities. In the face of such difficulties, it is particularly important that the family practitioner make a careful assessment of how these social forces affect the internal workings of the family (for example, structure, communication, interactional patterns, rules and belief systems, self-differentiation) and help the family members to view their problems in a broader social context. The technique of contextualizing personal problems can be very effective in reducing the sense of isolation and shame that results from the internalization of social toxins and traumatic events. Depending on the nature of the problems, the family practitioner may also assume the role of advocate; in that case, interventions might include resource referral, direct advice, coordination of services, and/or "macro" interventions at the organizational, community, state, federal or even, global levels. Our discussions of poverty and the family, migration and the family, as well as gay and lesbian families illustrate the stressful effects of outside forces.

- ***Stress at transitional points in the family.*** This refers to the normative changes a family experiences over time. These may result from developmental changes in family members (for example, a child reaches adolescence) and/or by changes in family composition (for example, a child gets married). A variety of family *stage models* have been proposed over time (O'Connell, 1972; Pollack, 1960; Rhodes, 1977). These view family development as a series of predictable stages (each with its own specific "developmental tasks"). Carter and McGoldrick (1989) view the family life cycle "as a process of expansion, contraction and realignment of the relationship system to support the entry, exit and development of family members in a functional way" (p. 13). In their view, the family is a basic unit of emotional development comprised of "the entire emotional system of at least three, and now frequently four, generations" (p. 6). Their traditional model, based on a two-parent, heterosexual middle-class family with children

TABLE 5.1

The Stages of the Family Life Cycle

Family Life-Cycle Stage	Emotional Process of Transition: Key Principles	Second-Order Changes in Family Status Required to Proceed Developmentally
1. Leaving home single young adults	Accepting emotional and financial responsibility for self	**a.** Differentiation of self in relation to family of origin **b.** Development of intimate peer relationships **c.** Establishment of self re. work and financial independence.
2. The joining of families through marriage; the new couple	Commitment to new system	**a.** Formation of marital system **b.** Realignment of relationships with extended families and friends to include spouse
3. Families with young children	Accepting new members into the system	**a.** Adjusting marital system to make space for children **b.** Joining in child-rearing, financial, and household tasks **c.** Realignment of relationships with extended family to include parenting and grandparenting roles
4. Families with adolescents	Increasing flexibility of family boundaries to include children's independence and grandparents' families	**a.** Shifting of parent–child relationships to permit adolescent to move in and out of system **b.** Refocus on midlife marital and career issues **c.** Beginning shift toward joint caring for older generation
5. Launching children and moving on	Accepting a multitude of exits from and entries into the family system	**a.** Renegotiation of marital system as a dyad **b.** Development of adult-to-adult relationships between grown children and their parents **c.** Realignment of relationships to include in-laws and grandchildren **d.** Dealing with disabilities and death of parents (grandparents)
6. Families in later life	Accepting the shifting of generational roles	**a.** Maintaining own and/or couple functioning and interests in face of physiological decline **b.** Support for a more central role of middle generation **c.** Making room in the system for the wisdom and experience of the elderly, supporting the older generation without overfunctioning for them **d.** Dealing with the loss of spouse, siblings, and other peers and the preparation for own death. Life review and integration.

Source: Adapted from Betty Carter and Monica McGoldrick, Eds., *The Expanded Family Life Cycle: Individual, Family, and Social Perspectives,* 3rd edition. Published by Allyn and Bacon, Boston, MA.

(Table 5.1) reflects their intergenerational perspective and consists of six stages of family development. To make the transition from one stage to the next, the family must undergo an emotional process that leads them to accept the need for the family system to transform. This transformation is called a "second-order change"—it involves a restructuring of the system itself. For example, when two people marry, they must commit themselves emotionally to the establishment of a new system. This allows them to form a boundary that separates them as a couple from each of their original family systems. The new system must establish its own rules, communication patterns, role structure, and so forth (Stage 2, Table 5.1). Each partner's original family system must also undergo a structural change that accommodates the addition of a new member and the inclusion of the couple as a subsystem (Stage 5, Table 5.1). In Carter and McGoldrick's view, individual family members are most likely to develop symptoms of emotional problems when the family is having trouble making the transition from one stage of family development to the next. When families are stressed at these transition points, the family practitioner's role is to help them make the second-order changes it needs to make so it can proceed along its natural developmental course. The difficulties a family experiences within a particular stage are alterable by "first-order" or more superficial changes in family behavior within its current organization.

- ***Stress from idiosyncratic problems.*** These refer to those serious, unexpected (nonnormative) problems that any family might face at any given time (for example, a family member's chronic illness, untimely death, unemployment, imprisonment, violence, substance abuse; handicapping conditions). Practitioners working with families must be alert to the challenges posed by such circumstances and to the risk that maladaptive transactional patterns may appear as the family attempts to cope with the need to adapt to these idiosyncratic sources of family stress. Our descriptions of the experiences of military and adoptive families illustrate the stress of idiosyncratic problems.

Families in Context: Effects of Socioeconomic and Sociocultural Variables

Much of the early foundational research on family systems tended to focus on white, U.S. middle-class families with children and two legally married heterosexual parents, as the norm against which all families were assessed. Thus, it has long been criticized for ignoring the impact of such variables race, ethnicity, gender, sexual orientation, socioeconomic status, and family form on family life and functioning and for starting "from a majority perspective (usually white, middle-class, male), comparing and searching for 'difference,' measuring the population of interest against some accepted norm and describing how it is different, exotic, or deviant" (Laird, 1993, p. 286).

Carter and McGoldrick (1989) responded to this criticism with the publication of *The Changing Family Life Cycle,* in which they explored alternate family life-cycle models based on these variations in context. They more fully explored the impact of oppressive social forces on families, in their 2005 edition, *The Expanded Family Life Cycle.* The following section explores the effects of several contexts (poverty, divorce, remarriage, gay and lesbian relationships, and adoption) on family structure and process (other "postmodern" family contexts are explored in Chapter 13, "Early Adulthood").

Socioeconomic Stress and the Family

Recognizing the risks for families burdened by economic insecurity, researchers in recent decades have called attention to the survival needs of families from the lower socioeconomic strata (Colon, 1980; Hartman & Laird, 1983; Terkelsen, 1980; Vosler, 1996). Some family theorists (Hartman & Laird, 1983; Terkelsen, 1980) have drawn on the work of Abraham Maslow (1954) in their examination of what is generally seen as the overriding purpose of family life: to support need attainment for all family members. Terkelsen (1980) referred to two basic kinds of needs: survival (for example, food, shelter, and protection) and developmental (for example, sense of psychological well-being). He believed that the family cannot support members' developmental needs unless, and until, survival needs are met.

Family Ecosystems Hartman and Laird (1983) use an ecological perspective to specifically examine the environmental resources to which families must have access to meet both survival and developmental needs. They underscore the need for practitioners to examine the social context in which the family is embedded to assess how the environment does, and does not, support adequate family functioning. Table 5.2 outlines the needs and resources they use as a basis to assess family functioning. Hartman and Laird (1983) also recommend the "ecomap" (see Appendix) as another valuable tool for assessing family well-being and for identifying sources of stress and social support. Here the social worker and family draw a diagram that creates a visual image of both formal and informal sources of support, whether or not relationships are conflicted, and the direction of energy flow in these relationships.

Social Class Discussions of social class in the United States are complicated for a variety of reasons. Dominant (and somewhat contradictory) U.S. discourse is that ours is a classless society in which all have equal access to upward mobility. This discourse does reflect an ideal on which the nation was founded, and many descendants of poor (often immigrant) families will testify to its truth. However, this discourse tends to mask the "shaping power" (Kliman & Madsen, 2005, p. 88) of social class—a phenomenon that is particularly complicated in this country by its "multiple relationships to economic and social phenomena, including race, ethnicity, religion, gender, sexuality, geography and mental and physical ability" (Kliman & Madsen, 2005, p. 89). Kliman and Madsen's

TABLE 5.2

Family Needs and Environmental Resources

Need	Resources
Nutrition	Adequate and varied food Clean air Pure and plentiful water
Shelter	Housing (space, light, warmth, privacy, and community safety)
Protection	Safe neighborhoods Police, fire, traffic control
Health	A clean environment Preventative, developmental, and rehabilitative health care Adequate, responsive, accessible medical system
Belongingness, intimacy, interpersonal connectedness	Lovers, kin, friends Neighbors, social organizations, interest groups
Communication and mobility	Access to resources Telephone, public and private transportation
Education and enrichment	Schools (proficient teachers, well-maintained buildings, equal opportunity, support services, etc.) Other resources—vocational, adult education Family life education The arts and recreation
Varied resources for the spirit	Religious organizations Opportunities to share meanings and values Preservation of and respect for cultural, ethnic, racial, and other kinds of "difference"
Autonomy, effectiveness, mastery (to experience oneself as a cause)	Gratifying work in or out of home Community participation Opportunities for initiating new experiences
Generativity	To contribute to the future

Source: A. Hartman and J. Laird, 1983, *Family-Centered Social Work Practice* (p. 160). New York: The Free Press, a Division of Macmillan, Inc.

description of some of the effects of social class cuts through the complexities and illuminates some simple realities that will be familiar to people at varying levels of the social hierarchy:

> Class position regulates access to disposable income. Preferential interest rates ensure that monied people can borrow liberally, without debt precluding retirement or inheritance. Class affects whether kin, neighbors, or paid caretakers help with children, the elderly, or sick family members. Class determines which adolescents drop out, work through college, help support the family, or expect parents to finance college, rent, and vacations. Some parents can remove lead from their homes; others can only pray that toddlers won't suffer neurological damage from eating lead paint chips, intensifying family needs through the life cycle. In 1996, 25% of all U.S. families had no health insurance (Knox, 1996), further stressing and shortening the lives of millions of working and unwillingly unemployed families. (Kliman & Madsen, 2005, p. 91)

Families and Macrosystemic Change Family research has increasingly begun to broaden its perspective to emphasize the interrelatedness of systems and to view families as inseparable from the economic, cultural, political, and historical contexts in which they exist. For example, Billingsley and Morrison-Rodriguez (1998) warn that structural social forces such as decreasing numbers of unskilled and semiskilled jobs, changing social mores, and punitive, ineffective social policies at the federal level "may accomplish what slavery could not—the destruction of the African-American family"(p. 33), and they advocate change at the macrolevel to offset what they see as a massive crisis for the African-American family as a source of strength and resilience for the black community (see Chapter 7, "Communities and Organizations").

Vosler's (1996) multilevel practice model also recognizes the inadequacy of current social institutions and policies in providing access to basic social support structures (for example, affordable housing, affordable health insurance, quality education, and child care) to lower socioeconomic status families. Vosler incorporated a developmental construction view that emphasizes the need to alter institutions and policies to make them more responsive to the needs of socially and economically disadvantaged families. Collection of specific data regarding a family's financial situation, community resources, and service gaps in terms of housing, transportation, and other basic support services as well as the agency's links to other services provides valuable information for program planning and policy changes at the community, state, federal, and even international levels (Vosler, 1999).

Poverty, Race, and the Family Life Cycle Before discussing any issues that face and affect families living in poverty, it is important to note that the poor are not a homogeneous group. There are as many variations in family structure and family circumstances among the poor as there are among the more affluent. Variations in the amount of time families have been poor, their level of upward (or downward) mobility, and their values and resources make it difficult to generalize about the effects of poverty on families. Still, there is a growing body of literature that documents the developmental, biological, and emotional risks associated with specific forms of socioeconomic disadvantage as well as the increasing numbers of U.S. families living in such circumstances. In fact, income level has been shown to have significant effects on the well-being of families, even when such variables as ethnicity and occupational status are controlled for (Huston, 1991). For further discussion of specific risks associated with poverty, see Chapter 7, "Communities and Organizations," Chapter 10, "Early Childhood," Chapter 11, "Middle Childhood," and Chapter 15, "Older Adulthood."

Hines (2005) noted that "family income does not equate with family competence" (p. 328), and that despite risks and hardships, families vary widely in their coping abilities and levels of resilience. However, she further noted that despite the variation in functioning, even the most resilient of the poor will face "innumerable barriers to transcending their concrete circumstances on a daily basis" (p. 329). Her model of the family life cycle of African-American families living in poverty illustrates possible adverse effects of economic, environmental, and social barriers faced by people living in what Kliman and Madsen (2005) refer to as the *underclass;* this term refers, not to all poor people, but rather to those who are chronically unemployed or whose income is generated in the underground economy. Although this model is based on the experiences of poor African Americans—"the most severely oppressed by virtue of poverty and racism" (Hines, 1989, p. 515), it has relevance for work with poor families from other racial and ethnic contexts, particularly if they have been poor for more than one generation. As Kliman and Madsen (2005) so aptly noted: "Deindustrialization and 'exported' manufacturing have brought families whose working class roots influence their life cycle patterns into the ranks of the underclass" (p. 93).

Hines observed several characteristics that may distinguish the life cycles of some poor families (especially those without other important social assets such as strong cultural and/or religious ties) from the life cycles of many middle-class families (across racial and ethnic groups), including the experience of chronic stress and untimely losses, obstacles to employment, more female-headed households, and a condensed life cycle, characterized by unclear delineation of transitions, role strain, and role overload.).

Chronic Stress, Untimely Losses, and Obstacles to Employment Poor families may be subject to a host of troubles in addition to poverty (for example, substance abuse, psychiatric disorders, untimely deaths of members, imprisonment). These may result in, among other difficulties, frequent changes in household membership and location, as well as frequent school changes for children. African-American families (both low and middle income) are more likely than any other group to experience racial discrimination in employment, housing, and education, as well as in their dealings with the criminal justice system (Billingsley & Morrison-Rodriguez, 1998). Any of these factors, alone or in combination, may serve to place additional strain on the family's coping capacities.

In addition, the poor face more obstacles and fewer opportunities to acquire employment. The last several decades have witnessed a steady decline in the number and availability of semiskilled and unskilled jobs in an economy that increasingly requires some form of higher education and technical expertise. The instability of their economic status may lead to a need for families to rely on institutional supports that may reinforce an already debilitating sense of powerlessness and frustration. Much has been written on the significance of work to one's sense of well-being (See, 1998; Wilson, 1996 cited in Billingsley & Morrison-Rodriguez,

1998, p. 31). Wilson sees a direct connection between work and family and community life; he attributes problems that plague inner-city ghettoes such as crime, family dissolution, poorly organized communities, and so on directly to the "disappearance of work" (p. xiii). Billingsley and Morrison-Rodriguez (1998) noted that lack of stability in employment is associated with decreased commitment to relationships such as marriage and parenthood.

Condensed Life Cycle, Female-Headed Households, and Life Cycle with Unclear Delineation of Transitions About 10% of U.S. children are born to a single parent who has never been married and does not have a partner. Sixty percent of births to African-American mothers in their twenties are to women without a partner; this figure for white women is 13% (U.S. Census Bureau, 2003). Approximately 60% of children living in mother-only families in the United States also live in poverty; this rate is higher for African-American mother-only families (Kirby, 1995).

Hines (2005) observed that members of chronically poor families tend to progress through the family life cycle in an accelerated manner—leaving home, finding mates, having children, and becoming grandparents earlier than do members of middle-class families. This truncated life cycle essentially consists of three stages: (a) adolescence/unattached adulthood; (b) coupling, bearing, and raising children; and (3) the family in later life. Because family members have less time to resolve the developmental tasks at each stage, they may be forced to assume roles for which they are developmentally underprepared and which are sometimes in direct conflict with their current developmental needs. This situation may lead to increased difficulties in proceeding through subsequent stages and may result in a family that is not adequately organized to meet its ongoing needs.

Grandparenting in Early Adulthood For example, there is a growing population of relatively young women of childbearing age who are becoming grandparents as their adolescent daughters have children. These women are often, but not always, African American, and either unemployed or among the "working poor" (See, Bowles, & Darlington, 1998). Rather than having their households convert, as expected, to single-generational families once their children are raised, these women find themselves in families that are expanding to include second and third generations. The problems are multiplied as some of these women are expected to take on full responsibility for raising their grandchildren (Henry, 1993, cited in See et al., 1998, p. 282). As See et al. (1998) point out, there is a historical tradition of rearing grandchildren by African-American grandparents as a means of economic assistance (Davis, 1995; Downey 1995; Woodworth 1994, cited in See et al., 1998, p. 282) in the past; however, these arrangements were seen as temporary until the parents became financially stable enough to resume caring for their children. Today, more and more grandmothers find themselves raising their grandchildren to maturity, with little support from the parents, who may be unable to parent for reasons of drug addiction, medical problems, or other issues (Minkler, 1992, cited in See et al., 1998, p. 282). In addition to the physical and economic burdens this situation presents (Minkler, 1994; Minkler, Driver, Roe, & Bedeian, 1993, cited in See et al., 1998, p. 283; Pinson-Millburn et al., 1995), See et al. pointed out the social and psychological consequences for these women who are "prematurely thrust into a new life phase of which they have no prior preparation" (1998, p. 285). They noted that when women are forced to extend the child-rearing stage of their lives, they will be less likely to focus on the developmental tasks that are generally associated with their chronological life stage (especially those associated with employment goals). This may create significant role confusion and role strain, as they attempt to assume two primary roles that have fundamentally different developmental tasks (those associated with entry into middle age and those associated with becoming a grandmother). For further discussion of issues related to grandparenting, see Chapter 14, "Middle Adulthood."

Having had their own children early, these women may have had to leave school, work in low-wage jobs, become dependent on public assistance, or otherwise postpone their personal goals; the pregnancy of their adolescent daughters may force them to repeat that sacrifice. The experience of a shortened childhood and then an abbreviated adolescence can inhibit resolution of stage-related developmental tasks for both the young grandmother and the adolescent mother and make subsequent developmental stages harder to navigate (See et al., 1998). This, combined with the potential for role overload and problems associated with underorganization of the family system (for example, poorly differentiated hierarchy and role structure) may render the family system less able to cope with both normative and nonnormative stressors.

Although the family life-cycle perspective provides a helpful framework for understanding poor families in that it allows one to understand how external stressors may exacerbate normative developmental pressures and unresolved generational issues, it does not account for the resilience seen in many poor families that allows them to cope with and, sometimes, thrive under extremely difficult circumstances.

Families and the Strengths Perspective In recent years, family practitioners and researchers have emphasized the utility of using a *strengths perspective* to understand and work with families. We refer the reader to Chapter 1 for a more comprehensive discussion of the value of this perspective. This approach originally grew out of a*sset-oriented* research developed, to a large extent out of work with African-American and female-headed families.

For example, Hill (1998) describes some of the fundamental values of African-based families that contribute to their resilience, including high respect for parents and parenthood, reverence for the elderly, the centrality of children, and an emphasis on the need for mutual support among family members. These resilient families are also headed by parents who maintain firm control over their children with caring, "uncompromising" (Hill, 1998, p. 57) discipline that supports strong character development in addition to correcting undesirable behavior. Hill also noted that the flexibility of the role structure in African-American families represents a major source of resilience. This adaptability manifests itself in patterns of shared parenting by husbands and wives, older siblings, extended family and nonblood relations; surrogate parenting in which relatives or fictive kin assume primary responsibility for rearing children (Denby 1996, cited in Hill, 1998, p. 56; Hill et al., 1993); and the sharing of work and household responsibilities between husbands and wives.

In addition, this flexibility of family roles may account in part for the fact that black single-parent families have been shown to be more resilient than white single-parent families (Benson & Roehlkepartain, 1993). Children in black female-headed families consistently show higher educational aspirations, higher rates of educational attainment, and less substance abuse and antisocial behavior than children raised by white single mothers (Benson & Roehlkepartain, 1993; Hill et al., 1993; Zill & Nord, 1994, cited in Hill, 1998, p. 56). Hines (2005) clarified the complex interplay of multiple factors in determining how well families fare in the face of extreme hardship:

> Single-parent family structures are not inherently dysfunctional, but they are particularly vulnerable because of poverty, task overload, and a lack of resources. More relevant than the structure of the single-parent family are the availability of other resources and the family's ways of functioning. Family adaptive strategies, when pushed too far, can become a vulnerability. For example, parental children can provide critical support to siblings, while developing self-esteem, and an enhanced sense of their own potential, if parents ensure that they assume only responsibilities that are within their capacities (Hines & Boyd-Franklin, 1996; Watson, 1998). But when parents abdicate responsibility to children who have inadequate skills, support, and power to meet the challenge, these children can easily become the object of their siblings' rage. The effort to take care of others may divert attention from their own developmental needs, leaving them ripe for frustration. Adaptive strengths are maximized when adults show sensitivity to the unique characteristics and needs of each child, avoid cutting children off from their fathers and paternal families, are clear about unacceptable behavior, and use positive, consistent discipline strategies. (p. 337)

Family Practice With Multi-Stressed Families Madsen (2007) explicates "four commitments" (p. 24) that form the foundation for the development of a therapeutic relational stance of *appreciative ally* with multistressed families:

- ***Striving for cultural curiosity and honoring family expertise:*** Here, Madsen encourages therapists to view each family as a "distinct culture" or "microculture" (p. 26). He emphasizes the need to approach clients with an "attitude of curiosity, seeking to learn about them while developing a keen sensitivity to the influence of broader macro-cultures" (p. 27) to understand how they perceive the world and how those perceptions affect their behavior and interactions.
- ***Believing in the possibility of change, and building on family and community resourcefulness:*** Here, Madsen points out that when we focus on family members' strengths, we reduce resistance and "evoke a sense of competence and pride that provides a stronger foundation from which to derive solutions to problems" (p. 32).
- ***Working in partnership and fitting services to families rather than families to services:*** Here, the nature of the relationship is determined collaboratively by the therapist and family, and this supports a process that draws on the resources of both. Madsen uses the model of "family-centered services" to illustrate this approach. Family-centered services generally refer to short-term, intensive services delivered in the home. Treatment addresses a broad range of

family needs and integrates traditional clinical interventions with systemically based concrete services as necessary. The whole family is viewed as the client, and families are actively involved in developing their treatment plans.

- ***Engaging in empowering processes and making our work more accountable to clients:*** Here, Madsen places emphasis on the need for therapists to make a "deliberate" (p. 39) choice to focus on techniques that empower clients, as opposed to ones that are disempowering. Acknowledging that helping professionals generally intend to act in ways that empower people, he makes a distinction between the *intent* of a therapist's actions and their *effects* (p. 39). He describes empowering approaches as those that "acknowledge support and amplify people's participation and influence in developing the lives they prefer" (p. 39); furthermore, he encourages the development of "accountability structures" (p. 42) that invite feedback from clients about their perceptions of the therapeutic process and the types of services being offered and developed.

Contextual Variations in Family Form

As noted earlier in this chapter, social and environmental changes may have a profound effect on families. In contemporary life, the form and function of the family has changed significantly for many people in Western, postindustrial societies. In this section, we will examine the following contemporary variations in family form: divorced and reconstituted families, adoptive families, gay and lesbian families, immigrant families, and military families.

Divorce and Reconstituted Families

Divorce The United States has the highest divorce rate in the industrialized world, with about 45% of U.S. marriages ending in divorce (Australian Bureau of Statistics, 2003; Statistics of Canada, 2003; U.S. Census Bureau, 2003; United Nations, 2001). It is important to note that divorce is not a single event in a family's life. Rather, it is a transitional process that leads to far-reaching changes in family roles, responsibilities, relationships, income, living arrangements, and so on (Berk, 2005). This transition typically leads to a state of crisis and disorganization of the family situation (Hope, Power, & Rodgers, 1999; Marks & Lambert, 1998). The situation may be particularly stressful for children (Amato & Booth, 2000). Although most children show an improved adjustment within two years of divorce, children and adolescents of divorced parents tend to score somewhat lower in academic achievement, self-esteem, social competence, and emotional and behavioral problems. In some cases, these difficulties, especially in the areas of sexuality and intimacy, may persist into adulthood (Amato, 2001; Wolfinger, 2000). However, research also shows that children's postdivorce adjustment problems can be mitigated when parents practice authoritative child rearing (see Chapter 10, "Early Childhood"), collaborate in child rearing, manage their stress well, and shield the children from family conflict. Ongoing contact with both parents is also very important for both boys and girls; in fact, research shows better adjustment for children living in joint-custody arrangements (Bauserman, 2002).

Other mitigating factors include a strong social support network, use of divorce mediation services, and regular child support payments by the noncustodial parent to relieve financial strain.

Carter and McGoldrick (2005) view the impact of divorce as a transitional crisis that disrupts the accomplishment of the family developmental tasks that are associated with the stage of the family life cycle in which the divorce occurs. From this perspective, the divorce creates a series of divorce-related adjustments that create a state of disequilibrium for all family members, including grandparents, siblings, and other extended family members. Optimally, the period of adjustment takes place over a period of two to three years (Carter & McGoldrick 2005) and involves completion of critical emotional tasks and changes in relationship status by all family members for the family to retain its equilibrium and to proceed developmentally at a more complex level (Carter & McGoldrick 2005). Carter and McGoldrick conceptualize this adjustment period as a series of additional phases of the family life cycle. These stages are depicted in Table 5.3. Peck and Manocherian (1989) noted that the divorce will alter each family life-cycle stage that follows it, so that each stage must be viewed with a dual perspective that includes the stage itself as well as the effects of the divorce. Carter and McGoldrick (2005) visualize the emotional processes that accompany divorce as "a roller coaster graph, with peaks of emotional tension at all transition points" (p. 376). These transition points are delineated in Table 5.4.

Blended or Reconstituted Families About two-thirds of divorced parents marry again (Hetherington & Kelly, 2003). Other parents may choose to cohabit without marrying. In any case, families that include a parent, stepparent, and children are referred to as blended or reconstituted families. The fact that half of all second marriages result in divorce (Hetherington & Kelly, 2003) testifies to the difficulties of negotiating the complex relationships and issues that arise in these families.

Carter and McGoldrick (2005) postulate that many of the difficulties faced by these families result from the failure of most people, including family practitioners, to understand that the rules and roles of the first family cannot be applied to the blended family; the new family requires an entirely new model of family that is able to accommodate its complex relationships, roles, and issues. In the absence of culturally established paradigms that clarify and validate the relationships of acquired family members, families are urged to accept the need for a new type of family structure that maintains permeable boundaries around members of various households (thus allowing children to move easily between family systems in accordance with visitation and custody agreements); works toward recognition of, and open lines of, communication among members of the various extended family networks; revises traditional family gender roles to allow birth parents to maintain ultimate responsibility for raising their children; and managing finances that may still be connected to the first family (for example, child support or alimony payments). Family practitioners can help families make the transition to the new family structure by helping them understand the predictable emotional processes and developmental tasks involved in this transition. Typically, these processes involve all members' fears of

TABLE 5.3

Divorce: Dislocations of the Family Life Cycle Requiring Additional Steps to Restabilize and Proceed Developmentally

	Phase	External Process of Transition Prerequisite Attitude	Developmental Issues
Divorce			
1	The decision to divorce	Acceptance of inability to resolve marital tensions sufficiently to continue relationship	Acceptance of one's own part in the failure of the marriage.
2	Planning the breakup of the system	Supporting viable arrangements for all parts of the system	**a.** Working cooperatively on problems of custody, visitation, and finances **b.** Dealing with extended family about the divorce.
3	Separation	**a.** Willingness to continue cooperative coparental relationship and joint financial support of children **b.** Work on resolution of attachment to spouse	**a.** Morning loss of intact family **b.** Restructuring marital and parental–child relationships and finances. Adaptation to living apart **c.** Realignment of relationships with extended family; staying connected with spouse's extended family
4	The divorce	More work on emotional divorce. Overcoming hurt, anger, guilt, etc.	**a.** Mourning loss of intact family; giving up fantasies of reunion **b.** Retrieval of hopes, dreams, expectations from the marriage **c.** Staying connected with extended families
Postdivorce Family			
1	Single-parent (custodial household or primary residence)	Willingness to maintain financial responsibilities, continue parental contact with ex-spouse, and support contact of children with ex-spouse and his or her family	**a.** Making flexible visitation arrangements with ex-spouse and his family **b.** Rebuilding own financial resources. **c.** Rebuilding own social network
2	Single-parent (noncustodial)	Willingness to maintain parental contact with ex-spouse and support custodial parent's relationship with children	**a.** Finding ways to continue effective parenting **b.** Maintaining financial responsibilities to ex-spouse and children **c.** Rebuilding own social network

Source: Adapted from Betty Carter and Monica McGoldrick, Eds., *The Expanded Family Life Cycle: Individual, Family, and Social Perspectives,* 3rd edition. Published by Allyn and Bacon, Boston, MA.

TABLE 5.4

Peak Emotional Transition Points for Divorcing and Postdivorce Families

1. At the time of the decision to separate or divorce
2. When this decision is announced to family and friends
3. When money and custody/visitation arrangements are discussed
4. When the physical separation takes place
5. When the actual legal divorce takes place
6. When separated spouses or ex-spouses have contact about money or children
7. As each child graduates, marries, has children, or becomes ill
8. As each spouse is remarried, moves, becomes ill, or dies.

Source: From Betty Carter and Monica McGoldrick, Eds., *The Expanded Family Life Cycle: Individual, Family, and Social Perspectives*, 3rd edition. Published by Allyn and Bacon, Boston, MA. Copyright © 2005 by Pearson Education. Reprinted by permission of the publisher.

emotionally investing in the new family; dealing with emotional reactions from the children, extended family, and former spouses; struggling with reactivated issues of guilt and loss of the first family; and coping with the ambiguity of the new family structure, roles, and relationships. These processes are outlined in detail in Table 5.5.

Adoptive Families Adoption agencies in the United States (and other Western industrialized countries) generally favor placing children with parents who are the age of most birth parents and who share the ethnic, racial, and religious background of the child. In recent decades, the numbers of healthy babies available for adoption has decreased (due in part to the legalization of abortion, more effective and widespread use of contraception, and decreased stigma of single parenthood), and the number of adults seeking to adopt has increased (due in part to increased interest on the part of older couples and single individuals, both heterosexual and gay/lesbian). More people are choosing to adopt babies from other countries, older children, and/or children who have, or are at risk for, developmental disabilities due to genetic, prenatal, or preplacement factors (Berk, 2005; Finley, 1999). Adoption contexts vary widely. Some children are placed in foster care until their birth parents' parental rights are terminated and a permanent adoptive placement is made. Others are separated from the biological parent at birth and immediately placed with their adoptive parents. In addition, several "openness" options are available to families, ranging from confidential, semiopen (or mediated), to fully open adoption. In open adoptions, adoptive parents and the adopted child interact directly or indirectly with the birth parent(s) via letters, e-mails, telephone calls, or visits. The frequency of contact is negotiated and can range from every few years to several times a month. In semiopen or mediated adoption, contact between birth and adoptive families is made through a mediator (for example, a social worker or attorney) rather than directly. In confidential adoptions, no contact takes place, and no identifying information is exchanged.

Although it has been documented that adoptees have higher rates of learning and emotional difficulties than other children (Levy-Shiff, 2001; Miller, Fan, Christensen, Grotevant, & van Dulmen, 2000), it is difficult to assess this data

TABLE 5.5

Remarried Family Formation: A Developmental Outline

Steps	Prerequisite Attitude	Developmental Issues
1. Entering the new relationship	Recovery from loss of first marriage (adequate emotional divorce)	Recommitment to marriage and to forming a family with readiness to deal with the complexity and ambiguity
2. Conceptualizing and planning new marriage and family	Accepting one's own fears and those of new spouse and children and remarriage and forming a stepfamily Accepting need for time and patience for adjustment to complexity and ambiguity of 1. Multiple new roles 2. Boundaries, space, time, membership, and authority 3. Affective issues, guilt, loyalty conflicts, desire for mutuality, unresolvable past hurts	a. Working on openness in the new relationships to avoid pseudomutuality b. Plan for maintenance of cooperative financial and coparental relationships with ex-spouses c. Plan to help children deal with fears, loyalty conflicts, and membership in two systems d. Realignment of relationships with extended family to include new spouse and children e. Plan maintenance of connections for children with extended family of ex-spouses(s)
3. Remarriage and reconstitution of family	Final resolution of attachment to previous spouse and ideal of 'intact' family Acceptance of a different model of family with permeable boundaries	a. Restructuring family boundaries to allow for inclusion of new spouse-stepparent b. Realignment of relationships and financial arrangements throughout subsystems to permit interweaving of several subsystems c. Making room for relationships of all children with biological (noncustodial) parents, grandparents, and other extended family d. Sharing memories and histories to enhance stepfamily integration

Source: From Betty Carter and Monica McGoldrick, Eds., *The Expanded Family Life Cycle: Individual, Family, and Social Perspectives,* 3rd edition. Published by Allyn and Bacon, Boston, MA. Copyright © 2005 by Pearson Education. Reprinted by permission of the publisher.

accurately, in part due to the heterogeneity of adoptive family situations and in part to a lack of accurate, comprehensive national data from which to draw conclusions (Finley, 1999). The differences noted have been attributed to a variety of causes. Problems with some genetic basis such as alcoholism, mental illness, and developmental disabilities may account for the birth mother's inability to care for the child, and the child may inherit a predisposition for the same problem. The circumstances of the birth mother's pregnancy may have exposed her to inadequate diet and medical care, excessive stress, and other factors that may have adversely affected the child's prenatal environment. Children who are adopted after infancy may show problems associated with attachment disorders resulting from difficult family relationships and/or child abuse and neglect prior to the adoption. In addition, lack of compatibility between an adopted child and his or her genetically unrelated adoptive parents may lead to increased family discord

(Berk 2005; Grotevant, Miller Wrobel, van Dulmen, & McRoy, 2001). Despite the risks, most adopted children develop well, and those with problems often show swift improvement (Johnson, 2002; Kim, 2002). Sensitive parenting and secure attachment in infancy have been found to predict cognitive and social competence at age 7 (Stams, Juffer, & van Ijzendoorn, 2002), and although late adopted children from troubled backgrounds show higher rates of severe attachment problems, many are gradually able to form trusting relationships with their adoptive parents. Evidence also suggests (Brooks & Barth, 1999) that transracially adopted children generally exhibit a healthy sense of identity as adults, as long as their adoptive parents allow for bicultural identifications through acknowledgment of, and exposure to, their birth heritage in childhood.

Finley (1999) noted that "adoptive family life is not inherently pathogenic, but that pathology may be found in some adoptive families, as it is in some of all family forms" (p. 363). He described what he sees as critical differences between adoptive and nonadoptive families, especially regarding the adoptive "triangle" or "triad." This triangle includes the adoptive parent(s), the biological parent(s), and the adopted child. Finley stated that "all members of the adoptive triangle are permanently present, if not physically, in the hearts, minds and fantasies of all members of the triad" (p. 363). In Finley's view, it is critically important that adoptive parents allow for and encourage free discussion of the adoption throughout the life cycle. This includes supporting the child's process of "adaptive grieving" for the birth parent (Winkler, Brown, van Kepper, & Blanchard, 1988); managing difficult emotions and behaviors through limit setting, guidance, and support; recognizing that the developmental challenges facing all members of the adoptive triad are normal and natural; and understanding and accepting the fact that the adoptive family structure is based on loss (Winkler et al., 1988). In fact, Winkler and colleagues (1988) feel that a major cause of dysfunction in adoptive families is related to denial of the differences between adoptive families and biological families. Rosenberg (1992) noted that it is important for adoptive families to understand the power of emotional and psychological connections, and to accept the significance of shared life experiences, as opposed to blood ties, as a foundation for permanence in their family relationships.

Gay and Lesbian Families Demo and Allen (1996) defined lesbian and gay families as "the intimate, enduring interactions of two or more people who share a same-sex orientation (for example, a couple) or by the enduring involvement of at least one lesbian or gay adult in rearing a child" (p. 416). These families are highly stigmatized, and discrimination against them is codified in law, religion, politics, and other institutions. At present, only six states recognize the legal right of same-sex couples to marry, and many other states have laws banning marriage between same-sex partners" (Lambda Legal Defense and Education Fund, 2009). Although some states recognize same-sex partnerships through either civil union or domestic partnership arrangements, these do not generally convey the full range of 1,138 legal protections, benefits, and responsibilities available to legally married couples by federal law (General Accounting Office, 2004); these include the right to make medical decisions for the spouse, inheritance rights, access to divorce custody and visitation rights, the ability to take out loans together, tax deductions, credits and exemptions, and so on. (Lambda Legal Defense and Education Fund, 1997–2005).

There has been very little research on structure and process in gay and lesbian families (Allen & Demo, 1995), and what little research that exists has tended to overemphasize both the differences between gay/lesbian families and heterosexual families on the one hand, and the similarities between gay male and lesbian families on the other (Laird, 1993). Demo and Allen (1996) noted significant diversity in both the structure and process patterns of gay and lesbian families "along central axes of social stratification—notably gender, sexual orientation, generation, age, race and ethnicity" (p. 416). For example, Kurdek (1995), in examining the interaction of gender and sexual orientation, found that gay male and lesbian couples are similar in that both tend to place a higher value on equality in their relationships than do heterosexual couples. On the other hand, there are also findings to indicate gender-based differences between gay male and lesbian couples; lesbian couples are consistently found to be more sexually monogamous in their relationships than are gay men (Kurdek, 1995). Kurdek also examined couples across gender and sexual orientation and found similarities among the four couple types studied (gay male, lesbian, heterosexual married, and heterosexual cohabiting) with regard to relationship satisfaction and stability.

Green (2007) discussed the ways in which societal and familial injustice may adversely affect the internal functioning of same sex couples. He pointed out that distressed couples, regardless of sexual orientation often struggle with similar problems. However, because gay and lesbian couples face unique challenges that result from antigay prejudice and discrimination, family therapists treating gay and lesbian couples must be careful to assess whether the presenting problems are related to these socially based challenges, or if the couple is struggling with more generic issues. Green (p. 120) focused on three particular challenges experienced by same sex couples:

- *Coping with external homophobia in families of origin and the larger society.* All same-sex couples face similar types of (external) homophobia from people and social institutions outside their relationship. As described earlier, their relationships are socially marginalized and often vilified. The potential for antigay discrimination or violence requires a high level of vigilance and is stress producing. Internalized homophobia occurs when gay/lesbian people turn these negative social attitudes against themselves; it is associated with a variety of mental health problems, including substance abuse, depression/suicidality, increased HIV risk-taking behaviors, and higher rates of concealed sexual orientation. Within the couple relationship, internalized homophobia may lead to seemingly meaningless arguments, problems with sexual desire or performance, and/or depression or withdrawal from the partner. Practice Example 5.2 illustrates how the therapeutic process may be used to address homophobia.
- *Resolving relational ambiguity in the areas of couple commitment, boundaries, and gender-linked behavior.* Because there are few visible role models and no historical social traditions or religious/legal frameworks that clearly define expectations and obligations for same-sex couples to follow, they must develop their own norms and define their own terms regarding both their commitment to one another and their boundaries with the outside world. Although this does,

to some extent, leave them freer to create relational patterns that are tailored to their individual needs (and many same-sex couples are able to create a mutually satisfying relational structure), it can present problems for couples if the norms, boundaries, and structure of the relationship remain vague.

- *Developing adequate social supports for the couple relationship (that is, a family of choice).* Relationships within the gay community are especially significant for lesbian and gay families who often find partners and friends to be more socially and emotionally supportive than families of origin and others in the wider community, who may represent sources of oppression and stigmatization (Crosbie-Burnett & Helmbrecht, 1993; Green, 2007; Johnson & Colucci, 2005). Ainslie and Feltey (1991), for example, found that women in lesbian communities tend to form support networks that perform many of the same functions as extended families based on marriage and blood relationships. Green noted that well-functioning same-sex couples tend to have strong networks of social support within the community; distressed couples, on the other hand, tend to be more isolated and should be encouraged to build and maintain a close-knit social system that supports them as a couple. The availability of such supports, however, may vary depending on location. Urban communities tend to have more gay-sponsored institutions than do smaller towns and rural areas; these may provide opportunities for diverse community members to find social support.

Increasing numbers of gay and lesbian people are opting to raise children. Many become parents through previous heterosexual relationships and more and more through adoption and reproductive technologies (Ambert, 2003; Patterson, 2002). Although there is limited research on gay and lesbian parents, and much of the existing research is based on small samples, findings consistently indicate that children in gay and lesbian families are as well adjusted as children in heterosexual families and can be distinguished from other children only by issues related to living in a society that may be largely nonsupportive, stigmatizing, and discriminatory (Berk, 2005). For example, children of gay and lesbian parents may experience teasing from their peers and rejection from the parents of their peers. (Morris, Balsam, & Rothblum, 2001). In some instances, this has been found to foster such positive character traits as empathy and tolerance (Ambert, 2003; Patterson, 2002).

Because most gay and lesbian families have a different structure (for example, families formed through partnerships that are not legally recognized, families without children, and families where children's parents are of one sex) than those families on which much of family theory has been based, Demo and Allen (1996) posit that "lesbian and gay families provide a fertile testing ground for family theories and simultaneously pose interesting and provocative challenges for dominant family theories" (p. 423). Furthermore, systematic study of gay and lesbian families may serve to increase our understanding of other "postmodern" families. In addition to questions related to the effects of egalitarian partnerships and gender flexibility, the issue of family resilience in the face of oppression may be a particularly valuable area for research. Gay and lesbian families are somewhat unique in that their right to exist is denied by many institutions of the dominant society. Questions regarding how this level of oppression may affect how members of gay and lesbian families

Increasing numbers of gay and lesbian people are opting to raise children. Although many have become parents through previous heterosexual relationships, others become parents through adoption or the use of various reproductive technologies.

negotiate their relationships to support mutual growth and development may help to illuminate new ways of relating that are positive and support resilience in other diverse, postmodern family forms (Demo & Allen 1996).

Families and Migration Migration has become normative for many people across the globe, and people migrate for a wide variety of reasons; some choose to leave their country of origin for work or study, whereas others are forced to flee from oppression, violence, and/or abject poverty. Whatever the reason, the stress involved in the process must not be underestimated—"indeed, immigration causes such long ranging and profound family changes that it creates an entire new life stage for all families that go through it" (Hernandez & McGoldrick, 2005, p. 170).

When working with immigrant families, it is, of course, critical to know the reasons for their migration—that is, their premigration experience—and what, if any, level of trauma was associated with that period. In addition, it is important to understand the meaning of the migration for the family; some families view it as a permanent process, whereas others maintain close connections with their country of origin, viewing the migration as a more temporary situation.

Regardless of the reasons behind the migration, all families face a complicated web of challenges once they resettle. These include adjustment to a new culture, changes in their socioeconomic status, and changes in their social support networks. How these challenges are met depends on a variety of factors. In addition to the reasons for the migration, the premigration experience and the family's experiences in their new context and variables such as age, gender, race, socioeconomic status, stage of family life cycle, and level of congruence between the

PRACTICE EXAMPLE 5.2

Addressing Homophobia as a Therapeutic Issue

Emma, a young professional woman in her early thirties, has been living with her lover, Angela, for the past 3 years. Emma has been in therapy for just over 3 months, initially presenting with symptoms of mild depression. She describes a close, but somewhat conflicted, relationship with her family of origin and has been "out" to them since her late adolescence. She describes her family's relationship with Angela as loving and accepting; the couple visits with them frequently, dining with them (and often, extended family members) at least once a week. Emma has a particularly warm and close relationship with her mother's first cousin, Gloria, who lives in a nearby town. During a session, she mentioned that Gloria had stopped by unexpectedly on Valentine's Day and that the visit had "stressed me out"—she explained that the Valentine's Day cards that she and Angela had exchanged that morning were on display on her mantle and "I didn't have time to put them away because I wasn't expecting Gloria to come by." She expressed some annoyance at Angela (who had apparently put the cards on the mantle) as well—"I've told her over and over again that she should keep the cards in the bedroom—just to avoid this sort of thing." Emma became quite defensive as the therapist began to explore the reasons for her stress and for her need to "hide" the valentines from her relative (especially, given that Gloria was well aware that Emma was a lesbian and that she lived with Angela). In a dismissive tone, she explained that she hadn't wanted to "upset" her cousin; she attempted to change the subject, stating that it was "no big deal." The therapist continued to explore the issue—why would Gloria be upset to see the cards? I thought she knew you were gay? Emma became increasingly exasperated as the therapist continued to keep the discussion focused on what she termed "such a meaningless issue." She explained that although her family knew she was gay, and that she and Angela were living together, she did not like to "rub their noses in it." When the therapist continued to explore the issue in the context of homophobia (both external and internalized), she defended her position (loudly) for several minutes, and then fell silent. When she began to speak again, her tone was soft and thoughtful—"I never really gave this a second thought. They know we're gay, but we never talk about it. They refer to Angela as 'my roommate'—after all this time. And I've been just so grateful that they let us come over together and don't reject us—I was willing to take whatever crumbs they threw me just so I could stay a part of my family."

values and norms of the culture of origin and the new context all serve as mediating factors in the adjustment process. (Hernandez & McGoldrick, 2005).

Adjustment to the New Culture The process of acculturation is a learning process that takes place over a period of generations in a family's life cycle (Ho, 1987; Inclan, 1985). Regardless of other circumstances, all people who migrate must come to terms with the differences in cultural norms between the culture of origin and the new culture. Cultural conflicts may produce stress on married couples (especially if women begin to embrace new gender roles that threaten the traditional family hierarchy); intergenerational conflicts are not uncommon, when children (who tend to acculturate more quickly) find themselves serving as interpreters of the language and culture for their parents. Again, the quality of this adjustment will depend on the interactions of all the variables discussed earlier; development of a pattern of biculturality (that is, adapting to and embracing the new culture, while maintaining connections to the old traditions) seems to support well-being by enriching the family's sense of identity and strengthening the skills needed to cope with current circumstances.

Changes in Socioeconomic Status Although the act of migration may provide the family with higher earnings and an improved standard of living, immigrant families must contend with a new social structure that has its own "hierarchy of power, privilege, and prestige" (Hernandez & McGoldrick, 2005). It is often the case that a family's socioeconomic status in the new culture represents a decline (at least initially) from their former status (Rogler, 1994). Socioeconomic factors affect most areas of family functioning. The consequences of ethnic prejudice and racism, xenophobia, and social invalidation, in terms of family members' self esteem and sense of identity, may lead to a sense of failure and isolation, domestic violence, and a host of mental health issues, including depression and substance abuse.

Changes in Social Networks Hernandez and McGoldrick (2005) pointed out that the loss of friends, family, communities, personal networks and cultural norms are sources of grief for immigrants. However, the pressures of coping with the new context may not permit a full, conscious grieving process; in this case, unresolved grief may become insidious. In the country of origin, most immigrants had a social network that fulfilled a variety of interpersonal functions; the task on resettlement is to create a new network to replace it. This is a time-consuming process, made all the more difficult by the fact that in the meantime, many interpersonal needs go unmet. This may place tremendous pressure on marital relationships, as spouses look to one another to fulfill functions previously handled by larger social networks. Loss of the peer group represents, for children, the loss of a major source of security; perhaps more significant, this loss occurs in a context in which parents, struggling to deal with their own losses, may be less available to provide support (Sluzki, 1992).

Hernandez and McGoldrick (2005) emphasized the need for therapists working with immigrant families to contextualize their experiences within the framework of the migration process to normalize their issues. They further advocate that families be helped to "locate problems within the larger sociocultural, economic and political context" (p.183) as a means of increasing social participation and a sense of empowerment.

Military Families In recent years, civilian mental health professionals have seen an increase in clients from military families (Kennedy, 2004). For them to provide these families with effective services, these professionals must understand a variety of contextual variables that are unique to the military: military culture, the unique stressors and challenges (and their associated mental health issues) faced by service members, and the transitional processes related to deployment (and military life in general).

Hall (2008) outlined the following characteristics of military culture:

1. *Authoritarian structure:* The world of the military is structured in a rigidly hierarchical manner, based on dominance and submission; Hall (2008) pointed out that this structure often (but not always) characterizes the internal workings of military families as well.
2. *Isolation from extended families and from the larger civilian world:* This isolation results from the high level of mobility of military families; because their location is inevitably viewed as temporary, families tend to remain disconnected from the local communities (whether or not they live on a military base) and to focus their attention and affiliation on the world of the military.

3. *Rigid class structure:* Military society is divided into two classes (ranks): officers and enlisted personnel. These essentially operate as separate subcultures, isolated from one another in a highly stratified social world.
4. *Parental Absences:* A common aspect of military life is frequent parental absence; since the early 1990s these absences may sometimes involve both parents. These comings and goings require continuous adjustment on the part of all family members. Although many families come to accept these changes as cultural norms, they may be experienced as highly stressful.
5. *Commitment to the military unit and mission:* The demands of the military require a near total commitment, with military members working long hours and forming close relationships to their team. Conflicts may occur if the commitment to the military member's unit is seen as taking precedence over the family, and maintaining this balance can be a continuous challenge.
6. *Disaster Preparation:* Military culture is permeated with the sense of being in harm's way, and deeply rooted in military culture is the understanding that a condition of service is that one may ultimately be required to sacrifice one's life for the country.

Mental Health Issues Marshall (2006), quoting an article in the *New England Journal of Medicine,* reported the results of a survey in which 17% of military members interviewed reported that they were returning from Iraq with symptoms of major depression, generalized anxiety, or PTSD. A report by the Mental Health Advisory Team III (2006) indicated that 14% of those soldiers interviewed reported experiencing acute stress, and 17% reported a combination of depression, anxiety, and acute stress. The total number of suicides in the Army rose from 60 in 2003 to 83 in 2005. Relationship issues at home or in theatre, legal actions, problems with comrades and command, and duty performance issues were found to be the strongest risk factors for suicide. Most soldiers reported job satisfaction, but from 2003 to 2006 there was an increase in discontent over the length of their deployments and the more dangerous combat environment. Soldiers who had been deployed multiple times were more likely to report higher levels of acute stress and more stress on their families.

Reports of child and spousal abuse have surged in recent years on many military installations, and in general, rates of domestic violence are higher in the military population than in the civilian population (Hall, 2008). Heavy alcohol use is a serious issue in the military, and rates of heavy drinking have increased significantly in the past decade. In addition, service members are, for a variety of reasons, at high risk for financial problems.

Stages of the Deployment Process As noted earlier, mental health professionals working with this population must have a well-developed understanding of the stresses on military families before, during, and after deployment. Several researchers have developed models that describe the effects of the deployment process; Pincas et al. (n.d.) divide the process into five phases: predeployment, deployment, sustainment, redeployment, and postdeployment. Each stage is time specific and characterized by emotional challenges that must be mastered by each family member. Although a detailed discussion of the stages of deployment is beyond the scope of this chapter, the model highlights the need for family members to be aware of the manifestations of conflicting feelings at each stage and the need for interventions that support communication, normalization of feelings, and patience for the process.

Strengths of Military Families No description of military families would be complete with an acknowledgment of the unique strengths that they develop despite, or perhaps because of, the many challenges they face (Rodriguez, 1984). These include the ability to accept and cope with frequent relocations as a social norm; resourcefulness and self-reliance, with lower levels of dysfunction than one might anticipate in light of the many stressors; evidence of lower rates of psychological problems for military children as well as higher scores on intelligence testing; increased awareness of people and global communities; and an empowering sense of personal and family pride of accomplishment and of service to a national mission.

Summary

At the beginning of the 21st century, we find that a number of combined social trends have resulted in a change in the way the concept of *family* is defined and have contributed to an enormous diversity of postmodern family forms, functions, and contexts. The way in which family is defined has great practical importance for social workers. In addition to influencing the practice models social workers use in dealing with family issues, the legal definition of family has a significant impact on local, state, and federal policies that affect families on every level.

We view the family as society's smallest social system—it adheres to most of the characteristics of other social systems and is inseparable from the economic, cultural, political, and historical contexts in which it is embedded. We have examined the impact of some of these contexts on families; in doing so, we have attempted to assume a broad perspective that allows for exploration of a wide variety of human roles and connections.

6 Group-Work Practice

Introduction

Individuals are members of many different groups, and human behavior is influenced by participation in these groups. The earliest group for most individuals is that of the family group, which Germain (1991) refers to as a "community subsystem." Other groups may include peer groups, organizational groups, and recreational groups. Each of these groups becomes the context and means for changing attitudes, interests, and behaviors. In other words, the group affects the individual's behaviors. However, the members and their social contexts are also powerful influences on the development of the group. "Person–group–environment" is a framework that emphasizes the interdependence of individuals in their families and other groups and in their relationships with the broader environment (Northern & Kurland, 2001, p. 49). Group work in the field of social work has its roots in social change and social justice. It was an integral service in settlement houses, Jewish community centers, and the labor movement, among other settings (Knopka, 1983). Although influenced by early social workers, these organizations were primarily concerned with "normal individuals" who were struggling with difficult socioeconomic conditions. A major contributor to group-work conceptualization during these early years was Wilbur Newstetter (1935), who defined group work as an educational process emphasizing (a) the development and social adjustment of an individual through voluntary group association and (b) the use of this association as a means of furthering other socially desirable ends (p. 291). It is concerned, therefore, with both individual growth and social results. Moreover, it is the combined and consistent pursuit of both these objectives, not merely one of them, that distinguishes group work as a process.

Group work solidified its identification with the profession of social work in the 1940s and established a professional organization—the American Association of Group Workers. The first group-work textbook, *Social Group Work Practice*, by Gertrude Wilson and Gladys Ryland, was published in 1949. Contemporary group-work practice has evolved from its legacy of debate between those who practiced in community agencies and emphasized social participation, social action, and problem prevention and those who practiced in hospitals and mental health centers and practiced therapy. Group-work practice now includes education, treatment, socialization, action, and just about any purpose that brings people together toward some common goal (Northern & Kurland, 2001; Toseland & Rivas, 2004).

The Association for the Advancement of Social Work with Groups (AASWG, 2006) is an international professional organization that has established Standards for Social Work Practice with Groups (see Appendix). They publish a newsletter—*Social Work with Groups*—that states the organization's mission as "advocacy and action in support of group-work practice, education, research, and publication . . . enhancing the quality of group life throughout the world" (AASWG, 2004, p. 1). The AASWG also promotes a Group Work Symposium each year at the Annual Program Meeting (APM) of the Council on Social Work Education.

Definition of a Group

A group can be defined as "a small face to face collection of persons who interact to accomplish some purpose" (Brown, 1991, p. 3). Groups are open, dynamic, human systems that involve mutual recognition, interdependence, and often psychological and social significance. A group should have a common problem, theme, or task and a commonality of purpose. However, it is the *mutual aid* that develops among group members that is the benchmark of group-work practice. William Schwartz (1961), who was a leading proponent of this concept, wrote: "The need to use each other, to create not one but many helping relationships, is a vital ingredient of group process" (p. 98). Mutual aid occurs when group members reflect on themselves and on the other person's situation—a process that benefits both the giver and the receiver. This relates to an appreciation of the inherent strengths of the group and the power of participatory democracy. This process challenges the group leader to consider the group as a whole first, and individual participants second, when initiating or responding to others (Gitterman, 2004; Middleman & Wood, 1990; Steinberg, 1997). The final component of mutual aid described by Schwartz (1971a, 1971b) is the *mediating function* that occurs between groups and the sponsoring institution and/or the larger social environment (as well as among the members of the group). Groups thus face challenges that come from within and challenges that come from without. The group leader helps the members keep an adaptive balance between the two (Schwartz, 1994). Northern and Kurland (2001) expound on the concept of mutual aid and wrote: "Group work demands 'depth of member participation' and a 'multiplicity of helping relationships'" (p. 155). They identified the following "dynamic forces of mutual aid" frequently identified as applicable to groups (p. 26):

- *Mutual Support:* A climate of both peer support and support from the leader.
- *Cohesiveness:* The mutual acceptance of members and commitment to the group.
- *Quality of Relationships:* When the relationship between the members and with the worker provides a blend of support and challenge.
- *Universality:* The realization that members share similar feelings and experiences reduces the sense of isolation and loneliness.
- *A sense of hope:* Identification with other group members' expectation of a positive outcome provides a sense of optimism.
- *Altruism:* Self-esteem and personal identity are enhanced as members learn they can extend themselves to others and offer help.
- *Acquisition of knowledge and skills:* Opportunities for self-expression and for risking new ideas beneficial to self-esteem.
- *Catharsis:* Expression of feelings and disclosure of ideas to others lessens anxiety and frees energy to work toward desired goals.
- *Reality testing:* The group becomes a protected place where members can compare feelings, opinions, and facts.

- *Group control:* Temporary group controls serve as a means toward the goal of individual control through behaving in accordance with the group's expectations; members reduce their resistance to authority, endure frustration, and accept necessary and fair limitations.

Group Norms and Group Roles

The *norms* of a group are those explicit expectations and beliefs shared by members concerning how they or others should behave under given circumstances. Norms can be *overt*—clearly stated—or *covert*—exerting influence on how members behave without being discussed. Norms develop as the group evolves and often reduce the need for structure and control by the group leader. They give groups a measure of stability and predictability by providing members with information concerning what they can expect from each other. In other words, norms define the range of behaviors that are acceptable in the group. In so doing, roles profoundly affect the group's capacity to respond to the individual needs of members as well as its ability to fulfill the purpose of the group. The extent to which members adhere to norms varies. Deviations from norms are not necessarily a bad thing because dissonance often allows for new ideas to emerge. The group leader, however, needs to understand the norms of the group and whether they are beneficial or detrimental to the group's well-being. Norms exert a great deal of influence over the group's response to situations. They also determine the extent to which the group offers its members positive experiences (Northern & Kurland, 2001).

Paralleling the idea of group norms is what Brandler and Roman (1999) refer to as manifest content and latent content (p. 185). *Manifest content* refers to the actual conversation that the group is engaged in (similar to the overt norms established by a group that are openly discussed). *Latent content* is what is not said but can be inferred (paralleling covert norms). Clues to latent content are often found in body language, silence, a feeling of tension in the room, humor, or affect that is not appropriate with content. The authors suggest that for the leader to remain alert to the latent content of a group, the following are necessary:

- The leader must have an understanding of her or his feelings.
- The leader must assess what the members of the group are feeling.
- The dynamics of the group population must be ascertained (for example, individuals who are mandated to attend a group may share a feeling of disempowerment).
- The group phase must be known. (See discussion of the phases of group development that follows.)
- The manifest content must be determined (what are people actually talking about?).
- Can any latent—or underlying theme—be understood?

Group roles are those behaviors that different group members assume. These may be formally assigned, or they may be informally based on the interests and abilities of different individuals. Members of groups often play different or multiple roles. Some roles are based on previous experiences with groups that people bring to the current group/environment. Roles can be divided into those that are product focused and those that are process focused. *Product-focused roles* help the group move toward its goals. Included among these roles are the *initiator* (proposes tasks to the group); the *information seeker* (requests facts or relevant information); the *clarifier* (interprets for the group); the *summarizer* (pulls together related ideas and offers a decision for the group to accept or reject); and the *consensus tester* (periodically checks with the group to determine whether a consensus is close (Napier & Gershenfeld, 1985, pp. 238–244, quoted in Schriver, 2004, p. 398). Some *process-focused roles* are the *encourager* (recognizes and gives opportunities to other members of the group); the *expresser* of group feelings (provides feedback on the mood of the group); the *harmonizer* (attempts to reduce tensions); the *compromiser* (tries to reconcile group differences); the *gatekeeper* (helps to keep all members participating in group discussions); and the *standard setter* (suggests standards for the group to use (Napier & Gershenfeld, 1985, pp. 239–244, 279–280, quoted in Schriver, 2004, pp. 398–399).

Northern and Kurland (2001) divide group roles into those that are *task oriented*—contributing to, or hindering, the group's purpose—and *socioemotional*—aiding in, or detracting from, the development of positive relationships between members. They also discuss the role of the *scapegoat*—the person on whom group members project hostility and negative feelings they may have about themselves. The scapegoat often acts in ways that elicit these feelings and consequent behaviors. The group leader must be aware when a member of the group is turning into a scapegoat, as this can easily lend itself to a bad situation for the scapegoated member and the group itself.

Leadership

Leadership can be defined as "the process of guiding the development of the group and its members" (Toseland & Rivas, 2001, p. 96). Schriver (2004) puts forth a functional definition of leadership that is simply "behavior that assists a group to achieve its goal." This idea of leadership replaces the concept of *hierarchy* with the concept of *equality* and aims to bring forth the potential for leadership that every person might have. *Functional leadership* can, therefore, emerge from a group. Individuals might have the *leadership traits*—personality characteristics—to lead others in a particular context. *Situational leadership* emerges from the requirements of a particular situation or expertise (a physician's services may be required on an airplane and in that context she or he becomes a leader). *Positional leadership* is created by the position that a person holds. The authority or influence comes from the position (the chair of a committee has positional leadership). There are also various types of leaders. *Authoritarian leaders* are those who control the behaviors of group members by making decisions and assigning tasks with little or no input from them. *Laissez-faire leaders* allow group members to do anything they wish, offer little direction, and try to exert minimal influence. *Democratic leaders* tend to discuss goals with the members, encourage their participation, and allow shared decision making (Gastil, 1994). Fiedler's (1967) *contingency model of leadership* recognizes that no one style of leadership is effective in every situation. The situational variables include the relationship between the leader and the members, the structure of the task, and the authority of the leader. He suggests two basic styles of leadership: *task-oriented* and *interpersonally oriented leadership*. This may be somewhat congruent with Northern and Kurland's (2001) suggestion that both a *socioemotional* and a *task theme* are operating in every group, to different degrees (see Stages of Group Development and the Role of the Group Leader).

Power and Authority

Leadership is closely related to the concepts of power and authority. *Power* refers to "behaviors of individuals that enable them to prevail in interactions with others, regardless of any social position they may hold" (Longress, 1995, p. 344). French and Raven (1959) recognized five bases of power: legitimate, reward, coercive, referent, and expert. *Legitimate power* is based on the right of one person to require and command compliance from another. *Reward power* involves the distribution of monetary, social, and other benefits to gain compliance. *Coercive power* derives from the capacity to physically or psychologically punish those who fail to comply. *Referent power* is based on identification, attraction, or respect. *Expert power* derives from the possession of superior ideas, skills, or abilities.

Authority is "power legitimated by appointment or election or power that accrues to individuals as a function of their position or role in society or the groups and organizations that make it up" (Longress, 1995, p. 345). *Charismatic authority* is based on the special characteristics of the individual. *Traditional authority* is based on institutional or social norms. *Rational-legal authority* is based on the power of laws or regulations that emerge from democratic processes.

Role of the Group Leader

A leader's role, although dependent on the type of group (see later sections of this chapter), is to identify evolving group norms and influence them in ways that create a positive ambience for change. Discerning the norms of a group can be difficult because they are often subtly imbedded in the group process and can be inferred only from the behavior occurring in the group. Leaders may be able to identify norms by asking the following questions:

- What subjects can and cannot be talked about in the group?
- What kinds of emotional expressions are allowed in the group?
- Do group members consider it their own responsibility or the leader's to make the group's experience a successful one?
- What is the group's stance toward the leader?
- What is the group's attitude toward feedback?
- How does the group view the contributions of individual members? What kinds of labels and roles is the group assigning to them?
- What is the group's pattern with regard to working on problems or staying on task? (Brander & Roman, 1999; Kurland & Salmon, 1998; Northern & Kurland, 2001; Toseland & Rivas, 2004)

A second major role of the group leader is to document and assist the group to document the incremental growth of each member. Another primary role is to observe evolving group behavior and to assess whether the emerging patterns of behavior undermine or support the therapeutic purposes of the group. The leader must demonstrate skill in engaging the empathy of the other group members for the situation of the person who is talking and sharing her or his experiences. Once the empathy is engaged, the group participants are able to recount situations involving their own experiences and offer suggestions and comments that derive from these experiences. Members of the group can take on different roles, and the leader must be able to have the ability to understand the behaviors manifested by individuals in the group and by the group itself. Identifying roles is vital because members tend to play out in growth groups the same roles they assume in other social contexts and need to understand the impact of dysfunctional roles on themselves and on others. Some members assume roles that strengthen relationships and are conducive to group functioning. By highlighting these positive behaviors, leaders enhance members' self-esteem and also place the spotlight on behaviors other members may emulate (Longress, 1995; Northern & Kurland, 2001; Toseland & Rivas, 2004).

Toseland and Rivas (2001) offer a "functional classification of group leadership skills" (p. 111). These include facilitating group process, data gathering and assessment, and action. *Facilitating group process* involves tasks such as attending and responding to group members, encouraging broad participation, focusing group communication, clarifying content, and guiding group interactions. *Data gathering and assessment* includes identifying feelings and behaviors, requesting information, synthesizing thoughts and feelings, and analyzing information. *Action-oriented skills* are reframing and redefining, modeling and coaching, confronting, resolving conflicts, and giving suggestions or instructions.

Co-Leadership

There are several benefits to having co-leadership (two leaders) facilitate a group: support; feedback; increased objectivity; training and professional development; opportunity to model communication, interaction, and resolution of disputes for group members; assistance with interventions and program activities; and help in setting limits and structuring the group experience. Co-leaders must communicate with each other about their leadership style, their strengths and weaknesses as leaders, their understanding of the group's purpose, their respective roles in the group regarding starting and ending, dividing responsibility for group content or intervention (for example, handling conflict), and how to handle the differences of opinion that may emerge during the course of the group (Toseland & Rivas, 2004). It is preferable to have this exchange immediately following the meeting when the co-leaders are most apt to remember what transpired and to plan for the next meeting. Co-leadership is time consuming and can be expensive for an agency. Models of co-leadership vary from those with equal status and experience to training models, where an apprentice is placed with a senior group practitioner to gain experience. The potential for role confusion and conflict is also present when there are two leaders in a group, especially when one is less experienced. This makes the importance of conversation about expectations and role important, especially for the person in training. When there is conflict between co-leaders, this can be damaging to the group. It seems more desirable to use a co-leadership model when there is a specific reason to have leaders as models who represent different points of view (for example, a male and a female co-leadership team may be an effective way to facilitate a male and female heterosexual group). Co-leaders are most effective when they complement each other's style, as opposed to when they are either too similar or too different (Brandler & Roman, 1999).

Pregroup Planning: Group Structure and Stages of Group Development

The pregroup planning stage of group work involves an understanding of the key structural components of a group as well as the stages or process of group development. This section will address these two aspects of groups.

Group Structure

Kurland and Salmon (1998) offer two models of group structure. One model is used when group composition is not predetermined and the other when group composition is predetermined (see Figures 6.1 and 6.2). Each model includes eight components: *social context, agency context, need, purpose, composition, structure, content,* and *pregroup contact* (p. 209). The models are intended to be used flexibly to guide the group leader's thinking. One area flows into the next, providing an opportunity to reconsider each item as the leader's thinking evolves. It is helpful to develop a group proposal during the planning stage that addresses each of the structural components of a group (see Appendix for an example of an outline for a task/treatment group proposal; Toseland & Rivas, 2004, p. 501).

FIGURE 6.1

Pregroup Planning Model (for use when group composition *is not* predetermined)

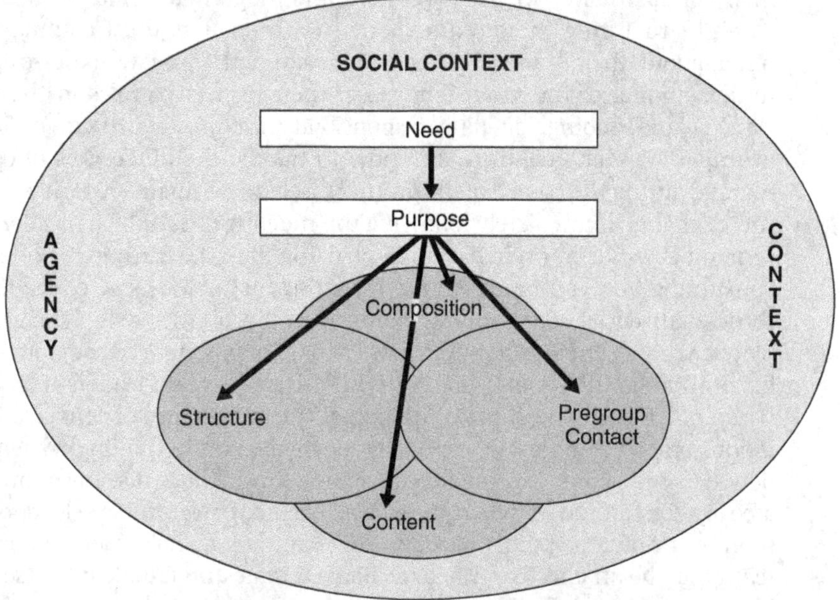

Source: R. Kurland and R. Salmon, *Teaching a Methods Course in Social Work with Groups*. Alexandria, VA: Council on Social Work Education. Reprinted by permission of CSWE Press.

FIGURE 6.2

Pregroup Planning Model (for use when group composition *is* predetermined)

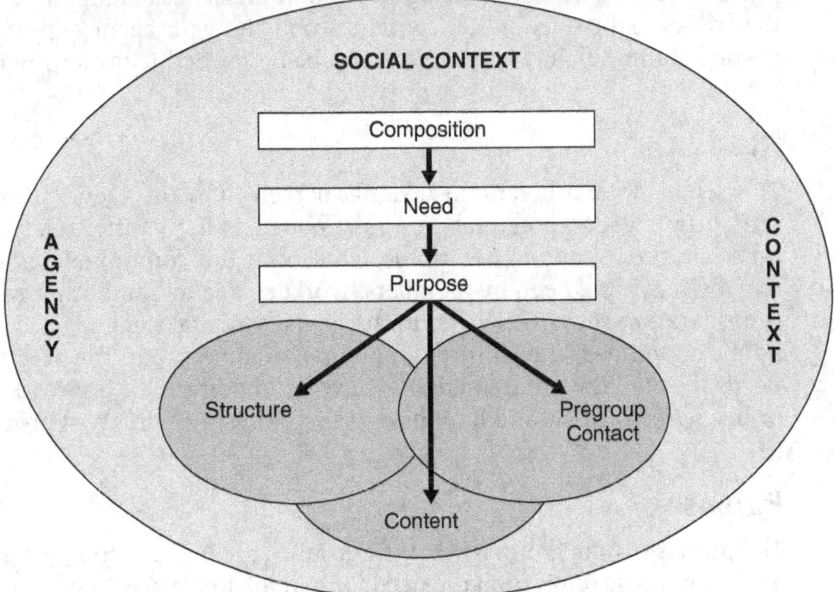

Source: R. Kurland and R. Salmon, *Teaching a Methods Course in Social Work with Groups*. Alexandria, VA: Council on Social Work Education. Reprinted by permission of CSWE Press.

Social Context

This area should include attention to influences such as the political environment, the geographic community, the agency climate, including policies that may affect services, and any cultural attitudes toward participation in groups. The personal and historical experiences that individuals bring to the group are also helpful. The impact of oppression or racism, for example, is going to influence the participation of the individual in the group. Small groups also link with systems outside the group (within the agency) or outside the agency (within the community or beyond) for various reasons, depending on the purpose of the group. In addition, groups are subject to the same confidentiality laws that govern social work practice with individual clients.

Agency Context and Sponsorship

Consideration must be given to the purpose of the agency (or host organization/setting for the group) and its philosophy toward working with groups. This includes the needs or problems of the population that the agency services, the purpose of the group as perceived by the agency, and resources that the agency is willing to commit to the group (for example, space, program aids, staff). Policies regarding reporting, accountability, evaluation, confidentiality, informed consent, intake, eligibility, fees, and staff workloads may have particular impact (Northern & Kurland, 2001, p. 115).

It is important that agencies do not support the development of groups for the wrong reasons (for example, to save money or to provide services to greater numbers of people in the absence of staff). A group should only be formed when it is the appropriate service for the clients being serviced. A final consideration is the relationship of the agency to the surrounding community and how the agency's place and reputation in the community impact on the group being formed (Northern & Kurland, 2001).

Need

This refers to the problems or needs as perceived by the agency administrators and staff, group leader, potential group members, and any other relevant persons. It is especially important to determine what both the commonalities and differences may be regarding need by members, workers, agency, and other relevant persons. Consideration should be given to the developmental stage (age), values, socioeconomic conditions, the culture of potential members, and the ability to meet these needs through the group modality. It is also important for the worker to realize her or his own strengths and limitations in working with different groups.

Purpose

The purpose of the group is what the group is hoping to accomplish collectively. The group's purpose flows from the need for it in the first place. The group leader and the members of the group must agree with the need and have a desire to meet that need. Individual members may have particular goals within the overarching common goal of the group. The purpose of the group differs from the content of the group. Purpose identifies the group's end, and content is the means to achieve the purpose (or end). A clear statement as to what the group hopes to accomplish—the outcome—is essential to the purpose of the group. A mechanism for determining whether the group purpose is being achieved is also important (such as feedback from various people). The purpose of the group should be clear and shared with the members at the time the group is discussed with them. The motivation and participation of members is greatly enhanced when they understand the group's purpose. Having a clearly stated purpose and being able to communicate that purpose to the group members avoids the possibility of "hidden agendas" by the leader or the agency. A *hidden agenda* is a goal that the leader or any group member wants to achieve that has not been directly voiced and shared with the group as a whole. Hidden agendas can be confusing and create problems in the group if they interfere with the stated purpose of the group. It is not ethical practice and is lacking in empathy for a leader to disguise or otherwise not honestly disclose the purpose of the group "up front" (Brandler & Roman, 1999).

After the purpose of the group is discussed, a contract between the leader and the member(s) should follow. A contract is a verbal or written agreement between two or more members of a group. The leader should contract with each individual member (if/when screening for group memberships take place) and again in the first session with the group as a whole. An example of a contract designed for a treatment group (discussed later) is shown in Practice Example 6.1.

PRACTICE EXAMPLE 6.1

Treatment Group Contract

As a group member I agree to:

1. Attend all group sessions.
2. Arrive on time for each group session.
3. Refrain from repeating anything that is said during group sessions to anyone outside the group meeting.
4. Complete any readings, exercises, treatment plans, or other obligations that I agree to in the group before the next group session.
5. Participate in exercises, role-plays, demonstrations, and other simulations conducted during group meetings.

As the group leader I agree to:

1. Be prepared for each group session.
2. Begin and end all group sessions on time.
3. Provide refreshments and program material needed for each session.
4. Discuss the group only with my colleagues at work and not outside the work context.
5. Evaluate each group session to ensure that the group is helping all members resolve their problems and is personally satisfying to all group members.
6. Provide members with appropriate agency and community resources to help then resolve their problems.

____________________ Group member   __________ Date

____________________ Group member   __________ Date

Source: From Ronald W. Toseland, Robert F. Rivas, *An Introduction to Group Work Practice*, 4th ed. Published by Allyn and Bacon, Boston, MA. Copyright © 2001 by Pearson Education. Reprinted by permission of the publisher.

There are some groups—involuntary or compulsory groups—that individuals are required to attend. Some examples might include recovery groups for substance abusers as part of probation, parenting groups for those who wish to regain custody of their children, and probation groups as a requirement for release from prison. In such groups, the sponsoring agency and worker may hold goals that are different from those of the members who are often resentful of having to attend. The worker's sensitivity in addressing both the purpose of such involuntary groups and engaging in some mutual discussion with the participants as to how the group might meet some of their needs despite their feelings about mandatory participation is important (Rooney & Chovanec, 2004).

Theoretical Framework

The theoretical framework of the group is directly related to the purpose of the group because it forms the conceptual basis for how the purpose will be understood and implemented. Some of the major theoretical models that can be used to guide group purpose include psychodynamic models such as Object Relations, Self-Psychology and Relational, Cognitive-Behavioral Theory, Narrative Therapy, and Multicultural Theory (Farber, 2002). When selecting a theory, attention should be given to the group members' developmental, sociohistorical, organization, political, and cultural contexts in addition to the purpose of the group.

Composition

Composition includes the numbers and characteristics of both the leader(s) and the members. For example, will there be one leader or co-leadership of the group (co-leadership of groups was discussed earlier in this chapter), and how many members will be in the group. Characteristics of group members include the degree of homogeneity/heterogeneity regarding age, sex, racial, ethnic, and religious background, socioeconomic level, behavioral characteristics, previous group experience, mental status, the nature of the problem(s), and any other issues that may affect the member's ability to share with others in the group. Brandler and Roman (1999) wrote: "A general rule for developing a group is to avoid selecting a single member of a group with characteristics greatly different from those of other members" (p. 116). This type of balance will help avoid tokenism in group composition. "*Tokenism* is the practice of giving the appearance of representation and access to resources or decision making without actually doing so" (Schriver, 2004, p. 405). Leaders of groups that include members from socially or racially oppressed groups must be sensitive to the impact this might have on participation and communication. The same factors used to determine group membership should be considered when assessing characteristics of the worker(s). Commonalities or differences between the worker(s) and the members will also affect the composition of the group (for example, if a person of color is leading a racially mixed group or if a white person is leading a racially mixed group, it could change the racial balance of the group).

Structure

Structure refers to the arrangements that are made to facilitate the group, such as the duration of the group and whether it will be a *closed group* or an *open group* that new members will be able to join on an ongoing basis. The length and frequency of each meeting should be determined as well. Other important structural issues are the meeting place, size of the meeting room, the physical arrangements in the meeting room, program supplies and/or equipment needed, fees, and confidentiality concerns. Groups that have open membership may frequently revisit the formative or beginning stage of group process. Tuckman's (1965; Tuckman and Jensen, 1977) model of forming, storming, norming, and performing was a helpful conceptual framework in understanding the group process in an open-ended after-school group at a therapeutic group program for children aged 8 to 13. The composition of this group changed as different children entered and exited the program. The first stage, *forming,* occurred when the children were building relationships with each other and acquainting themselves with the structure and norms of the group. The children who had been members of the group served (along with the group leader) as teachers of these group norms and as stabilizers of the group process. The groups *formed* and *reformed* each time a member departed or arrived. The group therefore could experience more than one stage at a time (*beginnings, middles,* and *endings*). Personal relationships were negotiated during the *storming* stage of group development, when the children competed for their role in the group. The *norming* stage occurred when the members of the group moved beyond the conflict and became more supportive and cooperative. The *performing* stage occurred when the group members realized they could accomplish things together and came to appreciate the power of the group to get things done (for example, to problem solve together to select a movie from several that were offered as choices).

Content

Content includes what will actually transpire or take place when the group meets. Content might include use of discussion, didactic material, arts and crafts, role plays, and a host of other medium. The importance of content is its ability to facilitate interaction among group members. A decision must be made as to who will plan the content of the group meetings and how this will be determined. Brandler and Roman (1999) include a glossary of group games and exercises that can be used with different populations and at different phases of group development. For example, during the *introduction circle,* the group leader asks the person immediately to her right to state her name and something related to the group purpose, such as why the person chose to come to the group. In addition, the leader asks the member another question directly related to the content of the group; for example, in a mothers' group, what the ages are of her children. The next person is asked to do the same and to repeat the name of the first person who spoke. If anyone has trouble remembering the names of those who spoke before her or him, the other members of the group are invited to help out (pp. 298–299). Brandler and Roman caution against using this exercise with young children or people with memory impairment, but otherwise feel it is a good exercise to identify who people are and why they are there. It provides a way to discuss group purpose and what the members hope to achieve.

Stages of Group Development and the Role of the Group Leader

The following is an overview of the stages of group development and the role of the group leader in each stage. Most groups progress through a series of predictable stages; however, a group may demonstrate the characteristics of more than one stage at any point in development. Understanding the stages of group development assists the leaders to anticipate the thematic behaviors characteristic of each stage and to recognize their significance. This knowledge helps leaders avoid errors, such as expecting members to begin in-depth explorations in initial sessions. Leaders must be able to identify functional and dysfunctional behaviors that emerge in early sessions and intervene to assist members to adopt behaviors that enhance the group's objectives. Without a clear understanding of the patterned behavior of a mature group, leaders cannot fulfill this role (Kurland & Salmon, 1998, pp. 213, 216–219). Northern and Kurland proposed that each stage of group development include both a *socioemotional theme* and a *task theme* that are included in the following descriptions (2001, pp. 47–48).

Planning or Pregroup Contact The group leader needs to consider both the criteria for group membership and the methods that will be used to recruit potential candidates. An assessment interview should take place with every individual prior to their joining the group (unless it has been determined with substantial reasons why this is not necessary). This interview should include a discussion of the group and what the potential members might expect from the first meeting. It is important to allow time for the candidate to ask questions and/or voice any concerns about participation. Timmer (1998) writes that one of the main reasons why a support group for teenagers with ADHD was problematic was that the leader did not conduct any individual screenings. Consequently, there were too many children whose behavior was oppositional and challenging to the leader. The way in which the group leader recruits members is important. Consideration must be given to who will make the initial contact with the potential group member as well as who will conduct the screening interview (for example, the person making the referral or the group leader). Referral sources must be acquainted with the purpose and structure of the group and the type of members the leader is interested in including. This can be a challenging task for the leader because starting a group can raise a host of issues. What happens if a referral is made to the group that the leader does not feel is appropriate? Will information be shared with the referral source? Finally, the timing of the screening interview in relation to the first group meeting is important. It is advisable to give members who have agreed to participate an opportunity to consider whether they want to join the group after the screening interview. Once the decision is made, it is a good time for the leader to individually contract with the member (previously discussed) about her or his participation in the group. A reminder call to each member is also advisable a day or two before the first group meeting.

Beginnings (Inclusion/Orientation) This stage is very important because it provides the foundation for the stages that follow. The norms, values, and purpose of the group (previously discussed) must be established, and commonalities need to be established as a basis for communication and cohesiveness.

Socioemotional Theme Inclusion, which includes engagement and members acting in ways to decide whether or not they will be included.

Task Members seek and receive information from the worker and other members and search for common ground and the potential meaning of the group for them. The members and the leader arrive at some contract or working agreement.

Role of the Leader The leader is active during this time as she or he defines and helps the members discuss the purpose of the group and what each hopes to gain from participation. Attention is given to help the members communicate and make connections with each other (and not just with the leader) but keep an appropriate distance as they get to know each other. It is important to acknowledge and allow the members to discuss any anxiety or concerns they may have about the group.

Lesser (2000) demonstrates this in a 12-week group for women that was conducted from a self-psychological theoretical framework (see Chapter 3). After introductions are made, she explores the members' feelings about joining the group: "I appreciate everyone taking a big chance with the unknown and coming here today. I know this wasn't easy. Beginnings can be hard, and meeting new people isn't always easy. Now that we all know each other's names, I'd like to ask each of you to try to share any particular concerns you had joining the group . . . you may find you share some common worries" (p. 37). Any group norms or rules should be clarified at this time regarding confidentiality and overall conduct in the group. The members should understand the purpose of the group and their role in it. Confrontations by the leader are rare in the beginning phase of most groups because the leader is focused on achieving a safe and stable environment. Effective confrontation generally requires a good deal of trust. However, any confrontation, whenever it takes place, should be as nonthreatening as possible to ensure that the individual member and the group as a whole will continue to feel able to talk about issues. The confrontation should be kept simple with a focus on what the worker is observing and not become defensive or judgmental.

Middles (Uncertainty-Exploration)

Socioemotional Theme Conflict and difference, particularly in relation to authority of the leader and the distribution of power among the group members.

Task Members explore the situation in relation to its hoped-for benefits, mutual expectations, and interpersonal relationships based on trust and acceptance.

Role of the Leader It is important for the leader to recognize the differences among members. This may be a time when group members test the leader and the group rules. The leader can facilitate this process while maintaining appropriate limits (for example, not letting people hurt each other either physically or verbally). This can be a very difficult time in groups, and the leader may need to confront members directly if they are hurtful or tend to stereotype others. The worker must point out when people are not listening or hearing each other and work to help members express anger appropriately. This includes encouraging members to support or question the comments and behavior of both the leader and of other members. If conflict becomes too threatening, it is the leader's job to regulate this and ensure that unacceptable behavior is not tolerated. Sometimes this necessitates individual conversations with group members to encourage them to express themselves in the group, to increase their understanding of something that may have occurred in the group, and to avoid having individuals feel intimidated or marginalized. Tropman, Johnson, and Tropman (1992) discussed the role of the *chairperson* of committee meetings, comparing her or his role to that of the conductor of an orchestra: "Just as an orchestra will perform badly with a poor conductor, a committee will perform poorly with an inadequate chairperson" (p. 85). The chairperson must see to it that the committee moves through the agenda with the full participation of members. This includes allowing enough time for dissenting viewpoints to be expressed as well as the ability to manage potential conflict in a productive manner so that the committee can reach decisions in a timely manner. Similar to other group leaders, the chairperson should maintain a neutral position. Giving up partisanship in favor of facilitating committee participation does not mean that the chairperson is not able to advance an opinion him- or herself; however, this opinion must not unduly influence the committee's decision-making process.

Middles (Mutuality Goal Achievement)

Socioemotional Theme Intensification of personal involvement, along with group identity. This includes empathy, mutual acceptance, self-disclosure, and respect for differences. The group is now able to allow for differentiation as well as integration.

Task Members work to maintain and enhance the group as a means for social growth and problem solving. Mutual aid is at its peak.

Role of the Leader The leader may begin to have a less-active role as the group proceeds, attempting to maximize group leadership and functioning. The leader is always evaluating where the group is and what the stresses and strains may be both in the group as a whole and for individual members. This involves an ongoing assessment of the attitudes, behaviors, relationships, motivation, and participation of each member. The group may need to reclarify goals and purpose as the group evolves, and the leader should encourage questioning and discussion. The leader continues to reach for threads of commonalities and interrelated concerns, helping members to see how they can help each other and identify common interests, concerns, and feelings. This is nicely demonstrated in session six of a ten-session play therapy group for children with problems in social skills. In an activity called "blindfold drawing" the children are instructed to take turns drawing something while blindfolded. His or her unblindfolded partner helps by giving materials, ideas, directions, and encouragement. The goal is to encourage the children to share, to work together toward a common goal, to take turns, and to do their share of the group work (Schaefer, Jacobsen, & Ghahramanlou, 2000, pp. 327–328).

Endings: Separation-Termination

Socioemotional Theme The members (and the worker) may be ambivalent about this as they prepare to leave the group and make transitions to other relationships.

Task The group works to complete unfinished business, review and evaluate the experience, and transfer gains into lives in the community.

Role of the Leader The leader's role during this phase of group development is to assess the group's progress toward the achievement of the group's goals and anticipate the responses of individuals to ending. Members may need help to express their feelings about ending and to discuss what they have gained and what ongoing goals they may have. It is important for the leader to share her or his observations of the group progress (not of individual members) and support their efforts to develop new relationships and experiences outside the group. This is also the time for the leader to be available for any individual members who may need help with their next steps. It may include communication with family members or staff who may need to be involved. It is important that the leader be aware of her or his own feelings about ending and, when appropriate, share with the group. In the termination phase of group play therapy with children who had been sexually abused, the leader used a sand tray to help the children move beyond their abuse and brighten their future orientation. He instructed the children to create the world as a grown-up, asking questions about the things they would like to do or the people they would like to have in their lives. Each child had the opportunity to describe the sand tray scene to the group. The leader then celebrated the accomplishments of the group by reviewing the different art projects they made, adding messages to a group poster, or passing hugs around the room. This group leader also presented transitional objects to the children that had some significance to the group (Hardaway, 2000, p. 286).

Types of Groups

The most common division of groups is between *treatment groups* and *task groups* (Toseland & Rivas, 2004). Northern and Kurland (2001) proposed that the distinction between these two categories can be a blurry one because, as previously discussed, all groups have both a socioemotional and a task component. Although we agree with the premise that all types of groups share certain commonalities, we feel the division into treatment and task groups is a helpful way to differentiate between two categories of group-work practice that can be contrasted in several significant ways. For example, in treatment groups, roles generally evolve as a result of interaction; in task groups, roles are often assigned. In treatment groups, self-disclosure is generally expected to be high, proceedings are kept strictly confidential (within the group), and success is based on members' success in meeting their treatment goals. In task groups, self-disclosure is low, proceedings may either be private or open to the public, and the success of the group is based on the accomplishment of a task or mandate, or producing a product (Hepworth, Rooney, & Larsen, 1997, p. 318). A third type of group is the *self-help group,* further distinguished from task and treatment groups by the fact that generally they do not have any professional leadership (Kurtz, 2004).

Task Groups

The main purpose of a task group is to accomplish a goal that is neither intrinsically nor immediately linked to the needs of the members of the group. The goal of a task group is generally one that affects a broader constituency and not just the members of the group. Members of task groups form a bond by working together on a particular mandate—or task—or producing a product. Members take on roles through a process of interaction and may also be assigned roles by the group. Assigned roles may include those of chair, team leader, or secretary. Communication is likely to be directed toward the leader and focused on the particular task the group is working on. These groups are also more likely to have formalized rules that govern how members conduct group business, such as agendas, parliamentary procedures, and minutes. Members of these groups generally have the expertise necessary to perform the mandated task. Self-disclosure is relatively infrequent, and although some of these meetings may be confidential, others are recorded in minutes and circulated to interested persons and organizations. Task groups are successful when they generate solutions to a problem, make decisions, develop a product, or make recommendations. Table 6.1 includes a selection of task groups that includes purpose, leadership, focus, bond, composition, and communication (Toseland & Rivas, 2004, p. 31). These task groups are grouped into three categories. Groups that are developed on the basis of *client needs* include *teams, treatment conferences,* and *staff development* groups. Groups that emerge from the *needs of an organization* are *committees, cabinets,* and *board of directors meetings,* among others. *Social action groups* or *delegate councils* are examples of groups that

TABLE 6.1

Typology of Task Groups

		Client Needs	
Selected Characteristics	**Teams**	**Treatment Conferences**	**Staff Development**
Purpose	To engage in collaborative work on behalf of a client system	To develop, coordinate, and monitor treatment plans	To educate members for better practice with clients
Leadership	Appointed to sponsoring agency	Neutral chair or chaired by member with most responsibility	Leader, supervision, consultant, or educator
Focus	Build team to function smoothly High member focus	Decision oriented Low member focus High client focus	Focus on staff members' needs and their performance with clients
Bond	Team spirit Needs of organization and client	Client system Treatment plan Inter- or intra-agency agreement	Continuing education needs Interest in client welfare Professional development
Composition	Often heterogeneous	Diversity by function, specialty, and expertise	Individuals with similar educational needs
Communication	Theoretically close, sometimes	Consideration of all points of view about the client system High disclosure	Leader-to-member Didactic and experimental instruction Member-to-member

Organizational Needs			
Selected Characteristics	**Committee**	**Cabinets**	**Board of Directors**
Purpose	To discuss issues and accomplish tasks	To advise an executive officer about future directions or current policies and procedures	To govern an organization
Leadership	Appointed or elected	Appointed by chief executive of an organization	Officers designated by bylaws and by subcommittee and approved by vote of the membership
Focus	A specific task or charge	The development of procedures and policies for organizational management	Policy making, governance, monitoring, fiscal control, fund-raising
Bond	Team spirit Needs of organization and client	Client system Treatment plan Inter- or intra-agency agreement	Commitment to the mission of the organization Service orientation
Composition	Interest in a task	Loyalty to the organization and the chief executive officer	Diverse members often selected for their status, power, influence in the community, expertise, representation of particular interest groups and constituencies
Communication	Relative to task Low member self-disclosure	Members present points of view based on their position in an organization To build a power base	Formal communication Parliamentary procedures Less formal in subcommittees Low member self-disclosure

(Continued)

TABLE 6.1

Typology of Task Groups (Continued)

	Community Needs		
Selected Characteristics	**Social Action Groups**	**Conditions**	**Delegate Councils**
Purpose	To devise and implement social change tactics and strategies	To exert greater influence by sharing resources, expertise, and power bases of social action groups with common goals.	To represent different organizations, chapters, or other units
Leadership	Indigenous leadership emerging from the groups Practitioners often is staffer or adviser	Often a charismatic or dedicated individual leading by consensus or elected by vote of the membership	Representatives appointed by the sponsoring organization
Focus	Consumer community, social justice	Building consensus and a partnership for maximum influence	Collective input and action Equality of representation Focus on larger issues, concerns, and positions
Bond	Perception of injustices, inequity or need for change	Interest in an issue Commitment to an ideological position	Larger purpose or community concern, rather than individual or agency concern
Composition	Based on common interest, shared purpose, and investment community	Loose, temporary confederation of groups or organizations working in partnership to achieve a common goal	Diverse by definition Represents interest of sponsoring organization
Communication	Internal member-to-member discussion Formulation and implementation of tactics and strategies for change High member self-disclosure in relation to social problems.	Formal or informal depending on type of coalition Less format in caucuses and subgroups Moderate member self-disclosure representing group interest	Provides a forum for communication among organizations Delegates are communication links between council and the sponsoring organization Low member self-disclosure

Source: From Ronald W. Toseland, Robert F. Rivas, *An Introduction to Group Work Practice,* 4th ed. Published by Allyn and Bacon, Boston, MA.

develop out of the *needs of the community.* Another type of task group—the *focus group*—is designed to collect in-depth, qualitative information about a particular topic or issue. Focus groups are used to clarify and enrich data collected during surveys or other research methods. They may be used by social service organizations to assess clients' satisfaction and/or opinions about services being provided. Meetings are semi-structured and require planning and attention to a specific agenda, recruiting appropriate participants, effective facilitation, and a clear and detailed analysis of the information obtained. It is useful for the leader to develop an interview guide with relevant questions. Leaders must be thoroughly familiar with the topics being discussed and have the ability to establish rapport quickly, to avoid jargon, to listen to each member's opinion, to flexibly use the interview guide, and to facilitate group dynamics that encourage the full participation of all present. Cooper and Lesser (2005) wrote about their use of *focus groups* in a research study they conducted in Jamaica, West Indies, to learn more about how the children who live in one crime-ridden community in West Kingston were affected by the violence. They planned to use the knowledge gained from these meetings to collaborate on the development of training for Jamaican human service providers who work with traumatized children. The researchers conducted three focus group meetings of stakeholders; each meeting lasted approximately an hour and a half. Participants agreed to be interviewed because they had strong, trusting relationships with the authors' Jamaican social work colleagues, some of whom were present during the interviews. The participants were invited based on their relevant experience, education, and/or leadership position in the community and in the field, for example, a school principal, social workers, and guidance counselors working with the children and parents in the affected communities. The researchers used a structured interview guide (see Practice Example 6.2) to keep the discussion focused on the salient points of the study.

PRACTICE EXAMPLE 6.2

Interview Guide for Focus Groups

1. Direct experience working with abused and neglected children
2. Jamaican view of child maltreatment, specifically child sexual abuse
3. Perception by children and families of treatment providers
4. Religious/cultural beliefs of children and families
5. Current treatment modalities, resources, and interventions
6. Cultural aspects that can be harnessed to promote change
7. Culture's effective use of support networks
8. Effects of care on children and families
9. Prioritization and actualization of family unification
10. Support networks for children and families
11. Perception by Jamaican social service system and families of core social work values such as self-determination and confidentiality
12. Unique Jamaican practice approaches that can be incorporated in U.S. to help culturally diverse clients

A useful technique in many task groups is brainstorming: a systematic set of rules to guide the group to generate creative ideas (Osborne, 1963).

Brainstorming A technique that is considered useful in many task groups is *brainstorming*. This is a systematic set of rules for generating creative ideas in a task group (Osborn, 1963). Brainstorming includes combining, rearranging, and improving ideas that have already been expressed. Members are encouraged to express any and all of their ideas, and criticism and judgment of any idea is discouraged. It is the leader's responsibility to explain how brainstorming works and to set a period of time for this exercise. During the brainstorming session, the leader writes the ideas on a flip chart and/or assigns someone else in the group to this task. Brainstorming is used primarily when the group wants to generate new ideas about a particular problem, not when the group faces a technical problem that requires systematic, organized thinking. The benefits of brainstorming include the sharing of ideas and decreased dependence on the leader as the single authority figure.

Groupthink Janis (1982) described the kind of thinking that can develop in groups when members are striving toward uniformity or conformity as *groupthink*. This occurs in situations when group norms become rigid and members lose their motivation to consider alternative course of action. Groupthink can arise when the leader does not encourage divergent views or open expression of ideas or when limitations or threats are placed on group members. Janis noted that groupthink was more likely to occur when the group was isolated, under the influence of directive leadership, or using unsystematic procedures for generating and evaluating decisions. Groupthink can be avoided by periodic division into separate smaller groups to work on specific tasks and reconvening to work out differences (Schriver, 2004, p. 396). Neck and Manz (1994) proposed *teamthink* as a way to avoid groupthink. Teamthink involves encouragement of divergent views, open expression of ideas, awareness of limits, recognition of each group member's unique contribution, and discussion of doubts.

Treatment Groups

The purpose of a treatment group is centered on meeting the members' socioemotional needs, such as *support, education, therapy, growth,* and *socialization.* Members bond on the basis of their common needs and common situations. Roles in the group develop through the process of group interaction and communication patterns are generally open. Members are encouraged to interact and talk with each other. These groups have flexible procedures for meetings, including a warm-up period, a time to work on members' concerns, and a time to summarize the group's work. Members are generally expected to share with the group on their own. Treatment groups are confidential and are successful to the extent that individuals feel they have met their personal goal for joining the group. Table 6.2 lists a selection of treatment groups: support, education, growth, therapy, and socialization (Toseland & Rivas, 2004, p. 23).

Treatment groups, specifically *therapy groups,* can be run from a number of theoretical perspectives. Each approach has different goals that affect both the stages of group development and the role of the group leader in each stage. Brabender (2002) and Farber (2002) discuss several approaches to group therapy: Ego Supportive, *Interpersonal, Object Relations, CognitiveBehavioral,* Eco-systemic, and *Problem Solving* that can be used with a variety of clients. The choice of a theoretical model is complex and consideration should be given to the group members' developmental, sociohistorical, organizational, political and cultural context, as well as the purpose of the group. Multicultural theory (see Chapter 3) provides a conceptual framework to assist the group leader in selecting the theoretical approach most congruent with the life experience of potential group members.

Self-psychology and narrative therapy (see Chapter 3) were the integrated frameworks for a 12-week group of aging women with significant and serious trauma histories, including physical and sexual abuse, experiences related to war, and death of infant children, conducted by a social worker in an outpatient treatment center. Posttraumatic stress disorder (PTSD) was diagnosed in each of these women following different medical procedures and/or experiences that triggered the flooding of memories from the past. Self-psychology promoted the significance of the group as a self-object for these women, providing empathic witnesses as they worked with traumatic memories during a vulnerable life stage. Narrative therapy empowered the women to share their past stories, reauthor these experiences, and face aging with integrity and grace. Self-psychological treatment concepts such as the self-object relational experiences of mirroring, idealizing, and partnering were woven with narrative techniques such as the definitional ceremony and use of therapeutic documents. These combined efforts provided the group members with comfort and empathy and allowed them to share and have others bear witness to some of their past traumas, contributing to achieving "ego integrity" (Erikson, 1959) during this final stage of life.

Support groups are another type of professionally facilitated treatment group; however, they are generally less structured and less formal. An example of such a group is described next.

Mutual Aid Groups for People with AIDS The need for support groups for people with AIDS and their families began in the 1980s, when the majority of these groups were composed of gay men. Discrimination and lack of knowledge precipitated the

TABLE 6.2

Typology of Treatment Groups

	Purpose of the Group				
Selected Characteristics	**Support**	**Education**	**Growth**	**Therapy**	**Socialization**
Purpose	To help members cope with stressful life events and revitalize existing coping abilities	To educate through presentations, discussion, and experiences	To develop members' potential, awareness, insight	To change behavior Connection, rehabilitation, Coping, and problem solving through behavior change interventions	To increase communication and social skills. Improved interpersonal relationship's through program activities, structured exercises, role plays, etc.
Leadership	A facilitator of empathic understanding and mutual aid	Leader as teacher and provider of structure for group discussion	Leader as facilitator and role model	Leader as expert, authority figure, or facilitator depending on approach	Leader as director of the group's actions or programs
Focus	The ability of the individual to cope with a stressful life experience Communication and mutual aid	Individual learning Structuring of the group for learning	Either member or group focus, depending on the approach Individual growth through the group experience	Individual members' problems, concerns, or goals	The group as a medium for activity, participation, and involvement
Bond	Shared stressful experiences, often stigmatizing	Common interest in learning skills development	Common goals among members Contract to use group to grow	Common purpose with separate member goals Relationship of member with worker, group, or other members	A common activity, enterprise, or situation
Composition	Based on a shared life experience Often diverse	Similarity of education or skill level	Can be diverse Based on members' ability to work toward growth and development	Can be diverse or can be composed of people with similar problems or concerns	Depending on location of group and purpose, can be diverse or homogeneous

Source: From Ronald W. Toseland and Robert F. Rivas *An Introduction to Group Work Practice,* 4th ed. Published by Allyn and Bacon, Boston, MA.

advent of a wide range of support groups among this population. In addition, the unique path of this pandemic prompted the scientific and health-care communities to establish community-based empowerment approaches to the provision of services for this population. Many AIDS-related health-care professionals supported the idea of establishing ongoing support groups for HIV-positive, asymptomatic individuals, and their family members. One such model of peer support is sponsored by the Long Island Association for AIDS Care. The model we are describing incorporates all HIV-positive populations, representing a cross section of people currently diagnosed with the illness. The support groups are ongoing, and the membership is continuous and stable. They meet once a week for 90 minutes, on the same night, and in the same location, generally a community facility such as a church. Rules of confidentiality are enforced (for example, what is said in the group stays in the group, and the names of group members are never disclosed to anyone). Applicants for these support groups are interviewed in 30-minute telephone screenings to determine whether they are appropriate candidates for the group they would like to attend. Individuals who are not appropriate for the group are referred for counseling elsewhere. Drop-ins and guests are not permitted because it is felt that confidentiality could be compromised. The groups are open-ended—new members may join at any time—and this format contributes to the continuity and long-term survival of the groups. New members are generally asked to make a commitment to attend the group for a specific length of time and to call in advance if they are not able to attend a meeting. These particular support groups are run by two agency-appointed facilitators. They are representative of the group's membership with regard to gender, ethnicity, and sexual orientation (for example, one facilitator may be heterosexual and the other may be gay). The facilitators generally approach the support groups as a democratic process. The facilitators of these support groups attend supervision meetings that help deal with the potential for burnout due to the difficult content of the group meetings. It also provides technical assistance for the handling of certain group dynamics (Barouh, 1992).

Self-Help Groups

The term *self-help* is used to emphasize the internal helping offered by group members to each other, as opposed to interventions by professional group leaders. Self-help groups generally assemble informally in different community settings, such as hospitals, churches, and community centers. The ethos of self-help groups is *empowerment* (whether psychological or social) that is achieved through the process of identifying the nature of the problem, joining with others, and educating oneself about achieving a solution(s); in other words, being potential help givers as well as help receivers. Some of the ways in which groups provide support between meetings include furnishing sponsors—persons who are available for in-between telephone contact and support-providing educational activities, advocating for members, and sponsoring events of interest. There are many self-help groups that serve people with chronic illness, and hospital and health facilities are frequent sites for these services (Wituk, Shepherd, Slavich, Warren, & Meissen, 2000).

Kurtz (2004) discusses several theoretical frameworks from the literature that can be applied to self-help groups. *Social support theory* (Killilea, 1982) suggests that individuals in crisis are partially protected from negative affects of stress when they are surrounded with human supports that include family, friends, or those who are similarly suffering. These support systems help to promote empowerment and mastery, offer guidance and advice, and provide validating feedback about emotions and behaviors (Zimmerman, 1995). *Cognitive behavioral theory* can be found in the reframing strategies used by many self-help groups. For example, Winterowd, Beck, and Gruener (2003) wrote about *chronic pain groups* in pain clinics that provide "opportunities for validation and support as well as for helping others" (p. 15). The groups are geared toward identifying cognitive and behavioral difficulties that might be influencing the participants' experiences of pain and their moods to enhance their functioning. *Reference group theory* (Powell, 1987) is applicable to understanding the cohesiveness many of these groups have, due in part to members' sharing similar issues. The most famous self-help group is probably Alcoholics Anonymous (AA), a 12-step fellowship, peer-led self-help group. The mission of all 12-step fellowships, including Narcotics Anonymous (NA), Gamblers Anonymous (GA), and Overeaters Anonymous (OA), among others, is to help the individuals who suffer from the particular condition. These groups accept referrals from professionals but do not otherwise involve them in their meetings. Self-help groups, perhaps more than any other type of group, is based on the notion of mutual aid as the curative factor.

Women's Groups

Schiller (1995) made a significant contribution to the group-work literature when she applied *self-in-relation theory* (see Chapter 3, "Cultural Relational Theory") to group therapy with women. She proposed a model that stresses how the importance of connection influences the way women approach conflict in groups. Stages 1 (*preaffiliation*) and 5 (*termination*) remain fairly congruent with other group models (Garland, Jones, & Kolodny, 1973; Johnson & Johnson, 1991; Tuckman & Jensen, 1977). Stage 2, however, *establishing a relational base with peers,* differs significantly from the phase of *power and control* that typifies other models and is characterized by the need women have to establish relationships with others like themselves. Women share experiences during this time and seek approval and connection that contributes to a sense of safety. Stage three, *mutuality and interpersonal empathy,* is an extension of stage 2 and moves into a greater ability to trust and share differences. Stage 4, *challenge and change,* is the time when the women are able to more directly question themselves, each other, and the leader. This includes greater ability to risk the direct expression of anger and disappointment due to the confidence they feel in firmly established relationships and connections among group members.

Persons with Disabilities in Groups

There are a variety of disabilities that a leader might encounter when working with groups of people. These group members may require some reasonable accommodation to effectively participate in the group and should be able to speak freely with the group leader and/or members about what these accommodations might be. They are entitled to specific rights under the law (see Chapter 18) with regard to their participation in groups. They have the right to expect that the group norms will recognize the value of diversity within the group and not discriminate against any person on the basis of their disability. Patterson, McKenzie, and Jenkins (1995, p. 79, cited in Schriver, 2004, p. 411) suggest "disability etiquette for a group." Their helpful guidelines follow.

- It is appropriate to acknowledge that a disability exists, but asking personal questions is inappropriate unless one has a close relationship with the person with the disability.
- It is important to speak directly to the person with a disability, even when a third party (for example, an interpreter) is present.
- It is appropriate to use common words such as *look* or *see,* for individuals with visual impairments, as well as *running* and *walking* with persons who use wheelchairs.
- It is appropriate to offer assistance to the person with a disability, but one should wait until it is accepted before providing the assistance. Clarification should be sought from the individual with the disability if the group leader is unsure of how or what type of assistance is needed.

Intergroup Dialogue

Intergroup dialogues "bring together members of two or more social identity groups that have a history of conflict or potential conflict" (Nagda & Auniga, 2003, p. 113). Small-group meetings are facilitated by a group leader over a period of weeks or months. The focus of group "dialogues" is to examine ways in which power, privilege, and oppression structure the experiences of social identity group membership(s). They engage the members in developing skills for engaging across differences (p. 113). Nagda and Zuniga (2003) focus on the importance of the dialogic learning process, differentiating between dialogue and debate and setting group norms and guidelines for participation. These authors acknowledge that the dynamics in intergroup dialogues may reflect issues parallel to interracial and ethnic conflicts in the larger society. They suggest an open and constructive discussion of these issues that can deindividualize the tensions, generate multiple perspectives, and result "in a deeper understanding of the impact of the social context on interpersonal and group conflicts" (p. 125). Zuniga (2003) describes a four-stage design that uses the "interconnected processes of sustained communication, critical social awareness, and bridge building as foundation principles" for intergroup dialogues:

Stage 1: Creating an environment for dialogue: Building a foundation for honest and meaningful interactions (two group sessions)

Stage 2: Situating the dialogue: Learning about commonalities and differences (two to three sessions)

Stage 3: Exploring conflicts and multiple perspectives about difficult topics (four to five sessions)

Stage 4: Moving from dialogue to action: Action planning and alliance building to advance advocacy and social justice (two sessions)

Technology-Mediated Groups

Meier (2004) and Kurtz (2004) write about a wide range of groups that are mediated by telecommunications technology, and we refer our readers to these resources for details. Examples of such groups are *computer-based self-help groups,* such as "chat room" discussions, newsgroup and discussion forums, and *telephone groups.* In telephone conference groups, the leader and group members call in from wherever they are at the scheduled time of the group meeting. Groups conducted over a speakerphone may involve some members meeting together in person who then talk, via speakerphone, with those who are not present in the room. Most of these groups have a participation of no more than six members to be most effective. A major advantage of such groups is that they are not dependent on geographic location or access to transportation. This is advantageous for many prospective group members who have chronic illnesses and disabilities or are otherwise incapacitated. However, technological problems are always possible when using these group mediums. This can be frustrating if a conversation is taking place and is suddenly interrupted. Keeping track of participation can be another obstacle. Perhaps the greatest challenge is forming the relational bonds that face-to-face conversation foster, with special attention to nonverbal expression, mood, and the many nuances that take place when people are together in the same room.

Summary

This chapter has provided a condensed version of the small group both as a context within which human behavior occurs and as an influence on its development throughout the life span. Group-work practice is synonymous with the history of social work and can serve a variety of purposes and populations in many different settings. And although it is not always *easy to be* a member of *a* group—it is almost impossible *never* to be a member of *any* group. Literally from birth to the end of life, human beings are interconnected and interacting with each other—whether in families, in organizations, in communities, or globally. Drumm (2006, pp. 20–21) delineates several principles that make a group a "social work group." These include (a) inclusion and respect; (b) mutual aid; (c) stage management; (d) facing and exploring conflict; (e) conscious development of the group's purpose; (f) breaking taboos by naming what is often difficult to discuss; (g) valuing activities such as music, writing and art; (h) problem-solving with the group members. The Internet and the World Wide Web have enabled even those individuals who are not at ease in group settings to join with others in cyberspace—the newest group setting—where human behavior and the social environment intersect.

7 Communities and Organizations

Communities are always the context, if not always the content, of social work practice.

HARDCASTLE AND POWERS, 2004, P. 5

Introduction

Communities and their various support systems (for example, formal and informal organizations and social networks) are considered to be macrosystems (as opposed to individuals and families, which are characterized as microsystems). They serve as "mediating" structures between the individual/family and the larger society, providing links to, and representations of, the wider culture. During childhood, the family serves as the individual's primary social environment; in adulthood, the individual's social world broadens considerably to include the wider community. As the individual participates in various sectors of community life (e.g., the economic, commercial, religious, educational, legal, health, and welfare organizations) he or she both shapes and is shaped by them.

In this chapter, we will attempt to provide a broad, integrated conceptual framework that recognizes the fact that communities and their subsystems are embedded in even larger, more complex systems that exert a profound influence on them. In Chapter 6, we examined how people respond to, cope with, adapt to, and shape the behavior of others with the intimate relationships of the family system. Here we will study these interactions in less-personal relationships, within the context of the wider social (macro) environment—that is, within formal organizations and informal networks such as neighborhoods, schools, work settings, or "other associations in which a person assumes a role as citizen, producer, consumer or client" (Mulroy, 2004). Our final task will be to examine the mutuality of connections among individuals, families, organizations, and communities and to explore how, together, they may accomplish goals that would not be possible by working independently.

Social Structure: Patterns of Social Interaction

The concept of social structure is based on the belief that the way people behave in social situations—their social behavior—tends to be patterned and organized. Human beings form *social institutions* to perform specific functions. For example, the family organizes people to perform survival functions such as reproduction and child care, safety, and economic security. Other social institutions—educational, economic, social welfare, religious, political, and so forth—perform other necessary social functions.

These institutions provide social relationships with order and predictability through the process of socialization and the appropriation of relevant social roles that enable people to work together to achieve their common purpose(s). Cultural values shape the expectations for behavior, or *norms,* within social institutions, and people are socialized to behave according to these norms (normative behavior) through the process of internalization.

Through the process of *social differentiation,* people are categorized on the basis of a range of socially defined criteria (for example, gender, race, religion, sexual orientation, physical attributes, or age). These differential categories may then be used to *stratify* people—that is, to create a hierarchy or vertical ranking of people that indicates their relative value in their society (*social stratification*). This may lay the foundation for *discrimination* (actions that deny equal access to social resources to less-valued members of the society) and *oppression* (the systematic restriction of opportunity through discriminatory practices); in effect, social structure determines how, and to whom, social resources will be allocated (Berger, McBreen, & Rifkin, 1996). The following section describes several social interactional concepts that are pertinent to an understanding of both communities and organizations.

Power, Oppression, and Patterns of Social Interaction

Power is the ability to enforce one's will on others and to control access to social resources (for example, money, education, housing, land, social acceptance, or weapons). Through various *institutional arrangements,* (socially agreed-upon, institutionalized patterns of status, power, privilege and wealth distribution), dominant groups in society (those who, by virtue of possessing culturally valued characteristics are "on top" of the vertical social hierarchy), may withhold power from those who, by virtue of their less-valued personal characteristics, are "on the bottom" of the vertical social hierarchy. This creates a context of oppression or disempowerment that may have serious negative implications for the emotional, social, and economic well-being of vulnerable groups.

Social exchange theory provides an important part of the conceptual foundation of community practice. Community practice is seen as taking place in an "exchange field" consisting of two or more parties who interact to exchange resources (Blau, 1964; Emerson, 1962; Homans, 1974). The act of exchange refers to the process of getting something one needs or desires from others by offering them something they need or desire. An exchange takes place only if both parties feel it will benefit them or, at least, not hurt them. In an exchange relationship, one has power when one controls the resources that someone else needs. If one needs a resource that someone else controls, one may engage in a variety of "power-balancing strategies" (Hardcastle & Powers, 2004, p. 40)—that is, look for other ways to accomplish one's goals either by looking for alternates that do not include the desired resource; finding something that one controls that is valuable to the "powerful" party; forming a coalition with others who may each have something the resource holder needs; or by working to deny the resource holder something it values.

Although power is very important in exchange relationships, it is not involved in every transaction. As people repeatedly exchange resources, they may begin to develop positive relationships; gradually over time these relationships may lead to the formation of networks, coalitions, support groups, and new organizations (Hardcastle & Powers, 2004). "Power as it is being lived and learned is neither fixed nor dynamic. It changes as the attitudes and behavior of any party change. This understanding of power offers enormous possibilities: it suggests that by conscious attention to the importance of one's own actions, one can change others—even those who, under the old view of power, appear immovable. All this allows us to discover new sources of power within our reach" (Lappe & DuBois, 1994, p. 54, quoted in Hardcastle & Powers, 2004, p. 42).

Social networks are comprised of people, groups, organizations, or other social units that are connected to one another through interactions and exchanges designed to help each meet their individual needs and objectives. Although members of a network may have different objectives, they share a belief that the network relationship will help them in their pursuits. Networks can be personal, professional, and organizational. Resources exchanged can be material (for example, money or clients) or nonmaterial (for example, information, validation, emotional support).

Social cohesion refers to the strength of ties between members of a social unit such as a community or network. Reciprocity and fair exchange foster cohesion; the more cohesive a unit is, the more frequent, intense, and durable are the relationships among members. Unequal distribution of power tends to threaten cohesion and may lead to greater opposition to the dominant group and instability of the network.

Social exclusion describes situations in which individuals or groups of people are excluded from participation in the life of the community or the wider society. For example, a public housing project or an adult home for the mentally ill may be viewed by its neighbors as separate or "outside" the community—here, a boundary is set up to exclude this entity from participation in community life.

Conflict theory assumes that every society is based on the "constraint of some of its members by others" (Hardcastle & Powers, 2004, p. 44), and that the unequal distribution of power and scarce resources among dominant and subordinate groups creates opposing interests that generate conflict. The result of this conflict is social change—the dominant groups seek to protect their dominance, and the subordinate groups push for change. This aspect of conflict theory is particularly relevant for community practitioners in that it provides a conceptual foundation for creating change and for facilitating the organization of oppressed people into activists who advocate for their own interests.

The Community: An Overview

The Community Defined

As is the case with many other social science concepts, *community* is a complex and multidimensional concept that defies a singular definition. Cohen (1985) found over 90 definitions of community in a review of the literature. Hillery (1955) noted that most sociological definitions of community include three common elements: geographic area, social interaction, and common ties. However, although communities are often connected to a territorial base, technological advances in electronic communication and physical mobility, as well as economic globalization, have made communities less dependent on clearly defined geographic boundaries (Hardcastle & Powers, 2004).

The term *community* implies people with social ties who share a sense of identity. For example, members of *communities of interest* (such as the *medical community*, the *gay and lesbian community*, the *disabilities community*) may share a social identity and ties without sharing a physical territory. In fact, residents can, and often do, share the same local space but hold widely differing identities, whereas people who aren't in physical proximity, such as undocumented immigrants or guest workers, may feel a stronger sense of kinship with people in their town of origin than with their new neighbors. Hutchison (1999), acknowledging that it is an evolving concept, defined community as "people bound either by geography or by network links (webs of communication) sharing common ties and interacting with one another" (p. 333). She further noted that all three of the aforementioned elements must be present for a community to exist.

Anderson and Carter (1990), drawing on the work of Chatterjee and Koleski (1970), Meenaghan (1972), and Gusfield (1975), described community as "a perspectivistic idea—that is, it is futile to attempt to understand a total community, but it is worthwhile to select issues or problems and then define community as it is relevant to these particular concerns" (p. 95). These authors view community as a social system, and they offer the following criteria for identifying its relational patterns. A community:

- Is a system intermediate between society and "microsystems."
- Has a consciously identified population characterized by a sense of belonging; that is, it is aware of itself and is part of its members' identities.
- Is organized and engaged in common pursuits.
- Has differentiation of functions.
- Adapts to the environment through energy exchange.
- Creates and maintains organizations and institutions to fulfill the needs of both subsystems and suprasystems.

Further, its members may or may not occupy common physical space, and its boundaries may or may not coincide with the boundaries of a political subdivision (city, town, or county; Anderson & Carter, 1990, p. 96).

Community Functions

Warren (1978) viewed communities in terms of their functions—that is, what do communities *do* and how do they affect their members? He proposed five social functions that communities fulfill for their members and that are important to the continuing existence of the community:

Production-Distribution-Consumption This is considered to be the most basic of all community functions and refers to the community's provision of basic goods and services that are seen to be desirable. Businesses, schools, religious organizations, governmental offices, health-care providers, and others carry out these functions for the community and its members.

Socialization This refers to the process through which the community's various *institutions* (for example, families, schools, churches) transmit shared values, behavioral expectations, and knowledge to members.

Social Control This refers to those processes that communities use to ensure that members conform to community norms for behavior, role expectations, values, and so forth. This function may be carried out by families, religious institutions, social welfare organizations, courts, police, and others.

Social Participation This is an essential community function that allows for community members to participate in the life and administration of their community. It may be carried out through various informal networks or groups, voluntary organizations, religious institutions, and so forth.

Mutual Support This is how communities provide help to members when their individual and family needs are not met through their own personal resources. It may be fulfilled by formal organizations, such as social welfare organizations and religious institutions, and/or informal organizations and networks, such as friends, neighbors, kin, and/or other affiliations.

Community Competence

A community is generally thought to be competent when it is able to deal effectively with the broad range of needs and problems that face its members and the community as a whole (Cottrell, 1976; Fellin, 2001; Germain, 1991). Competence is enhanced when members feel identified with, and committed to, their community, are able to communicate effectively with one another, and have a high level of participation in community decision making (Hardcastle & Powers, 2004).

In addition to the maintenance of internal cohesion, community identification, mutual aid, and social participation, competent communities maintain effective connections with the larger social, economic, and political environment to ensure their access to needed resources:

> A community that strives toward self-direction achieves and maintains beneficial connectedness to the outer environment. It is committed to, and engaged in, protecting itself against the loss of resources, self-direction, competence and relatedness imposed by external or internal forces of coercive power.
>
> Pinderhughes' transactional conception of disempowerment (1983) suggests that weak connections to the larger environment, or its failure to provide needed resources to a community, entrap the members and set in motion a malignant process by creating powerlessness in the community. The more powerless a community is because of denial of resources and services, the more its families are hindered from meeting their needs and from organizing to improve the community so that it can provide them with more support. The more powerless the family is, the more its members are blocked in their attempts to acquire skills, to develop self-esteem, and to strengthen the family, and the more powerless the community becomes. (Germain, 1991, p. 43)

Community Subsystems: Formal and Informal Structures

Communities are comprised of a variety of social groups that serve as support systems for their members. These may be formal or informal in nature. Informal systems include families, as well as such social networks as friends, neighbors, kin, and coworkers. These may serve as valuable environmental resources that help people cope with life stressors by providing emotional support, information, advice, and mutual aid in the form of money, child care, housing, and other help as needed. Through the process of meeting people's need for social connection and recognition, these networks also contribute to members' physical, mental, and social well-being (Berkman & Syme, 1979; Nukolls, Cassell, & Kaplan, 1972). In contrast to more formal support systems, these informal networks develop naturally, as people participate in the life of the community and form personal relationships with one another.

Formal systems are created to accomplish a specific purpose. Voluntary associations such as clubs, formed groups, and churches, as well as more structured organizations such as schools, workplaces, corporations, social agencies, health centers, and government service offices, all fall into the category of formal systems, although they are characterized by varying levels of *formalization* or structure. For example, self-help groups often start out as informal systems, but these eventually tend to grow larger, and as they expand, they frequently begin to adopt a more complex structure of roles and authority and hence, greater *formality.*

Auspices of Formal Organizations

Formal human service organizations are established under three general auspices:

Public organizations are established and run by federal, state, or local governments. They are supported by tax revenues. The executive officer of public human services organizations is often a political appointee, and lower level staff are civil service employees. These agencies are legally mandated to serve all who are eligible and generally have little or no flexibility in terms of what services they provide.

Voluntary, nonprofit organizations are legally incorporated as nonprofit corporations and are subject to laws that govern charities. These organizations vary widely in size and are governed by volunteer boards of directors. Funding sources also vary—these may include private philanthropies, government service contracts, and/or government insurance programs such as Medicare, private insurance companies, and/or through the operation of related businesses, such as stores. These organizations typically show more flexibility with regard to services, policies, and workplace rules because they are self-governed and not subject to the political considerations that influence public organizations.

Private, for-profit organizations are privately owned, either by an individual, a partnership, investment group, or stockholders (for example, private practitioners, corporations that own health-care facilities such as hospitals, nursing homes, and rehabilitation facilities). Their primary goal is to make a profit, through the provision of services, so the need for business generation exerts a strong influence on service delivery.

Transnational organizations are a more recent development. With continuous advances in technology, and the ever-increasing integration of world economic systems, the postmodern era has witnessed expanding patterns of transnational migration. These have resulted in the development of social needs that are global in nature and that require interventions that rely on international cooperation, as well as organizations whose auspices transcend national boundaries (Gibelman & Furman, 2008). Currently, a variety of international, national, and local organizations (both public and private) exist that serve to assist immigrants and refugees to negotiate the migration process. Although a more extensive discussion of such agencies is beyond the scope of this book, we have included online resources at the end of this chapter that provide more information on this subject. Although few social work services are currently truly transnational, the field of international or global social work is gaining recognition as an increasingly valuable and necessary field of practice. Furman and Negi (2007) envision the eventual development transnational alliances of social workers who collaborate to provide effective premigration services (in the sending community) and postmigration services (in the receiving community). Such transnational organizational networks would facilitate the coordination of services necessary to maintain client well-being across national boundaries. They further suggest that current international social work networking groups (for example, the International Association of Schools of Social Work) might be effective forums for developing such alliances and sharing expertise and knowledge.

Formal Organizations as Social Systems

Formal organizations share the same characteristics and operate under the same basic assumptions as all other social systems. These properties are discussed in the following sections, as they relate to organizations. (See Chapter 1 for more detailed discussions of social systems; also see Chapter 1, Practice Example 1.1, for a description of systemic concepts as they apply to formal organizations.)

Goal Direction

Formal organizations, like all social systems, exist to fulfill a purpose. Holland (1995) defines formal organizations as "formalized groups of people who make coordinated use of resources and skills to accomplish given goals or purposes (p. 1788, quoted in Gibelman & Furman, 2008, p. 22). In human service organizations specifically, those goals generally involve "promoting and enhancing the well-being of the people they serve" (Holland, 1995, p. 1787, quoted in Gibelman, 2008, p. 22).

Traditionally, human service organizations articulate their reason for existence, and what they seek to accomplish, through a formal, broadly stated *mission statement* as well as more specifically articulated *goals and objectives.* The organization's *mandates* codify what it is required to do according to its charter, articles of incorporation, or, for public agencies, to the law (Bryson, 1989).

Organizational Structure

As is the case with all social systems, formal organizations develop a structure that allows them to carry out their functions and accomplish their goals. Organizational structure refers to the "actual arrangements and levels of an organization in regard to power, authority, responsibilities and mechanisms for carrying out (organizational) functioning and practices" (Skidmore, 1990, p. 97). Most formal systems are characterized, to one extent or another, by hierarchical levels of authority, specialized roles in which occupants are replaceable; relationships based on what people do, as well as rules, policies, and procedures that govern organizational behavior (Germain, 1991). Subsystems develop as a means of carrying out the work of the organization. These may include structures for governance, staffing patterns, and/or work divisions, units, or departments (Gibelman & Furman, 2008).

Traditional Organizational Structure: Bureaucracy and Scientific Management Today, the term *bureaucracy* has become almost synonymous with *formal organization*. The concepts of bureaucracy and scientific management, as models of organizational structure and management, evolved during the Industrial Revolution and represent attempts to increase productivity, efficiency, and profits. Bureaucracies are distinguished by several characteristics, including a hierarchical structure of authority that is spelled out by a stable, comprehensive system of rules and regulations; extensive record keeping, or *red tape;* and specially trained, salaried career managers who run the organization and have the authority to hire, fire, and move personnel from one position to another (Pugh, Hickson, & Hinings, 1985; Shafritz & Ott, 1987). They rely on principles of *scientific management* designed to increase efficiency (getting the most accomplished with the smallest amount of input) and effectiveness (achieving the goals of the organization). These principles include analysis and standardization of work tasks and close monitoring of workers by managers who are responsible for planning, decision making, and evaluation of how tasks are to be carried out (Fisher & Karger, 1997). These so-called rational frameworks for organizational management were adopted as a means of controlling fraud and maximizing efficiency. Today, the term *bureaucracy* has become almost synonymous with "formal organization", and most social service systems have, to a greater or lesser extent, a bureaucratic structure.

Informal Structures in Formal Organizations To cope with problems of functioning in organizations, agency personnel develop informal networks of interpersonal relationships. These strongly affect the organization's operation as well as its culture. *Organizational culture* refers to the pattern of assumptions, values, rules, and norms that emerge among members of an organization; this pattern develops slowly over time, is generally unspoken, guides the behavior of agency personnel within the organization and with external systems, and determines, to a large extent, the overall quality of organizational life (Daft, 2008; Hellriegel & Slocum, 2007).

Both managerial and nonmanagerial staff need to develop a good understanding of the organization's informal structure and culture if they are to function effectively. Informal networks can either sabotage or support new programs and policies, and an understanding of these structures can reveal alternative sources of power that are not reflected on the formal organizational chart, informal communication networks, as well as ways to informally influence organizational decision making.

Adaptation and Maintenance of the Steady State: Rational and Nonrational Processes in Formal Organizations

As was discussed in Chapter 1, every social system must be flexible enough to continuously adapt to changing internal and external demands to remain functional and accomplish its goals, while maintaining its identity. As goal-oriented systems, bureaucratically structured organizations attempt to operate rationally to fulfill their official purpose. Although the bureaucratic form officially represents an attempt to rationally organize the operation of decision-making processes, it tends to work best "when information is clear, and when resources are readily available" (Hardcastle & Powers, 2004, p. 35). On the other hand, these rational processes tend to break down as the organization attempts to contend with complex variables that are beyond its control (for example, its political and institutional environment, the complexity of client needs, insufficient revenues and resources, intra-organizational conflict). In other words, in the face of competing internal and external interests and pressures, what the organization actually does may or may not coincide with its officially stated goals. As pressures multiply, there may develop less-rational, defensive processes that operate to undermine the delivery of services in several ways. For example, a hierarchical and highly centralized decision-making structure may create too much distance between the organization's decision makers and its clients, thereby making it difficult to be flexible enough to meet changing client needs. Rules and procedures may become increasingly rigid with time, and in a process known as *goal displacement,* they may begin to serve to maintain the status quo, rather than to fulfill the agency's original mission. Social work staff may be themselves struggling with conflicts between their professional norms/values and their agency's norms and policies (Germain, 1991).

Formal Organizations: Changing Paradigms

Several contemporary management trends challenge the traditional bureaucratic structure, as they attempt to increase organizational adaptiveness and flexibility. Many of these contemporary trends specifically target the hierarchical authority structure of bureaucratic organizations and advocate for more participatory frameworks that serve to redistribute power from management, to the workers who provide services directly to clients. For example, the use of teams of workers who are responsible for service provision is thought to be an effective means of promoting organizational responsiveness to changing demands, thereby increasing its viability over time. As teams work to identify issues, problem-solve, set goals, and evaluate their own progress, they assume some of the power traditionally given to individual managers (Fisher & Karger, 1997; Kirst-Ashman & Hull, 2008).

Fisher and Karger addressed the issue of "escalating managerialism" (1997, p. 155) by urging that social welfare organizations adopt more ideological social constructions to guide their policy making and programming decisions. Along these lines, they recommended a rethinking of workplace productivity demands, with quantitative evaluations of productivity replaced by more qualitative assessments that give greater weight to the achievement of worker and client goals.

Additionally, in response to the changing demographics of U.S. communities, contemporary organizations have been placing increased value on multicultural competence in their staffing patterns, policies, procedures, and practices. This stands in stark contrast to the traditional bureaucratic structure that values conformity over diversity. Some examples of these more dynamic, contemporary trends and methods are described next.

Total Quality Management (TQM) Total Quality Management is one of several approaches that exemplify the ways that management can be used to empower employees and improve the quality of services to clients. Here, the role of manager is seen as that of facilitator, director, and overseer (Deming, 1986). Although management retains overall responsibility for production, the company relies heavily on worker input and participation in decision making and problem identification. Kirst-Ashman & Hull (2009) describe several foundational concepts of TQM:

- Clients are viewed as customers; services are focused on clients' needs and their perceptions of the effectiveness of service provision.
- Feedback from clients is actively sought and used as a means of improving services.
- Quality improvement is a primary organizational goal.
- Employees who directly serve clients are granted broad powers of decision making.
- Teams of employees are given primary responsibility for service provision; cooperative (vs. competitive) relationships among team members are supported and emphasized.
- An organizational culture that values teamwork, cooperation, flexibility, and autonomy as the path to excellence is nurtured.
- Top management displays a strong commitment to the TQM approach.

The Learning Organization This type of organization represents a related trend designed to empower workers and increase the organization's ability to adapt to changing demands. Here, staff at all levels are empowered to identify and resolve problems. This enables the organization to continuously develop and grow and meet its goals more effectively (Aldag & Kuzuhara, 2005; Daft, 2008). The learning organization is characterized by several foundational concepts (Kirst-Ashman & Hull, 2009):

1. Power is distributed among all staff instead of being concentrated at the top.
2. The organization encourages and supports employees to take risks, be creative, and share knowledge.
3. Greater emphasis is placed on the effectiveness of service provision, as opposed to the process. In other words, service provision is less governed by specific rules and more by outcomes. Client feedback is actively solicited as a means of evaluating services.
4. Multidisciplinary collaboration and teamwork is encouraged and supported; teams are given authority to continuously make improvements as necessary.

Again, this contrasts with more bureaucratic structures that tend to support maintenance of the status quo.

5. Information sharing and open communication across the organization is encouraged as a means of increasing adaptiveness.

Culturally Competent, Antiracist Organizations The notion of antiracism and multicultural competence has it roots in the growing understanding that clients from nondominant social groups are often poorly served or underserved by traditional mental health and other social welfare organizations that are primarily Eurocentric in nature. In his discussion of the need for organizations to adapt to an increasingly diverse workforce and client base, Minors (1996) noted:

> Like other living creatures, organizations use energy to preserve their integrity or university. They treat staff, volunteers and clients who are different in much the same way that biological organisms treat viruses and bacteria. Organisms use their resources to isolate or expel intruders, even when the intruders help them respond to serious threats and, over time, very few organisms survive without adapting to the environment. Similarly, over time, very few organizations are successful without changing in response to internal and external forces. (p. 196)

Multicultural competence has been defined as "an ability to provide services that are perceived as legitimate for problems experienced by culturally diverse persons" (Dana, Behn, & Gonwa, 1992, p. 221) As it applies to organizations, this concept refers to a set of agency practices (including the direct practice paradigms utilized by individual practitioners), policies, formal structures, and staff attitudes and behaviors that enable the system as a whole to work effectively in a diverse cultural context (Kirst-Ashman & Hull 2009) and to provide access, appropriate services, and positive outcomes for all groups served by the agency. Organizations are considered to be culturally competent when they are staffed at all levels by people from diverse backgrounds, provide ongoing training, and ensure a high level of skill in providing culturally competent services, work to promote social justice, and participate in research that contributes to our understanding of how best to serve clients from diverse backgrounds (Corwin, 2006; Diller, 1999).

It is safe to say that social welfare organizations exist on a continuum of functioning, with regard to their competence in this area. Minors (1996) delineates stages in an organization's progression toward becoming culturally competent; these range from *discrimination* (refers to organizations and services that are monocultural and racist; these support the maintenance of power by traditionally dominant social groups); *nondiscrimination* (refers to organizations that are moving toward the development of a more inclusive structure, although on a superficial level, they recognize differences, they are committed to a universalist view that minimizes the significance of cultural differences at a deeper level); and *antidiscrimination* (these recognize and seek to change the traditional power differentials among social groups; they actively work to eliminate all forms of oppression at the individual, organizational, and societal levels).

Although there are varying models that describe pathways that lead to organizational multicultural competence (or antiracism), they all emphasize a developmental process and common goals (Golembiewski, 1995; Minors, 1996; Sue et al.,

1998; Valverde, 1998). Corwin (2006) suggests that if an organization is to make the changes necessary to achieve a desirable level of cultural proficiency, it is essential that there be a strong commitment to this goal by its top leadership. She has identified several other critical components of an overall strategy to achieve organizational cultural competence. These include the development of a written mission statement of long-term goals and specific plans for achieving them, as well as the designation of a group that is empowered to analyze the agency's structure, culture, policies, procedures and so forth and to translate its findings into the development of appropriate programs and practices. This culturally based needs assessment must include recommendations for how to recruit and retain diverse staff at all levels and how to institutionalize programs that support diversity training and culturally appropriate services. If the effort is to be successful, the organization must recognize and utilize the assets and resources of the community it serves, encourage a high level of community involvement in all levels of assessment and change, and institute mechanisms to maintain that collaboration over the long term (Adams & Krauth, 1995; Delgado, 1998; Green, 1999; Sue et al., 1998). Practice Example 7.1 illustrates an incremental change initiated by one social worker and how this contributed to client well-being. Practice Example 7.5 illustrates the development of a culturally competent, community-based clinical program.

PRACTICE EXAMPLE 7.1

A Step in the Direction of Multicultural Competence

A social work intern, placed at a mental health clinic whose mission statement includes a commitment to "creating an environment in which individuals of color experienced themselves as an integrated and valued part of the community," noticed that the artwork displayed on the clinic walls portrayed middle-class, Eurocentric themes that did not reflect the cultural identity of the agency's client population. Noting that the clinic had already made great strides toward its goal of multicultural competence and being aware of the powerful impact of one's physical environment, she proposed that the agency begin to display more racially and ethnically inclusive artwork as a means of helping clients "feel more mirrored, valued, and embedded in their social world."

In developing her proposal, she recalled a recent experience with a client whose family had moved to the mainland U.S. from Puerto Rico:

"The room that I was using for the session was a room that is normally inhabited by someone who has an interest in Puerto Rico. This was made obvious through the objects placed throughout the room. Most significant was a large detailed map of Puerto Rico. I was in the midst of doing the diagnostic with this client. He was tired, and I was having some difficulty in involving him in the therapeutic process of the diagnostic. Suddenly, he started questioning—whose room we were in, why this person had a map of Puerto Rico, etc. Then the client began to use the map to tell his story—where he grew up, what was significant about the different locations on the map, what it is like for him when he goes back to visit, and more. There are potentially connecting, enriching, and validating clinical experiences that are available through having inclusive artwork. It can offer a variety of important opportunities: a way for the client to be the "expert" in the context of the relational power differential between therapist and client; it can also bring therapeutic content right into the room."

Organizational and Community Connections to the Wider Environment

As is the case with all social systems, communities and organizations are embedded in larger, more complex systems "as part of an ecology of shifting resources and constraints" (Mulroy, 2004, p. 78). It is important, therefore, to understand the external issues that are critical to both organizations and communities, assess the interrelationships of these issues and how they affect a particular agency's mission, goals, resources, and operations and a community's overall competence. These macro influences include such factors as the market economy, globalization, patterns of immigration, and institutional arrangements such as international real estate investment, financial lending decisions, national or regional labor market demands, broad policies on such social issues as immigration and health care, changing federal priorities, and so forth (Mulroy, 2004). Chapter 1, Practice Example 1.1, illustrates the impact of macro factors (that is, changes in federal policy) on the functioning of a single organization.

Structural Linkages in Organizations and Communities

Roland Warren's (1978) work on horizontal and vertical linkages clarifies the need for communities to strengthen both internal and external relationship networks. *Horizontal* linkages refer to relationships with systems within the community; *vertical* linkages refer to relationships and interactions between the community and the outside world. The nature of the linkages between the community and its various organizational subsystems is an important area to assess when engaging in community practice—that is, does this organization have a vertical or horizontal connection to this community? Horizontally linked organizations exist on the same level as the community; their center of authority and decision making are at the community level. Here, the health and well-being of the community are important to the functioning of the organization (and vice versa). The locus of decision-making authority in vertically linked organizations is located above the community level—it may be centered at the regional, state, federal, national, and even international levels (Hardcastle & Powers, 2004). Therefore, a particular community's health and well-being have little significance to the functioning of the vertically linked organization, whose domain includes many different communities; because decision making is more removed from the individual, the decisions that the organization makes may not necessarily benefit (and, in fact, may harm) members of any one community or another.

If a community's organizational structure is primarily vertical, it will be characterized by greater fragmentation of social relationships, few definable geographic and social boundaries for community functions, more explicit social contracts, and a higher degree of interaction among entities that are two or three levels removed from one another (Hardcastle & Powers, 2004).

An *Organization in Environment* Perspective

Mulroy (2004) presents an "*organization in environment*" approach that "seeks to capture the dynamic nature of complex events and relationships external to an organization's boundaries as they continuously emerge, intertwine and evolve" (p. 93). She emphasizes the importance of understanding how macro factors directly affect people's lives and views a commitment to social justice as the critical frame for understanding this influence. This model rests on an ecosystemic view of the social environment in which communities and organizations are viewed as parts of larger systems, or spheres of influence, "that helped to create institutional barriers of the past" (p. 77). In addition, it views organizations as dynamic forces that have the ability to reverse the inequities built into larger societal systems and, in doing so, to strengthen the communities within which they reside. Figure 7.1 depicts this model, illustrating how, as communities and organizations are affected by larger social forces (particularly those driven by globalization and associated public policies), they can work to find solutions "to help break down or change oppressive institutional barriers in the larger society" (Mulroy, 2004, p. 81).

FIGURE 7.1

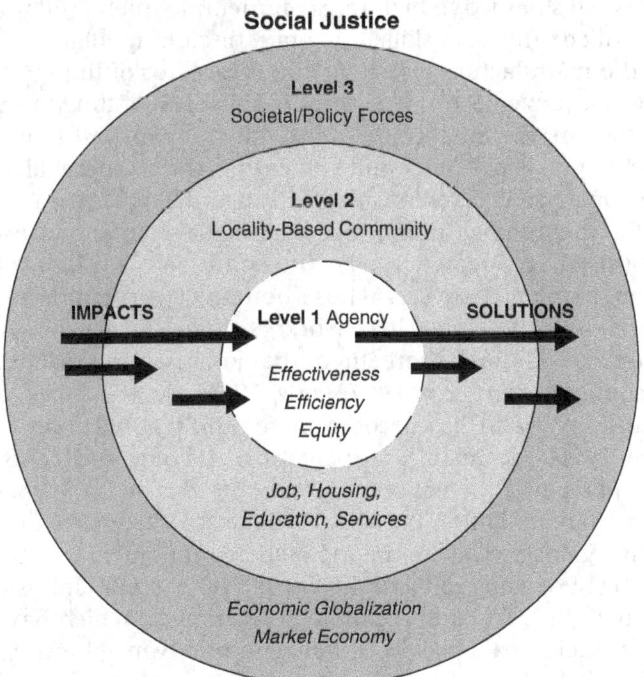

Source: Mulroy, E. (2004). Theoretical perspectives in the social environment to guide management and community practice: An organization in environment approach. *Administration in Social Work, 28*(1), 77–96.

The Changing Macro Context for Community Life

Over the past 50 years, profound changes in U.S. society have significantly affected community life. To understand the postmodern community as a context for social work practice, one must first recognize the broad social changes that have occurred in the environment in which these communities are embedded. We will review, in the following sections, some of the most significant of these changes. In later sections, we examine the impact of these changes on community life and the implications of these changes for community-based social work practice.

Structural Changes in the Economy

The U.S. economy has undergone a profound restructuring, shifting its emphasis away from manufacturing and farming and toward personal, professional, and entertainment services, information, technology, and e-business. Many trends have converged to create, especially since the 1990s, a growing economic inequality among the U.S. population. The loss of many well-paying manufacturing jobs has been accompanied by a rise in the number lower-paying service industry jobs. This has led to high rates of unemployment and underemployment among unskilled and semiskilled people (including older people who once worked in the manufacturing sector), and this sector of the economy is expected to remain weak (Levy, 1995). U.S. corporations, responding to shrinking markets and lower cost international competition, have downsized to increase efficiency, reducing managerial positions and increasing the vulnerability of white-collar workers to job loss. In addition, the contingent workforce is expanding; from 1988 to 1992, the number of new jobs classified as temporary rose approximately 30 percent (Reskin & Padavic, 1994). The contingent workforce includes temporary workers, part-time workers whose hours vary according to employer need, and independent contractors. These workers generally lack job security and fringe benefits; there is widespread agreement that job insecurity will remain an issue in this new economy (Bernstein, 1997; Levy, 1995).

The nation's wealth has become increasingly concentrated at the top. For example, in 1999, the middle 60 percent of income recipients in U.S. society owned 48.5 percent of the nation's wealth; this was down 5.1 percent from 1980 (U.S. Census Bureau, 2001). Between 1983 and 1998, approximately 88 percent of real income gains accrued to the top 20 percent of income recipients, with only about 12 percent of gains going to the bottom 80 percent (Johnston, 2003). Some of this inequality is related to technological changes, which have created a division between highly paid positions that require advanced technological skill and lower-paid positions, which have been *deskilled* through advances in technology. Economic inequality has been exacerbated by the trend, over the last 30 years, toward more regressive tax policies at both the federal and state levels, whereby wealthy citizens pay proportionally less in taxes than they did previously.

Globalization

The past two decades have witnessed a rapid increase in economic globalization worldwide. With globalization, the social power of capital and corporations increases, with a simultaneous decrease in the social power of labor and nation-states (Gray, 1998; Mishra, 1999). For example, the expectation for social responsibility on the part of transnational corporations has been reduced, as government regulations have been significantly weakened. Pressure for lower taxes on the very wealthy and on corporations and for low-wage labor increases with globalization (Gray, 1998; Johnston, 2002a, 2002b).

Demographic Changes

Economic restructuring has led to a population shift in the United States away from the industrial Northeast and Midwest, toward the Sunbelt of the south and the Southwest (for example, to California, Florida, and Texas). Most of the U.S. population now lives in 39 metropolitan statistical areas of one million people or more, as opposed to smaller cities and rural communities (U.S. Census Bureau, 2001). Most of the most recent growth of these metropolitan statistical areas has occurred in the regions beyond the traditional suburbs. These enlarging metropolitan statistical areas generally have no common, regional government that is responsible for coordinating activities among the many smaller villages, towns, and cities that are included in their geographic territory. This seems to have led to a situation in which communities are increasingly segregated by social class and, often, by race and ethnicity (Scott, 2002), and this situation is thought to inhibit upward social mobility (Massey, 1994). At the same time, the United States is becoming increasingly diverse, both ethnically and socially. Projections indicate that there will be no majority ethnic population in this country by the year 2060.

Technological Changes

The technological advances that have revolutionized modern information, and communication access and processing have narrowed the distances among people, organizations, and communities (Hardcastle & Powers, 2004). People are increasingly relying on electronic linkages to satisfy the need for social and emotional support and to reduce the sense of isolation (Uncapher, 1999).

Poverty

Even before the severe economic downturn in 2008, American working families were losing ground economically; median family incomes showed declines several times since the turn of the new century. Poverty, of course, continues to worsen as the economy shrinks and unemployment rates and food and fuel costs rise. The working poor have been hardest hit by the current crisis, as working full time in the current economy does not guarantee that one will avoid living in poverty. For example, a full-time worker who is paid the minimum wage will earn less than $15,000 a year (www.itwd.rutgers.edu/PDF/Brief-OnlineLearningProgram.pdf).

Poverty cuts across all ethnic groups; however, although most poor people in the United States are white, black and Hispanic households are proportionally overrepresented among the poor. For example, according to the Children's Defense Fund's State of America's Children Report (2008), the poverty rates for African-American children are more than three times those for white children. The demographics of poverty tend to break down along racial and ethnic lines—the majority of poor, non-Hispanic white people live in either rural areas or in metropolitan statistical areas, while poor black families tend to reside in central cities (Frey, 1990).

Since the 1960s, women and children have come to represent an increasing proportion of the poor in the United States. The poverty rate for children below age 6, rose from 15.3% in 1969 to 22.7% 1996 and is currently increasing (Children's Defense Fund, 2002). According to census data collated by the National Women's Law Center in Washington, D.C., about 15 million American women were living in poverty in 2006. Poverty rates are highest for women of color, single mothers, and older women. Poverty rates for African-American and Latina women are about twice as high as those for white women. Approximately one in five elderly women and one in three single mothers (www.womensenews.org) are living in poverty. Twenty one percent of working single mothers are poor; this is double the percentage for families headed by single fathers and four times that of families with children headed by a married couple (U.S. Department of Labor, 2002).

Changes in the Social Welfare System

As the United States became increasingly industrialized in the 19th century, it gradually became clear that its existing social institutions (for example, the family, religious organizations, economic and political systems) were inadequate to meet the dependency needs of all its citizens in a market-based economy. The social welfare system (and the profession of social work) developed in an attempt to meet those needs, first, through private service organizations, and later, with social welfare programs run by local governments as well. The social welfare system grew considerably at the time of the Great Depression when the federal government began to assume responsibility for various aspects of social welfare (for example, the Social Security program). A second period of growth occurred in the 1960s with the federal government's War on Poverty, and by 1988, the combined social welfare expenditures by the government at the local, state, and federal levels totaled approximately $85 billion a year—an increase of over $60 billion a year since 1950 (Popple & Leighninger, 1993). Over the past quarter century, there has been an effort to reduce the amount of government spending in this area, and this effort has excited a great deal of controversy over the very nature of the social welfare system:

> . . . since the 1980s we have seen federal, state and local human services policies move toward reduction, competition, divestiture and privatization of public programs. These changes are accompanied by the rhetoric, if not always the reality, of returning power, responsibility and control to state and local governments and the private sector for welfare and social services and an increase in personal and family responsibility. The federal government's role and responsibilities for welfare and human services probably are undergoing their greatest transformation since the New Deal of the 1930's. (Hardcastle & Powers, 2004, p. 8)

Historically, there have been two dominant and competing conceptions of social welfare: residual and institutional perspectives (Wilensky & Lebeaux, 1965). Essentially, the *residual* approach views the social welfare system as a backup system or safety net that provides temporary, emergency aid to dependent people when other social institutions (for example, the family, the economic system, and religious organizations) are unable to do so. The *institutional* approach, on the other hand, views the social welfare system as a social institution designed to provide ongoing preventative aid to citizens before other social institutions fail to do so. In this view, families and religious and economic institutions are inadequate to deal with the complex issues presented by a fragmented, rapidly changing modern world. Our current social welfare system reflects both perspectives, although each has predominated to one extent or another at different times in our history. Although the residual perspective is older, the expansion of the social welfare system in this country from the Great Depression through the 1960s, reflected an institutional approach (for example, the Social Security and Medicare programs). By the 1980s, federal policies toward social welfare began to reflect a residual perspective (for example, welfare reform, proposed changes to the Social Security system), as services were, and continue to be scaled back.

Privatization and commercialization have become major trends in social welfare. Underlying these trends is the assumption that the allocation and provision of social services are best determined by economic market forces (Gibelman & Demone, 1998; Moe, 1987; Morgan, 1995; Salamon, 1997); This market-oriented approach has increased competition for public funds within the human service field. Initially, competition for public funds was limited to the not-for-profit sector, as agencies of varying sizes competed with each other for government contracts (in an era of reduced government spending for social services). Gradually, the not-for-profit agencies began to face competition from the private, for-profit sector as well (Mulroy, 2004).

The trend toward privatization has been particularly difficult for small, community-based nonprofits, especially those with a social justice mission (Fabricant & Fisher, 2002). Facing mounting pressure to prove short-term results, and finding it difficult to compete economically with large corporations, many of these agencies have had to limit themselves to providing services to only the neediest clients (Gibelman & Demone, 2002).

Large, well-resourced private and commercial enterprises (often without ties to local communities) have greatly benefited from the trend toward privatization. These agencies have been increasingly involved in providing educational, health care, and human services, often in the form of packages of services purchased by government agencies (for example, welfare-to-work job training programs, Medicaid billing, management information systems, as well as case management and direct services to clients; Frumkin & Andre-Clark, 2000). Currently, approximately one-third of the social services market is now in the hands of the profit sector, and this trend is projected to continue (Hardcastle & Powers, 2004).

Privatized, for-profit human service organizations have been criticized as being unresponsive to the needs of the poor (who are often unable to pay for services) and to social work's commitment to social reform (Fisher & Karger, 1997). Fisher and Karger suggest that part of the reason professional social workers have been flocking to private practice in recent years has to do with workplace problems in social agencies, such as restricted professional autonomy, rigid schedules, and shrinking resources, which lead to longer work hours, larger, more difficult caseloads, and restrictions on practice that limit satisfaction for both the professional and the client. They urge the adoption of more progressive organizational management frameworks for social welfare organizations as a partial remedy for the trend toward privatization They call for more participatory management frameworks (as described earlier in this chapter), large-scale professional unionization, worker-owned cooperatives, and employee-owned organizations.

The Changing Face of Communities in the Postmodern Era

It has been suggested that the significance of the societal changes described earlier is that as we let go of our traditional notions of community, we find that new forms of community are developing and that we are participating differently in community life (Berger, 1998; Kirchhoff, 1999; Ladd, 1999; Oldenburg, 1999; Wellman, 1999). Wellman proposed that people in modern Western societies now live in what he terms "loosely coupled" communities (1999). No longer bound by geographic location, people are forming more narrow and specialized ties to a variety of diverse social networks instead of committing to one broadly supportive, tightly knit community. This form of association is certainly supported by electronic linkages in cyberspace communities—here, members perform many of the same functions as do informal networks in face-to-face communities (Wellman & Gulia, 1999).

In general, as people become more and more mobile (and able to reduce their isolation through cyberspace), their relationships to their neighborhoods and towns change. Viswanath and colleagues (2000), in a study of local community ties using length of stay as a variable, found four types of neighborhood residents. They define *natives* as those who have lived in the community for over 5 years and who are unlikely to move away. *Relocators* have also lived in the neighborhood for over 5 years, but these residents are likely to eventually move somewhere else. *Settlers* have lived in the neighborhood for less than 5 years but plan to stay, whereas *drifters* (who have also resided in the neighborhood for less than 5 years) are very likely to move. They note that there is a tendency for conflict to arise among community members who have varying levels of commitment to the community (Viswanath, 2000).

Changes in Community Functions in the Postmodern Era

The traditional community functions described earlier in this chapter have all been significantly influenced by changes in the broader social context (Warren, 1978). The following section reviews some of the most significant changes in these community functions.

Production-Distribution-Consumption As the U.S. and world economies become increasingly globalized, the structure of our communities becomes more and more vertical—that is, organizations that are significant to community functioning are increasingly based outside the community. In other words, facilities that provide direct services to the community may be physically located in the community but may represent one of many such units controlled by a distant, central location. For example, the local pharmacy may be one part of a large chain of stores that are centrally controlled by a physically remote corporate headquarters. Corporate decisions regarding the local store's functioning (for example, store hours, delivery policies) may have little to do with community needs. Similarly, in a city composed of many small diverse communities, the school system may be controlled by a central board that regulates curriculum for all local schools. As a result of the centralized decision-making process, aspects of the curriculum may conflict with a specific community's ethnically and/or religiously based system of values and norms. If unrecognized, such conflict may compromise the school's ability to teach, student performance, and even school funding.

Socialization In the past, socialization was considered to be the responsibility of the family, religious institutions, informal peer groups, and to some extent, the educational system. Although these social institutions do continue to perform this function, other institutions, such as the national and global media and the Internet, are becoming more influential, as children spend more time on the Web, watching television, and consuming other forms of media. In effect, the local community and its structures are exerting less control over socialization as larger, more remote, vertical (and often proprietary) national and global structures assume more control. The values that are imparted by these institutions are not necessarily those of the community—because a shared value system strengthens community members' internal control over their behavior, the weakening of these ties tends to necessitate the need for the imposition of stronger external controls to regulate members' behavior (Hardcastle & Powers, 2004).

Social Control As noted, as community cohesion is undermined by the weakening of a shared community value system and by a move toward increasingly vertical structure, it becomes more and more necessary to rely on external sources of control to maintain social order. As communities become more differentiated and heterogeneous, the formal rule of law and legal contract are replacing the more traditional and informal methods of maintaining order through socialization processes: "External social controls represent a failure of socialization" (Hardcastle & Powers, 2004, p. 105).

Social Participation This community function is essential if a community is to be healthy and competent to meet its multiple needs—in other words, the different parts of the community must collaborate, share power, and share decision-making and problem-solving responsibilities as they work together to address community issues and needs. Community competence is enhanced when there is community-wide participation in decision making. In Hardcastle and Powers's words:

> Civic participation has become more remote and fragmented with industrial society's separation of work from home, extension of the community's physical geographic boundaries and movement to a contract society. Social interaction and participation is more complex and distant, intricate, socially isolating, and detached. Tertiary social

> structures of larger and more impersonal communities have replaced direct integrating and bonding social interactions. Town meetings, informal face-to-face discussions, and debates as consensus-building modes of political interacting have been replaced by political parties, extensive media political advertising, political action committees (PACS), public opinion polls, impersonal media talk shows, and the virtual reality and chat rooms of the Internet. These allow politicians to bypass the mediating structures of associations, include grassroots political parties, and appeal directly to the voters. The mass-marketing approach reduces the mediating function, reciprocity, and community accountability mechanisms. Participation in these more impersonal and technological modes may be virtual but contribute little to the social investments, social capital, and reciprocity necessary for a community's social cohesion (2004, p. 106)

Mutuality Informal networks of friends, neighbors, and family still represent the first line of support for people when they are in need. However, as communities have become more complex, people are increasingly relying on more formal organizations to assume this function. For example, as the number of dual-earner families increases, more and more young children are cared for in day-care centers and other forms of early childhood education and care. Elderly people who need assistance to live independently are increasingly relying on formal (often, for-profit) health and welfare agencies to provide in-home assistance or other specialized *assisted living* arrangements. The general decline in shared identity and community cohesion has a particularly significant impact on the mutuality function. Absent a sense of identification among people, provisions for mutual support increasingly depend less on community cohesion and more on vertical structures and social control measures such as state and federal taxation. Hardcastle and Powers (2004) emphasize the importance of social participation, especially on the part of the poor, in fostering social solidarity and social networks that serve to promote mutuality and reciprocity in community functioning.

Community Macropractice: Skills and Strategies

Although micropractice will remain an important aspect of social work practice, community practitioners are in increasing demand. The number of neighborhood associations in the United States and worldwide have been increasing in the last 20 years, with community practitioners working to effect change, identify community assets, and link groups to work together for common purposes (Hardcastle & Powers, 2004).

Community practice on the macrolevel is generally thought to include community organization and development, social planning, and social action. Hardcastle and Powers define community organization and development as "the practice of helping a community or part of a community such as a neighborhood or a group of people with a common interest to be a more effective, efficient and supportive social environment for nurturing people and their social relationships" (2004, p. 3). They define social planning as "the development and coordination of community agencies and services to meet community functions and responsibilities and to provide for its members" (p. 4). They define social action as the "development, redistribution, and control of community statuses and resources, including social power and the alteration of community relations and behavior patterns to promote the development or redistribution of community resources" (p. 4).

Tropman, Erlich, and Rothman (2001) link specific community practice strategies and tactics to specific types of community problems. For example, if the practitioner's assessment indicates that *community cohesion* is inadequate, he or she would use a community development strategy designed to engage people and to encourage involvement and participation around a community-based task. The goal of such a strategy would be to increase a sense of connectedness among members as they work; here, the task itself is much less relevant than the process of becoming "a community in creation" (2001, p. 4). If community assessment indicates a reasonably good sense of community cohesion, the practitioner needs to assess *community capability. Capability,* in this context, refers to the community members' ability to do things together as a community. The practitioner would utilize a social action strategy designed to help members mobilize and act to accomplish a common goal. Here, the accomplishment of the task is the primary goal, although the process of learning to mobilize and act is also important. As a community becomes more capable, the practitioner must begin to consider the issue of *community competence.* Competence refers to not just to the community's ability to act, but further, its ability to act *effectively* on its own behalf. This requires a strategy of social planning—in Tropman, Erlich, and Rothman's words: "Planning is associated with competence, because planning works ahead of problems in a proactive way, rather than responding to problems in a reactive way" (2001, p. 4). At this point in the community intervention, the accomplishment of the task is paramount, with the strengths gained from the process considered a secondary gain.

Community Building

Hardcastle and Powers define community building as "engaging a community to improve itself" (2004, p. 122). The idea of community building requires an approach that recognizes the interconnections among individuals, families, organizations, and communities, as discussed earlier, and the need to link micro- and macropractice strategies. Support for families and children, a commitment to racial equity, and respect for cultural diversity, a strength-based perspective, and an acknowledgment of the need to forge broad partnerships within the community are critical elements for successful community based practice (Walsh, 1997). The strengths-based perspective, so central to this approach, guides the practitioner to help community members identify priorities, community assets, and opportunities and to mobilize them to use these to facilitate collective change (Chaskin, Brown, Venkatesh, & Vidal, 2001; Checkoway, 1997).

This approach is particularly helpful when dealing with impoverished or otherwise disadvantaged communities, in that it empowers members to determine and promote their own interests (Turner, 1998). As has been discussed, in the postmodern era, communities face the challenge of reversing patterns of oppression and unequal power distribution in traditional communities (Schriver, 2004). Practice Example 7.2 illustrates the concept of community building strategies to empower the GLBT population, a marginalized group, to effect positive social change.

PRACTICE EXAMPLE 7.2

Community Building for Lesbian, Gay, Bisexual, Transsexual, and Transgender Youth

Supporting Our Youth (SOY) is a grassroots program that builds community for lesbian, gay, bisexual, transsexual, and transgender youth in Toronto. The program provides a variety of arts, cultural, recreational, and employment training activities, a mentoring program, and a housing program. For example, Fruit Loopz is a popular cabaret that showcases the creative talents of queer and trans youth; The Rainbow Book Club and Pink Ink Literary Café provides young people with opportunities to explore their sexual and gender identity through literature and poetry. The Bill 7 Award provides scholarships to students who have been rejected by their families because of their sexual orientation or gender identity. SOY also sponsors summer programs in theater and visual arts that provide employment training and skill building. The Mentoring and Housing Program tailors traditional mentoring models to fit the special needs of queer and trans youth whose ties to their families are often tenuous or completely severed. For example, homeless youths who are matched with a mentor may be helped to access permanent subsidized, nonprofit housing or may, in other cases be placed in an adult mentor's home. A supper club/drop in provides street-involved youth with contact with adults who share similar sexual and gender identities. The program was started in 1998, and its development illustrates a broad range of community-building tactics and strategies. These will be discussed later in this section, but first, it is important to understand the societal and community contexts for lesbian, gay, bisexual, transsexual, transgender, and queer people in Canada during the time period in which the program evolved.

Societal Context

By the end of the twentieth century, lesbians and gay men had achieved gains in legal protection and rights that were unprecedented in Canadian history. Equal rights in housing, employment were solidly protected in the human rights code of the federal government and of most provinces. Lesbian and gay relationships were granted most of the same rights and responsibilities as common-law couples. Large and visible gay and lesbian communities existed in most large cities, and smaller cities and rural towns were increasingly home to lesbian and gay groups and organizations. At the same time, problems remained. Outside of urban areas, many gay men and lesbians remained closeted, schools continued to be unsafe environments for queer youth, and many religious groups and political parties remained opposed to equality of rights for lesbians and gay men; transgendered and transsexual people were (and are) denied protections and rights based on gender identity.

As the gay and lesbian community became more visible, young people began to recognize their struggle with sexual orientation and gender identity at younger and younger ages. The difficulty of dealing with social stigma, while also dealing with the difficult developmental issues of adolescence, is compounded by the adolescent's continued financial and emotional dependence on their biological families. As ties with the biological family become strained or are totally severed, due to homophobia, many young people migrate to large urban centers in search of acceptance. Unfortunately, because of the high cost of living and lack of affordable housing in these urban centers, many end up either living on the street, or otherwise marginalized.

Community Context

Although Toronto's mainstream social welfare system already had a range of services for marginalized and street-involved young people, the specific issues and needs of queer and trans youth were generally not addressed by those programs (for example, the relationship between sexual orientation/gender identity and an individual's substance abuse or the dangers facing a queer or trans person living in a youth shelter due to homophobia and associated violence. Although Toronto had a large, visible gay and lesbian community, most of the social and recreational activities were adult-oriented, making it difficult for youth to find their place there.

In 1991, a group of (primarily gay and lesbian) health care and social service workers in Toronto formed the Coalition for Services for Lesbian and Gay Youth to advocate for the development of specialized services for gay and lesbian youth, within the existing health and social welfare system. Despite the lack of a formal structure and a clear mandate, within a few years, that group's efforts toward raising community consciousness had resulted in a number of service initiatives in Toronto. For example, by the mid-1990's, the community had established a gay-positive youth substance abuse program, a transitional school program for young people facing discrimination in their regular schools, and several professionally facilitated coming-out groups. In addition, mainstream agencies began offering specialized training to help staff deal more effectively with these young people, and openly gay and lesbian counselors were increasingly available. However, just as awareness was growing about the need for services for lesbian, gay and bisexual youth, the neo-conservative Ontario government began to dramatically reduce overall spending for health-care, social services, public housing, education and other support programs. As efforts to resist these cutbacks met with little success, the Coalition looked for ways to develop services that did not rely on government support.

Community Building Initiative

Needs Assessment and Feasibility Study

The idea for SOY emerged in 1997 when the Coalition consulted with a broad spectrum of the community in an effort to identify the needs of gay, lesbian, and bisexual young people and to assess the level of support the community might provide. The initial needs assessment and feasibility study indicated wide support for a grassroots community effort that focused on recreational, cultural, and arts activities, employment and skill-building activities, and access to safe, affordable housing and positive adult mentors. It also identified many potential challenges, including competition for scarce resources (the AIDS crisis had depleted the adult gay community of much of its human, financial, and social capital), difficulties involved with motivating gay and lesbian adults to participate and engage with young people (a fairly comfortable adult gay community tended to avoid contact with young people because of the stereotype that depicted them as predatory pedophiles), and the difficult task of reaching the most marginalized groups in the target population (youth of color, trans youth, and street-involved youth) . SOY's successful development was based on principles of community building such as the encouragement of grassroots participation, an asset-based approach that encouraged grassroots participation, nurtured diverse skills, encouraged the formation of broad partnerships and coalitions, and created a progressive organizational structure with a participatory management style.

Identifying and Mobilizing Community Assets to encourage grassroots participation and to form broad-based partnerships and coalitions

Using the results of the needs assessment and feasibility study, the Coalition applied for and received, operating funds from the Ontario Trillium Foundation. It began operating in 1998 under the sponsorship of the Central Toronto Youth Services (CTYS)—a child mental health center located within the gay and lesbian community. CTYS provided SOY with free office space, administrative support, and nonprofit status (enabling the program to access grant money and tax-deductible donations). From the beginning, SOY placed a high value on outreach and promotional activities designed to reach diverse groups—among other things, they developed a Web site, brochures and a newsletter, distributed flyers and posters, used paid advertising. Their visibility enabled them to access increasing amounts of fiscal, human, and social capital—they have been able to

(Continued)

recruit volunteers and to access funds and support from a variety of community organizations and businesses, foundations, and corporate donors. With the active participation of adult and youth volunteers in every aspect of organizational functioning (volunteers initiate, develop, implement, and evaluate program initiatives with support from paid staff), SOY has been able to maintain and nurture deep roots in the gay and trans communities of Toronto.

Asset Building and Progressive Management

The program's organizational structure is fairly informal—it is overseen by a Community Advisory Board consisting of volunteers who lend their expertise and advice, but who have no formal authority. A small group of paid staff are ultimately responsible for overall program operation and fund raising, however, the bulk of their work revolves around recruiting volunteers and supporting volunteer efforts at developing and implementing program initiatives. Volunteers are encouraged to participate in every aspect of organizational functioning—the program has a strong commitment to helping the volunteers expand their expertise by giving them broad responsibilities and autonomy, along with guidance and support. The program's flexibility and lack of commitment to any particular form of activity has allowed it to undertake a broad diversity of initiatives and thus to remain responsive to the needs of the community—programs targeted for specific ethnic and racial groups, or groups with special interests (such as environmentalism) have come to fruition through strong community and volunteer support.

The community building principles upon which SOY was founded, have broad applicability for social workers involved in community based practice. In Lepishak's words:

> The basic principles of SOY, however, are transferable to other queer and trans communities, as well as to other groups that are marginalized or oppressed. They includes shared community understanding of needs; significant and diverse community involvement in visioning and direction setting; ownership by those involved in carrying out the work; as much attention to process as to outcome; and sufficient financial and other resources to undertake the work. (Lepishak, 2004, p. 97)

Source: B. Lepishak, 2004, "Building Community for Toronto's Lesbian, Gay, Bisexual, Transsexual, and Transgender Youth," *Journal of Gay and Lesbian Social Services* 16(3/4), pp. 81–97.

Assets and Capital: Economic, Social, Cultural and Human Resources for Community Building The assessment, use, and development of community assets is fundamental to the success of all community-building efforts. The term *assets* is closely related to the term *capital,* and we will use these interchangeably to refer to those resources or strengths that are available to empower the community. Assets (or capital) may refer to such tangible resources as money, housing, and small business (economic capital), or to more intangible social and spiritual strengths such as the potential for political influence and relationship building; the norms and networks of civic engagement that support community participation; and the practical knowledge, skills, and talents possessed by members of the community (human, social, and cultural capital). Cultural assets may be neglected by social workers who may have limited understanding of cultural processes that differ from those of their own cultural background. However, these may be rich sources of support for community-building enterprises, and it is advisable for practitioners to extend their efforts toward identifying these resources. For example, Delgado (1997, 1998) stresses the potential benefit of identifying assets that represent cultural institutions outside the realm of social welfare and governmental systems. He describes how nontraditional assets such as herbal shops, laundromats, and beauty parlors may become sources of active leadership and participation in community-building efforts. In many cultures, religious institutions serve as support systems for community members when they are in need. For example, Garrison (1978) found that ministries of small Pentecostal churches were sources of a wide range of support services (from providing emergency financial aid to rehabilitating drug addicts) for Puerto Rican women in New York City. The African-American Church has been a center of social cohesion and social control in black communities since the time of slavery (Germain, 1991). The past and future role of the African-American Church is discussed in more detail later in this chapter (see Practice Example 7.5).

Hardcastle and Powers (2004) discuss several ways that assets may play a role in community practice. *Asset building* refers to the development of such tangible assets as housing, small businesses, and financial investments. For example, Habitat for Humanity is a not-for-profit organization that uses local organizations to coordinate the efforts of volunteers who help families build their own homes and homes for others. Each family provides a designated number of hours of labor toward the building of their home, in exchange for a no-interest mortgage. Other asset-building enterprises work to encourage financial independence for community members through support for small business development and other forms of tangible wealth creation such as targeted training and education programs and matched savings accounts for designated purposes, such as home buying or college savings. *Asset claiming* is another community-building strategy that focuses on helping people to identify and access resources to which they are entitled, such as tax credits and other sources of money. It also refers to campaigns that promote social and economic justice, such as the living wage movement. Here, coalitions of progressive organizations seek to help the working poor by pressuring for local ordinances and legislation to raise the pay of low-wage workers. *Asset identifying and mobilizing* refers to the identification, nurturing, and use of underused social capital in communities. In other words, the community builds on those tangible and intangible assets that already exist in its midst (for example, voluntary associations, physical spaces, individual talents and skills, indigenous leaders, and small businesses). In fact, the very act of identifying resources sometimes seems to motivate community members to work together for change (Onyx & Bullen, 2000).

Building Interorganizational Connections in Community Practice

Interorganizational Relationships A great deal of community macro practice has to do with creating and maintaining relationships among various community groups and organizations. Interorganizational theory is based on the idea that all organizations are subunits of larger networks of organizations and community groups, and that the relationships among these subunits are crucial to each one's ability to survive and thrive (Hardcastle & Powers, 2004). Within these networks, each organization establishes a *domain*—that is, a "territory" based on its mission and goals. An organization's domain may include any combination of client population, problem area, source of resources, catchment area, type of treatment, and so forth. Although there may be some overlap among certain aspects of the domains of different organizations within the network, there must also be a degree of separateness as well for each organization to maintain its identity.

Each organization also has a *task environment;* this refers to the other agencies, groups, and individuals with which an organization must interact to accomplish its goals (Thompson, 1967). The task environment is the part of an organization's environment that most directly affects its functioning, and it includes the following: sources of financial resources, space and labor and equipment, regulatory, accrediting or other authoritative bodies, sources of referrals, clients, providers of services the organization needs to perform successfully, and competitors (Hasenfeld, 1983, pp. 61–63; Thompson, 1967).

Interorganizational Collaboration Recent decades have seen a significant increase in the formation of collaborative ventures among community organizations. As society has become more complex and more vertically integrated, power is increasingly exercised by networks of organizations whose interests are compatible. Through a variety of interorganizational arrangements, these networks have been very successful at mobilizing their resources to influence public policy as a means of expanding and consolidating their power. On a global, national, state, and, increasingly, local level, such collaborations have served to protect elite corporate interests and to ensure their position in the structuring of social power (Hardcastle & Powers, 2004).

On a local level, networks of community-based associations can serve as mediating structures that help the community resist pressure from these larger forces; recent decades have seen a significant increase in the formation of such collaborations as partnerships, alliances, joint ventures, coalitions, and consortia. These have been found to be a very effective way for social workers to proactively address a range of environmental barriers that serve to constrain their ability to accomplish their goals, especially within a social justice context (Mulroy, 2004). As agencies bring their unique perspectives on community issues, they are able to explore their differences and greatly expand their vision of how problems may be addressed and resolved. (Gray, 1989). Alter and Hague (1993) contend that this growing number of interorganizational collaborations actually represents an evolutionary change in the way organizations are structured; they predict that at some point in the future, collaborative networks will represent the new institutional form.

Of course, the process of forming a successful collaborative network of organizations is a complex one that takes time to evolve. Patience for this process seems to be a key factor in developing one's skills in collaboration (Mulroy & Shay, 1998). Alter (2000) describes the early phase of this process as one of identifying potential partners and working to overcome resistance to change. Here, it is important for practitioners to understand the distribution of power within the community, as well as its structure of vertical and horizontal linkages. She describes this as a dynamic and gradually evolving process of formal and informal interactions among individuals and groups.

Building Bridges Between Micro- and Macropractice

There has been a long-standing controversy in the social work literature about whether the community should be seen as the target of, or the context for, social work practice (Fisher & Karger, 1997; Hardcastle, Wenocur, & Powers, 1997; McDonald, Billingham, Conrad, Morgan, & Payton, 1997; Sviridoff & Ryan, 1997). Despite claims to an ecological perspective that recognizes the transactional nature of the person–environment relationship, there has persisted in the social work profession a great divide among practitioners who specialize in direct individual/family practice and those who practice from a more *social* perspective and specialize in enhancing the health of the community.

Although traditionally associated with such macropractice activities as community development and organization, social action, and social planning, there has recently been a rethinking of the meaning of community practice that broadens its scope to include direct practice with individuals and families (Fisher & Karger, 1997; Schriver, 2004; Wells & Gamble, 1995). This school of thought offers a fresh perspective for understanding the interrelationships of the many elements of community life as well as the implications of these interrelationships for individual and collective well-being.

Hardcastle and Powers pointed out that direct service social workers are, in fact, engaging in community practice whenever they refer clients for community services, access community resources, and advocate for policies and programs to improve their clients' lives. They define community practice as "the application of skills to alter the behavioral patterns of community groups, organizations and institutions or people's relationships and interactions with these entities" (2004, p. 3).

They stress the need for the direct service social worker to view him- or herself as a "community social caseworker" (p. 426)—one who formulates a biopsycho*social* (our italics) construction of the client's problem, performs a community assessment with the client, and then uses community skills to network with, and access, community resources as part of an overall intervention strategy (Fisher & Karger, 1997; Hardcastle & Powers, 2004). Direct service practitioners will increasingly need community practice skills, including social action, as they try to work in an increasingly fragmented community with the growth of managed mental health care and with more and more pressure for efficiency, evidence-based practice, and cost cutting (Asch & Abelson, 1993).

Contextualized micropractice emphasizes the importance of helping individuals to understand the *social* reasons for their personal problems, as well as the importance of primary and secondary resources (family, neighbors, and friends), and of the community resources that are available to help them (Fisher & Karger, 1997; Hardcastle & Powers, 2004; Lightburn & Sessions, 2006).

PRACTICE EXAMPLE 7.3

Contextualized Micro-Based Practice for Women with Chronic Mental Illness

A social worker in a community mental health clinic facilitates a small socialization support group for Latina women with chronic mental illness. All the group members are poor, all receive Medicaid or Medicare insurance benefits, and none speak English fluently. At least one member is homeless, several others live in adult homes, and the rest rent single rooms in boarding houses or live with relatives. When mental health services for the poor were threatened by significant funding cuts at the state and local level, the social worker helped to shift the focus of the group from personal issues toward a more public analysis of their concerns. She helped to raise their collective consciousness by educating them about how policy issues and the political arena affected their lives, enabled unregistered members to register to vote, provided information about polling locations, and provided support for 100% member participation in the voting process during that critical period, and thereafter. One or two group members went on to become actively involved in an advocacy group that worked for the advancement of the rights of the mentally ill; these members helped maintain the group's growing social awareness and inclination toward civic participation over time.

Underlying this emphasis is the recognition that at some level "all social work is political" (Hardcastle & Powers, 2004, p. 428), and its ultimate goal must be to empower clients by helping them understand the contextual and structural factors that shape their problems (Fisher & Karger, 1997; Hardcastle & Powers, 2004; Lightburn & Sessions, 2006; Swartz, 1995). In other words, contextualized practice is "grounded in a macro-conceptualization of problems" (Fisher & Karger, 1997, p. 50) that helps clients to see the links between their personal problems and wider societal ills and uses the community and its informal and formal networks to provide social support for change: "For example, the devastation of AIDS results not simply from the virus, but from homophobia, poverty, racism and the lack of adequate health care for all but the most affluent. While it is important to help sick people by connecting them to welfare agencies and health care personnel, it also remains important to seek to combine individual intervention with structural work around AIDS" (Fisher & Karger, 1997, p. 47). Practice Example 7.3 illustrates the concept of contextualized micropractice.

> When there is disorganization, crime, violence, loss of resources, or a break in the ties to the outside and to institutions on the inside, families often reflect that with their own internal struggles (although many families do much better than one would expect under such conditions). But even more pointedly, it is highly unlikely in this complex, rapidly changing world that any family can meet its commitments for the socialization, security, guidance and protection of children without support from the larger community. . . . Environments that are harsh because of poverty, diminished resources, isolated families, inadequate medical care, environmental toxins, neglect, poor nutrition and violence are tough on a little persons' brain. Chronic unrelenting stress can lead to brain cell death and can impede in a very direct way the ability of a small child's (or even older children's) cells to

> regenerate broken or disorganized connections. The miracle is that in such environments some children do make it and do better than anyone could have possibly expected. We know too little about them, but if they do make it, we have to at least consider the possibilities of strong, determined and competent parenting or caretaking; extended family involvement, sources of support, guidance, and respite in the community such as child care or a tutoring program at a church, after school programs, the involvement of a caring, concerned non-familial adult; supportive peer relationships or a sanctuary like a library or park—it is hard to say what it might be. (Lightburn & Sessions, 2006, p. 57)

Community-based clinical practice is grounded in the understanding of this fundamental interdependence between the well-being of individuals and communities—that is, how the health of one profoundly influences the other.

> Community-based practitioners seek an infusion into clinical mental health practice of the values and perspectives of "community"; an integration of interventions that build on the healing powers of the collective, of belonging to a group that contributes to a social identity and provides opportunities for a meaningful, contributing social role. At the same time, community based clinicians recognize that the highly specialized knowledge base developed in "the clinic" is extremely useful in "the community" as well, enhancing the capacity of individuals, families and communities to support the health of all. Community-based clinicians work to render this knowledge usable within neighborhood and outreach settings, often hosted by professionals in related disciplines." (Lightburn & Sessions, 2006, p. 4)

There is mounting evidence suggesting that when mental health services are provided in traditional clinic or office-based settings, they fail to reach a substantial portion of at-risk and vulnerable clients in need of services. This is due, in part, to the fact that clients facing multiple risks may not understand how such services may help them and, in part, to the fact that traditional mental health theories and practices tend to be Eurocentric in nature (see Chapter 1) and are therefore to some degree "culture-bound" in terms of their effectiveness. Clinic-based mental health practitioners have been slow at best to adapt their practices to better engage diverse populations, and financial constraints have restricted their ability to provide the kinds of systemic activities necessary to address the problems many at-risk clients face (Lightburn & Sessions 2006; Sue, 2001). Recognition of the limitations of traditional systems of delivery of mental health services, of the effectiveness of early intervention and prevention services, of the increasing level of psychosocial stressors and severity of symptoms of emotional disturbance in the American populace, the increasing diversity of the U.S. population, and the erosion of a sense of community in American life have all contributed to the growth of community-based clinical practice (Lightburn & Sessions, 2006).

A defining characteristic of community-based clinical practice refers to the relocation of the mental health delivery system out of traditional medical/psychiatric settings into community-based settings where other types of services are delivered. By "integrating mental health principles into the fabric of community life" (Lightburn & Sessions, 2006, p. 29), by providing services in such neighborhood-based settings as early childhood programs, family support centers, school-based mental health programs, and community care programs for the elderly, practitioners can reach clients who are otherwise unlikely to access traditional mental health services for a variety of reasons.

Community-based clinical practice has been particularly successful with client populations who experience multiple risk factors that challenge healthy development (Lightburn & Sessions 2006). For example, poor children are at higher risk for poor mental health outcomes because they are often exposed to cumulative sources of stress such as greater exposure to violence, family turmoil, dangerous neighborhoods, poor-quality schools and day care, as well as threats in the physical environment such as poor air quality, lead paint, and so forth (Evans, 2004, Linver, Fuligni, Hernandez, & Brooks-Gunn, 2004). High rates of emotional health issues and commission of violent acts, including suicide, among American youth have been well documented (Achenback, Domenci, & Rescorla, 2003; Garbarino, 1999; Jenkins & Bell, 1997; McWhirter, McWhirter, McWhirter, & McWhirter, 2004). Furthermore, research suggests that early identification of risk and protective factors with timely targeted intervention can mitigate against the development of violent and other forms of disturbed behavior. Community-based clinical practice lends itself to an ecological understanding of such problems, with an emphasis on multilevel preventive strategies.

In addition, clients facing multiple risks are also often involved with several different service systems (for example, child welfare, educational, and health-care systems), and this may seriously undermine any one practitioner's efforts to help. In such complex situations, practitioners must increasingly rely on strengths-based, culturally competent, and collaborative models of practice if they are to ensure equitable outcomes for all the clients they serve. The provision of mental health services in a community-based setting can allow for collaboration among professionals with clinical knowledge in various disciplines and nonprofessionals with knowledge of the local community. Such collaborations greatly increase understanding of the client's problems and strengths and allow for multilayered, coordinated plans for intervention that support recovery and resilience, as opposed to merely treating symptoms (Carter & McGoldrick, 2005; Lightburn & Sessions, 2006). Practice Examples 7.4 and 7.5 illustrate principles of community-based clinical practice.

PRACTICE EXAMPLE 7.4

Community-Based Clinical Practice with Traumatized Foster Children

In 2003, a long-established urban family services agency created the Foster Care-Mental Health Partnership Project to bridge the gap between foster care agencies and mental health services for children with a history of trauma. Long-standing issues of fragmentation of services between those systems had severely limited access for foster children to appropriate mental health services, especially trauma-focused assessment and treatment. It was felt that this lack of access to necessary services was a major contributing factor to situations in which traumatized children experienced multiple foster care placements and disrupted relationships, extended lengths of stay in care, and poor prognostics.

The Project partnered four mental health agencies with four foster care agencies. Each mental health agency established a licensed clinic on site at its partnering foster care agency. In addition to locating appropriate mental health services to traumatized foster children in a familiar environment, the partnerships serve to improve coordination of mental health and foster care services. Mental health therapists participate in case conferences at the partnering foster care agency; they work closely with foster care case workers to maintain stability within the foster homes, expedite permanency planning, and address problems as they arise. The following case example illustrates many of the benefits of the Project's model of care.

Cristina is a 13-year-old adolescent girl who was placed in foster care with two of her siblings, as a result of a finding of parental neglect. The foster care agency referred Cristina to their partner agency's onsite mental health clinic because she had been sexually abused while in her birth mother's care and was showing symptoms related to posttraumatic stress disorder and intermittent explosive disorder. The onsite mental health clinic prescribed medication to help Cristina control her anger and provided her with weekly trauma-based psychotherapy sessions with a clinical social worker. Cristina's foster mother, Ms. Martinez was juggling many appointments at the foster care agency for Cristina and her siblings, and the onsite location of the mental health clinic made it easier for her to follow through with Cristina's psychotherapy.

Over time, it became clear that the children's visits with their birth mother were becoming increasingly contentious. The birth mother publicly blamed Cristina for the family's turmoil, and her siblings rejected her in support of their mother.

In reaction to the family situation, Cristina's behavior became increasingly oppositional, disrespectful, and angry at the world. Her teachers complained about her irritability and provocative behavior toward her classmates. Her foster mother, Ms. Ramirez, was growing more and more frustrated, and soon, Cristina was only hearing negative criticism from the significant people in her life. In her psychotherapy sessions, the child appeared defeated and unmotivated. The situation deteriorated to the point that Ms. Ramirez officially requested that the foster care agency remove Cristina from her care within 10 days.

Cristina's psychotherapeutic goals went far beyond helping her build skills to cope with her difficult life situation. Her environment provided constant negative triggers that impeded the healing of her wounded spirit; clearly, without significant positive changes in her environment, Cristina's well-being would remain seriously compromised.

The partnerships between the foster care and mental health agencies played a critical role in enabling all involved to collaborate and advocate effectively on Cristina's behalf. The psychotherapist and foster care caseworker worked closely with each other in an attempt to keep Cristina in the foster home by increasing their support of Ms. Ramirez. Together, they facilitated provision of crisis intervention services so that psychotherapeutic work could occur at home, with the child and foster parent together. They worked intensively with Ms. Ramirez to help her understand how the dynamics of Cristina's home and school environments triggered her negative responses, and this enabled behavioral interventions in the home that built on Cristina's strengths and achievements.

In addition, the therapist's observations of Cristina's interactions with her birth mother at agency visits provided the data necessary to support the caseworker's claim that the mother's poor judgment rendered her unable to provide the nurturing and protective support that were essential for Cristina's well-being. The therapist wrote letters to the court, cosigned by Cristina's psychiatrist, advocating for temporary suspension of visits with the birth mother, due to their negative effects on the child's emotional and behavioral functioning. She also recommended continuation of Cristina's psychotherapy and placement in Ms. Ramirez's home, citing the child's need for a stable environment. The therapist's physical presence at the foster care agency enabled her to confer with foster care

(Continued)

agency staff during this written appeal process, such that all were informed and supportive of these recommendations. As a result, the court suspended parental visits for 6 months, in an effort to give Cristina time to stabilize.

Today, Cristina's visits with her birth mother are still suspended. She and Ms. Ramirez share an emotional connection that enables Cristina to seek her foster mother for help when she recognizes elevated anger. Cristina actively seeks praise and reward from Ms. Ramirez through recognition of moments in which she can use her coping skills to keep her anger in control. Schoolteachers are sending home award notices for Cristina's daily displays of helpful, respectful, and compliant behaviors. Cristina is aware of her progress and the hard work she has performed to stabilize herself. During a recent session she asked her therapist, "Do I make you proud?" Her therapist smiled in response.

PRACTICE EXAMPLE 7.5

Community Building and Community Based Clinical Practice in the African-American Community: The Role of the African American Church in Providing Culturally Relevant Services

Community Macro-Practice and the African-American Church

Billingsley and Morrison-Rodriguez (1998) use a systems perspective as a model to explain how the various parts of African-American communities can be mobilized to serve as mediating structures between the African-American family and the wider society, whose practices and policies often serve to weaken it. They describe three forces in modern society that contribute to family breakdown, as they "assault" (p. 38) the African-American family. Briefly, they refer to economic forces (for example, the loss of millions of unskilled and semi-skilled jobs, in part, related to rapid technological changes); social forces (for example, increased social acceptance of premarital sex, divorce, and pregnancy without marriage, tolerance for fathers who do not fulfill parental responsibilities); and the force of racism (for example, discrimination in work, housing, education and the criminal justice system puts additional pressure on families already stressed by social and economic forces). These issues are also discussed in Chapter 5, "The Family in Society".

The authors' essential premise is that the African-American Church, as a mediating structure between families and the wider society, is ideally situated to assume an activist role "to remind the larger society and its government structures of their responsibility toward African-Americans, whose forced labor established the economic might of the United States" (p. 37). They suggest that as the strongest and most prized institutions in the African-American experience, the family and the Church mutually influence one another.

The African-American Church has fulfilled multiple roles for the community outside of its basic spiritual function (for example, social service center, financial institution, social advocate, educational and entertainment center) and has guided the African-American community through two reform movements: the abolition of slavery and the Civil Rights Movement. Over time, the African American Church's autonomy has permitted it to assume a leadership role in confronting the power structure on policies that are detrimental to families; in times of crisis, African-American people have often turned to the church for advice, assistance and leadership. Billingsley and Morrison-Rodriguez (1998) suggest that the African-American community now faces another challenge: "ensuring the survival of the African-American family in the maelstrom of social and technological change taking place on a global scale" (p.40). These challenges include fostering the commitment to marriage and responsible parenthood, diminishing the number of births to single mothers, encouraging responsible sexual behavior among young people, reducing domestic violence, and providing economic and social assistance to at risk families.

They further suggest that in this modern crisis, the African-American Church may need to develop new types of knowledge and resources, in order to be an effective agent for change. Although some churches fall into the "activist" category, many more (mostly small and rural) will require substantial assistance in the form of education and material support to enable them to confront the stressors that their communities are facing. Since they are likely to be among the only resources for families in poor communities, it is critical that these smaller churches be supported to assume an activist role. In order to confront this modern crisis effectively, these churches will need "knowledge of social welfare policy and politics, family dynamics and child development, economic and micro enterprise development, public-private capital creation, job training and job readiness, asset building and many other strategies which promote family wholeness and economic self-sufficiency" (p. 45). Organized groups of African-American churches, such as the Congress of National Black Churches, can be of assistance by providing information about the available opportunities (such as family focused public-private partnerships and new sources for funding, such as "charitable choice" provisions) as well as the pitfalls, of current policies. Social workers are also in a position to help churches learn about program development, economic management and program evaluation and accountability. Armed with this knowledge, churches can learn to demonstrate the effectiveness of their programs and to attract external social and economic support.

Providing Community-Based Clinical Services in the African-American Community: Partnering with the African-American Church

Queener and Martin (2001) also acknowledge the central role of the African-American Church (as well as the importance that religion and spirituality have in the lives of many African-Americans), and they present a culturally appropriate, community-based model for the delivery of mental health services within African-American communities. The African-American Counseling Team (AACT) attempts to address the underutilization (and inappropriate utilization) of mental health services in the African American community, by using an African-centered approach and partnering with the African-American Church to deliver services.

The team utilizes techniques that draw on theories of development that are incorporated with positive features of African-American culture. Unlike traditional psychotherapy, "African-centered" models view spirituality as a central component of healthy development.

For example, Queener and Martin (2001) describe a model of psychotherapy, developed by Meyers (1988), called "Belief Systems Analysis". Here, the client is encouraged to adopt a worldview based on what are referred to as optimal belief systems (these are based on communalism, intrinsic self- worth, self knowledge, the union of opposites and the integration of the spiritual with the material) vs. sub-optimal belief systems (based on materialism, competition, externally determined self-worth, dichotomous thinking and individualism). In this model, optimal belief systems are considered to be supportive of spiritual growth and healthy development. Therapy is considered to be successful when the client is empowered to define reality for him/herself, bases his/her self-esteem on intrinsic factors and draws on a spiritual foundation of patience, positive beliefs and faith.

Despite the important role played by the clergy as indigenous helpers in the African-American community (Cook, 1993), Queener and Martin (2001) point out that collaborations between the Church and the mental health community tend to be quite rare for a variety of reasons. They view such collaborations as important ways to provide culturally relevant services and urge practitioners who are interested in serving the African-American community to examine their own beliefs about religion and spirituality, and to work to forge meaningful professional relationships with clergy.

(Continued)

The Akron Unity Partnership (AUP) is a coalition of African-American Churches in northeastern Ohio that works to mobilize private and public resources in the interest of community development. Members of the AUP clergy, recognizing the limitations of both traditional mental health delivery systems within their community, and of their own training to manage the mental health needs of their parishioners, formed the African-American counseling team as a means of better meeting the community's needs in this area. The AACT provides culturally appropriate, direct clinical services to parishioners and non parishioners of all ages, consultation and advocacy services to community agencies to enhance their services, educational and preventive services, as well as culturally appropriate research using parishioners as study participants.

Collaboration between the AACT and the AUP clergy occurs at multiple levels of service delivery. AACT's appointment clerk has an office In an AUP church, so the client's first contact with the mental health system is made through a trusted community organization. A high degree of collaboration is built into the clinical process. The same client may be receiving pastoral counseling from his/her pastor while receiving clinical services from a mental health provider; clergy may accompany clients to their mental health sessions, and there is ongoing consultation between pastoral and mental health counselors as necessary. In addition, as part of educational and preventive services, AACT offers life skills workshops to parishioners on such topics as stress management, anger management, self-esteem, coping with loss, etc. The workshops are often presented as part of regular bible study meetings, and may be co-facilitated by both the pastor and mental health practitioner; clients benefit from hearing the same message from both a theological and mental health perspective. The churches promote AACT services through the use of brochures, discussion during sermons, direct referrals, and including clinicians in a variety of church activities. Clinicians too, utilize various church services as adjuncts to therapy.

The black church has guided the black community through two reform movements: the abolition of slavery and the civil rights movement.

Source: A. Billingsley and B. Morrison-Rodriguez, 1998, "The Black Family in the 21st Century and the Church as an Action System: A Macro Perspective." In Letha A. (Lee) See (Ed.), *Human Behavior in the Social Environment from an African American Perspective* (pp. 31-47). Binghamton, NY: The Haworth Press, Inc.; J.E. Queener and J.K. Martin (2001). Providing Culturally Relevant Mental Health Services: Collaboration between Psychology and the African-American Church. Journal of Black Psychology, Vol. 27 No 1 Feb. 2001.

Summary

In this chapter, we have attempted to provide the reader with a broad-based integrated framework that recognizes the mutuality of connections among individuals, families, organizations, and communities, as well as the profound influence exerted on them by the larger systems in which they are embedded. We have examined several sociostructural concepts that are relevant to community functioning and have explored both traditional and progressive perspectives related to definition and functioning of communities and their subsystems. The community, as a context for social work practice, has changed greatly over the past 50 years in response to profound changes in U.S. society. The social work profession is currently faced with the challenge of understanding these trends and using that understanding to think of new ways to practice most effectively. This will increasingly require a contextualized view of client situations that clearly acknowledges and accepts the importance of the social change aspect of social work and better integrates micro- and macropractice perspectives.

8

Spiritual Development

Carolyn Jacobs, MSW, PhD

Dean and Elizabeth Marting Treuhaft Professor, Smith College School for Social Work

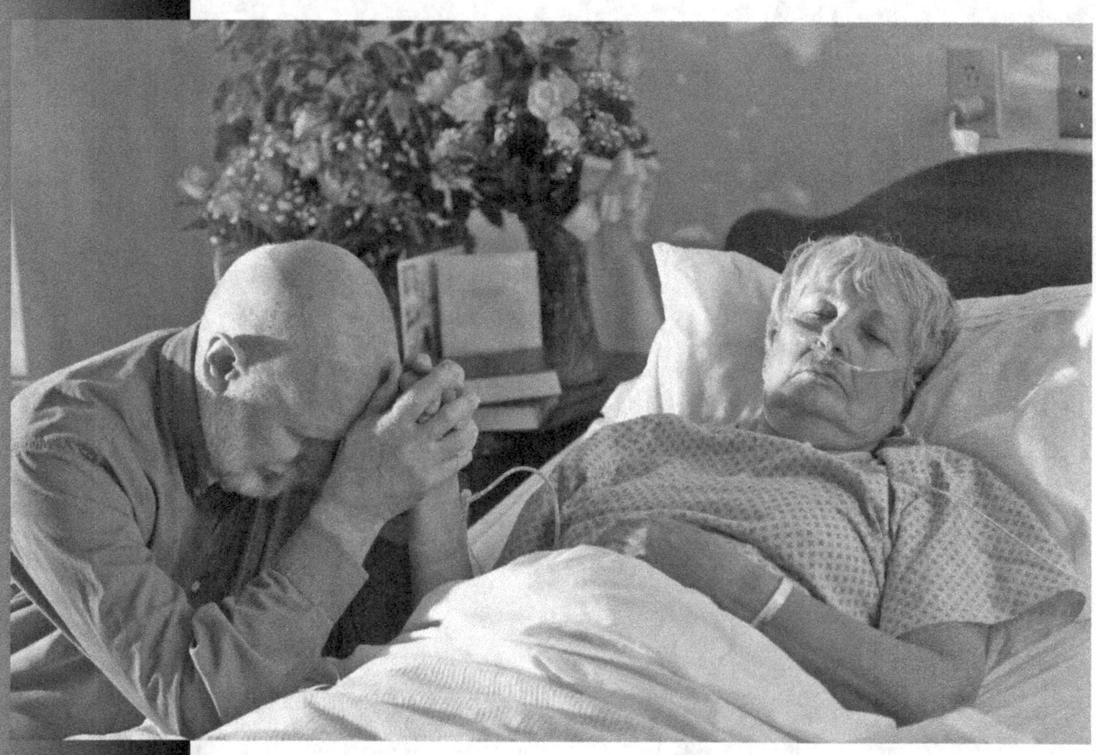

. . . it is a maxim in contemplative traditions that one needs help from others in the course of one's spiritual pilgrimage. But this maxim is not complete without its corollary; helping others is a part of being a pilgrim. Taken together, these understandings reflect the two commandments upon which Jesus said all the Law and the Prophets depend, loving God totally and loving one's neighbor as oneself. This in turn reflected the Hebrew mandate recorded in Leviticus, "You shall love your neighbor as yourself. I am the Lord." "True happiness," says an old Hindu scripture "consists of making others happy." This is also the foundation of the Buddhist Bodhisattva vow that affirms that one will not attain final liberation "until all sentient beings are saved." Put another way, service to others is at once a means and an end of spiritual growth.

(May, 1982)

Introduction

This chapter examines the complexity of spiritual identity development through the life cycle. It includes definitions of spirituality, cultural diversity and spirituality, feminist spirituality, family and community, life cycle focuses on spiritual development, and the role for the social worker and spiritual assessment. The book, *The Secret Life of Bees* (2002), by Sue Monk Kidd, will provide a text with examples to explicate the complexity of ideas in spiritual identity development and assessment. The story provides examples that illustrate the complexities of spiritual development in a cultural context with feminist spiritual images. Excerpts from the book will be used throughout the chapter. The following overview of the book provides useful background for the reader.

The Secret Life of Bees is set in the American South in 1964. Isolated on a South Carolina peach farm with a neglectful father, 14-year-old Lily Owens has spent much of her life longing for her mother, Deborah, who died amid mysterious circumstances when Lily was 4 years old. To make matters worse, her father, T. Ray, tells Lily that she accidentally killed her mother.

Lily is raised by Rosaleen, her African-American nanny. When Rosaleen attempts to exercise her right to vote, she is attacked by three white men and thrown in jail. Lily is determined to save Rosaleen and finally escape her own father as well. Seizing the moment, she springs Rosaleen from jail, and the two set out across South Carolina in search of a new life.

Their destination is Tiburon, South Carolina—a town they know nothing about except that in a box once belonging to Lily's mother, there is a cryptic picture of a black Virgin Mary with the words "Tiburon, South Carolina" written on the back. They are taken in by three black beekeeping sisters who worship the Black Madonna. It is here, surrounded by the strength of the Madonna, the hum of bees, and a circle of wise women, that Lily makes her passage to wholeness and new life.

Definitions of Spirituality

During the last decade, the media has explored the significance of religion and spirituality in the lives of people. The December 7, 1997, *Sunday New York Times Magazine* cover story was "God Decentralized, a Special Issue." On the cover was the statement that Americans are still the most religious people on the planet, but these days, they are busy inventing unorthodox ways to get where they are going. Spirituality is surfacing everywhere—in the workplace, in leadership, in recovery, in education. Years later, the September 5, 2005, edition of *Newsweek*'s cover story was "Spirituality in America—Our Faith Today." The story explored the questions of what we believe, how we pray, and where we find God. A survey reported that 79 percent of those polled described themselves as "spiritual," and 64 percent said "religious" (Marty, 2005b, p. 48). In the U.S. population, one finds that there are those who pursue their search for meaning in traditional religious denominations, some of which may include spiritual practices outside their traditional religion as integral to their search (for example, Catholics and Jews who incorporate Buddhist meditation in their spiritual practice while maintaining their primary religious identity). There are others who see the essence of their religious tradition as service to others and join with those across religious traditions to share lives characterized by the spirit of activism, and finally there are those who shun organized religion and find community in following popular spiritual teachers, retreats, and/or alternative spiritual practices (p. 65). It is critical that social work reflect the diversity of society's spiritual worldviews (Hodge, 2003a, 2003b).

The literature provides many ways of defining spirituality as scholars focus on separating religion from spirituality. A humanistic–phenomenological spirituality includes definitions framed by several authors. Elkins and colleagues defined spirituality as "a way of being and experiencing that comes about through awareness of a transcendent dimension and is characterized by certain identifiable values in regard to self, others, nature, life, and whatever one considers to be the Ultimate" (1988, p. 10). Pearlman and Saakvitne identified four dimensions of spirituality: "orientation to the future and sense of meaning in life, awareness of all aspects of life, relation to the nonmaterial aspects of existence, and sense of connection with something beyond oneself" (1995, p. 63). Buchanan and colleagues presented two orientations regarding spirituality and religion: intrinsic and extrinsic. "Spirituality or intrinsic being the reliance on an internal authority, meaning that the expert is the individual, truth is derived from individual experience, and great value is placed on personal insight" (2001, pp. 436–437). Religion or extrinsic being is associated with institutionalized beliefs and attitudes where truth is held by religious leaders, sacred texts, and institutions (pp. 436–437). Finding a generally acceptable definition of spirituality challenges one to include a range of understanding that is often beyond boundaries of explanation. It asks that we be open to the many ways and expressions of meaning-making in the lives of individuals. Openness to a pluralistic perspective on the meaning of spirituality invites one to explore inclusive descriptions rather than univocal definitions (Schneiders, 1993, pp. 394–406). As a result, the following definitions are offered in the spirit of providing ways to hold narratives in service of meaning making for the individual, group, or community.

It has been said that religion is for those who live in fear of going to hell, whereas spirituality is for those who have been there. When working at the interface between the two in the context of social work, it is important to distinguish between religion and spirituality. Social forms or shared beliefs and rituals define a specific religion. Personal experiences or themes of connectedness to others and the universe define spirituality. Often there is a disjunction of the spiritual from the religious in both the popular media, discussions, and research. There seems to be a perspective rising from conversations and studies that spirituality expresses the desire to engage in practices and communities that touch the heart rather than the socially accepted religious rituals, dogma, and celebrations, which are in the external world and may not touch the inner world or lend one to acts of mercy and justice in the external world.

Individual suffering and oppression based on group membership may stimulate discussions of spirituality. The experience of suffering moves people to seek meaning and comfort either within or outside of their current religious tradition. Distinguishing the differences in religious and/or spiritual beliefs and practices allows a deeper understanding of their impact on the individual's psychological functions and ways of making meaning out of life's circumstances (Canda & Furman, 1999, p. 37; Joseph, 1988; Lovinger, 1984; Lukoff, Lu, & Turner, 1992).

Definitions of religion and spirituality abound in the literature (Cornett, 1998; Doka, 1993; Hugen, 1998; Kilpatrick & Holland, 1990; Lewandoski & Canda, 1995). Canda and Furman offer definitions of both: "Spirituality relates to a universal and fundamental aspect of what it is to be human—to search for a sense of meaning, purpose and moral frameworks for relating with self, others and the ultimate reality. In this sense, spirituality may express through religious forms, or it may be independent of them. Religion is an institutionally patterned system of beliefs, behaviors and experiences, oriented toward spiritual concerns, and shared by a community and transmitted over time in traditions" (1999, p. 37).

Constable (1990) stresses that spirituality may or may not include belief in a *monotheistic* God. It is one's personalized experience and identity pertaining to a sense of worth, meaning, vitality, and connectedness to others and to the universe. It incorporates faith—one's pattern of response to uncertainty inherent in life where the limits of material and human effectiveness are exceeded. It pertains to one's relationship with ultimate sources of inspiration, energy, and motivation; it pertains to an object of worship and reverence, and it pertains to the natural human tendency toward health and growth.

Spirituality involves a picture of human persons and their capacity to act, to know, to will, to reflect, and to meditate. It is a broad picture of relationships and obligations with other human beings and with a transcendent other. It is not limited to a theistic, atheistic, animistic perspective of the transcendent other. Others speak of spirituality as "heart knowledge," where wholeness, meaning, and inner peace occur. Spirituality is a sense of being at one with the inner and outer worlds (Lindsay, 2002; Thompson, 1992). Griffith and Griffith provide definitions of religion and spirituality that are most applicable to this chapter: "Religion represents a cultural codification of important spiritual metaphors, narratives, beliefs, rituals, social practices and forms of community among a particular people that provides methods for attaining spirituality, most often expressed in terms of a relationship with the God of that religion" (2002, p. 17). "Spirituality is a commitment to choose, as the primary context for understanding and acting, one's relatedness with all that is. With this commitment, one attempts to stay focused on relationships between one's self and other people, one's physical environment, one's heritage and traditions, one's body, one's ancestors, and a Higher Power, or God. It places relationships at the center of awareness, whether they are relationships with the world or other people, or relationships with God or other non-material beings" (pp. 15–16).

Spirituality in social work has been related to three dimensions of practice. The first dimension concerns clients. Social workers must recognize the spiritual needs of each person and, moreover, recognize that these needs are inextricably related to the growth and development of the whole person. To ignore this aspect of human life is to ignore people in their wholeness. A second dimension concerns the roots of social service agencies. Historically, most agencies were founded under religious auspices. In all religious traditions, service to others is intrinsic to spiritual practices. The third dimension is related to individual social workers. As social work moves toward holistic and strengths-based models of practice, it cannot ignore the spiritual dimensions of human life. The profession and individual social workers have begun to acknowledge that spirituality is a quality and capacity of the social worker (Canda, 1988; Joseph, 1988).

Social work education has acknowledged this relevance in the most recent Council on Social Work Education's educational policy (2003), which contains a statement on the importance of diversity content in social work curriculum paying attention to theory and practice that includes both religious diversity and spiritual development.

Cultural Diversity and Spirituality

Culture can be defined as "the shared understandings people hold, that are sometimes, but not always, realized, stored and transmitted in their language," that characterize a family, a workplace, a region, or a people of a particular ethnicity (Quinn, 1991, p. 57). Cultural diversity can be expressed in behaviors and in meanings. Behaviors are discerned based on observable variables such as family structures, child-rearing practices, food, and roles in rituals surrounding life events such as birth and death. Meanings and values within those observable variables are more subtle and complex. They are often discerned in the context of metaphors. Each culture encourages the use of certain metaphors and discourages the use of others. Cultural values, beliefs, and behaviors evolve and are transmitted over time.

The influence the roles that institutional rules, poetic traditions, and social situations play in the human social group are important in understanding cultural diversity and spiritual practices. Which metaphors can be experienced as real is largely governed by constraints from family, ethnic, and religious traditions (Griffith & Griffith, 2002).

Spirituality is essential to understanding many cultures as it provides values and beliefs that provide particular patterns, guides, interpretations, and ways of making meaning out of life's circumstances. Some example are ethnic groups such as Haitians or Puerto Ricans, where spiritualists play a significant role in making meaning of life's circumstances; religious healers in Southeast Asian communities or *chrandesimos* in Mexican communities; and charismatic Christian and Pentecostals who are represented in all ethnic groups. Exploring indigenous healing practices and beliefs provides an important source of information in understanding human growth and development across cultures. Understandings of God, spirits, and other deities and their relationship to individuals and groups are defined in cultural contexts.

Levels of religiousness and meanings of spirituality differ around the world. In certain parts of northern Europe, religion is seldom used as a way of coping with stress. Among Americans, religiosity and social support appear to be greater among African Americans than in Caucasian Americans. Although research on the relative importance of religion as a coping mechanism has been explored, it is important to note that one is mindful of the variability within the group (Cohen & Koenig, 2003). With the following general thoughts, one must never overlook the individual's perspective on what are the meanings of their cultural heritage and spiritual practices. When engaging people from diverse cultures, it is important to make efforts to understand cultural explanations and belief systems around behaviors as part of assessment and intervention. Respecting diversity leads to developing alliances and cooperation in implementing intervention strategies. The perspectives on development from non-Western and Western cultures have different focuses. Non-Western societies value the importance of the collective and community as essential in healthy development. In those cultures, early development of intimacy is valued over independence. Western societies emphasize individualism or early independence as the goal in their cultural definition of healthy development. It is important to note that Western models of mental and physical illness ignore the religious or spiritual aspects of culture, whereas Eastern, African, and Native American cultures view religious and spiritual beliefs and practices as essential dimensions of individual and community development (Walker, 2005).

Where there is a sociocultural history of enslavement, both psychological and physical, and of racial discrimination, one may find spiritual traditions that emphasize narratives of struggle against, and triumph over, systems of exploitation. There is a strong sense of the communal experience of rituals such as "drumming, dancing, the use of trance as catharsis and call-response that encourages active participation in worship." An Afrocentric perspective on spirituality would view spirituality as "a vital life force that animates us and connects us to the rhythms of the universe, nature, the ancestors, and the community. A full realization and acceptance of the fact that our spiritual force is a primary drive leads to bonding with community in ways that alleviate psychological suffering caused by centuries of oppression" (Wheeler, Ampadu, & Wangari, 2002, p. 73). In any assessment or understanding of individual or community health or dysfunction, one must consider the role of religion and/or spirituality in contributing to the positive or negative impact that spiritual or religious practices or beliefs might have on the health of individuals and the community.

In *The Secret Life of Bees*, the personification of Mary is shaped by Catholicism and the African-American experience of the Daughters of Mary. Here the characterization of a feminine divinity, drawn from the experience of slavery, offering compassion, hope, and healing, is deeply rooted in the historical cultural experience of the African-American women in the novel. The creation of rituals and acceptance of the ways in which the community becomes a place and resource for individual growth, development, and healing are crucial in understanding the importance of spirituality in human development. Although fictional, these characterizations in *The Secret Life of Bees* represent the meanings attached to images of strong women, the creation of healing communities, a richly developed feminist spiritual practice, and strong religious commitments in the African-American culture.

Feminist Spirituality

Sandra Schneiders (1993, p. 396) defines feminist spirituality as, "Essentially a reclaiming by women of the reality and power designated by the term 'spirit.' It involves not only reappropriating the power of spirit but rehabilitating bodiliness as the immanent medium of the transcendent, and finally reintegrating all that has been dichotomized by patriarchal dualism."

The term *connectedness* has profound meaning for those concerned with feminist spirituality. New images and symbols, such as webs and networks, weaving and dancing, and circles and spirals are important in exploring feminist spiritual narratives and the ways of making meaning. The rediscovery of the *Goddess*, the feminine universal divine, gives energy to transforming hierarchical structures of religion to participative and inclusive communities. Erlichman has identified several components of her working definition of feminism and feminist therapy that can be integrated with definitions of spirituality. Of particular relevance are consciousness raising, cultural competency (i.e., understanding race/ethnicity, class, diversity); listening and being heard; finding one's voice; nonhierarchical models, roles, and relationship; understanding the affect of oppression, including racism, sexism, homophobia, and classism (2001, p. 39).

Feminist spirituality is concerned with the reintegration of the historical splits of mind, body, and spirit in our discussions and work with the individual. There is a concern with reempowering women and with nonhuman nature. There is a commitment to the intimate and intrinsic relationship between personal spiritual growth and transformation and a politics of social justice. This commitment faces simultaneously inward and outward. This mirrors society in that women must experience themselves as fully human daughters of divinity and its bearers in this world, and the world must reintegrate what has been dichotomized, empower that which has been marginalized and abused, and liberate that which has been constrained and enslaved (Schneiders, 1993, pp. 400–401). An empowerment framework offers a holistic perspective that shares feminist theological concerns with difference, merging spirituality and social action, and the role of faith in resisting oppression (Tangenberg, 2003).

Family and Community

Families develop distinctive patterns of child rearing, norms for communication, and rituals to deal with life events such as births, marriages, losses, and deaths. The meaning and socialization of a child in a family is defined by the spiritual worldview of the family. Rites of passage, religious attire, participation in secular celebrations, or celebrations of other religious groups are determined by a family's spiritual worldview.

The role of the child based on gender and birth order, the child's special relationship with members in the religious community, the extended family's role in child care and socialization, issues of authority, and methods of discipline are shaped by the spiritual worldview (Pellebon & Anderson, 1999). As children grow older, their interpersonal relationships are often influenced by their parents' spirituality. The values and beliefs of those who interact with their children are often assessed based on the parents' spiritual worldview. With adolescence comes less parental control over the child's spiritual worldview. Cognitive, physical, and social changes allow for increased information and exploration regarding different ways of knowing and making meaning of life events. At this stage the family competes with information from the larger society and with the peer group for the adolescent's beliefs and values. Young adulthood sees the potential for an individual's spiritual worldview to become internalized based on their intuitive and logical construction. They may engage the struggle regarding in-group and out-group relations, sexuality, or conformity of personal behaviors to their spiritual beliefs as they encounter the larger society as mediated through communities. Older adults in the family may be reexamining firmly established religious commitments and spiritual practices based on crises related to transitions for other family members or their own health and life challenges as they face their own mortality (Pellebon & Anderson, 1999). Communities are the larger social system in which families and individuals negotiate their religious and/or spiritual practices. Communities provide spaces for expression of commitment, collaboration, and a sharing of diverse talents and gifts (Brown & Isaacs, 1994, pp. 508–517).

In relation to spirituality, religious institutions and spiritually oriented groups bind communities together in ways that are characterized by commitment, opportunities for social interaction, and common ties as expressed in beliefs and values.

It is important to note that what holds a community together is a sense of shared meanings that entails spirituality (Dokecki, Newbrough, & O'Gorman, 2001). There is a psychological and spiritual sense of community that is increasingly represented in religious institutions where the spiritual, psychological, and social needs of families are met. Although these community institutions most often have fuller development in protestant megachurches, one can also find elements of this holistic approach to meeting the needs of families in other parishes, temples, and synagogues. The resources provided for the members may include recreational fitness facilities and programs; spaces for psychoreligious educational programs for children, parents, and elders; self-help groups; and spaces for meditation, religious services, and celebrations. They often provide pastoral counseling and a range of social services. Their members experience feelings of connectedness and mutual belonging that arise from a sense of belonging, shared goals, values, rituals, and actions. There is an important link between families and communities where their spiritual needs are attended to in the context of shared values and perspectives on meeting other human needs. It is essential in competent social work practice that one consider and assess the potential religious and spiritual resources available to individuals and families.

Spirituality and Life-Cycle Stages

Where is God? As 7-year-old Peter lands after his first cross-country airplane trip, he is musing about not having seen God as he flew above the clouds. His grandfather chose to ignore the question, leaving the 7-year-old perplexed with what had been a clear Sunday school teaching that God was in heaven above the clouds.

Spirituality and the life span can be examined from the perspectives of cognitive development, faith development, and object relations. Although one may think that airplane flight creates the first crisis of belief for this 7-year-old African-American boy, one needs to understand how cognitive development influences religious understandings.

A review of Piaget's conceptualization of children's cognitive stages and Elkind's research on cognitive religious development provides a context for understanding stages of religious development in children (Hood, Spilka, Hunsberger, & Gorsuch, 1996, pp. 44–68). Piaget's conceptualization of children's cognitive stages presents the ways children think about their world throughout their life span: from the birth *sensorimotor* or *practice intelligence stage* (birth to age 2), to the *preoperational* or *intuitive intelligence stage* (ages 2–7), to the *concrete operational stage* (ages 7–12), to the *formal operational stage* (age 12 and up). At the formal operational stage, the child is capable of complex abstract thinking involving the hypothetical solutions to problems. Elkind's (1971) research on cognitive religious development supports a Piagetian progression of religious understanding. In the 1960s Elkind did three separate studies of Jewish, Catholic, and Protestant children focusing on their understanding of their religious identity and ideas. He found considerable age-related cognitive similarity in children's responses to questions of identity across the three religious groups. For example, in the 5-to-7-year age range (comparable to Piaget's late preoperational stage), where children live in an egocentric world, unable to see things from others' perspectives, children seem to think denominational affiliation is absolute, having been ordained by God, and therefore it cannot be changed. A few years later (ages 7 to 9), the age of Piaget's early concrete operational stage, religious ideas are indeed concrete. Religious affiliation is to be determined by the family into which one was born and includes nonhuman beings.

Fowler's (1981) stages of faith development are congruent with Piaget's and Elkind's stages. Fowler and others have described stages moving from *primal faith* in utero and during the first few months of life to *intuitive/projective faith* (early childhood), where the child becomes aware of the sacred, of prohibitions, and the existence of morality. The *mythical/literal faith* of the latency age corresponds to the Piagetian stage of concrete operations. The *synthetic/conventional faith* of early adolescence relates to formal operational thinking. The *individuative/reflective faith* of late adolescence or young adulthood moves one from reliance on external authorities to authority within the self, leading to consciously chosen commitments. *Conjunctive faith* of midlife or beyond unfolds the integration of opposites, an opening to the multiple perspectives of a complex world. Finally, *universalizing faith,* which occurs at an unspecified age, involves a oneness with the power of being and a commitment to love and justice (Fowler, 1991). The empirical evidence of stages of faith development is still in the early stages of research and is limited in its generalizability (Munk, 2005). Given the scarcity of formulations that draw on both cognitive and moral development, Fowler's work is useful when extending the life-cycle discussion to include spiritual dimensions of development with cognitive development for children.

Another way of exploring spiritual development is through an *object relations* framework. Ana-Maria Rizzuto (1979) applies an object relations framework for understanding the complexity of religious and spiritual experiences in individual development. From conception and the story of the family into which they are born, the person is provided a beginning perspective on the development of a God representation throughout the life span. This representation in the mind of the parents forms the mythology about the meaning of the child in the life of the primary caregivers. Often the birth of a child calls for a religious ritual (circumcision, baptism) that physically and spiritually marks a child's relationship to God (Rizzuto, 1979). Toddlers whose primary caregivers provide an environment where they are present at regular Friday *Shabbat* services, share prayer before meals and at bedtime, attend weekly church services, and participate in religious rituals according to their particular traditions develop a sense of the sacred and Holy One. They experience, name and reexperience, reembrace, and rename this transcendent other as they develop. Children learn God language through their environment (Yust, 2003). Most children complete the Oedipal cycle with at least a rudimentary God representation untouched as they continue to revise parent and self-representations during the life cycle. If the God representation is not revised to keep pace with changes in self-representation, it soon becomes asynchronous. Ideas of God as a Santa Claus figure or as an all-knowing and judging parent may not be useful when the adolescent or adult needs a compassionate and merciful God representation to negotiate a major loss or crisis. Untransformed early images of God may be experienced as ridiculous or irrelevant, or even threatening or dangerous. Each new life crisis or landmark—illness, violent attack, abuse, death, graduations, promotions, falling in love, birth of children, catastrophes, natural disasters, wars—provides opportunities for remembering some once highly relevant or feared aspect of the God representation (Rizzuto, 1979, pp. 1–84).

Munk (2005) and Stokes (1990) discuss the changes in faith that occur more during periods of transition, change, and crisis than during times of relative stability. The stages of middle to late adulthood as adolescents move out to school, work, and adult relationships; the experiences of losses of significant relationships through separations and death; and the impact of retirement. Erik Erikson (1959/1980) addresses spirituality during his final stage of development: integrity versus despair. Here it is believed that the individual's task is to come to terms with reviewing one's life as it nears the end (Munk, 2005).

God, psychologically speaking, is an illusory transitional object. God comes into existence in transitional space. Winnicott (1982) says that religion is located in that illusory intermediate area of experience that helps throughout life to bridge inner and outer realities. He defines that transitional domain as the space where art, culture, and religion belong. It is the place where one's life finds the full relevance of one's objects and meaning for oneself (Rizzuto, 1979, p. 206).

Spirituality and Mindfulness

Mindfulness practices provide resources and strong connections for attending to spirituality and social work practice. Although the origins of mindfulness-based practices are in Buddhism, there are many secular adaptations and uses of mindfulness practices in stress management, mindfulness-based stress reduction, and psychotherapy (Benson, 1975; Kabat-Zinn, 1990; Linehan, 1993). Germer, Siegel, and Fulton cite that mindfulness as it relates to social work practice can be defined as "the awareness that emerges through paying attention on purpose, in the present moment and not judgmentally to the unfolding of experience moment to moment." They have defined mindfulness in relation to psychotherapy as (1) awareness, (2) of present experience, (3) with acceptance. They view these distinct components as "irreducibly intertwined in the experience of mindfulness." Mindfulness has been defined as moment-by-moment awareness and attention (Germer, Siegel, & Fulton, 2005, pp. 6–7).

Epstein (1995) discusses bare attention as allowing things to speak for themselves as if seen for the first time, distinguishing any reactions from the core event. It allows both the social worker and the client to fully focus on the present moment and to hold the past events and present experience of trauma in a way that enables the client to gain insight and engage in the process of adaption and change.

In *The Secret Life of Bees,* one can see through August's relationship with Lily the importance of mindfulness and of bare attention. "She didn't say, 'Come on now, stop your crying, everything's going to be okay,' which is the automatic thing people say when they want you to shut up. She said, 'It hurts, I know it does. Let it out. Just let it out.' So I did. With my mouth pressed against her dress, it seemed like I drew up my whole lifeload of pain and hurled it into her breast, heaved it with the force of my mouth, and she didn't flinch. She was wet with my crying. Up around her collar the cotton of her dress was plastered to her skin. I could see her darkness shining through the wet places. She was like a sponge, absorbing what I couldn't hold anymore. Her hands felt warm on my back, and every time I paused to sniff and gasp for a little air, I heard her breathing. Steady and even. In and out. As my crying wound down, I let myself be rocked in her breathing" (pp. 238–239).

August's capacity to pay attention to the moment and to use herself to allow Lily's experience of trauma to surface provides an excellent example of how awareness, acceptance, and staying in the present moment leads to healing. Acknowledging the pain and suffering, staying in the painful remembering, and mindful breathing are all examples of mindfulness that social workers can use in their work.

Developing the capacity to pay attention or listen to the client can be strengthened by using meditation techniques that enable one to focus on breath and increase awareness of sensory experiences. These techniques are useful for both the social worker and the client. There are many possibilities for developing the capacity to pay attention in the process of developing empathy and awareness of countertransference issues (Germer, Siegel, & Fulton, 2005; Kabat-Zinn, 2005; Rubin, 1996; Sorenson, 2004).

God from an object relations perspective has never been seen and cannot be proven to be real. Those who believe in God experience God as a fully intimate object that has total knowledge of them, even those deep dimensions of self that are not known to the individual or other people. The transitional space allows an unchallenged space of communication between the believer and his or her experience of God. Prayer becomes the way of communication and may be experienced in traditional and nontraditional ways (Rizzuto, 1979; Winnicott, 1982).

A Hasidic student asks his teacher, "I have a question about Deuteronomy 6:6 that says, 'And these words, which I command you this day, shall be upon your heart.' Why is it said this way? Why are we not told to place them in our heart?"

The teacher responds: "It is not within the power of human beings to place the divine teachings directly in their hearts. All we can do is place them on the surface of the heart so that when the heart breaks they drop in" (Dombeck & Karl, 1987).

This particular assessment story fits well with the theoretical orientation of object relations. Dombeck and Karl (1987) used the following question in this multifaceted model for taking a religious history.

Questions for a Religious Community

Placement within a Religious Community Here one determines a person's place in a religious community. Religious affiliation? Changes in religious affiliation? When did changes take place? What is the level of present involvement? What is the relationship with the religious or spiritual leader and the faith community? These questions focus on what is placed on the heart. Using Rosaleen in *The Secret Life of Bees* as an example, we learn that she grew up in the church but stopped going. In her home, "she had a special shelf with a stub of candle, creek rocks, a reddish feather, and a piece of John the Conqueror root, and right in the center a picture of her mother, propped up without a frame" (Kidd, 2002, p. 29). Lily's church experience included an admonition against Catholics. When she discovered that her mother had a Catholic connection, she was pleased with this sense of rebellion against her Protestant religious background.

The questions regarding one's place in a religious community allow us to understand the particular belief systems and dogma that provide a context for understanding the various meanings of life events and human development.

Personal Meanings Attached to Symbols, Rituals, Beliefs, and Divine Figures

This set of questions focuses on the spiritual resources that have been internalized by the individual. What religious practices are most meaningful? When, and in what ways, does one feel close to the divine? What does one pray about? When? Where? What gives special strength and meaning? These questions center on what has dropped into the heart.

> "How come you put the Black Madonna on your honey?" I asked. I'd been curious about this from day one. Usually people got in a rut putting honey bears on them. "I wish you could've seen the Daughters of Mary the first time they laid eyes on this label. You know why? Because when they looked at her, it occurred to them for the first time in their lives that what's divine can come in dark skin. You see, everybody needs a God who looks like them, Lily." (Kidd, 2002, pp. 140–141)
>
> "Well," August said, going right on with her pasting, "you know, she's really just the figurehead off an old ship, but the people needed comfort and rescue, so when they looked at it, they saw Mary, and so the spirit of Mary took it over. Really, her spirit is everywhere, Lily, just everywhere. Inside rocks and trees and even people, but sometimes it will get concentrated in certain places and just beam out at you in a special way." (Kidd, 2002, p. 141)

The questions centering on what has dropped into the heart provide information and metaphors for that area of transitional space where the individual interacts with phenomena that can be used to organize responses and give meaning to life events. The transformation of symbols, rituals, beliefs, and divine figures was a profound example of resilience and capacity to create that which was waiting to bring life and hope. Rosaleen's special shelf affords a glimpse into the meanings attached to symbols from her Southern African-American heritage and the importance of her mother in her life. With the image of the Black Madonna, Lily discovers the importance of having a God who looks like each person. The examples of resilience and creativity give hope to all who encounter the depth and significance that personal meanings can bring forth.

Relationship to Religious Resources

This focuses on those internal objects that are used in understanding and making meaning of one's responses. What is the relationship with God? How does God feel about you? How had the relationship changed? How is God involved in your problems? Has there ever been a feeling of forgiveness? The following excerpts from *The Secret Life of Bees* illustrate how forgiveness, healing, and transformation occur.*

> Above me, black Mary was flecked with honey and seemed not at all surprised. I lay in the emptiness, in the tiredness, with everything—even the hating—drained out. There was nothing left to do. No place to go. Just right here, right now, where

*From *The Secret Life of Bees* by Sue Monk Kidd, copyright © 2002 by Sue Monk Kidd. Used by permission of Viking Press, a division of Penguin Group (U.S.A.) Inc.

> the truth was. I told myself not to get up in the night and walk across the floor unless I wanted to cut my feet to smithereens. Then I closed my eyes and began to piece together the dream I wanted myself to have. How a little door in the black Mary statue would open up, just over her abdomen, and I would crawl inside to a hidden room. This was not all my imagination, as I had glimpsed an actual picture of this in August's book—a statue of Mary with a wide-open door and, inside, all these people tucked away in the secret world of consolation. (p. 260)
>
> "Our Lady is not some magical being out there somewhere, like a fairy godmother. She's not the statue in the parlor. She's something inside of you. Do you understand what I'm telling you?" "Our Lady is inside me," I repeated, not sure I did. (p. 288)
>
> "When you're unsure of yourself," she said, "when you start pulling back into doubt and small living, she's the one inside saying, 'Get up from there and live like the glorious girl you are.' She's the power inside you, you understand?" "And whatever it is that keeps widening your heart, that's Mary, too, not only the power inside you, but the love. And when you get down to it, Lily, that's the only purpose grand enough for a human life. Not just to love, but to persist in love." (p. 259)
>
> I feel her in unexpected moments, her Assumption into heaven happening in places inside me. She will suddenly rise, and when she does, she does not go up, up into the sky, but further and further inside me. August says she goes into the holes life has gouged out of us. This is the autumn of wonders, yet every day, every single day, I go back to that burned afternoon in August when T. Ray left. I go back to that one moment when I stood in the driveway with small rocks and clumps of dirt around my feet and looked back at the porch. And there they all were. All these mothers. I have more mothers than any eight girls off the street. They are the moons shining over me. (p. 302)

At this point in religious history, the focus is on what heals or cripples the heart. One is concerned that internal objects that cripple may need to be engaged in a more psychologically oriented process than a spiritually oriented process.

In metaphorical language, Dombeck and Karl (1987) assessed what has been placed on the heart, what has or has not dropped in when the heart breaks, and what heals or cripples the heart in times of crises. Starting with a wide concentric circle, they started with the person's placement within a religious community with its social, cultural, and political contexts. Exploring personal meanings provides an opportunity to gain valuable information about cherished beliefs and spiritual practices. Finally, by identifying the healing or crippling nature of one's relation to the religious and spiritual resources, we are better able to assess the impact of God representations on the individual's development and functioning. Here one explores the bond, range of affects, ambivalence, and important internal dialogues with God images.

In any spiritual assessment the social worker must be aware of what normative spiritual experiences are within the client's spiritual worldview. When the social worker is unsure, consultation with religious leaders from the client's traditions is important in understanding the appropriate expressions of spirituality and ways of making meaning within the client's religious tradition (Hodge, 2004).

Au (1989) developed an exercise to help clients identify the impact of a relationship to God as a significant internal object by having clients express the God of their childhood with a drawing, symbols, or word. A second expression would be the image of God today. After finishing the two images, clients should note what the juxtaposition of the two images gives rise to in terms of insight questions and feelings. Clients may also explore how these images affect their daily life and decisions. The value of this exercise is that it allows us to understand the power of early representations that may need to be revisited and revised to maximize one's functioning at a current state of life.

Several techniques or tools such as life reviews, history, genealogies, life maps, and genograms from spiritual perspectives can assess the positive or negative implications for spiritual and religious practices. They are useful across theoretical perspectives on human growth and development. Life reviews provide opportunities to resolve earlier conflicts with significant others and God. In addition to the life review, a spiritual genealogy that charts a client's spiritual family tree can add to the life review for ongoing work. Spiritual histories allow exploration of the religious traditions of primary caregivers, one's spiritual beliefs and practices, along with the degree of integration within the faith community. Spiritual turning points are useful in understanding an individual's belief regarding the power of external and internal forces in life (Fiori, Hays, & Meador, 2004). Spiritual life maps allow for a pictorial depiction of one's spiritual journey. Genograms allow for the exploration of the relational dimensions of spirituality. They can highlight spiritual resources, significant relationships, and other spiritually based information that may be significant for the assessment and intervention phases of social work with individuals and families (Bullis, 1996; Dunn & Dawes, 1999; Hodge, 2001, 2003a, 2003b). One can adapt these techniques or tools to fit most practice intervention strategies. Spiritual suffering requires an ongoing assessment. It is not the social worker's responsibility to solve spiritual problems or concerns but to create a holding environment to nurture and support the client's exploration (Abram, 1997; Applegate & Bonovitz, 1995). People respond to and perceive their environment according to their inner structures and levels of organization. A social worker's primary responsibility is to obtain as clear an idea of the client's inner structure as possible (Vaughn, 1991).

Spiritual assessment based on a strengths perspective uses engagement, continuous collaboration, advocacy, and supportive termination to generate a holistic profile. It requires that the social worker actively engage in a relationship that positions the client as an expert on his or her life situations. Puchalski (1999) provides a useful and simple assessment tool for a spiritual history.

FICA: A Spiritual Assessment

FICA is an acronym that can be used to structure an interview.

F: Faith or beliefs. What is your faith or belief? Do you consider yourself spiritual or religious? What things do you believe in that give meaning to your life?

I: Importance and influence. Is your belief important in your life? What influence does it have on how you take care of yourself? How have your beliefs influenced your behavior during this illness or crisis? What role do your beliefs play in regaining your health?

C: Community. Are you part of a spiritual or religious community? Does this support you, and how? Is there a person or group of people you really love or who are really important to you?

A: Address. How would you like me, your health-care provider or social worker, to address these issues in your health care or our work together?

We may learn more by asking questions regarding what nourishes or supports a person's spirit, and by being open to hearing a range of responses, including specific religious rituals, as well as experiences of nature, music, poetry, and relationships. Whatever the assessment tools or questions, the essential dimension is our capacity to be fully present to the client's spiritual quest for meanings.

With an emphasis on strengths and resources rather than on symptomology and problems, the pressing question is not what kind of life one has had, but what kind of life one wants. It is at this juncture that spirituality emerges as a life force. Life strengths and support are not fixed, nor can they be evaluated once and then used as an ongoing standard. In the context of strengths assessment, spirituality often emerges as a stabilizing force that helps to maintain a person's sense of balance in the wake of change, difficulty, doubt, and death. Assessment from a strength perspective invites us to ask questions that provide definition to thematic life strengths and values that constitute a person's sense of self in the world.

Summary

Spirituality can become increasingly important at specific stages of people's lives—births, terminal illness, losses, deaths, and celebrations. Techniques of rituals, prayers, meditation, or scripture may bring feelings of joy, comfort, and peace that should be accepted and understood as signs of healing. In *The Secret Life of Bees,* the Daughters of Mary's celebration of the Feast of the Assumption affords a communal experience of breaking the chains of oppression as experienced by African Americans and women and moving toward a celebration of transformation and life.

It is important to acknowledge that religious dogma can be a contributing factor in the development of pathology, or it can be a means of explaining some emotional problem by some religious groups. The assessment requires collaborative work between spiritual guides/professionals and mental health professionals to clearly discern/diagnose which dynamic is in process. Complications in spiritual experiences can be confused with mental illness; what some would assess as spiritual desolation, others might assess as psychological depression. From a strengths perspective, spiritual practices may be used to heal and facilitate growth in the individual—for example, the role of spirituality in 12-step programs, prayers for healing, Buddhist meditative practices, Reiki, and other forms of body/mind/spirit practices. It is important to distinguish among these many nuanced perspectives on religion and spiritual practices when one is working at the interface of social and psychological development.

This chapter began with May's quote, which reflects the social worker's role in attending to their own spiritual journey while providing service to others. The importance of the social worker's *spiritual competency* in conducting a spiritual assessment cannot be overlooked. It is a more specific form of cultural competency and "is composed of three components: (a) knowledge of one's own spiritual worldview and associated biases; (b) an empathic understanding of the client's spiritual worldview; and (c) the ability to develop intervention strategies that are appropriate, relevant and sensitive to the client's spiritual world view" (Sue, Arredondo, & McDavis, 1992, p. 481). Hodge concluded that four principles can be seen as building blocks in a foundation for spiritually competent practice. First, demonstrate respect for a client's spiritual autonomy by exhibiting respect for clients' spiritual beliefs, values, and practices and their right to refrain from discussing their spirituality. Second, become a cultural anthropologist by demonstrating curiosity and interest as they seek to allow clients to guide them toward a fuller understanding of their worldviews. Third, exhibit sensitivity to the biases people of particular faiths often encountered in the larger culture. Fourth, monitor religious countertransferance, which is especially important for those social workers who have rejected their family of origin's faith and may have clients from these faiths (Hodge, 2004, p. 40). Spiritual competence in social work practice requires a commitment to these preceding four principles and to developing a contemplative or meditative practice such as mindfulness. It is important that social workers attend to their spiritual practice to be aware of how their worldview facilitates or blocks the social work relationship.

9 Infancy

Introduction

During the last half-century, there has been a remarkable expansion of our understanding of the infant. Advances in infant research have yielded findings that demonstrate even newborns and very young infants are extraordinarily capable human beings. This chapter will examine the current state of knowledge regarding the infant's biopsychosocial development, as well as the many areas where understanding continues to elude us.

We will view infant development from an ecosystems perspective, in which behavior and growth are seen as the outcomes of transactions between innate, genetically influenced, biologically based endowments (for example, temperament; sensory–perceptual and cognitive capacities; genetically guided maturation; inherent motivations; and behavioral systems) and a complex social and physical environment.

The Inherent Nature of the Infant

It is now widely accepted that infants are born with many qualities and capacities that provide the foundation for their future development and that, virtually from birth, they are capable of actively participating in shaping their own experiences. The following section will examine those innate infant characteristics that are most salient to our purposes and is not intended to be an exhaustive discussion.

Sensory–Perceptual Capacities

Infants are equipped at birth with fairly well-developed sensory-perceptual systems that allow them to experience most forms of sensory stimulation available to human beings (Kagan, 1984). In fact, certain senses appear to be at least partially active in utero (DeCasper & Spence, 1986; Mistretta & Bradley, 1977). At the time of birth, infants can see, hear, smell, taste, and respond to touch, pain, and positional change (Bertenthal & Clifton, 1998; Kagan, 1984).

Vision Newborns are able to see objects fairly well from a distance of 8 to 10 inches (responding best to sharp contrasts in light and color), can visually track slow moving objects, and can distinguish between certain visual patterns (Kagan, 1984). By 2 to 3 weeks after birth, infants are capable of imitating facial expressions. The visual apparatus matures rapidly during the first 6 months. Development in this area then slows down, reaching full maturity by age 4 (Kellman & Banks, 1998).

Hearing Research has shown that the fetus is responsive to sound in utero, and within days of birth, infants demonstrate the ability to discriminate between sounds. For example, infants just days old show a preference for the sound of their mother's voice over that of another woman (Snow & McGaha, 2003), and they can distinguish between different speech sounds (such as "pa" and "ba"), as well as between certain musical notes (Kagan, 1984). In the early months, infant vocalizations reflect the full range of sounds used by all known human languages. As infants increasingly become attuned to the inventory of sounds used in the language of their immediate environment, they begin to limit their vocalizations to reflect those sounds only, gradually losing the capacity to produce the full range of sounds (Bornstein, 1995; Cheour et al., 1998; Kuhl, 1999).

Taste and Smell The ability to discriminate by taste and by odor is also present at birth (Mistretta & Bradley, 1977). Newborns react differentially to salty, bitter, sour, and sweet tastes (Newman & Newman, 1999), and within days of birth show a preference for the odor of their mother's milk over that of another woman (MacFarlane, 1975).

Touch The sense of touch is especially important for human development. Distressed infants (and adults as well) are often soothed by being held, rocked, and stroked gently. From an early age, infants may show a preference for certain holding positions and types of touch. Very young infants use sucking as a self-soothing technique, and within months, infants use sucking and mouthing to explore objects.

Cross-Modal Perception This is an innate capacity, observable in earliest infancy, which is built into the infant's perceptual and cognitive systems (Kuhl & Meltzoff, 1982; Meltzoff & Borton, 1979). It refers to the fact that all the senses together form an interconnected system that allows information to be transferred from one sense to another. For example, if one is given a quarter to feel, but not see, one might easily conjure a visual image of a quarter, thereby allowing one to identify it visually. In a now-classic study of nursing newborns, MacFarlane (1975) placed a pad soaked with their mother's milk on one side of their heads, and pads with another woman's milk on the other. The infants consistently turned their heads toward the mother's milk. In addition to demonstrating recognition of the mother's scent, it appears that the mother's scent activated the infant's visual system and created anticipation of some visual stimulation. In another study, infants just weeks old, were blindfolded and given a pacifier of a particular shape to suck. They consistently discriminated that pacifier from another of a different shape when the blindfold was removed (Meltzoff & Borton, 1979). This demonstrates the infant's capacity to make cross-modal connections between touch and sight to recognize shape (Stern, 1985).

The ability to transfer information among the various senses increases over the first few years of life, and it is considered an important prerequisite for future social, cognitive, and linguistic learning and development. Deficits in sensory–perceptual integration skills may result in difficulties with language development, learning disabilities, attention deficits, and other problems in childhood (DeGangi, 2000; Stern, 1985).

Innate Motivational and Behavioral Systems

The Sociable Behavioral System There is strong evidence to indicate that human beings are born with a biologically based motivation to seek out, maintain, and control social interactions with other human beings—that is, to be "sociable." This tendency is thought to have evolved as a necessary adaptation for survival (being in the company of others provides a measure of safety from predators; social involvement also increases one's ability to gather food and to find or create shelter; Eisenberg 1966). The organization of this motivation is referred to as the sociable (or affiliative) behavioral system (Bowlby, 1969/1982).

Ample evidence of this sociable behavioral system can be seen almost from birth, with newborns showing a remarkable capacity to orient themselves to social stimulation and to respond to the behavior of other humans (Bowlby, 1969). For example, infants appear to be innately attracted to the visual pattern of an oval with two spots placed as "eyes." Stern (1977) believed that this implied that a scheme of the human face is somehow encoded in the genes, thus biologically predisposing the infant toward attraction to that form. According to Siegel (1999), primates have been shown to have neuronal groups in their brains whose functions are to respond to faces and facial expressions. Face-to-face interaction is therefore seen as an important mechanism for the kind of interactional stimulation necessary for early brain development (Davies, 2004). It is well documented that newborns prefer looking at the human face above all else, and some infants are capable of imitating facial expressions within weeks of birth. Newborns are also especially responsive to the sounds and intonations of the human voice, and shortly after birth, they can be seen to quiet down and attend to softly spoken speech (Marvin & Britner, 1999). By the age of 4 to 6 weeks, most infants begin to smile in response to pleasurable external stimulation. This "social smile" is most easily elicited by the sight of the human face and by the sound of the human voice (Stern, 1977).

The Attachment Behavioral System Closely linked to the sociable behavioral system, but distinct and more specific (Bowlby, 1969/1982), is the attachment behavioral system. Although the goal of sociable behaviors is to bring the child into contact and interaction with other people in general, the goal of attachment behavior is to maintain close proximity to a specific person—in other words, the primary caregiver (usually, but not always, the biological mother). This does not imply that the child is capable of forming *only* one attachment; in fact, most infants are thought to form attachments to more than one familiar person during the first year. In most cultures, the biological parents, grandparents, older siblings, aunts, and uncles generally serve as attachment figures, although the infant tends to prefer one principal attachment figure over the others (Van IJzendoorn & Sagi, 1999). Attachment theorists believe that, like the sociable behavioral system, the attachment behavioral system evolved in humans as a means of survival. The feature that distinguishes the attachment system from the more general sociable system is that the goal of the attachment bond is to offer protection, a sense of security, and comfort. This is not the case with other social ties. The attachment figure, by definition, is one whom the child perceives as more competent and therefore able to provide the protection the child needs to survive.

Almost from the moment of birth, newborns are prepared to bond with their caregivers. The release of hormones immediately after birth causes a heightened state of alertness in infants for 20 to 30 minutes postpartum when they may have their first opportunity to bond with their mother. It is thought that this period of heightened alertness may have evolved to promote mother–infant bonding (Lagercrantz & Slotkin, 1986).

Very young infants quickly begin to differentiate their primary caregiver from other people. Newborns, just 2 days old, can discriminate their mother's face and scents from those of strangers, and as early as 3 days postpartum, they show a preference for their mother's voice over other sounds and the voices of others. Through repeated interactions over the first weeks and months, infants learn to recognize their primary caregiver by face, scent, touch, and voice. Through this process, infants gradually form what is known as an "attachment bond" with at least one caregiver by the end of the first year. This process will be discussed in greater depth later in this chapter, as the quality of the attachment bond is thought to have broad implications for future development (Cassidy, 1999).

Temperament

Temperament refers to innate, biologically based traits that affect how a person responds to the environment. Although it is accepted that infants are born with a particular temperamental style that predisposes them toward certain mood states and styles of reacting, temperament theorists differ with regard to what specific traits most accurately represent inborn temperament; what biological processes (for example, physiological processes, genes, prenatal conditions) are responsible for an individual's temperament; whether, and for how long, temperamental traits may persist through the lifespan; and, perhaps most important, what, if any, influence inborn temperament exerts on later development.

Temperamental Traits The research of Thomas and Chess (1977, 1986) is among the best-known and comprehensive explorations of temperament. These investigators identified nine temperamental traits: activity level; how easily the child adapts to change; the child's tendency to approach versus withdraw from unfamiliar stimuli (for example, new demands, new foods); level of distractibility; regularity of biological functions (such as eating and sleeping); persistence and attention span; quality of mood; intensity of emotional reactions (positive and negative); and the child's threshold of responsiveness to sensory stimulation. They believe that individual differences of expression of these traits are constitutionally grounded, present, and identifiable from early infancy, persist at least into early childhood, and operate in transaction with the social environment to codetermine the child's experience (in other words, they affect how the child responds to others and in turn, how others respond to the child).

Thomas and Chess also identified three patterns of infant temperaments: easy, behaviorally inhibited (slow to warm up), and difficult. Forty percent of the infants sampled displayed *easy* temperaments. These infants showed age-appropriate persistence and ability to attend, adapted easily to change, and generally displayed a positive mood. They demonstrated a positive approach to new and unfamiliar situations. They were moderately active and mildly to moderately sensitive to sensory stimulation, and their emotional reactions (positive and negative) were mildly to moderately intense. They showed regular patterns of sleeping and eating and, overall, made their parents feel quite competent.

Behaviorally inhibited infants comprised 15% of the sample. These infants appeared to be more sensitive to new stimuli and to withdraw emotionally when confronted with unfamiliar experiences. If permitted to adjust slowly, without pressure, they gradually adapted and showed positive interest in the (now more familiar) new experience. Their activity level tended to be low, and their emotional reactions (positive and negative) were of low intensity. Overall, these infants might be described as cautious, sensitive, and shy.

Ten percent of infants displayed what Thomas and Chess refer to as a *difficult* temperament. These children had intensely negative reactions to new or unfamiliar experiences and were negatively persistent, resistant, and slow to adapt to change. These children displayed generally negative mood states, with intense emotional reactions and oversensitivity to stimulation and irritability. Sleeping and eating patterns tended to be irregular. The challenges these children present may lead parents to feel frustrated and less than adequate.

Other temperament theorists regard temperament as a set of genetically inherited characteristics that serve as a precursor of later personality traits (Buss & Plomin, 1984; DeFries, Plomin, & Fulker, 1994; Plomin & De Fries, 1985). Buss and Plomin (1984) identified three critical traits that represent inborn, genetically determined temperamental traits: emotionality, activity, and sociability. From their perspective, personality and temperament in infancy are the same. With age, these inherited "seeds" of personality become increasingly differentiated in response to central nervous system maturation and the child's unique experiences with his or her particular social environment. Also supporting this perspective is Tellegen's research at the University of Minnesota, which provided strong evidence of some genetic grounding for such adult personality traits as the sense of well-being, alienation, traditionalism, social closeness, vulnerability to stress, risk aversion, achievement, and social potency (Coleman, 1986).

Kagan (1984) takes a slightly different approach to temperament, viewing it as characterized by one major dimension: behavioral inhibition to the unfamiliar. He has found that behavioral styles at either extreme of this dimension (for example, *inhibited/shy* or *bold/sociable*) characterize approximately the top or bottom 10 to 15% of children along this continuum; further, these traits tend to persist well into childhood and, possibly, through adolescence and adulthood, depending on the nature of the individual's transactions with the social environment (Kagan, 1998).

Physiological Underpinnings of Temperament Recent findings have allowed researchers to identify and locate several "emotion-motivation" systems in the lower, subcortical areas of the brain that are thought to be related to temperament and personality development (Derryberry & Rothbart, 1997; Posner & Rothbart, 2000). These systems are presumed to express genetically determined differences in *reactivity* or the ease, speed, and intensity of becoming activated by a relevant stimulus. When activated, these *emotion-motivation systems* in the brain produce an emotional reaction (physiological arousal) and an emotional expression (such as crying, yelling, laughing), as well as a tendency to either approach or avoid the stimulus. The individual's particular emotional and behavioral reaction is governed by a complex interplay of activation and inhibition among these systems (Leseman, 2002).

Kagan (1998) believes that the temperamental styles of extreme inhibition or disinhibition are related to individual differences in arousal of the amygdala (a brain structure that controls avoidance reactions). For example, in behaviorally inhibited children, the amygdala is easily aroused by novel stimuli and produces such physical indicators of stress as increased heart rate (Snidman, Kagan, Riordan, & Shannon, 1995), higher concentrations of cortisol in saliva, and elevated blood pressure (Gunnar & Nelson, 1994). In disinhibited children, the same stimuli produce minimal excitation of the amygdala. On electroencephalograms, shy, inhibited children show higher levels of activity in the right cortical area (a section of the brain associated with negative emotion). Uninhibited, sociable children show higher activity in the left cortical area (associated with positive emotion; Calkins, Fox, & Marshall, 1996; Fox, Calkins, & Bell, 1994).

Despite differences in theoretical models regarding the dimensions, sources, and developmental relevance of inborn temperament-related behavior, few dispute the idea that infants are born with some form of constitutionally grounded characteristics, and that these represent at least a part of the developmental equation. In any case, identifying and assessing an infant's innate disposition is certainly helpful in understanding his or her internal responses to environmental stimulation, particularly within the context of the development of the attachment bond by the end of the first year of life.

Developmental Maturation in Infancy

Although in many species the brain is fully developed at birth, the human brain takes years to reach full maturity. During the last 2 months of gestation and the first 2 years after birth, the brain grows most rapidly through the production of synapses and dendrites. During this period, the brain goes from 25% of its eventual adult weight (at birth) to 75% of adult weight (by age 2), and this development provides the foundation for the increasing elaboration and complexity of the functioning of the central nervous system and for the maturation of skills in all areas of human functioning.

Neurobiological Maturation

All aspects of human functioning (for example, sensory-perceptual and cognitive abilities, physical motor skills, and emotional responsiveness) are organized via the process of synaptogenesis that occurs during this period. Synaptogenesis refers to the linking of neurons—the wiring process through which neurons establish connections with each other by sending out long branches or dendrites. When these dendrites reach the neuron they are aiming for, a synapse or connection forms that allows neural impulses to travel from one neuron to another. Neurons produce chemicals called neurotransmitters, which help impulses to travel between neurons. This process of dense branching of dendrites allows neurons to communicate with one another in a coordinated way and creates a control system that manages all aspects of human behavior. As these connections are established, myelin sheaths form around the dendrites, facilitating faster transmission of neural impulses over time. As more neurons become myelinated, the person exhibits new abilities and higher-level capacities for organizing experience (for example, walking, cognitive advances). Waves of chemicals that promote the interconnections of nerve cells (trophic factors) are released region by region, so that different areas of the brain are connected to each other sequentially—with one layer of brain tissue maturing before another—until the entire brain is mature. As noted in Chapter 2, the pace of this process is genetically programmed, but the specific nature of the developing brain is profoundly influenced by the person's transactions with the environment (Nelson, 2000). By the time a child reaches the age of 2, the number of synapses (or connections between neurons in his or her brain) reaches adult levels. By ages 4 through 10, the number of synapses in the child's brain surpasses adult levels. The number of synapses then begins to drop, decreasing to typically adult levels by about age 16 (Blakeslee, 1995).

During this period of rapid growth, the brain exhibits a high degree of plasticity, and the influence of the environment on the organization of brain functions is striking. Experience strengthens those neural connections that are used. Those that are not used eventually atrophy and are pruned away. Thus, the newborn brain comes equipped with a set of genetically based rules for development and for how learning takes place, which is then shaped by experience. By the time the production of trophic factors declines in adolescence, the brain's basic structure is more or less formed. Because the maturation process is so powerfully influenced by experiences with the environment, human brains resemble each other in terms of their overall structure and interconnections but are different in terms of their fine connections (Blakeslee, 1995).

Recent research has focused on the existence of critical periods for development of brain systems that regulate emotional growth. For example, there is evidence (some based on magnetic resonance imaging technology) to suggest that the brains of children exposed to relational trauma during the early years of life are smaller overall and show other abnormalities that are thought to affect future emotional cognitive and social development (De Bellis et al., 1999). Chronic early trauma related to severe disturbances in the infant's relationship with the primary caregiver seems to affect the development of the individual's stress response system, causing it to secrete higher levels of stress hormones in response to perceived danger (De Bellis et al., 1999; Perry, 1994) and to be activated even when no real threat exists (Perry, 1997). Perry (1997, 2002a, 2002b) believes that this type of early trauma causes the more primitive lower and midbrain areas to overdevelop and the limbic and cortical structures (responsible for higher level functions) to be underdeveloped. The impaired brain functions resulting from early relational trauma may interfere with development in many ways: concentration, motivation, and the ability to accurately read environmental cues (Perry, 2002a, 2002b; Schore, 2001) may all be affected; high levels of anxiety, difficulty sleeping, and in severe cases, symptoms of attention deficit disorder and hyperactivity may be seen (Perry, 1997).

Many questions about the brain's development remain to be answered. In addition to the issue of critical or sensitive periods for the development of different regions of the brain, cognitive neuroscientists are particularly interested in the particular processes by which experience influences the development of the brain's circuitry and whether those circuits are subject to change later in development. (See Chapter 2 for further discussion of neurobiological development.)

Attachment

Decades of research have yielded solid evidence to support the view that the quality of the child's attachment relationship with at least one primary attachment figure (usually the biological mother) has a significant effect on the child's ability to develop age-appropriate cognitive and socioemotional skills in childhood and adulthood (George & Solomon, 1999). Furthermore, problems in the organization of this attachment relationship have been shown to be related to behavioral and mental health problems in children and adults (George & Solomon, 1999).

The Caregiving System Although infants are innately predisposed to bond with their caregivers, the type and quality of the bonds they form are dependent on the quality and nature of the environments in which they are raised. Many postpartum reactions of mothers operate in synchrony with those of their newborns (Simpson, 1999). For example, hormonal activity immediately after delivery creates feelings of elation in the mother and serve to predispose her to emotional bonding. Observations of mothers' interactions with their newborns reveal behaviors (apparently unlearned) that seem designed to promote bonding. Furthermore, these behaviors largely transcend culture. For example, mothers in all cultures position themselves about 8 to 10 inches from their young babies. This coincides with the distance at which newborns are best able to see. In their interactions with their infants, mothers typically use "baby talk" and high-pitched sounds; they slow down the pace of their speech and accentuate certain syllables. Young infants clearly prefer this pattern of speech, as it is probably well suited to the development of their auditory systems. From birth, the stimulation the mother provides through soothing, touching, feeding, gazing, and sharing emotions activates the development of connections in the parts of the brain that will be responsible for socioemotional communication and bonding (Perry, 2002a). Many theorists (for example, Bowlby, 1984; Stern, 1977) believe that the caregiving behavioral system is, like the attachment behavioral system, to some degree biologically preprogrammed to ensure (from an evolutionary perspective) the protection of the young. This assumption may help to explain why most adults (as well as adolescents and older children), even those without previous experience with babies, tend to respond to infants in fairly predictable ways. Many have suggested (Lorenz, 1943; Stern, 1977; Suomi, 1995) that certain characteristics of the infant (for example, physical features, emotional expressiveness) may actually serve to elicit these partially innate, stereotypic behaviors.

Purposes of the Attachment Bond Davies (2004) outlined four primary functions of attachment, which are described next.

Regulation of Affect and Arousal When infants become distressed for whatever reason (for example, they may be hungry, tired, frightened, experiencing pain, or desiring interaction), they communicate their distress by exhibiting attachment behaviors designed to draw a caregiver to them. For the newborn, these distress signals are limited to a few behaviors, such as fussing, looking anxious, and crying. In later infancy, with the developmental advances in motor skills (for example, reaching, crawling, and walking), the child's repertoire of attachment behaviors increases to include raising the arms, following, seeking hugging, and climbing on the lap. These behaviors activate the caregiver's "caregiving behaviors." These may include soothing the infant with soft vocalizations, picking the infant up, stroking, rocking, feeding, changing, playing, or anything else that is needed to alleviate the distress. When the attachment–caregiving systems are well organized and functional, the caregiver's responses to the infant's signals of arousal and distress will be fairly prompt and accurate, resulting in a reduction of the child's distress and state of physiological arousal (for example, decreased rate of respiration and heart rate, reduction in bodily tension). This synchrony is crucial to, and characteristic of, a "secure" attachment relationship. Over time, through repeated interactions in which the caregiver is able to accurately read the infant's signals and provide soothing, the infant learns and internalizes strategies to soothe him- or herself (in other words, to self-regulate). This provides the beginnings of a sense of competence. The sense of competence, as it relates to attachment and future development, will be more fully explored later in this section.

Provision of a Sense of Security and Protection The synchrony that is characteristic of a secure attachment relationship provides the infant with a sense of security and protection. When the caregiver is able to read the infant's distress signals accurately, the infant develops what Erikson (1963) referred to as a sense of "trust" and what Newman and Newman (1999) defined as "an experiential state of confidence that their needs will be met and that they are valued" (p. 169).

Communication and Expression of Feelings As the attachment relationship develops, it becomes the mechanism by which the infant learns to communicate and to express and identify emotions; indeed, it is the context within which all psychological development occurs (Gianino & Tronick, 1988; Stern, 1985; Tronick, 1989; Tronick & Weinberg, 1997). This relational view of psychological development is based on the assumption that children and adults construct the meaning of their experiences through their interactions with others (Tronick & Weinberg, 1997). In the case of the infant, the primary relationship context for development is that with the attachment figure(s).

The infant's ability to feel and express emotions has an important interpersonal function—it is the way in which infants communicate their needs, intentions, and reactions. Again, when the caregiver is generally able to understand and accurately respond to the infant's emotional communications, a secure attachment develops and provides a context that will support the infant's healthy development (Tronick & Weinberg, 1997). Here, infants develop a sense of themselves as effective and competent (in other words, they learn that they are able to communicate effectively and to get what they need to feel better). Although attachment theorists generally emphasize the need for caregivers to respond to infant signals with well-timed, well-matched (or accurate) responses that effectively meet the infant's needs, it is becoming increasingly clear that even in the most secure relationships, this type of "synchrony" is not always present, nor is it always possible (Spencer, 2000). In reality, "transactions between infant and parent show moment-to-moment variability in the degree of synchrony, attunement, and mutual responsiveness" (Davies, 2004, p. 10). Minor "mismatches" between the infant's signals and the caregiver's responsiveness occur regularly, and it is believed that another distinguishing characteristic of the secure attachment relationship is the ability of the pair to effectively *repair* these mismatches as they occur. In this way, the infant learns that he or she can effectively cope with temporary misunderstandings and minor frustrations and feels free to communicate a full range of feelings. For example, a mother may be occupied with the care of an older child when the infant begins to feel lonely and to desire attention. The infant may begin to signal a desire for interaction using his or her—usually effective—strategy of smiling, cooing, and kicking his or her feet to attract the mother's attention. When it becomes clear to the infant that the preoccupied mother is not responding, the infant may begin to fuss and, eventually, to cry loudly until his or her need for attention is satisfied.

Infants typically begin to use their first words by the end of the first year of life, although precursors of language skills can be seen almost from the moment of birth. Newborns, just weeks old, can discriminate between sounds as their parents talk to them and vocalize using a variety of sounds during the early months. By 6 months of age, the brain matures enough to make it possible for the child to make more complex consonant–vowel babbling sounds (Locke, 1993). Parents reinforce and encourage these vocalizations by responding verbally; gradually the infant's babbling starts to sound increasingly like the parents' speech sounds. As the infant matures, communication exchanges are practiced as the parent talks to the baby and labels objects during play, caregiving, and joint-attention activities. By about 10 to 12 months, infants usually begin to say their first words, although their receptive language skills are more advanced. As the infant's cognitive development permits the use of language as intentional communication, the context of the parent–child relationship becomes the context for true language learning (Bloom, 1998).

Provision of a Safe Base for Exploration In the early weeks and months, the caregiver takes a more active role in maintaining proximity and tending to the infant's needs. By about the age of 4 to 6 months, as maturation of the central nervous system brings forth improved motor skills and increased cognitive awareness, infants become increasingly able to actively participate in controlling interactions with the caregiver (Stern, 1977). They also become interested in exploring physical objects in the environment. Bowlby and other attachment theorists believe that the urge to explore (exploratory behavioral system) and to have an effect on the environment is an innate motivation that, like the attachment system, provides a survival function by helping the child learn about the workings of the environment. Bowlby believed that the exploratory and attachment systems operate in a complementary fashion and that the link between the two systems evolved to allow the child to explore and learn about the environment while being protected by the caregiver. Ainsworth (1963) first described the young child's use of the attachment figure as a "secure base from which to explore" (in Cassidy, 1999, p. 8). This is a central concept in attachment theory, and it refers to the fact that the child derives the confidence to explore the environment through his or her confidence in the attachment figure. In other words, if a child feels secure in the belief (based on experience with and knowledge of the attachment figure), that the attachment figure will be attentive and responsive when and if the child needs to be protected, the child will then feel secure enough to explore and experiment with the environment. If (again, based on experience) the child feels unsure about the likelihood that the attachment figure will be available to protect him or her, he or she may be reluctant to explore because his or her energy will be devoted to making sure the attachment figure is available and remains attentive.

Security of attachment has been linked to the young child's ability to develop a sense of efficacy and competence, self-direction, and positive self-concept. Robert White (1971) called this inborn motivation the urge for "effectance," and he believed it was satisfied by exploration and by acting on the environment in such a way as to produce desired effects—to make happen what one wants to happen. Through repeated experiences of acting effectively, the child begins to develop a sense of competence. This sense of competence (the belief that one can take desired action and influence outcome) is essential to the development of self-esteem and a positive self-concept.

The infant's successful interactions with the environment increase feelings of efficacy and competence. Parents can support such success by structuring the infant's activities, providing hands-on assistance, encouraging efforts, and expressing pleasure at the infant's accomplishments. Bruner (1985) described the process parents use for facilitation of infant development as "scaffolding." Here, parents provide support (like a scaffold) for the infant's motor, cognitive, and emotional tasks until the infant is developmentally ready to accomplish the task autonomously. For example, when the infant first begins to develop the motor skills necessary for standing and taking steps, parents provide physical support to compensate for the child's lack of balancing skills to help the child walk. Their physical support and positive responses to his or her efforts provide a "scaffold" for the child to practice a skill he or she cannot perform alone. The physical support helps the child practice the actual activity; the positive emotional encouragement reinforces and actually increases the child's motivation to master this and other tasks.

Phases of Attachment Development Bowlby suggested that the attachment behavioral system develops in four phases. The first three of these occur in the first year of life, with the fourth phase beginning after the age of 12 months. Please see Table 9.1.

Patterns of Attachment The quality of attachment varies from one caretaker–infant pair to another, and the quality of that relationship determines the infant's working model (in other words, expectations of caregiver responsiveness). Variations in the quality of individual attachment relationships may be associated with any number of factors, including temperamental *mismatches* between parent and child; disabilities that affect the child's ability to respond positively to usually effective caregiving behaviors; extraneous stressors such as poverty, parental mental illness, and/or substance abuse; and marital discord, which may affect the parent's ability to respond adequately to the infant's signals.

A delicate balance exists between the infant's exploratory and attachment behavior systems (Ainsworth, 1967, 1978). In other words, if the infant feels anxious or threatened in some way while exploring the environment, he or she

TABLE 9.1

Phases of Attachment Development

Phase	Time Frame	Description
Phase 1	Birth to 3 months	Infants engage in a variety of behaviors, including sucking, rooting, grasping, smiling, gazing, cuddling, crying, fussing, and visual tracking, which serve to maintain closeness with a caregiver or to bring the caregiver to the infant. These behaviors do not appear to be aimed at a specific person. It is through repeated interactions that infants first begin to learn what to expect from the caregiver(s). If the caregiver's responses are well attuned and synchronous with the infant's signals, then stable patterns of caregiver–infant behaviors start to establish themselves. Gradually, the infant begins to rely less on crying and more on smiling and gazing to draw the caregiver in.
Phase 2	3 to 6 months	Maturational advances in cognitive and motor skills allow the infant to assume greater control in initiating, maintaining, and terminating interactions with the caregiver(s). Most notable is the infant's demonstration of preference for a few familiar caregivers over strangers. This new skill is probably related to maturation of the central nervous system, which provides for gradual improvements in active memory (Kagan, 1984). Infants begin to greet these familiar caregivers with smiles or with termination of crying; they may vocalize more in their company and may cry when the caregiver leaves.
Phase 3	6 to 12 months	A true attachment begins to form. This coincides with important motor, cognitive, and communicative maturational advances. Motor development during this phase is dramatic. By the age of 6 months, most infants are able to reach for and grasp nearby objects. The infant undergoes rapid maturation of motor skills and control of the body, which lead to sitting, improved balance, crawling, standing, cruising, and by around the age of 12 months, walking. Babies are better able to explore their environment and take greater control of their activities. They can now actively seek out the attachment figure whenever they wish by crawling, climbing, or following. Maturation of the central nervous system, especially the prefrontal cortex, also leads to significant cognitive advances (Kagan, 1984). After about 6 months of age, the nature of the child's play and social interactions begins to change, and the parent–child relationship begins to focus on "joint-attention" activities in which the parent and infant increasingly share experiences of objects or situations (Davies, 2004). These activities are important vehicles for the parent to communicate understanding and clarification of the infant's feelings and reactions. Also around this age, cognitive advances in the infant's ability to understand cause-and-effect relationships lead the infant to begin to become more of an initiator in interactions with the parent. The infant's behavior becomes increasingly "intentional" as he or she becomes increasingly able to generate plans and to take action to satisfy his or her desires.

(Continued)

TABLE 9.1

Phases of Attachment Development (Continued)

	Between 8 and 12 months of age, the infant's "active memory" improves significantly (Kagan 1984). Active memory refers to the ability to retrieve the past, to notice a relationship between the past and present, and to begin to try to predict consequences. Infants can now hold mental representations of objects and people in their memories. Prior to about age 7 months, when an object is out of the infant's sight, it is also "out of his/her mind." By about 7 months, infants begin to search for objects that have been hidden from them, indicating the ability to remember the object and perhaps the spot in which it was hidden. Piaget (1952) referred to this new ability or concept as "object permanence." These maturations in memory functions also seem to underlie two attachment-related behaviors that emerge in infants at about 9 months of age, regardless of culture: ***stranger anxiety*** (i.e., the infant reacts with distress to the sight of an unfamiliar person) and ***separation anxiety*** (i.e., the infant reacts with increased distress when the caregiver leaves). Because the child now maintains memories of objects, people, and situations, the sight of a stranger may be distressing because the stranger's face does not match the "scheme" the child now holds in his/her mind of the faces of familiar people. With regard to separation, memories of past separations and the distress they caused seem to be activated, as the child can now recognize and anticipate the immediate signs that a parent is about to leave. Babies vary in how they express their distress with regard to separation and strangers. This is probably due, to some extent, to temperamental factors and, particularly in the case of stranger anxiety, to contextual factors (e.g., is the caretaker nearby; how does the caretaker respond to the strange; how often is the child exposed to strangers). Reactions to separation may lead initially to attempts to locate the caregiver, then to protest, to experience despair, and then, if the separation is prolonged, to detach (Bowlby, 1960). Consistent with the ability to form mental representations, the infant develops his/her first "working models" of the attachment relationship. Here, the infant holds in his/her mind the knowledge (based on experience) of what he/she can expect in terms of caregiver responsiveness. Specific characteristics of a caregiver and patterns of expectations about how a caregiver will respond to the infant's actions are organized into a complex attachment scheme—the internal, mental representations of the anticipated responses of a caregiver or an "internal working model" (Bowlby, 1969; 1982). Also consistent with the ability to form mental representations is the infant's growing understanding, near the end of the first year, that others have their own perspective and intentions. This understanding underlies the emergence of another behavior by the end of the first year: social referencing. Here the infant begins to "read" the caregiver's attitudes in situations in which the infant feels uncertain and needs help in assessing its dimensions.

Phase 4	12 months and beyond	Children will actively seek connection with the attachment figures when they feel a need for closeness. Children may ask the attachment figure to play, to read to them, to hug them, or simply ask to accompany the attachment figure to the supermarket. These behaviors will be especially prominent when children they are experiencing some form of unusual stress such as illness, and family discord. Children with secure attachments feel confident that closeness to their attachment figures will reduce their distress.

will tend to cease exploration and activate attachment behaviors (in other words, seek proximity to the caregiver). Assessments of the quality of the infant–caregiver relationship must necessarily take into account caregiver responsiveness to the child as well as the timing and effectiveness of the child's display of attachment behaviors. For example, if a child is in a dangerous or distressing situation, it is adaptive for him or her to cease exploration and seek proximity to the caregiver. If the situation is reasonably secure, that same behavior might be considered maladaptive.

Ainsworth (1967, 1969) pioneered the study of individual differences in quality of attachment. She developed the Strange Situation method for assessing infant–caregiver relationships. Here, the infant was introduced to several increasingly stressful events, including an unfamiliar laboratory with a stranger who interacted with the child and two brief separations from the mother. The idea behind this experiment was that the stressful situations would activate the child's attachment system and that the child's behavior would reveal his or her expectations about the caregiver's availability and responsiveness. The child's ability to balance exploration of a new environment with a need for comfort from the caregiver was also assessed. Ainsworth distinguished three basic attachment patterns from her research: *secure* attachment (the ideal), and two forms of *anxious* attachment: avoidant and resistant. A fourth *anxious* pattern, *disorganized* attachment, is also now being used. These four patterns of attachment are described in Table 9.2.

Recently, another method of assessing attachment patterns, the attachment Q-Sort, has been developed. Here, the child is assessed according to a set of 90 indicators of attachment-related behaviors. Information is provided by a parent or other well-informed caretaker, and a score is computed that indicates whether a child is securely or insecurely attached (Waters, Vaughn, Posada, & Kondo-Ikemura, 1995). Results of Q-Sort assessments generally correspond well with those of the strange situation method.

Culture and Attachment Although there are wide cross-cultural variations in approaches to infant care and in how attachment behavior is expressed, the development of an attachment behavior system is considered universal. Parental consistency and responsiveness, as well as the child's use of the parent as a secure base, are considered important for the development and assessment of security of attachment across cultures (Posada et al., 2002; Waters & Cummings, 2000).

TABLE 9.2

Patterns of Attachment

Attachment Pattern	Behavior during Strange Situation	Parent Characteristics	Infant Characteristics
Secure	Actively explored environment and interacted with stranger while parent was present. Decreased exploration and sometimes showed distress on separation. On reunion, pleased to see caregiver, sought contact and was easily soothed.	Emotionally responsive, available, and loving.	Cry less than other infants. More apt to cooperate with parent's wishes. Show better adjustment in toddler and preschool years.
Anxious resistant	Tended to maintain close contact with caregiver even before separation occurred and showed difficulty using parent as a secure base for exploration. On separation, was very distressed and on reunion, sought contact with caregiver but was difficult to soothe.	Inconsistently responsive to infant's signals. Sometimes ignore distress signals and at other times, appear to intrusively insist on contact with the infant, despite infant's lack of apparent interest. Seem to enjoy close contact with their infants but do not necessarily provide it in response to the infant's needs	Because they cannot accurately predict parent's responsiveness, they are unable to use parent as a secure base for exploration. Seem preoccupied with parent at the expense of developing other interests. In later stages their ability to develop an autonomous sense of efficacy and competence is compromised.
Anxious avoidant	Played independently regardless of the mother's presence; showed physiological signs of distress, but no outward signs of distress when she left; ignored her when she returned.	Seem to reject their babies, frequently ignoring them and speaking about them in negative terms. Tend to respond angrily and impatiently to the infant's signals of distress and spent less time holding and cuddling their babies than other mothers	Seem to focus their attention on exploring the outside world; defensively avoiding attachment behaviors and signals of distress to avoid rejection. As toddlers, show higher levels of aggression and hostile interactions with other children.

Disorganized	No clear strategies for dealing with distress, separation and reunion.*	Mothers tend to have serious deficits in maternal behaviors and exhibit a variety of problems, including abusive tendencies, depression, and other mental illnesses. Tend to be unavailable and unpredictable.	Seem confused and fearful with inconsistent and unpredictable behaviors.*

*More research is needed to accurately assess this pattern.

Source: Based on descriptions of secure, anxious-resistant, and anxious avoidant patterns from Ainsworth et al., 1978, information on disorganized pattern is based on Main and Solomon (1990).

Questions have been raised, however, about the usefulness of the Strange Situation method as a measure of attachment behaviors across all cultures. Kagan (1984) believes that some findings of insecure attachment in the strange situation method may actually reflect culturally based differences in either temperament or child-rearing practices. For example, he found (Kagan, Kearsley, & Zelazo, 1978) that, when compared with Caucasian infants, Japanese infants tend to show higher rates of inhibition and fearfulness. In addition, Japanese infants are rarely left in the care of strangers; thus, the strange situation may be much more stressful for them than for infants who are more accustomed to maternal separations (Takahashi, 1990). This may explain why Japanese infants exhibit higher rates of anxious attachments when assessed by this method. Additionally, it has been suggested that cross-cultural assessments would yield more accurate results if investigators focused more on the wider social networks in which most people (Western and non-Western) live, by changing their perspective from the attachment dyad to the attachment network (Van IJzendoorn & Sagi, 1999). This might control for greater diversity of family forms and child-rearing practices when assessing attachment patterns.

Alternate Pathways for Attachment in Contemporary Life

The past several decades have brought about enormous social changes with respect to families and family functioning. We will explore some of these changes (for example, working mothers and substitute child care, late adoption, and assisted reproductive technology) from the rather narrow perspective of attachment in infancy and childhood. Unfortunately, our discussion will raise more questions than it answers.

Substitute Child Care

With approximately 70% of mothers of young children now working outside the home, questions about how early substitute caregiving (group or individual) may affect early attachment has been hotly debated for years, and this debate continues to the present moment. A study by the National Institute of Child Health and Human Development (NICHD, 1997, 1998) indicated that it is important to consider the quality of both substitute and parental care as opposed to viewing the substitute care in isolation. Apparently, infants are least likely to be secure when there are deficits in parental sensitivity and responsiveness combined with poor-quality or frequently changing child-care arrangements. Recent surveys rated 86% of U.S. day-care centers as poor to mediocre in quality, with only 8% rated as excellent (Zigler & Hall, 2000). A recent NICHD study (2002) of children in day-care found that an early start (within the first few months after birth), high intensity (30 or more hours per week), and long duration (up to 4½ years) of use may have negative effects on children's social-emotional outcomes, regardless of quality of day care or quality of parenting. These effects included higher rates of insecure attachments and externalizing behavioral problems, as well as problems with peer relationships and poorer parent–child relationships. It has been postulated that because young infants require a high degree of sensitive and responsive one-on-one care and are more vulnerable to stress, even high-quality day-care situations (with about three other babies present) may be less than adequate (Shonkoff & Phillips, 2000).

These findings have been disputed by many scholars, who suggest that further research is necessary to determine if these results reflect permanent changes or temporary fluctuations in children's psychological functioning, and that these results do not necessarily represent clinical behavioral problems, but rather a socially acceptable level of independence and assertiveness. Clearly, more research in this area is indicated before policy implications can be clearly assessed.

Adoption and Assisted Reproduction

The past two to three decades have also witnessed major changes in patterns of adoption (Hersov, 1994) and in the use of assisted reproduction techniques for conception. Fewer adoptions involve healthy newborns and young infants and increasingly involve older children, many of whom have special needs. International adoptions and transracial adoptions are also growing more common. In addition, some families participate in "open" adoptions that allow for continuing contact with the biological parents; increasing numbers of adoptees are also locating and meeting their biological parents when they reach adulthood. Studies of severely deprived children adopted from poor-quality Romanian orphanages showed that those children who were adopted early, especially prior to 6 months of age, showed few attachment problems when assessed at age 6 years. Those adopted later, at 2 years or more, showed much higher rates of severe attachment problems (Rutter, Kreppner, & O'Connor, 2001). Similarly, later adopted children with histories of abuse and/or neglect and multiple placements were found to have difficulty forming relationships and to have, in general, poor developmental outcomes. Less is known about the effects of both "open" adoptions and the adult adoptee's search for biological parents (Rutter & O'Connor, 1999).

Again, many important questions remain to be answered: What effect does adoption have on the child's working models of attachment? How does the adoptee's "relationship" with the biological parent (known or unknown) affect these working models? Does transracial adoption affect the child's working models (Phoenix & Owen, 1996; Tizard & Phoenix, 1993)?

As more children are born via assisted reproduction techniques such as in vitro fertilization, egg donation, sperm donation, and surrogate motherhood, it will be important to learn more about the consequences of these technologies for attachment. For example, a child born through assisted reproduction may have as many as three to five parents. The question of how this might affect the child's working models and sense of self warrants study (Rutter & O'Connor, 1999). Although there is some evidence to suggest that, all else being equal, these children are not at greater risk with respect to their relationships (Golumbok, Cook, Bish, & Murray, 1995), empirical research would be helpful in discerning how and when to best explain such technologies to the child.

Summary

Advances in research over the past 30 to 40 years have greatly expanded our understanding of infant development. We now know that most babies come into the world equipped with well-developed sensory–perceptual systems; basic motor, cognitive, and language functions; rudimentary personalities or temperaments (based on patterns of emotional reactivity); and genetically based biopsychological motivations and behavioral systems (for example, attachment and exploratory). These innate endowments provide infants with not only the foundation on which future development is built, but also with the ability to actively participate in shaping their own experiences to some extent. On the other hand, recent research also makes it clear that infant development is not primarily internally driven but is equally regulated and shaped by external forces. That is, children's innate potentials must receive *nourishment* from their environment to fully develop. For example, the attachment relationship with at least one primary caregiver represents the fundamental environmental context for infants, and the quality of that relationship has a significant impact on the development of age appropriate socio-emotional and cognitive skills during infancy and childhood. A secure early attachment relationship predicts more successful adaptation in later childhood; securely attached children tend to show better overall social and problem-solving skills.

Any number of factors, either internal or external to the infant, may adversely affect the security of the primary attachment relationship. For example, a disability or illness may impair the infant's ability to clearly signal needs or to respond to normally effective caregiving. On the other hand, external stressors such as poverty, marital discord, substance abuse, or mental illness may, either directly or indirectly, prevent the parent from providing the sensitive, responsive caregiving needed to establish a secure attachment bond. Finally, temperamental "mismatches" between parent and child may lead to dysfunctional transactions that interfere with attachment security.

Neurobiological research findings also support the notion of a transactional model for infant development, as well as the significance of the primary attachment relationship. The first 2 years of life represent a period of rapid brain growth. During this time, the brain exhibits an extremely high degree of plasticity, and the environment plays a major role in the shaping of the brain's circuitry. For example, there is now some evidence (some based on magnetic resonance imaging technology) that early severe disturbances in the primary attachment relationship may result in abnormal brain development, for example, smaller size, disturbances in the stress response system, and underdeveloped cortical structures and overdevelopment of more primitive lower and midbrain functions (Perry, 1994, 1997, 2002b; DeBellis et al., 1999; Schore, 2001). These abnormalities are thought to result in a variety of symptoms seen in children who have experienced early trauma (for example, impaired concentration and motivation, high levels of anxiety, sleep disturbances).

Although the importance of a secure attachment based on parental consistency is universally valued across cultures (Waters & Cummings, 2000; Posada et al., 2002), cultures differ widely in how they provide infant care, in the child-rearing practices they employ to prepare their children for adulthood, and in how attachment behavior is expressed. Within our own culture, major social changes with respect to families and family functioning, including working mothers and substitute child care, transracial adoptions and adoptions of older children, and assisted reproductive technology, have raised new issues and questions regarding attachment development and expression in an ever-widening range of circumstances.

10 Early Childhood: The Toddler and Early School Years

Introduction

We define "early childhood" as the period of life from ages 1½ to 6 years of age. This encompasses what are commonly referred to as the "toddler" (ages 1½ to 3) and "early school years" (ages 3 to 6)—periods that are often examined as two distinct developmental stages. During the toddler years, children undergo rapid advances in motor, cognitive, emotional, social, and language skills and experience a strong, biologically based urge to be autonomous and in control of their actions. Erikson's (1963) psychosocial crisis of autonomy versus shame and doubt reflects the developmental challenges for this age group.

With continued rapid developmental progress in all areas, children gradually become less egocentric, more self-controlled, and more aware of the complexities of reality. There emerges, during the early school years, a powerful motivation to absorb and assimilate new information and to make connections between experiences, as children begin to realize that there is much they do not know (Davies, 2004). The early school-age child's seemingly relentless curiosity and endless questions about almost everything reflect a strong urge to understand how the world works, and these underlie Erikson's psychosocial crisis of "initiative versus guilt."

During early childhood, the number of synapses and the branching of neuronal circuits in the brain continue to increase steadily. The myelination process, begun in infancy, also continues, insulating the neuronal circuits that link different parts of the brain. This process allows the child to better integrate information from a variety of sources. As a result, one sees improved integration of perceptual, physical, and cognitive functions, greater speed of thought, and a developing self-awareness (Nelson, 2000).

Biological–Psychological Development

Neurobiological Development

Between the ages of 16 and 24 months, a burst of growth in the cortical areas of the brain, particularly in the left temporal lobe, may account for the improvement in memory and information-processing skills that are necessary for advances in language such as learning large numbers of words and linguistic structures (Johnson, 1998). The reticular formation (a structure in the brain stem responsible for maintaining alertness and consciousness) sends neural fibers to other areas of the brain and begins its myelination in early childhood. Circuits in the sensory and motor areas become myelinated, and this allows for continued improvement in perceptual and motor skills and in the integration of the two (Nelson, 2000). Functions located in the right and left hemispheres of the brain are increasingly integrated during the early school years with advanced myelination of the corpus callosum (a structure that links the two hemispheres). The process of myelination of the fibers linking the cerebellum (a structure that assists in control of body movements and balance) with the cerebral cortex is completed around age 4 (Tanner, 1990) and is probably related to the substantial gains in motor control in children of this age.

Motor Development

Motor skills improve rapidly during the toddler years. One- and 2-year-olds may struggle to control gross motor movements; by age 3, activities such as walking, running, climbing stairs, and riding a tricycle are accomplished with relative ease (Davies, 2004). With greater integration of brain functions, physical coordination improves, and toddlers spend much time engaged in a variety of gross and fine motor activities. In addition to pleasure, these activities provide important opportunities for mastery and thus make significant contributions to the toddler's self-concept. Improved motor skills also allow for more autonomy in "activities of daily living." For example, with increases in control of their hands and in eye–hand coordination (in other words, the ability to guide the hands with the eyes), toddlers become adept at feeding themselves with a spoon, fork, and cup; as they gain control over their bowel and bladder musculature, they become ready for toilet training. Finally, the advances in gross and fine motor control allow for greater access to a wide range of opportunities for exploring the environment.

These motor skills continue to develop at a steady pace during the early school years. Children become stronger and more coordinated and can perform increasingly complex gross motor skills, such as skipping, hopping, throwing a ball, or pumping a swing, with a well-organized set of movements. Eye–hand coordination improves enough to allow for cutting with scissors and such preacademic skills as drawing simple shapes and recognizably human figures, as well as (in some cases) the ability to write letters and numbers. Improved fine motor skills allow for greater independence in such activities as dressing (for example, buttoning and zippering).

Cognitive Development

Along with the improvements in motor skills that allow for physical access to a wider environment, cognitive advances during this period provide toddlers with important tools for understanding how the world works. By the age of 2, (the outer limit of what Piaget, 1952, referred to as the "sensorimotor period"), toddlers generally exhibit a good grasp of the cognitive concepts gained in infancy. They are able to use these as a foundation on which to gradually build the more complex cognitive concepts necessary for the logical, abstract forms of thought used by older children. They begin to progress beyond evoking simple mental images (representational thinking) toward increasing use of symbols to represent objects and other environmental stimuli (symbolic thinking). For example, toddlers increasingly play "pretend," using one object to represent another (for example, pretend that sand is food they can "feed" to a doll); they are also aware that objects have names, and they begin to use words to represent more and more things. Memory continues to improve, as do problem-solving skills and the ability to formulate simple, action-oriented goals and plans (for example, to plan to put a puzzle together or to look for a toy that is out of sight).

Cognitively speaking, children from about 2 to 6 years of age (encompassing both the toddler and early school-age periods) are in a period of transition. As they consolidate and build on the cognitive foundation developed in infancy, they gradually (with acknowledged variation in timing, due in part to biology and in part to experience) move from a rather "magical" orientation to a more logical understanding of the workings of the environment. Piaget (1952) referred to this period as the "preoperational stage" of cognitive development. During the early part of this life phase, young children's ability to objectively understand reality is impeded by such developmental limitations as egocentrism (in other words, the view of oneself as central and causative; the inability to take the perspective of others); a limited ability to determine causality and predict consequences; difficulty distinguishing between thought and action (thus a belief that feelings may cause things to happen); and difficulty viewing more than one dimension of an object or circumstance at a time.

During the early school years, as brain functions continue to mature, children begin to grasp the more complex cognitive concepts that underlie the capacity for logical thought; thus they are able to perceive reality more clearly. Egocentrism gradually diminishes during this period, so that children at ages 4 or 5 are often able to see another's point of view; by 6, the capacity for nonegocentric thought is much more consistently available (Davies, 2004). Through repeated experiences, combined with expanding language skills, early school-age children enlarge their knowledge base. They begin to see similarities between experiences, to make associations, and to form increasingly complex categories (for example, they begin to sort by color, size, and shape). With the ability to perceive similarity comes the ability to discern differences, and this provides the cognitive foundation for their growing self-awareness, their beginning awareness that other people have their own feelings, thoughts, and intentions, and their ability to discern cultural expectations. Children of this age develop a beginning capacity for seriation (the ability to order objects by particular characteristics), and this ability continues to develop through childhood. For example, 5-year-olds may, with effort, be able to order objects by length (for example, shortest to longest); however, the ability to order by volume is often not possible until about age 12 (Zastrow & Kirst-Ashman, 1997). Despite these advances, early school-age children still tend to rely less on reasoning and more on observable surface qualities (in other words, appearance alters perception) to interpret reality; by the time they enter the middle-school-age years, most have a grasp of the concept of conservation (in other words, matter is neither created nor destroyed despite changes in form) and are able to use logic to understand changes in appearance.

Language Development

There is a great leap in language learning starting at about age 18 months. Working vocabulary jumps from less than 50 words at age 18 months to about 1,000 words by age 3. Children generally begin to use two- and three-word sentences by around age 2; by age 3, they can construct longer, more complex sentence structures that make appropriate use of personal pronouns, prepositions, and plurals. Between the ages of 3 and 4, intelligibility of speech generally improves and by age 5, advances in vocabulary and grammatical skills are sufficient to allow the child to increasingly rely on language rather than action as their primary means of communication.

The use of words as a primary means of communication is momentous and has important implications for many areas such as development of a sense of self and advancement of cognitive skills. More information about the influence of language will be highlighted throughout this chapter in the context of other aspects of development.

The Emerging Sense of Self

Around the age of 18 months, toddlers begin to develop a clear sense of themselves as autonomous beings with their own thoughts, feelings, and intentions. This is accompanied by a strong urge to assert control and do things for themselves, often without regard for their actual level of competence or incompetence as the case may be. By age 2, with improvements in active memory and other cognitive skills, toddlers are far less distractible than they were at age 1, and this allows for greater persistence in pursuing independent action.

Paralleling the shift to cognitive self-awareness, toddlers gradually become aware of, and interested in, the thoughts, emotions, and intentions of others. By age 2, toddlers develop "self-consciousness," meaning they can now begin to imagine how others see them. Although they do not seem to be aware of social comparisons (in other words, being better or worse than others), they are, at this stage, sensitive to the positive and negative reactions of others (Newman & Newman, 1999). This leads to the experience of new emotions such as enjoyment of praise from other people and feelings of pride in their accomplishments, and on the other hand, shame and embarrassment about failure or from incurring the disapproval of others (Davies, 2004). The urge to assert control and the developmental advances noted earlier underlie Erikson's (1963) psychosocial crisis of autonomy versus shame and doubt.

Imitation and the Autonomous Self During the toddler years, imitation becomes a primary mechanism for learning and for the development of a sense of autonomy and self-control. Toddlers, motivated by the drive for mastery and competence, imitate almost everything they observe; in this way they acquire a vast array of skills that pave the way for greater autonomy (Newman & Newman, 1999). As adults perform tasks, express feelings and attitudes, and act according to their moral value, their toddlers, through observation and imitation, become socialized into their family's (and, by extension, their community's and culture's) way of life. In addition to advancements in such skill areas as household activities, language, and self-care, the imitation of caregiver behaviors allows toddlers to develop skills that satisfy their need for social competence (Kuczynski, Zahn-Waxler, & Radke-Yarrow, 1987).

By the end of the toddler period, children have a fairly well established sense of themselves as autonomous individuals. Older toddlers frequently use the pronouns "I," "me," and "mine" (as well as "he," "she," and "we"); they can describe internal psychological states such as emotions, desires, and intentions; and they have incorporated a beginning awareness of gender identity ("I am a girl" or "I am a boy"). During this stage, the self-concept is highly dependent on the sense that one is competent and loved (Newman & Newman, 1999).

Attachment and the Sense of Self Much of young children's sense of self is derived from experiences in the attachment relationship. For example, the views children develop of themselves are based, in large part, on how the attachment figures regard them (Thompson, 1998). When parents have been consistent and effective in helping the child feel safe, cope with anxiety and frustration, and evaluate potentially dangerous situations, the child gradually internalizes these abilities as part of her or his working models of self (Davies, 2004).

The Sense of Self in an Expanding Social Environment Although children in early school age continue to depend on the actual attachment relationship for security and support, advancements in symbolic thinking allow them to begin to derive comfort simply by thinking about the caretakers (Bretherton & Munholland, 1999).

During the early school years, children's worlds generally begin to expand to include influences beyond the family (for example, friends, neighborhood, school, television). This wider range of social exposure, combined with the cognitive advances described earlier, contributes to a significant expansion of the child's sense of self during this period. As children become more capable of understanding the perspectives of others, and as their memories, language skills, and capacities for logical and abstract thinking improve, they begin to recognize cultural norms and values, social roles (including gender-related issues), and behavioral and moral expectations. The beginning capacity to make associations among experiences and to assimilate new information expands their knowledge base and stimulates a seemingly insatiable curiosity about the workings of the world. Erikson (1963) refers to this urge to actively investigate and understand the environment on a conceptual level as "initiative." Children of this age may express initiative in a host of ways (for example, asking questions; taking things apart to see how they work; exploring their own (and sometimes, their friends') bodies; experimenting with different behaviors just to observe the consequences; drawing; painting; or building things. Whereas the toddler is motivated toward simple physical exploration of the environment, the child in early school-age strives to actively manipulate the environment on a more conceptual level (Newman & Newman, 1999).

The Emerging Self Concept This is the time of life when children's self-concepts become increasingly differentiated. According to Damon and Hart (1988) the self is initially viewed by the early school-age child as a collection of categorical identifications or concrete, observable characteristics and typical behaviors and activities (for example, I have brown eyes; I am a Catholic; I have a baby sister; I like to draw) that seem to have little significance to the child outside the fact that they exist. In other words, during this phase of life, children tend to define themselves according to their observable attributes. The self becomes increasingly complex and enhanced through the child's identification with the parents and other significant people. The process of identification is much more global than the toddler's simple imitations of behavior in that through identification, the child incorporates valued characteristics of the parent as part of him- or herself.

Identification and the Sense of Self Identification allows the child to maintain a feeling of closeness to the parents even when they are not present. The feelings of security the child derives from this sense of closeness support her or his ability to function more independently and to tolerate the physical separations from the parents that are necessary for further development. A significant outcome of the parental identifications of early school age is the development of the idealized self-image, referred to in psychoanalytic theory as the ego ideal. Here, the child internalizes a set of positive standards, ideals, and ambitions that represent the ways she or he would like to be, based on the values of the parents and the culture (Newman & Newman, 1999).

Gender Identity and the Sense of Self It is during early childhood that children begin to conceptualize gender as one dimension of their self-concept. According to Kohlberg (1966), the process of understanding one's gender involves four developments that occur sequentially during this phase of life. By the age of about 2½, children can correctly label themselves and other children as boys or girls and can use other gender-related labels (for example, brother, sister) accurately. Somewhere between the ages of 4 and 7 (Serbin, Powlishta, & Gulko, 1993), children learn that one's gender is a stable and constant characteristic that does not change as one grows older, or as one changes dress or hairstyles. This understanding generally develops as children learn that gender has a genital basis and/or as they internalize social norms relating to gender. By age 5, most children understand that gender does not change as do other characteristics such as height and weight (Szkrybalo & Ruble, 1999). Once children become aware of gender labels, they begin to identify with the same-sex parent, to specifically attend to the characteristics their culture associates with gender, and to develop basic gender categories or schemas (Bem, 1981) that strengthen gender-typed self-images and behaviors as they are incorporated into the child's self-concept. During early childhood, children's beliefs about gender-appropriate behavior become stronger and are often applied quite rigidly. This is likely due in part to environmental factors and in part to young children's cognitive limitations (for example, difficulty integrating conflicting information; Berk, 1999).

Questions regarding the origin of differences between the behaviors, preferences, and self-concepts of boys and girls remain and continue to be actively debated. What is not disputed is that differences exist, and that over time, the self-concept becomes *gender-typed.* Hormonal activity accounts in part for behavioral differences observed between boys and girls and for children's tendency to prefer playing with same-sex peers. As a result of higher levels of androgens (male sex hormones), boys as a group tend to show higher activity levels, greater impulsivity, and more overt aggression, whereas girls tend to be more fearful, sensitive, compliant, and relationally aggressive (Eisenberg & Fabes, 1998; Feingold, 1994; Geary, 1998; Saarni, 1993). Sex-based differences in play styles are similarly affected by hormonal activity (Macoby, 1998), with girls frequently preferring calmer, quieter activities than boys. As children begin to interact more with peers in early childhood, they begin to show preferences for playmates with compatible interests and behavioral styles.

In addition to biologically based differences, much evidence exists to support the notion that the child's social environment serves to promote gender-typed behaviors, especially for boys. Research has documented differences in parental expectations (Brody, 1999; Turner & Gervai, 1995) as well as differential parenting practices for boys and girls (Leaper, 1994; Kuebli, Butler, & Fivush, 1995). Supporting the view that environmental forces affect gender-typing, researchers have found that children whose parents exhibit nonstereotypic gender role behavior are less gender-typed themselves (Turner & Gervai, 1995; Tenenbaum & Leaper, 2002; Weisner & Wilson-Mitchell, 1990). Along the same lines, children with opposite-sex older siblings show less gender typing, presumably because they have had more experience with "cross-gender" activities and values.

Preschoolers' propensity for playing with same-sex peers also reinforces gender-typed behaviors (Martin & Fabes, 2001) and leads to different styles of social interaction (Leaper, 1994; Leaper, Tenenbaum, & Shaffer, 1999). For example, boys tend to play in larger groups and to use commands and physical force to influence playmates. Girls, on the other hand, tend to prefer playing in pairs and tend to rely on persuasion, concern with the friend's needs, and acceptance as a means of influence. As friendship groups become more segregated, boys and girls begin to inhabit two distinct social worlds with differing beliefs, interests, and behaviors (Macoby, 2002). By age 4 children are three times as likely to prefer play with same-sex as opposed to opposite-sex peers. This pattern is seen across cultures (Berk, 1999) and continues through childhood (Benenson, 1993; Martin & Fabes, 2001).

Self-Regulation (Self-Control) and Moral Development Especially during the toddler years, children's burgeoning sense of themselves as individuals with minds of their own, and their determination to assert themselves, often lead to behaviors that appear irrational, negative, and out of control. This is due to the fact that despite their desire to control themselves (behaviorally and emotionally), toddlers do not yet have well-developed capacities for self-regulation, and they are easily distressed for a variety of reasons (Davies, 2004). See Table 10.1 for an overview of common sources of stress for children in early childhood. In addition, the young toddler's developing physical skills and urge to explore invariably lead to the need for parents to limit their behavior in the interest of safety.

The period of early childhood represents the beginning of moral development in that the child gradually develops first, self-control, and then, over time, the ability to internalize parental standards and expectations. It is during this time that parents begin to raise their expectations for behavior and to teach what is, and what is not, considered to be acceptable behavior. Many developmental advances converge to prepare the child for such instruction, including a beginning awareness that others have their own separate perspectives; development of a rudimentary sense of time and the concept of future; improved memory; improved capacity for empathy; improved understanding of cause-and-effect relationships; a heightened interest in deviations from norms (Kagan, 1984); and a newly emerging capacity for self-evaluation and goal formulation. Despite these cognitive advances, the toddler's sense of right and wrong remains relatively primitive and is motivated primarily by the wish to obtain the parents' approval and to avoid punishment. Although toddlers become increasingly aware of their parents' standards and expectations, they rely heavily on the external controls imposed by the parent because of their limited internal controls (Emde & Buchsbaum, 1990). Toddlers begin to use psychological defense mechanisms such as projection to help them self-regulate. In general, it has been found that those

TABLE 10.1

Sources of Stress for Children in Early Childhood

Difficulty in understanding what is happening. For toddlers, egocentrism and magical thinking can cause misunderstandings and distortions that cause anxiety. Although early school-age children demonstrate better reality testing, this is unreliable, especially in times of stress.

Difficulty in communicating. This is especially true for toddlers, who can think better than they can speak.

Frustration over not being able to do what they can imagine.

Conflicts between wanting to be on their own versus wanting parent's help.

Separation or threat of separation from caregivers.

Fears of losing the parent's approval and of being unloved, rejected, or abandoned. This issue arises frequently for toddlers, whose desires and behaviors often conflict with the parents' expectations. Another common source of distress is the fear of losing the parents' love to a new sibling, given that many families have their children within 2 or 3 years of each other.

Reactions to losing self-control. It feels frightening and overwhelming to lose control of one's impulses. Early school-age children are much better able to control themselves than are toddlers; however, the experience of loss of control is equally distressing for children in both phases. Distress over the results of aggressive behavior or thought may be intensified by the child's egocentricity, which leads him/her to think that others have the same feelings and thoughts toward him/her. Other forms of loss of control, such as lapses in toilet training, may be equally distressing to a young child struggling to control dependency wishes.

Distress related to rejection by peers. This is particularly distressing to children in early school age, for whom the role of peers and friends becomes increasingly significant. Children become more aware of how they are perceived by peers and more sensitive to rejection, teasing, and exclusion. Still hampered by egocentricity and a limited ability to evaluate the intent of others, the young child may experience insults as if they are true and react with strong feelings of humiliation and anger.

Source: D. Davies, 2004, *Child Development: A Practitioner's Guide* (2nd ed.), (pp. 212 and 288–289). New York: The Guilford Press. Adapted with permission.

children who demonstrate the ability to comply with parents' wishes in toddlerhood tend to develop adequate internal controls by age 6 (Kochanska, Aksan, & Koenig, 1995).

Like toddlers, children in early school age continue to depend on the attachment relationship for help with regulation of feelings and impulses (most notably, in times of stress); however, they make substantial progress in their ability to exert internally based self-control. Children commonly use rather primitive psychological defense mechanisms such as *projection, displacement, denial,* and *regression* to help with self-regulation during this phase. They gradually begin to internalize parental expectations and limits; eventually these become part of the child's own self-concept. In fact, during this phase, children begin to use the social skills learned in the attachment relationship in their dealings with peer conflicts. As they use these strategies successfully, children feel a greater sense of control, increased self-esteem, and tend to experience greater popularity with peers (Dunn, Cuttling, & Fisher, 2002).

The child's progress in the development of internalized self-control is made possible, in part, from cognitive developments that occur during this phase. Improvements in the ability to categorize experiences allow the child to make generalizations that serve to minimize distress through a sense of familiarity. For example, a child who has attended group day care may feel less apprehensive about beginning school than a child who has not had that experience. Along similar lines, improvements in memory allow the child to recall not only rules and expectations for behavior, but also the consequences of previous actions; they are then able to use these memories to make choices about future behavior.

Other developmental advances converge to promote the process of internalization of moral standards. Competent use of language furthers the young child's ability to self-regulate in several ways. The ability to make "good" choices is reinforced, as children use words to remind themselves of rules and to guide their behavior. Increased ability to use language allows for communication of desires and needs in a way that others easily understand, thereby reducing a major source of frustration. In addition, language allows the child to begin to replace actions with words. Putting strong feelings into words serves to diffuse some of their intensity; in addition, the act of announcing one's intentions serves to delay action momentarily and may afford the child an opportunity to consider the consequences of an action.

As knowledge and awareness of moral expectations increase through interactions in which behaviors are either rewarded or punished/ignored, children begin to internalize them and to make moral judgments about their own feelings, wishes, and impulses. Identification with parents and their values reinforces this process, as does the child's increasing motivation to have friends. By about age 5, children are able to explain the reasons for their moral judgments. Such moral reasoning relies on the child's increasing ability to empathize and to see another's perspective. The capacity to feel guilt (a painful, negative emotion that follows the belief that one has thought, felt, or done something wrong) develops sometime between the ages of 3 and 4. In Kagan's view, this capacity emerges as a direct result of a new cognitive "talent" (1984, p. 175)—the child's recognition that she or he has the capacity to choose how, and how not, to behave. By about age 6 the process of internalization of morality results in the formation of the conscience or superego. This, together with the "ego ideal," forms the internal locus of control for moral behavior.

By the ages of 5 or 6 children can manage their emotions fairly well. "Emotional competence" has been defined as the ability to express one's feelings without being overtaken by them, the ability to recognize feelings (one's own and those of others), and the ability to consciously control one's emotions (Saarni, 1999). Emotional competence in early school age predicts good peer relationships and good school adjustment in the elementary school years (Denham et al., 2003).

Sociocultural Development: A Transactional View

Recent theory and research clearly indicate that early child development (as well as that of other life phases) is more or less equally driven and regulated by internal as well as external factors.

The notion that early childhood may represent a sensitive period for the development of a host of basic cognitive, language, and socioemotional skills (and problems) is reinforced by studies of brain functioning (Cicchetti & Tucker, 1994). From a neurobiological perspective, the early years of life are characterized by a high degree of plasticity that makes this a time of both tremendous adaptability and vulnerability to environmental experiences (Leseman, 2002). Some (Pianta, 1999) have even suggested that the child's adaptation and competence during the early years is *primarily* a property of systems that are *external* to the child. Although attachment relationships within the family continue to represent primary contexts for development, the importance of larger social forces (for example, poverty, neighborhood violence) must not be overlooked (Huston, 1991; Masten, 1992; Radke-Yarrow et al., 1995). Although these social ills may affect young children through their impact on the family (regardless of quality of attachment), one must also recognize their influence on child development (Pianta, 1999). In Pianta's words, "It is difficult even for the most well-tuned physiology to regulate itself in the context of home environments that are unpredictable or violent (e.g., Cummings et al.). . . . In a larger sense, the distributed nature of competence means that children are only as competent as their context affords them the opportunities to be" (1999, p. 98).

On the other hand, evidence also supports the fact that internal factors exert influence on early childhood development. Right from the start, children show internally based differences (for example, distinct "personalities" or temperaments; basic capacities in the areas of communication, cognition, and perceptual-motor skills; innate biopsychological needs and motives). Additionally, neurobiological growth, coordination, and consolidation processes develop according to genetically programmed timetables. "These processes both facilitate the development of ever more complex skills in task-activities and social interaction, but also constrain what at a given age and in a given period of time can be appropriated by the child through activity and social interaction" (Leseman, 2002).

The following section will explore the ways in which transactions among developmentally driven internally based motivations (for example, the desire for social interaction with peers); internally based individual differences (for example, temperament, disabilities); important environmental contexts (for example, family, peers, school); and social forces (for example, poverty, abuse, sociocultural status) may affect the young child and her or his developmental path.

Peer Relationships and Play

The child's social world expands significantly during early childhood. Peer interaction becomes increasingly important and occurs primarily through various forms of play.

Peer Relationships As children increasingly value spending time with peers and gaining their acceptance, they are motivated to develop skills in perspective taking, sharing, and negotiation as means of maintaining their friendships (Piaget, 1951). In fact, resiliency research indicates that having friends serves as a protective factor for children, while not having friends puts them at risk (Werner, 2000).

In addition to supporting the development of social skills, friendships help children cope with such developmental transitions as starting school. Children with friends in kindergarten show better attitudes toward school and better academic performance overall (Ladd, 1990, 1999). From early childhood on, the quality of children's relationships with peers is considered to be an important indicator of their overall level of adaptation and social and emotional competence. By the time they enter middle childhood, children are expected to have developed the skills needed to form stable friendships. Difficulties in peer relationships during early childhood strongly predict later mental health problems (Kazdin, 1992; Loeber, Green, & Lahey, 1990).

Play Children's play behaviors develop significantly from the ages of 3 to 5 years. The simple, repetitive sensorimotor play activities of infancy (for example, banging a xylophone with a stick) progress to more functional play (in other words, using objects such as toy cars as they are meant to be used) and/or more constructive sorts of activities that involve creating things (for example, drawing, building with blocks). These activities may be solitary, or children may engage with others in parallel play (in other words, alongside other children but in separate activities); in associative play (engaged in separate activities from peers but with mutual interaction such as sharing toys, commenting on each other's activities); or in cooperative play (in other words, interacting with peers on a common activity such as building a house with blocks).

Two new types of play emerge during these early years. As children become more interested in cooperative play, they begin to participate in group games (for example, Hide and Go Seek or Red Light–Green Light) that involve simple rules, physical skills, and a degree of coordination and cooperation. These provide experiences in perspective taking and role reciprocity and may pave the way for participation in more advanced team sports in middle childhood.

Advancements in cognition that allow children to represent an action in memory and then copy what they remember leads to the development of "pretend" play. As symbolic thinking advances and children understand that they can give objects "pretend" meanings, "make-believe" or "pretend" play becomes increasingly complex. Children's play progresses from solitary imitation of familiar activities (for example, pretending to vacuum the floor) to planned organized activities involving other children (or adults) roles, props, and agreed-upon stories.

Theories as to the significance of pretend play vary; however, few would disagree that such activity is more than an amusing pastime. Piaget (1962) believed that pretend play allowed the child to make sense of experience by allowing for mental manipulations not possible in reality. Vygotsky (1978) saw such play as involving a cognitive process in which the child is free to practice skills she or he has yet to master in "real life" (in other words, *zone of proximal development*). Erikson (1972) saw the value of pretend play in supporting social and personality development. In his view, the dramatization of psychological struggles (for example, anger at parents; jealously toward siblings) provides relief from tension and affords children the freedom to explore confusing or distressing experiences without the pressures of having to make themselves understood through language or to adhere to social expectations for behavior.

Temperament

The role of temperament should not be overlooked when examining development in early childhood. In Kagan's view, the temperamental biases toward inhibition, or lack of inhibition to the unfamiliar, tend to be preserved from infancy to adulthood. This is due in part to its biological base and in part to the fact that "many moments of every day are punctuated by interactions with other people that require a decision to withdraw or to participate. Each time one chooses either course, the relevant habit is strengthened, making this disposition an intimate part of each person's character" (1984, p. 69).

Temperament and Goodness of Fit Kagan noted that parents (and others) respond differently to inhibited and uninhibited children, and that each child's behavior is ultimately "a joint product of the child's temperament and the adult reactions" (p. 70). For example, children classified as *behaviorally inhibited* seem cautious and shy and tend to withdraw emotionally in response to the stress of novel situations. Parents and other adults may reinforce this inhibited behavior by overprotecting the child and restricting autonomy (Messer & Beidel, 1994). On the other hand, if parents combine patient and firm support for participation, with acceptance of the child's need to "warm up" to the unfamiliar experience, the child is likely to become actively involved, thereby increasing the sense of autonomy and strengthening coping skills.

Thomas and Chess (1977) used a transactional, "goodness of fit" model to explain how the interaction between temperament and parenting style may affect a child's behavior and development. For example, a parent with an active, outgoing disposition may feel frustrated, disappointed, and perplexed by a cautious child who uses withdrawal to cope with stress. The parent may, with the best of intentions, try to push the child to participate prematurely, thereby increasing the child's distress and need to withdraw (as well as increasing the risk for later development of anxiety-related disorders). This would not be considered a "good fit," and the parent might benefit greatly from help in understanding why her or his well-intentioned helping style seems to overwhelm and "shut down" the shy, timid child.

On the other hand, in Western middle-class families, children with difficult temperaments are at higher risk for later behavior problems. This is presumably due to a poor fit between the child's temperamental style and cultural expectations. These children have been found to receive less sensitive caregiving in infancy (Van den Boom & Hoeksma, 1994), and as they grow, frustrated parents may resort to inconsistent and/or punitive reactions that inadvertently reinforce the child's negative behavior (Berk, 1999).

In essence, the "goodness of fit" model emphasizes the need for child-rearing environments in which adaptive functioning is supported by recognizing each child's temperamental needs and tailoring parenting strategies to best suit them; here, parenting strategies build on the child's strengths to help them master developmental challenges (Berk, 1999).

Temperament and Culture The role of cultural "fit" is also important when examining temperament and child-rearing practices. For example, temperamentally impulsive, nonanxious children from low-income Puerto Rican families are not at risk for later behavioral problems, presumably because parenting practices in these families favor treating such children with patient acceptance (Gannon & Korn, 1983). In China and other parts of Asia, shy, restrained behavior is valued and seen as a sign of advanced social development (Chen, Rubin, & Li, 1995), whereas in Western cultures, the same behavior is often viewed as a sign of social incompetence. In a study of Canadian and Chinese children, Chen and colleagues (1998) found that Canadian mothers were less accepting than Chinese mothers of their shy children—they punished them more frequently and were less encouraging of achievement. Chinese mothers showed the opposite reaction to shy children, providing more encouragement of achievement and less punishment.

Temperament and Parental Discipline Strategies Kochanska (1993, 1997; Kochanska, Aksan, & Koenig, 1995) found that child temperament influences the effectiveness of parental discipline strategies. For example, she found that temperamentally inhibited children are highly sensitive to expressions of disapproval. These children generally respond to mild discipline (for example, reasoning suggestion, gentle requests) with adequate moral internalization and conscience development (Kochanska, 1997; Fowles & Kochanska, 2000). Being very susceptible to anxiety, these children are easily overwhelmed by more intense forms of discipline and/or too much power assertion. In contrast, mild disapproval does not make impulsive, nonanxious children uncomfortable enough to stimulate moral internalization, and frequent use of power assertion tends to be counterproductive, in that it creates resentment that interferes with the child's ability to process the adult's messages (Kochanska, 1993; Kochanska, Aksan, & Koenig, 1995). For these children, it is more effective to provide consistent, more directive discipline that focuses on rewarding good behavior and avoiding situations that tend to provoke difficult behavior. In addition, a secure attachment relationship is vital to conscience development in nonanxious children. Kochanska (1997) posits that for children who do not respond with discomfort to commonly effective disciplinary strategies, a close relationship with the attachment figure provides an alternate pathway for moral development (in other words, the child is motivated by the desire to maintain close, loving ties to the caregiver).

Disabilities

This section will examine several disorders, the early signs of which may become apparent in early childhood. We will view these from a developmental perspective, viewing early signs and symptoms as they relate to the period of early childhood. We direct the reader to Chapter 2, "Neurobiological Underpinnings of Human Development," for a more comprehensive discussion of each of these disabilities.

Learning Disabilities Early signs of various learning disorders may become apparent during early childhood. Young children may show deficits in speech and language development, reasoning abilities, and other capacities necessary for the acquisition of early academic skills. These deficits may be accompanied by problems in the development of motor, social, and/or self-regulatory skills.

For example, children with sensory integration disorders may be more vulnerable to hyperarousal; thus, in early childhood, they may experience more difficulty developing strategies for self-regulation (Davies, 2004). This problem may have particular impact on the development of what is referred to as "effortful control." Most children show a beginning capacity for effortful control by around age 2. Children with sensory processing difficulties, however, may find themselves easily overstimulated by situations that would not overwhelm a less-reactive child, and they generally need adult intervention to help decrease arousal (De Gangi, 2000).

Increased awareness of genetic and developmental risk factors as well as the availability of brief screening tests make early identification of children at risk for some learning disabilities possible. However, in reality, many children with learning disabilities only receive services after they have failed, in elementary school, to learn to read. Many are either retained in grade, mainstreamed with long-term remediation, and/or assigned to special education classes.

Attention Deficit Hyperactivity Disorder Although many parents report signs of attention deficit hyperactivity disorder (ADHD) in their children as far back as infancy or even from before birth, referrals for diagnostic evaluation of this disorder are typically initiated during early childhood (or later). This is probably because symptoms of the disorder often become more obvious when children enter school (or preschool) and are expected to follow directions and coordinate their social behaviors with other children.

Typically, the first symptoms of ADHD to be noticeable are *hyperactivity* and *impulsivity* around the age of 3. By age 5 (or later) symptoms of inattention may become more prominent (Hart et al., 1995). Parents of preschoolers with ADHD have described their children as continuously moving and unresponsive to praise and punishment (Weiss & Hechtman, 1993). Alessandri (1992) found preschoolers who met the criteria for this diagnosis were more restless and distractible than their typically developing peers; in addition, they engaged in less constructive and cooperative play.

Typically, these young children show difficulties in modulating their behavior in response to varying situational demands (Abikoff, 1985; Barkley, 1996). By the very nature of the disorder, young children with ADHD are unable to cooperate and be productive in preschool settings, and their disruptive behavior puts them at high risk for expulsion from such programs (Blackman et al., 1991). This situation serves to compound the risks associated with this disorder in that, having been denied the opportunity to work on the preacademic and social skills needed to adapt to the structure of school, these children are at increased risk for future school failure. Without appropriate school and home-based intervention, many of these behavioral problems will persist (and often escalate) when the child is faced with the increasing demands and expectations of elementary school (Campbell, 1990; Olson & Hoza, 1993). Not surprisingly, these children are at increased risk for later diagnosis of other externalizing behavioral problems (Abikoff, 1985; Barkley, 1998), such as oppositional, defiant, and conduct disorders.

In light of the risks associated with the disorder, it is strongly recommended that children receive early intervention designed to prepare them for kindergarten (McGoey, Eckert, & DuPaul, 2002). However, early differential diagnosis is complicated by the fact that many other conditions (for example, sensory impairments, language disorders, learning disorders, mental retardation, emotional, psychiatric, or behavioral disorders) may mimic the symptoms of ADHD. Information gathered from parents, community service providers, and experts in the field (Eckert, McGoey, & DuPaul, 1996) indicate a lack of appropriate resources for this group; specifically noted were strong needs for interventions designed to educate parents and service providers about the disorder as well as direct services to children designed to improve behaviors and academic performance. Given the current state of the literature, practitioners have little specific information with which to guide their interventions with preschool-age children who show symptoms of this disorder. However, some general guidelines can be extrapolated from current research (McGoey, Eckert, & DuPaul, 2002). At present, most professionals agree that treatment for children with ADHD should involve a well-coordinated combination of interventions, possibly offered over a long term. These interventions generally include use of psychostimulant medication, parent support, and training in behavior management techniques as well as classroom interventions to manage behavior in the classroom (Barkley, 1998; Hinshaw, 1994).

Autism As noted in Chapter 2, autism is the most severe (and well-researched) subtype of the pervasive developmental disorders (PDD) and is characterized by impairments in social interaction and communication impairments in social interaction and communication skills as well as narrowly focused, unusual, and stereotypic patterns of behavior and interest. Autistic children often exhibit problem behaviors in response to demands that stress their capacities in the areas of language comprehension and expression, sensory processing, and ability to tolerate change. Early childhood programs that are highly structured, consistent, and predictable tend to reduce frustration and stress and may help to prevent many of these challenging behaviors from emerging in the first place.

However, children are often not diagnosed with autism until after the age of 3 or 4 because the primary symptoms involve difficulties in areas (for example, peer relationships) that do not typically develop before then. Because of the perceived value of early intervention in preventing many of the potential difficulties associated with this disorder, experts in the field are encouraging recognition of signs and symptoms that may be present at age 2 or earlier.

For example, at about the age of 18 months, typically developing children begin to develop increasing awareness of their own thoughts and feelings, as well as those of other people. These capacities form what is referred to as a theory of mind, or metacognition, and they pave the way for future social and moral development by allowing for the development of empathy. This increased capacity for empathy allows the child to relate to others with increasing sophistication, intuiting the intentions, desires, thoughts, and feelings of others and guiding her or his behavior in prosocial ways.

As early as age 2, autistic children show deficits in capacities related to metacognition and theory of mind (Baron-Cohen, 2001). They tend not to establish joint attention (for example, call someone's attention to something by using such techniques as pointing) or to imitate the motor movements of others (Charman et al., 1997). They seem relatively unaware of the feelings and intentions of others (Klinger, Dawson, & Renner, 2003) and engage in significantly less cooperative, functional, and pretend play than other young children (Hughes, 1998). Current thinking suggests that these signs of atypical development be addressed through early intervention services whether or not a definitive diagnosis has been made.

The Child-Rearing Environment

Despite the broadening of young children's social life, the child-rearing environment remains their most significant developmental context. It is generally agreed that effective child rearing requires parents to adopt a child-focused perspective, often at the expense of their own egocentric concerns (Leseman, 2002). Beginning with Diana Baumrind (1967, 1971) research on parenting has shown three significant assessment criteria that help distinguish parenting styles: (a) acceptance and involvement, (b) control, and (c) autonomy granting (Gray & Steinberg, 1999; Hart, Newell, & Olsen, 2002). Table 10.2 describes the ways in which

TABLE 10.2

Characteristics of Different Child-Rearing Styles

Child-Rearing Style	Acceptance and Involvement	Control	Autonomy Granting	Effects on Children
Authoritative	Warm, attentive, and sensitive to the child's needs	Makes reasonable demands for mature age-appropriate behavior, and consistently enforces and explains them	Permits the child to make decisions in accord with readiness	High sense of competence, show positive mood, good self-control, ability to persist on tasks in early years. In later childhood, show high self-esteem, maturity, and good school performance (Baumrind & Black, 1967; Herman et al. 1997; McAdoo, 1997; Mackey, Arnold, & Pratt, 2001)

(Continued)

TABLE 10.2

Characteristics of Different Child-Rearing Styles (Continued)

Authoritarian	Cold and rejecting; frequently degrades child.	Coercive style; make many demands by yelling, commanding, and criticizing	Makes decisions for the child; rarely listens to child's point of view	Show more anxiety and negative mood; lower frustration tolerance. Boys tend to show higher levels of anger and defiance; girls tend to be more dependent and overwhelmed by challenging tasks (Hart, Ladd, & Burleson, 1990; Nix et al., 1999; Thompson, Hollis, & Richards, 2003)
Permissive	Warm but tend to be inattentive or overindulgent	Makes few demands	Allows child to make inappropriate decisions for child's age	Show higher levels of impulsivity; tend to be demanding and dependent on adults; show less ability to persist on tasks; lower school achievement; and higher levels of antisocial behavior (Barber & Olsen, 1997; Baumrind, 1971)
Uninvolved	Emotionally detached	Makes few demands	Shows indifference to child's point of view or decisions	Show lower levels of self-regulation; problems with school; higher levels of anti-social behavior in adolescence (Aunola, Stattin, & Nurni, 2000; Kurdek & Fine, 1994)

different parenting styles vary according to these criteria and the impact of each style on child development. Based on the positive child outcomes, the authoritative model is thought to be the most adaptive.

Culture, Social Class, and Child-Rearing Style Although there is widespread agreement on the benefits of an overall authoritative child-rearing style, variations across cultures and socioeconomic classes suggest that there are group-based differences in parental motivation and children's perceptions of their parents' behavior that may alter the negative consequences of more controlling, authoritarian parenting styles. These styles therefore may be adaptive to particular cultural values and family circumstances (Berk, 1999). For example, Chinese parents report that they are more demanding (Berndt et al., 1993) and place a higher value on control than do Caucasian-American parents; however, here control reflects the parents' concern, involvement, and commitment to instill culturally based values of self-discipline, respect for elders, and socially desirable behavior (Chao, 1994; Lin & Fu, 1990). Along similar lines, Latin American and Asian Pacific Island families demand respect for strong paternal authority and combine this with an extremely high degree of maternal warmth and affection to instill in their children strong feelings of family identification and loyalty (Fracasso & Busch-Rossnagel, 1992; Harrison et al., 1994).

Socioeconomic status and the social context in which poor families may live (for example, high-crime neighborhoods, unsafe housing) may also demand a more controlling and forceful child-rearing style to keep children safe and to prevent them from becoming involved in antisocial activities. In fact, some recent studies have shown that the use of more controlling child-rearing strategies is associated with better adjusted young children in ethnic minority families from lower socioeconomic circumstances (Baldwin, Baldwin, & Cole, 1990; O'Neil & Parke, 1997).

Parental Discipline Strategies Parents use a variety of strategies to help shape the child in the direction of parental expectations. The American Academy of Pediatrics (1998) defines the term *discipline* as the "system of teaching and nurturing that prepares children to achieve competence, self-control, self-direction and caring for others." That organization lists three elements that must be present for a discipline system to be effective. Here, effectiveness is demonstrated by long-term internalization of moral values as evidenced by the child's ability to behave acceptably even when the parent is not there.

The following sections will address the impact of the child-rearing environment as it relates to each of these elements.

Attachment As children enter the early school-age years, those with histories of secure attachment exhibit better frustration tolerance, more positive affects, and better problem-solving skills (Kochanska, 2001) than do children with insecure attachments. They also show better internalization of their parents' rules and expectations, based on positive identifications (Kochanska, Aksan, & Koenig, 1995). In early school age, these children are more likely to turn to their adult caregivers when they are distressed or frustrated (Vondra, Shaw, Swearingen, Cohen, & Owens, 2001). They tend to be assertive (as opposed to aggressive) and to seek attention in positive ways (Bradley, 2000). They appear to have internalized the belief that their self is worthy of help and that help will be available when it is needed (Sroufe, 1989, 1990).

Children with histories of insecure attachment tend to have greater difficulty in developing self-regulation, presumably because they have not experienced adequate soothing from caregivers and, as a result, have not internalized effective regulatory strategies as part of their working models of self. As a result, they tend to be highly reactive to stressors and to respond with feelings of helplessness, anxiety, and frustration. These children show more anger and physical aggression than their securely attached counterparts, and because the attachment relationship is not viewed as an effective source of soothing, they tend not to rely on the attachment figure for help when they are under stress (Vaughn & Bost, 1999). Additionally, their sense of mastery, competence, and self-esteem may be compromised by their difficulties in persisting in the face of frustration and impairments in their ability and interest in pursuing independent exploration and goal-directed activity. Young children with histories of insecure attachment may avoid separations from caregivers at the expense of exploration; they may reverse roles with the parent, attending to the parents' needs instead of engaging in age-appropriate activities; or their exploratory behavior may show a quality of recklessness (Lieberman & Pawl, 1990). It has been postulated that such difficulties may be related to increased anxiety about caregiver responsiveness and/or internal working models of "learned helplessness"—a belief that their efforts will not result in success (Aber & Allen, 1987; Lieberman & Pawl, 1990; Seligman, 1975).

Strategies for Teaching and Strengthening Desirable Behaviors Parents may actively support their young child's development in any number of ways. According to Davies (2004), because so much of the world is unfamiliar and confusing to young children, adults spend a lot of time helping them understand and cope with their experiences. This may involve setting clear limits; using language to help the child understand his or her feelings and experiences; providing distraction, reassurance, advice; and serving as a model for socially appropriate behaviors and as a mediator and social reference between the child and new people or experiences. Preparing young children in advance for what to expect in novel situations, and offering choices when appropriate options exist, may increase their sense of control and reduce the uncertainty that leads to distress, provide valuable coping strategies for potentially difficult situations, and impart information about expectations and norms of social behavior. Davies sees these parental behaviors as "a cognitive and affective dimension of providing a secure base" (2004, p. 197), and he noted that as situations repeat themselves and become more familiar, the child's anxiety begins to decrease because he or she is better able to determine what is going to happen and to generalize this information to other situations. Other proactive techniques such as the use of praise and other positive affects in reaction to desirable behaviors ("Good Sharing!"; "Nice Manners!") may serve as powerful motivators for continued efforts and for helping the child understand that he or she is moving in the right direction.

Strategies to Eliminate Undesirable Behaviors Undesirable behavior generally refers to behavior that is either unsafe or noncompliant with reasonable expectations of adult caregivers and interferes with positive social interaction and self-discipline (American Academy of Pediatrics, 1998). Depending on the circumstances, the behavior may require immediate intervention to keep the child safe; at other times, the undesirable behavior may best be handled by waiting and discussing the situation when emotions have subsided. Some undesirable behaviors need a consistent consequence to prevent the behavior from generalizing or alternative responses, such as removal of attention. In many cases, especially in toddlerhood, the best course is to avoid situations in which the behavior is likely to occur.

Inevitably, during early childhood, there will arise situations in which the child refuses to comply when a parent insists on a particular behavior, and a specific disciplinary technique will be necessary. According to Newman and Newman (1995), for a disciplinary technique to be effective in helping the child to internalize moral expectations and change future behavior (regardless of the presence of an authority figure), it must interrupt or inhibit the undesirable behavior; it should point out a more acceptable form of behavior; it should explain why the behavior is considered inappropriate; and it should stimulate empathy for the victim of the unacceptable behavior. These techniques are generally characterized as "inductions" and reflect the "authoritative" parenting style (see Chapter 14). Mild forms of power assertion, such as "time-out" and withdrawal of privileges, as part of an overall authoritative child-rearing style, can also be effective in reducing undesirable behaviors and do not carry the negative side effects associated with harsh, physical punishment.

School Readiness and Later School Achievement

In 1989, the federal government created a national educational agenda for improving U.S. schools, stating as its first goal that all U.S. children would start school ready to learn. Achievement of this goal is now thought to depend, to a large extent, on early identification and intervention for children who are at risk for school failure. This includes children who either have, or who are thought to be "at risk" for developing, handicapping conditions, as well as children from culturally or economically disadvantaged backgrounds. (See Chapter 18, "Social Policy Through the Life Cycle.")

School Readiness and Children with Disabilities Because early intervention has been shown to have a significant positive impact on the development of children with or at risk for disabilities, many experts (although recognizing the validity of concerns about premature labeling and the complexities of differential diagnosis) strongly encourage the earliest possible recognition of signs and symptoms of developmental problems to facilitate appropriate and timely intervention. (See Chapter 18, "Social Policy Through the Life Cycle.")

Early identification programs are designed to detect children who are considered "at risk" for either having, or developing, handicapping conditions. In preschool children, early identification should involve assessment of "at-risk" indicators (for example, prematurity, low birthweight, prenatal drug–alcohol exposure, chromosomal anomalies, neurological conditions), systematic observations of the child as well as the use of standard screening tests. If the early identification process indicates developmental deficits, it is recommended that the child be referred for more comprehensive assessment and follow-up services. Intervention services should be tailored to meet the child's individual needs and the availability of a continuum of programs and services is considered critical for success (National Joint Committee on Learning Disabilities, 1985). Some children and some disabilities may require special education over the long term, and early intervention services are seen as part of a continuum of care. In other cases, the goal of early intervention is to mitigate or avoid the need for special education services as the child moves to elementary school.

School Readiness and Children from Culturally and/or Economically Disadvantaged Backgrounds Although neither low socioeconomic status nor membership in an ethnic minority group directly causes children's developmental delays or lowered school success, both are associated with increased vulnerability to a higher accumulation of risk factors that are potentially damaging to children's intellectual development and later school achievement (Leseman, 2002). Poverty is an especially significant indicator of risk for children under the age of 6 because early development is so strongly entwined with environmental context (Duncan, Brooks-Gunn, & Klebanov, 1994). In addition to higher levels of risk accumulation, research (Bus, Leseman, & Keultjes, 2000; De Jong & Leseman, 1998; Gottfried, Fleming, & Gottfried, 1998; Leseman & Van den Boom, 1999) has found lower levels of cognitive and language stimulation, decontextualized language use, and home literacy practices in families with low incomes and from nonmainstream cultural groups; additionally, these factors have been shown to have direct, negative effects on children's preparation for, and ultimate success in, school.

The consensus of opinion seems to be that investment in early childhood education programs for all children, but particularly those at risk for eventual academic problems, may produce broad, long-term individual and social benefits (Slavin et al., 1992, 1994, 1996). For example, current research indicates that children who participate in high-quality early childhood education programs tend to show better reading and math achievement scores in the later grades, lower rates of special education placements, higher rates of high school completion, less juvenile delinquency, less teenage pregnancy and levels of psychosocial stability, college attendance, and economic independence (Leseman, 2002; Slavin et al., 1992, 1994, 1996).

However, implementation of a successful broad-based system of service requires that certain important issues be recognized. First, the category of children classified as at risk are not a homogeneous group and, therefore, have varying needs for intervention. For example, immigrant families with little education and low incomes may provide very good contexts for the development of secure attachments and social and emotional skills. However, their low level of literacy and home language might indicate the need for educational support (Leseman, 2002). Also, certain characteristics of program design appear to be significant in terms of positive outcomes. Although more research is indicated, current studies seem to support the notion that a relatively intensive, early starting (around age 3), multisystemic approach that combines a child-focused, developmental preschool with parent involvement, education, and psychosocial support is most apt to produce positive outcomes over the long term (Yoshikawa, 1994). In addition, quality of service is also significant to results. Measures of quality include, among other factors, sensitive, responsive caregiving, a stimulating physical and educational environment, professionally trained and reasonably paid staff, as well as a favorable staff–child ratio (Leseman, 2002). The issue of continuity of services is also important to success. Currently, in the United States and elsewhere, early childhood education and care consist of a kind of patchwork of services that varies in quality and approach and operates under different regulations. Also worrisome is the problem of transition to elementary schools of varying quality and the impact this has on children's ability to maintain gains obtained through early intervention. These are areas that require further research, although some promising strategies are being tested worldwide.

Summary

The early childhood period is seen as a period of transition from the egocentric, magical world of the dependent infant into the child of the middle years, who thinks more logically, has a broader perspective, and is aware of the world as a complex place into which she or he must fit. Developmental advances in toddlerhood allow the child to begin to understand the workings of the environment and to express the self as an autonomous being. Erikson's (1963) psychosocial crisis of autonomy versus shame and doubt reflects the toddler's need to develop mastery and self-control. The early school years bring challenges that provide opportunities for the development of a more complex sense of self that includes a gender identity, a moral code, and any number of other recognizable characteristics. Erikson's (1963) psychosocial crisis of initiative versus guilt reflects the child's need to actively investigate the nature of the world with curiosity and creativity, thereby providing opportunities for an elaboration of the sense of self as well as a sense of competence and social acceptance. An examination of the issues related to child rearing, harsh treatment, socioeconomic and sociocultural disadvantages, and individual differences in such areas as temperament and ability illuminates the continuing dependence of the child in early school age on the caregiving environment, as well as the potential that exists for negative resolution of Erikson's psychosocial crises. The less-than-optimal results of a poor fit between the young child and her or his various developmental contexts reflect, at their core, Erikson's conceptualizations of shame and guilt.

11 Middle Childhood

Introduction

Middle childhood is a relatively longer period than infancy, toddlerhood, or the preschool years. It extends from age 6 to ages 11 or 12. This is a time when children increasingly enter the world outside the family and take on new challenges. Psychological and social competence become important benchmarks in the development of self-esteem and skills that, in turn, set the stage for the adolescent years. Dubois and colleagues present four core areas that constitute the internal structure of both psychological competence and social competence for children: cognition, behavior, emotions, and motivation. The authors stress that each of these four "domains of influence" (2003, p. 403) must be understood within the context of the child's environment. The strengths of one dimension may serve to protect children against the negative consequences for mental health associated with the weaknesses in another dimension. Consideration of both the psychological and social domains of human development helps facilitate holistic case conceptualization and treatment planning. Figure 11.1 illustrates the social and psychological aspects of positive mental health in each area.

Additional tools that have been used to understand the child within the context of his or her environment are the genogram (McGoldrick & Gerson, 1985;

FIGURE 11.1

Quadripartite Model of Mental Health, Revised

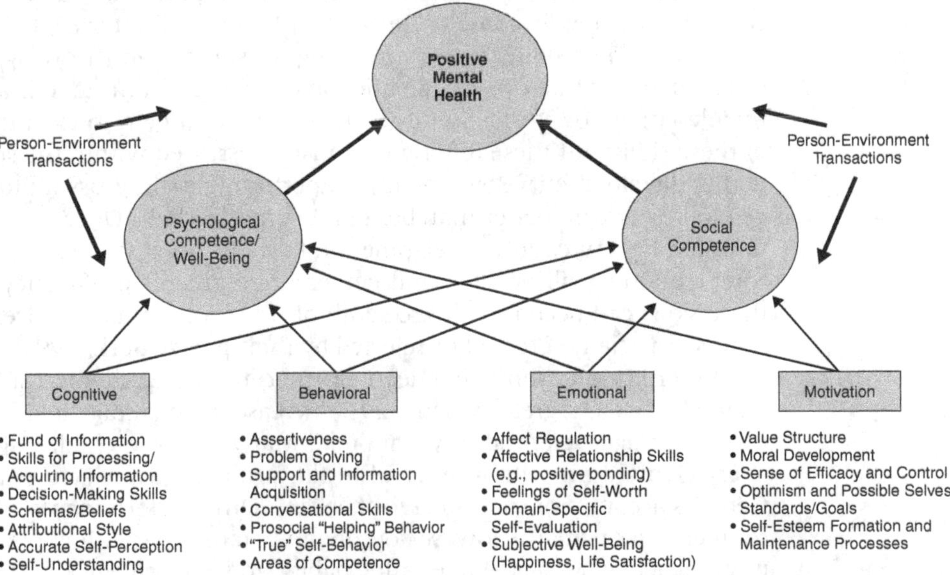

Source: D.L. Dubois, R.D. Felner, E. M. Lockerd, G. R. Parra, and C. Lopez, 2003, "The Quadpartite Model Revisited: Promoting Positive Mental Health in Children and Adolescents." In M. A. Reinecke, F. M. Dattilio, and A. Freeman (Eds.), *Cognitive Therapy with Children and Adolescents: A Casebook for Clinicians* (2d ed.), (pp. 402–434). New York: Guilford Press. Reprinted with permission.

McGoldrick, Gerson, & Shellenberger, 1999); the eco-map (Hartman, 1978); the social network map (Tracy & Whittaker, 1993); and the culturagram. The *genogram* is a diagram of the child's nuclear and extended family and relevant identifying information. The *eco-map* presents the family's connection with the surrounding environment. The *social network map*, a more detailed version of the eco-map, illustrates the types of support available to a family and the resources that could compensate for gaps in those resources. Finally, the *culturagram* is a family assessment tool that demonstrates the effect of ethnicity and culture on children (Congress, 1994). This tool is particularly helpful in understanding children from diverse ethnocultural backgrounds and countries (Webb, 1996) and can also be helpful in understanding the child's (and the family's) ethnic identity development. (See Chapter 4 for further discussion of identity development; examples of these tools are provided in the Appendix.)

Biological and Physical Development

Children continue to grow and mature during the middle-school years, but at a slower rate than earlier childhood. Children average 2 to 3 inches per year of growth during the middle-childhood years and roughly 3 to 5 pounds of weight gain per year. Boys are somewhat bigger than girls during most of these years. Girls begin to develop the secondary sex characteristics associated with puberty during the later years of middle childhood. Boys are more likely to begin developing secondary sex characteristics during early adolescence. The stability of the earlier years of middle childhood, including emotional self-regulation and self-control, may now become more erratic (Robbins, Chatterjee, & Canda, 1998).

Gross motor skills, such as climbing, running, and throwing, and fine motor skills, such as hand–eye coordination and writing, continue to improve during the middle-childhood years. Some gender differences seem to exist in the maturation of these skills, but these differences must be assessed within the sociocultural context of development. Boys usually outperform girls in gross motor skills, and girls generally perform better than boys in fine motor skills. Of course, there are exceptions, and every child's development follows its own unique course. The fact that some children will develop and demonstrate greater proficiency with various of these skills can become a source both of pride for certain children and shame for others, especially if teased or rejected by their peers (Berk, 1999, 2003).

Recent studies show that nearly 25 percent of U.S. children suffer from obesity, defined as weight greater than a 20% increase over average body weight, based on the child's age, sex, and physical build. Many of these children go on to become overweight adults with a range of health problems associated with the condition. Genetics account for some degree of obesity. Other determinants are the social environment, particularly low socioeconomic status, parenting practices, degree of physical activity, maladaptive eating habits, and excessive television viewing, which promotes sedentary behavior, as well as encourages snacking (Berk, 2003).

Psychological Development

Erikson (1950) referred to middle childhood as the stage of *industry versus inferiority* when the child masters developmentally appropriate achievements or feels compromised if he or she struggles (see Chapter 3). Although self-esteem is a core element of psychological well-being during these critical years, children are learning and growing in many areas. There may be some children who have difficulties in one or even several areas of development but are excelling in other areas. Recent research (Davies, 2004) supports the significance of "domain-specific" knowledge and skills during the middle-school years. This is a shift away from Piaget's (1936/1952) research, from which he posited that knowledge and skill developed "across domains." Current research is significant both for understanding that children may not be able to transfer a particular knowledge or skill, and for appreciating that children may be able to master something in one area that brings a sense of self-esteem and accomplishment. For example, John, a bright 12-year-old with significant learning disabilities and central auditory processing problems, loves to play chess. He cannot, however, transfer the reasoning and problem-solving skills he uses successfully when playing chess to other areas of his academic and social life.

Freud (1905/1957) felt that middle childhood, referred to as the *latency period* in psychoanalytic theory, was a time when the sexual and aggressive drives are relatively quiet. For example, Freud felt the *sorting behaviors* associated with the child's love of collections during this time was an attempt to keep the sexual and aggressive impulses at bay (Schamess, 1996b). During middle childhood, drives are now directed, both physically and cognitively, toward the mastery of skills (Bornstein, 1951). By middle childhood, children have generally developed a range of defenses. The term *defenses* has its roots in psychoanalytic theory and refers to "unconscious automatic responses that enable us to minimize perceived threats or keep them out of our awareness entirely" (Walsh, 2003, p. 199). Valliant (1995) felt that defenses were inherently adaptive responses necessary for children to cope with personal, social, and environmental stresses. Coping strategies—or defenses—may change depending on the context or situation, making a given coping ability adaptive at certain times and maladaptive at others. Seen in this context, defenses contribute to the child's growth and must therefore be understood within the overall context of child development. Two other important ways to think about defenses during middle childhood are to remember that coping efforts may be "problem-focused" or "emotion-focused" (Walsh, 2003, p. 201). *Problem-focused coping* is centered on ways to change the environment. Children need adults to intervene actively on their behalf during the earlier years of middle childhood with decreasing intensity as the child matures. *Emotion-focused coping* addresses the meaning a particular situation has for a child and the ways in which she or he handles it. An overview of the defenses of middle childhood are presented in Table 11.1.

TABLE 11.1

Defenses in Middle Childhood

- *Repression.* Involves the elimination or "forgetting" of unacceptable feelings, impulses, or thoughts from conscious awareness.
- *Sublimation.* Avoiding direct awareness of aggressive impulses and sexual curiosity through "neutral" activities such as games, collecting, projects, creativity, and (general) interest in things outside the self.
- *Reaction formation.* Turning an impulse or wish into the opposite. An example is the transformation of preschooler's intense interest and curiosity about sex differences to the school-age child's tendency toward sex segregation.
- *Displacement in fantasy.* Impulses that would be negative, aggressive, intrusive, or antisocial if acted out are experienced "at a distance" through fantasy. Displacement in fantasy can involve either the child's own fantasizing or her enjoyment of TV shows and movies where impulsive, aggressive behavior is depicted.
- *Isolation.* Involves repressing the affect connected with a thought so that the thought has a "neutral" quality. Very frequently school-age children can describe a stressful event in a matter-of-fact tone but have trouble answering when asked how they *felt* about it. This is isolation at work.
- *Doing and undoing.* Expression of negative impulse, followed immediately by its opposite. A child who is angry with her parent—either directly or privately—undoes the impulse by being oversolicitous, apologetic, or spontaneously saying, "I love you, Mom."
- *Turning against the self.* Involves punishing the self for having a forbidden impulse. In response to anger toward a parent, for example, the child feels guilty and "beats himself up" by condemning himself.

Source: D. Davies, 2004, *Child Development: A Practitioner's Guide* (2nd ed.), (p. 372). New York: Guilford Press. Reprinted with permission.

Cognitive Development

The idea of intelligence is central to all models of cognitive development. This includes appreciation for the biological, social, experiential, motivational, and emotional aspects of human development. The executive function of the brain develops during middle childhood, although executive skills do not reach complete development until late adolescence (Flavell, 2000). Kagan characterized executive functions as "skills in approaching and thinking about problems." He included the following as executive functions: (a) ability to articulate a problem and generate ideas about how to solve it; (b) knowing cognitive strategies that help in problem solving and when to use them; (c) having a more flexible approach to problem solving; (d) a longer attention span; (e) better control of anxiety; (f) the ability to monitor one's own performance; (g) faith in one's ability to think about problems; and (h) awareness of one's shortcomings in thinking about problem solving (1984, cited in Davies, 2004, pp. 365–366).

We refer the reader back to Chapter 2 to Dr. Russell Barkley's (1997) model of executive functions. It is important to note that because executive functions develop during the middle-school years, children with disorders such as ADD and/or other types of executive function disorders may begin to exhibit more difficulties as the demands for these types of functions increase. These children may need environmental accommodations, modifications in expectations, and parental support to achieve mastery and feel successful.

Select examples of the types of tasks requiring executive skills in the middle-school years are as follows: Ages 6 and 7—follow safety rules, raise hand before speaking in class, bring papers to and from school; ages 8 to 10—keep track of belongings when away from home, complete homework assignments of up to 1 hour, plan simple school projects (such as a book report); ages 11 and 12—use a system for organizing schoolwork, plan and complete longer-term projects that may require a timetable, follow a school schedule that involves changing teachers, classrooms, or schedules (Dawson & Guare, 2004, p. 9).

Gardner presents a definition of intelligence as "the ability to solve problems, or to fashion products, that are valued in one or more cultural or community settings . . . human cognitive competence is better described in terms of a set of abilities, talents, or skills . . . called 'intelligences'" that may more closely approximate some of the strengths that children with "jagged cognitive profiles" bring to the learning environment (1993, p. 15). Gardner developed a set of seven "multiple intelligences":

- *Linguistic intelligence:* Ability to use language as a form of expression and communication (such as poets or writers).
- *Logical-mathematical intelligence:* This includes logical and mathematical ability as well as scientific ability. Much current IQ testing is based on linguistic and logical-mathematical intelligence through its testing of verbal and mathematical skills.
- *Spatial intelligence:* The ability to form a mental mode of a spatial world and to be able to maneuver and operate using that model (for example, engineers, sculptors).
- *Musical intelligence:* The ability to appreciate and use music as a form of expression (singers, composers).
- *Bodily-kinesthetic intelligence:* The ability to solve problems or to fashion products using one's whole body, or parts of the body (dancers, athletes).
- *Interpersonal intelligence:* The ability to understand other people and what motivates them, how they work, how to work cooperatively with them (salespeople, politicians, clinicians).
- *Intrapersonal intelligence:* A capacity to form an accurate, truthful model of oneself and to be able to use that model to operate effectively in life (1983, pp. 8–9).

Piaget introduced the concept of *concrete operations* to define cognitive development during the middle-school years (1936/1952; Piaget & Inhelder, 1969). He classified the components of operational thought into several categories of skills. *Reversibility* allows children to reverse, or undo, an action in their mind. *Compensation* is the skill that enables children to focus on more than one aspect of something at a time. *Conservation* skills involve the ability to understand that properties of an object do not change when their appearance is altered. *Classification* skills include the ability to group objects into categories according to their characteristics. *Combinational* skills involve the ability to manipulate numbers in addition, subtraction, multiplication, and division. This is a shift from action to thought as the child is increasingly able to use logic. Logical thinking requires an ability to distinguish between the subjective, which allows children to have a clearer understanding of causality (Davies, 2004; Newman & Newman, 1995; Robbins, Chatterjee, & Canda, 1998). One of the most pronounced developmental changes during the middle-childhood years is the child's developing capacity for self-observation, generally based on comparisons with others. This includes identification with the expectations and values of the child's parents, family, and peers. The child's evaluation of his or her own success is important in developing self-esteem. Because middle-school children are oriented toward the concrete—as opposed to psychological (more abstract)—explanations for their actions or the actions of others, social comparison can put children at risk and lead to psychological and social problems. Although children in the middle years of childhood are more capable problem solvers than they were during their earlier years, a limitation of concrete operational thinking remains. "Children think in an organized, logical fashion only when dealing with concrete information that they can perceive directly. Their mental operations work poorly with abstract ideas—ones not apparent in the real world" (Berk, 2003, p. 242). Piaget felt that brain development combined with experiences in a varied external world should lead children in all cultures and societies to reach the concrete operational stage. Some research studies have suggested, however, that this may not be the case. The forms of logic proposed by Piaget may be more heavily influenced by training, context, and cultural conditions than previously thought (Artman & Cahan, 1993; Ceci & Roazzi, 1994; Rogoff & Chavajay, 1995).

Vgotsky (1934/1986) felt that human cognition was inherently social and language based. It is language, developed during the earlier years, and increasingly sophisticated during the middle years, which actually helps to provide the older child the ability to organize things mentally rather than by using concrete items. Experience remains important, however, as the child has only a limited ability to engage in hypothetical thinking and may also have trouble grasping new information that he or she has not experienced before (O'Connor, 2000, p. 115). Moreover, it is important to appreciate that language itself is influenced by the experiences in the environment (for example, children who are raised in families where caregivers talk or read to them on a regular basis). Vgotsky felt that children speak to themselves for self-guidance; he felt language was the foundation for all higher cognitive processes, including controlled attention, deliberate memorization and recall, categorization, planning, problem solving, abstract reasoning, and self-reflection (Berk, 2003, p. 257). Language also contributes to self-regulation because children can substitute words for action or find ways to talk to themselves. This speech, called *egocentric speech* by Piaget, is now called *private speech*. Children with learning difficulties have higher rates of private speech than other children, which may be a way they compensate for impairments in cognitive processing and attention that make academic tasks more difficult for them (Friedburg & McClure, 2002).

Piaget (1945/1951, 1963) felt that play bridged the gap between the child's concrete experience and abstract thought, making the symbolic function of play noteworthy. Play represents the child's attempt to organize his or her experience and gives concrete form to the child's inner world. As Landreth wrote, "A major function of play is the changing of what may be unmanageable in reality to manageable situations through symbolic representation, which provides children with opportunities for learning to cope by engaging in self-directed exploration" (2002, p. 12). The child's increasing ability to substitute thinking, words, and fantasy for impulsive actions is demonstrated through play (Davies, 2004, p. 336). Vgotsky (1933/1978) regarded make-believe play "as a unique broadly influential zone of proximal development in which children advance themselves as they try out a wide variety of challenging skills" (Berk, 2003, p. 259). As children create imaginary situations, they learn to act in accord with internal ideas and not to respond only to external stimuli. Children use object substitutions during this process (for example, pretending that a group of blankets are a fort). As they do this, children learn that thinking is separate from actions and objects and that ideas can be used to guide behavior. Pretend play also encourages that children act against their impulses as they observe the rules of the game. In this way, they come to understand social norms and expectations.

Children who are raised with two languages (bilingual) may be advanced in cognitive development, particularly in the areas of selective attention, analytical reasoning, cognitive flexibility, and concept formation. Children generally become bilingual either by acquiring both languages at the same time in early childhood or by learning a second language after mastery of a first one. When school-age children acquire a second language after they already speak a first one, it generally takes them 3 to 5 years to become as competent in the second language as native-speaking peers. As children get older, the ability to acquire fluency in a second language becomes more difficult and is generally enhanced by the opportunity to be immersed in the language, such as living in another country (Bialystock, 2001; Bialystock & Hakuta, 1999).

Moral Development

Children develop a sense of right and wrong (which continually matures) during the middle-school years. They are conscious of what is socially acceptable and what they must do to fit into their peer group. Children also begin to distinguish between acts that are morally wrong and behavior that does not adhere to social expectations; for example, hitting may be a moral violation, but not listening to the teacher's direction is not conforming to what is expected (Davies, 2004).

Freud (1923a) felt that it was the process of resolving the Oedipal conflict that caused the child to develop a superego (or conscience). Briefly summarized, it is the parental (father–aggressor) prohibition against the child's sexual wishes toward his mother that is incorporated internally to form his superego. Freud felt that without the threat of castration, girls have less-developed superegos than boys.

Piaget (1932/1965) offered a cognitive explanation for the development of conscience. Initially the child responds to rules—external factors—in a specific, concrete manner. This period, roughly lasting from ages 5 to 10 years, was called *heteronomous morality.* Children's moral understanding during this stage is limited by the power of adults, particularly parents, to insist that children comply with rules and a child's cognitive immaturity, which limits their capacity to consider other perspectives (Berk, 2003). Gradually the child moves from following the letter of the law to appreciating the spirit of the law. Finally, at the end of the middle-childhood years, Piaget felt that children had the cognitive ability to conserve rules and expectations in the absence of external prohibitions (Altman, Briggs, Frankel, Gensler, & Pantone, 2002). This "*internalized conscience*" (Davies, 2004, p. 336) assists the child with impulse control and personal responsibility and allows the child to judge his or her own behavior and to experience an internally based negative self-evaluation (O'Connor, 2000, p. 117). In creating linkages between moral rules and social conventions, the ideas of justice develop. The youngest middle schoolchild, for example, has an idea of fairness based on equality. This standard of fairness is called *reciprocity.* The slightly older middle schoolchild has an understanding that someone who worked harder than the others might deserve special merit. Finally, the oldest middle schoolchild is able to give special consideration to those who are disadvantaged (Kohlberg, 1969). Piaget referred to this more advanced understanding as *ideal reciprocity,* a realization that rules can be flexible and revised to consider individual circumstances (Piaget, 1932/1965).

Along with an internalized conscience and set of moral rules, feelings of guilt, shame, anxiety, and self-blame often come. We want children during these years to develop a healthy conscience that allows them to take responsibility and begin to understand the importance of following parental and social rules. We must, therefore, be alert to being too hard on children (especially during the earlier years of middle childhood, when the internalized conscience is in its infancy). Children will often avoid talking about problems during this period because the problems are associated with being bad. The conscience is internalized, and so the badness is experienced as being inside the child. It is important to also remember that conscience is not only developmental but also based on the child's adult and peer influences and the environment to which he or she is exposed.

Kohlberg (1981) developed a system of moral development based on six stages that he felt were contingent on the stages of cognitive development put forth by Piaget (see Table 11.2).

Carol Gilligan (1982) challenged the male-oriented premise of Freud's idea that the superegos of females are less developed than those of males and offered a model of development that differed from Kohlberg's as well. She proposed that women are psychologically oriented toward relationships and interdependence, which make their moral development different, but not less than that of men. Gilligan's three stages of female moral development are based on *principles of care*—in contrast to *principles of justice*—and include (a) *orientation to self*—this is a survival orientation during which the individual concerns of emotional and physical survival are primary; (b) *morality of care*—conventional care when the person defines actions as being right or correct based on self-sacrifice and responsibility for the care of dependent and unequal other; and (c) *morality of nonviolence*—integrated care when the individual is able to consider the needs of others as well

TABLE 11.2

Stages of Moral Development

The Preconventional Level
Stage One: The punishment and obedience orientation: Children are focused on fear of authority and avoidance of punishment.
Stage Two: The instrumental purpose orientation: Children become more aware of different perspectives, but this is based on reciprocity.

The Conventional Level
Stage Three: The "good-boy"–good girl" orientation of the morality of interpersonal cooperation: Children want to obey rules because to do so promotes harmony.
Stage Four: The social-order-maintaining orientation: Child considers the larger perspective of societal laws.

The Postconventional or Principles Level
Stage Five: The social-contract orientation: Children regard rules as being more flexible.
Stage Six: The universal ethical principle orientation: Self-chosen ethical principles of conscience now guide actions.

Source: L.Kohlberg, 1981, *The Philosophy of Moral Development.* San Francisco, CA: Harper and Row.

as of oneself (Walsh, 2003, p. 161). Gilligan (1982) wrote: "The moral imperative that emerges repeatedly in interviews with women is an injunction to care, a responsibility to discern and alleviate the 'real and recognizable trouble' of this world . . . women's insistence on care is at first self-critical rather than self-protective . . . in the development of a postconventional ethical understanding, women come to see the violence inherent in inequality" (pp. 99–101). Walker (1984) disputed that moral development was sex related at all. He felt that there was not only one focus (such as a principle of care or a principle of justice) and advocated a "win–win" approach to solving moral conflict as the highest stage of human development.

Gender Development

Gender has been defined in Chapter 4. In this section, we address gender development during the middle years of childhood. Kohlberg (1969) felt that children learned the concept of *gender constancy* (the awareness that gender cannot be changed) by going through a series of stages. The first, *gender labeling,* occurs when children label their own sex and that of others correctly. The second stage, *gender stability,* occurs when children have at least a partial understanding of the *permanence of gender* (in other words, the gender or sex of a person does not change if they dress in men's or women's clothing). Gender constancy occurs when children become certain of the situational consistency of sex. Mastery of gender constancy is associated with cognitive development, notably the skill of conservation, and develops at approximately ages 6 to 7. Carver, Yunger, and Perry (2003) discussed the gender identity challenges faced by children during middle childhood. Children are now relinquishing earlier components of gender identity—intergroup bias and felt pressure for gender conformity. They are consolidating a new kind of gender identity—a sense of *gender typicality*. These gender developments are based on both biology and cultural expectation. Schriver (2004) wrote that the socialization experiences of the child in the home, school, and community significantly influence the developmental process. Van Wormer, Wells, and Boes (2000) concur with Schriver. They pointed out, for example, that in middle childhood children are often exposed to homophobic comments about gay and lesbian people. Words such as *fag* and *gay* are often used in a derogatory manner, and although children may not always know exactly what the words mean, they somehow understand that it is something they can say to hurt another person. A group of children who deserve special note are those—later self-identified as transgendered—who may be struggling with the development of gender identity in middle childhood. In toddlerhood and the preschool years, cross dressing and cross-gender behaviors are often tolerated. However, as children advance into middle childhood, they are expected to conform to traditional binary categories of gender—male and female. This could create feelings of confusion and an internalized sense of deviance for those who cannot quite fit into their assigned genders. Most children recognize at some point during the middle years of childhood that cross dressing is not socially acceptable, and they are therefore driven into a secret world. Cross dressing—more an expression of gender during middle childhood—often becomes entangled with sexuality during puberty, creating greater confusion for these youngsters. Children who are exposed to nontraditional role models and experiences as well as traditional ones may develop a wider range of gender role behaviors and greater clarity about their own gender (Gagne, Tewksbury, & McGaughey, 1997).

There is an accentuation of gender differences in late childhood and early adolescence (ages 11–13). Girls begin to use nonconfrontational means to express anger and aggression, referred to as *social aggression* or *relational aggression* (Crick, Casas, & Nelson, 2002). This type of behavior blurs the lines of friendship and contributes to rumors, social ostracization, character defamation, and feelings of betrayal. Girls who repeatedly use tactics of relational aggression are bullies. Their tactics are verbal rather than physical, but the result of ongoing assaults such as this lay the seeds for depression, eating disorders, and self-harming behaviors. Boys are less socially sophisticated and more likely to engage in both verbal and physical types of aggression. Aggression and social rejection in middle childhood have a poor prognosis for adjustment during adolescence.

Racial and Ethnic Identity Development

Models of racial and ethnic identity development were presented in Chapter 4. In this section we would like to make some points related to the development of ethnic and racial identity during middle childhood. More sophisticated cognitive abilities contribute to the fact that children during middle childhood are (or become) aware of racial differences and the social rejection or discrimination that some children are exposed to. Parents and community are of a particular significance in racial and ethnic identity development during this time. They often provide protection and support from racism and prepare children to cope with hostilities they may experience from others who discriminate against them or view them in a negative light. The identity development of children who experience racial discrimination can be problematic. The socialization patterns nurtured in family and community that foster individual and group identity will have a significant and positive impact.

For those children who may require counseling services during middle childhood, working with someone from their own racial and ethnic group may be preferable, to instill positive ethnic socialization. This is especially true for disadvantaged children, who may not be exposed to this role modeling in their own homes or communities, for example, children who live in foster homes. Jackson and Westmoreland (1992) make important observations regarding the racial identity development of African-American children in placement with white foster-care parents. These children can be doubly affected: first, by feeling abandoned by their black families and deprived of the opportunities for identity development they would have provided; and second, growing up in a white family and community without racial role models. Jackson and Westmoreland cited a study by Helms (1990) that found that black children who had been adopted by white parents often developed reference group identities that were similar to their adoptive parents. It is important to raise children who may be adopted by parents of a different race or culture (or from another country) with a "bicultural identity" that can incorporate positive feelings and experiences about their own heritage as well as the heritage of their adoptive parents.

Parental Influences: The Importance of Attachment

The child's attachment history during the earlier years exerts influence during this time. "Quality of attachment during the first two years continues to differentiate between children through the end of middle childhood" (Davies, 2004, p. 345). At the onset of middle childhood (roughly age 6), attachment to parents may actually increase from what it had been during the preschool years in response to entry into school. The daily separations may now be longer. The new cognitive demands on the child may cause strain and even anxiety.

The child's individual temperament shapes his or her interactions with parents. Children are influenced by language stimulation in the home and by their parents' emotional reactions, communication style, tolerance, and responsiveness to the child's needs. Parents function as managers of their children's social environment. They influence children's social competence and acceptance by peers in several ways: (a) through face-to-face interactions with the child and other family members; (b) providing children with direct social information such as coaching and emotional advice; (c) facilitating contact with other children; (d) engaging their children in organized activities; and (e) monitoring their children's friends and whereabouts.

Relationships with parents serve as a model for future relationships. Children develop working models of expectations about relationships based on the qualities of the parent–child relationship, seeking out new relationships in ways that reinforce prior beliefs. A child's middle years can be profoundly affected by a parent's substance abuse; by physical, emotional, or sexual abuse; and by depression and anxiety disorders in members of the family, particularly the parents. Interactions with siblings are also important, and abuse by older siblings can often be very harmful, particularly if minimized by parents (or others), who may not understand the seriousness of the situation (Altman et al., 2002, p. 57). A woman in her early thirties talked about the chronic verbal abuse she was subjected to by an older sister, later diagnosed with bipolar disorder. Her parents did not understand that the older sibling had crossed over the line of the occasional taunting of a younger sister but was engaging in persistent verbal assaults that left this woman feeling vulnerable and unprotected in her home. Attachment to parents (and older siblings) during middle childhood, although significant, begins to decrease as the child develops in self-confidence and mastery of skills and begins to shift attachment needs to peers.

Attachment to Peers

The change in social reference from the family to the peer group begins in middle childhood and is "a pivotal aspect of the transition from early childhood to adolescence" (Costanzo, Miller-Johnson, & Wencel, 1995, p. 97). Peers are one of the main contexts in which children learn to evaluate their competence. As peers increasingly become the child's reference group, they provide new sources of belief. The two forms of appraisal that come from peers are *comparative appraisal* and *reflected appraisal.* "In comparative appraisal, the child employs others as benchmarks for the evaluation of his or her own abilities and traits, particularly competency-related attributes . . . reflected appraisal is the process by which children become attentive to the attitudes of others toward them" (Costanzo et al., 1995, pp. 98–99). Latency aged children can develop distorted and rigid comparison standards. Negative social/self-comparisons can become self-perpetuating and lock children into certain roles vis-à-vis their peers.

Acceptance is important, and there may be multiple processes by which children are accepted or rejected by peers. For example, social behavior plays a powerful role in determining whether a child will be accepted or rejected. Children often desire to be popular among their peers and become keenly aware of who the popular children are. Children in middle school will often speak of the "popular group." Popularity refers to how well the peer group likes or dislikes an individual. Friendship, which also becomes important during the years of middle childhood, is a mutually reciprocal relationship between one or more children based on common interests and concrete activities. It is entirely possible to have friends, but not be popular. Although it may also be possible to be popular, but not to enjoy true friendship, this is a more abstract concept (generally developed during adolescence) that does not help the child in middle school who feels the pang of not being popular. What peers think of them becomes increasingly important to children during these years and becomes internalized and part of self-identity. Children have a need to be with those with whom they identify; children who are "different"—in any number of ways—stand out and may be rejected or ridiculed. For example, children who have cognitive delays, those who struggle with impulse control, or show odd mannerisms, such as those associated with obsessive compulsive disorder or Tourette's syndrome, are often at risk for rejection by their peers. Children with physical disabilities and chronic health problems can also be seen as different from peers during these years (see Chapter 10). Children will need support and encouragement from sensitive adults during this often difficult time as they struggle to find their own place. During these middle years, children often practice how to resolve things between and among each other with less need of interference by adults, including parents and teachers. Some adults, therefore, may struggle with when it is appropriate to intervene. They either become overinvolved in their children's relationships with their peers or remain too uninvolved when attention is needed and children are unable to resolve difficult situations.

Sociocultural Developments

Social, cultural, and economic factors affect the development of children during the middle years and lay the groundwork for opportunities or lack of opportunities during adolescence and adulthood. Costanzo et al. discuss how variations in socialization processes affect the developing behavioral and affective responses of children (1995, p. 84). The community or neighborhood is critical to children during middle childhood in molding experience and shaping adjustment to the social world. They are affected by who lives in the neighborhood and how safe the streets are, as children are more prone to victimization than adults. Children who live in poorer communities may face overcrowded schools and less access to specialized services such as computer technology, diagnostic testing, or recreational activities. Children who are disadvantaged socioeconomically are at higher risk for certain illness such as rheumatic fever, meningitis, gastroenteritis and parasitic diseases, anemia, and growth retardation. Many of these conditions produce delays in the development of cognitive skills. Cognitive delays have also been attributed to poor nutrition, which is often symptomatic of inadequate maternal education or resources. Vision and hearing problems are more prevalent among low-income children. Dental hygiene is often deficient due to poor access to prophylactic dental care. Pediatric AIDS and the rates of injuries (such as car injuries caused by not using car seats or seat belts) are highest among disadvantaged children. We cannot overestimate the extent to which relationships with people and environments support or inhibit progress through middle-childhood development. Children will be as competent as their context affords them the chance to be. The Search Institute (2004) identified

40 developmental assets for middle childhood that contribute to healthy development. Those referred to as *external assets* included family support, a caring neighborhood, a caring school climate, a community that values children, creative activities and child programs, and positive adult role models. Rapid growth in skills is tied to physical, emotional, and social adjustment. Caregivers and other aspects of a child's environment provide psychological nurturance and physical care. Endowment can sometimes overcome the deprivations of some social contexts, whereas the reverse can be true as well. Nevertheless, no environment, however optimal, can completely compensate for the deficits that some children are born with (consider, for example, children with pervasive developmental disorders). However, it is clear that a child's environmental context can mitigate the impact of certain deficits in endowment or emphasize the child's difficulties (Palombo, 2001, p. 145).

School Influences

Davies (2004) suggests that the years between 5 and 7 to 8 are a transitional phase of middle childhood due to the tendency children at this age have to vacillate between egocentric thinking and more advanced cognitive skills. Nowhere does this present more of a challenge to youngsters than the school setting, particularly the first and second grades. Schools are primary contexts for socialization among this age group. It is an institution that all children and families have contact with. The influence of school on children's development is pervasive. The school is an extension of the family in terms of educational and socialization functions. However, there are differences in how this occurs. The greatest difference is that the school relates to children on the basis of organization and achievement. The relationship between a teacher and his or her students is more impersonal than between family members. Systematic evaluation is a part of the school experience. Completing assigned tasks and other responsibilities are given greater significance than generally occurs in families. Adjusting to these changes is what the transition from home to school is about for most children. Children with problematic development in the areas of social skills, cognitive problem solving, and academic self-efficacy are highly susceptible to negative reinforcement exchanges in the school environment. Such interaction patterns place youth at increased risk for truancy, delinquency, and psychological problems. Generally, in an adequately nurturing school/classroom environment, the child's anxiety decreases, and school adjustment proceeds without further problems. This may not be the case with children who may have traumatic family backgrounds, life stresses (such as coping with parents' divorce), or a range of other factors. We must also consider teachers or schools that place developmentally inappropriate expectations on children in the ever-increasing measurement of achievement by standardized testing. Excessive homework can keep children away from recreational activities and create stress within families. Children may develop anxiety that can interfere with their school adjustment. Many school districts conduct screenings in kindergarten to determine whether there are any significant developmental or cognitive lags that should be addressed. Although these screenings clearly identify some difficulties, more extensive testing may be needed to detect learning disorders that can plague children through their academic careers and become the root causes of many problematic behaviors.

The Carolina Abecedarian Project is an example of an early educational program for children considered high risk for school failure based on social and economic variables. Children were enrolled in a child-centered prevention-oriented intervention program in a day-care center from infancy to age 5. This intervention operated 8 hours a day for 50 weeks a year and included an infant curriculum to enhance development and parent activities. A second intervention was provided in elementary school—the children in kindergarten received 15 home visits a year for 3 years from a teacher who also prepared a home program to supplement the school curriculum. The results of these interventions showed significant positive effects on intellectual development and academic achievement, which were maintained through age 12 (4 years after the intervention ended at age 8; Campbell & Ramey, 1994). An example of another successful program—the Primary Mental Health Project (PMHP)—was designed for early detection and prevention of school adjustment problems among children in primary grades. Carefully selected, trained, and closely supervised nonprofessionals work to establish caring and trusting relationships with the children and act as liaisons to parents and teachers. Program evaluation studies showed significant improvements in children's grades, achievement test scores, and adjustment ratings by teachers (Cowen et al., 1996; Office of the Surgeon General, n.d.).

The transition from elementary to middle school is a difficult—if not the most difficult—transition that children face during their academic years. It occurs in tandem with puberty when many changes are already taking place. Some children make the transition in sixth grade, others in seventh grade, and still others as young as in fifth grade, depending on the school district. The older K–8 system seems to work better for most children because friendships are not disrupted (which often happens when children go to another school), and older children can take a leadership place in the school hierarchy, rather than being the youngest in a new school environment.

Bullying/Cyberbullying

Bullying Bullying typically occurs between sixth and eighth grades. Bullies and their victims both seem to have difficulty adjusting to their social environment, and both experience difficulty making friends (Nansel et al., 2001). The U.S. Secret Service and U.S. Department of Education (2002) did research that showed that almost three quarters of those involved in shootings as adolescents (both within schools and/or their communities) had experienced bullying or felt threatened or attacked by others over long-term periods, generally beginning in middle school. The attackers were all boys, and all had exhibited some kind of worrisome behavior prior to the shootings. Among children who are the victims of bullies, depression and anxiety were prevalent. A national online survey among 3,420 students aged 13 to 18 and 1,011 secondary school teachers that studies harassment in schools found the most common reason for being harassed is appearance. The second common reason for harassment is sexual orientation. Other reasons for harassment include race, ethnicity, gender, disability, and religion (www.harrisinteractive.com). Schools have become more proactive around the issue of bullying; however, greater attention must be paid to social relationships and interactions in the school setting. Although educators often feel this is not the domain of schools, this could not be farther from the truth. A caring school climate that includes relationships with teachers and peers in a safe environment contributes to the healthy development of the middle schoolchild (Search Institute, 2004). The best approach to creating this atmosphere seems to have everyone in the school work together to change the school norms (Crawford, 2002). School can be a place where adjustment difficulties are maintained and reinforced or become the place for shaping and providing opportunities for the development of cognitive, affective, and social skills. Educators need to design school environments that accommodate individual differences in style of learning and socialization. For example, in some middle schools, cafeteria seating is set up in small groupings with the children themselves making decisions about where they will sit and with whom they will socialize during lunch. Based on knowledge about social hierarchies, this is not the ideal situation. It might be better to encourage a system of rotation that limits the potential for exclusionary behaviors. Adults must actively intervene to encourage positive social skills and inclusionary behaviors. Twemlow and Sacco (2008) suggest that staff and students must prioritize the need to make an antibullying program successful. In school, all children have the right to feel they have a place that is secure and free from social harassment, and that adults will intervene when necessary to ensure that this happens.

Cyberbullying Bullying has taken on new forms in contemporary culture. Vulgar images, mean messages, and private information are being released and sent through e-mails, cell phone texts, Web pages, blogs, and instant messaging. This form of bullying reaches children in their homes. Cyberbullying presents a challenge to both parents and educators. Schools are often unclear whether this form of bullying falls within their domain of authority, and parents are even less clear how to address the often anonymous but cruel form of victimization. Guidance counselors, teachers, social workers, psychologists, and other adults who work with children should be knowledgeable about cyberbullying and work together with parents and the community at large to protect children from this latest form of harassment (Sturgeon, 2006).

Special Education

In 1975 the Education of All Handicapped Children Act, (Public Law P.L. 94–142) was passed (now known as Individuals with Disabilities Education Act [IDEA]). This legislation guaranteed children between the ages of 3 and 21 years the right to a free appropriate public education in the least-restrictive environment. Some of the disabilities covered under the law include visual disabilities, learning and communication disorders, pervasive developmental disabilities, health disorders, attention deficit and disruptive behavior disorders, and emotional disorders (which include mood disorders, anxiety disorders, and schizophrenia). After diagnosis and classification, these children are eligible for individual education plans (IEP) implemented and monitored by the school's special needs department (see Chapter 18 for further discussion of this legislation). Classification of a disability occurs after a comprehensive evaluation. This is a significant point because many disabilities will only be diagnosed if the appropriate testing is done. Table 11.3

TABLE 11.3

Components of a Comprehensive Evaluation

Type of Evaluation	Areas That May Be Assessed	Staff Who Might Conduct Evaluations
Physical examination	Vision, hearing, physical development, medical needs, and physical factors that affect school progress.	School physician Nurse practitioner Physician's assistant
Psychological assessment and psychological evaluation (as deemed necessary by the school psychologist)	General intelligence, learning strengths and weaknesses, instructional needs, social interactions, and relationships.	School psychologist
Social history	Social development, current social interactions, factors within home, school, and community that may contribute to student's difficulties.	Social worker Guidance counselor School psychologist School administrator School nurse
Observation in the classroom	Performance in the current educational setting, relationship to teachers and other students, learning styles, and attention span.	School administrator Teacher Reading specialist Guidance counselor CSE member School psychologist
Appropriate educational revaluations	Educational achievement, strengths and weaknesses, vocational and academic needs.	Teacher Reading specialist Guidance counselor Vocational counselor
Assessments in all areas Relating to the suspected disability	Specific assessments relating to health, vision, hearing, social-emotional development, general intelligence, communication skills, motor abilities, and academic performance.	School nurse Speech therapist Audiologist Physical therapist Occupational therapist Specialist with knowledge in area of suspected disability
Vocational assessment	Possible areas of future employment; work-related skills, interests.	Counselor Psychologist Work site evaluator Vocational counselor Rehabilitation counselor

Source: N. B. Webb, 1996, *Social Work Practice with Children* (p.195). New York: Guilford Press. Reprinted with permission.

depicts the components of a comprehensive evaluation. It is important to remember that diagnosis of childhood mental disorders is not always straightforward or easy to make. We must determine whether the child's symptoms of behaviors are occurring with an unexpected frequency or at an unexpected point in development and/or lasting for an unexpected length of time.

Components of a Comprehensive Evaluation Children may be having difficulties for a variety of reasons, and it is important to correctly identify the cause(s), particularly with regard to special needs, as soon as possible. Consideration of developmental principles enhances our understanding of various problems children may be having. Proper assessment includes the assessment of biology and psychosocial influences, which are reciprocal. Those children with more obvious differences or disabilities (such as autism, mental retardation, or deaf-blindness) are more easily identified, and school accommodations are made to ensure their education. Unfortunately, children with less obvious differences (such as auditory processing or nonverbal learning disabilities) may go unnoticed. These conditions can, of course, also be the problem, or the child can have more than one condition. Many children in their middle years come to the attention of mental health personnel and school adjustment counselors as a result of disruptive behaviors in the classroom. In fact, *disruptive disorders,* such as *oppositional defiant disorder* and *conduct disorder,* seem to be a collection of behaviors rather than a coherent pattern of mental dysfunction. They are frequently found in children who suffer from ADHD (see Chapter 2). The Office of the Surgeon General (n.d.) reports the following:

- *Oppositional defiant disorder (ODD):* This disorder is characterized by a persistent pattern of disobedience and defiance toward authority figures, including parents, teachers, and other adults. Children with this condition often engage in behaviors such as fighting and arguing, being purposely annoying or hurtful to other people, refusing to comply with the requests of adults, blaming others for their mistakes, and testing limits. Oppositional defiant disorder can be (is not always) a precursor of conduct disorder.
- *Conduct Disorder:* Conduct disorder is more serious than oppositional defiant disorder and is generally diagnosed in children in their later middle years and adolescence. These children behave quite aggressively by fighting, bullying, intimidating, physically assaulting, sexually coercing, and being cruel to people or animals. Vandalism; setting fires; theft; early tobacco, alcohol, and substance use and abuse; and precocious sexual activity are not uncommon behaviors in children (and adolescents) diagnosed with conduct disorder. These behaviors are serious enough to interfere with all aspects of school and social adjustment, including learning. Children with an early onset of conduct disorder are at high risk for development of adult antisocial personality disorder.

Parents need help to understand the law and to ensure that their children get the appropriate services to assist in their education. This may be especially true for immigrant parents, parents who do not speak English, and parents from poor and working-class families who may be intimidated by the language of the law. Although learning disabilities may be underdiagnosed in some children, other children are overrepresented in classes for the learning disabled. These often include children whose first language is not English as well as normal but underachieving culturally and racially diverse children (Davies, 2004). It is important to appreciate that schools and most testing instruments have a Eurocentric focus.

Children from different racial and ethnic groups may have problems adjusting to this focus as opposed to problems with learning or with behavior. Social class can also play a role in determining those who are labeled as learning disabled because children from poor and working-class families may not be exposed to the same range of experiences as those from more socioeconomically advantaged families. Schools must develop multicultural educational models and ensure that testing is culturally relevant and sensitive (Schriver, 2004). Dudley-Marling (2004), writing from a social constructivist perspective, emphasized that learning and learning problems occur in the context of human relations and activity. "It takes a complex system of interactions performed in just the right way, at the right time, on the stage we call school to make a learning disability" (p. 482). "The essential question in response to the appearance of a learning difficulty is 'What's going on here?'" (p. 488). Solutions then involve the patterns of interaction between students, teachers, and the school environment in addition to appropriate instructional support and direction (p. 489).

Maltreatment during Middle Childhood

The effects of maltreatment during middle childhood can continue from previous years of abuse or neglect but can also correlate with this new developmental period in the child's life. Age appears to be a risk factor for children 7 to 11 years of age, as there is an increase of maltreatment during the middle-school years. This may be due to an increase in reporting as children are increasingly involved with others outside the family during these years, particularly with the onset of school. Maltreated children often have difficulties with school adjustment and academic achievement. Many of these children have lower language and intellectual functioning, particularly if the abuse began in early childhood. These children are more likely to have learning disabilities, to have behavioral problems, and to be in special education classes. Specifically, maltreated children often have difficulties in using appropriate emotional responses in interpersonal situations. Many have poor self-esteem, suffer from depression, and are at high risk for suicide. Abused children tend to struggle with anger, aggression, and impulse control during the middle years of childhood and into adolescence. Another consequence of maltreatment is ADHD or ODD. There are several kinds of maltreatment.

Physical Abuse

This type of abuse involves the battery of a child. Features that might indicate the presence of physical abuse include parental reluctance to give a clear history of the child's injury, a history of the injury that appears to be inconsistent with the actual injury, a history of the injury that is incompatible with the child's developmental capability, an inappropriate response by the parents to the severity of the injury, and a delay in reporting the injury or getting treatment for the child. Children who have been physically abused may also show physical signs of injury or pain related to their injuries. Shame and fear may contribute to the child's social difficulties and isolation when the child feels it is necessary to make excuses for injuries (U.S. Department of Health and Human Services, 2003).

Sexual Abuse

Sexual abuse or molestation includes exposure, genital manipulation, sodomy, fellatio, and coitus. Vaginal penetration by an unrelated person constitutes rape. If the adult is biologically related, the term is *incest.* Each of these abuses is a distinct type of maltreatment with very serious and specific behavioral and psychological manifestations during middle childhood. Physical signs of sexual abuse in children 7 to 11 years of age can include vaginal or penile discharge; sexually transmitted disease; nightmares and sleep disorders; tearing around the genital area, including the rectum; visible lesions around the mouth or genitals; the presence of semen in oral, anal, or vaginal areas; bite marks on or around genitals; and repeated cystitis (inflammation of the bladder), especially in girls (Scannapieco & Connell-Carrick, 2005, pp. 175–176).

Sexual abuse can cause children to have distorted ideas about sexuality. Their behavior often becomes sexualized as well, including excessive masturbation, engaging in sex talk with other children and adults, and engaging in sex play with other children. They may show a heightened awareness of sex and sex acts that are often manifested in their play with dolls or pets or in drawings. Many of these children are also at risk for acting out sexually on other, younger children. There is great difficulty in the attachment relationship if the perpetrator of the sexual abuse is the child's parent or primary caretaker (Scannapieco & Connell-Carrick, 2005). Many sexually abused children have cognitive distortions and perceive themselves as different from other children. They suffer from feelings of shame and even guilt as they often blame themselves in some way for the sexual abuse. Many sexually abused children exhibit symptoms of *posttraumatic stress disorder,* such as difficulty sleeping, difficulty concentrating, anxiety, aggression, and depression. Sexually abused children have difficulty making friends due to their compromised trust in other persons, the burden of carrying the "secret" of the abuse, and feeling different from their peers (Fiering, Taska, & Lewis, 1998; Finkel, 2000; Finkelhor, 1995; Kress & Vandenberg, 1998).

Neglect

Neglect is defined as a failure to meet a child's basic physical and medical needs, emotional deprivation, or desertion. Some indicators of neglectful behavior toward children in the middle years can include leaving a school-aged child alone for long periods of time; leaving children aged 9 or younger to baby-sit children ages 5 or younger; children drinking or using drugs with parental approval or encouragement; lack of medical attention for serious illness; not obtaining required immunization shots; and lack of identified medical or psychological services that pose a substantial risk for the child (Scannapieco & Connell-Carrick,

2005, pp. 171–172). Signs of neglect in school-age children may also include poor school attendance, poor hygiene, inappropriate clothing, and bad relationships with peers and adults. Failure to seek appropriate health care and follow up with routine school requirements can also often be a sign of neglect. It is sometimes difficult to distinguish neglect from poverty, and it is important not to further stigmatize children and families who may be struggling due to lack of resources (U.S. Department of Health and Human Services, 2003).

The risk factors for child maltreatment during the middle school years are multiple and varied. The parents, caregivers, and families of these children often have problems of their own, including low self-esteem, antisocial personality, paternal psychopathology, serious mental illness, cognitive deficits and distortions, poor impulse control, and substance use. Many are low income, and there is often unemployment in the home. Although child maltreatment occurs in all socioeconomic groups, most of these parents and families are socially isolated with few social supports. It is important to protect children and balance their protection with parental rights and supportive assistance to families who may be going through difficult times. Child welfare is a complex topic and one that will be covered in more detail in Chapter 18.

Summary

The years of middle childhood provide opportunities for growth and development in so many areas, often making the boundaries between normal and abnormal less distinct. Children's behavior is ever-changing, complicating clinical presentation and suggesting fluidity between and among different diagnoses. Children move beyond their families during these years and begin to take their place in the world of school, peers, and various social arenas. It is important for children to develop a sense of competence in their developing abilities, which sets the stage for self-esteem and autonomous coping. The internalization of values and the development of a conscience become increasingly important and are precursors to the adolescent years, when teenagers must rely on internalized norms to govern their behavior. Children develop social perspective during these years. This important skill influences their ability to be less self-centered and to empathize with others. Children also begin to learn that self-esteem is based both on the ability to please oneself and to get along with others. This important balance will continue to challenge children through adolescence and into early adulthood, but the seeds are laid during the middle years of childhood.

12 Adolescence

Introduction

Adolescence has been described as a cultural phenomenon because of its origins in late 19th-century changes in the economic and social structure of U.S. society (Germain, 1991). The concept of adolescence was created when the need for advanced education produced a greater economic dependence on parents during the period between puberty and the time when an individual achieved economic and social independence. Two important factors were introduced by formal and extended schooling. The first is the longer delay in achieving economic self-sufficiency. The second is the prolongation of social experiences that take place in school and/or community contexts that are institutionally separated from adult life (Cole & Cole, 1996, p. 710). Environmental-learning theorists and those who take a cultural-context perspective accept the universality of adolescence as a period of transition between childhood and young adulthood. However, they feel that adolescence exists as a "prominent stage of development only in societies where young people reach biological maturity before they have acquired the knowledge and skills needed to ensure cultural reproduction (Schlegel & Barry, 1991; Whiting, Burbank, & Ratner, 1986, cited in Cole & Cole, 1996). This extended period (between the ages of 12 and 19) became formally defined as adolescence: "the phase of life beginning in biology and ending in society" (Lerner, Villarruel, & Castellino, 1999).

Adolescence involves two significant transition points: the transition to early adolescence from childhood and the transition from late adolescence to adulthood. The substages of adolescence are early adolescence, which generally corresponds to the middle-school years (11–14 years); middle adolescence (15–18 years) to the high-school years; and late adolescence (18–21 years) to college or entry into the workforce. There is no other period of the life cycle, except infancy, during which such rapid changes in the individual take place: biologically, psychologically, cognitively, and socioculturally (Steinbeng, 1996).

Figure 12.1 depicts a contextual model of adolescence developed by Holmbeck and Shapera (1999), which illustrates the biopsychosocial nature of this developmental period. This model highlights many of the points that we will discuss in this chapter. The factors presented in the model, as well as those we will discuss, are interrelated. As Holmbeck and associates point out: "The primary developmental changes of adolescence impact on interpersonal contexts, that in turn impact on the developmental outcomes of adolescence" (2000, p. 358). In addition, Shirk (1999) also considers that there are developmental norms, as well as both reasonable and inappropriate departures from those norms, that must be assessed.

Biological Development

Adolescence is marked by the rapid changes initiated by puberty. Pubertal changes occur during early adolescence by a steady process of changing hormonal activity resulting in the maturation of physiological mechanisms (for example,

FIGURE 12.1

Developmental Contextual Model of Adolescence

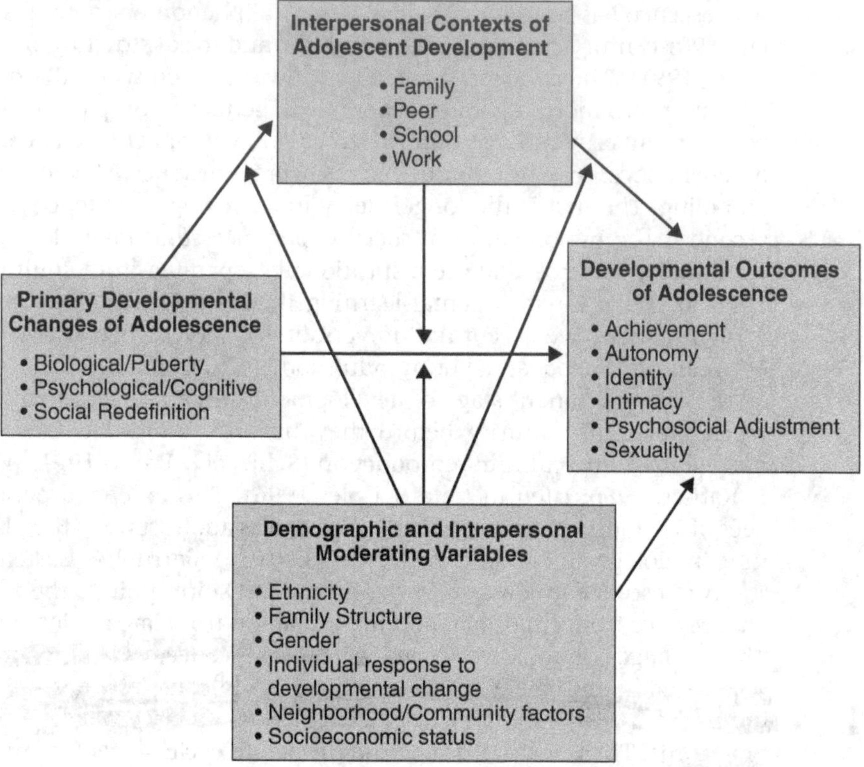

Source: C.N. Holmbeck and C. Shapera, "Research Methods in Adolescents." In P.C. Kendall, J.N. Butcher, and G.N. Holmbeck (Eds.), *Handbook of Research Methods in Clinical Psychology* (2nd ed.), (pp. 634–661). Hoboken, NJ: John Wiley & Sons Inc. Copyright © 1999 Holmbeck and Shapera. Reprinted with permission of John Wiley & Sons, Inc.

reproductive capacity), a growth spurt, and the development of secondary sex characteristics. The main hormones concerned with growth in adolescence are the pituitary growth hormone, sex hormones (testosterone and estrogen), and the pituitary gonadotropic (sex-gland-stimulating) hormones. *Testosterone* is the male sex hormone and is responsible for most of the growth in the adolescent male during this time. This includes acceleration in the growth of the testes and scrotum. The time of first ejaculation of seminal fluid generally occurs about one year after the beginning of penis development. The female sex hormone is called *estrogen* and is secreted at puberty by the cells of the ovary, which causes growth of the uterus, vagina, and breasts. Pubertal development in girls also involves growth in height and body proportion weight, an increase in body fat, and the appearance of pubic hair. *Menarche*, or the first menstruation, is not the start of puberty and may actually occur several years after the first signs of puberty. The average age for menarche is 12 to 15 years. Ovulation is not consistent during this time, and girls are not considered fertile until about 80% of their menstrual cycles include ovulation. Dysmenorrhea—the experience of painful menstruation—occurs in approximately 33% of adolescent females once ovulation occurs. This is a spasmodic uterine or lower abdominal and back pain during the first 12 to 14 hours of the menstrual flow. It often disappears after the female reaches 24 years of age, when the uterus is mature, or after the birth of a baby. The pelvic bones of a young girl do not grow to a size large enough to successfully carry a baby to term until they are about 17 (Ashford, LeCroy, & Lortie, 2006).

The most rapid pubertal changes occur during early adolescence. Maturity generally occurs 1 to 2 years earlier in girls than in boys. Girls often experience social and emotional difficulties and may be self-conscious about the changes they are experiencing. Early maturation in boys is generally viewed by themselves and others in a more favorable light. By middle adolescence most pubertal changes have occurred. The timing of these pubertal changes relative to one's peers, and the responses of the adolescent's family and peers to the changes, are important variables in the youth's overall adjustment during this time (Call, 2001; Laursen, Coy, & Collins, 1998; Paikoff & Brooks-Gunn, 1991; Sagrestano et al., 1999; Weisz & Weersing, 1999).

Although the biological changes that occur during puberty are universal, some cultural factors influence this time of life as well. For example, adequate food and nourishment result in earlier onset of puberty. Eating disorders, prevalent in contemporary Western society, generally begin in early adolescence and often continue well into adulthood. Due to the serious nature of this problem, eating disorders will be discussed in a separate section in this chapter.

Psychological Development

The psychoanalytic study of the period of adolescence began in 1905 with Freud's then-controversial *Three Essays on the Theory of Sexuality.* Freud described puberty as the time when infantile sexual life takes final form. According to Freud, boys and girls now enter the psychosexual stage of development when adolescents experience a reawakening of aggressive and sexual impulses that had been relatively dormant during middle childhood—the *latency period* of psychosexual development (Berzoff, Flanagan, & Hertz 1996). Jones, a leading psychoanalytic scholar and disciple of Freud's, wrote, "Adolescence recapitulates infancy . . . the precise way in which a given person will pass through the necessary stages of development in adolescence is to a very great extent determined by the form of his infantile development" (1922, pp. 398, 389). For psychoanalytic theorists, the biological and the psychological are intertwined. Youngsters at this stage of development are often flooded with new, socially unacceptable sexual and aggressive feelings that require time for processing. Psychoanalytic theory postulates that "the upholding of a steady equilibrium during the adolescent process is in itself abnormal" (Freud, 1905/1953, p. 139)—a comforting thought to those who witness this tumultuous stage. The defiant types of adolescent behavior may be seen as attempts to regain emotional stability.

Anna Freud (1936a, 1936b) wrote about the struggles of the ego during adolescence to master the tensions developing from these feelings. In normal circumstances, the ego and the superego alter to accommodate the maturing forms of sexuality (see Chapter 3). Difficulties arise, however, when the ego is either too immature to handle the developing sexual impulses or the id impulses overcome the ability of the ego to negotiate the profound changes taking place during this period. In this case, conflict produces the development of neurotic symptoms (see A. Freud, 1936a, b). Anna Freud (1936b) explained the reluctance of the adolescent to engage in therapy (still seen today) as resulting from the adolescent's preoccupation with the present, with little energy left to engage in either the past (with which analytic theory is concerned) or with the therapist. Anna Freud felt it might be better to work with the parents of adolescents rather than the adolescents themselves during this difficult time. The parents often need help and guidance as their son or daughter goes through this difficult stage. We have come to understand over time that this intrapsychic process is made more complex by a host of variables, including socioeconomic conditions, gender conflict, racial identity development, and the various neurobiological and attachment issues described elsewhere in this book.

Erikson (1959) referred to adolescence as a stage involving the major task of identity development. He described it as a "second toddlerhood." During the first toddlerhood the young child negotiated with the parent for increasing individuality and a transition to self-reliance. During adolescence, the youngster strives to maximize individuality and control while struggling with the reality of a dependent position. According to Erikson, "a new life task presents a crisis whose outcome can be a successful graduation, or alternatively, an impairment of the life cycle which will aggravate future crises . . . each crisis prepares the next, as one step leads to another and each crisis also lays one more cornerstone for the adult personality" (1959, p. 254). The four earlier developmental crises that adolescents must rework are (a) establishing trust in the larger world as opposed to the primary caregiver(s); (b) establishing autonomy (choosing one's path in life rather than as the toddler exercising his will; (c) taking initiative (setting goals for what one might become, initially expressed as pretend play during early childhood); and (d) industry, which brings independence and taking responsibility for one's goals and for the quality of one's work. The tasks that the adolescent faces are (a) creating an expanded self-concept; (b) increasing self-direction and independence from the parents while maintaining mutually satisfying relations with them; (c) establishing same-sex and opposite-sex friendships and preparing for adult commitment to a sexual partner; (d) maintaining group affiliations and learning social interdependence; (e) building vocational interests and readying oneself for pursuing them; and (f) building a set of moral values (Germain, 1991, p. 354).

Erikson (1959) felt that the danger of this developmental stage is *identity diffusion* or *identity confusion* as opposed to the development of a secure identity. He felt that adolescents must resolve their identities in both the individual and the social spheres, or establish "the identity of these two identities" (Erikson, 1968a,

p. 22). This identity-forming process depends on how adolescents judge others, how others judge them, how they judge the judgment processes of others, and their ability to make use of the social categories available in the culture when they form judgments about people (Cole & Cole, 1996). Erikson's ideas about the mental processes involved in resolving the identity crisis of adolescence fit with Piaget's ideas of formal operational thinking.

Kegan (1982) suggests that many of the identity-related tasks that Erikson discusses are more appropriate to mid- and late adolescence. He offers a stage called *affiliation versus abandonment* that more directly represents the identity conflicts of early adolescence. This stage coincides with the theme of being accepted or rejected by others—a salient one among middle-school children. Marcia (1983) also differentiated the identity tasks of early adolescence from mid- and later adolescence. She referred to the need of the youngster to disconnect from the internalized parent, that is, beginning to define one's own interests and attitudes from those of one's parents. Marcia identified four patterns of coping with the task of identity formation during adolescence (1983, cited in Cole & Cole, 1996, p. 699). These are described next.

- *Identity Achievement:* Adolescents who display this pattern have gone through a period of decision making about their choice of occupation, or political, or religious commitment.
- *Foreclosure:* Young people who display this pattern take over patterns of identity from their parents.
- *Moratorium:* This pattern is displayed by adolescents who are experiencing an identity crisis.
- *Identity Diffusion:* Adolescents who manifest this pattern have tried several identities without being able to settle on one.

Elson felt that adolescents were vulnerable to "disorders of the self," which become manifest in "low self-esteem, lack of goals, immobilization, or in dangerous acting out behavior, such as substance abuse, delinquency or perversions" (1986, p. 94). Erikson (1968a) posited that youth in the United States and other democratic societies were particularly vulnerable to this identity conflict because they are exposed to many choices and freedoms. Identity diffusion occurs less often within the context of rigidly proscribed roles (although other struggles may be more salient for youth in these situations).

Sexual Identity Development

Erikson's theory of identity development is based on heterosexual identity development, with successful resolution for the adolescent being the ability to establish intimacy with an opposite-sex partner. Other authors write that sexual identity is often unsettled at the start of adolescence, and many adolescents will engage in sexual experimentation with both male and female partners (Hunter & Hickerson, 2003; Van Wormer, Wells, & Boes, 2000). In fact, in many cultures, adolescent homosexual behavior is only rarely viewed as an expression of lifelong sexual identity (Savin-Williams, 1995). It is viewed as a way for young men to learn about sex, part of the ritual of becoming a man within the context of separating the sexes. Later, adolescents display a higher correspondence between sexual behaviors and sexual identity. In our dominant heterosexual society, adolescents may use heterosexual attractions as the benchmark against which to understand their same-sex attraction. However, they must then begin the process of developing a gay, lesbian, or bisexual identity or attempt to preserve a heterosexual identity. This can be a very difficult time because the developmental tasks include both the internal coming-out process (the process of recognizing and expressing sexual identity to oneself) and the external coming-out process (disclosure of a gay identity to other gay people; identifying oneself to heterosexual others, such as parents and close family members; and going public at school, work, or in the community (D'Augelli, Hershberger, & Pilkington, 1998; Moses & Hawkins, 1982; Szymanski & Chung, 2001; Waldner & Magrueder, 1999). Savin-Williams wrote: "One of the most important developments in the life of a lesbian, bisexual, or gay male youth is how she or he comes to the point of self identification" (1995, p. 168). This recognition can be a source of inner turmoil and identity confusion because the adolescent can no longer assume a heterosexual identity but also knows that homosexuals are stigmatized. Most families of gay and lesbian adolescents are heterosexually oriented, making it difficult if not impossible to socialize their teen family member to what life will mean for them (Hunter & Mallon, 2000, p. 231). A poignant example of the struggle gay youth face was recounted by a 15-year-old boy. After the initial relief of disclosing that he was gay to his parents and their acceptance of him, this young man said to them: "Now that I don't have to worry about your acceptance, I realize I have to worry about acceptance from the rest of the world."

Kleinberg writes about the difficulties young lesbian women face in disclosing their sexual identity to their parents, particularly their mothers. She wrote: "Disclosure is an ongoing process that forces a woman to struggle with the needs of the other people for whom she cares . . . among lesbian women who choose to come out to their parents, the foremost reason is a desire to share their lives and their identity with their parents and hence to feel better connected to them" (1986, p. 1). This has been demonstrated in clinical practice with adolescent girls who are developing a lesbian identity. There is a keen desire on the part of these young women to tell their mothers and to feel accepted by them.

Current research indicates that self-labeling occurs at a relatively young age, but revealing that identity only to select and supportive others is optimal for psychological well-being (Andersen, 1998; Hunter & Hickerson, 2003; Savin-Williams, 1995). Overall, one of the best predictors of self-esteem among lesbian youth, who seem to be a special group in this regard, is early recognition of homoerotic attractions. This may partially be due to the fact that the prohibition for girls to behave in a gender atypical manner is less severe than for boys. For example, many adolescents may be particularly sensitive to how they are perceived by male peers. Terms used to label nonheterosexual behavior are often destructive to gay adolescent males. Males may also face a greater fear of physical harm because male adolescents as a group are more likely to engage in assaultive behavior than their female counterparts. The choices are not optimal. Passing is difficult because it fosters low self-regard, acting-out behavior, and low levels of interpersonal intimacy. Where, for example, do these youth go to socialize and/or discover who else is like them without possibly exposing themselves to ridicule or even harm? Without appropriate opportunities for peer dating and socialization, gay adolescents may resort to transient and anonymous sexual encounters with adults. They may also give up the hope of ever having the opportunity to be in committed relationships with members of their gender, often resulting in self-esteem problems and feelings of being unlovable to anyone (Fontaine & Hammond, 1996; Friend, 1998). Gay youth have been found to attempt suicide at a rate two to three times higher than other adolescents. This is due to the societal discrimination that often translates into self-hatred based on internalized homophobia. A significant number of adolescent runaways are gay and lesbian youth who have been thrown out by families (Kulkin, Chauvin, & Percle, 2000; Morrison & L'Heureux, 2001; Rotheram-Borus & Bradley, 1990; Rotheram-Borus, Hunter, & Rosario, 1994; Rotheram-Boris, Rosario, & Koopman, 1991; Van Wormer, Wells, & Boes, 2000).

Youth of color may face additional difficulties in developing their sexual identity and orientation because they must integrate these with their ethnic, cultural, and racial backgrounds as members of communities that may be at odds with each other. Gay and bisexual African-American and Latino male youth who attend the Hetrick-Martin Institute in New York City discussed the pressures they face when they come out to their communities. For example, they may experience racism in the gay community and homophobia in their ethnic or racial community (Kunreuther, 1991). On the other hand, the racial and ethnic background of a gay, lesbian, or bisexual adolescent can be a supportive factor. These youth can often gain support from the sexual minority communities that the cultural community is not able to give. It is often the case, however, that families, religious organizations, and peer groups put youth of color in a position of "choosing" one support over another, making it difficult to achieve an integrated sense of identity. Cohler and Hammack (2007) suggested the theoretical lens of life course theory to understand the significance of history on the development of the adolescent's emerging personal narrative about sexual identity. They offer two competing narratives of gay identity in contemporary society that adolescents must negotiate. The narrative of struggle and success focuses on the struggle for identity and the creation of a positive, "minority culture" within a larger stigmatizing, heterosexual society. The narrative of emancipation reveals how gay youth are experiencing their life stories in the absence of antigay prejudice and conflict regarding their sexual orientation. These divergent narratives of gay adolescence exist simultaneously and contribute to the variability in gay youth development (p. 54).

Although little research has been done on this topic, transgendered youth face enormous challenges during this stage of development (see Chapter 4). Gagne,

Tewksbury, and McGaughey examined the coming-out experiences of 65 masculine to feminine transgenderists. Although these accounts were retrospective—and could therefore be reconstructed biographies (1997, p. 16)—feminine behaviors and feelings of being or wanting to be girls created confusion for these individuals as young children and adolescents, particularly when they received messages that they could not act that way.

For this group of adolescents, falling in between the gender binary of masculine and feminine often resulted in the assumption of homosexuality. For many transgenderists the first display of feelings that are later labeled as transgendered come in the form of cross dressing. Cross dressing, especially during adolescence, becomes an accessible means of gender exploration. The message to these youngsters is that their behavior is deviant. This was clearly illustrated in the case of a 14-year-old boy, who was brought for counseling by his distraught parents, who on more than one occasion had found "items of his mother's clothing" in his dresser drawers and who had discovered their son dressed in his mother's clothing. Such messages drive transgendered adolescents into a secret world, where feelings about what is "natural" are held in private (Gagne, Tewksbury, & McGaughey, 1997, p. 24). Feelings of shame are often present because finding role models and formulating an identity outside the gender binary is almost impossible. Therefore, they may look for companions and role models through online bulletin boards. Although such encounters can prove helpful in some ways, these adolescents are vulnerable and at risk for victimization by adults who can exert power and influence over them.

Ethnic and Racial Identity Development

Adolescents who are members of racial and cultural minority groups may face ethnic identity concerns that are central to their overall identity formation process. Phinney and Alipuria (1990) found that ethnicity was rated as significantly more important to overall identity by minority groups compared with Caucasian groups. Although part of this significance may be related to discrimination, another aspect is the challenge these youngsters experience in reconciling often conflicting values between the minority group and the majority or mainstream cultures. In her popular book, *Why Are All the Black Kids Sitting Together in the Cafeteria?*, Beverly Tatum addressed how adolescents of color begin to think about their identities (1997, p. 49). Tatum says, "It's not uncommon to find adolescents of color actively exploring identity, which manifests itself in styles of dress, patterns of speech, music, and who they hang out with in the corridors of their schools" (Tatum 1997, quoted in Sparks, 2004, p. 49). She also pointed out that this type of identity exploration can cause misunderstanding and potential conflict when happening in the presence of others who may not have done that type of identity exploration. For example, most white people have not had to give much thought to skin color, unlike persons of color (Gibbs, 2003).

Phinney (1989) conducted studies with adolescents from various ethnic backgrounds and, based on his research findings, proposed a three-stage developmental model of identity. The first stage, *unexamined ethnic identity,* begins with lack of awareness about one's identity. The youngster's thinking about ethnic identity during this stage is concrete with minimal conflict. The second stage is called *ethnic identity search,* when youth engage in a period of exploration to learn more about their group. This period may involve some discomfort due to awareness of conflict and is often initiated by an encounter in which the adolescent has an unpleasant experience based on ethnic/racial background. During this stage, some adolescents adopt an oppositional identity and reject the speech, dress, and behaviors associated with white America. The last stage is *achieved ethnic identity,* which is assumed to lead both to positive attitudes regarding one's own ethnicity and to a sense of belonging. This developmental approach posits that ethnic identity will vary with age; younger adolescents would be expected to have a less clear and committed sense of their identity.

Adolescents from racial and ethnic groups that experience racism and discrimination are particularly vulnerable to suicide. Latina females have a 21% rate of suicide attempts; African-American and non-Latina white females have rates of 10.8 and 10.4%, respectively. Adolescent males overall have lower rates of suicide than other adolescents (Cooper & Lesser, 2005, p. 21). It is noteworthy that research on the higher rates of suicide among Latina girls has been linked to the demands placed on these youngsters in acculturating to a dominant culture that presents definitions of women's roles that are different from those familiar to the immigrant Latina mother. This results in a strain in the mother's capacity to be a mentor to her daughter and a concurrent strain for the daughter, who may struggle to balance traditional cultural sex roles and the acculturated roles of U.S. society (Zayas, Kaplan, Turner, Romano, & Gonzalez-Ramos, 2000).

Cognitive Development

There have been various approaches to understanding the cognitive development of adolescents. Piaget (1969, 1972) thought that adolescence was a time when formal operational thinking emerges and adult reasoning can take place. The novelty that characterizes adolescent thought starts around age 11 or 12 (when final growth spurt occurs in the frontal lobes of the brain) and does not reach its point of equilibrium until about age 14 or 15. The *amygdala,* which governs emotional responses, expands in adolescence. During this period the concrete logic is detached from the objects themselves so that it can function on verbal or symbolic statements without other support. The adolescent is developing the ability to manipulate ideas, as opposed to objects. This leads to an understanding of abstract theories and concepts (Piaget, 1969, p. 105). Cognitive functions such as problem solving, maturity, and insight are therefore still developing in adolescents (Ashford, LeCroy, & Lortie, 2006, p. 392).

Early adolescence also involves a cognitive shift that enables youngsters to see themselves and others in a more realistic way, replacing the parents' perception of reality they were previously dependent on. Middle adolescence lives in the present with little interest in childhood or adulthood. At this stage, peers are the primary sources of support. Teenagers in middle adolescence tend to be moody, cognitively creative, and emotionally passionate. Later adolescence (beginning at ages 18 and 19) is a time of consolidation and looking toward the future. Teenagers are now able to see family and friends in more balanced ways and are less preoccupied with themselves. They reconnect with family as they become aware of what they value from their parents and want in the relationship.

Information-Processing Approach

A second theory of cognitive development is the *information-processing approach* (Keating, 1990; Klahr, 1982; Klahr & Wallace, 1976; Siegler, 1996). This approach holds that development is a continuous process in which limitations on cognitive capacities are gradually overcome, long-term memory capacity gradually increases, behaviors are routinized, and strategies are developed to link input more effectively to output. If the input is not attended to, it will disappear in a matter of seconds; if attended to, the input will be stored temporarily in short-term (working) memory, where it can be retained for several seconds. This short-term memory input can be combined with memory of past experiences (long-term memory) or it can be forgotten. Short-term memory is continually monitored by control processes that determine how the information temporarily held there is to be applied to the problem at hand. Control processes also determine whether a piece of information in short-term memory needs to be retained or can be forgotten (Cole & Cole, 1996, p. 357).

Keating (1990) described five ways in which adolescent thinking is different from that of middle childhood. The first is that adolescents are thinking more about alternative possibilities that may not readily be apparent. The second is the ability adolescents have to think ahead more often and systematically than younger children. Third is the cognitive ability to think through hypotheses and contemplate a wider range of scenarios. Fourth, adolescents can think about their own thought processes and to engage in *second-order thinking*. This is the ability to think in terms of rules and to hold two different rule systems in mind and consider each of them. Finally, adolescents have the ability to think beyond conventional limits and consider and debate issues such as morality, politics, and religion (Keating, 1990). Described from an information-processing perspective, Keating (1990) and Moshman (1998) proposed that the following cognitive changes occur during adolescence: (a) increase in the ability to remember, process, and organize information; (b) development of a knowledge base; and (c) ability to cognitively self-regulate. Other theorists have proposed that verbal exchanges and socially relevant cognitions, such as empathy skills, verbal communication, understanding of other people's behaviors, the role of affect, and the many ways in which the adolescent interacts with her or his social world, are also important contributions to cognitive development during this life stage (Guerra, 1993; Nelson & Crick, 1999; Shirk, 1999).

Cultural-Context Approach

Another approach to understanding the cognitive development of adolescents is put forth by those theorists who take the *cultural-context approach* (Chi, Glaser, & Rees, 1982, Linn, 1983). They suggest that new modes of thought become prominent as adolescents prepare to adopt adult rules; however, these thoughts vary depending on the context of the adult activity. These theorists do not feel (as Piaget did) that all cultures have contexts that require formal operational thinking.

According to the cultural-context perspective, what is universal is the ability to think systematically about systems and what varies are the contexts within which such ability will be used. In his later writings, Piaget (1972) also conceded that the acquisition of formal operations may be context specific, casting some doubt on his former theory (Piaget & Inhelder, 1969) that formal operational thinking was a totally systematic pattern that is routinely used during adolescence (Cole & Cole, 1996, p. 682).

Cognitive development during adolescence affects the development of attachment. The capacity for formal operational thinking characteristic of this period allows the teenager to construct, from experiences with parents and other caregivers, such as extended family members, a more consistent view of the self apart from interactions with others. Views of oneself in attachment relationships now become more internally based and less centered on a particular relationship. Formal operational thinking also provides adolescents the opportunity to compare relationships with different attachment figures and to an attachment ideal. Of course, this increased capacity brings with it the realization that parents may be deficient in ways previously not considered by the younger child. This presents another arena for conflict with parents, who are now viewed more critically, until the adolescent is able to consider that attachment needs can be met from other relationships.

Kohlberg (1969, 1984) discussed the development of *moral reasoning* during adolescence. In the latter stage of moral development (see Chapter 11 for Kohlberg's stages of moral development), reasoning shifts from upholding the expectations of one's family and other immediate social groups to upholding the expectations and laws of society. This is called "conventional reasoning"—when youngsters begin to recognize the existence of shared standards of right and wrong. This type of thinking takes place during midadolescence. Kohlberg (1984) felt that this type of moral thinking depends on the ability to engage in formal operational reasoning: in particular, the ability to consider simultaneously the various factors relevant to moral choices. During the postconventional stage (which Kohlberg felt only about 10% move into by young adulthood), moral reasoning is based on principles more so than the actual "letter of the law" (Kroger, 2000).

Sociocultural Developments

An important aspect of adolescence is developing a sense of belonging in the larger sociocultural world and a sense of connection to cultural and family traditions. In many cultures, puberty rites are initiated during this time. There seems to be a general ambivalence on the part of both society and the adolescents themselves in our culture regarding the role expectations of youth. This is illustrated by the different ages at which one is considered adult enough to obtain various privileges or incur certain consequences. For example, there have been many dissenting opinions over if and when juveniles who commit violent crimes should be tried as adults. There are differences (sometimes even among states in our country) regarding the legal age to drink, obtain a driver's license, go into the military, vote in an election, or serve as a juror. Marcia (1983) argued that socially sanctioned rites of passage are not always conducive to the disorganized ego state of early adolescence. She feels these can inhibit self-definition in adolescents. Family, peers, and the school and community environments also each provide opportunities for belonging and for change. We will discuss some of these in the following sections.

Parental Influences: The Changing Significance of Attachment

It is not easy to parent an adolescent. Parents need to recognize their son or daughter's expanding intellectual capacity. They must accept their teenager's desire for independence, peer friendships, dating, and recreational activities away from the family. They must begin to relinquish some parental control and rely more on communication and discussion in establishing standards for conduct (Holmbeck, 1996). Parents need to recognize and appreciate how important their role is during this developmental stage. *Authoritative* parenting is needed to monitor, supervise, and provide guidance to adolescent children. An example of authoritative parenting is setting appropriate curfews, knowing where the adolescent will be, and with whom she or he will be. *Authoritarian* parenting, which provides too little independent thinking, might interfere with a youngster's need to spend time with peers and away from family (for example, not allowing the adolescent to go out with friends at all). *Permissive* parenting, which provides too much independent thinking, puts the adolescent at risk. An example of this type of parenting would be the parent who does not know where the youngster is for long periods of time or does not either know or like their child's friends but allows their son or daughter to spend time with them nonetheless. Tensions between adolescents and their parents may arise during this time affecting the adolescent's education, vocation, values, and emotional separateness and connectedness.

There are particular strains on families during adolescence. Generally, parents are approaching or are in middle age when their children are adolescents. They may be experiencing loss of sexual activity just as the adolescent child exhibits a budding sexuality and attractiveness. One or both parents may be experiencing stress in their work. Some parents may try to experience success through their child or convey messages of disappointment that affect the teenager as he or she is making future vocational plans (Germain, 1991). It is imperative that adolescents remain affectively tied to their parents, while attaining "emotional autonomy" from "child-like dependencies on parents" (Holmbeck et al., 2000, p. 354). Blos (1975) and others (Josselson, 1994; Kroger, 2000; Quintana & Lapsley, 1990) discussed adolescence as a second *separation-individuation process*. Although the task of the first separation-individuation process was to internalize the image of the primary caretaker (Mahler, 1963), the task for the adolescent is to relinquish the internalized representation to enable more autonomous functioning. Allen and Land address the "goal-corrected partnership" the adolescent must negotiate with each parent "in which behavior is determined not only by the adolescent's current needs and desires, but by the recognition of the need to manage certain 'set goals' for the partnership" (1999, p. 321). A successful balance of efforts to attain autonomy and maintain the relationship in adolescent–parent interactions when there are disagreements may be a stage of attachment security in adolescence. Adolescents are learning how to function with greater social, cognitive, and emotional autonomy (Allen & Land, 1999). Adolescents are moving away from being receivers of caregiving and developing strategies for approaching other kinds of attachment relationships (for example, with peers, romantic partners, and eventually perhaps as caregivers to others).

Parents need to adjust their own attachment relationships with their adolescent to help their growing child learn how to live independently. The central function of the attachment relationship with parents during this life stage is providing a secure base for the adolescent child while she or he explores the often wide range of emotions involved in pursuing independence. Values often clash because the adolescent is trying to establish a set of values that is different from those of her or his parents. Achieving appropriate separation while remaining emotionally connected thus presents difficult interlocking life tasks for both parents and adolescents. Weingarten, in writing from a postmodern narrative perspective, addresses the critical role a therapist can play during this time. She feels therapy provides an opportunity and a context for bringing adolescents and their parents together: "A parent and adolescent can benefit from hearing each other's stories, and that each may be a resource for change for the other" (1997, p. 311).

Attachment to Peers

Relationships with peers take center stage during adolescence. Sullivan (1953) felt that it was crucial to have intimate friendships during childhood and adolescence to discover a healthy sense of identity. The ability to understand others by sharing themselves helps to define the attributes that make them unique. The cognitive, developmental, and social changes that take place during adolescence make it possible for peers to serve as attachment figures for each other when separating from the primary attachment figures (the parents or caregivers). This process involves a transformation from the more hierarchical attachment relationships with parents to more equal relationships among peers. Peer-based relationships generally begin in pre- or early adolescence. Adolescents tend to choose friends from their same social class and racial groups, and these are often slow to change. Cross-sex friendships also become more common during adolescence, often putting lesbian, gay, bisexual, and transgendered youth at risk for verbal and physical harassment. Friendships, therefore, may reflect the adolescent's status and reputation and provide some information about the adolescent's overall behavior.

Self-esteem among adolescents is often related to the status of their crowd. In his study of high school peer relations, Coleman (1980, 1990) identified a "leading crowd" comprised of students highly envied or regarded by their classmates. The self-esteem among these high-status groups (across a number of schools) was higher than the self-esteem within groups further down the status hierarchy. The characteristics of the students in the high-status elite groups included peer popularity, control over extracurricular activities, school leadership positions, and positive regard from adults (Brown, 1991; Brown & Gilligan, 1992).

When viewed within the context of attachment, peer pressure can be seen as a reflexive desire to please peers, just as the adolescent had once pleased parents (during earlier developmental phases). Elson (1986) writes from a self-psychological perspective and discusses the important *twinship* and *partnering self-object* needs that are prominent during adolescent peer relationships (see Chapter 3). These include a sense of identification and emotional support, which helps alleviate shame and embarrassment among youth of this age when others are making the same mistakes.

Peer relationships can be disrupted during a crisis in an adolescent's life and become a source of stress and pain. Consider that children with ADHD, learning disabilities, and mood disorders often have social problems (see Chapter 2). This may partially be due to the fact that adolescence is a time when the capacity for empathy and more complex social encounters occur, and these areas are often difficult for youth with these problems.

Peers are an important bridge to the development of romantic relationships that may involve sexual interest. During adolescence, the sexual and attachment systems each push toward the establishment of the intense relationships previously maintained with peers. Here we see a confluence between the biological and attachment systems (Kupersmith & Dodge, 2004). Adolescents learn how to express and deal with their sexual identities in discussion with friends (Cole & Cole, 1996). For all the reasons discussed, interactions with, and acceptance by, one's peers are crucial to identity formation during adolescence.

As teenagers become more involved with peers and romantic relationships, their interactions with siblings, similar to those of parents, tend to decline. However, sibling attachments are also influenced by relationships with people outside the family, which can influence the degree of emotional support they may seek from their brothers and sisters.

School Influences

The field of *developmental contextualism* (Vondracek & Porfeli, 2002; Walsh, Galassi, & Murphy, 2002) suggests that making an adolescent's environmental context more supportive may buffer any discomfort in the family. Nowhere is there a more likely arena for this to occur than in the school setting, where adolescents spend a good portion of their day. Schools present one of the main contexts where the developmental adjustments of adolescents are pronounced. Stress on children increases during the transition from middle school to high school as the expectations for academic performance and personal responsibility for one's actions increases. Germain (1991) includes school underachievement, failure, and dropout as factors associated with the development of risk behaviors in adolescents. In addition to dropping out from school entirely, Richman, Bowen, and Woolley (2004) define school failure as "inclusive of poor social and academic performance while a student is in school." Although the school dropout rates are declining, there are still approximately 23% of adolescents who leave high school without receiving a diploma. In addition, many of those who remain in school are not functioning adequately or are leaving without the appropriate knowledge or technical abilities. These students generally face lower individual and family incomes, higher unemployment, earlier involvement in sexual intercourse, higher risk of sexually transmitted disease, increased likelihood of school-age pregnancy, increased use of and demand for social services, increased crime, reduced political participation, and higher health-care costs (Manlove, 1998, cited in Richman, Bowen, & Woolley, 2004, p. 133). A higher proportion of white students (91.2%) graduate from high school, followed by black students (83.5%), and Latino students (63.4%). Many Latino students face the additional challenges of immigration status and language during their high school years, which may contribute to the lower rate of high school graduation among this group (Urban Institute, 2004).

Schools can provide both an opportunity for prevention of problems as well as focused intervention when they occur. Therefore, schools must be vigilant in their efforts to ensure that they provide a safe learning environment for all youth. Many adolescents have challenging and problematic socialization experiences in schools where they feel unprotected by adults and the school's inability to regulate behavior. Social or relational aggression among girls in the school setting has been on the rise for several years. This type of exclusionary behavior often leads to the development of eating disorders, self-injurious behavior, and depression among those youth who find themselves consistently on the periphery of groups. Adolescents need to have connections with teachers and school-based counselors to whom they can turn before problems escalate. Spencer (2000) and Whitney-Thomas and Maloney (2001) write that forming relationships with adult teachers (as well as other supportive adults) often furnishes adolescents with social capital or a context to observe and practice basic social roles. These support systems must be meaningful and accessible. Rylance (1998) and Whitney-Thomas and Maloney (2001) report that merely having counseling services available for students at schools does not address the needs of students who fail to ask for help (and may be most often in need of services). In addition, findings from the *National Longitudinal Study on Adolescent Health* (Resnick et al., 1997) found that family and school connectedness reduced emotional distress, early sexual activity, substance abuse, violence, and suicidal behavior. Both parents and school personnel must raise questions regarding the supportive people in the adolescent's life who are able to provide advocacy and resources when needed. Adolescents should not be exposed to harassment of any kind, whether based on race or ethnicity, sexual identity or orientation, learning difficulties, or social status. Children with learning disabilities are particularly vulnerable to developing low self-esteem as they struggle to achieve academic success (Elbaum & Vaughn, 2003). These students are often described as not trying hard enough when often they are trying quite hard. They may attempt to cope with their shame by giving an air of not caring about school and by giving up. This may be easier than to have peers who are performing better see their struggles. Children need opportunities to excel in different areas to realize their full potential and make a contribution to their school and to society. This includes recognition of nonacademic classes such as music, art, and theater. All too frequently these programs have been cut or eliminated in school districts strapped for funding and under increasing pressure to produce results on standardized tests. High schools often sponsor elite varsity teams, but no opportunity for interested, less-athletic students to have the chance to play a team sport. Schools must encourage and support the diverse talents of all adolescents rather than reinforcing social hierarchies. Corbin discusses the importance of collaborative relationships among social workers, counselors, and teachers to move from student-level interventions (based on problems presented by individual students) to "interventions involving students, caregivers, teachers, and the larger school community-systemic interventions" (2006, p. 327).

The Carnegie Council on Adolescent Development (1989) offered some goals directed at educational institutions to prepare youngsters for life in the 21st century. They stressed the importance of trust between educators, advisors, and youth in middle schools; reengaging families in the education of young adolescents; building trust between young adolescents and school-based health-care programs; encouraging early adolescents to take part in various community social service programs; and encouraging early adolescents to learn how to participate in a social democracy (Kroger, 2000, p. 41). Schools can take a leadership role, for example, in organizing voter registration and voter encouragement among adolescents who are eligible to vote for the first time while in high school. Instructors in history and civics have the opportunity not only to educate students about the political process in the United States but also to help empower them to become part of the electoral community. Schools must be able to provide students with stability and participation within a safe and supportive context. For this to occur, the demands of the school must fit with the capabilities of the individual student and provide a range of expertly staffed, unstructured youth activities that can serve as a developmental context (Larson, 2000). This balance contributes to care and support as opposed to risk and stress (Battin-Pearson et al., 2000; Richman, Bowen, & Woolley, 2004; Williams, Ayers, Van Dorn, & Arthur, 2004).

Community Influences

Another important domain of influence for adolescents is the community in which they reside. Three risk factors relevant to our discussion of community are delinquency, crime, and violence; substance use and abuse; and unsafe sex, teenage pregnancy, and teenage parenting (Call, 2001).

Delinquency, Crime, and Violence Adolescent violence is of major concern. Research has shown there is a reciprocal relationship between the actions of the adolescent on the context and the actions of the context on the adolescent (Call,

2001; Lerner, 1999). Juvenile delinquency is defined as "illegal acts committed by persons under eighteen years of age, including some acts that if committed by someone eighteen or older, would not be illegal (status offenses)" (Federal Bureau of Investigation [FBI], 2000). The most serious of these are violent crimes such as forcible rape, robbery, aggravated assault, murder, and nonnegligent manslaughter. The next level of seriousness involves burglary, larceny, motor vehicle theft, and arson. Other delinquent acts include offenses such as forgery, vandalism, gambling, driving under the influence, drunkenness, disorderly conduct, vagrancy, and status offenses such as running away and violating curfew (Williams et al., 2005). Several risk factors contribute to the rate of juvenile delinquency among adolescents. The first includes community risk factors, and the second are interpersonal or individual risk factors. Neighborhoods characterized by poverty and high-density living present great challenges to adolescents and their parents. Poor minority youth are at a disadvantage and often indulge in risky behaviors. Adolescents in suburban and rural areas, including those from affluent communities, are also at risk because access to money without concomitant responsibility can be problematic. Rural adolescents are at risk for psychosocial distress due to loneliness, lack of mental health resources, and a changing socioeconomic environment. These changes may include underemployment, poverty, and inadequate housing (Herrenkohl et al., 2000). Many adolescents join gangs to satisfy a need for connectedness, attachment, and identity. Gangs can be differentiated from peer groups on the basis of their delinquent activity. Huff defines a gang "as a group of individuals who interact frequently with each other, are frequently and deliberately involved in illegal activities, share a common collective identity expressed through a gang name, and typically express that identity by adopting certain symbols or claiming control over certain 'turf' " (2001, p. 4). There is increasing availability of drugs and firearms in many communities. Communities need to provide recreational outlets for adolescents, including access to sports, music, theater, and other activities where they can form peer relationships with positive adult role models and mentors. Unfortunately, too many of our communities get caught up in competing interests and shut youth out of organized activities at a time when they need most to be involved (Ashford, LeCroy, & Lortie, 2006; Williams et al., 2005).

Interpersonal risk factors include family conflict, lack of parental supervision, and excessive or inconsistent punishment. Three of the strongest correlates of conduct disorder in adolescents are poor parental supervision, lack of parental involvement in the youngster's activities, and parental antisocial personality disorder. Individual risk factors include early onset of problem behaviors, low commitment to school and academic failure, physiological abnormalities, rebelliousness, temperament, cognitive and neuropsychological deficits, and hyperactivity (Larson, 2000; Williams et al., 2005).

Substance Use and Abuse The beginning of some substance use (generally alcohol, marijuana, and/or tobacco) generally occurs sometime during adolescence. Initiation of any of these substances by the ninth grade is a strong predictor of lifetime substance use.

Alcohol abuse among adolescents remains high. The most recent figures from the Monitoring the Future Study (Johnston, O'Malley, & Bachman, 2005), a long-term survey of the behaviors, attitudes, and values of U.S. secondary school students, college students, and young adults, reports that up to 72% of high school seniors had used alcohol at least once in the previous 12 months. Twenty-two percent had used marijuana and 2% used hallucinogens in the past month. Thirty-one percent had used tobacco (cigarettes), 15% tried inhalants, and 19% smoked marijuana. The use of "gateway drugs" such as alcohol, cigarettes, inhalants, and marijuana is common among youth between the ages of 13 and 14 (Jenson, 2005, p. 185). Many youth who experiment with these types of drugs proceed to drugs such as cocaine, amphetamines, and heroin as they get older. Substance abuse is a major cause of accidents, illness, and death among adolescents. It also causes problems within the family and can lead to school failure and delinquency.

Contextual factors, as well as individual, biological, and psychological, factors play a role in the trajectory of substance abuse among adolescents. Among the high risk factors for substance abuse are low drinking ages and low taxes on alcoholic beverages; neighborhood factors previously discussed; family alcohol and drug use; poor family management practices; school failure; association with drug-using peers, as well as rejection by conforming peers; family history of alcoholism; and ADHD (Jenson, 2005, p. 188). Expectations and role modeling from families, peers, school, neighborhood, and other settings can influence whether adolescents begin to drink. They can also be influential points of intervention (Search Institute, 2004). Holder and colleagues (1997) identified five community intervention tactics to address the problem of substance abuse among adolescents: (a) community mobilization, (b) responsible beverage service, (c) reducing drinking and driving, (d) controlling underage drinking, and (e) limiting alcohol access.

It is noteworthy that there is often co-morbidity of substance abuse with other disorders during adolescence. Prevalent among these are anxiety disorders and other mood disorders, such as bipolar disorder, dysthymia, and major depression. Children with social phobia may be at high risk for substance use/abuse during this developmental stage as well (Beidel & Morris, 1995; Clark, 1993; Myers et al., 2001).

Parents, educators, and health and mental health-care providers need to be proactive in screening and assessing adolescents in settings where substance abuse problems may be present, as adolescents typically do not identify themselves as substance abusers. They need to know what the youth is using, for how long, and what effect the substance is having on his or her mood and behavior. Knight, Sherritt, Shrier, Harris and Change (2002) reviewed the CRAFFT test, a brief screening device developed for use among adolescent medical patients. The CRAFFT questions (p. 609) are listed next:

C – Have you ever ridden in a CAR driven by someone (including yourself) who was "high" or had been using alcohol or drugs?

R – Do you ever use alcohol or drugs to RELAX, feel better about yourself, or fit in?

A – Do you ever use alcohol or drugs while you are by yourself, ALONE?

F – Do your family or FRIENDS ever tell you that you should cut down on your drinking or drug use?

F – Do you ever FORGET things you did while using alcohol or drugs?

T – Have you gotten into TROUBLE while you were using drugs or alcohol?

Despite limitations of the study, these authors found strong evidence that the CRAFFT test provides medical providers a "practical means of quickly identifying adolescent patients who need more comprehensive assessment or referral to substance abuse treatment specialists" (p. 613). This is a tool that can also be utilized by social workers and other mental health clinicians working with adolescents. Table 12.1 depicts a list of variables to consider when conducting an assessment of adolescent substance abuse.

Unsafe Sex, Teenage Pregnancy, and Teenage Parenting Adolescents are at a higher risk for acquiring sexually transmitted infections (STIs), including two bacterial infections: *Neisseria gonorrhea* and *Chlamydia trachomatis*. These two conditions are often asymptomatic and therefore go undetected and untreated. In females, they can lead to pelvic inflammatory disease, which puts women at risk

TABLE 12.1

Traditional Consent Domains for Determining Level and Nature of Intervention

Drug abuse problem severity

- Onset of initial drug use; onset of regular (for example, weekly or more frequent) use of drugs.
- Frequency, quantity, and duration for specific drugs, with an emphasis on the preferred drug; both recent (for example, the previous 6 months) and lifetime use should be covered.
- Review of signs and symptoms of abuse (in other words, hazardous and harmful use) and dependence (de-emphasis on withdrawal symptoms).
- Reasons for use (for example, social, coping, psychological).
- Personal consequences due to drug use, including social, emotional, family, legal, school, HIV/AIDS risk behaviors, and physical.

Risk and protective factors

- Personal adjustment (for example, self-image, conventionality of values, delinquency proneness, psychological status, school affiliation, learning abilities).
- Peer environment (for example, peer drug use, peer norms, abstinent role models).
- Home environment (for example, family togetherness, parenting practices, parental drug use behaviors and attitudes, sexual/physical abuse, sibling drug use behaviors, family norms, and expectations about drug use).
- Community and neighborhood characteristics (for example, population density, level of crime, socioeconomic status).

Source: K. C. Winters, 2001, "Assessing Adolescent Substance Use Problems and Other Areas of Functioning: State of the Art." In P.M. Monti, S.M. Colby, and T. A O'Leary (Eds.), *Adolescents, Alcohol, and Substance Abuse: Reaching Teens through Brief Interventions*. New York: Guilford Press. Reprinted with permission.

of reproductive loss, including infertility and entopic pregnancy. Syphilis, another bacterial STI, is on the rise among adolescents. Viral STIs among sexually active adolescents include genital herpes, genital warts, and HIV (Centers for Disease Control, 1995a, 1995b, 1999a, 1999b, 2000a).

Several behaviors put adolescents at risk for contracting STIs. They may be more likely to have multiple partners (concurrent or sequential) rather than a single long-term relationship. Adolescents tend either not to use contraceptives or to use nonbarrier methods (such as withdrawal). Early initiation of sexual intercourse and unprotected oral sex also contribute to incidence of STIs among this age group. The immunological and physiological immaturity of the urogenital tract in young adolescent females makes them high risk for STIs. Adolescents who are sexually abused are at risk of STIs transmitted by their abusers. These adolescents may also be more likely to engage in behaviors that put them at further risk of contracting STIs (Alford, Huberman, & Moss, 2003; Amaro, 2000).

Adolescents often feel that high-risk sexual behaviors are a way to enhance their sense of connection with others, elevate their status in their peer group, challenge authority, or assert their autonomy. Efforts focused on delaying sexual initiation, diligent contraception use, sex education, assertiveness, and decision-making training all provide alternatives to adolescent childbearing and parenting and the occurrence of STIs in this population (DiClemente, 1992; Germain, 1991; Rounds, 2004).

Another risk factor associated with sexual activity during adolescence is pregnancy. Pregnancy is not in itself a problem but becomes one when it occurs within a context that could prove to be harmful to the adolescent or the baby. There are several options when teenage girls become pregnant: to have the baby and raise the baby, either as a single mother or with the baby's father, married or unmarried; to have the baby and put the baby up for adoption; or to terminate the pregnancy. The rate of single motherhood is higher among Latina and African-American adolescents than European white teens because of fewer economic, educational, and social opportunities. To prevent teenage pregnancy among these youth, greater attention must be given to expand the options of those living in poverty and/or not achieving in school. Adolescent parents are at greater risk than adult parents to engage in abusive parenting interactions or neglect their infant's emotional needs. Their thought processes and social awareness are egocentric, peer oriented, and not conducive to empathic parenting. Even when teenage mothers recognize their babies' cues, they do not necessarily respond appropriately because of their limited knowledge of child development. Greater difficulties often arise during the toddlerhood and preschool years when more complex parenting skills are required.

Disability and Chronic Illness in Adolescence

For the adolescent, being different from one's peers in ways other than those they choose can be psychologically demanding. In a research study that examined self-definition in a sample of adolescents with and without disabilities,

Whitney-Thomas and Maloney examined how young people developed a sense of themselves. The students with disabilities had the most difficulty expressing their self-definition. Those with the greatest struggles were the least able to identify their own need for help and use it when offered. The authors concluded that these teens would benefit from the most intensive intervention in the areas of self-definition and coping with issues of mental and physical health (2001, p. 387). Self-blame is common among adolescents, and adolescents may wonder why they are the ones going through a particular struggle. Coming to terms with the random nature of illness or disability evokes feelings of anger, sadness, and despair. Chronic illness and disability can complicate the adolescent's relationships with parents and peers.

Adolescents may need help to follow medical treatments that might interfere with lifestyle. They must also be encouraged by parents and health-care providers to take part in decision making and not surrender total autonomy. Adolescents with physical and visual disabilities may face problems in dating and sexual expression. Questions regarding reproductive capacity may come up during this time. The adolescent's temperament as well as his or her support system (including family peers, school, and community) can shape illness behaviors, along with the type, extent, and rapidity of the disease process. (For a more thorough account of chronic illness and disability, see Chapter 17.)

Depression and Anxiety in Adolescents

We discussed the neurobiological underpinnings of depression in Chapter 2. Developmental differences in presentation complicate the recognition of depression and other mood symptoms in adolescents. Youngstrom, Findling, and Feeny make this important point: "Current approaches involve searching for the same diagnostic symptoms but recognizing that they may interact with developmental factors to produce new forms of expression" (2004, p. 63). For example, hypomanic or manic symptoms (as in bipolar disorder), such as hypersexuality, gambling, or compulsive spending, may be less expressed among adolescents due to the societal constraints during this developmental phase.

Depressed adolescents often have co-morbid diagnoses (more than one disorder occurring simultaneously). They may be depressed and have anxiety or they may be depressed and abusing drugs. Symptoms of depression in adolescents include low self-esteem, poor body image, self-consciousness, inadequate coping, academic difficulties including truancy and school dropout, argumentativeness, slowed onset of thinking, delayed onset of puberty, antisocial behavior, risk taking such as unsafe sexual activity, substance use, vandalism, and generally, a fair amount of irritability (American Psychiatric Association, 2000). Between the ages of 12 and 15 years, girls show higher rates of depression than boys, and this trend continues into adulthood. The reasons for this may include girls' reactions to pubertal changes influenced by societal expectations, which differ for girls than for boys. Suicide peaks at midadolescence and is the third-leading cause of death in this age group, making depression a significant medical problem. Risk factors for suicide among adolescents include disruptive behaviors, substance abuse, previous suicide attempts, presence of firearms, discovery of pregnancy, legal problems, peer rejection, social isolation, poor school adjustment, and overall hopelessness. Suicidal adolescents also feel they are isolated within the family and often view themselves as expendable. As previously discussed, gay youth and adolescents from racial and ethnic groups that experience racism and discrimination are at high risk. A thorough evaluation of suicide is important when working with depressed adolescents (see Cooper & Lesser, 2005). Family counseling and intervention are also important to enhance family problem solving and conflict resolution so that blame is not directed toward the suicidal adolescent. It is noteworthy that threats of self-injury may appear to be (or indeed be) manipulative at times. However, this is a seriously maladaptive coping strategy when, combined with the adolescent's developmental impulsivity and compromised judgment, can prove fatal. It is important to check the adolescent's level of self-control when expressing suicidal ideation (Friedberg & McClure, 2002). It is always advisable to ensure, with the cooperation of parents or other adults, that items that may pose risk be removed (pills, guns, knives, etc.). Threats or acts of self-harm (or harm to others) should always be taken seriously (Curry & Reinecke, 2003).

Five spheres of functioning are affected when adolescents experience anxiety: physiological, mood, behavioral, cognitive, and interpersonal. Many medical conditions can mimic anxious complaints, and a doctor's involvement is crucial. Anxious adolescents often worry about their capacity to cope and often expect the worse to happen, resulting in avoidance. Anxious teens need help to face their fears and develop competency in taking charge of their anxiety and finding adaptive ways to cope. Anxiety can have enormous developmental implications for adolescents and can undermine their future goals (for example, pursuing educational and career opportunities). It can also impair relationships with peers (Friedberg & McClure, 2002, p. 219). Anxiety can also play a major role in the onset of substance use/abuse as adolescents turn to drugs and alcohol to attend social events (Albano, 2003; Barrett & Shortt, 2003; Kendall, Aschenbrand, & Hudson, 2003; Kendall, Chu, Pimentel, & Choudhury, 2000; March, 1995; Weisz et al., 2003).

Cognitive-behavioral therapy has been considered beneficial in the treatment of adolescents who suffer from depression and anxiety because it emphasizes the cognitive processes involved in the development, maintenance, and modification of behavior. Because these cognitive processes are still in flux, adolescents may be more amenable to cognitive therapy (see Chapter 3 and Freidburg & McClure, 2002; Kendall, 2000; Reinecke, Dattilio, & Freeman, 2003 for further discussion of cognitive-behavioral therapy with adolescents). Other authors (Elson, 1986; Palombo, 2001) feel *self-psychology* (see Chapter 3) may be effective with adolescents because it underscores the significance of the nonverbal process in psychotherapy. The hallmarks of self-psychology are empathy, affect attunement, and cognitive understanding on the part of the therapist. This is particularly significant with young adolescents who often give a host of nonverbal clues without uttering a word. The therapist must be attuned to what may be happening in the life of an adolescent and conduct a comprehensive assessment, attending to neurobiological as well as psychological, cognitive, and sociocultural factors.

Depression is a significant medical problem for adolescents: suicide is the third leading cause of death for individuals in this age group.

Self-Harming Behaviors

Self-harm is defined as "intentional self injury or self mutilation without suicidal intent" (Abrams & Gordon, date). Self-harming behaviors include the use of knives or razors to cut the forearms, wrists, or legs; scratching; burning; self-hitting; hair pulling; and bone breaking. Other terms used to describe these behaviors include self-mutilation, self-cutting, deliberate self-harm and self-destructive behavior (Zila & Kiselica, 2001). The relationship between self-injury and suicidal behavior is complex and not fully understood. The major point of differentiation between the two is intent. Suicidal ideation, gestures, and the completed act of suicide involve the wish to terminate life or the intentional cessation of life. The intent of self-injury is to alleviate distress; however, people who engage in self-harming behaviors may be at higher risk for suicide ideation and/or suicide attempts. This may be particularly significant when self-injurious behaviors no longer provide the affect regulation they once did.

Adolescents who engage in self-harming behaviors may be expressing feelings or needs they cannot identify or express. These behaviors may represent a way of managing chaotic home or school environments. They may also be an internalized response to a sexual or other traumatic experience that allows the youngster to organize feelings and express suffering. They can represent an external attempt to control internal dissociation processes. Most cases of self-injury seem to be precipitated by a situation involving a subjective threat of abandonment or rejection by significant others. The attack on the self is often preceded by intense hurt, rage, and a wish to retaliate against the uncaring other. It is significant that the adolescents are often not able to make any connection between the precipitating event and their self-harming behavior. The act replaces a more direct form of communication, turning the feelings and actions on the self while withdrawing from the interpersonal reality of the situation (Guralnik & Simeon, 2001, p. 187)

Self-harming behaviors may have different meanings for adolescents from different racial and ethnic groups. A study of suicide among Latina adolescents (Turner, S.G. Kaplan, C.P Zayas, L. & Ross, R.E. (2004) demonstrated an attachment disruption between these girls and their mothers who grew up in another country, causing an intergenerational clash about cultural expectations. Straker (2006) feels that self-cutting represents more than an attempt at self-soothing. She believes it is an attempt to put in place the elements involved in building a self-structure. These include mirroring, the establishment of a boundary, and the substitution of verbalizing feelings with signs that are literally cut into the flesh.

Self-harming and self-injury are self-destructive behaviors that need attention; however, they are also an indicator that the adolescent is struggling with other issues that need exploration. Psychodynamic therapy combined with cognitive and behavioral exercises that alter distorted belief and offer new coping skills can empower youngsters who self-injure.

Eating Disorders

"An eating disorder is present when a person experiences severe disturbances in eating behavior, such as extreme reduction of food intake or extreme overeating, or feelings of extreme distress or concern about body weight or shape" (National

Institute of Mental Health, 2008).The etiology of eating disorders is thought to be multiply determined, including biological, cognitive, psychological, and socioenvironmental factors. The two most common eating disorders that occur among adolescents, primarily girls, are anorexia nervosa and bulimia nervosa. Both include an attempt to achieve weight loss through restricting the intake of food. Bulimia nervosa often includes binge eating, followed by self-induced vomiting or laxative abuse (Cooper, Todd, & Wells, 2000; Fairburn & Wilson, 1996). Adolescents who develop eating disorders often do not view their weight loss, however excessive, as problematic. The difficulties the teenagers have in managing their emotions and life events become associated with distorted body perceptions and beliefs about how they look. The adolescent gains a feeling of control over her body, replacing the loss of control over emotions and events. Unfortunately, what often happens is that the adolescent loses control over her body, and the eating disorder now controls the adolescent. Surrey emphasizes that disturbances in eating reflect the message society gives "especially to young girls . . . about eating and about equating beauty with thinness" (1984, p. 6). She feels there is a "cultural inconsistency between pathways of self development for young girls and cultural values which stress self development through learning how to eat" (pp. 6–7).

Another type of eating disorder is binge eating (BID), a disorder that may be separate from bulimia nervosa. Eating episodes involve an unusually large amount of food and a sense of loss of control of the eating episode. There are no significant gender differences related to this disorder, and it includes a more ethnically and culturally diverse group of adolescents (www.interscience.wiley.com, retrieved, 9/22/2008). A complete discussion of this serious condition is beyond the scope of this chapter; however, treatment approaches include psychodynamic, cognitive-behavioral, family therapy, psychoeducation, psychopharmacology, and various group approaches such as body perception groups and cognitive therapy groups. Issues such as shame and underlying feelings of depression and low self-esteem must be addressed. The restoration of weight, however, must be seen as a critical factor in treatment and one that is not open to negotiation (Bowers et al., 2003; Garner & Garfinkel, 1997; Treasure, Schmidt, & van Furth, 2003). A family therapy approach developed by Christopher Dare and Ivan Eisler at the Maudsley Hospital in London offers a promising approach to the treatment of anorexia. The premise of this model is that a patient in acute starvation stages of anorexia will not be able to use insight until a process of refeeding has occurred, and the family is the best context within which this should occur. The therapist empowers the family to take on the responsibility for nurturing their child back to health, providing support to them during this process (Lock, 2001).

Obesity is another type of eating disorder rising in prevalence among children and adolescents. Although all eating disorders are generally thought to involve the interaction of multiple biological and experiential factors that mutually influence each other, some cases have a definable organic onset. Treatment of any adolescent with an eating disorder requires collaboration with a physician and a nutritionist (Bowers et al., 2003; Cooper, Fairburn, & Hawker, 2004; Fairburn & Brownell, 2002).

Adolescents in Military Families

Children who reach adolescence in military families face some particular challenges related to the stages of predeployment, deployment, and postdeployment that directly affect their relationships with parents, peers, and community. Huebner and Mancini (2005) pointed out that adolescents may experience changes in their relationship with the parent who is leaving as well as the parent who remains. Delayed reactions are not uncommon. During the deployment stage, adolescents may have conflicting feelings such as pride and anger. In addition to their own life stage stressors such as school and friends, teens may now have increased emotional burdens such as worrying about the deployed parent's safety. They may also be expected to take on additional chores to help their parents or younger siblings at home. The adolescent's world continues in the absence of the deployed parent. Reengagement can be exciting as well as challenging, especially when the parent resumes responsibilities as an authority figure in the home. These authors stress the importance of parents being in open communication with their adolescent children about what the deployed parent will be doing, about their worries and fears, and to be honest in answering any questions they may have. In addition to stresses related to deployment, adolescents in military families may move frequently. This presents challenges in being part of a peer group. Formal support systems such as groups for teens living in military families are especially helpful. Other supports include teachers, guidance counselors, and friends.

Summary

Adolescence is a critical time "when one's developmental trajectory can be dramatically altered in positive or negative directions" (Holmbeck et al., 2000, p. 336). In addition to the enormous intraindividual changes occurring and the opportunities these present for both adaptation and maladaptation, influential contextual changes are taking place as well in the family, with peers, at school, and in the community at large. Schulenberg, Maggs, Steinman, and Zucker write that "the meaning of developmental transitions originates in the interaction of physical maturational processes, cultural influences and expectations and personal values and goals" (2001, p. 24). Regardless of gender, class, culture, and historical period, adolescents face developmental transitions in biological, psychological, and cognitive development; relationships with parents and peers; sexuality; school; and work. The changes youth experience can dramatically affect those around them and can influence how they manage and resolve the developmental issues of identity formation, sexuality, and emotional and economic autonomy.

13 Early Adulthood

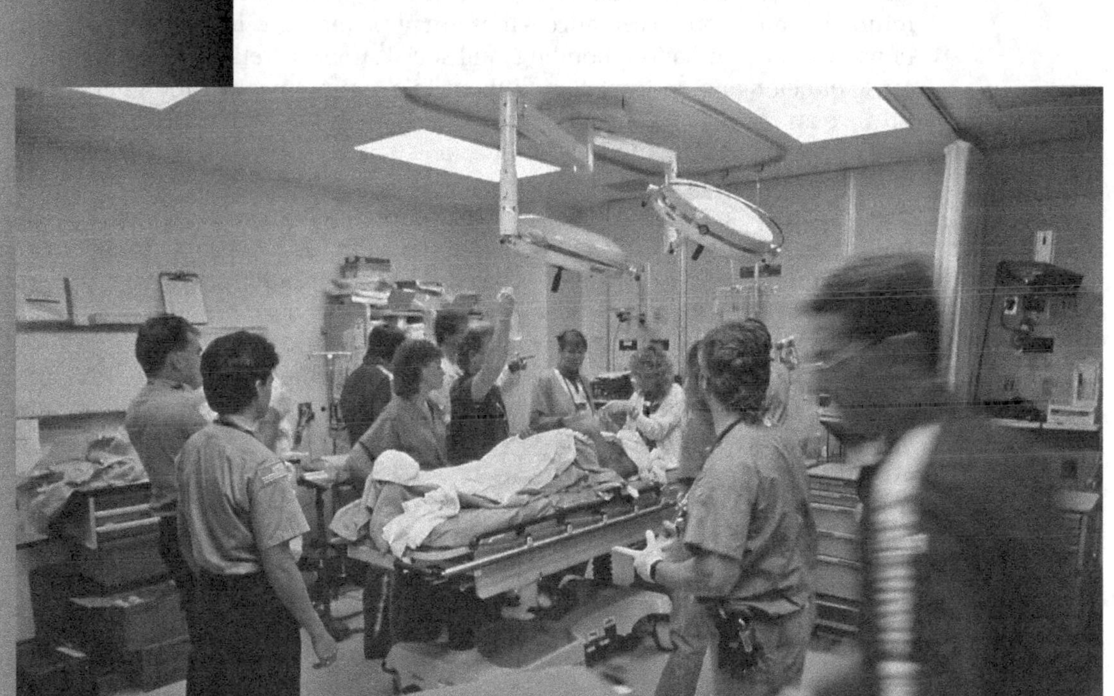

All that has gone before can be seen as preparation;
all that follows can be viewed as actualization.

Newman and Newman, 1999

Introduction

As individuals make the transition to adulthood in Western postindustrial societies, two overarching themes achieve particular significance. These are *love* and *work* (Freud in Erikson, 1950; Levinson, 1996; Smelser 1980). In this context, *love* is broadly defined to include attachment relationships (relationships that have significance to one's sense of security such as with romantic partners, parents, siblings, and children); intimate relationships (relationships in which partners feel a sense of mutuality, affection, acceptance—these may or may not include attachment relationships); and affiliation, bonding, and social support (relationships that provide a sense of belonging, mutual commitment to a common cause and interactions that nurture an individual's sense of well-being; Hutchison 1999). *Work* also refers to a range of activities, defined by Smelser as "whatever heights of purposeful, organized mastery of the world they are capable of reaching" (1980, pp. 4–5). The concept of work in Western capitalist societies has generally referred (since the Industrial Revolution) to *paid* employment done as a means to attain personal advancement. We will however, broaden the concept to include what the Puritans meant by work, when they developed the first American settlements: "an expression of devotion to family, community and society" (Hutchison, 1999, p. 246). This definition includes a diverse range of activities, including volunteer and domestic work (work done without pay for the common good) as well as paid employment (work performed for compensation in an effort to advance oneself or one's family economically, or as a means to grow and learn; in some cases, this type of work also contributes to the common good). The practical enactment of these themes, including issues involved with the balancing of work and family relationships, will be examined in greater detail later in this chapter.

There begins, during the early adulthood period, a gradual decline in self-absorption as one is increasingly drawn to establish intimate relationships with people outside one's family. Erikson conceptualized this process as the psychosocial crisis of intimacy versus isolation—here, one "is ready for intimacy, that is, the capacity to commit himself (*sic*) to concrete affiliations and partnerships and to develop the ethical strength to abide by such commitments, even though they may call for significant sacrifices and compromises" (1963, p. 263). Isolation, the negative counterpart of intimacy, results in significant psychological strain, as one may feel unable to attain, through relationships, that sense of mutuality, support, and connectedness that is critical to the psychological well-being of social creatures such as human beings.

The psychosocial crisis of intimacy versus isolation is enacted within the context of a social world in which cultural demands exert pressure on the individual to assume particular roles at particular times. In fact, from the perspective of social role theory, adulthood is primarily characterized, and shaped, by the many intricately woven roles an individual assumes with age. In this view, one's social roles provide structure and meaning to one's life, as well as new experiences that provide opportunities for personality and behavioral change and growth. The most common new role experiences for young adults involve entering the workforce, choosing a mate, and becoming a parent. The assumption of these roles is generally accompanied by some degree of normative psychological distress as young adults struggle to develop coping mechanisms to adapt to their changed circumstances (Pearlin, 1991).

As is true for all phases of life, the importance of context must not be underestimated in examining an individual's developmental experiences. The concept of the *life course* provides a model of development and functioning that recognizes the transactional nature of human functioning and the "indeterminate nature of non-uniform pathways of psychosocial development and social life" (Germain, 1991, p. 150). Differences in experience that emerge from racial, ethnic, religious, and socioeconomic background, gender socialization, sexual orientation, ability and disability, as well as power differentials and oppression all affect one's life path and must be given considerable weight in any assessment of functioning. It is a fact of modern life that traditional timetables for many of life's transitions are becoming less predictable, and often, less age-dependent. Increased numbers of people are postponing (or choosing to avoid altogether) marriage; with improved technology and increasing life expectancy, middle-aged people are becoming parents for the first time; elderly children are becoming caregivers for their elderly parents, and job and career changes are increasingly common throughout the course of adulthood. Expected and unexpected transitions and life events occur and recur throughout the life course. However, over time, the capacity to adapt and change direction becomes somewhat limited by the paths already taken (Hamilton, 2000). It follows, then, that adults will exhibit less flexibility than will children. Nevertheless, Bowlby's observations regarding child development ring true (albeit to a lesser extent) when applied to young adults: "The course of subsequent development is not fixed. . . . It is this persisting potential for change that gives opportunity for effective therapy" (1988, p. 136).

Biological and Psychological Development

Many physical capacities, such as strength, endurance, energy level, and sensory (except for visual acuity) functioning, reach their peak in early adulthood (Craig, 1999, Meisami, 1994). The brain reaches its maximum size and weight during early adulthood. Although many people show mature brain wave patterns in their early 20s, many others show increasing patterns of maturity into early adulthood (Friedman, Berman, & Hamberger, 1993; Scheibel, 1992). Although Piaget concluded that cognitive development is largely completed by the close of adolescence, more recent research indicates that there may be qualitative changes in cognition during early adulthood. In this section, we will examine the developmental changes that occur in various aspects of biological and psychological functioning during the period of early adulthood.

Health and Safety

For the most part, early adulthood represents a period of good health, and young adults have the lowest death rate for all adult groups (Craig, 1999). However, lifestyle (for example, diet, exercise, drug use) and life circumstances (for example, race, class, and life events) may have a significant effect on health and mortality rates for this age group. Death from AIDS and accidents pose significant threats to individuals in this age group (U.S. Bureau of the Census, 1997). For black males, the rate of death from homicide and police shootings is more than double the rate for all men from the ages of 25 to 44 (Craig, 1999).

Fertility

Fertility also peaks during early adulthood; women in this age group have the highest fertility rates of all women of childbearing age in United States (Hamilton et al., 2005). Although fertility remains relatively stable for women between the ages of 25 and 38, it begins to gradually decline by age 30, and after age 40 there is a rapid decline in the number, regularity, and quality of ova released and fertilized. In 2004, U.S. women ages 25 to 29 had the highest birthrates (116 births per 1,000 women), followed by women ages 20 to 24 (102 births per 1,000 women). During the same year, Hispanic women had the highest fertility rates, followed by non-Hispanic black women and Asian women (Hamilton et al., 2005). The general trend, however, shows that American women are delaying childbearing. For example, birthrates for women between ages 30 and 34 have increased from 62 births per 1,000 women in 1980 to 96 births per 1,000 women in 2004; in the same time period, birthrates for teens ages 15 to 19 declined by more than half (Hamilton et al., 2005). Male fertility also peaks during early adulthood. However, despite the fact that as men age their seminal emissions tend to contain fewer viable sperm, male fertility tends to remain more stable into later adulthood (Troll, 1985).

Cognitive Functioning: Postformal Thought

As noted previously, there is evidence to suggest that there are qualitative changes in cognitive functioning during early adulthood. These changes are exhibited by what Labouvie-Vief (1990) refers to as postformal thought. This type of thinking is characterized by the integration of logical processes associated with formal operational thought, with more flexible, relativistic, and interpretive ones. Labouvie-Vief (1990) suggests that this level of thought may be especially adaptive for understanding the complexities and subtleties of modern society.

Schaie also examined postformal thought, but he focused on how the utilization of information changes throughout adulthood, rather than on the qualitative changes in cognition (Schaie, 1977/1978, 1993, 1994; Schaie et al., 1989; Schaie & Willis, 1993). Schaie proposed five stages of cognitive development. He suggests that throughout childhood and adolescence, the primary cognitive task is to acquire information and cognitive structures that allow one to understand the world and prepare one for the future. He refers to this as the *acquisitive stage*. During early adulthood, people apply their intelligence to accomplishing their personal, family, career, and social goals—for example, job or career choice and selection of a life partner. He refers to this as the *achieving stage.* As people progress to the later stages of early adulthood and middle adulthood, they enter what Schaie refers to as the *responsible stage.* Here, the individual's primary concerns revolve around their personal family and career situations. As middle adulthood progresses, many, but not all, people enter the *executive stage* in which they assume a broader perspective that leads them to focus attention beyond their personal situations and toward an interest in societal institutions (for example, volunteer groups, charities, religious organizations, or local governments). Thinking once again begins to focus inward during late adulthood (the *reintegrative stage*), as people tend to become more concerned with issues that relate to their personal concerns. It is notable that Schaie's adult stages seem, in many ways, to provide a parallel, cognitive component to Erikson's psychosocial crises of adulthood (intimacy versus isolation, generativity versus stagnation, and integrity versus despair).

Intelligence

Sternberg (1985) proposed that intelligence is comprised of three elements, each of which is important to one's ability to perform different activities. *Componential intelligence* is important for such activities as the analysis of data to solve problems and relies on the person's ability to choose and implement formulas and to utilize information to develop rational problem-solving strategies. This type of intelligence is correlated with academic success and is measured by traditional IQ tests. However, this type of intelligence is not highly correlated with success in other aspects of adult life (Wagner & Sternberg, 1991; Sternberg & Wagner, 1993). *Experiential intelligence* refers to one's ability to apply the benefit of past experience to solve current problems. *Contextual intelligence* involves the ability to successfully meet the challenges of everyday life. Also called *practical intelligence,* this aspect of intellectual functioning seems to best predict overall success in adult functioning in such areas as career advancement, positive social relationships, and good health (Epstein, 1994; Epstein & Meier, 1989).

Sociocultural Functioning: Development in Context

As noted earlier in this chapter, themes of love and work tend to predominate during adulthood. Young adults are increasingly drawn to form intimate relationships outside their families of origin, and it is during early adulthood that most people enter the world of work. We will, in the following section, examine these themes in greater depth, especially as they relate to contemporary contexts.

Changing Relationship with the Family of Origin

Carter and McGoldrick view the phase of young adulthood as the beginning of a new phase of family life. In this view, "the completion of the primary task of coming to terms with their family of origin most profoundly influences who, when, how and whether they will marry and how they will carry out all succeeding stages of the family life cycle. Adequate completion of this requires that the young adult separate from the family of origin without cutting off or fleeing reactively to a substitute emotional refuge. Seen in this way, the *young adult* phase is a cornerstone" (1989, p. 13).

Young adulthood is seen as a time to establish one's life goals and to differentiate oneself from the emotional life of the family of origin. In other words, young adults must emotionally come to terms with "what they will take along from the family of origin, what they will leave behind and what they will create for themselves" (Carter & McGoldrick, 1989, p. 13). There is a need to shift to a less hierarchical style of relating between the parents and the young adult, toward an adult-to-adult style that allows for mutual respect and acceptance. These tasks apply to both men and women, although the women's need to establish themselves outside the caregiving role has only been recently recognized. Issues of gender socialization may influence and distinguish some of the problems faced by men and women as they move through this phase. Specifically, Carter and McGoldrick (1989) warn that women may tend to prematurely cut off the process of self-definition in favor of finding a mate, whereas men may overemphasize the role of work in establishing their identity, at the expense of committing to intimate relationships. It should also be noted that cultural factors will also play a major role in how this phase (and all phases of family system development and functioning) is enacted.

Forming Intimate Relationships: Marriage, Cohabitation, and Serial Monogamy

Despite many variations in the type and timing of intimate relationships in modern society, young adulthood is generally the time when men and women begin to form emotionally close, sexually intimate relationships that involve shared interests and activities and some degree of commitment. The majority of young people report that they hope to eventually marry and in fact, most do. According to the U.S. Bureau of the Census (1997), only 14% of men and 10% of women had not married by the ages of 40 to 44. For most adults, having a satisfying marriage is the most important indicator of well-being—in a longitudinal study of single young adults and those who married and remained married for 7 years or more, the married people showed a greater sense of well-being and fewer mental health problems than those who remained single (Horwitz et al., 1996). In recent decades, however, a number of social, economic, and political trends (for example, changing sexual mores; demands for higher levels of skill and training in the workplace; the changing role of women in society) have influenced the traditional patterns of marriage and childbearing. Perhaps the most significant and far-reaching change is that young people are marrying (and having children) at later ages than in previous generations. For example, the percentage of never-married women between the ages of 20 and 24 rose approximately 40% from 1960 to 1996. The increase in never-married men was approximately 28% during the same time period (U.S. Bureau of the Census 1976, 1997).

In addition to the postponement of marriage, there has been an increase in the number of committed, unmarried couples (both heterosexual and gay/lesbian) living together without legally marrying and in the number of people engaging in *serial monogamy*—those forming monogamous relationships without a commitment to a shared future and/or marriage. Some of these relationships will lead to a legal marriage, some not. In the case of lesbian and gay couples, legal marriage is generally precluded as an option by law. In light of these social changes, our discussion of the characteristics of intimate relationships will encompass all committed relationships, including legally married heterosexual couples and committed, cohabiting (heterosexual or gay/lesbian) couples.

Romantic Love and Readiness for Commitment In Western societies, unlike many traditional and/or collectivist societies, romantic love is considered to be the basis for a committed relationship and/or legal marriage. Whatever the status of the intimate partnership (legally married, heterosexual couple, cohabiting heterosexual, or gay/lesbian couples), the experience of romantic love brings the relationship partners feelings of elation and heightened self-esteem. The loss or preclusion of the fulfillment of romantic love may lead to depression, loss of self-esteem, and feelings of isolation.

The commitment to an intimate relationship (particularly to a legally sanctioned marriage) generally represents a change in status and role, as well as a significant life transition for both partners. Becoming a couple can enrich one's development by bolstering one's self-concept and self-esteem. On the other hand, it may serve to be a source of increased stress and anxiety. Carter and McGoldrick (1989) view the process of becoming a couple as more than just the joining of two individuals. Rather, they use a multigenerational model that envisions this as a process of transforming two family systems, while creating an overlapping third system. They view the failure to adequately deal with the need to renegotiate family status as a primary reason for marital failure. (For further discussion of the stages of family development and of marital failure, see Chapter 5.)

The process of becoming a couple presents many challenges, all of which may be seen as part of the development of a new family system with its own rules, narratives, role structure, and so on. These tasks include, among others, the balancing of each partner's individual needs and customs with the need to establish an identity as a couple. This process involves the need to reach agreement about the nature of the couple's relationship to family and friends, the balancing of work and personal needs and demands, the allocation of life tasks, conflict management, and the acceptance of difference and of each partner's imperfections (which become increasingly obvious through the process of becoming a unit). The way in which young adults cope with these challenges will vary, depending on many factors, including readiness for the relationship; level of intimacy and mutuality within the relationship; each partner's personality, attachment, and communication styles; and cultural patterns, as well as each partner's readiness to commit to a long-term relationship.

Readiness to commit to a long-term relationship appears to be a significant factor in relationship stability. For example, in a study of couples in lasting marriages, those who described themselves as happily married described a strong commitment to the marriage and a willingness to tolerate difficult situations by confronting problems and working on resolving them (Lauer & Lauer, 1986). An individual's readiness to make this type of commitment may be related to their religious, social, and/or cultural values. There is also evidence to suggest that one's ability to commit to an intimate relationship is related to the achievement of a stable sense of identity. College students who have achieved identity have been found to also have the most intimate relationships, whereas students rated to be identity confused are the least able to form intimate relationships and show the highest levels of isolation (Craig-Bray, Adams, & Dobson, 1988).

Attachment and Adult Relationships During the past two decades, the relationship between an adult's *attachment style* and his or her experience of romantic relationships have gained increasing amounts of research attention (Brennan & Morris, 1997; Brennan & Shaver, 1995; Hazan & Shaver, 1987; Jones & Cunningham, 1996; Shaver & Hazan, 1988). Generally speaking, this research has supported the notion that there are links between a person's early attachment experiences and attachment style (secure, avoidant, and ambivalent) and his or her adult relationship styles, although more research in this area is clearly indicated (Feeney, 1999). For example, Levy and Davis (1988) found evidence to support connections between secure attachment and better relationship functioning. There is also evidence to support links among attachment styles and expressions of intimacy, passion, commitment, dependence, and anxiety within adult relationships (Feeney & Noller, 1990; Feeney, Noller, & Callan, 1994; Levy & Davis, 1988), as well as among attachment styles and regulation of affect, negative emotions, and conflict management (Feeney, 1999). For example, Kobak and Sceery (1988) found that securely attached adults were better able to handle their negative feelings in constructive ways than were those classified as avoidant (these tended not to acknowledge negative feelings) or ambivalent (these tended to heightened expression of negative feelings accompanied by high levels of distress and anxiety.)

Environmental Factors Environmental factors may also play a significant role in a person's readiness for commitment. For example, the combined pressures of oppression, social stigma, and lack of social recognition may exert powerful influences on the lives of gay and lesbian couples. Socioeconomic and issues of racism (described in detail in Chapters 5 and 7), coupled with high levels of crime and substance abuse in urban areas, seem to have contributed to reduced commitment to relationships on the part of African-American men (Billingsley & Morrison-Rodriguez, 1998; Raley, 1996). Structural changes in the U.S. economy have had a profound impact on couples and families. This will be further explored later in this chapter.

The Parenting Role

The addition of a child represents a significant transformation of the family, as it moves from a two-member to a three-member system. This requires personal changes within the parents, as they gradually adjust to their new roles and status, and as they attempt to integrate these new roles with their roles as spouses. As with all other normative transitions, some degree of stress is to be expected as the new parents' usual routines are disrupted, role expectations and responsibility for various tasks are reassigned, the skills involved with infant care and child rearing are learned, relationships with extended family and friends are adjusted to accommodate their new status as parents, and new family norms and values develop

(Germain, 1991). The couple's ability to adapt to these changes may be influenced by any number of factors, including each adult's attachment history, state of physical and mental health, the level of mutuality present in the couple's relationship, availability of social support, and other environmental resources, including financial security. Although the transition to parenting is not, in all cases, smooth, most people eventually find that they develop adequate coping skills, and that the necessary family transformation is accomplished. If this does not occur, it becomes more likely that serious repercussions, including marital breakdown, insecure parent–child attachment, and/or abuse and neglect may result (Germain, 1991).

The Decision to Delay Childbearing In recent years, there has been a tendency for couples to delay childbearing until they have been married for a few years. This decision may be related to many factors, including career considerations, financial security, and/or the desire to feel certain about the strength of their relationship before adding children to the family. For women, the delayed entry into parenthood has been found to be related to level of education, career commitment, and income level (Newman & Newman, 1999). In a study of fathers 30 years old or above, Cooney and associates (1993) found that older fathers tended to have more positive feelings toward, and to be more involved with, their children than did their younger counterparts. This may be related to the fact that being farther along in their careers, these fathers may feel more confident and less conflicted about balancing the demands of work and family.

The Decision to Remain Child-Free The decision not to have children is becoming more common in Western industrialized countries, where women are becoming more educated and are achieving higher levels of career success and commitments. Although social attitudes toward couples who opt for this choice are becoming more accepting, these couples may be subject to negative stereotypes (for example, they may be viewed as selfish, poorly adjusted, and less fulfilled than couples with children) and pressured to change their minds, especially from other family members (Somers, 1993). Somers found that couples who decide not to have children tend to be well-educated urbanites who hold nontraditional sex role standards.

Infertility Other couples find that they are unable to have children, despite their desire to do so. *Infertility* (the inability to conceive a child after one year of trying) appears to be on the rise. From 1988 to 1995, infertility rates increased by approximately 25% (Lemonick, 1997). This problem often represents a significant source of stress that may result in lowered self-esteem, diminished sexual satisfaction, and increasing social isolation (Sabatelli, Meth, & Gavazzi, 1988). Some couples resolve this issue by accepting, and adjusting to, the fact that they will not have children; others choose to adopt, and still others opt to seek medical treatment for infertility. Infertility treatments may include use of fertility drugs, artificial insemination, in vitro fertilization (fertilization outside the uterus), sperm injection (a form of in vitro fertilization in which the sperm is injected directly into the egg), use of donor eggs and/or donor sperm or a surrogate mother (a woman who is impregnated by the infertile woman's husband's sperm, carries and delivers the baby, and then returns the baby to the infertile couple at birth). The enormous financial costs and low rates of success of these treatments, as well as the associated feelings of loss of control, disappointment, and invasiveness, may make these treatments more stressful than the actual medical condition (Newman & Newman, 1999). In addition, many ethical issues related to infertility treatments have arisen. For example, what is to become of excess embryos that are created during the process of in vitro fertilization but not implanted in the woman's uterus? What are the rights of the surrogate mother who decides not to return the child? What are the rights and/or responsibilities of the sperm or egg donors? How and when should a child be told about the circumstances of his or her conception?

On the other hand, studies have shown that children conceived through artificial insemination and in vitro fertilization showed no significant differences with respect to social and emotional development when compared with adopted children and children conceived naturally (Golombok et al., 1995). The same study showed that parents of children conceived through assisted reproduction techniques showed higher levels of positive involvement with their children and lower levels of stress than parents of both naturally conceived or adopted children.

Entering the World of Work

Most young people begin to work when they leave school and, usually, before they commit themselves to intimate relationships and/or parenthood. For most, economic security depends on employment in the workforce. In addition to the obvious economic functions of work, one's occupation, particularly in this country, has a significant impact on one's social status, social life, and sense of personal identity (Feldman, 1997) and on lifestyle in general. In fact, researchers have found that there are two primary sources of satisfaction and motivation related to work: extrinsic motivation and intrinsic motivation (Singer, Stacey, & Lange, 1993; Stohs, 1992). *Extrinsic* work factors include salary, status, work environment (including coworker relations and adequacy of supervision), stress levels, opportunities for advancement, and other employment practices. *Intrinsic* work factors include one's assessment of one's competence and achievement, interest and challenge, and other sources of personal satisfaction. Workers who report high levels of intrinsic satisfaction from their jobs tend to report more job satisfaction and higher levels of involvement and identification with their work (Craig, 1999). In addition, job satisfaction has been found to be higher when workers have some influence over the nature and performance of their jobs (and over other people), as well as when the job requires a variety of different skills (Steers & Porter, 1991).

The changes in the nature of the workplace in U.S. society were discussed in Chapter 7. Many of these changes (for example, the globalization of the economy, the higher educational and training standards for entry-level positions in many jobs and careers, and the fast-paced changes in the type of work available) have injected higher levels of uncertainty into the process of choosing a career, finding work, and remaining employed.

Dual-Earner Families One of the most far-reaching effects of these economic changes has been on young families (especially those who have low incomes), as it has become increasingly necessary for both adults in the family to work.

In 1996, 60.5% of women with young children (under 3 years of age) were employed outside the home—this represented an increase of 27.5% since 1975 (U.S. Bureau of the Census, 1997). Although some of these increases are due to the fact that more women are choosing to work, many other women do so out of economic need. Many (but not all) of the issues related to these *dual-earner* families discussed next will apply to most dual-earner families, regardless of economic circumstance.

Although this family structure has benefits, it also presents many challenges. When both parents work outside the home, traditional family roles must be reshaped. Because the dominance of this family form is a relatively recent phenomenon, couples may have few role models to help guide them as they attempt to perform basic family functions (for example, child care, shopping, cooking, cleaning) and to create new paradigms for family life. Piotrkowski and Hughes pointed out that "the dual-earner family is a team short of players; these are really three job families (if we count housework and childcare provision) and with children, there are simply not enough hands to do the work" (1993, p. 200).

Piotrkowski and Hughes (1993) also pointed out that a primary context for all, or most, dual-earner families is the basic imbalance of power between workplace and home—that is, families adapt to the demands of the workplace more than the workplace adapts to family concerns. This context is powerfully influenced by social class. In addition to affecting monetary and other forms of remuneration, control over such issues as work schedule, time off, and flexibility of boundaries between work and home tends to increase as one rises up the occupational ladder. For example, dual-career families in the upper socioeconomic classes tend to have jobs that offer a higher level of autonomy and financial rewards than most other jobs. This situation may facilitate the integration of work and family roles, in that these families may be able to afford household help, quality child care and to take time off to attend to issues related to their children's lives and care. Low- and middle-income families, however, have fewer resources with which to balance work and family responsibilities and therefore may find even normative family issues to be sources of great stress.

Family-friendly workplace policies such as paid family leave with health care, provisions for sick children, flex-time, company-supported child care, and childcare vouchers can greatly support family functioning. Although there is increasing awareness of the problems of dual-earner families on the part of employers, relatively few workplaces provide adequate employee benefits in this area, and those tend to be large rather than small employers (Hayghe, 1988 as cited by Piotrkowski & Hughes, 1993, p. 190).

Public policy also exerts a powerful influence on most dual-earner families, especially those policies that govern the availability of affordable, high-quality child care and family leave and health care. Compared with Western European countries of similar economic status, the United States is notoriously regressive in the provision of policy supports for families (Davies, 2004; Zigler & Lang, 1991). For example, in the year 2000, the United States spent approximately 2.5% of its gross national product (GNP) on family support programs, compared to Sweden, which spent close to 15%, and France, which spent almost 9% (UNICEF, 2000). Other developed countries in the West provide family supports, such as paid paternity and maternity leaves, affordable high-quality, out-of-home child care as needed, child allowances, and universal health care. In contrast, federally guaranteed (since 1993) family leave in the United States is unpaid and not universally available. Furthermore, the United States provides no universal guarantee for the provision of health-care benefits and has traditionally depended on the private sector for provision of these benefits. With enormous increases in the cost of health care, fewer and fewer employers are offering affordable family health coverage, and the number of uninsured families in the United States today is growing.

In addition, with no national policy to ensure the availability of affordable high-quality child care, one of the greatest challenges facing dual-earner families is arranging for the care of their children while the parents are at work. Although the overall amount of available child care has increased in the past two decades, this expansion has generally occurred in services that are affordable only to those at the upper end of the socioeconomic ladder. The quality of child care in the United States is highly variable, with low-income and working-class children generally receiving lower quality (both formal and informal) care (Davies, 2004), and with many families forced to rely on a tenuous patchwork of arrangements to cover such contingencies as work schedules, emergencies, child's illness, and school holidays. In addition to increasing stress on family functioning, this situation can also create serious obstacles to employment for families with low incomes.

Another context that strongly influences the balancing of family and work life is gender inequality (Thompson & Walker, 1989 as cited in Piotrkowski & Hughes, 1993, p. 191). Because women are generally paid less than men, the husband's job frequently takes priority in families. Women, for example, are often the ones to take days off from work to care for a sick child or deal with family emergencies. Despite many changes in women's roles in society, traditional attitudes still exert influence on families' approach to family work. With women tending to take on the bulk of household duties, they essentially find themselves with two jobs—one paid, the other unpaid (Hochschild & Machung, 1990).

There is some evidence of change in this area. In a review of the research, Pleck (1990) found that men had been increasing their share of family work, although this tended to be in the area of child care, and not in the less interesting household chores. In addition, how family work is accomplished varies by ethnicity and social class. African-American couples, for example, traditionally share responsibilities for child care, domestic functions, and paid employment (Hill, 1998). In the words of Piotrkowski and Hughes:

> Practitioners serving dual-earner families with problems may find it difficult to see their embeddedness in an inhospitable social context. Dual-earner families themselves often do not understand the extent to which the stresses they experience are normative and result from lack of support. Men and women in contemporary dual-earner families grew up with traditional views about family and work roles that provided a blueprint for how to be a family. But the influx of women into the labor force, the new feminism, and the rise of the dual-earner family as a dominant family structure for two-parent families with children has introduced uncertainty into how to be a viable family. Not only are dual-earner families faced with additional task demands, for which old solutions do not work,

> but they also lack clear socially prescribed and supported roles for accomplishing basic family functions. Contemporary dual-earners are struggling to construct new relationship "bargains" for how to be a family. Thus, what the practitioner sees is a family groping for solutions to normative dilemmas where few models for solving them exist. The fact that most dual-earner families manage is a testament to their resourcefulness and strength. (1993, p. 201)

Contextual Variations

Chemical Substance Abuse

The abuse of alcohol and other drugs is a problem of such major proportions, and far reaching consequences, that social workers in every field of practice are likely to encounter it as a treatment issue in one form or another. Chemical substance abuse is often found to be a related factor in such presenting problems as marital discord, school failure, decreased workplace productivity, automobile accidents and fatalities, felony arrests, domestic violence, rape, sexual and physical abuse and neglect of children, and homelessness, as well as a host of medical and health conditions. In fact, the magnitude of the problem of alcohol abuse in our society has led Krestan and Bepko (1989) to advise clinicians to assume that there is an alcohol-related problem in every family "until thorough assessment proves otherwise" (p. 483).

Krestan and Bepko (1989) use a family life-cycle model to illuminate the clinical issues involved in treating alcohol problems:

> Alcoholism typically represents a progressive sequence of events that may continue through several successive life cycle phases. If drinking begins in an early developmental phase, dysfunction may be obvious, or it may remain more insidious, and consequently, go unidentified. Non-problematic drinking may arise early in the life cycle and become dysfunctional in later phases and tend to resolve itself in later ones (Vaillant, 1983 as cited by Krestan & Bepko, 1989, p. 483). Dysfunction for the individual and family occurs *over time* and its pace is different for different individuals and families. Frequently, the pacing and intensity of dysfunction are related to life cycle stresses occurring at the onset of problematic drinking. For instance, drinking frequently becomes problematic for women at such developmental points as menopause or at life-cycle stages such as early marriage or early parenthood that stress role concept and adjustment. (p. 483)

These authors also emphasize the intergenerational impact of alcoholism on families, as well as the need for clinicians to be cognizant of the tendency of families affected by this problem to develop a pattern of rigid denial of the individual's problematic drinking and its affect on family functioning.

Binge Drinking on College Campuses Binge drinking (consuming five or more alcoholic drinks in a row) among college students gained increased attention during the past decade, especially after a series of well-publicized deaths on college campuses. As this kind of heavy drinking has gained social acceptance, it has been incorporated into a wide variety of college rituals and celebrations (Newman, 1999). Wechsler et al. (1994), in a national survey of over 17,000 college students, found that nearly half of their sample had engaged in binge drinking on at least one occasion during the 2-week period prior to completing the survey. In addition, they found that frequent binge drinkers were 7 to 10 times more likely to suffer physical injuries, damage property, have unprotected sex, or drive under the influence of alcohol. In fact, alcohol-related injuries are a leading cause of death among college students (McGinnis & Foege, 1993).

Among young adults, full-time college students who are not living with their parents and who are members of fraternities or sororities report higher levels of binge drinking than do high-school seniors, young people who do not attend college, and those who attend community colleges (Gfroerer et al., 1997; Johnston et al., 1997). Risk factors for heavy drinking among college students include biobehavioral vulnerability (Wechsler, Dowdall, Davenport, & Rimm, 1995), a family history of alcohol problems (Sher, 1994), a history of conduct disorder or delinquent behavior (Jessor, Donovan, & Costa 1991), and peer pressure (Bauer 1994). Although most young people are able to emerge relatively unscathed from this period of heavy drinking, early adulthood is clearly a time of life when one is particularly vulnerable to the kind of stressors that are commonly associated with the abuse of alcohol and other chemical substances.

Impact of Chemical Substance Abuse on the Developmental Tasks of Early Adulthood

The problem of chronic alcohol abuse may complicate the young adult's ability to accomplish many of the developmental tasks of early adulthood (as well as those of other life phases). The differentiation of self from one's family of origin is often seen as a central task of early adulthood, as its accomplishment has a strong influence on the developmental tasks and life choices that one makes (for example, solidification of a sense of identity, choice of a partner, work decisions) throughout adulthood (Krestan & Bepko, 1989). When alcoholism is an issue in any family (regardless of which family member exhibits the problem drinking), the presence of dysfunctional boundaries, a rigid and inappropriate role structure, and other maladaptive interactional patterns within the family system tend to make self-differentiation a problem for all family members. The young adult who has been raised in such a family

> . . . may have developed the skills to survive within the family system without having developed the skills to separate from it. Where alcoholism is found in the young adult's family of origin, one of these potential solutions to the problems of differentiation tends to predominate. The individual may become alcoholic or otherwise addicted himself or herself, assuming a pseudo-differentiated stance; he or she may perpetuate a family role of over-responsible functioning and marry an alcoholic; or he or she may simply become cut off from the family emotionally. (Krestan & Bepko, 1989, pp. 489–490)

The young adult's ability to form a committed, intimate relationship may also be affected by alcoholism. In addition to interfering with boundaries, roles, and rules within the couple system, alcoholism may lead to dysfunctional interactional patterns that interfere with the couple's ability to adequately cope with conflict related to intimacy, difference, and power issues. The addition of children to such a system tends to bring on more difficulties, as the family system tends to be unable to adequately meet the children's developmental dependency needs. Children in such families may attempt to cope with the family dysfunction and disorganization by taking on rigid, inappropriate roles that are related to either overfunctioning or underfunctioning behavioral patterns; the resultant sense of grief and loss may lead to depression and social isolation and other serious problems (Krestan & Bepko, 1989).

Treatment of Chemical Substance Abuse It is important to note that treatment interventions during this phase of life may significantly mitigate the harmful effects of problem drinking. For example, Marlatt et al. (1998) found that brief intervention utilizing cognitive-behavioral and motivational techniques, provided to high-risk college students in their freshman year, was successful in significantly reducing both drinking rates and the harmful consequences of alcohol consumption. In a 2-year follow-up, they found that those individuals who had received the intervention also showed significantly greater reductions for both harmful consequences of alcohol consumption and for alcohol dependence. Although the consequences of problem drinking are by no means restricted to the stage of early adulthood, successful treatment during this phase of life may provide significant future benefits by helping individuals develop the skills needed to successfully negotiate and accomplish the developmental tasks of subsequent life stages (Krestan & Bepko, 1989).

Gay and Lesbian Young Adults: Coming Out

According to Schope (2002), gay individuals must continually decide whether or not to disclose their sexual orientation to other people in their lives (Schope, 2002). Although it is commonly believed (Cain, 1991 as cited by Schope, 2002, p. 2) that the failure to disclose sexual orientation indicates that the individual has not dealt with his or her internalized homophobia, and that disclosure to others is an indication of positive identity formation and self-acceptance, it is also true that such disclosure presents enormous risks of rejection and discrimination, as well as exposure to a wide range of factors that are beyond the gay individual's control (Shidlo, 1994 as cited by Schope, 2002, p. 2). Schope (2002) noted that the decision of whether or not to disclose one's sexual orientation involves the need to calculate potential gains and losses. Furthermore, this decision represents an ongoing task that must be reconsidered in every new situation and with every new acquaintance (Rothberg & Weinstein, 1996 as cited by Schope, 2002, p. 2). When the decision is made not to disclose, the individual will find him- or herself in an ongoing struggle to control information and behaviors that might expose that person's sexual orientation (Bowes, 1996 as cited by Schope, 2002, p. 2). Although the advantages of disclosure are very significant (for example, it eliminates the need to hide and fabricate; it is related to less fear of harassment, less anxiety, higher self-esteem, and the ability to build a protective support network), these benefits cannot be realized unless the reaction to the disclosure is positive (Schope, 2002). As a result of these many risks, Schope (2002) found that gay and lesbian individuals are selective in disclosing their sexual orientation. Although most are able to disclose to their friends, many remain closeted with their parents, siblings, coworkers, and neighbors. Schope

(2002) also found that residence in urban areas was associated with being open about one's sexual orientation in all aspects—in fact, many gay and lesbian people move to cities to live more openly. Willingness to disclose is also highly correlated with age (Schope, 2002), with younger people being more open and less willing to compartmentalize their lives than were those of previous generations. Schope concludes that this development indicates that as more and more gay and lesbian people become freer to disclose, it will become less and less necessary for them to use their energy to manage and control information to hide their sexual orientation. In this case, they will be increasingly free to direct their energy toward healthier pursuits. (For additional discussion of issues related to gay, lesbian, and transgendered individuals, see Chapters 4, 5, and 7.)

The Impact of Disability in Young Adulthood: Sexual and Reproductive Issues

Cole and Cole (1993) present an overview of sexual and reproductive issues experienced by people with physical disabilities. These authors point out a necessary distinction between early onset disabilities (acquired prior to sexual maturity) and acquired disabilities (those acquired after sexual maturity). They suggest that early onset disabilities generally "affect sexual development in terms of the language of sex, privacy, self-exploration, sex education and personal learning" (1993, p. 242). For example, the authors point out that physical disabilities in childhood may limit the development of both psychosexual and social maturity, as children with disabilities are often denied many of the natural opportunities for privacy that allow other children to spontaneously explore their bodies and indulge their natural sexual curiosity. In addition, these children do not often experience the feelings of security and intimacy that other children experience through the sense of touch. "Many children with disabilities experience far more 'handling' than tender loving caresses" (p. 244).

Opportunities for socialization, so important to growth and development in adolescence, are often restricted for the child with a physical disability. In these situations, children with physical disabilities are often restricted to the role of spectator, and this serves to further restrict their psychosexual growth and development.

Disabilities that are acquired in early adulthood (after the onset of sexual maturity) present another set of challenges. The affected person's plans, goals, and expectations for gender role enactment and sexual identification as a man or a woman may all be interrupted by the onset of the disability. Cole and Cole distinguish between acquired disabilities that are stable (for example, a spinal cord injury) or progressive (for example, multiple sclerosis). Although each represents a traumatic event, the stabilization of a disability may allow the individual to assume some control during the process of adaptation. Progressive disabilities, on the other hand, present a more complex picture in that the unpredictability of these conditions make it difficult to develop a sense of control, much less to plan for the future. This lack of certainty serves to "complicate the usual challenges of relationships and family living" (1993, p. 249) when young people are involved in the process of dating or planning a family. With some disabilities, sexual activity and pleasure may be maintained by adapting intimate behaviors to accommodate the physical condition. On the other hand, more severe physical losses (for example, a man with a spinal cord injury) may present a multitude of concerns, from erectile dysfunction and serious concerns about fertility, to worries about one's ability to participate in parenting activities, and about social acceptance in one's role as a man or a woman (Neistadt & Freda, 1987; Rabin, 1980 as cited by Cole & Cole, 1993, p. 249). In addition, partners of people with disabilities may find themselves in the roles of both caregiver and intimate partner. This may cause conflicted feelings for both partners and may add to the stress in the relationship:

> Persons socialized in contemporary American culture are surrounded by traditional societal messages about parenting and disability (Hahn, 1981). It is imperative that health care practitioners avoid falling into the trap of stereotypical responses of pity, avoidance, infantilization, and excessive attention to persons with disabilities. Independence, personal esteem, positive body image and positive sex messages should be emphasized. Silence from the medical community concerning disability, sexuality and reproductive issues relays the stronger message of rejection and repression and gives the impression that parenting is not to be considered. This approach is not helpful. (Cole & Cole, 1993, p. 230)

Domestic Violence

Dwyer and colleagues define *domestic violence* as "violent acts perpetrated on a partner in a relationship, in the presumed safety and privacy of the home" (1996, p. 68). They further note that this type of violence "involves the unjust exercise of force to dominate, abuse or coerce another" (p. 68). Domestic violence is the leading cause of injury to women ages 15 to 44, and victims are not limited to any one social class or racial or ethnic group (Smith, 1989 as cited by Dwyer et al., 1996). According to Dwyer and colleagues (1996) there are three traditional causal theories of domestic violence, described next.

Individual or psychological models generally attribute domestic violence to personal characteristics of the abuser and, to some extent, to the victim. These characteristics include poor self-control, low self-esteem, mental illness, substance abuse, and the ability to ascribe blame (on the part of the perpetrator) or to internalize blame (on the part of the victim). Gondolf and Fisher (1988 as cited by Dwyer et al., 1996) use the concept of *learned helplessness* to describe the behavior of victims of domestic violence. In this view, the abuse reduces the victim's sense of control and eventually leads her (or him) to stop trying to leave the situation. Dutton and Painter (1993 as cited by Dwyer et al., 1996) suggest that traumatic bonding—that is, the formation of a powerful emotional bond between two people in which one partner abuses the other—may explain some of the behavior of victims of domestic violence.

Sociological models look to social structures, particularly the family, to explain how domestic violence is permitted and encouraged among partners. These models pay particular attention to the role of family structure, family stress, and the intergenerational transmission of violent patterns to explain how these transactions occur.

Sociostructural models are based largely on feminist theory, and they focus on variables of gender inequality, social acceptance of violence, and patriarchy as root causes of domestic violence. These models view domestic violence as a form of male social control over women that is embedded in the historical inequality of power distribution between men and women.

Dwyer and colleagues (1996) recommend the adoption of an *ecological model* to conceptualize the abuse of women. Such a model would acknowledge the complexity of the issue by providing a framework for integrating the various theoretical models described earlier and for providing a unifying strategy for intervention. This framework would provide a flexible model that would allow for consideration of psychological, sociological, and sociostructural factors in assessing and treating domestic violence.

Summary

The period of early adulthood represents the time of life when individuals begin to actualize the skills and knowledge developed during childhood and adolescence. Themes of love and work predominate as young adults begin to differentiate themselves from their families of origin and prepare themselves to commit to the world of work and intimate relationships. Traditional timetables and expectations for age-graded behaviors have largely disappeared in modern society. More young people are postponing (or rejecting altogether) marriage and childbearing as they attempt to adapt to a world that provides less security and greater demands than ever before. We have also explored how contextual issues related to economic status, chemical substance abuse, sexual orientation, disability, and domestic violence may affect the development and functioning of young adults, especially as these relate to the developmental crisis of intimacy versus isolation (Erikson, 1963).

14 Middle Adulthood

Introduction

Midlife begins at age 40 and extends to age 60, a span of 20 years. However, this stage of life is an artifact of urban industrialized society and as such is promoted by authors such as Weisner and Bernheimer (1998, p. 216) as a "cultural category" that brings unique challenges and problems. The most extensive exploration of midlife in our nation's history—a 10-year MacArthur Foundation Study on the quality of life in middle age—compared respondents ages 40 through 60 to both older and younger adults. The findings show that although one's sense of purpose begins to drop with age, self-acceptance and mastery over one's circumstances go up. Adults at midlife are typically characterized both by a new perspective of who they are and a new perspective about their world. This often involves expectations about what they want to accomplish with the remaining half of their lives and different satisfactions in living. This stage of life is characterized more by personal and social factors, rather than biological maturity (as earlier developmental phases had been). The roles and tasks of midlife are often numerous and diverse. They may include, for example, changing jobs or careers, relinquishing parental involvement with older adolescent and young adult children, or beginning a family (Ashford, LeCroy, & Lortie, 2006, p. 509). Well-being is actually heightened at midlife due to "maximal role complexity." This research supports Erikson's (1958) findings about social responsibility being important in the middle years. Qualities such as mastery, autonomy, and the strength of relationships are the buffers to midlife stress. Such behavior has positive effects on one's physical health as well. The quality of social relationships is a powerful predictor of how long one lives, the incidence of illness, and recovery rates from illness (Brim, Ryff, & Kessler, 2004). This chapter will address how the middle years influence major life roles and, simultaneously, how those roles influence human development. We will examine how intra-individual developmental experiences, sociohistorical era, and other relevant contextual factors influence individuals in their middle years of adulthood. Franz categorizes these changes as being *universalistic* (age or stage related), *normative* (typical change(s) in response to a life event), and *idiosyncratic* (unique to each individual; 1997, p. 49).

Physiological Changes

Women

Menopause is the major biological occurrence for women in the middle years of their lives. It occurs when the ovaries stop functioning and no longer produce the hormones *estrogen* and *progesterone*. The average age of menopause is 51.4 years, and the majority of women reach menopause between 45 and 55. It is a gradual process that can take 5 to 20 years. Menopause is considered to have ended when a woman has not experienced a menstrual cycle for 1 year. Hormone levels begin to drop during the period preceding menopause, referred to as *premenopause*.

During this time, the menstrual cycle may become irregular; there may be a decreased monthly flow and increased spotting; and symptoms of premenstrual tension, such as breast tenderness and fluid retention, may occur. Women who go through menopause prior to age 50 are at greater risk for developing medical conditions such as heart disease and *osteoporosis* (Ashford, LeCroy, & Lortie, 2006; DeAngelis, 1997). A major symptom of menopause is the hot flash, when a wave of heat rises from the woman's chest to her neck, face, and arms, lasting from a few seconds to a minute or more. These flashes generally occur at night and can interfere with sleep. Another effect of estrogen loss is thinning and drying of the vaginal membranes and an increase in the frequency of urination and stress incontinence. The sexual response cycle—desire, excitement, and orgasm—is also affected by aging and menopause. Erotic interest often increases for women in the desire phase of the sexual response cycle. When estrogen declines, the *testosterone* in women's bodies can have greater influence, which continues to be produced during menopause. In the excitement phase, the lack of estrogen can lead to problems with vaginal dryness, making the sexual experience a negative one. During orgasm, women have no *refractory period* and can have multiple orgasms (Ashford, LeCroy, & Lortie, 2006; Boul, 2003).

The cessation of menstruation is a natural part of the life cycle. However, the drop in estrogen during this time also results in a drop in *endorphins,* substances in the brain that make you feel good and, therefore, can cause depression. The insomnia associated with hormonal changes may also contribute to depressed mood as well as to irritability and a decreased ability to handle stress. Due to the increased longevity of most women, the risk to health, general well-being, and quality of life due to lowered estrogen levels, *estrogen replacement therapy* is now considered a medical option for postmenopausal women (Grodstein, Manson, Colditz, Willet, Speizer, & Stampfer, 2000; Huffman & Myers, 1999; Nelson, Humphrey, Nygren, Teutsch, & Allan, 2002; Saucier, 2004). There are, however, many questions and concerns regarding this treatment, particularly whether it contributes to an increase in the risk of breast cancer or cancer of the uterine lining.

Other physiological changes associated with the middle years of adulthood for women may include loss of a youthful appearance and a loss of energy. Banister points out that these perceptions are also grounded in cultural meaning. In our society, women are often made to feel they are less attractive than when they were younger. The physiological changes of midlife may prove to be stressful, but they also provide an opportunity for women to challenge cultural stereotypes and redefine their identity according to their own standards (Belsky, 2007). Midlife may also signal a new responsibility to engage in self-care activities and make more "self-enhancing life choices" (1999, p. 533), although this is complicated by other roles and responsibilities that also emerge during this stage of life (see later sections of this chapter).

Men

The term *male menopause* has come into popular usage; however, it is important to understand that because men do not menstruate, there is no male menopause equivalent to female menopause. Although there are subtle changes in hormonal levels for men during midlife, nevertheless, "by 50 years of age most healthy men can expect to have retained some 90% of their circulating sex steroid hormones" (Boul, 2003, p. 6). During the middle years of sexual life, the main focus for men seems to be on sexual dysfunction or impotence rather than changes in hormone status or reproductive ability. It is difficult to determine whether sexual dysfunction is in any way related to hormone status. In fact, studies propose that factors associated with smoking, obesity, alcohol, depression, heart disease, prostate failure, and socioeconomic factors seem more likely (Aytac et al., 2000; Sullivan & Reynolds, 2003). It is also possible that, in the case of heterosexual men, for example, the decline in male libido is reflective of decreased opportunity due to menopausal problems being experienced by female partners. Declining rates of sexual activity could affect loss of libido for all men (for example, due to shame and fear of performance). The sexual response cycle is different for men than for women. As men age, their sex drive—desire—generally declines. This is affected by a drop in the male hormone, testosterone—excitement phase. The physiological reaction to excitement or stimulation results in blood engorgement of the genitals. Men in midlife may require both psychological and tactile stimulation for orgasm to occur. This last phase of the sexual response cycle changes dramatically with age, particularly between the time between one orgasm and the physical ability to achieve another orgasm. The midlife male may need as long as 24 to 48 hours between orgasms (Ashford, LeCroy, & Lortie, 2006; Boul, 2003).

Cognitive Functioning

Intellectual functioning is generally stable in midlife; however, much depends on the extent to which intellectual capacities are exercised. Schaie (1994, 1996) and Willis and Schaie (1999) participated in an extensive research project on intellectual functioning in midlife—the Seattle Longitudinal Study. Data from this study indicated that adults achieve peak performance on complex higher-order abilities, such as inductive reasoning, spatial orientation, and vocabulary, during midlife. Processes such as perceptual speed and numerical ability begin to decline during the early middle years. Miller and Lachman studied factors that might contribute to high levels of performance during midlife, using control beliefs, or the extent to which individuals feel able to affect their performance, as a potential predictor of cognitive performance. Their research consistently showed that "those who feel they have greater control over their cognitive performance are able to achieve higher levels of performance than those who do not" (2000, p. 71). The authors caution, however, that control beliefs need to be considered within the context of socioeconomic variables, health status, and particular tasks; for example, control beliefs may be more relevant than they would be for tasks in which age-related declines are less evident and successes are more common (p. 72). Several researchers contend that adult cognitive functioning must be assessed differently from people in earlier life stages. The type of intelligence may change, but the degree of intellectual ability does not. The research of Garden, Phillips, and MacPherson (2001, p. 479) on middle aging and the executive functions of the brain provides evidence that adults 53 to 64 years old show deficits in performance on structured laboratory neuropsychological executive tests. They are, however, unimpaired on more realistic and open-ended planning tasks—"real-world" executive skills such as those involved in handling a hectic work schedule or cooking a meal (2001, p. 479). Myers (2001) felt that *crystallized intelligence*—the individual's accumulated knowledge—actually increases with age. *Fluid intelligence*—the individual's ability to reason abstractly—decreases with age. The focus in the middle years, therefore, should be not on how information is acquired, but on how information is used (Schaie, 1994; Willis, 1989). Social and abstract cognitive skills have greater prominence, and these are related to the roles individuals in midlife are called on to assume. For example, adults in midlife are generally assuming greater family and community responsibilities than younger adults, who may be more focused on beginning careers and families. Neugarten described midlife as a "period of maximum ability to handle a highly complex environment" (1968, p. 97).

Psychological Development

The first major theorist of adult development was Carl Jung (1930/1983), who himself experienced a major upheaval at midlife following his separation from Freud. Jung divided psychological development into two phases. Childhood to age 40 is a time when the ego gains mastery. This first stage of life is preparation for the second half of life, when people may become more intrapsychically attuned. This involves coming to terms with mortality—a task that extends beyond the psychological and into the spiritual—or into the pursuit of meaning. People begin to question their commitments and become increasingly receptive to previously suppressed or neglected aspects of their personality. Jung felt the midlife years are characterized by separation and loss, as each phase of life has a quality of death and rebirth and brings a new dimension to the person. The goals of successful midlife, according to Jung, are completion of *individuation* and *transcendence*. It is the realization of the first goal that makes the second one possible.

Erikson (1950, 1958) expanded on Jung's focus on the inner, offering a view of the restructuring of personality in a less ego-centered way. "The moving out of oneself allows moving into others, which expands the personality and revitalizes the ego" (Dziegielewski et al., 2002, p. 68). Erikson defined the critical task of midlife as the avoidance of self-preoccupied stagnation and the achievement of generativity, a concern for guiding and nurturing the next generation, or advancing causes that benefit society. He wrote: "In the middle years, once intimacy has been achieved and maintained, and as sexual vigor begins to wane, caring for others, for products, and for ideas does eclipse earlier needs and ego investments" (Erikson, cited in Hoare, 2002, p. 32). Intimacy is the first "we" stage. It depends on a well-grounded ego identity and an "I" that is formed to such an extent that its ideological convictions are comparatively solid. It is not "identity versus identity confusion" as the dialectic that must be resolved prior to intimacy with another. It is "identity against cynicism." Cynics repudiate intimacy because it is antithetical to engage genuinely and deeply with a loved one, all the while questioning the other's goodness and intentions (Hoare, 2002).

Erikson did not believe (as Freud had) that development ceased in childhood. He felt there were opportunities for growth and development throughout all life's stages. Erikson revised some of his views on adulthood as he passed through that stage himself. He moved away from the concept of "identity" as a circumscribed crisis during adolescence. Instead, he felt "a benchmark to the late adolescent, identity is both the gateway to and the cornerstone content of adult development" (Hoare, 2002, p. 31). Erikson also changed his concept of "integrity" to *integrality* and called this the ability to maintain a sense of wholeness in the face of bodily and sometimes mental and physical deterioration. Erikson felt that midlife adults live in two present-tense worlds: the current adult world of mature life and the prior childhood world that lives inside the psyche "in a vivid or vague, truthful or vastly restructured form of childhood" (p. 31). Wisdom is a midlife goal because it is a time when one can still influence resolutions through guidance and leadership. In later life, individuals have achieved an individual wisdom, but they are in less of a position (in our society) to pass that on. Finally, Erikson replaced wisdom with faith as the final form of achievable, existential hope (Hoare, 2002).

Midlife Crisis

The term *crisis* comes from Eriksonian theory. It means there is a heightened concern and a need to make a choice. It is not associated with a breakdown or any particular stage of life. Jacques (1965) felt midlife presented many challenges that could become "crises" because it is a time of change from an external to an internal focus that provides wisdom for later years. The negative attitude toward the age of 40, which also suggests a "crisis"—and the perception of older ages as even worse—is almost exclusively a trait of Western cultures. Western culture does not provide guidelines for this stage of life. Therefore, these feelings may lead to an impulse to act out and experience feelings and emotions similar to those felt previously (Clark & Chwiebert, 2001; Kruger, 1994).

Levinson (1978, 1986) felt a midlife crisis was actually a normal phase of life. He noted that transitional periods such as the middle years of adulthood are when established life structures are discarded or revised and new life structures are created. The tasks are to accept the losses of the end of a time period, to review the past, and consider the possibilities for the future. Lachman feels that stressful life events and transitions form the context through which the "dialectic between development and loss occurs" (2001, p. 208). This understandably results in a common experience of agitation during the middle years. For example, Levinson (1978, 1986) wrote about the "*empty nest syndrome,*" describing the feelings of women, whose primary career was that of wife and mother, when their youngest child leaves home. In more contemporary times, midlife may represent a time when women can resume careers or prepare for new ones. Unemptied nests may bring more tears than empty nests.

Midlife transition may be a term better suited to the middle years of adulthood than *midlife crisis.* The psychological purpose is the transformation of consciousness. Stein and Stein (1987) describe three phases of *midlife transition:* destructuring, liminality, and restructuring. Destructuring involves a shift or change of focus at this time of life. The period of *liminality* is marked by moods expressed as being lost in a deep woods or wandering alone in the desert. The unconscious is active and produces vivid and powerful dream images that can ultimately be useful in bringing about *restructuring.* Factors predicting well-being at midlife include income, friends, good health, high self-esteem, lack of self-denigration, a benign superego, goals for the future, a positive life narrative, the belief that one has a right to a life, positive midlife role models, and positive feelings about one's appearance (McQuaide, 1998).

Sociohistorical Context

Havighurst (1973) felt that the particular ways in which personality changes during midlife are affected by one's resources for expansion and growth, the cultural restrictions that one needs to overcome, and the opportunities available. Erikson (1958) had a biopsychohistorical approach to adult development. He used the term "historical relativity" to consider the ways in which adults of different eras consistently thought, felt, and were motivated to behave, how they supported self and family, and how they adapted to their new positions in the social structure. Erikson produced six images of what that adult is and might become within her or his sociohistorical context (cited in Hoare, 2002).

- *Prejudiced adult:* The construct of the prejudiced adult is a powerful identity image. Erikson believed people had both individual identities and group identities. Group identities can take cohesiveness to the extreme of exclusivity and superiority over other groups. Erikson felt that prejudice represented identity immaturity and showed impoverished adult development. Unlike Freud, who thought prejudice resulted from intellectual narrowness ("psyche intellect equation"), Erikson felt that prejudice was "an inability or disinclination to engage the affect and mind so that it can reside within the social perspective and view of another" (a "psyche-empathy-normative equation") (Hoare, 2002, p. 63). The experience of receiving and handing out rejection or prejudice increases with advancing age. It is easier to avoid rejecting others when one is treasured at some level in home life, at work, and in the community and is oneself not prejudicially restricted from such inclusion.
- *Moral, ethical, spiritual adult:* By middle age, superego development has taken hold, and people often fear they are not as good as they should be. Principled behavior defines advanced adult identity. Ethical adults are those who in most instances affirm judiciously instead of negating arbitrarily.

- *Playing, childlike adult:* Playing adults are engaged, adaptive, and resilient. Play represents the freedom of adult roles and role latitude.
- *Historically and culturally relative adult:* A deep interest in the past becomes evident in the middle years of life. The historically, culturally relative adult is a highly abstract, cognitively developed person who lives in history and yet knows the self as residing in one era in the total flow of time.
- *Insightful adult:* Insight is the principled developmental tool that moves adults to the ethical level of behavior. Insight depends on, but occurs after, knowledge in the learning sequence. Insight takes us beyond knowledge. Neugarten (1968) raised the point that the social environment of a particular generation will influence the social timetable of when people accomplish major life tasks. For example, during World War II many couples delayed marriage and childbearing until after the war, resulting in the postwar "baby boom." Since the 1950s the median age at first marriage has increased for both men and women. Childbearing is extending into the 40s and 50s, so some people in midlife may be becoming parents for the first time and raising very young children. The point is that it is difficult to generalize about people in midlife.

Race and Culture

Persons of color may experience particular challenges during midlife due to the cumulative stress of discrimination and oppression. This includes the energy expended by parents to both educate about and protect their children from racial slights (see Chapter 11 on middle childhood and Chapter 12 on adolescence), particularly as they approach adolescence (Elman & O'Rand, 1998). Several authors describe the unique challenges facing four ethnic/racial groups in the United States. African Americans face social conditions that are detrimental to self-improvement, such as discrimination and racism. As a group, they are more likely to come from poverty, which results in related health disorders. Hypertension in the middle adult years is a widespread phenomenon among African Americans of all income levels. African-American men have a higher incidence of illnesses that result in death at an earlier age than their white counterparts, making it more likely that African-American women will be widowed earlier. Asian Americans face language problems and the pressure of the *model minority* stereotype. *Acculturation* leads to value conflicts between younger and older generations. Native Americans have problems that are rooted in their history of discrimination and broken promises. They face poor academic achievement, high unemployment rates, language problems, and prejudice. Latino Americans are also challenged by language, as many immigrants speak only Spanish, frequently resulting in poor academic and social progress. They also cope with discrimination and prejudice (Ashford, LeCroy, & Lortie, 2006; Brice, 2003; Gatson & Porter, 2001).

Non-English-speaking adults and illiterate adults (Ashford & LeCroy, 2010) are two other groups who may face additional challenges in midlife related to discrimination in employment. Consider the woman in her early fifties who immigrated from the former Soviet Union, where she worked as a chemical engineer and now works as a caregiver for the elderly and infirm in the United States. Or, the woman in her early sixties who helped support her family as a housekeeper and is embarrassed when she is asked to complete forms at her primary care physician's office because she cannot "spell too well."

Intimate Relationships in Midlife

The middle years of adulthood hold both promise and challenge with regard to romantic and intimate relationships with a primary partner. For some heterosexual couples, marital satisfaction may increase when children leave home. For others, it can bring an end to the main goal they shared. The majority of middle-aged adults consider their spouse or partner to be their closest friend and the person with whom they are most intimate. Their friendship includes enjoyment, acceptance, trust, respect, mutual assistance, confiding, understanding, and spontaneity. There may be a move from the more passionate love of the younger years to an affectionate or companionate love that includes having another person near and enjoying deep, caring feelings for the person. Another phenomenon that often characterizes the middle adult years is that men and women tend to feel less tightly bound to traditional gender roles than before.

Divorce

Some marriages do not work, and marital separation and divorce are not uncommon among couples in the middle years of adulthood. The national rate of divorce grew about 10% in the 1990s, although it is currently showing some signs of ebbing. Many reasons can contribute to the decision to divorce, including communication problems, finances, and shifting cultural views that lead to the couple growing apart in interests or life goals. Lack of common sexual values in a marriage can also create problems and can lead to extramarital affairs, although interestingly, most research suggests that marital affairs are often more related to psychosocial needs. Women's economic gains have also contributed to divorce rates as they have entered professional and managerial careers that provide economic security to leave a marriage or support a family (Kilborn, 2005).

Widowhood

Women are more likely to become widows during midlife than men are to become widowers, because women live an average of 8 years longer than men. Nearly one quarter of married women are widowed in their 40s and 50s: roughly one third are white women and two thirds are black women. Men who die in their middle years of life and their widows are disproportionately from lower educational and occupational statuses. Older widows tend to have obsolescent work skills, and younger widows often have children at home, leaving widowed women with few economic resources. Consequently, these women often have incomes that are below the poverty line.

Parenting in Midlife

Parenting occurs within the trajectory of life span development. More specifically, Blieszner, Mancini, and Marek (1996) consider midlife parenting to be located at the intersection between individual development and family experience. They view it through the lens of previous parenting and personal development experience and as a precursor to late-life parenting and old age experiences. Transition in the lives of children influence the centrality of the parent role as well. Children are generally in adolescence when parents reach midlife. Parents experience more economic problems during their children's adolescence because teenage children cost more. These changes lead to conflict and power struggles between adolescents and middle-aged parents. For those midlife adults whose children are young adults, parents must now shift their relationship from one of parent–child (for example, from protectors and financial providers) to one of parent–friend. The nature of these changes is influenced by the characteristics of the child, the parent, the larger sociocultural system, and the historical period. For example, social class (as indicated by the level of education achieved in the earlier years of life) and the extent to which midlife parents experienced upward social mobility during their formative years influence their psychological and social well-being. It may moderate whether parents are challenged by the growing autonomy of their adolescent children or when adult children overtake their parents' achievements. It is noteworthy that some individuals become parents for the first time in midlife (after age 40), which introduces another set of joys and challenges.

Briefly stated, there are greater health issues for both the mother and the developing fetus with women who have children after age 35. The risk of infertility substantially increases, as women are born with a given number of ovum (eggs) and do not produce additional ovum throughout their lives. Some couples who choose to have children in their middle years and are not able to conceive have increasingly turned to donor insemination and adoption, particularly international adoption (see Chapter 5 on family development for a fuller discussion of this important topic).

Erikson considered parenting to be the most common expression of generativity. He felt that through generativity, defined as "primarily the concern in establishing and guiding the next generation" (1963, p. 267), adult lives become meaningfully integrated into modern social institutions and societal endeavors designed to ensure the continuity of things deemed worth preserving from one generation to the next. Parents see evidence of their children's accomplishments, including educational achievements, occupational pursuits, and personal and interpersonal qualities. Parents are contributors to how their children's lives unfold; therefore, the stakes for parental self-evaluation are high (Ryff et al., 1994). This may be particularly true for parents of children with mental health problems, learning disorders, chronic illnesses, and/or developmental disabilities. Seltzer, Floyd, and Hong described how the "atypical caregiving challenges that these parents face may cause stress and threaten their physical and mental health" (2004, p. 187). They use the term "accommodative coping," which involves "flexibly adjusting one's goals in response to a persistent problem." Accommodative coping is based on a life course gradient—lowest among individuals in their 30s, peaks between the ages of 52 and 57 (midlife years), and levels off and declines thereafter. Life course timing of the child's diagnosis, lack of control over the caregiving context, and the need to make major life accommodations are all factors that put these parents at risk for health and mental health problems during their middle years of life (p. 194).

Generativity finds its ultimate motivational sources in cultural demand and inner desire. The former refers to society's expectations that men and women should devote increasing personal resources toward the maintenance and advancement of the next generation as they move through young adulthood and into middle life. The latter captures what Erikson (1963) called *the need to be needed,* suggesting that generativity springs from two sources: the communal need to be *nuturant* and the *desire* to do something that transcends death. This gives rise to a conscious *concern* for the next generation. Concern may stimulate generative *commitment,* and generative *action* may include behaviors that involve creating, producing, maintaining, cultivating, or nurturing. The personal meaning of the complex relations among *demand, desire, concern, belief, commitment,* and *action* is determined by the person's narration of generativity, or the subjective story the adult creates about proving for the next generation. McAdams (1990) refers to this as the *"generative script"*—an inner narration of the adult's own awareness of where efforts to be generative fit into her or his own personal history, into contemporary society and the social world he or she inhabits and in some cases within the scope of society's own encompassing history. The generative script is an important part of the larger life story that an adult constructs about her or his identity (McAdams, 1990, 1993).

Grandparenting in Midlife

Many adults become grandparents in their middle years, generally between the ages of 50 and 65, with an average age of 47 (Connor, 2000). However, grandparents can be anywhere from 30 to well into their 80s or even 90s (Santrock, 1997).

Although it is a role eagerly anticipated, and highly valued in the life cycle, few empirical studies exist on the role of grandparenthood. Two notable exceptions follow. In a study of 70 middle-class grandparents, Newgarten and Weinstein

(1964) observed five styles of grandparenting: formal, fun seeker, distant figures, surrogate parents, and mentors. Based on data from a 1983 NIA-supported national survey of 510 grandparents, Cherlin and Furstenberg (1992) observed three styles of grandparenting: (a) remote, characterized by a relationship with little contact; (b) companionate, characterized by an emotionally involved, friendly relationship; and (c) involved, characterized by behavior similar to that of the parental role. Grandparents between the ages of 45 to 60 appear to be more willing to give advice and to assume responsibility for caregiving and discipline of grandchildren than grandparents aged 60 and older (Santrock, 1997).

Whatever the particular style of grandparenting, grandparenthood is profoundly meaningful. Kivnick (1983) conceptualizes five dimensions that are believed to be shared to some extent by all grandparents: (a) centrality, where grandparenthood is a central part of the individual's life and meaning; (b) valued elder, where grandparenthood is characterized by the traditional concepts of the respected and wise elder; (c) immortality through clan, where grandparenthood is a way of achieving immortality through procreation; (d) reinvolvement with personal past, where the individual's life review is assisted by being a grandparent; and finally (e) indulgence, where an attitude of lenience and indulgence is expressed toward the grandchild. Grandparents are able to share their experience in child rearing, reflecting a person's influence across generations. This new role offers new opportunities and new learning. It can lead to self-reflection on one's own parenting history, which can be a source of stress as well as of accomplishment. Becoming a grandparent can replace impending retirement and concern over the loss of status, especially in contemporary times, when grandparents have often been called on to assist working—dual-income—adult children. It is important to note, however, that some of these grandparents may be considerably younger (in their 30s) if, for example, they had children as teenagers and their adolescent children are now becoming parents. In such cases, grandparents may be taking care of both the teenage mother and her child, often while being the primary financial support for them as well.

Surrogate Grandparenting

Kelly (1993) discussed several issues that relate to a particular group of grandparents—surrogate grandparents (those who are raising their grandchildren)—that can cause additional stress during midlife. It is estimated that surrogate parenting describes about 5.5% of all grandparent experiences. The growth in grandparent custody of grandchildren is correlated with the 1979 change in state and federal laws for foster care (see Chapter 18 on policy through the life cycle). These laws gave priority to out-of-home placement with next of kin (Fuller-Thompson & Minkler, 2002). Lugaila (1998) used Current Population Reports from the U.S. Census Bureau to examine household living arrangements. He found that the phenomenon of grandparents caring for grandchildren crosses all ethnic and racial groups but was particularly prevalent among African Americans. Hayslip and Kaminski (2005) reviewed the literature and found that grandparents assume the parental role in times of crisis, sometimes because a parent has become ill or has died, but more often when the adult child has become incapacitated in their parental role due to HIV/AIDS infection, substance abuse, incarceration, and/or catastrophic events. Gross (2002) describes two grandmothers—ages 51 and 59—who were thrust into the role of child rearing when their daughters died in the terrorist attack on the World Trade Center. These grandparents may be caring for younger grandchildren, who need a lot of care and attention, at the same time that they are caring for aging parents. They may be isolated from their peers who are no longer raising young children, and they may not quite fit in with those who may be significantly younger. Hammer and Turner wrote: "Grandparents tie the present to the past as well as to the future and thereby provide the crucial links between generations" (2001, p. 106). They may also face the additional worry about the grandchild's parent (their son or daughter), economic burdens, and feelings of self-doubt or poor self-esteem related to the problems their own children are having as adults and as parents. The grandparents may worry about becoming ill or living long enough to care for their children and grandchildren. Based on data from the 1992–1994 National Survey of Families and Households, Fuller-Thompson and Minkler (2000) found higher rates of depression and multiple chronic conditions among caregiving African-American grandparents as compared to noncaregiving African-American grandparents. They note that some African-American women with custody of grandchildren often face a particularly painful situation. Where once such grandparents would have turned to church and community for support, they may now find themselves isolated due to the stigma attached to their adult child's HIV/AIDS status. Social work intervention might begin with reenlisting the church and community in support of grandparents by reducing the fear and stigma surrounding HIV/AIDS. Another important role for social workers is the development of community-based caregiver support groups that are culturally sensitive and build on the strengths of the African-American grandparents (Fuller-Thomson & Minkler, 2000). The American Association of Retired Persons (AARP) has established formal support networks for grandparents raising grandchildren.

Filial Maturity

At the same time that midlife adults may be renegotiating their roles with adolescent and/or young children, they are also dealing with changing relationships with increasingly aging parents. For adults who are parents, caring for their own parents—perhaps over a long period of time—can become increasingly demanding. Blenkner (1965) theorized that the parent-caring experience was a developmental milestone in the life of individuals generally occurring in their middle years. She called this *"filial maturity"*—the change in perspective that allows the adult caring for an aging parent to meet caregiving needs in an adult–adult reciprocal relationship. Because the adult children can view their parents as individuals apart from the parenting role, they have a new opportunity for personal and psychological growth, easing the burden of caregiving. Adult children work this through after an initial *filial crisis,* when they first take on the care of their aging parents. Cicirelli (1983) expanded on these concepts and introduced another one.

Filial anxiety refers to the emotions emanating from the *filial crisis.* Filial maturity occurs when adult children have worked through previous relationship issues that were ignored during the years when family members were busy living independent lives. "When adult children no longer see their parents as protectors but rather as needing protection, they must shift their own identity toward consolidation of an adult sense of self and individuation" (Sherrell, Buckwalter, & Morhardt, 2001, p. 387). This developmental achievement can be reflected in the quality of the child's caregiving for the parent. Caring for an aging and frail parent can offer some restitution for previous limitations in the parent–child relationship and allow individuals to assume the full role of adult in their own minds as well as in their family of origin (Eckert & Shulman, 1996; Greenberg, 1994). The amount and time of caregiving for a parent offers the opportunity for working on internal issues or, conversely, for stagnating and even regressing. It is a last chance—a *third separation individuation*—in which more realistic internalizations of oneself and one's parents can evolve. It can bring a resolution of earlier life issues because there is a realization that life and time are finite and that what occurs in the present between the parent and child is all that will be. Reengaging with one's parents in midlife can result in unique intrapsychic and interpersonal changes (Neugarten, 1968).

Nydegger (1991) expands on Blenkner's discussion of filial maturity and describes it as an intergenerational or ongoing process that occurs simultaneously for adult children and their parents in middle age as they enact their respective roles in relation to each other. The adult children acquire filial maturity through *filial distancing*—becoming emotionally independent of their parents—balanced with *filial comprehending*—understanding parents as persons with their own needs. Simultaneously, parents are acquiring *parental maturity*—distancing and encouraging their children to become independent adults. As they care for their aging parents, they are also modeling filial maturity to the younger generation. This is how intergenerational values concerning caregiving are transmitted and contribute to ensuring that their own caretaking needs will be met when they are in their later years (Blieszner, Mancini, & Marek, 1996).

Gender Differences in Midlife

Gender differences are particularly pronounced in the middle years of adulthood, although as Lesser and colleagues wrote: "One of the hallmarks of the baby boomer generation, now at midlife, has been the re-envisioning of traditional gender roles" (2004, p. 80). A major difference across socioeconomic and racial categories is that men are often focused more on their one primary role in midlife—work. Women's roles in midlife are characterized by multiple roles, and women may therefore be dealing with more role strain and role conflict. McQuaide recognized this phenomenon when she described women as having "two voices within them . . . a voice that speaks for the family and the voice that speaks for the career" (1996, p. 38). In U.S. society, the care of aging parents often falls more on daughters than sons, placing women in positions of role overload (for example, as mother, grandmother, caregiver for aging parents, employee, spouse). See Figure 14.1.

FIGURE 14.1

Four Major Social Roles of Woman

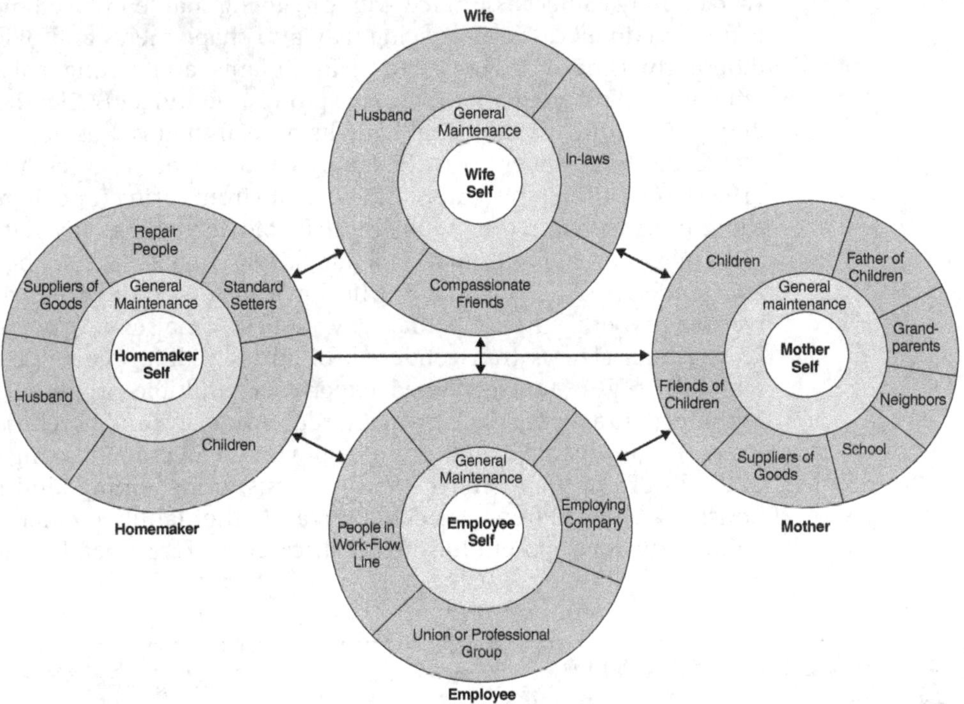

Source: Adapted from J.B. Ashford, C.W. LeCroy, and K.L. Lortie, 2005. *Human Behavior in the Social Environment: A Multidimensional Perspective* (3rd ed.), (p. 554). Belmont, CA: Thomson Brooks/Cole.

Men who are in their middle years, although perhaps not as frequently as women, also find themselves in the role of caring for aging parents. This may be especially true for men who are divorced, remarried, with a sick spouse, those who have never married, gay men, or those who do not have sisters. The life course role identity perspective (Elder, 1992, 1996) views caregiving as a role in the life course that one is likely to enter and exit once or several times during adulthood. Lemme (1995) used the phrase "caregiving career" to refer to caring for children, caring for elderly parents and relatives, and providing care for a dependent husband. It is important to consider the developmental timing of transitions to the caregiver role, the intersection of other roles in relation to the caregiver role, and the changing historical context for the caregiver role (Elder, 1992; Moen, Robinson, & Fields, 1994). Role identity theory predicts that the more competently and easily a person is able to fulfill all the internalized, normative, behavioral expectations related to all of her or his social roles, the more likely it is that he or she will exhibit high self-esteem and well-being (Stryker, 1980; Wells & Stryker, 1989). There are, however, role strains that affect the health and mental health of adults in midlife who are caring for aging parents. When role conflict occurs, especially on a frequent basis, decline in self-esteem can occur. Most contemporary work environments are not organized to facilitate employees' fulfillment of family responsibilities, be they young children or aging parents. Employed women have more work–family conflict associated with caregiving than employed men, although this is not true in all cases. Caregiving may also shape men's and women's retirement differently (similar to how caring for infants and young children may shape employment differently for these two groups; Dentinger & Clarkberg, 2002; Marks, 2005). Thus, the psychological benefits of filial maturity as described by Blenkner would be more evident if work–family conflict were also less problematic. Roots (1998), recognizing the strains that emanate from caring for children and caring for aging parents, referred to adults in their middle years as *"the sandwich generation."*

There is another group of individuals who may face challenges in midlife that are gender based—individuals who have lived a part of their lives as men or women (whether heterosexual, gay, lesbian or bisexual) before they came to know themselve as transgendered, often in midlife (Devor, 2002). Individuals who identify as transgendered experience multiple forms of marginalization. Many people are poor, lacking in affordable housing and psychosocial community support. They would benefit from help with the decision making process involved in disclosure of their gender identity status, transitioning, and re-working relationships with children, grandchildren and other family members. (see Chapter 4 on identify development for further discussion of transgenderism).

PRACTICE EXAMPLE 14.1

Mrs. L

Mrs. L is a 51-year-old woman who has responsibility for her elderly mother (92), who until recently has been able to live alone in her home. She also works part time as a medical receptionist, is a wife and the mother of three children, one of whom has ADHD. Mrs. L's husband, age 52, also has an elderly mother (age 89), who recently had a fall, and while she is recovering in a rehab facility, Mr. and Mrs. L are trying to make some decisions regarding both the immediate care of Mr. L's mother following her discharge from the rehab facility as well as for Mrs. L's mother. Mrs. L visits her mother every day, does grocery shopping, and provides personal care assistance for her. Both of their parents are reluctant to leave their own homes or go to a nursing home facility. The stress has caused Mrs. L to have migraine headaches and panic attacks. At the suggestion of her primary care physician (PCP), she sought counseling for stress and support. She is a member of the "sandwich generation." Working within an transtheoretical framework (combining supportive ego psychology and cognitive behavioral therapy), the social worker developed a treatment plan with Mrs. L to decrease symptoms of depression and anxiety (including panic attacks); to maintain communication with her husband about their needs as a couple in midlife (helping Mr. and Mrs. L to support each other during this time); holding family meetings so that the children could be involved (as appropriate) in discussions regarding the changing priorities of their intergenerational family over the course of the life cycle. Additional goals would include counseling for Mrs. L's daughter related to this adolescent girl's challenges related to ADD and coordination and advocacy with the girl's school to provide appropriate accommodations related to her learning.

Lesbian, Gay, and Bisexual Midlife Development

Sociohistorical context is a particularly relevant factor in appreciating the life course and stage of the gay community in their middle years—they grew up before or during the gay liberation movement of the 1960s and 1970s. "Coming out" and gaining acceptance was a long and difficult process for these individuals, made more arduous by the AIDS epidemic of the 1980s. Hopcke (1992) coined the term "AIDS-induced midlife" to describe gay men who confronted mortality at an earlier stage of development and went through the psychological and spiritual transformations congruent with that process. This generation experienced profound bereavements due to the multiple losses of friends, partners, and colleagues to the HIV epidemic. This, for many of these individuals, represented a second major loss of "family," as many of them (but certainly not all) had diminished relationships with families of origin. Many enter midlife HIV-infected and sustain the greatest mortality attributable to AIDS. Some of the individuals experience "survivor guilt" and problems with anxiety and depression attributable to the tragedies associated with HIV/AIDS in their communities (Kertzner, 2001; Kertzner & Sved, 1996). Due to the fact that they were further stigmatized by the health and mental health communities to which they turned for help during this difficult time, many gay men in midlife were pioneers and leaders in the creation of services for gay persons with HIV/AIDS. Hunter and Hickerson (2003, p. 354) applied Erikson's concept of "generativity" to these individuals, who not only cared for the sick but also spearheaded the effort to curtail the epidemic for the next generation (2003, p. 354). For these reasons, the current generation of gay men in midlife is arguably different from past and future generations.

Friend (1990, 1991) addressed three constructs that contribute to well-being in gay men and lesbians in their middle years: affirmative, conforming, and passing. Affirmative older lesbians and gay men had constructed a positive identity by rejecting the view of the larger culture. Conforming individuals were not well adjusted within the heterosexual community nor had they affiliated with the gay and lesbian community. Those who passed accepted their sexual orientation but capitulated to the heterosexist ideology. Herdt, Beeler, and Rawls (1997) also stress the significance of the historical context in which an individual lives as a major determinant of midlife adjustment, especially as it affects those who conformed or passed. They may have faced fear of disclosing gayness, legal and inheritance problems, and loss of ill partners to relatives unable to accept their relationship. Discrimination in the workplace and housing were real factors, which, along with internalized homophobia, contributed to their living a dual life, however incongruent. Horn (1994) described the concept of the *"lavender ceiling,"* pointing it out as being both imposed and self-imposed (discriminated against if found to be homosexual; holding themselves back from advancement due to fear of exposure of their homosexuality). They did not have visible role models or other cultural resources. Future generations of gay men and lesbians may face fewer of these particular challenges in their middle years with continuing medical advances against HIV/AIDS and the evolution of some legal rights such as domestic partnerships, parenting rights, and the adoption of antidiscrimination legislation (Kertzner & Sved, 1996). Nonetheless, given the pervasive influence of homophobia, continued efforts will undoubtedly be necessary to continue the struggle for civil liberties.

Kimmel (1978) noted the interlocking oppressions of being gay and aging in a culture that stigmatizes both. Gay men, for example, contend with what Brown, Cook, Sarosy and Quarto (1997) described as "accelerated or premature aging" as a result of loss of the physical attractiveness of their younger years. Sarosy believes that the difficulties gay, lesbian, and bisexual young adults face in negotiating a heterosexually focused world may result in some coping abilities that serve them well in the middle years of adulthood. The mastery of stigma developed slowly throughout the lives of these individuals, and the coming-out process provided opportunities to develop resilience as well as taxed coping resources. In other words, midlife and the entire process of aging may be less problematic because their major developmental crisis or transition may have occurred when they were coming to terms with their sexual orientation. In a study conducted by Brown and associates (1997), lesbian women felt that being middle aged paled in comparison to facing their sexuality and coming out to family, friends, and society. By the time most of these women were in midlife, they were relatively clear about their identities. They had experienced loss of family, community, and social acceptance early in life. High levels of independence from families resulted in "families of friends" for support (Brown et al., 1997). Nonetheless, anger and feelings of vulnerability related to stigma and homophobia may also be present in midlife. These may include estrangement from families and loneliness around family-centered holidays, the importance of youthful attractiveness, and dealing with life events such as the raising of children and the illness and death of a long-term partner without institutional frameworks like legal marriage or inheritance laws.

Kimmel described six "social-sexual patterns" among gay males and lesbians: (a) heterosexual marriage with or without periodic homosexual relations following or followed by a gay lifestyle; (b) celibacy with homosexual affectional orientation; (c) raising children, including adopted children; (d) long-term gay friend/lover relationship(s); (e) gay lifestyle with no long-term sexual relationships; and (f) bisexual lifestyle without marriage (1978, p. 118). When gay persons, for example, have been in long-term heterosexual marriages, they may struggle with tasks usually associated with adolescence instead of with midlife (Hunter & Hickerson, 2003, p. 361). In contrast with younger generations today who may have children through donor insemination, midlife gay and lesbian persons who have children generally had them within heterosexual marriages. They may feel alienated and different in the gay community. They also face the additional challenge of disclosure to their children and perhaps for single lesbian or gay individuals the task of raising their children within a lesbian or gay relationship, often without the same social supports enjoyed by heterosexual parents (Laird, 1996). If mothers or fathers are coming out as lesbian or gay in midlife, their teenage children may react negatively to this divergence from the norm in sexual orientation. The relationships that gay and lesbian individuals engage in may have been modeled on heterosexual relationships. The words *butch* and *femme*, for example, are complex metaphors that refer to the "masculine" and "feminine" roles modeled in heterosexual relationships. The feminist and lesbian feminist movement rejected these roles. Contemporary couples do not generally adopt these types of dichotomous roles but instead reflect the general cultural shift into more egalitarian roles (Laird, 2000). The relationship quality has been shown to be higher when both individuals are open about their sexual identity, intensifying the link to each other. However, open affection for each other has also risked harassment and threats, making it difficult for couples to be consistent in when, where, and to whom they will be open.

Philosophical Issues

Midlife brings a new set of tasks that focus on the meaning of one's life and existence. Individuals evaluate goals and roles determined in their earlier years. There is a review of life partnerships. There may be a sense of emptiness for the old pleasures that can cause dissatisfaction with the current lifestyle. There may also be a decreased sense of competition and aggressiveness. Flanigan (1992) has written on the interesting topic of forgiveness during the midlife years. She has identified several stages involved in forgiving: claiming the injury, blaming the injurer, balancing the scales, choosing to forgive, and the emergence of a new self. Enright (2001) also identified several stages in the process of forgiveness: uncovering anger, deciding to forgive, working on forgiveness, and discovery and release. People who are able to forgive seem to achieve inner peace that results in positive self-esteem and other physical and mental health benefits. Empathy motivates forgiveness and is more likely to occur if the offender offers an apology.

Work in the Middle Years

Adult life during the middle years continues to include a good portion of time at the workplace, whatever the occupation or profession. Work gives direction to an overall lifestyle. Work determines one's socioeconomic status, which involves where people live, with whom they socialize, what schools children attend, and a general sense of self-identity. Fox developed a *spirituality-of-work* questionnaire (1994, pp. 309–310) that focuses on bringing *life* and *livelihood* together. It includes questions such as, (a) Do I experience joy in my work? (b) Do others experience joy as a result of my work? (c) What do I learn at work? and (d) What is sacred about the work I do? Some people may change careers or jobs in midlife, some by choice and others because jobs may end. When adults in midlife lose their jobs, it can result in economic, psychological, and social hardship. This can include anger, guilt, and shame. Joblessness affects not only the individual but the entire family as well (Ashford, LeCrog, & Lortie, 2006, p. 510; Newman & Newman, 2002).

Individual differences play a significant role in determining whether a person experiences career adjustment difficulties in midlife. These include job stress, job dissatisfaction, burnout, and midcareer change. An interesting concept related to the midlife work years is that of *"professional obsolescence,"* defined by Ashford,

LeCroy, and Lortie as "the use of information, theories, and technology that are less useful in performing tasks than what is currently available in one's field of practice" (2006, p. 486). Adults in midlife may, therefore, need additional and ongoing training to remain current in the workplace. Men whose feelings of confidence and identity are derived from their work role may begin to question their personal worth when they retire from paid employment. Those who retire in their 50s and early 60s tend to either have health problems or have sufficient resources to retire and wish to enjoy nonremunerative activities such as travel, recreation, or volunteer work. Retirement due to health is more common among working-class men. In general, working-class men may not experience retirement as positively as middle- and upper-middle-class men because they lack the financial resources that men in higher economic classes enjoy. Working-class women (wives) are more likely to work for economic reasons, and a major factor in the morale of women in midlife is the degree of consensus between husband and wife on how occupational and family roles are to be meshed (Ashford, LeCroy, & Lortie, 2006). Sex discrimination affects the career advancement of women. Women make less money and are concentrated at the lower end of the organizational hierarchy. Women's lives tend to be organized around events in the family life cycle, so that unlike those of male counterparts, their careers are often interrupted and then resumed or terminated.

Summary

The middle years of life are complex when individuals engage in a process of reassessing, renegotiating, reevaluating and restructuring their lives. They are a time of conflicting demands marked by both change and continuity. The physical, psychological, cognitive, and social challenges require flexibility and adaptation as appearance alters and roles and relationships both within the family and the larger society shift. The middle years of adulthood occur within a historical context, and today's generation of midlife adults have grown up with the label "baby boomers"—a legacy from parents who have come to be called "the greatest generation" due to their struggles through a depression and World War II. Baby boomers, unlike the previous generation, came of age during a socially progressive era that included civil rights legislation and advances for gay and lesbian individuals. Some also saw combat in Vietnam—a war that divided the nation. They have weathered a major health epidemic—HIV/AIDS—that has affected many as they now face another stage of life. They are parenting children who are coming of age in a sociohistorical era with great technological advances that make worldwide communication a simple task. Wagenseller (1998) talks about being spiritually renewed at midlife. This includes having the capacity to penetrate the meaning of the obstacles we may meet, to appreciate the value in the troubles that befall us, and to be open to life's unanticipated turns. Erik Erikson, in his sixth decade of life, felt that *wisdom*—which he had originally attributed to the final stage of life—should actually not be last among life's accomplishments. He decided that wisdom must be achieved earlier if mankind is to survive its destructive tendencies—wisdom must be achieved in midlife.

15 Diversity in Older Adulthood

Ann Roy, PhD
Professor, Springfield College School of Social Work

Introduction: Trends and Concepts

Professional social workers are concerned with human behavior across the life span in all its psychological and social manifestations. Social workers who choose the profession of gerontology, "the study of multiple processes of aging" (Reisch & Gambrill, 1997, p. 144), focus on older adulthood.[1] Because older adulthood encompasses a wide range of ages and levels of functioning, a common age grouping used by the U.S. Census Bureau and found in the gerontological literature is young-old (65–74), middle-old (75–84), and oldest-old (over 85; Hutchison, 1999). It should be noted, however, that in light of the fact that "[b]etween 1900 and 1996 overall life expectancy increased nearly 30 years, from 47.3 to 76.1" (Quadagno, 2002, p. 78), and that many of us can expect to live 100 years and beyond, these categories may have become less meaningful. Why might this be so? It is apparent that the health and well-being of many adults in the sixth decade bears a closer resemblance to adults in middle rather than old age, thus lessening the utility of these age categories.

The starting point of any gerontological discussion begins with the recognition of the rapidly changing societal context within which we find ourselves at the beginning of the 21st century. Two major trends are destined to alter our fundamental understanding of aging: (a) the demographic change anticipated in the United States, specifically, the 20% increase in persons age 65 and over between 2004 and 2030 (Moody, 2002), which will affect all major institutions in the United States, and (b) the fast-paced rate of scientific discoveries that have implications for an extended and productive human life span. Following a brief look at these trends, we will explore themes relevant to older adulthood and their implications for social workers and the social work profession.

With respect to the demographic trend, about 13% of the U.S. population were aged 65 and over in 2004. By 2030, when this figure reaches 20%, all institutions in the United States will feel the impact. The majority of today's institutions (for example, elementary and secondary schools, higher education, corrections, private nonprofits, and the corporate sector) primarily meet the needs of young and middle-aged adults, whereas institutions in 2030 will be compelled to address the needs of older adults. The phenomena of great numbers of adults reaching age 65 will have a major impact on the Social Security system, and especially on Medicare, our only universal health care program for adults 65 and over. The rapidly escalating costs of new medical technology and pharmaceuticals, in conjunction with the dramatic increase in the number of recipients, is projected to jeopardize the solvency of Medicare by 2020, at which time the program will only

[1]A number of names are used in the gerontological literature to denote older persons. Some commonly used names are "seniors," "elders," "the elderly," "aged," "older adults," "aging baby boomers," and "senior citizens." Unfortunately, some terms for older persons in the popular media are pejorative and should not be used. Because each appellation conveys a slightly different shade of meaning, wherever possible, we will refer to persons 65 and over simply as "older adults," and the period of older age as "late adulthood." We believe that use of such phrases avoids an ageist bias.

be able to cover 79% of hospital inpatient costs under trust fund reserves (in other words, Medicare Part A, Health Insurance trust fund; TIAA-CREF Public Affairs, 2005). As well, it is expected that this dramatic demographic change will affect the average age of retirement, the number of years spent in retirement, and the nature of retirement years (for example, how retirees divvy up their time in terms of leisure and volunteer activity, part- and full-time work, and travel). Social Security, Medicare, and retirement will be addressed in more detail later.

It is our view that another far-ranging influence of this large contingent of older adults will be their impact on society's "perception of aging and the aged" via media portrayals, advertising, and consumer marketing. Although of lesser importance than the looming issues of Social Security and Medicare, the pervasive nature of media influence, advertising, and marketing can be expected to influence normative behavior (for example, consider the correlation between the ban on cigarette advertising, and the reduction in the rate of smoking and acceptability of smoking). Similarly, consider public discussion on the topic of sexuality in older adults, a long-standing taboo. A case can be made that the influence of media and marketing (with schemes that now include scenes of older adults enjoying the benefits of an impotence drug, a significant problem related to chronic health conditions among older adult males) may help encourage acceptance of sexuality in elders. This example, and surely others yet unknown, will alter our perceptions of older persons.

Not only can we anticipate a change in attitudes toward older adults through the impact of media, marketing, and advertising, but consumer goods themselves can also be expected to change dramatically. To illustrate, the American Association of Retired Persons (AARP), one of the largest organizations representing older persons, is collaborating with a large home retail business to develop a "seal of approval" program for products that are safer and will accommodate needs of older persons. Elder-friendly products might include safer bath and electrical mechanisms (AARP Home Depot link, 2004). In the future, with large numbers of vigorous older adults maintaining high visibility in society, institutional accommodations for older adults will become the norm, and the impact, by sheer force of numbers alone, will reverberate throughout all social and economic institutions in the United States.

With respect to scientific advances, there is a concept in gerontology known as the *compression of morbidity* (Fries, 2002). This idea was first proposed in 1980 by a theorist named James Fries. "Compression of morbidity" captures a long-standing controversy in the field of aging. The essence of the debate is: Will we trade off longer life expectancy for additional years of disability, or will longer life be accompanied by only a brief period of illness? This is an important piece of epidemiological knowledge, as most of us would not wish for longer life if we had to endure added years of disability and illness. According to Fries, "[T]here are increasing data on the ability to move infirmity farther into the life span, shortening its overall duration. A theoretical framework for intervention into these serious problems, the compression of morbidity, is emerging" (Fries, 2002, p. 345). Hayward, Crimmins, and Saito's (1998) report findings are consistent with Fries's theory. They report that, along with the dramatic decline in heart disease in the 1980s, active life expectancy increased, particularly in men. They suggest that as the overall population reduces risky health behaviors, we are likely to see a further increase in active life expectancy.

In gerontology, as in the social work profession, the concept of *diversity* is important (Germain & Bloom, 1999). Diversity entails the multiplicity of cultural, ethnic, race, class, religious, and sexual orientation differences that exist between and within societal groups. In addition to our common understanding of diversity, gerontologists conceive of diversity as the variation among older persons in terms of health status, work history, and overall life experience. Still other factors include the influence of historical period and cohort effects and how they contribute to diversity among older adults (Germain & Bloom, 1999). This is to say that based on the great variability among older adults and how they experience the later years of life, one should avoid generalizations. Nevertheless, generalizations are inescapable as we capture the rapidly expanding body of knowledge in gerontology.

The Biology of Aging

The National Institute of Health (NIH) established the National Institute on Aging (NIA) in 1974 to study the biological and social aspects of aging. It is clear that some combination of heredity, environment, and lifestyle interact to produce what we know as aging. Numerous biologically based hypotheses for why we age have been proposed over the years. These include, but are not limited to, growth hormones, metabolic processes, genetic mutations, and cross-linking proteins (National Institute on Aging [NIA], 2002). Scientists explain that it is the slow-down in cell division and eventual cell death that brings about the visible and invisible signs of aging; graying hair, changing metabolism, decline in muscle mass, and other common physical manifestations of older age. More recent scientific explorations are beginning to clarify pieces of the aging puzzle. We will briefly look at two biological theories of aging: genetic and biochemical.

Genetic Theories Animal studies, with many parallels to human physiology, have successfully extended life span in fruit flies, nematodes (roundworms), and mice. For example, one genetic explanation posits that when certain genes linked to aging mutate, they fail to produce a protein found to limit life span. Scientists have been able to manipulate these age-related genes so as not to produce this protein, and consequently, they have extended the healthy life span of roundworms and fruit flies (NIA, 2002).

According to National Institute on Aging:

> The genes isolated so far are only a few of what scientists think may be dozens, perhaps hundreds, of longevity- and aging-related genes. But tracking those down in organisms like nematodes and fruit flies is just the beginning. The next big question for many gerontologists is whether counterparts in people—human homologs—of the genes found in laboratory animals have similar effects. (2002, p. 10)

Biochemical Theories In terms of the biochemistry of aging, oxygen appears to play a vital role not only in cell health, but also, curiously enough, in cell death. How so? One by-product of metabolism is *free radicals* (an oxygen atom with one unpaired electron). Left unchecked, free radicals attack and damage cell DNA, a process linked to degenerative diseases and many signs of aging. Although the body has ways of lessening free radical damage through antioxidants (for example, vitamin A, vitamin E, and cell enzymes), some free radicals are still able to damage cell DNA (NIA, 2002). Free radicals can also be produced by tobacco smoke and sunlight, thus providing biological evidence for the impact of environmental factors on aging and the importance of healthy lifestyle choices. Social work intervention here might include education and raising public awareness around lifestyle choices made in the young and middle-adult years that will affect the quality of the later years.

Leonard Guarente (2004), a biotechnology researcher at the Massachusetts Institute of Technology, predicts that within a decade we may have the capability to slow down human aging, perhaps adding 20 to 30 healthy years to an individual's life expectancy. Students of history should be reminded of Ponce de Leon's search for the Fountain of Youth in the New World. He discovered Florida, but alas, no Fountain of Youth (Moody, 2002). Although we may welcome the prospect for a long, healthy life, it is the societywide ramifications of such an evolution that are most extraordinary. Indeed, all areas of human endeavor will be compelled to address the challenges and opportunities presented by increased longevity.

Poverty and Ethnicity

In 1998, the ethnicity of older adults was as follows: 85% non-Hispanic White, 8% African American, 5% Hispanic, 2% Asian Pacific Islander, and 0.4% Native American, representing 32.4 million persons age 65 and older (Quadagno, 2002). However, there are striking disparities in wealth and income among these diverse groups of older Americans. Why might this be so? A partial explanation follows. One of the most important wealth-building mechanisms available to the majority of U.S. citizens is that of home ownership, where current federal taxes are reduced and equity accrues. A home purchase in early adulthood encourages the building of equity throughout the working years and, as such, becomes a highly valued asset during retirement. In the mid-twentieth century, minorities experienced the dual discriminatory practices of *redlining,* which prohibited loans to minorities, and *restrictive covenants,* which prevented minorities from living in white Protestant neighborhoods. Thus, many African Americans, persons of Hispanic and Asiatic origin, and others arrived in older adulthood with no home of their own (the Federal Housing Authority supported these practices between 1934 and 1949; Quadagno, 2002). As a consequence, minorities bring far fewer assets into older adulthood as compared to their white counterparts. Furthermore, due to "cumulative disadvantage" (see following definition), older minority adults often live on impoverishment-level Social Security benefits. In fact, many minority older adults must continue to work to sustain themselves and their families (Quadagno, 2002).

Health Care and Ethnicity

The majority of older adults have benefited from the 1965 establishment of two government health programs: *Medicare,* a universal health-care federal program for persons age 65 and over that provides coverage for hospitalization and doctor visits, and *Medicaid,* a means-tested state/federal program that provides health coverage for the poor. Subgroups of older adults, however, experience considerable barriers in their attempts to access health care. As Ford observed,

> The cumulative effects of poverty, segregation, discrimination, racism, official neglect, and exclusionary immigration laws, experienced over a lifetime, sometimes for generations, have left their mark on the older members of minority groups now living in the United States. Generally poorer physical health and greater disability, compared to that of White persons of the same age and gender, give mute evidence of disadvantages endured. (1999, p. 1)

Disparities in health care have been noted, for example, in a report by Sherman (as cited in National Association of Social Workers [NASW], July 2005a), where Hispanic and African-American women were much less likely than white women to receive hospice care or be treated with pain management. In other research, based on a sample of 472 low-income, predominately Hispanic and African-American women with breast or other gynecological cancer, it was found that although 24% were moderately to severely depressed, they were far less likely to be treated with antidepressants or supportive counseling as compared to middle- or upper-middle-class women with a similar type of cancer (Ell's study, as cited in NASW, July 2005b). And, according to a Kaiser Family Foundation study:

> Minority Americans are twice as likely to be uninsured as whites and minority Medicare beneficiaries are more likely than whites to have no supplemental insurance. African American and Latino beneficiaries report problems accessing specialists and health care. Disparities continue to exist in relation to screening, diagnosis and therapeutic interventions for African American elders. (Administration on Aging, 2005, p. 3)

The preceding studies illustrate, among other things, the adverse impact of race, gender, and ethnicity on the equitable distribution of health-care resources.

What other factors might affect access to health care? Consider what would happen if one were to reach older adulthood with the following life course: an eighth-grade education with a series of low-paying, unskilled jobs, the experience of substandard housing, a lifetime of poor nutrition, and years of isolation from mainstream society either by virtue of geography or illiteracy. This scenario is consistent with the theory of *cumulative disadvantage,* whereby persons who begin life with advantages tend to accumulate them throughout a lifetime, and persons who begin life with few advantages tend to fall behind, resulting in systematic inequalities (Quadagno, 2002). It is clear that lifelong disparities, and the emergent marginalization and impoverishment, take an egregious toll on older minorities with early death from chronic disease and untreated health and mental health conditions. Poverty, then, is another factor limiting access to health care among older adults.

Because Medicare covers hospital stays and doctor visits, it provides a safety net for older adults' health-care needs. The drawback is that even with Medicare, there remains a financial gap in coverage that unduly burdens the poor. Specifically, as of this writing, Medicare does not provide coverage for prescription drugs,[2] nor can the

[2]The Medicare Prescription Drug Act was implemented in January 2006 as Medicare Part D. However, according to a Families USA study as cited in *The Republican* (Medicare official touts drug plan, 2005), states may drop their dual-eligible candidates as a cost-saving measure. Because Medicaid provides other benefits to the poor above and beyond drug coverage, this move represents a setback for poor elders.

poor afford Medicare premiums, deductibles, and copayments. The solution is to have low-income Medicare beneficiaries enroll in Medicaid. In fact, 6 million Medicare beneficiaries are enrolled in Medicaid, yet this represents only one-half of older adults on Medicare who are eligible for Medicaid (Perry, Kannel, & Dulio, 2002).

According to a 2002 study of low-income older adults, underenrollment in Medicaid is due to misperceptions about Medicaid, including a lack of awareness of the Medicaid program itself, confusion as to who is eligible, and the long and burdensome enrollment forms (Perry & Dulio, 2002). Social workers should be alert for opportunities to educate Medicare beneficiaries who might be eligible for Medicaid. Valuable, too, would be organizing and promoting community outreach to inform low-income seniors of Medicaid benefits and the details of enrollment conditions (Quadagno, 2002).

Rural Elders

Approximately 30% of all persons over 65 live in rural areas. Rural culture places a high value on independence, self-reliance, and natural helping (Germain & Bloom, 1999). According to Weber, rural older adults, as compared to their urban counterparts, are at a higher risk for poor physical and mental health, chronic illness, low income, poor nutrition, and poor housing (1976). Although isolated rural areas of the country have always been in short supply of mental health and medical services and skilled practitioners (for example, nurses, social workers, and physicians), elders have traditionally made good use of natural helping networks of relatives, neighbors, and friends (Germain & Bloom, 1999) to fill that gap.

Social-Psychological Perspectives on Late Adulthood Development

Stage Theory

In Chapter 3 you were introduced to Erik Erikson's eight-stage theory of psychosocial development. With the addition of a ninth stage, Erikson explored, but did not fully develop, psychological and social behavior in late adulthood. Nonetheless, Erikson's ninth stage is an attempt at theoretical development of late adulthood—a period neglected by developmental theorists (Robbins, Chatterjee, & Canda, 1998). According to Erikson, the most important task to be resolved in later life is that of coming to terms with inevitable physical decline. Moreover, he posits that many of the ego qualities that evolved from earlier stages are paralleled in old age. Thus, from the ability to trust, developed in infancy, is derived the ability to appreciate human interdependence in older adulthood. From industry, developed in stage four, comes the ability to maintain a sense of effectiveness in life, and from intimacy—in stage six—is derived the ability to come to terms with ways to express love (Robbins, Chatterjee, & Canda, 1998).

Levinson, Darrow, Klein, Levinson, and McKee (1978) explored the life cycle. Their focus was on adulthood using a developmental model consisting of four overlapping eras, including late adulthood between 60 and 85. Similar to Erikson, Levinson and associates feel that late-life adults must come to an acceptance of deterioration, "coming to terms with the process of dying and preparing for his own death" (1978, p. 38), and find "a new balance of involvement with society and with the self" (p. 36). Some theorists focus on developmental tasks to be mastered in late life. Havighurst (as cited in Robbins, Chatterjee, & Canda, 1998) defined six such developmental tasks of later maturity:

1. Adjusting to decreasing physical strength and health
2. Adjusting to retirement and reduced income
3. Adjusting to death of spouse
4. Establishing an explicit affiliation with one's age group
5. Adopting and adapting social roles in a flexible way
6. Establishing satisfactory physical living arrangements (p. 208)

Disengagement Theory

The lasting importance of *disengagement theory* is its place in gerontological history as the first theoretical explanation for social-psychological responses to aging among older adults. Disengagement theory was based on a study of 172 adults between the ages of 50 and 70, conducted between 1956 and 1962 and known as the Kansas City Study of Adult Life. Cumming and Henry (1961) theorized that as people aged, they naturally withdrew from society by reducing the number of social roles and ties to others. This is consistent with the sociological perspective known as functionalism. One of the tenets of functionalism is that social systems must find a way of "minimizing potentially disruptive behaviors" (Parsons, 1951, p. 30). Thus, disengagement theory was viewed as an appropriate and beneficial response of an older person preparing for death and beneficial for society, as it reduced the disruption caused by death. This theory has been challenged, for example, by the work of Neugarten, Havighurst, and Tobin (1968). Also using data from the Kansas City Study of Adult Life noted earlier, these researchers found that life satisfaction was correlated with a high level of engagement in numerous social roles. Further, they stated: "We regard personality as the pivotal dimension in describing patterns of aging and in predicting relationships between level of social role activity and life satisfaction . . . there is no sharp discontinuity of personality with age, but instead an increasing consistency" (1968, p. 177).

Activity Theory and Its Close Relative, Continuity Theory

Activity theory posits that successful aging requires that middle-aged level of social involvement be sustained for as long as possible into older age. Havighurst's (1968) study (N = 159 adults age 50–90) tends to support activity theory. He found that a high level of activity, as compared to a low level of activity, was related to greater contentment. He also found that personality type was related to life satisfaction and cautioned that neither disengagement theory nor activity theory provides a complete explanation for successful aging. *Continuity theory* argues that older adults continue to use coping styles they have used throughout their lifetime. It includes the idea that one's personality and approach to life's challenges remain much the same over time. Thus, as with activity theory, those who were actively engaged earlier in life remain so, and those who tended toward passivity likewise maintain this attitude. It also includes the idea that older adults cope by substituting new roles for roles lost later in life (Atchley, 1985). Overall, it is an optimistic view of aging as a continuous process of adaptation and coping. As Atchley stated: "Continuity is an adaptive response to both internal and external pressures" (1985, p. 238). This theory is consistent with social work's *strengths perspective,* emphasizing, as it does, one's capacity to make life adjustments by drawing on tried coping skills and forging new and meaningful roles.

Social Construction Theory

A more recent view of aging, derived from *symbolic interactionism, phenomenology,* and *ethnomethodology,* is known as *social construction of aging.* This theory argues that aging is a socially constructed phenomenon whereby the individual's self-conceptions about aging arise through interaction with the social environment (Dannefer & Perlmutter, 1990). According to Dannefer and Perlmutter, "Human beings participate in the construction of their own personhood, their own conditions of life, and their own social world. . . . It may provide the means to reverse or compensate for some debilities, including some assumed to be an ontogenetic part of aging" (1990, p. 116).

In the preceding discussion we presented recent demographic trends; introduced biological theories of aging; introduced the concepts of poverty, health care, and ethnicity and their impact on older adults; and introduced several theories of social-psychological development in older adulthood. Amid the uncertainties ahead, one thing appears certain: As the enormous cohort of middle-aged adults moves into older adulthood, it will change the very nature of the aging experience. Indeed, is it not time to rethink our idea of what it means to age when 80-plus-year-olds, provided with simple muscle-building exercises, no longer require walkers (NIA, 2002), and when we observe men and women in their seventh and eighth decades sitting on the U.S. Supreme Court, ruling on the great issues of the day? This is a critical moment for the social work profession whose presence in the community provides a wonderful opportunity to develop innovative interventions to meet the needs of older adults in the years ahead.

Physical and Mental Health in Older Adults

Physical Health

According to the National Institute on Aging (2002), changes that occur during normal aging vary widely among older adults. More specifically, organs or the organ system show different rates of decline among older adults. The following findings are taken from a well-regarded, longitudinal study known as the Baltimore Longitudinal Study of Aging that began in 1958 and continues today (as cited in NIA, 2002). As we age, the heart muscle becomes thicker, and the amount of oxygen it consumes during exercise declines. The arteries also tend to get stiffer, placing a further strain on the heart, and the lungs' breathing capacity declines by 40% between the ages of 20 and 70. Among older adults, the kidneys are less able to remove wastes from the blood, and the bladder's capacity diminishes (NIA, 2002). Osteoporosis is a thinning of the bones through mineral loss that is common in women at the time of menopause but affects older men as well. Sight and hearing changes are also common, and beginning as early as one's 40s, it becomes difficult to read material at close range. After 50, we are all susceptible to glare, and it becomes more difficult to hear at higher frequencies. To conclude on a positive note, the Baltimore Longitudinal Study of Aging found that the adult personality remains consistent throughout older adulthood, and that it is the exception, rather than the rule, for an individual to have a radical disposition change (NIA, 2002). This latter finding is consistent with continuity theory, a developmental theory discussed earlier.

Chronic Conditions Most older adults develop one or more chronic conditions. The degree to which chronic conditions affect one's daily life depends on a host of factors, including, but not limited to, genetic endowment, environmental conditions, and access to good health care. Osteoporosis, mentioned earlier, is at the root of much disability in older adults. It is a major cause of fractures of the hip that often results in a need for long-term care.

Social Work Intervention Social workers can provide education and support for their older clients and encourage known preventive measures such as the use of calcium, Vitamin D, and weight-bearing exercise, the combination of which has been shown to reduce frailty in older adults (NIA, 2002). Heart disease, stroke, and cancer are the leading causes of death in the United States and are more likely to occur in older-age cohorts. Each condition has lifestyle implications. That is, poor health behaviors, including the failure to get routine screening exams, partially explains the development of heart disease, stroke, and cancer. Therefore, appropriate social work intervention would call for the social worker to encourage the older adult to maintain a regular routine of screening exams, eliminate smoking behavior, increase his or her exercise, and maintain a nutritious diet, thereby lowering his or her risk of dying prematurely.

Mental Health

As in the general population, mental health issues are common among older adults. They range from minimally disruptive and highly treatable, to severe and persistent and quite resistant to treatment. The following discussion will focus on issues of particular relevance to older adults.

Depression and Anxiety Just as depression and anxiety affect younger persons, older adults struggle with similar mental impairments. When diagnosed in an older adult, therapy and medications (alert to adverse affects from multiple drug interactions) may be called for. Suicide in persons 65 and over is a widespread problem, and unlike in younger cohorts (Germain & Bloom, 1999), older adults who desire to commit suicide show great determination and provide few indications as to their intentions. Major depression is thought to be the underlying cause (Quadagno, 2002) of suicide in older white males, but remains underdiagnosed by health practitioners.

Alzheimer's Disease We will devote considerable attention to this devastating illness as it is one of the most feared and disturbing conditions of older age with potential for a major impact on families and institutions in the years ahead. *Dementia* is correlated with older age and characterized by severe diminution in cognition. There are a number of types of dementias, but by far the most prevalent is *Alzheimer's disease.* According to Beaver and Miller (1992), neurologists concur that over one half of the dementias known as *senile dementia* or *chronic brain syndrome* are, in fact, cases of Alzheimer's that have begun at a later age. Currently, 4.5 million persons in United States are afflicted with Alzheimer's disease, and this figure is expected to grow to 14 million by the year 2050 (Alzheimer's Association, 2005a).

Three Stages of Alzheimer's Disease Gorman describes three stages in Alzheimer's progression. The first stage lasts 2 to 4 years and is characterized by mild symptoms of forgetfulness, where the person cannot remember the name of everyday things and lacks good judgment; the second stage lasts 2 to 8 years and is characterized by moderate symptoms, such as difficulty in name recall, becoming easily lost, increased confusion, anxiety and personality changes, and a reduced ability to perform activities of daily living. The third stage lasts 1 to 3 years and is characterized by severe symptoms where the person's ability to acquire new information is destroyed, as is the ability to recognize family or friends (Gorman, 2002). Other behavioral and/or psychiatric symptoms include irritability, anxiety, and depression, and in the last stage, physical or verbal aggression, pacing, yelling, delusions, and hallucinations may be experienced (Alzheimer's Association, 2005b). Even in this last stage, where the spoken word is meaningless and death is the endpoint, persons with Alzheimer's respond to touch, eye contact, and music (Gorman, 2002).

The first medications to treat the cognitive symptoms of Alzheimer's disease were approved in the early 1990s by the U.S. Food and Drug Administration (FDA). These medications were from a class of drugs known as *cholinesterase inhibitors,* one of two classes of drugs currently approved by the FDA for the treatment of Alzheimer's disease. Cholinesterase inhibitors maintain *acetylcholine* levels in the brain, a chemical that helps the brain cells communicate with one another. One such cholinesterase inhibitor is *Donepezil* (whose trade name is Aricept), the administration of which is now standard treatment for most patients (Alzheimer's Association, 2005c). Donepezil must be closely monitored for side effects, but clinical trials have shown modest improvement on tests of memory and thinking.

Although medications can be effective in controlling some of the behavioral and psychiatric symptoms of Alzheimer's disease, it is recommended that medication be used in conjunction with behavioral or environmental interventions. For example, social work intervention for agitation might include providing a soothing environment, reducing environmental triggers, and monitoring comfort levels of the client. Antidepressants and antipsychotics are also helpful in treating the behavioral symptoms of Alzheimer's disease (Alzheimer's Association, 2005b).

Most persons with Alzheimer's are cared for at home by a spouse, adult child, or sibling, and caregiver burden can become an issue. The strain of caregiving is aggravated by the fact that it is often the responsibility of an older adult child or spouse confronting age-related challenges of their own. Furthermore, for the family caregiver, it is the severe personality changes that are often the most troublesome manifestation of the disease and most destructive of the quality of family life (Alzheimer's Association, 2005b). As Berman and Rappaport observed: "The caregiver needs the opportunity to mourn once again the loss of the demented relative. This is essential because, long before dementia proves fatal, a psychological death occurs with the deterioration of the personality of the patient" (1985, p. 68). Clearly, the social worker must address the needs of both patient and caregiver. An overall social work approach is well described by Berman and Rappaport:

> The social treatment of demented people and their families . . . requires a full range of social work skills, including counseling and support; resource referral; case management; grief work; family therapy and group work; patient, professional and community education; political action and advocacy; program development and research. These tasks require strength, stamina, flexibility, and creativity as we apply our helping skills to both patients and their caregivers who carry such depleting and draining social responsibilities. (1985, pp. 69–70)

Recent Breakthrough Studies on Prevention of Alzheimer's Disease The first Prevention of Dementia Conference was held in 2005, in Washington, D.C. During the conference, the Alzheimer's Association reported on a number of exciting new research studies. For example, studies show that risk factors for Alzheimer's disease include low levels of education, early-life gum disease, lack of social stimulation, extreme worrying, stroke, and low physical activity (Alzheimer's Association, 2005a). Other studies noted protective factors, including high level of fruit and/or vegetable juice consumption (thought to be related to the polyphenols in juice, chemicals that may protect the brain); high level of education (thought to stimulate neuronal growth); and social activity (thought to be mentally stimulating; Alzheimer's Association, 2005a). In fact, so much recent progress has been made (according to one geriatric physician attending the conference), that it may be possible to prevent Alzheimer's disease within the next 5 to 10 years (Alzheimer's Association, 2005d).

Prevention Intervention Many of the risk factors noted earlier relate to lifestyle choices. As such, social workers with expertise in brain function, human behavior, addressing the needs of the community, and who are committed to working with persons at high risk for Alzheimer's (for example, the poor and the poorly nourished) are well positioned to offer an important community resource. One might envision, for example, patterning a social work prevention program after the one directed by Elizabeth Edgerly, a psychologist with the Alzheimer's Association. This program, entitled "Maintain your Brain" (June 21, 2005), provides free, preventative classes around the country.

The Frail Elderly

The frail elderly are older adults in need of care due to declining physical and or mental abilities. These are persons with many of the conditions mentioned earlier, including, but not limited to, congestive heart failure, painful rheumatoid arthritis, severely reduced eyesight, and/or dementia (such as Alzheimer's disease), who find their activities of daily living (ADLs) severely limited. Nursing-home care is often the only viable solution for long-term care of the very frail elderly. Although 5% of elderly are in nursing homes at any given time, it is estimated that about 10% of older adults with similar ADL care needs reside in the community and are cared for by their families (Germain & Bloom, 1999). It should be noted that although frail elders are a relatively small proportion of all older adults, they represent great numbers among the oldest-old cohort, requiring high levels of geriatric care and very large health-care expenditures. The challenge for social work in the decades ahead will be to address the substantial health and mental health-care needs of our frailest older adults.

Contemporary Contexts

We need not wait until the older adult population explodes to comprehend that the text of public discourse must now turn to the needs of an aging society. Indeed, the drums have begun to beat for Social Security and Medicare reform, healthcare reform, and long-term care reform. The following discussion will focus on issues vital to society and of particular relevance to older adults.

End of Life Issues

Advanced Directives The circumstances of death in the United States have shifted dramatically from the early 20th century, when persons died in their own homes, to the present day, when most older persons die in medical or medical-related institutions. Hutchison views today's attitude toward death as "death denial" (1999, p. 280). Perhaps in response to a lack of control over the circumstances of one's death, the last 20 years has witnessed the growth in popularity of advanced directives. There are two types of advanced directives: the *living will,* a document stating the extent to which one wishes to prolong life with technology, and *Durable Power of Attorney for Health Care,* a document that assigns a close relative or friend to act on one's behalf should one become medically incapacitated. Unfortunately, advanced directives are often neglected in the crisis atmosphere of a patient's final hours, either because the directives are not known to exist, cannot be located in a timely fashion, or are overridden by family members. At present, no more than between 4% and 20% of persons complete advanced directives (Moody, 2002).

The use of advanced directives is intended to avoid the type of dispute illustrated by the contentious and highly politicized battle over the court-ordered removal of Terri Schiavo's feeding apparatus—a tube that had been keeping Ms. Schiavo alive in a persistent vegetative state. The case served to heighten society's awareness of the "right-to-die" issue and became a conservative rallying point, as various constituencies attempted, but failed, to halt the court order (National Public Radio, 2005). A related issue is that of assisted suicide. Oregon is the only state where an individual may choose to end his or her own life under controlled circumstances (Quadagno, 2002). Although a right to die has been affirmed in Oregon, it is a controversial issue that resulted in a challenge by the second Bush administration asserting that Oregon's doctor-assisted suicide law is a violation of the Controlled Substances Act (Right to Die, 2005).

Death and Dying in American Society The concept of death and dying was brought to the forefront of public discussion with the 1969 publication of *On Death and Dying* by Elisabeth Kübler-Ross. Based on her observations of patients diagnosed with a terminal illness, Kübler-Ross identified five psychological reactions experienced by persons facing death: denial, anger, bargaining, depression, and acceptance. She believed that a dying person moved through each stage in a step-by-step manner (Kübler-Ross, 1969), and if sufficient time existed prior to death, this progression would occur among all dying persons, whether young or old (Hutchison, 1999).

Though widely popular, Kübler-Ross's findings are not without controversy. For example, Marshall (1990) objected to her assertion that dying persons across all ages respond to the prospect of death as described. But as Kübler-Ross's sample was mostly young and middle-aged persons, a legitimate question arises regarding the generalizability of her framework to older adults. There is, as well, a lack of professional agreement regarding the stages she described. For example, Feifel observed "that just as there are multitudinous ways of living, there are numerous ways of dying and grieving. Despite the equanimity of sorts that it offers, and a prevailing chic, the hard data do not support the existence of any procrustean stages or schedules that characterize terminal illness or mourning" (1990, p. 540).

On an optimistic note, Kübler-Ross found that, irrespective of how an individual responded to the dying process, some sense of hopefulness was maintained until death. As she so eloquently stated: "It is this glimpse of hope which maintains them through days, weeks, or months of suffering. It is the feeling that all this must have some meaning . . . if they can only endure it for little while longer" (1969, p. 123).

Others have studied the reactions of older adults, in particular, to the prospect of death (Butler, 1963; Kalish, 1968; Peak, 1977). Peak observed three types of responses among older dying persons: "(1) those who face the prospect of death and handle it by active means within their capacities; (2) those who completely block out ideas of death; and (3) those who spend much time and energy trying to avoid the fears and anxieties it excites" (1977, p. 214).

Butler (1963) developed the idea of *life review,* or a reinterpretation of life experiences and past conflicts with the potential for both positive and negative outcomes. It is thought to be a common occurrence among older persons and to exist across cultures (Hutchison, 1999). Life review is similar to Erikson's eighth stage of ego integrity versus despair, whereupon the end of life calls forth a sense of self-acceptance or self-rejection. According to Butler, "Such reorganization of past experience may provide a more valid picture, giving new and significant meanings to one's life; it may also prepare one for death, mitigating one's fears" (1963, p. 68). Marshall observed that the life review is a social process and that "people who reported social reminiscence—that they talked a lot about their own past with other people—were more likely to demonstrate success in the process" (1986, p. 140). Hutchison (1999) also noted possibilities for spiritual renewal in the life review process as one searches for meaning in one's own existence.

A social work approach presents itself in terms of a theoretical application using Erikson's eighth-stage theory of ego integrity versus despair, and the more applied concept of life review. For example, a social worker might encourage a client's life review while being available to further explore persistent areas of conflict with a goal of *accepting one's life* as often joyful, sometimes troubled, but always of one's own making. Social workers might also conduct *reminiscence groups* in long-term care facilities. These groups serve many purposes from enjoyable recreation, promotion of socialization skills, to exploration of stressful past life events that may need further individual follow-up by the social worker (Ebersole, as cited in Beaver & Miller, 1992).

More broadly, social workers who care for the older dying person and their family members bring compassion, professional knowledge, understanding of death and dying, and perhaps most important of all, an acceptance of one's own mortality and openness to one's own struggles and fears about death (Scott, 1977). Social workers must remain attuned to the range of normal emotions that occur in the course of human dying. Should a client express anger toward her- or himself, family, or the social worker, the social worker needs to recognize the normality of this response and be able to continue to work with the older dying person as yet a living human being who continues to discover levels of meaning throughout the dying process (Scott, 1977).

Sadly, as Kalish has observed, there are those who find despair at life's end. He described older persons who experience a self-perceived social death. He stated: "The self-perceived socially dead individual has accepted the notion that he is 'as good as dead,' or that he is, for all practical purposes, dead, or that his role has ceased" (1968, p. 254). This experience is related to social isolation, anxiety about growing dependence on others, and/or the diagnosis of a terminal illness. Social workers can provide a much-needed intervention in such cases. For example, the social worker might work with an older client toward the goal of reduced social isolation by encouraging meaningful human relationships, whether it be reconnecting with estranged family members or seeking out other rewarding social relationships. Assisting one's client in the working through of past conflicts is also invaluable. So-called *social death* is the one death that is reversible (Kalish, 1968). On the other hand, when a sense of social death is precipitated by a diagnosis of a terminal illness, no finer use of gerontological social workers can be found than among those employed within the hospice movement, to be described next.

Hospice Care One response to the perceived inhumanity of the dying process has been the growth of the *hospice movement.* Hospice is a compassionate form of end-of-life care for persons with a terminal illness. It stresses palliative care, relief of chronic pain, and "the value of the meaningfulness of life . . . resulting in the prolonging of living rather than dying for many terminally ill persons" (Feifel, 1990, p. 540). Begun in the United States in 1974, hospice encourages a peaceful death free of pain (Quadagno, 2002). What is unique about hospice care is that it seeks to compassionately address the needs of both the dying person and the grieving family members, unlike the focus of most medical interventions. A study by Resse and Raymer (2004) found that social work practice in hospice lowered anxiety among patients, which, in turn, contributed to a reduction both in the number of crisis hospitalizations and hospice costs. It should be noted that although hospice is a place where social work practitioners can make a profound difference in the way in which an older person experiences death, the trend has been to elevate nursing services and underutilize social work services.

According to Havighurst (as cited in Robbins, Chatterjee, & Canda, 1998) a developmental task of late maturity is "adjusting to the death of a spouse" (1998, p. 208). Research appears to demonstrate that men and women respond differently to the death of a spouse. Germain and Bloom (1999) found that women cope well 2 years after the death of a spouse, whereas men are more likely to die. The grief response is thought to weaken the immune system, making men and women more susceptible to disease. In addition, men have traditionally been dependent on their wives for tasks of daily living such as meal preparation, arranging medical visits, and social connections (Germain & Bloom, 1999). Without the support of a spouse, male health appears to deteriorate rapidly, resulting in a high mortality rate in widowers.

Long-Term Care

Only about 5% of older adults reside in a long-term care facility at any given point in time. It would be misleading, however, not to follow up with a relevant and perhaps more troublesome figure: The likelihood of any individual 65 and over residing in a nursing home before death has been estimated to be as high as 40% (Moody, 2002). The message is that if we are privileged to live a long life, each of us has a substantial chance of spending some period of time, however brief, in a nursing home. In 2002, the U.S. government began collecting data from 3,500 nursing homes, including such measures as untreated bedsores, use of restraints, and incidences of pain. A recent report based on this data (U.S. Department of Health and Human Services, 2004) found that fewer residents were being held in restraints, and residents themselves reported fewer incidents of pain. This vital information on caregiving in nursing homes can now be accessed via the World Wide Web (www.medicare.gov). The purpose of continuous monitoring is to bring nursing homes into compliance and thereby improve treatment of residents.

Still, 20% of nursing homes failed to meet established criteria, indicating substandard care of our most vulnerable older adults. We can only conclude that although public pressure has resulted in improvements in long-term care facilities, most institutions have a long way to go to provide optimum care that respects the autonomy and dignity of the individual. It is, therefore, understandable that fear of nursing homes is prevalent, and most families go to great lengths to avoid this difficult decision. Nonetheless, contrary to widespread belief, even when it becomes necessary to place a frail elder in a nursing home, families do not abandon their older members, but rather, continue to care for them and maintain a high level of contact with their beloved family member.

In the early 1990s, the state of Ohio responded to the growing desire of older adults to be cared for in their own homes and the increasing costs associated with nursing home care. The state of Ohio addressed these issues by implementing a statewide program known as PASSPORT. It is administered by Area Agencies on

Aging (AAA) and provides a Medicaid waiver for the aged and disabled to be cared for in their own home. Applebaum, Mehdizadeh, and Straker (2004) conducted an 8-year longitudinal research study examining Ohio's long-term care use trends. Overall, results showed that more elders were being cared for at home rather than in long-term care facilities. A new trend observed in the Ohio data was that home care is prevalent even among the oldest-old cohort. This is a reversal of past trends and consistent with national trends (Applebaum, Mehdizadeh, & Straker, 2004).

A growing number of alternative housing arrangements are available for older adults, some of which are still in the planning stage. The following are examples of the range of public–private arrangements that should become common in the future: "naturally occurring retirement communities; leisure-oriented and continuing care retirement communities; board and care homes; adult day care and respite services; home sharing; assisted living and medical care in residential settings" (Moody, 2002, p. 18). One housing arrangement known as "continuing care retirement community" (CCRC) is growing in popularity. According to Sherwood, Ruchlin, Sherwood, and Morris: "CCRCs incorporate a continuum-of-care perspective" (1997, p. 2). This housing arrangement includes services to address deteriorating health of older adults and the need for long-term care. A positive feature of CCRCs is that they allow for "aging in place" (1997, p. 2). However, as social workers we should be concerned that high entrance fees and monthly payments limit accessibility to only the wealthiest of older adults.

Elder Abuse

A disturbing though not uncommon social issue among families and caregivers of older adults is that of elder abuse. In addition to physical and sexual violence perpetuated against older adults, elder abuse includes verbal threats and intimidation, financial mishandling of monies, and/or neglecting to meet the care needs of the older person (for example, not making wheelchairs and other equipment available, failure to administer medications properly, and/or failure to provide nutritional meals). Although there have been more reports of elder abuse in recent years, similar to the increase in reporting of domestic violence, there is no evidence that the rate of elder abuse is increasing. A higher rate of reporting reflects a greater awareness of elder abuse as a social problem, the enactment of the Federal Older Americans Act that authorizes each state to provide ombudsman programs to act on behalf of abused elders (Germain & Bloom, 1999), and less tolerance generally for any type of domestic violence.

Although it is estimated that only a small proportion of older adults (less than 2%) suffer abuse outside institutions, this is probably an underestimate. It is apparent that elder abuse often goes unreported due to complicated family dynamics, including the reluctance and embarrassment of parents to report abuse at the hands of their adult children. The major cause of elder abuse appears to be high stress among family caregivers and sometimes a prior pattern of family violence. According to Wetle and Fulmer:

> Dependency relationships in families change as one member becomes increasingly dependent on the family for care. The health professional may be unaware of longstanding patterns of interaction among family members. The stresses of family

> caregiving may exacerbate a relationship that has always been characterized by verbal and physical abuse. In some cases, changing dependency relationships may turn the tables, and the previously abused may become the abuser. (1995, p. 108)

Ethical dilemmas arise when the social worker strives to adhere to the principle of autonomy, as well as to the law's requirement of protection from harm. For example, Bergeron and Gray (2003) described ethical conflicts that may arise for social work facilitators of caregiver support groups. Caregivers themselves may be older and in poor health, trying to meet the demands of a frail family member. Ostensibly, the purpose of the support group is to relieve stress associated with caregiving. What happens, however, when the facilitator suspects abuse? He or she faces issues of confidentiality for group members and reporting requirements established by the enactment of the Federal Older Americans Act (Germain & Bloom, 1999). Bergeron and Gray suggested that social work group facilitators be thoroughly versed in their state's elder abuse laws. They also urge social workers to discuss with each group member behaviors deemed "exceptions to confidentiality" (2003, p. 102). Finally, although social workers should monitor caregiver stories, remaining alert to possible abuse situations, at the same time they should provide opportunities in private for group members to preserve their dignity when abuse is suspected (Bergeron & Gray, 2003).

It should be noted that reporting elder abuse (Bergeron & Gray, 2003) has been made difficult by the fact that state laws governing the report, investigation, and intervention on behalf of the abused victim vary widely. For example states vary in terms of mandated versus voluntary reporting of suspected elder abuse; states vary in terms of actions to be taken by a reporter, some requiring the victim's permission, others requiring the victim's permission *except* when the victim is incapacitated, and still others requiring no permission from the victim whatsoever.

Social workers in long-term care institutions offer mental health and direct-care services, as well as provide vital communication between residents and family members. Social work roles are varied, from the maintenance of safety standards and provision of proper clothing, to advocacy for higher-quality food and other necessities, counseling for anxious family members, and therapeutic intervention with depressed or otherwise distressed residents. Thus, the social worker may assume the broker, advocate, and counselor role within the nursing home setting.

It is well documented that nursing homes are the site of many cases of elder abuse. Elder abuse in nursing homes includes both verbal and physical assaults such as pinching, slapping, and using restraints to control patients (Foner, as cited in Quadagno, 2002). The underlying cause of abuse appears to be the structure of long-term care institutions that rely heavily on underpaid, low-skilled, and poorly trained aides. Furthermore, due to the need to care for groups of highly dependent persons, nursing homes implement numerous bureaucratic efficiencies (for example, all residents will be readied for meals at 8 a.m., noon, and 5 p.m. sharp; all residents will be seated in the day room; all residents will be bathed, dressed, and toileted at the appointed hour of 8 p.m., and other rigid routines), often at the expense of residents' need for thoughtful and compassionate care. In most cases, elder abuse perpetrated by nursing home aides is not intentionally cruel (Foner, as cited in Quadagno, 2002), but a result of a number of factors that contribute to increased workload stress: high patient-to-staff ratio, high turnover and high absenteeism among direct-care staff, and lack of background checks resulting in repeated hiring of persons with criminal histories of abuse.

Social workers provide valuable leadership and training for nursing home aides (certified nursing assistants) engaged in the difficult task of providing daily care for residents. Training may be in the form of educational modules reviewing basic human behavior, psychology, and the types of behaviors to expect from residents at various stages of Alzheimer's disease, for example. Social workers may teach behavioral interventions appropriate for older adults suffering from dementia and provide hands-on demonstrations on how to redirect behavior, or soothe agitated residents.

For example, a common condition among Alzheimer's residents is known as "sundowning," whereby a person becomes agitated and fearful of shadows cast at sunset. The social worker may assist the nursing home staff in establishing an appropriate environmental setting through well-designed furniture arrangements, décor, and homelike routines and offer therapeutic interventions to reduce the effects of sundowning. The social worker also helps to reduce abuse by providing support and encouragement to the front-line nursing home aides—workers so poorly rewarded in terms of remuneration or respect for such essential caretaking.

Another important way abuse can be prevented is through the implementation of an ombudsman program whereby ombudsmen facilitate complaints against the facility by residents and family members and monitor quality of care (Quadagno, 2002). We note that the National Association of Social Workers (NASW) has recently called for social workers to become more politically active (NASW, 2005c). Therefore, consistent with the goals of our national organization, we urge social workers to work with their legislators and advocate for aides in terms of better pay and benefits, the provision of continuing education, and higher staff-to-patient ratios in long-term care institutions. Perhaps then nursing home aides themselves would no longer have to live a bare-bones existence; in turn, we would hope to see a reduction in the anger sometimes misdirected toward the vulnerable nursing home resident.

Of course, the approaches mentioned to reduce elder abuse entail a substantial financial investment on the part of nursing home owners, boards of directors, and indirectly, taxpayers. At present, the public does not appear to place a high priority on financial support for nursing homes, as illustrated by recent cuts in Medicaid funding, the federal/state program that funds beds for poor nursing home residents. On July 1, 2005, for example, the governor of Massachusetts, Mitt Romney, signed a $23.8 billion state budget (Romney trims, signs budget, 2005) that eliminated $43 million in Medicaid money for nursing homes. The sad fact remains that many nursing homes are able to provide only minimal standards of care to the detriment of our frailest citizens.

Retirement

Within the next 15 years, nearly all baby boomers will exit the workforce to spend a period in retirement that, for some, will rival the number of years spent in the workplace (Moody, 2002). During President George Bush's administration, we saw a vigorous political debate on how to re-structure Social Security. The solvency and basic structure of the United States' most enduring old-age security system was at stake (TIAA-CREF, 2004). For 70 years Social Security has greatly reduced poverty among older adults and provided middle-class retirees a guaranteed, albeit small, source of financial support.

Currently, the Obama administration is battling a major recession, and for now, the contentious issue of Social Security smolders in the background. It is, however, helpful to recall the arguments on each side. One side proposed to restructure the Social Security program through privatization. This was envisioned as a voluntary program whereby individuals would divert a portion of their Social Security payroll tax into a privately owned account (for example, conservative stocks and treasury bonds). The thinking was that a private account in the stock market would result in a higher rate of return as compared to that which is provided by Social Security (TIAA-CREF, 2004). The opposing side sought incremental changes that would keep Social Security solvent without changing its basic structure. Some examples put forth were the amount of taxable income could be increased to include persons with incomes above the present cap of $90,000 to capture more dollars; the age at which full retirement benefits are provided could be raised; and/or benefits of wealthy seniors could be reduced in light of their otherwise strong financial position (TIAA-CREFF, 2004).

In terms of public approval of partial privatization of Social Security, a CNN/*USA Today*/Gallup poll of 1,010 adults conducted in February 2005 (CNN/*USA Today*/Gallup, 2005) found that 55% think that private accounts are a "bad idea." Interestingly, two thirds of those polled believe that wealthier Americans' benefits should be limited and workers with incomes above $90,000 should pay Social Security taxes on all their wages (CNN/*USA Today*/Gallup, 2005). The Social Security debate highlights profoundly different political ideologies, pitting neoconservatives who have never favored Roosevelt-era social programs, against liberals who view Social Security as a basic right. Before the Social Security Act became law in 1935, many older adults were impoverished, and frail older adults were at the mercy of their families and almshouses. The social work profession's Code of Ethics is consistent with the view that Social Security is a right, particularly for the frail old and other vulnerable citizens.

In a national Retirement Confidence Survey conducted in 2004, it was found that although most workers expected to have a comfortable retirement, only 58% had begun saving for retirement. Financial advisors (TIAA-CREF, 2004) urge baby boomers to save more for retirement, and not to count on Social Security to finance any more than one third of their retirement needs. Without adequate savings (TIAA-CREFF, 2004), many baby boomers will be compelled to continue working full or part time during their retirement years. Others, though financially secure, will choose to remain in the workforce as long as they are healthy. For many, retirement is seen as a time for reviving creative interests left behind in one's youth, developing new interests, and traveling. On a more problematic note, there exists a vision of retirement (fueled by media advertising) that conveys a carefree lifestyle, perfect health through medicine, and the idea that "the good life" is within reach of all. Advertisers fail to note that only the healthiest and wealthiest older adults have the means for such a rosy retirement scenario.

Retirement planning poses great challenges to older adults. First, they must acquire financial resources to support 20 to 30 years of retirement. Second, they must plan for the possibility of long-term care. Retirees are concerned about the quality of a potential nursing home placement, along with the difficult financial burden it might impose. A major misperception is that Medicare will pay for long-term care. The confusion lies in the fact that Medicare *will* provide up to 100 days of nursing home rehabilitation for an older adult discharged from an acute-care hospital. Medicare will not, however, provide long-term care for that older adult.

As social workers we should be concerned by the fact that most preretirement planning is done by large corporations reaching only the advantaged older worker (Moody, 2002):

> Programs typically reach only the more educated and well-off older people, for whom financial planning makes obvious sense. But poor people also need education about the benefits and entitlements for which they may be eligible, particularly if they are forced to retire early because of ill health. Minority group members report that preretirement planning is not relevant to their needs and concerns (Torres-Gil, 1984). Early retirement among minorities, instead of being a sign of wealth, is often a sign of disability. (Standford, Happersett, and Morton, 1991, p. 283)

Social workers could provide an invaluable service by offering clients and communities preretirement planning that includes long-term care. They could also provide a public service by spreading the word that if you are poor, Medicaid (see earlier discussion) will provide financial support for long-term care, and if you are among the middle class, financing long-term care is a personal responsibility. Notwithstanding its intended purpose, Medicaid is often used by middle-class adults to finance long-term care. This is a controversial use of a federal program intended for the poor citizens (Quinn, 2001).

In 1965 the Older Americans Act (OAA) established the Administration on Aging (AoA). The AoA, through 10 regional offices, has been responsible for the establishment of a complex network of programs and services nationwide for older adults (Carlton-LaNey, 1997). Another organization that advocates for older adults at the local level is the Area Agency on Aging (AAA), a community-level resource for programs and services.

PRACTICE EXAMPLE 15.1

Saving for Retirement: Advice from the Experts

The root of a secure retirement is financial resources. Financial advisors ask us to view Social Security as "one leg" of a three-tiered financial base required for financial security in retirement (Cutler, 1997). The other two legs are (a) Traditional pensions (known as "defined benefit plans," where an employee's pension is based on a salary/length of employment formula) or 401(k), 403(b) employer based retirement plans (known as "defined contribution plans," where an employee puts pretax monies into a fund and the employer often matches a certain percentage) and (b) other savings, for example: IRAs (Individual Retirement Accounts); CDs (Certificates of Deposit); MMAs (Money Market Accounts); and regular bank savings accounts. Two urgent messages from financial advisors (TIAA-CREF, 2004) are (a) save early and as much as you are able to take advantage of the "magic of compound interest" and (b) it is never too late to begin a savings program, even if one is near retirement.

The American Association of Retired Persons (AARP) is the largest and most politically active body working on behalf of older adults today. The AARP has a powerful lobby in Washington and is a testament to the older adults' vital interest in having a say on the issues of the day that affect their lives and the lives of their cohorts. Though one must be at least age 50 to join, the AARP is a good source of information for younger social workers interested in older adults. Mature social workers may also find this a personally rewarding organization in which to belong. The AARP, however, is not without controversy. For example, in 2004 the AARP supported the addition of a controversial Medicare D prescription drug program. Critics claim that behind AARP's support is their connection to pharmaceutical advertising dollars. Nonetheless, that AARP is a highly influential advocate for older adults is evidenced by the fact that AARP is on record as being opposed to the second Bush administration's initiative on private Social Security accounts, boding ill for the future of such accounts.

Finally, let us note that the social work profession has begun some major initiatives on aging, with perhaps the most comprehensive to date being the establishment of the John A. Hartford Foundation of New York. Founded in 1998, the John A. Hartford Foundation provides competitive grants for schools of social work and social work faculty to encourage commitment to the development of relevant gerontological curriculums at the baccalaureate and master's degree level, as well as to stimulate major research initiatives in aging—an encouraging sign, indeed.

Five Emerging Issues

HIV/AIDS

Demographics According the Centers for Disease Control and Protection (CDC, as cited in Emlet & Shippy, 2008), 20% of persons with HIV/AIDS are age 50 and above. This figure includes persons who were diagnosed early in their lives and "aged in" to the older demographic, along with persons who were diagnosed with HIV/AIDS as older adults. And although the overall infection rate of HIV/AIDS is decreasing, the rate among persons over 50 is increasing. The face of HIV/AIDS is also changing. How so? The fact is that although the majority of HIV/AIDS infections are in men, nearly 27% of HIV/AIDS infections in 2004 occurred in women. Furthermore, older women are at an increasing risk of contracting HIV/AIDS through heterosexual contact, and African-American and Hispanic men are contracting HIV/AIDS at a faster rate than Whites, primarily by means of intravenous drug use (Mack & Ory as cited in Emlet & Shippy, 2008).

HIV/AIDS and Age Status As a social work student of human behavior and the environment, and as we discuss HIV/AIDS and *age*, the term "double jeopardy" should come to mind—the fact that HIV/AIDS and *age* are both stigmatized in our society (Emlet as cited in Robinson, Petty, Patton, & Kang, 2008). And, indeed, studies show that older adults with HIV/AIDS are at a disadvantage within the health-care establishment where a majority of resources have been directed toward a younger population. Older HIV/AIDS adults, as compared to younger HIV/AIDS-infected adults, are diagnosed less often, are diagnosed later in the disease progression, are treated less often, and have poorer medical outcomes. In a study by Shippy and Karpiak (as cited in Robinson et al., 2008) older HIV/AIDS respondents reported difficulty accessing services on two levels. That is, when they attempted to seek help at an AIDS service organization, they felt that their age put them at a disadvantage. On the other hand, when seeking help from non-HIV services, they felt that their HIV status put them at a disadvantage. Furthermore, when we include the fact that there are a disproportionate number of older persons of color living with HIV/AIDS, it is clear how truly vulnerable this group is, requiring cultural, political, and clinical social work skills to address their unmet needs.

Notwithstanding the preceding discussion, because so little research has been done on older HIV/AIDS-infected adults, the possibility should be entertained that age, rather than a hindrance, might in fact confer some "special resilience" in those with the disease (Robinson, et al., 2008). For example, in a long-standing support group of gay HIV/AIDS-infected adults, group members who were diagnosed with HIV/AIDS later in life appeared to have stronger problem-solving skills and better coping skills (Robinson et al., 2008) as compared to members who were diagnosed early in their lives.

Older Adults Ignored Why have older adults been given much less attention in terms of HIV/AIDS? First, HIV/AIDS began in a young population, and for over two decades HIV/AIDS has been associated with the young, gay male population. Second, due to a narrow, stereotypic view of sex and what is age appropriate, few in the medical establishment have given much thought to HIV/AIDS among older adults, thus stymieing HIV/AIDS prevention for older adults. Finally, with the advent of *highly active antiretroviral therapies* (HAART), HIV/AIDS has become a chronic illness with the result that even more numbers of HIV/AIDS-infected adults are living longer and aging into an older demographic (CDC, 2003).

Social Support Research on quality of life for persons living with HIV/AIDS, similar to research on other chronic illnesses, indicates the importance of social support. For example, Heckman, Kochman, and Sikkema (as cited in Emlet & Shippy, 2008) found that the presence of social support was linked to feelings of validation and a reduction in risky sexual behavior. In a study of 307 adults, Lee and Rotheram-Borus (as cited in Emlet & Shippy, 2008) found that social support was associated with better coping skills and higher survival rates. Robinson et al. (2008) also found that in a qualitative study of a long-running HIV support group, the group provided "a sense of belonging, mutual support, like-mindedness, and the need for information" (p. 123).

Emlet (2006) conducted a cross-sectional study to compare the social networks of young HIV/AIDS adults to those of older HIV/AIDS adults. For both groups, family and friends were the largest source of support. For gay or lesbian adults, friends were the largest source of support, confirming other research showing that the "family of choice" is an important component of social networks among HIV/AIDS-infected adults in the gay community. Emlet also found that older males, as compared to younger males, more often lived alone, and older persons of color were the least likely to have strong social support. Too, HIV-infected older persons of color were often unaware of HIV services offered in the community, and as a consequence, they were found to have used HIV community services less often than their white counterparts. Finally, he found a negative correlation between social support and stigma, indicating that the greater the social support, the less the feeling of stigma (2008).

Social Work Interventions The conclusion to be drawn from the preceding studies is that persons with HIV/AIDS who are socially isolated are more at risk than persons who are embedded within a social network. Social support plays a key role in promoting healthy functioning among old and young adults alike. The implication for social workers is that by understanding the relationship between HIV/AIDS status and age, race, ethnicity, and gender—all factors that may increase the risk for older HIV/AIDS-infected clients—we can intervene to counteract social isolation. One place to begin is by administering a brief social support scale to detect whether or not a client is socially isolated. This opens the door for discussion about concerns the client may have about HIV/AIDS, and thereby normalizes the issue for one's client. Also, social workers should be familiar with the various services funded through the Older Americans Act and the Ryan White CARE Act (Emlet, 2008). Services available through the Ryan White CARE Act may be accessed through http://www.hab.hrsa.gov/programs.htm. Another practical resource to identify services in every community around the United States is *Eldercare Locator*. This is a national toll-free directory provided by the U.S. Administration on Aging and can be accessed through www.eldercare.gov.

In addition to direct service, community intervention is important. This may consist of providing HIV/AIDS information and material at senior centers as well as conducting prevention and educational programs that specifically address the needs and sensitivities of older adults. Essential topics to cover in an HIV/AIDS program for older adults include (a) dispelling myths concerning transmittal of HIV/AIDS, (b) use of condoms, and (c) who is at risk for HIV/AIDS (Emlet & Poindexter, 2004). Social workers should also use their advocacy skills on behalf of the older persons with HIV/AIDS. By informing themselves of antidiscrimination laws, social workers can promote the equitable treatment of older persons with HIV/AIDS (Levy-Dweck, 2005) and help ensure that social justice prevails.

Other HIV/AIDS Issues In a study of knowledge and attitudes on HIV/AIDS (sample of 160 community-residing older adults), Hillman (2007) found that although older women had a greater basic HIV/AIDS knowledge than older men, they: (a) failed to see that HIV/AIDS had any relevance to themselves, (b) did not understand the particular risk that HIV/AIDS posed to older women, and (c) reported social stigma toward persons with HIV/AIDS. Risks for older women include reduced efficaciousness of AIDS medicines, higher mortality rate, and a higher rate of contracting HIV/AIDS in a sexual encounter as compared to a younger woman (due to the greater likelihood of abrasions during intercourse providing an entry for HIV). Furthermore, although the women in the study understood that condom use prevents HIV/AIDS, this knowledge may not necessarily indicate a greater personal use of condoms. Why might this be so? One theory is that, among older men and women, the tradition of male dominance in the sexual arena remains prevalent. This, in turn, may result in a woman's feeling of powerlessness to influence her partner's decision to use a condom (Hillman, 2007).

Primary care physicians and other health-care professionals who treat older women are an important source of the dissemination of HIV/AIDS prevention and intervention information. In the course of patient care, they can provide opportunities for discussion of HIV/AIDS and, among other things, the importance of condom use (Hillman, 2007). Unfortunately, health-care professionals often perpetuate the very same stigmatization of persons with HIV/AIDS as is seen in the wider society. Thus, two important roles for the hospital social worker are (a) to provide health-care professionals with a supportive environment where honest and open discussion is encouraged around HIV/AIDS to overcome avoidance and/or stigmatization of older patients with HIV/AIDS, and (b) to encourage physicians and other health-care professionals to use evidence-based practice as defined by McNeece and Thyer (as cited in Emlet, 2008) as "the integration of the best research evidence with clinical expertise and client values in making practice decisions" (p. 144). Given the importance of "client values" within this definition, a health-care professional cannot provide the best possible treatment if there is any vestige of negativity associated with HIV/AIDS patients.

Addiction in Older Adults

Demographics Along with the aging of the population, there has been a concomitant increase in alcohol and illicit drug use among older adults. It is estimated that 30% of all cases of alcoholism occur among persons age 60 and over (Center for Substance Abuse Prevention [CSAP], as cited in Andrews, 2008). According to Hanson and Gutheil (2004), community prevalence rates for problem drinking among older adults vary from a low of 5% to a high of 15%. With the aging of the baby boomers (born between 1946 and 1964) it is anticipated that along with alcohol abuse, illicit drug use will increase dramatically. A study by Gfroerer, et al. predicts that between 1999 and 2020, 5 million persons aged 50 and over will need substance abuse treatment (as cited in Andrews, 2008). Older substance abusers are not a homogeneous group; rather, gender, race, and socioeconomic differences exist. For example, being male is associated with alcohol abuse. That is, men are more likely to drink heavily than women across all age groups. Too, it appears that whites are heavier consumers of alcohol than other racial groups, although African-American men between 50 and 59 have higher rates of heavy drinking as compared to similarly aged white males (Jackson, Williams, & Gomberg, as cited in Hanson and Gutheil, 2004).

Greater Sensitivity to Substances Interestingly, an older adult metabolizes alcohol as about as efficiently as a younger adult. The difference is that in an older adult, there is a diminished amount of body water with which to reduce blood alcohol concentration levels (BAC). Thus, an older adult may consume a much lower level of alcohol as compared to a young person, but end up with a similar blood alcohol concentration (National Institute on Alcohol Abuse and Alcoholism [NIAA], 1998). This means that it takes a much lower quantity of alcohol to produce a problematic response. As well, the older adult exhibits greater sensitivity to alcohol, over-the-counter drugs, and prescription medications, and there is evidence that older adults misuse psychoactive prescription medications such as hypnotics. This misuse has been associated with increase in illness and mortality (Blow, Oslin, & Barry, 2002).

The most common way health-care professionals diagnose problematic drinking or other substance abuse is through use of the *Diagnostic and Statistical Manual of Mental Disorders,* Fourth Edition (*DSM-IV*). In the case of older adult abusers, however, the criteria used in the *DSM-IV* are often not appropriate and must be modified for an older adult. To illustrate, how would the *DSM-IV* criteria specifying difficulty with occupational tasks apply to an older adult who has retired? On the other hand, financial competency or ability to engage in social activities is still appropriate (Blow, 1998).

Treatment Considerations A number of treatments have been found efficacious for addressing issues of substance abuse in older adults. The Center for Substance Abuse Treatment (CSAT, 1998) recommends three short-term approaches: (a) brief intervention to investigate a potential problem and motivate an individual to take constructive action, (b) intervention where family or friends gather around the client to verify the problematic nature of the person's substance behavior, and (c) motivational intervention to empower a patient to solve his/her own problems. For a somewhat longer-term approach (i.e., at least six sessions), a social worker might consider some form of brief therapy, including cognitive-behavioral therapy, group therapy, brief humanistic and existential therapies, brief psychodynamic therapy, and short-term family therapy (CSAT, 1999).

Alcohol Use among Frail Elders and Nursing Home Residents In a study on homebound frail elders in the community, 4% of the sample (*N* = 148) were found to be problem drinkers. Also troubling was the fact these frail elders averaged about five medications each and they were found to mix medications with alcohol (Emlet, Hawks, & Callahan, 2001). Health-care professionals often miss the correct diagnosis of alcoholism when an elder presents with conditions that mimic the effects of alcoholism (e.g., memory loss due to alcoholism can easily be mistaken for Alzheimer's disease). Social workers need to advocate for frail elders by informing and educating health-care providers of the particular needs of elders who abuse alcohol. Pharmacists should also be alerted to the issue so that they might be aware of any contraindications with a patient's prescription medication and his/her use of alcohol (Emlet, Hawks, & Callahan, 2001).

High levels of alcohol-related problems have been reported among institutionalized populations. For example, problem drinking, heavy drinking, and alcoholism have been reported among residents of veteran's hospitals (Joseph, Atkinson, & Ganzini as cited in Klein & Jess, 2002). Though few studies have been done on alcohol use in nursing homes, it has been estimated that as many as one half of nursing home residents have alcohol-related problems (Joseph as cited in Klein & Jess, 2002). Klein and Jess (2002) conducted a study of nursing homes and their policies and practices on use of alcohol by residents. They interviewed administrators of 111 intermediate-care facilities and found a variety of alcohol policies—from the "no alcohol allowed" policy to the daily ritual of the cocktail hour. Some institutions require a doctor's orders to consume alcohol; others merely have "standing orders." Some nursing homes allow alcohol consumption only on special occasions, some only when residents are off-campus. As in society at large, institutional alcohol policies are conflicted in their approach to the use of alcohol. That is, is alcohol a psychoactive drug in need of regulation? Or, is alcohol a social beverage meant to be enjoyed? In fact, alcohol is both. This explains some of the difficulty nursing home administrators have in maintaining consistent alcohol policies. Klein and Jess recommend that social work educators provide more curriculum on the role of alcohol and older adults in nursing home settings. As well, they suggest that schools of social work provide more field placements in nursing homes so that graduate-trained social workers can provide staff training in the benefits and detriments of alcohol and in the use of alcohol screening techniques (2002).

Increase in Use of Illicit Drugs Although alcohol is by far the most widely abused drug, cocaine and heroin are also abused by a small segment of older adults. It is thought that most older adults who use illicit drugs tend to have begun early in life and continued into old age. Illicit drug use is expected to increase with the aging of the baby boom generation, a generation that has been more open to the use of cocaine and other illicit substances than the current one (Andrews, 2008; Blow, Oslin & Barry, 2002). The numbers of persons in need of substance abuse treatment will go from 1.7 million in 2000 to 4.4 million by 2020 (Gfroerer, 2002). This increase in demand will mean that resources in the substance abuse treatment system must shift to accommodate the needs of aging baby boomers.

Another group in which illicit drug use is expected to increase is among older Latinos. By 2050, 17% of the U.S. older population will be Latino. In 2002–2003, The National Survey on Drug Use and Health (NSDUH) found that 1.55% of Latino adults age 50 and over reported illicit drug use (Substance Abuse and Mental Health Services Administration [SAMSHA], 2005). According to Andrews (2008), "the number of older adults with a substance abuse problem is expected to increase more quickly among Latinos than among any other ethnic group of older adults" (p. 91). Delgado (as cited in Andrews, 2008) noted that Latinos face many barriers to treatment, one of which is the stigma associated with seeking mental health services in the Latino community. Andrews (2008) conducted a qualitative study to assess older Latinos and their patterns of substance abuse. She used two groups of key informants, social work researchers in gerontology and substance abuse treatment providers. Andrews found that the majority of key informants felt that the older Latino population will experience an increase in substance abuse similar to what is expected among aging baby boomers. The challenge will be to provide age-specific and culturally competent treatment administered by bilingual and bicultural social workers with whom an older Latino can identify.

The Older Veteran

Posttraumatic Stress Disorder Older adults who have experienced war often face difficult challenges as they age. In World War II and the Korean conflict, soldiers who appeared mentally traumatized were said to have shell shock or battle fatigue. In the aftermath of both wars, many traumatized veterans did not receive psychiatric treatment for their condition, and some aging veterans experienced delayed-onset *posttraumatic stress disorder* (PTSD; Ruskin & Talbott as cited in Owens, Baker, Kasckow, Ciesla, & Mohamed, 2005). That is, persons who appeared to have functioned well in multiple aspects of their lives, may, in older adulthood, experience a resurgence of complicated feelings regarding their war experiences. In severe cases this takes the form of posttraumatic stress disorder (PTSD). According to Sherwood, Shimel, Stolz, and Sherwood (2003):

> In 1980, the term posttraumatic stress disorder or PTSD became the official designation to describe emotional and behavioral responses to psychological trauma. Major symptoms include: re-experiencing through intrusive recollections, flashbacks and nightmares, anxiety, depression, numbing of affect, cognitive and memory alterations, physical complaints, sleep disturbances and excessive irritability. Additionally hypervigilance and exaggerated startle response may be present. (p. 75)

Some researchers estimate that 1 million older veterans currently experience PTSD symptoms (Snell & Padin-Rivera, as cited in Owens et. Al., 2005), and although many veterans receive treatment within the Veterans Administration health-care system, the majority are treated by private physicians, hospitals, and nursing homes. Unfortunately, older veterans being treated in nonveteran settings are likely to be misdiagnosed with, for example, alcoholism or antisocial personality as the primary diagnosis rather than the correct diagnosis of PTSD. Why would this be the case? Because, in general, although the health-care record may note the veteran's military history, its significance in the client's life is ignored. Rather, it tends to serve as just one more bit of information for insurance purposes (Sherwood et al., 2003).

The gerontological social worker must approach the veteran with thorough knowledge of the normal aging process. This includes understanding that the losses concomitant with the aging process can trigger PTSD. Events such as retirement, illness, moving, or the loss of a spouse, may engender old feelings of sadness and mourning associated with death during combat. Furthermore, dramatic and highly publicized events such as September 11 terror attack on the World Trade Center and the February 2003 Columbia Shuttle Crash may also trigger symptoms of PTSD such as helplessness and anxiety (Sherwood et al., 2003). Ideally, as a social worker working with older adults, when you learn of a new client's military history, far from being merely a means to assess insurance coverage, this fact should serve as a starting point for asking sensitive, direct, and relevant questions that will allow you understand the relationship of your client's experience with war trauma and current presenting issues.

According to Dalenberg (as cited in Sherwood et al., 2003) listening to a veteran's painful and horrific stories can be very difficult for the clinician. There is an understandable tendency for the clinician to avoid discussions that have the potential to arouse strong emotions. This is the time when peer and supervisor support is essential as a way for the social worker to process his or her own countertransference issues and remain open to the older veteran. In addition to individual therapy, other interventions for older veterans who experience trauma-related symptoms include case management, group therapy, couple or family therapy, psychoeducation, psychopharmacology, and concrete services (Allen and Bloom, as cited in Sherwood et al., 2003).

Programs Serving Older Veterans Several types of organizations serve the health-care needs of older veterans. In terms of preventive health care, Keyhani et al. (2007) were interested in examining which organizational structures best address the preventive health-care needs of veterans. In their study, they defined prevention as a male veteran receiving: (a) an influenza vaccination, (b) a pneumonia vaccination, (c) cholesterol screening, and (d) prostate screening. The researchers then compared three types of organizations: the Veterans Health Administration (VHA), Medicare HMO (managed health-care organization), and Medicare FFS (fee-for-service) in terms of the four preventive measures listed earlier. They found that the VHA provided significantly more preventive services as compared to either Medicare HMO or Medicare FFS. The authors noted that since 1995, the VHA has upgraded its system with electronic records, incorporated performance measures, and emphasized service integration (Keyhani et al., 2007). Still, although this study sheds a positive light on the Veterans Administration, when we recall the widely reported decrepit conditions of the Walter Reed Army Medical Center in Washington, D.C. (Swift action promised at Walter Reed, 2007), it is clear that there is much room for improvement in the way we treat our veterans. As social workers, we must advocate for the comprehensive, physical, and mental health treatment of all veterans, young and old alike.

Another veterans' issue is long-term care housing. *Assisted living* (a form of group housing offering help with activities of daily living) has become a popular form of housing for older adults. In terms of programmatic approaches to housing, *assisted-living facilities* have the potential to be cost effective as well as provide autonomy for the resident (Kane, as cited in Hedrick et al., 2007). In the past, because Medicaid (the government health-care insurance program for the poor) did not cover *assisted-living facilities,* such facilities were affordable only to high-income persons. Now, although most states provide Medicaid funding for assisted living, the number of *assisted-living facilities* for low-income persons remains quite small.

Between 2002 and 2004, the U.S. Department of Veterans Affairs authorized a pilot study to determine the feasibility of funding veterans in community assisted-living facilities (Hedrick et al., 2007). The study was known as Assisted Living Pilot Program, or *ALPP,* and enrolled 743 veterans whose demographics included: average age (70 years), gender (male), race (Caucasian), and marital status (single). The veterans were placed in one of three types of facilities: *adult family home* (a private family dwelling consisting of six or fewer residents), *adult residential care* (a community-care facility consisting of seven or more residents), or an *assisted-living facility* (a community-care facility consisting of individual apartments with services purchased based on need). The researchers found that by including different types of housing arrangements, they were able to match a veteran's level of need to an appropriate community-based facility. For example, the *adult family home* admitted more impaired veterans, whereas *adult residential care* and *assisted-living facilities* admitted generally higher-functioning veterans (e.g., the latter facilities were less likely to admit veterans with behavioral problems such as aggression or wandering or health-care needs such as tube feeding). The conclusion of the study was that with support from the Veterans Administration, a broader range of community-based living arrangements could be made accessible to low-income veterans, thereby improving their quality of life (Hedrick et. al., 2007).

The veteran population over the age of 85 is exploding (now over 1 million), and thus, long-term care is a particularly pressing issue (Shay & Burris, 2008). In light of this growing need, the Department of Veterans Affairs (VA) and its Office of Geriatrics and Extended Care (GEC) held a conference in March 2008 in McLean, Virginia, to bring together experts in geriatric health and long-term care. The purpose of this conference was to strategize a more flexible, coordinated approach to long-term care of veterans. A number of models of care that show promise were discussed, one of which addressed support for family caregivers. This is an important issue because it is estimated that there are 34 million family caregivers in the United States responsible for caring for persons over age 50 (Stone, 2008). Furthermore, it is well established that caregiving exacerbates stress and increases the likelihood of serious health problems in the caregiver. Among other programs to address caregiver burden (Shay & Burris, 2008), the VA has instituted *caregiver assistance pilot programs* at eight VA sites. The focus of these pilot programs is on education, skill-building, 24-hour respite, and the use of technology.

Other Veteran Issues Older veterans face a range of issues; most are common to older adults, but with the added component of having seen combat. A study by Rosenheck and Koegel (1993) sought to understand whether homeless veterans differed in some way from homeless nonveterans. The researchers conducted a secondary analysis of three surveys of male homeless veterans (there are so few older women veterans who saw combat that most studies do not include women, as more women see combat we expect that future research will include older women veterans). The researchers found that other than demographic differences (i.e., older veterans were more likely to be white, married at some point, and better educated), all other characteristics of homeless veterans were similar to those of nonveterans. Thus, homeless veterans could not be differentiated from homeless nonveterans in terms of employment history, housing stability, criminal history, physical health, and/or mental health. The authors suggest that the many beneficial programs established by the Veterans Administration for homeless veterans, such as outreach, housing support, and benefit enrollment, would also be of value to the homeless nonveteran (Rosenheck & Koegel, 1993).

Earlier in the chapter we discussed the complicated and difficult issue of elder abuse. Abuse, unfortunately, is also a problem among older veterans. It is important to understand both the characteristics of both victim and perpetrator. According to Kosberg (as cited in Moon, Lawson Carpiac, & Spaziano, 2006) most victims are older white women, often with history of intergenerational conflict, problem drinking, and isolation. The majority of perpetrators are family members, either a spouse or an adult child. The perpetrators share similar characteristics such as substance abuse, financial dependency, history of childhood abuse, and a lack of understanding and sympathy for the elder victim. There is also a growing body of *caregiver burden* literature that demonstrates the vulnerability of caregivers, particularly when dealing with dementia of a family member.

So how do these characteristics compare to older veterans who are abused? (again, because older combat veterans are nearly all men, the research is limited to males). Moon et al. (2006) conducted a secondary analysis of medical records and social work referrals of 575 veterans who received services from Veteran Affairs Geriatric Outpatient Clinic in Los Angeles. They found that 5.4% were abused as reported by Adult Protective Services. This abuse, as also evident in the general population, was perpetrated by family members. The most commonly reported type of abuse was financial abuse and neglect (including self-neglect). The two most common dispositions were to remove the elderly victim from his domicile to a nursing home and to establish conservatorship. If the victim had dementia, both interventions were likely—a nursing home placement along with conservatorship. During their study of veteran elder abuse, the researchers noted two significant problems in terms of service coordination for veterans. That is, 35% (N = 11) of the abused veterans did not receive any follow-up treatment after having been reported by Adult Protective Services. Also troubling was the fact that no counseling was offered to the family member(s) who perpetrated the abuse. There is a growing consensus that if elder abuse is to be stopped, both the victim and the abuser must be treated (Brownell, Berman, & Salamone, in Moon et al., 2006.)

Ethnicity and Social Work Practice with the Older Adult

Earlier in the chapter we discussed ethnicity in terms of poverty and health status in the United States. Now we will consider ethnicity in terms of how the social work practitioner might best address the needs of older African Americans and Hispanics. Currently, African Americans are the largest older minority population, composing 8% of ethnic minority elders. African Americans 65 and over are expected to grow by 150% by the year 2030 as compared to the non-Latino white population, which is expected to grow by 91% (Burnette & Kang, 2003). Earlier in the chapter we referred to "accumulative deficits," that is, due to years of past discrimination, low socioeconomic status, low educational levels, and limited access to good health care, great numbers of African Americans find themselves facing older age with serious chronic illness and far fewer resources as compared to their white age-mates.

Let us look at what social work has to contribute by way of meeting the needs of older African Americans. Foremost, the knowledge of institutional racism and discrimination that social workers acquire in their policy and other graduate courses provide the basis for understanding and sensitivity to the great reluctance and mistrust many African Americans have with respect to the medical establishment. This mistrust is based on a sad reality. For example, studies show

> Structural factors such as institutional racism may affect the quality of health care services offered to older Black women. For example, older Black women with chronic conditions may receive poorer health care than older White

> women, even when medical services are being delivered to patients covered by government insurance and critical demographic variables are controlled. (Gornick et al.; Schneider, Zaslavsky, & Epstein as cited in Chadiha & Adams, 2003, p. 155)

Thus, social workers working with African-American elders must find ways to lessen the perceived threat. This may be accomplished by encouraging open discussion of concerns the client might have, including any negative incidents experienced in the course of past medical intervention. Second, the social worker can offer to accompany the older African-American adult to his/her initial office visit and determine for themselves that the client's physician is a culturally competent geriatrician. This would go a long way toward reassuring the elder, as well as assuring that the African-American client is accorded all due respect and receives medical treatment according to "best practices."

Another important issue in culturally competent work with older African Americans is that of self-health care. Among African Americans, self-health care is widely employed when deciding how to treat symptoms of chronic illness. Self-health care refers to "the participative roles that laypersons play in shaping the processes and outcomes of professional care—roles that extend to self-management of chronic health conditions" (Ory, DeFriese, & Duncker as cited in Burnett & Kang, 2003, p. 124). Although self-care has been associated with folk medicine, traditional, and lay interventions, studies show that most self-care is effective (Eisenberg et al., as cited in Burnett & Kang, 2003). Burnette conducted a self-care study by examining the daily health diaries of 144, nonrandomly selected, older African Americans, each with at least one chronic illness, and recruited from three senior centers. Results showed that even when older African-American participants experienced serious symptoms (e.g., chest pain, diarrhea, and swelling) most turned first to lay or informal self-care solutions rather than to the medical establishment (as cited in Burnette & Kang, 2003).

Thus, social workers practicing culturally competent social work would be well advised to understand this important aspect of the African-American approach to health care. This approach is highly compatible with the *NASW Code of Ethics.* How so? As the social worker provides supportive self-care strategies to help an older person manage his/her chronic illness, he/she is cultivating the ultimate purpose of self-care—the continued autonomy and empowerment of the older adult.

Now let us turn to the second largest minority group of older adults, namely, Hispanics. According to Min (2005), "the number of older people of any Hispanic origin will increase from 5.0% in 2000 to 27.8% of the total older population in 2050" (p. 348). Throughout their lives, many older Hispanics faced the same barriers as African Americans—discrimination, low socioeconomic status, low educational levels, low employment across a lifetime, and restricted access to health care. This has resulted in fewer resources late in life and poorer health as compared to their white age-mates. Cultural practices are also an important consideration for Hispanic elders. Following is an example in the preventive health-care field to illustrate the role of culture.

In 2001, Maramaldi conducted a study of breast cancer follow-up appointments among low-income older white and Latina women (as cited in Maramaldi & Guevara, 2003). He found that although Latina women expressed more trust in their doctors than did older white women, Latina women were less likely to return for a follow-up appointment regarding a possible malignancy. Why would this be the case, especially after the Latina women in the study had expressed such trust in their doctor? Maramaldi provided two interpretations. The first is that although Latina women may indeed have trusted their doctor on the initial visit, as time went by, and there was less contact with the medical establishment, the salience of culture-based beliefs may have taken hold. Specifically, a more fatalistic outlook that includes the belief that life events happen outside ones' self—that events are in the hands of God (Chavez and Hubbell as cited in Maramaldi & Guevara, 2003)—may have taken precedence over the doctor–patient relationship. The thinking among the Latina women might have been: Why does it matter if I return for a doctor's appointment, as whatever is to happen is not under my control? Another interpretation according to Marin and Gamba (as cited in Maramaldi & Guevara, 2003) is that Latinos' prefer to avoid confrontation, and the Latina women in the breast cancer study may have given an acquiescent response, but behaviorally, that did not indicate that the Latina women would return for their follow-up visit.

It is evident that social work with Hispanic elders entails not only gerontological knowledge, but use of a cultural lens through which the social worker might find the best way with which to engage an older Hispanic adult. Schools of social work have an important role to play. Schools can ensure that the needs of older Hispanic Americans are met by encouraging the development of bilingual/bicultural social workers committed to gerontology.

To conclude, we will discuss an older adult population about which relatively little has been written—older Chinese adults. Today, as older Chinese immigrants come to the shores of America, they face daunting language and acculturation challenges, as did the Chinese Americans who immigrated many decades before. We know from the literature that there is an alarming incidence of suicide among older adults in China (Chou & Chi, 2005; Yip, Chi, Chiu, Wai, Conwell, & Caine, 2003), and that older Chinese Americans have a higher suicide rate than older whites (Liu & Yu, as cited in Dai, et al, 1999). According to Desjarlais, Eisenberg, Good and Kleinman (as cited in Dai et al., 1999), the prevalence of suicide is particularly high among older Chinese women. Despite its public health significance, attempted suicide among late-life Chinese is said to be underresearched (Tsoh et al., 2005). Roy, Cooper, and Lesser (2008) conducted a pilot study on depression and help-seeking behavior among Chinese elders in Boston and Guangzhou (a city in southern mainland China). The excerpts in Practice Example15.2 describe the pilot study findings. These findings have been incorporated into a larger funding request to the Hartford Foundation to explore in depth the phenomenon of depression in older Chinese adults.

PRACTICE EXAMPLE 15.2

Chinese Elders, Depression, and Help-Seeking: A Pilot Study

The sample consisted of 100 older Chinese adults, 50 from Boston and 50 from Guangzhou, China. Because we used a convenience sample of elders selected from senior centers, the findings are not generalizable to older Chinese adults in Boston or Guangzhou. Data were collected using questionnaires and focus groups, constituting a "mixed methods design" approach to research. Comparing demographic variables from the Guangzhou and Boston sample we find the following: (Note: Percentages have been rounded to the nearest whole percent.) The Guangzhou group had more men (36% vs. 30%), were older (mean age 78 vs. 76), and reported more years of higher education (29% vs. 24%). In terms of health status, elders in Guangzhou reported poorer health: that is, 35% ($N = 18$) reported "poor" to "very poor" health as compared to 14% ($N = 7$) of Boston elders who reported poor health. Again, it should be noted, that the majority of elders in both Guangzhou and Boston reported "good" to "excellent" health with 65% ($N = 33$) of Guangzhou elders reporting "good" to " excellent" health and 86% ($N = 43$) of Boston elders reporting "good" to "excellent" health.

Our main quantitative question was: How do levels of depression compare between Chinese elders in the Boston and Chinese elders in Guangzhou, China? We found that Guangzhou elders were more depressed (using Geriatric Depression Scale cutoff score of 11 or greater) as compared to Boston elders. That is, we found that in the Guangzhou group, 29% ($n = 16$) were depressed as evidenced by their score on the GDS, as compared to 9% ($n = 5$) in the Boston group. A Fisher's Exact Test (used in place of a Chi Square when the expected cell size is small, 2-tail $p = .025$) revealed that there was a statistically significant difference ($p \leq .05$) in depression between the two samples, indicating that the differences in depression between Boston and Guangzhou were likely not due to chance (Roy, Cooper, & Lesser, 2008).

In addition to the administration of the GDS, we used a semistructured interview guide to obtain qualitative data from the same groups of elders described earlier. The semistructured interview guide was administered by our Chinese-Canadian Research Associate. Permission was obtained to audiotape the group-based interviews. Examples of the questions included in the semistructured interview guide were as follows: (a) How do you know when you are feeling sad? (b) How do you show it? (c) If a man is depressed, what would he show? and (d) If a woman is depressed, what would she show? All focus group meetings were recorded on cassette tapes and translated and transcribed after our return. We applied the grounded theory approach to the data analysis as described by Strauss and Corbin (1990). The primary technique used was open coding, which involved constant comparisons to conceptualize. The coded data were then categorized into the resulting themes. The following are an example of themes identified: (a) recognizing and expressing unhappiness, (b) trouble expressing negative feelings, and (c) gender difference in expression of unhappiness. We found both differences and commonalities in meaning between the Chinese in Boston and the Chinese in mainland China. Descriptions of negative feelings and behaviors seemed more intense and hostile among the mainland Chinese elders. They more frequently used words such as *scold, fight, humiliate,* and *conflict* than their Boston counterparts. Those living in Boston had more familiarity with mental health services and acknowledged the value of mental health practitioners. Those in China had less exposure and were more skeptical. They spoke of "not having the habit" (Roy, Cooper, & Lesser, 2008, p. 82) of seeking counseling and raised issues of cost concerns and the quality of the help provided. Both groups had limited appreciation of the role of the social worker, although those in Boston did view their helpfulness in delivering concrete services.

Older Gays and Lesbians and the Issue of Late-Life Caregiving

The topics addressed earlier in the chapter on HIV/AIDS are critical to the older gay and lesbian community. Why is this so? Because, notwithstanding the fact that new incidents of HIV/AIDS are occurring at a higher rate among intravenous drug users and their partners, the gay community still has the highest HIV/AIDS prevalence rates. Thus, as the gay community ages, many of the lingering issues of managing a deadly chronic illness remain as new health and caregiver issues emerge. Lesbians stood with their gay brothers early on in the fight for gay/lesbian rights. They became caregivers of those who suffered and died of the terrible scourge that was HIV/AIDS illness during the 1980s and early1990s (Grossman, D'Augelli, & Dragowski, 2007). Perhaps no other issue is as important to all older adults, heterosexual or homosexual, as the answer to the question: Who will care for me when I can no longer care for myself?

This concern is even more pressing to members of the gay and lesbian community, who may have moved away from family and relatives earlier in their lives to become a part of a more accepting community of gay, lesbian, and bisexual and transgender adults (the GLBT community). Traditionally, it is the family who provides the majority of care to older ill or frail adults. To whom does the GLBT community turn when they are in need of caregiving? The answer lies in the network of nonbiologically related friends developed in response to society's homophobia and discriminatory practices. This is sometimes referred to as a "family of choice" (Beeler, Rawls, Herdt, & Cohler, as cited in Grossman, D'Augelli, & Dragowski, 2007). Although same-sex marriage is now legal in Connecticut, Iowa, Massachusetts, and Vermont, and society's views on homosexuality have moderated somewhat, the current cohort of older adults lived during a time of great intolerance and hostility toward homosexual persons.

It is understandable, therefore, that many older GLBT members fear and mistrust traditional institutions. For example, Quam and Whitford's study (as cited in Johnson, Jackson, Arnette, & Koffman, 2005) found that gay men felt that being homosexual made aging more difficult, including such things as relationship formation, loneliness and fear of being discriminated in health care, housing, and long-term care. On the other hand, some writers suggest that being gay or lesbian is a benefit in terms of the aging process. According to Lucco, being gay provides older adults with the following benefits: "acceptance from a larger community; more awareness of planning for the future such as finances; and stress of being in a minority classification enhanced the psychological and spiritual dimensions of life" (as cited in McFarland and Sanders, 2003, p. 70). A small study by McFarland and Sanders (N = 59) showed that the two main concerns among GLBT elders were lack of a caregiver were they to need assistance with physical or mental health later in life and a lack of financial resources to assist them as they age. In this same study, respondents overwhelmingly reported that they would not consider using nursing homes or long-term care. When asked about the barriers to service they expected to encounter as they grew older, the following were reported: (a) discrimination in the health-care system, (b) a lack of understanding from service providers, and (c) the limited legal rights of their partner.

So back to the question of who will care for the older gay/lesbian adults? Most likely, it will be a member of the gay/lesbian community. An alternative solution is to encourage the development of service providers with enlightened and socially just ideas about the delivery of services. As Lucco reported in his study, the majority of gays and lesbians were interested in a planned retirement housing facility that specifically addressed the needs of gays and lesbians (as cited in McFarland & Sanders, 2003). The following is a good example of this new approach to services. SAGE Metro St. Louis (CSWE news Briefs, 2009) is a newly developed outreach organization for the purpose of educating the community about the needs of older GLBT adults. The organization's short-term goals are to: (a) provide a social network for GLBT seniors, (b) create a referral system of mainstream agencies that are open to the GLBT community, and (c) conduct individual needs assessments. SAGE Metro St. Louis is also training staff who work for community agencies serving older adults so that they can be alert to the special needs of the GLBT community, an often hidden community in St. Louis.

Social workers can play an important role in educating the community. For one, they can advocate at the legislative level for antidiscrimination laws to be applied to all caregiving institutions. Second, social workers can provide community education and training that addresses the needs of gay/lesbian older adults by encouraging community service providers to promote "gay friendly" environments. Such environments are absolutely essential to serve the needs of many older gay/lesbian adults who have not disclosed their sexual orientation and exist uneasily beneath the radar. One particularly relevant issue is to value and recognize the importance of a person's gay or lesbian life partner. Therefore, it is important that the social worker be sensitive to the barriers that the partner faces such as ineligibility for health insurance and lack of hospital visitation rights. It also includes being aware of the often problematic relationship that exists between older gays/lesbians and their children and/or parents, who may or may not know of their family member's orientation (McFarland & Sanders, 2003).

Summary

This chapter sought to illuminate important issues in the lives of older adults and those who love and care for them. We have tried, as well, to show its relevance and applicability to the social work profession. As there is still much to discover about the biopsychosocial mechanisms of "why we grow old," gerontological social work can be expected to grow in the forthcoming decades. Social work with older adults enhances the vitality of all communities, but it is especially needed in our underserved regions. The challenge for social work is to understand the totality of the aging experience through sensitive cultural lenses and to enrich the aging experience for our most vulnerable aged—the poor and frail. We believe that living "the good life" should be available to all Americans, not reserved for the wealthiest few.

16 Trauma and Development

Introduction

Freud wrote, "The essence of a traumatic situation is an experience of helplessness on the part of the ego, in the face of an accumulation of excitation, whether of external or internal origin" (1926, p. 81). There are two components to a traumatic experience, the objective and the subjective. It is the subjective experience of the objective events that determines whether an event is traumatic (Allen, 1995, p. 14). Allen (2001, p. 10) conceptualizes *trauma* as a *chronic physical illness* that requires not only treatment but also ongoing self-care. We agree with those authors, who describe trauma within the framework of developmental psychopathology—a concern with the origins and course of individual pathways to adaptation and maladaptation—because "at any age, trauma affects developmental pathways" (Cicchetti, 1984; Wapner, 1995). We therefore feel that it is important to include a chapter on this specialized topic for our readers.

Types of Trauma

Traumas may take the form of an unusual event or a serious of continuous events that subject people to extreme, intensively overwhelming, perceived, or experienced threats to oneself or others. Traumas are classified in a number of ways. They can involve events that are short term and unexpected. These experiences are generally recalled in detail and often leave the individual with complex memories of the event(s). Traumas can include either a *series of traumatic events* or exposure to a *prolonged traumatic event*. Memories of these experiences are frequently unclear because of dissociation (to be discussed in a later section of this chapter). Trauma may involve *directly experienced* and/or *vicariously experienced* events. Finally, traumas may be *accidental*, such as airplane and car crashes; *natural disasters*, including catastrophes such as floods or earthquakes; and those *deliberately caused by humans*. This last group includes acts of violence, child abuse, combat, and ritual or cult abuse that usually cause greater victimization, often cause feelings of shame, guilt, and worthlessness, and may lead to longstanding interpersonal and characterological problems (Meichenbaum, 1994). Allen writes that attachment trauma in childhood (see later section on this topic) is particularly problematic because it "not only generates extreme distress but also, more importantly, undermines the development of mental and interpersonal capacities needed to regulate that distress" (2001, p. 10).

Acute Stress Disorder

A condition referred to as *acute stress disorder* can occur if a person has been exposed to a traumatic event in which both of the following were present: The person experienced, witnessed, or was confronted with an event or events that involved actual or threatened death or serious injury or a threat to the physical integrity of self or others; and the person's response involved intense fear, helplessness, or horror. Acute distress disorder is diagnosed when the disturbance lasts for a minimum of 2 days and a maximum of 4 weeks and occurs within 4 weeks of the traumatic event (American Psychiatric Association, 2000).

Posttraumatic Stress Disorder

Posttraumatic stress disorder (PTSD) is a more serious condition and is diagnosed when the duration of the disturbance (same as the symptoms identified in acute stress disorder) is more than 1 month. PTSD is *acute* if the duration of the symptoms is less than 3 months and *chronic* if the duration of the symptoms is 3 months or more. See the *Diagnostic and Statistical Manual of Mental Disorders* (*DSM-IV;* American Psychiatric Association, 2000) for the complete criteria for both acute stress disorder and PTSD. Traumatic events can cause long-term changes in affect, behavior, physiological functioning, and mental health for some, but not necessarily to all who are exposed to them (Allen, 2001).

Assessment of Trauma

The following mediating factors are important in assessing an individual's reaction to a traumatic event: the characteristics of the trauma; the characteristics of the individual's reactions to the trauma (for example, evidence of dissociative responses); pretrauma factors (whether there was prior victimization or multiple traumas); recovery factors (successful coping; family and social supports; Allen, 2001; Meichenbaum, 1994; Webb, 1999). Table 16.1 illustrates a tripartite assessment model developed to guide the clinician in assessing trauma in children (Webb, 1999). We feel this model can be adapted to the assessment of individuals across the changing context of human development. It is important to appreciate also that the resolution of trauma may never be entirely complete. Trauma may be reawakened at each new stage of the life cycle, where it will continue to be reconstructed, bringing new aspects of the individual's experience to light (Herman, 1992).

Neurobiology of Trauma

PTSD is associated with a range of neurobiological and physiological changes. Terror alters the chemical functioning within the brain. This altered chemical functioning creates a heightened sensitivity to triggers that in turn create nonadrenaline surges. These surges create hyperactive arousal states that stimulate the survival response. The survival response systems include the following: *limbic system* (memory, learning, and emotion); *endocrine system* (metabolism and blood pressure); *autonomic nervous system* (gastrointestinal); and *immune system*

TABLE 16.1

Tripartite Model for Assessment of Trauma

The Nature of the Crisis Situation

a. Psychosocial and environmental problems
b. Anticipated versus sudden crisis
c. Single event (Type 1 trauma) versus recurring (Type 2 trauma)
d. Natural disaster, accidental disaster, deliberately caused disaster
e. Solitary versus shared experience
f. Proximity to the crisis
g. Presence of loss factors
    1. Separation from family members
    2. Death of family members
    3. Loss of familiar environment
    4. Loss of familiar role/status
    5. Loss of body part or function
h. Presence of violence
    1. Witnessed and/or experienced
    2. Element of stigma
i. Presence of life threat (to self/family/others)

Individual Factors

a. Age
    1. Developmental level
    2. Cognitive level
    3. Moral level
    4. Temperamental characteristics
b. Precrisis Adjustment
    1. Home
    2. School
    3. Interpersonal
    4. Medical
c. Coping style/ego development/resilience
d. Past experience with crisis
e. Global assessment of functioning (DSM Axis 5)
f. Specific meaning of crisis even

Factors in the support system

a. nuclear family
b. extended family
c. school
d. friends/community
e. culture/religion

Source: N. B. Webb, 1999, *Play Therapy with Children in Crisis: Individual, Group, and Family Treatment* (2nd ed.), (pp. 4–5). New York: Guilford Press. Reprinted with permission.

(thymus, spleen, lymph nodes, skin, etc.; Brohl, 1996, pp. 44–45). Neurocognitive problems in adults resulting from PTSD include disturbances in memory (see section on traumatic memories) learning, attention, and concentration. Several authors have identified PTSD as causing neurocognitive developmental delays in children (Cicchetti, 1984; Terr, 1988;Van der Hart, 1989). These include delays in preoperational and operational thinking, selective encoding of memories, verbal restrictions, visual and auditory perceptual distortions, visual hallucinations, lags in motor development, knowledge of self and others, the capacity to self-correct, and increased occurrence of ADD in abused children.

Trauma as a Chronic Illness and a Developmental Disorder

Trauma is also a risk factor for becoming a person with disabilities. Complex trauma of childhood in which an individual experiences physical, sexual, and emotional abuse and/or neglect over an extended period of time has been associated with an excess rate of a number of physical, potentially disabling chronic illnesses in adulthood, including fibromyalgia, autoimmune disorders, chronic pelvic and gastrointestinal problems, irritable bowel syndrome, and cardiovascular illness. These individuals are also at risk for substance abuse, cigarette smoking, disordered eating, and avoidance of physical activity (Brown, 2008, pp. 187–188). Adults with PTSD often meet the criteria for co-morbid psychiatric disorders such as major depression, substance dependence, and anxiety disorders. These conditions all put the person with a history of trauma at financial risk, as many live on disability payments. See Practice Example 16.1: Ruth.

PRACTICE EXAMPLE 16.1

Ruth

Ruth is a 41-year-old woman, married, who has a history of incest that began when her father sexually abused her at age 2 and continued until she was a young adolescent. She also suffered physical and emotional abuse from her father. Her mother, who Ruth felt knew what was happening but was too ashamed or afraid to intervene, turned away from her daughter. Her parents divorced during her adolescent years. Ruth grew up believing that she was responsible for the abuse, for her parent's divorce, and ultimately for their unhappiness. Ruth had a difficult adolescent and young adult trajectory, becoming involved with substance use (including alcohol, cocaine, and heroin). She also developed fibromyalgia, which, combined with her major depression and PTSD, disabled her from working for a period of 8 years when she was on disability. Ruth found her way to counseling and was able to slowly begin the process of recovery from her childhood abuse, recognizing that she was not to blame for what occurred. Nonetheless, life is challenging for Ruth. She was able to find employment after completing an associate's degree at a community college and is now trying to form friendships. She hopes one day to have a relationship with a man she can trust and who will understand her journey.

Traumatic Memories

Memories of traumatic experiences are different from memories of ordinary life events or situations. Extreme emotional arousal may interfere with *hippocampal memory functions,* thus encoding traumatic memories differently in the brain than ordinary memories. *Glutamate* is the main *excitatory neurotransmitter* in the brain. Dopamine, serotonin, norepinephrine, and GABA are the inhibitory neurotransmitters in the brain. Organized perception requires a balance between the two. Trauma creates high levels of glutamate that results both in impaired perception at the time of trauma as well as an altered coding of memory. During conditions of high arousal *explicit memory (autobiographical memories explicit to the self)* may fail, and the person may be left in a state of *speechless terror* when words fail to describe what occurred. There may, however, be no interference with *implicit memory* (when people are influenced by past experience without any awareness that they are remembering; Schacter, 1996, p. 161). This results in a condition called *alexithymia* in which the person may experience an emotional reaction but be unable to articulate the reason for acting as she does (Van der Kolk, 1994). It is this "phobia of memory" (Janet, 1919/1925, p. 661) that splits off traumatic memories from ordinary consciousness. The neurobiological systems that support implicit and explicit memory and that generally operate in tandem (thus producing meaningful, emotional memories) are dissociated by psychological trauma. Consequently, they operate independent of each other; in other words, implicit memories may be unaccompanied by any explicit understanding or representation of the events in which they occurred (Allen, 2001). A major problem associated with the integration process involves failures in encoding (a process of establishing a coherent account of what is occurring at a given time). Problems in encoding then lead to difficulties in consolidation (neurobiological process whereby information that is encoded becomes resistant to disruption), storage, and retrieval (Allen, 2001). In other words, traumatic memories do not serve any social function. They are consolidated in sensory, rather than semantic, representations. Trauma narratives can be understood as attempts to make sense of these dissociated, fragmented memory imprints (Van der Kolk, 1998). The lack of integration of traumatic memories is thought to be the leading cause of the development of complex biobehavioral change following traumatic events (Van der Kolk, 1996a, 1996b).

Auerhahn and Laub discuss several *forms* of *traumatic memory* that can follow massive psychic trauma. They have organized the different *forms of memory*—or states of "*knowing*"—according to psychological distance from the traumatic experience. These range from "*not knowing* to *screen memories* (these involve the substitution of true, but less traumatizing, memories for those that cannot be brought to mind); to *fugue states* (in which events are relived in an altered state of consciousness); to retention of the experience as *compartmentalized, undigested fragments of perceptions* that break into consciousness (with no conscious meaning or relation to oneself); to *transference phenomena* (the traumatic legacy is lived out as one's inevitable fate); to a *partial, hesitant expression* as an overpowering narrative; to the experience of compelling, *identity-defining* and *pervasive life themes* (conscious and unconscious); to its organization as a *witnessed narrative;* to its use as a *metaphor* and vehicle for *developmental conflict;* and finally, to *action knowledge* (in which knowing becomes consciously sequential and determines subsequent action)" (1998, p. 23). Rashkin (1999) discussed the *"phantom transmissions"* of traumatic memories, giving the example of parents who survived the Holocaust as children. The child of the now-grown adult (parent) inherits a secret traumatic situation—or *phantom memory*—of something that has occurred and cannot be undone. In essence, the wounds of the past are transmitted to the child without memory. One of the legacies of massive trauma is the erasure of memory. The child also inherits the imperative to suppress any desire to know or understand the origin of the secret to maintain the parents' (survivors') and family's integrity.

False Memory Syndrome (FMS)

The name "false memory syndrome" was given to memories of sexual abuse by their parents by adult children who confronted their parents about these early experiences of abuse after being in therapy. Many of these parents claimed they were innocent and brought charges against the therapists, referring to the recalled memories of sexual abuse as "false creations . . . born of the patients' suggestibility and their therapists' leading questions" (Ashford & LeCroy, 2010, p. 571). Although some ineffective therapeutic practice may have contributed to parents being falsely accused of sexual abuse of their children, incest remains a problem that cannot be ignored. The entire family bears the burden of intrafamily sexual abuse. Sheinberg and Fraenkel (2001) wrote about the inherent complexities of working with individuals and families in which incest has occurred and caution against reducing this emotional issue to one of confronting and punishing the parents. Davies and Dalgleish (2002, cited in Ashford & LeCroy, 2010, p. 571) commented, "Efforts to bridge the gap between victims of abuse and victims of false memory may help discover a balanced truth."

Trauma and Dissociation

Dissociation is the disengagement from the external environment and attending instead to the inner world of one's psyche. Dissociation at the moment of the trauma has been shown to be an important concomitant for the development of full blown PTSD. This occurs when engagement (or attachment) is too painful and the individual retreats. Unfortunately, this relational style makes the person vulnerable to posttraumatic flashbacks because grounding in current reality is so compromised. Patients whose history include both sexual and physical abuse at a young age and over a sustained period of time show the greatest degree of dissociative behaviors. Although utilized as a coping mechanism, the painful irony is that dissociation actually undermines coping because it robs the individual of the adaptive aspects of affects, including appropriate grief (Wiley, 2001). Two phenomena associated with dissociation are important to highlight: *depersonalization,* which refers to feelings of unreality associated with the internal world and the self, and *derealization,* or feeling as if the external world is unreal. Extreme detachment can go beyond depersonalization and derealization and involve a total unresponsiveness and disorientation that can go on for hours at a time. This description goes beyond the defense of dissociation in which the ego prevents the intrusion of history and therefore creates a boundary that serves a protective function. This profound level of detachment involves a trauma-induced condition of ego regression, to a state of inner *objectlessness*. An example of this occurred in counseling sessions with a middle-aged woman who been sexually, physically, and emotionally abused by her father throughout her childhood (from ages 3 to 12). There would be times during the sessions when she would be absolutely still and unable to speak with a distant look on her face. This represented an absence of object representation (refer to Chapter 3 for a review of object relations theory) that leads to a void and a rupture of the self (Krystal, 1968).

Treatment of Trauma

The overall goals of any therapy involving the treatment of trauma are straightforward. They include the *deconditioning* of anxiety and altering the way the individual views herself and her world by reestablishing a feeling of personal integrity, safety, and control. It is important to appreciate that there is no inherent gain in remembering trauma unless the individual's life is invaded by traumatic intrusions from the past. The treatment of trauma is complex and generally involves attention to a number of factors. These include providing an environment that encourages a reparative process of safety and trust; symptom reduction and stabilization; the opportunity for interpersonal control, mastery, and adaptive coping skills; promoting avenues of self-expression; restructuring of trauma-related cognitive and personal schemas; restitutive emotional experiences; the deconditioning of traumatic memories and responses (implicit memory needs to be made explicit autobiographical memory); and the reestablishment of social connections, hope, and optimism for the future. In other words, to be fully engaged in the present, traumatized individuals must find a way to gain control over their emotional responses and place the trauma in the larger perspective of their lives. Massive defenses must relax so that dissociated aspects of experience do not continue to intrude into life experiences thereby continuing to retraumatize the already traumatized individual (Van der Kolk, 1996).

The theoretical approaches to treating trauma are varied. Included among them are *psychodynamic psychotherapy* (Herman, 1992); *narrative constructivism* (Meichenbaum, 1994); *cognitive behavioral therapy* (Follette, Fuzek, & Abueg, 1998); *eye movement desensitization and reprocessing* (EMDR; Shapiro, 2001); *dialectical behavioral therapy* (DBT; Linehan, 1993); *group therapy, psychopharmacology,* and *psychoeducation* (Foa, Keane, & Friedman, 2004; Litz, 2004; Pearlman & Saakvitne, 1995). Whatever approach is used, it is important to provide the patients with a cognitive framework for understanding their often incomprehensible symptoms and the specific approach to treatment (again focusing on containment of traumatic symptoms and affect regulation first). Traumatic memories can be stored as behavioral reenactments. These behavioral memories are spontaneous expressions of trauma-related behaviors in everyday activities and relationships (Van der Kolk & Van der Hart, 1989, 1991). Bowlby's (1988) work on attachment has also provided a substantial body of knowledge related to the type of attachment relationship the patient will bring into the treatment relationship. It is, therefore, important to be vigilant about the complex ways in which trauma may repeat itself in the therapeutic relationship.

Herman (1992) describes "stages" of trauma in a psychodynamically rooted therapy, which we illustrate with vignettes from clinical practice.

Safety

The therapist must offer a sense of safety and security for the individual to feel secure enough to discuss traumatic material. Meichenbaum goes so far as to say that "the art of questioning is the most critical skill for therapists to develop" when working with people who are traumatized due to their heightened sensitivity and fear (1994, p. 125). He offers eight categories of interview questions: (a) questions that allow the client to tell her story at her own pace; (b) questions that assess the impact of the traumatic event; (c) questions that help the client reframe the event and her reactions; (d) questions that enlist the client's strengths and coping abilities; (e) questions that generate coping efforts and solutions; (f) questions that establish collaborative treatment goals; (g) questions that help the client develop a different perspective; and finally, (h) questions that can be raised with important persons in the client's life when or if others are seen conjointly with the client. See Practice Example 16.2: Chris.

Remembrance and Mourning

The work of remembering and reconstructing the traumatic memory is what turns the memory from something that is horrifying into a personal narrative that the individual can integrate into her life, shifting from the role of victim to survivor. The therapist is a "witness" to the person's story and provides validation for the loss that the individual has experienced and now grieves. It is not necessarily the opportunity for disclosure, but the type of therapeutic reaction to such disclosures that may be of most benefit to the client. It is the patient, not the therapist,

PRACTICE EXAMPLE 16.2

Chris

Chris, a woman in her early 50s, had been physically and emotionally abused by her mother throughout her childhood years. Divorced, and in recovery from alcohol abuse for 3 years and in a relationship that she felt was "not right" for her, Chris felt she was ready to talk about her childhood. She wanted to be able to be in a "good relationship" and felt that her childhood history was getting in the way. Despite this patient's desire to talk, the therapist moved slowly, inquiring about Chris's current life, her ability to raise three children she was proud of, and her accomplishments at her job. In this way, the therapist not only got to know Chris better, but also gave Chris the chance to get to know the therapist better, allowing her to make sure this therapist was the person she felt safe enough with to talk about her frightening experiences as a child.

CASE PRACTICE EXAMPLE 16.3

Chris

As Chris told her story, she cried frequently and clearly was expressing a deep and profound sadness for the little girl (she was) and the childhood she never had. Chris realized that she had many inner strengths as a child, including a keen intellect, a compassionate heart, and a spirit that enabled her to stand up to her mother. As she told her story, Chris began to understand that her mother had serious psychiatric problems and was most likely episodically psychotic. She realized that she was more vulnerable to the abuse than her younger brother because she was the female child, and her mother clearly felt competitive and threatened by this lovely, precocious daughter. She also realized that her brother also fared better because she often protected him from her mother's wrath (that was directed at him on many occasions). Chris often stepped in and took the "punishment" as a result. As Chris understood these childhood events through her adult eyes, she began to appreciate her strengths and gain in confidence and self-esteem.

who reconstructs the traumatic memory; however, the therapist can facilitate this process by empathic attunement to what the patient may be experiencing in the present as she recounts her story (Lindy, 1996). See Practice Example 16.3: Chris.

Reconnection

During this phase the survivor faces the task of creating a future. The client may need to examine aspects of her own personality that render her vulnerable to exploitation, but only after it has been clearly established that the perpetrator alone is responsible for the crime(s). The therapist needs to be mindful of the client's feelings of shame and guilt during this process. It is important to help the client find ways to reconnect with other people at this time and restore familial, social, and occupational functioning as much as possible. See Practice Example 16.4: Chris.

CASE PRACTICE EXAMPLE 16.4

Chris

Chris could now see that she was not a "bad person" and didn't merit the abusive treatment she had received as a child. She began to talk about the qualities she hoped for in a partner and that she deserved to be treated with respect. Chris also realized that she had so little trust in people (including her ex-husband) that she "tested" them by being provocative and/or nonresponsive to their attentions to her. She recognized how this had originated in her relationship with her mother—an untrustworthy caretaker—but also how it now contributed to her difficulties in having a good relationship. She became less fearful of intimacy because she now understood that she was not "bad" and no longer had to fear that someone would one day discover that and either become abusive or leave her. A year after terminating therapy, Chris called her therapist to let her know she had met a "wonderful man" and that they were planning to be married.

Trauma and Substance Abuse

Trauma and substance abuse are frequent co-occurrences. There are three dominant hypotheses proposed to explain the consistent findings regarding PTSD and substance use comorbidity (Chilcoat & Menard, 2007, pp. 9–28).

1. Self-medication hypothesis suggests that individuals with PTSD use psychoactive substances in an attempt to control painful symptoms.
2. High-risk hypothesis identifies drug use as a high-risk behavior that increases an individual's risk of exposure to trauma.
3. Susceptibility hypothesis proposes that drug users become more susceptible to PTSD following trauma exposure.

The link between PTSD and substance abuse is also affected by the type of trauma, the specific PTSD symptoms, and the type of substance abused. The two sides of substance abuse, intoxication and withdrawal, are related to PTSD symptoms, but in different ways (Allen, 2001, pp. 205–206). Alcohol and opiate withdrawal, for example, often mimics PTSD arousal symptoms, for example sleep loss, nightmares, increased anxiety, and increase in intrusion of traumatic cognitions (Chilcoat & Menard, 2007). Psychostimulants act as pharmacological stressors with neurophysiological effects similar to those of environmental stressors, making stress-sensitized clients with PTSD poor candidates for stimulant use. PTSD assessment should ideally occur after the addicted individual has completed withdrawal.

Trauma and PTSD most often precede rather than follow substance abuse, and changes in PTSD symptoms affect substance abuse more often than the reverse. The relationship between trauma and substance abuse is one of a vicious cycle, with one disorder serving to sustain the other, making each of them more severe in the presence of each other and complicating the treatment of the other. For example, treatment of substance abuse may increase symptoms of PTSD, and assessment and treatment of PTSD may exacerbate substance abuse. The best course of action is to conduct a concurrent evaluation of substance use (SUD) and PTSD, evaluating the urges to drink or use drugs; difficulty concentrating; feeling as if a traumatic event is recurring; reexperiencing, avoidance, or arousal symptoms; and actual drinking or drugging behaviors (Read, Bollinger, & Sharkansky, 2007). Consideration should be given to the stigma and shame associated with each of these disorders, as these may influence the client's report of both trauma and substance use. Conducting the assessment in a sensitive, respectful manner, with knowledge of both the commonalities and differences between these two disorders as well as the way they affect one another is crucial, as lack of trust in the provider can be another barrier to effective assessment. An integrated treatment protocol that includes psychoeducation, identification of high-risk stressors, and coping with relapses in substance use should follow (Allen, 2001, pp. 210–211).

Trauma and Children

The symptoms of trauma in children differ from those described for adults because traumas of childhood occur during a time of incomplete development. They must therefore be recognized and understood within their developmental context. Table 16.2 provides a guide to the signs of traumatic stress in children according to their age. (See Chapters 9, 10, 11, and 12 on infancy, early childhood, middle childhood, and adolescence for a perspective on how traumatic symptoms deviate from normal development.)

TABLE 16.2

Signs of Traumatic Stress in Children

Age Range	Traumatic Reactions
Preschool (ages 1–5)	Uncontrollable crying, regressive behavior, confusion, irritability, eating problems, separation fears and excessive clinging to caretakers, running aimlessly, trembling with fright, lack of response to attention, heightened arousal and confusion, generalized fear, nightmares and sleep disturbances, startle response, fussiness, physical sensations, "freezing" (sudden immobility of body), grief, somatic symptoms
Middle Childhood (ages 5–11)	Sleep problems, weather fears, headache, nausea, visual or hearing problems, distractibility, fighting and aggressive behaviors and angry outbursts, concerns about safety, repetitious traumatic play and retelling, feelings of responsibility and guilt, loss of interest in activities, generalized fear, specific trauma-related fears, giving close attention to parent's anxieties, school avoidance, marked regressive behaviors, cognitive confusion, generalized fear, helplessness and passivity, difficulty identifying feelings, anxieties about death, startle response, separation anxiety, withdrawal
Early Adolescence (ages 11–14)	Withdrawal, isolation, memory gaps, depression, suicidal ideation, aggressive behaviors, substance abuse, lack of self-care (bathing), appetite disturbance, self consciousness, trauma-driven acting out, excessive activity and involvement with others, retreat from others to manage inner turmoil, rebellion at home or school, life-threatening reenactment, accident proneness
Adolescence (ages 14–18)	Confusion, withdrawal, isolation, antisocial behavior (i.e., stealing), substance abuse, hallucinations, distractibility, obsessional thinking, withdrawal into heavy sleep or night frights, depression, eating disorders, trauma-driven acting out (i.e., cutting), retreat from others to manage inner turmoil, threatening reenactment, accident proneness

Source: Adapted by J. Lesser from "Terrorist Attacks and Children." National Center for Post-Traumatic Stress Disorder. www.ncptsd.org/facts/disasters/fs_children_disaster.html. Retrieved September 3, 2004.

Trauma-Related Disturbances in Children

Children who experience and/or witness events that overwhelm their capacity to understand or cope with them are at great risk for developing PTSD as well as other serious disturbances. Eth and Pynoos offer a classification of the types of disorders that can develop in response to particular "catastrophic" events (1985, cited in James, 1989). Table 16.3 gives the reader a snapshot of these problem behaviors. Trauma can exercise a pervasive impact on child development and be an antecedent to many serious emotional disorders. It is, therefore, imperative that clinicians working with children conduct a comprehensive developmental assessment with specific attention to the role that trauma may have played in the child's life.

Child Maltreatment

Children exposed to repeated abuse (including physical, sexual, and emotional; see Chapter 11 on middle childhood, where these terms are defined) face the formidable developmental task of trying to find a way to develop a sense of trust and safety with caregivers who are untrustworthy and unsafe. The child, therefore, "takes the bad object into himself—internalizes it—and protects himself from the reality of an extremely bad environment and creates a reality of a tolerable environment" (Cooper & Lesser, 2005, p. 84). As Herman asks: "Without the inner structure of caring parents, how can one survive . . . is there life without father and mother?" (1992, p. 193). This inner badness, although preserving the relationship with the parent(s), does so at the child's expense, causing him to form a stigmatized identity that becomes a part of the child's personality structure, often persisting into adult life. The child tries hard to camouflage this inner sense of badness, often with valiant attempts to be good. Saunders and Arnold suggest that splitting may occur at any point through the latency period of childhood in the lives of children who have been chronically or seriously abused (1991, p. 3). They state that splitting, previously described in the psychoanalytic literature as a defense (Kernberg, 1976), may "reflect an internalization of the child's actual experience, thereby representing more of a *repetition phenomenon* than a defensive one." These children often present with what appear to be attachment relationships to their abusive caretakers, but we need to be careful not to confuse attachment relationships and trauma bonds. A trauma bond is the internalized set of expectations and cues that a child develops when an adult intermittently harasses, beats, threatens, or abuses the child (DeYoung & Lowry, 1992; Dutton & Painter, 1981). The attachments formed in such situations manifest themselves in positive feelings and attitudes by the children for the maltreating or abusing adult caregivers. The help provided to these children will be more effective if the helpers are aware of the psychological dynamics that characterize the relationship they had with their abusers. A prerequisite for *reconnection* or *reattachment* is helping the children mourn the loss of the attachment figures. Many times, families, helpers, and even the larger culture collude with abused children in avoiding the work of mourning and in suppressing their

TABLE 16.3

Common Psychiatric Disturbances Found among Children in Selected Catastrophic Situations, in Relative Frequency of Occurrences

		Disasters			Child Molestation			Physical Abuse
Rank		***DSM-III disorder***	**Rank**		***DSM-III disorder***	**Rank**		***DSM-III disorder***
1	313.21	Anxiety disorder, avoidant disorder	1	308.20	Posttraumatic stress disorder, acute	1	313.00	Overanxious disorder
2	309.12	Anxiety disorder, separation-anxiety disorder	2	309.81	Posttraumatic stress disorder, posttraumatic stress chronic	2	313.21	Anxiety disorder, avoidant disorder
3	307.46	Sleep-terror disorder	3	300.29	Simple phobia	3	307.46	Sleep-terror disorder
4	313.00	Overanxious disorder	4	313.82	Identity disorder	4	308.20	Posttraumatic stress disorder, acute
5	300.29	Simple phobia	5	313.81	Oppositional disorder	5	309.81	Posttraumatic stress disorder, chronic
6	300.22	Agoraphobia, without panic	6	300.02	Generalized anxiety	6	309.40	Adjustment disorder
7	308.20	Posttraumatic stress disorder, acute	7	309.24	Adjustment disorder with anxious mood	7	314.01	Attention-deficit disorder with hyperactivity
8	309.81	Posttraumatic stress disorder, chronic	8	300.81	Somatization disorder	8	300.29	Simple phobia
9	314.01	Attention-deficit disorder with hyperactivity	9	300.22	Agoraphobia, without panic	9	305.00	Functional neurosis
10	314.80	Attention-deficit disorder, residual type	10	309.00	Adjustment disorder residual type	10	313.82	Identity disorder

Source: From *Post-Traumatic Stress Disorder in Children,* 1985. Washington, D.C., American Psychiatric Association. Reprinted with permission.

grief due to our own inability to tolerate the child's distress and story and the feelings of guilt, helplessness, and shame evoked in us by the child's pain (James, 1989, 1994). James, recognizing the complexity involved in the treatment of children who have been traumatized due to child abuse, developed a framework (Table 16.4) of nine "traumagenic states" outlining the dynamics, psychological impact, and behavioral manifestations of trauma (1989, pp. 23–26).

TABLE 16.4

Traumagenic States

1. Self-blame

Dynamics:

Cognitive development: A child thinks a person is good or bad. If a good adult does something bad, the child blames himself.
Excitement: Child may experience part of the trauma as physiologically thrilling and therefore believes he must have wanted it to happen.
Payoff: Child experiences material or emotional reward.
Compliance: Child did not actively resist his aggressor, so blames self.
Purification: Child keeps image of aggressor positive and blames himself so he can continue to have loving feelings toward the aggressor.
Role reversal: The child is parentified; he assumes the caretaker role in the family and blames himself when something goes wrong.
Identification with aggressor: Child associates emotionally with role of aggressor and blames self as part of this identification.
Timing: Child associates something he did with onset of traumatizing event and blames self.
Control: Child blames self to create illusion he can stop the traumatizing event when he chooses.
Assignment: Child is told by others he is to blame and believes it to be true.

Psychological Impact:

Guilt, shame, belief that self is bad.

Behavioral Manifestations:

Isolation, attempts to rectify, remediate, self-punishing acts, self-mutilation, suicide, substance abuse, sabotaging achievements due to belief of self-unworthiness.

2. Powerlessness

Dynamics:

Helplessness: No one and nothing was able to protect the child or halt the event.
Fear: Experienced fear, often repeatedly.
Isolation: Assistance, support, and a different perspective from others are unavailable.
Vulnerability: Child's personal boundaries invaded, often repeatedly.
Disbelief by others: Child unable to make others believe his experience.

Psychological Impact:

Anxiety, fear, depression, lowered sense of efficacy, perception of self as victim, need to control, identification with aggressor, experiencing part of self as being split off (dissociation).

Behavioral Manifestations:

Nightmares, phobias, toileting problems, delinquency, pseudo maturation, agitation, withdrawal, retreat to fantasy world, running away, school problems, vulnerability to subsequent victimization, obsessive and age inappropriate caretaking of others, aggressiveness, bullying, suicidal ideation, and gestures.

(Continued)

TABLE 16.4

Traumagenic States (Continued)

3. Loss and betrayal

Dynamics:
Violation of trust: Child had expected he would be protected and cared for.
Exploitation by others: Child is used by adults or older children.
Physical and/or emotional loss: Loss of significant part of child's world such as parents, sibs, other significant people, pets, home, school, community, often in conjunction with other traumatic events.

Psychological Impact:
Numbing of emotions, denial, suppressed longing, guilt, rage, distrust of self and others.

Behavioral Manifestations:
Somatic reactions: Recurrent anxiety dreams, regressive behaviors, withdrawal, inability to attend, leading to learning difficulties, emotional disconnecting, avoidance of intimacy, apathy, indiscriminate clinging, hoarding, explosive aggression, elective autism.

4. Fragmentation of bodily experience

Dynamics:
Physically overpowered: Child witnessed or experienced physical injuries, pain, and intrusion.
Loss of control: Child told and /or experienced nonownership of her body.
Senses overwhelmed: Powerful sensory stimuli linked with pain and physical violation.
Confusion: Child given incomprehensible reasons for physical assault.

Psychological Impact:
Loss of body integrity/control, denial, self loathing, fear, helplessness.
Experiences part of self as being split off, repression, loss of confidence.
Loss of concept of personal future.

Behavioral Manifestations:
Elicits protection from others, anesthesia of body parts, disowns body, hysterical seizures, dangerous risk taking, eating/sleeping disorders, somatic complaints, extreme aggression, withdrawal/excessive daydreaming, dissociation.

5. Stigmatization

Dynamics:
Blame: Child blames, denigrated, humiliated.
Shocked reaction: Family and community respond to event with horror.
Secrecy: Child pressured not to tell about traumatic event.
Damaged goods: Child treated as if permanently damaged.

Psychological Impact:
Guilt, shame, lowered self-esteem, feels different from peers, self-loathing.

Behavioral Manifestations:
Isolation.
Avoidance of achievement/success.
Compulsive drive to achieve, but never experiences self as good enough.
Substance abuse.
Self-destructive behavior.

6. Eroticisation

Dynamics:
Reward: Child rewarded for inappropriate sexual behavior.
False information: Child given false information about sexual behavior and morality.
Learning: Child learns she has power and is valuable as a sex object.
Imposed fetishism: Physical parts of child given inordinate attention by adults.
Conditioning: Conditioning of sexual activity with negative emotions and memories.

Psychological Impact:
Preoccupation with sexual issues; confusion about sexual identity; confusion about sexual norms; confusion of sex with love and caregiving or care getting; negative association to sexual activities and arousal sensations; positive association to exploitative sexual activities.

Behavioral Manifestations:
Sexualization of affection, sexual preoccupation, compulsive aggressive or sadistic sexual behavior, precocious sexual activity, sexual victimization of self or others, responds to neutral touching as a sexual approach.

7. Destructiveness

Dynamics:
Survival: Child believes destructive behavior necessary for his survival.
Identification with aggressor: Child associates emotionally with aggressor and imitates destructive acts.
Punishment: Believes he deserves punishment and acts in ways that cause him to be hurt, by himself or by others.
Mastery: Behavior is an attempt to understand and cope with experiences.
Revenge: Child wants retribution against those he sees as responsible for the trauma.

Psychological Impact:
Reinforces self-blame, guilt, shame; frightening loss of impulse control; confusion regarding self-concept; confusion regarding values, morals, addictive cycle, destructive or abusive acts relieve tensions caused by destructive or abusive acts.

Behavioral Manifestations:
Child engages in destructive violent or sexualized behavior toward self, other people, animals, objects, withdrawal, preoccupation with revenge fantasies, dangerous risk taking, ritualistic reenactment of all or part of traumatic events, compulsive secret play, elicits abuse from others.

8. Dissociative Disorder

Dynamics:
Predisposition: Biopsychological capacity to dissociate.
Insufficient protection: Child experiences lack of internal/external resources to cope with experience.
Overwhelming terror: Environment chronically and inconsistently infused with traumatic events.
Modeling: Behavior observed in several generations; parents' dissociative response become models for child.
Reinforcement: Dissociative splitting is approved by others and provides relief from pain.
Pain phobic: Thought of physical or emotional pain overwhelms child with fear.

(Continued)

TABLE 16.4

Traumagenic States (Continued)

Programming: Child taught to self-divide through constant reference (e.g., "You are two people").
No restorative experience: Lack of soothing; child blocked from processing feelings related to trauma by secrecy and/or not being allowed to express anger, fear, neediness, etc.

Psychological Impact:
Fragmentation of personality; inconsistent and distorted development; depersonalization; feels alienated from others; encapsulates intense emotions.

Behavioral Manifestations:
Spontaneous trance states, dual identity, denies witnessed behavior, peculiar forgetfulness patterns, odd variations in skills, schoolwork inconsistent, sudden mood and behavioral shifts, self-destructive.

9. Attachment Disorder

Dynamics:
Unavailable attachment figure: Caregiver unable or unwilling to form emotional attachment to child; multiple generic caregivers.
Negative response cycle: Child's increased anxiety from unmet needs. Leads to driven negative expression of need and conflict; caregivers respond punitively; and child's anxiety increases.
Distancing: Child rebuffs attempts at emotional closeness due to distrust and a felt need to protect self with distancing.
Discontinuity and loss of caregivers: Caretaking is unpredictable and viewed by the child as capricious.
Unmet needs: child's unmet needs for closeness and human connection not responded to or unpredictably met. Reciprocity does not occur, so child does not experience self as being pleasurable or lovable
No pleasure in relationships: Child unable to invest emotionally in receiving care and nurturance.

Psychological Impact:
Cannot trust needs will be met; cannot find comfort or security in relationships; isolated, lonely, depressed, low self-esteem, lacks secure base from which to explore the universe, unable to develop a sense of mastery.

Behavioral Manifestations:
Cling, rage reactions, learning difficulties, overcontrolling with peers and adults, emotional detachment, lack of emotional reciprocity, engages in social interactions that block and avoid emotional closeness and vulnerability, will engage in relentless and repetitive demands for caregiver attention while not experiencing satisfaction or comfort from interactions, nonresponsive to affectionate caring, lack of spontaneity, rigid, lacking in warmth, does not turn to adult in times of need; rejects adults' efforts to soothe him, child suppresses own emotional responsiveness and instead imitates behaviors of others, sabotages potentially gratifying situations.

Source: Reprinted with the permission of The Free Press, a Division of Simon & Schuster Adult Publishing Group, from *Treating Traumatized Children: New Insights and Creative Interventions* by Beverly James.

Play Therapy in the Treatment of Traumatized Children

Play is the language of children, and therefore, the implementation of any treatment plan, within any theoretical framework, must involve play therapy. The definition of play therapy and several theoretical models were presented in Chapter 3. The purpose of play therapy with children who have been traumatized is to help them reach some sense of closure about the event(s) (Gil, 1991). The play therapist should ensure that the verbal or interpretive content of the play therapy session(s), including observed play themes, are relevant to the goals of treatment. Attention should be directed to the affect, play themes, and behavior that occur as a result of play therapy interventions. O'Connor (2000) offers a categorization of the different levels of play that includes attention to the role of corrective events, interpretation, and problem solving at different stages of the child's development:

Level One (Ages 0–2) The therapist works to create an experience with the child that can undo what he or she experienced. This new experience can hopefully then be generalized to the outside world. It is important to involve caregivers as much as possible during this developmental phase so as not to confuse the caregiving role. *Play materials:* baby bottle, baby blanket, baby powder, stuffed animals.

Level Two (Ages 3–5) Interpretation is now added to corrective experiences in the playroom. The therapist comments on the child's behavior. *Play materials:* interactive pretend toys (such as telephones, toy dishes, and pretend food); dollhouses, schoolhouses, and other pieces of equipment that represent different environments, art materials; play dough and clay; therapeutic coloring books; sand tray.

Level Three (Ages 6–10) Therapy now becomes a blend of corrective experiences and interpretation. The child thinks concretely and feels most comfortable playing; however, he or she is now capable of processing his experience using language. *Play materials:* small pretend toys (such as animals, dolls, cars) and their settings (home, school, etc.), artwork, clay, construction toys (such as Legos), board games.

Level Four (Ages 11–13) Children move between concrete and abstract thinking at this stage of development. They are able to utilize "talk therapy," but may also want to be involved in some activity at least some of the time during the counseling session. Activities are geared toward alleviating the child's anxiety rather than being therapeutic in themselves.

In addition to the materials suggested earlier, consider including props or sets that specifically pertain to the situation the child is currently dealing with (for example, a schoolhouse or a courtroom). Remember also that these props can be constructed from simple items such as cardboard boxes. Consider collapsible dollhouses and puppet stages or mobile playrooms that can be carried to different settings (see O'Connor, 2000, and Schaefer and Reid, 2001, for additional suggestions regarding play materials and activities). Children often have competing drives to both achieve mastery over the traumatic memories but also to avoid these memories. The therapist therefore walks a clinical tightrope in helping children disengage from the trauma (and the traumatic memories) without pushing them beyond their ability to handle their emotions (Gil, 1991). Practice Example 16.5 of counseling an 8-year-old boy following his mother's death after a prolonged and serious illness illustrates this struggle.

PRACTICE EXAMPLE 16.5

David

This is David's fourth session following the death of his mother from cancer. Described by his father at home as vacillating from being withdrawn and uncommunicative to having angry outbursts of temper, David does not bring up the topic of his mother during his visits. He has also told the therapist that he does not like going to the groups (his father has taken him to a bereavement group for children who have lost parents) because they (the group leaders) ask the children to draw pictures or tell stories. "Even when they aren't asking us to do them about our parents, I know that's what they want." The therapist makes a decision to follow David's lead and asks him how he would like to spend his time when he visits with her. David would like to "play card games." The therapist spends the next eight sessions playing different card games with David. In the middle of one of these games in the ninth meeting with David, he tearfully tells the therapist that he "used to play cards with his mom and that's why he likes to play cards with me."

A final point regarding traumatic memories in children is taken from Gil, who suggests that the concept of "traumatic memories" be replaced with that of "traumatic expectations" (1991, pp. 11–17). This is because traumatic experiences greatly influence a child's view of the world, especially in the areas of safety and security, risk and injury, and protection and intervention.

Trauma and the Military

Many men and women return home from military duty with posttraumatic stress disorder (PTSD). This can be related to what Shaw (2007, p. 24) defines as the acute traumatic moment, or "the sudden conscious awareness of overwhelming feelings of helplessness to cope (internal danger) before the fear of injury and death (external danger)." This unmasking of the illusion of safety represents a traumatic moment when the individual becomes aware of the incongruity between the illusion of safety and the reality of one's vulnerability to an imminent and pressing danger. The awareness of this new reality represents a psychic trauma, with a continuum of responsiveness that varies from a brief traumatic moment to a sustained traumatic experience. With increasing exposure to combat, there is progressive and prolonged exposure to war-related trauma, multiple traumatic moments that are drawn out over time. Veterans who return from Iraq or Afghanistan often have feelings of helplessness, have seen death, have personally killed, and been subject to life-threatening attacks and the threat of being killed. Such experiences have contributed to "intrusive recollections." that evoke a "posttraumatic emotional response,"typically one of fear or helplessness, that can lead to certain behaviors, including for example, suicide, danger to others, and substance abuse. Tick (2005, p. 5) in his powerful book *War and the Soul,* feels that PTSD is not best understood or treated as a stress disorder with regard to the effects of war. He refers to it as an "identity disorder and soul wound, affecting the personality at its deepest levels" (p. 97). This author, who has worked with war veterans for over 25 years, feels that "for the survivor's soul to heal, he or she must revisit the experience of war in a way that tells the truth and frees the heart from bondage to the past" (p. 198). Tick believes that in contrast to stress reduction strategies that counsel avoidance of disturbing memories, healing of veterans with PTSD can only occur when they are helped to relive memories and their accompanying feelings so that they may be expressed and relieved. "This imaginal return is a key factor in addressing PTSD appropriately as an identity disorder" (p. 194). Treatment involves helping the veteran to disown war and violence, reaffirm the original call to service, and restore the moral fiber that is undone in combat. The techniques used to accomplish this include storytelling, healing journeys, grieving rituals, meetings with former enemies, soul retrieval, initiation ceremonies, purification, and the nurturing of an identity from veteran to warrior. Tick wrote: "With such restoration, the healed veteran embodies high qualities of decency, honesty, kindness, compassion, and cooperation along with strength, courage, clear-mindedness, and vision" (p. 199). Finally this author believes that therapists need to be more open and self-disclosing with veterans than with almost any other group of clients, including what their therapist did during war and/or how they feel about it and about veterans. Of course, as with all clients, assessment and an appropriate course of treatment must be done individually and as soon as possible after the veteran returns home (Friedman, 2006).

Trauma and Aging

Posttraumatic symptoms can emerge in aging individuals following absence or remission for a significant number of years—referred to as a "latency period." Although the cause for the emergence or reemergence of symptoms is not scientifically determined, it may be related to the overall developmental tasks of this stage of life "mourning for losses, giving meaning to past and present experiences; accepting one's past and present states; reestablishing self-coherence and self-continuity; and achieving ego integration" (Aarts & Op den Velde, 1996, p. 368). Erikson described the task of the final stage of life as being between ego integrity and despair. Ego integrity involves "the ego's accrued assurance of its proclivity for order and meaning . . . the acceptance of one's one and only life cycle as something that had to be and that, by necessity, permitted of no substitutions" (1951, p. 241). Clausen (1986), who wrote about aging from a life-span perspective, felt that *memory* is the vehicle for moving toward ego integrity as it plays a pivotal role in the organization of a person's identity. *Reminiscence* is an important developmental process in the later adult years. It is also important in the resolution of trauma (described earlier). Sternberg and Rosenbloom (2000) wrote about adults who were child survivors of the Holocaust who often claim that a sense of sadness never left them. Separation continues to evoke powerful feelings for them. Many have only fragments of memory, which can be traumatic but serve a healing function as well. However, if trauma occurs early and lasts for several years (as it did for many of these survivors) and then does not abate (due to new traumas that occurred in the postwar years), the structures required for an integrated, mature personality are shaken to the core. Even the preverbal memories of a "vulnerable existence" are encoded, often requiring only a

PRACTICE EXAMPLE 16.6

Mrs. P

Mrs. P is a 70-year-old woman diagnosed with PTSD. As a young woman Mrs. P was a German refugee during World War II. She experienced multiple traumas including rape by Soviet soldiers and the loss of both parents. Mrs. P was never treated. PTSD was diagnosed following a medical experience that triggered the memory of being raped. From the time of that procedure, Mrs. P was flooded with wartime memories long forgotten. Her trauma memories were intermingled with feelings of guilt over Germany's role in the Holocaust.

touch, a smell, or a sound to be reactivated. Nonetheless, these individuals often feel a strong need to bear witness to the atrocities they endured. The act of giving testimony helps link fragments of memory and put life events in chronological order (Sternberg & Rosenbloom, 2000, p. 15). Lifton (1979) attributed this documentation of the past as "symbolic immortality"—the survivor's memories become a heritage they leave to the following generations as well as a memorial to their lost families and prewar lives (Mazor et al., 1990, p. 12). Later adulthood is a difficult stage of life for those who suffered early trauma. The ability of the emerging fragility and dependence on others for care and the experience of losses may exacerbate posttraumatic symptoms and traumatic memories, sometimes even after decades of adequate coping (which may have included denial, repression, concentration on work, and/or raising a family). The ability of trauma survivors to ward off trauma-related memories and associated affects inevitably decreases with aging. It is therefore important not to omit questions about childhood trauma from intake with older adults. The historical factors that might have informed the nature of trauma exposure for members of particular age cohorts; for example, wars, health epidemics, and so forth must also be considered (Brown, 2008, p. 127).

It is also important to consider that some older adults may have been perpetrators of abuse during their young years. These individuals may have been valued members of the family. Conversely they may be ostracized from their families due to past offenses or now in their declining years become abused by their former targets, completing the cycle of violence in the family. (See Chapter 15 on older adulthood.) See Practice Example 16.6.

Trauma and Culture

Traumas that occur in the context of cultural or social upheavals create profound discontinuity in the order and predictability that culture has brought to daily life and social situations. It profoundly alters the basic structure, not just of the individual, but also of the cultural system as a whole. DeVries defines culture as "a protective and supportive system of values, lifestyles, and knowledge, the disruption of which will have a deleterious effect on its members" (1996, pp. 401–402).

Cultural trauma occurs when an entire culture experiences a historical, geographical event caused by the same persons or events (Jenkins, 2001). When cultural protection and security fail, the individual's problems are proportional to the cultural disintegration. Cultural trauma, therefore, may be viewed as a combination of the severity of the stress and the supportive capabilities of the environment. The neurological underpinnings of human behavior presented in Chapter 2 extend to culture and the process of enculturation that occurs from birth. Castilli discusses the importance of "neural networks" resulting from a combination of genetics and culture, which affect cognitive processing and result in a person from a particular cultural background or country of origin organizing the world in a certain way (1995, p. 23). Consider the implications of this understanding for immigrants and refugee populations, who often enter the new country of residence and must undergo an acculturation process following numerous losses (or possible traumas) that they may have endured in their country of origin. Strong attachments to people and the lifestyles these attachments provided can lead to a deep sense of loss when the life of the culture is disrupted. The loss of those persons and the disintegration of that cultural system become traumatic (Alexander et al., 2004). Lesser and Eriksen discussed the challenge of cross-cultural counseling with a 17-year-old Vietnamese adolescent who came to the United States at age 8 with an older sister and her husband on a refugee boat, leaving his mother and other siblings behind. They wrote: "The journey from Vietnam was treacherous and the overcrowded boat nearly capsized several times." Then, the client and his family "resided in refugee camps for two years prior to moving to a northeastern city" (2000, p. 30). When working with clients with these types of trauma histories, we must be careful of ethnocentric diagnostic systems that could impose a worldview that may violate the cultural survival of the survivors. Individuals can erroneously be labeled as having psychiatric disorders when their symptoms may reflect, for example, a profound suffering that is culturally determined. These individuals may be suffering from cultural bereavement, not from PTSD—or they may be suffering from both (Eisenbruch, 1991). Practice Example 16.7 illustrates another example that presents a dilemma in making a culturally relevant diagnosis when the clinical picture is complex.

PRACTICE EXAMPLE 16.7

Mrs. G

Mrs. G, a Latina woman in her early 40s, talked about what coming to the United States (15 years ago) from Puerto Rico was like for her and her husband. Mrs. G left behind her close, extended family and found profound discrimination in her new community. She was suddenly "an outsider" and an outsider who was "untrustworthy." Mrs. G coped by "praying" and "living a good life," but it was "painful" and "very stressful." She developed many health problems, including chronic fatigue and a series of somatic symptoms that doctors referred to as "hypochondria." A culturally sensitive clinical evaluation would consider the effects of cultural and racial trauma on Mrs. G.

Tseng and Streltzer, in describing the impact of cultural factors on mental health, differentiate between "major psychiatric disorders" (such as schizophrenia and bipolar disorder), which have prominent biological determinants and where "cultural factors may effect the phenomenology of, reaction to, and management and outcome of the disorder," and "minor psychiatric disorders" (for example, adjustment problems) that may be more directly tied to "psychological and contextual factors where culture may have more of a direct impact" (1997, p. 9). Cultural trauma is not just the result of a group experiencing pain. It is the result of this acute discomfort entering the core of the collectivity's sense of its own identity—it is community-identity disrupting (Alexander, 2004, p. 10). With trauma, certain cultural patterns are activated. For example, on the group level, social bonding becomes a regression to nationalism and conservatism, paranoia replaces trust, and aggression may occur in place of nurturance and support (DeVries, 1996). Helplessness and isolation are the core experiences of psychological trauma. As empowerment and reconnection are the core experiences of recovery from trauma, it is often helpful to have a formal cultural acceptance of the traumatic experience. The reestablishment of symbolic places and culturally proscribed behaviors is important to reinstate members of the community in role functions appropriate to their places in the life cycle. Individuals need to be reconnected with their ordinary supportive networks and engage in activities that include a sense of mastery and a vision of the future. These cultural roles, shared values, and historical continuity act as stress managers; otherwise, *social extrusion* and stigmatization may result as a cultural defense against the unwanted stories of trauma. When this occurs, a dissociative, delusional process in response to trauma takes hold. The three keys to understanding trauma and traumatic reactions within a community and cultural context are legitimizing the individual communication of distress, facilitating the mobilization of resources embedded in community life (indigenous social support), and maintaining resources and support after the immediate crisis has ended (for example, self-help healing alternatives and professional counseling, if necessary; DeVries, 1996).

A poignant example of this last phenomenon is occurring in Kingston, Jamaica, where the combination of organized crime, gang warfare, an illegal gun trade, and a constant flow of guns and deportees is responsible for what has turned into a paramilitary culture (Mitchell, Scarlett, and Amata, 2001, p. 87). Women and mothers interviewed in a research study on the effects of violence on children in a community in West Kingston, Jamaica (Cooper & Lesser, 2005) spoke of "children killing children" and the level of fear that they live with in their communities. One mother described seeing her son gunned down in the street in front of her eyes. This woman also carried the scars of a knife attack against her. Jamaica is among the countries with the highest incidence of violence against women worldwide and the highest incidence of sexual assault, incest, and domestic violence (Planning Institute of Jamaica, 2003). This relational pattern between men and women and adults and children contributes to the development of psychopathological reactions and personality disturbances (Crawford-Brown, 1999, 1997; Kamsner & McCabe, 2000;

Lambert, Lyubansky, & Achenback, 1998). Enormous efforts are being made in Jamaica to address the impact of poverty, drugs, and the subsequent violence so that the problems do not become chronic (Stamm et al., 2004; see Chapter 6 for further discussion on this topic).

Cultural Countertransference

Perez-Foster cautions the mental health clinician to be aware of "*cultural countertransference,*" which she describes as a "complex and interacting set of culturally derived personal life values; academically based theoretical/practice beliefs; emotionally driven biases about ethnic groups; and feelings about their own ethnic self identity" (1998, p. 42).

Particularly in cross-cultural counseling and interventions, if we are not sensitive to cultural countertransference, we run the risk not only of a misinformed assessment of the problems being presented, but also to possibly retraumatizing our clients. Empathy and understanding are not enough, and there can be a challenging line between attributing *too much* to race and *not enough* to race. Basham advises to approach the client with a "not-knowing stance" (2004, p. 299). We feel that such a stance, combined with empathy, understanding, multicultural competence, and attention to racial identity development form the foundation for such a position. Clinicians from a background similar to their clients must also be mindful of cultural countertransference because their assessment could be biased by subjectivity. The models of identity development presented in Chapter 4 are helpful guides to practitioners who are working toward greater understanding of cultural countertransference.

Racial Trauma

We give special attention to racial trauma given the pervasive "personal, cultural and institutional implications for our daily lives . . . and its daily impact on interpersonal relationships" (Tatum, 1993, p. 2). Bass discusses the "intergenerational transmission" (2002, p. 274) of cultural and racial trauma—a result of slavery and its aftermath—that has psychologically, economically, and physically affected the African-American community (Saville, 2003). Eyerman (2003) writes about the impact of the racial trauma of slavery on the formation of African-American identity from the end of the Civil War to the Civil Rights Movement. He describes slavery as "collective memory . . . a form of remembrance that grounded the identity-formation of a people" (2001, p. 60). Reid, Mims & Higginbottom (2005) introduced the term "Post-traumatic Slavery Disorder" (PTSlaveryD) to describe the economic, cultural, political and psychological impact slavery has had on African Americans. Miliora (2000) introduced the phrase "depression of disenfranchisement" to describe the effects of cultural racism on self-esteem, confidence, and ambition. She stresses the importance of validating some expression of anger with clients who have suffered discrimination and helping these clients develop coping skills that constructively channel that anger. Brown (2008) discusses the notion of "invidious comparison of harm" (p. 84), a concept that describes "how dominant cultural norms of scarcity of resources lead to competition among individuals and groups for scare emotional resources with that scarcity expressed as a competition for 'who had it worse.'" This is an important concept to consider when working with individuals whose parents or grandparents or ancestors may have suffered from sociocultural trauma. It is sometimes helpful to bond with others who have similar historical legacies, for example, recommending a support group for children or grandchildren of Holocaust survivors. Practice Example 16.8 illustrates how racial trauma affected one man's identity.

If the therapist had not directly addressed the issue of racial trauma, Mr. L may nonetheless have talked about his experiences with racism. We believe, however, that good clinical practice includes attention by the therapist to the impact of racial traumas. Self-esteem and identity problems, compounded by traumatization, may enhance the severity or breadth of life problems experienced by the ethnic minority patient (Gusman et al., 1996). Having said this, it is important to also remember that Mr. L—along with countless other African-American people—learned to cope in his own way within his "strong family and community relational networks that function independently of European American influences" (Allen, 1996, p. 210). The therapist must also be mindful of the strengths and resources different oppressed groups have historically used to deal with racial trauma. These include family and community networks and in many cases, a strong affiliation with spirituality and religious institutions. (See Chapter 8 on spiritual development for further information on this topic.)

PRACTICE EXAMPLE 16.8

Mr. L

Mr. L is an African-American man in his late 50s, suffering from major depression following the breakup of a relationship with a Latina woman he hoped to marry. It was important that the therapist be sensitive to the likely possibility that this man may have experienced some type of racial discrimination growing up in the South in the 1950s. This legacy would be the psychosocial backdrop to his current midlife loss. The therapist, a white woman in her early 50s, asked directly about Mr. L's childhood and early adult years as an African-American man and whether he felt racism had affected his life. This point of inquiry opened the door to Mr. L's description of the many losses and injuries to his self-esteem he suffered as an African-American man. He described being called names, being seen as stupid, and enduring many instances of racial discrimination during his early adult years. He said, "things are better now ... but they were real bad back then." As therapy progressed, Mr. L expressed anger, feeling his entire life could have been different "if he wasn't a black man" or "if black men weren't hated or feared so much ... when I was younger." He also saw how his experiences with racism had colored his relationships, including the one that had just ended in which his girlfriend felt he "lacked motivation." Mr. L said that he had "given up" and was "tired" and willing to accept his life as it was: "She wanted more ... more than I guess I wanted."

The Helpers

Trauma is a complex phenomenon that affects people of all ages, across all cultures and classes, in a variety of ways, and at different developmental stages of life. We have learned much about the impact of trauma on people and how to help them recover from devastating experiences. The treatment of trauma is essential to the recovery of individuals, families, communities, and countries. Social workers face a high rate of professional contact with traumatized people. They may experience emotional fatigue and strain, such as empathetic withdrawal and empathetic enmeshment. Figley (1995, 2002) refers to this condition as "compassion fatigue. Figley (1999, p. 10) also described a related condition that affects those who work with traumatized individuals—secondary traumatic stress (STS), or "the nature, consequent behaviors and emotions resulting from knowledge about a traumatizing event experienced by a significant other. It is the stress resulting from helping or wanting to help a traumatized or suffering person." In a recent research study (Bride, 2007) designed to investigate the prevalence of secondary traumatic stress in a sample of social workers, the results indicated that "social workers engaged in direct practice are highly likely to be secondarily exposed to traumatic events through their work, many social workers are likely to experience at least some symptoms of STS, and a significant minority may meet the diagnostic criteria for PTSD" (p. 63). Lifton (2005) and Tyson (2007) refer to those who bear witness to the stories of combat survivors as "distant survivors" who also need to make meaning out of the trauma experiences they are hearing. This concept of "shared trauma" encompasses the symptoms described in compassion fatigue, secondary traumatic stress disorder, and vicarious traumatization and also addresses the effects of primary traumatization of the therapist from the experience of collective shared trauma (Tyson, 2007, p. 185). Clinicians who are unaware of their compassion fatigue are at risk for experiencing a lack of empathy with their combat survivor clients and unable to help them negotiate the social isolation and disconnection from others that often plagues returning soldiers. A more severe way in which trauma treatment may affect the therapist is called vicarious traumatization. This is a phenomenon in which the therapist may experience many of the same symptoms that the client experiences, for example, reexperiencing, psychic numbing, avoidance, anxiety, and depression, often at subclinical levels (Pearlman & Saakvitne, 1995).

As a result, the importance of self-care cannot be overemphasized. We offer some suggestions gleaned from the literature that could be helpful to therapists in such situations: Recognize the emotional, cognitive, and physical signs of stress reactions; do not limit clinical practice to work with trauma victims; limit overall caseloads; engage in self-care behaviors such as vacations, exercise, mindfulness, and other relaxation activities' and practice self-compassion (Germer, 2009) when recognizing one's limitations in helping the client (Figley, 2002; Meichenbaum, 1994; Lifton, 2005; Tyson, 2007).

Summary

This chapter has attempted to consolidate some of the major issues in understanding trauma from a biopsychosocial perspective. Charney (2004) cautions us not to focus only on stress-related psychopathology. He has worked to develop psychobiological models of resilience to extreme stress to understand why some individuals are able to cope with minimal psychopathological consequences. He identified 11 possible neurochemical, neuropeptide, and hormonal mediators of psychobiological response to extreme stress and related these to resilience and vulnerability. The neural mechanisms of *reward* and *motivation* (hedonia, optimism, and learned helpfulness), *fear responsiveness* (effective behaviors despite fear), and *adaptive social behavior* (altruism, bonding, and teamwork) were found to be relevant to the character traits associated with resilience. Charney concluded that the opportunity now exists to bring the advances of the neurobiological basis of behavior to facilitate the prediction, prevention, and treatment of stress-related psychopathology (p. 195).

We also encourage our readers to consider the varied ways that knowledge of trauma and development can be integrated with knowledge about larger systems. This will hopefully further contribute to creative and multifaceted approaches to prevention, treatment, and socioenvironmental interventions for persons of all ages. Working with individuals who have been traumatized involves coordination among mental health professionals, clergy, teachers, doctors, lawyers, law enforcement officials, and often, protective service workers. It is important to develop partnerships with key community agencies and indigenous community leaders. No two people will assist those who have been traumatized in exactly the same way. The treatment of trauma involves different people who come together at a particular point in time. Together they take a journey in which some are the helpers and some are the helped, but all are transformed in some unique way.

17 Chronic Illness and Disability

Introduction

This chapter provides an overview of the impact of disability and chronic illness on individuals in society. We include information about the type and range of conditions that challenge many people. In doing so, we hope to contribute to effective and sensitive social work practice with this population. The terms *disability* and *chronic illness* are often associated and/or used interchangeably. Illness can cause a disability, a disability can cause an illness, or the two may occur together. Many impairments are *progressive* or *episodic*, or directly related to the effects of a chronic illness. For many chronic illnesses and conditions, the impact may be similar to that of relatively stable impairments. Disruptions to self-identity may also be shared between people who become chronically ill or have impairments later in life. A great degree of fear can accompany chronic illness, particularly an illness that may be progressive. There may also be a level of uncertainty about what one might be able to do at given points in the future. Further uncertainties are introduced by symptoms or conditions such as pain that are not visible or easily communicated to others. Individuals need assistance and support as they use a range of problem-based and emotional approaches to retain a sense of competence and mastery. We hope that including a chapter on chronic illness and disability in this book provides a framework for assessment that views disability and chronic illness from a biopsychosocial, strengths-based perspective.

Definition of Disability

The earliest or traditional view of disability was that the individual with a disability was supernatural—either evil or "possessed" and therefore deserving of her or his plight due to sinful behavior—or divine, taking on the role of a shaman and being holy or revered. This view evolved through the years into the societal conceptualization of disability. This perspective eliminated the supernatural aspect but retained the idea that people with disabilities are "different" and there is a *stigma* attached to this difference. The word *stigma* evolved from the Greeks and referred to bodily signs designed to expose something unusual and bad about the moral status of the signifier. In contemporary times, stigma is applied to the disgrace itself more than to the bodily evidence of it. It refers to an attribute that is deeply discrediting, and on this assumption, stigmatized individuals are discriminated against in a variety of ways. Goffman wrote about this process: "An individual who might have been received easily in ordinary social intercourse possesses a trait that can obtrude itself upon attention and turn those of us whom he meets away from him, breaking the claim that his other attributes have on us . . . he possesses a stigma, an undesired differentness from what we had anticipated" (1963, p. 5).

The term *ableism* is used to refer to bias against persons with disabilities. This bias continues to appear in both the attitudes and behaviors of those individuals who are the temporarily able bodied (TAB), a term introduced by disability rights activists to describe people who have not yet experienced disability (Brown, 2001, p. 181). Internalized ableism also affects people with disabilities, leading to self-devaluation and devaluation of others with disabilities and competition for scare resources. It can be difficult to define what constitutes a disability.

The *medical* model defines disability from a functional limitations perspective, and the focus of disability is on a physical, behavioral, psychological, cognitive, or sensory difficulty situated within the person. The medical model distinguishes between the terms *impairment, disability,* and *handicap.* The World Health Organization (2006) defines these conditions as follows. *Impairment* is a disturbance in body structure or processes that is present at birth or results from later injury or disease, a loss or abnormality of psychological, physiologic, or anatomical structure or function. *Disability* is a limitation in expected functional activity due to an underlying impairment, a restriction or lack of ability to perform an activity within the range considered normal for human beings. Disabilities may affect daily life skills; having full range of movement; having intact senses (vision, hearing, smell, taste, balance, and touch); communicating with others (speaking and writing); learning and working; using mental processes (thinking, concentrating, and problem solving); interacting with others; and developing and maintaining relationships. A *handicap* is a social disadvantage experienced by people as a result of impairment or disability that occurs because they do not meet social expectations for performance. Handicaps can include social obstacles (people's negative attitudes or behaviors), personal obstacles (lack of information about one's own disability and resources), physical obstacles (such as inaccessible buildings, parks, or transportation), and resource obstacles (such insufficient money, insurance, personal care assistants, employment, training, housing, or recreation). The *economic* or *work limitation* definition of disability is congruent with the medical model. It concerns whether an individual is able to function in a paid-for-work capacity. The economic or work limitation is dependent on doctors and other medical and mental health professionals to diagnose and describe the nature of the disability. The *sociopolitical* conceptualization describes disability as the function of social, economic, and political forces working together. The problems experienced by people with disabilities are seen as being caused from being members of an oppressed minority group who are denied equal rights. Society "makes disability" when it creates structures that limit people's opportunities and access to resources, and language is a powerful tool that aids in that process. Language can be used to express attitudes toward people with disability in a positive way, or it can be used to reinforce discriminatory perceptions. The phrase "people with disabilities," for example, instead of "disabled people," is a linguistic shift that identifies the person first, not the disability (Altman, 2001; Barnartt, 1996; Brzuzy, 1999; Higgins, 1992; Jaeger, & Bowman, 2001).

Types of Disabilities

There are a number of different ways to group disabilities. One way is by *activity limitation* (National Institute on Disability and Rehabilitation Research, 1992). Another is by *causative condition,* such as impairments (which limit function) and diseases and disorders (which may also limit function but are caused by underlying conditions). Access Unlimited (1999), a disability organization that monitors access and accommodations for persons with disabilities, suggests a specific system of categorization: (a) physical impairments; (b) hearing impairments; (c) vision impairments; (d) learning disabilities; (e) speech impairments; (f) attention deficit hyperactivity disorders; (g) cardiovascular or circulatory conditions; (h) mental, psychoneurotic, and personality disorders; (i) traumatic brain injury; (j) respiratory disorders; and (k) diabetes, epilepsy, and other conditions. We have chosen to use Rolland's (1988, 1989) system of grouping chronic illness and disabilities into three categories as a conceptual framework for our discussion of select conditions. The first category—*progressive, permanent disabilities*—is characterized by an ever-increasing degree of severity and impairment. This category includes conditions such as diabetes, arthritis, and Parkinson's disease. The second category—*constant* or *permanent disabilities*—includes those that essentially remain the same throughout the life span (although they can sometimes progress). Included among these are spinal cord injury, blindness, and deafness. The final group—relapsing or episodic syndromes—is disorders such as multiple sclerosis and systemic lupus erythematosus. Episodic but permanent disabilities can be unpredictable and include periods of unusual activity interspersed with periods of disability. Many of these conditions bring with them a state of *chronic pain* that underscores the challenging interplay between biological processes and psychological and experiential factors. We have therefore decided to include a category on chronic pain in this section as well.

Progressive, Permanent Conditions

Diabetes Diabetes (*diabetes mellitus*) results from the body's inability to make the hormone insulin. There are two types of diabetes. Type I—insulin-dependent diabetes mellitus (IDDM)—typically develops during childhood (between ages 10 and 14). Type II diabetes—noninsulin dependent diabetes (NIDDM)—typically starts in adulthood and increases substantially as a function of age. Type I diabetes greatly affects the lives of those who have it. Individuals must follow a complex regimen of diet, exercise, and insulin injections. The individual needs to keep the blood glucose balanced. Too much insulin can cause hypoglycemia (overcorrection), and too little insulin can cause hyperglycemia. Diabetes can be exacerbated by pregnancy and can cause severe problems for both the mother and the developing fetus during pregnancy. Whites are more likely than nonwhites to develop Type I diabetes. Nonwhite groups are particularly at risk for Type II diabetes. Obesity, diet, and inactivity are risk factors for Type II diabetes (Mackelprang & Salsgiver, 1999).

Cancer The term *cancer* actually refers to more than 100 diseases that are characterized by malfunctioning DNA, resulting in rapid cell growth. The body normally regulates the growth and division of its cells. When cancer develops, this regulation is disrupted, and cancer cells continue to grow and divide uncontrollably, forming new abnormal or malignant body cells. This process creates a growing mass of tissue known as a *tumor* or *neoplasm*. Although cancer typically forms a tumor, not all tumors are malignant. It is the continued, inappropriate, and lack of normally programmed cell death that makes a growth malignant. Cancer cells will spread or *metastasize* from the initial tumor locally or to distant areas of the body through the blood stream or the lymphatic system. Some cancers grow rapidly; others grow slowly. Although cancer can develop almost anywhere in the body, the cancers most frequently diagnosed in the United States include skin cancer, prostate cancer, breast cancer, lung cancer, and colorectal cancer. The symptoms of cancer vary from none at all to include fatigue, unexplained weight changes, fever, pain, or a lump that seems to be growing (Bessell, 2001; Greer, 1995; Moorey & Greer, 2002).

A common but insufficiently recognized complication of cancer is sexual dysfunction (Schover, 1998). These problems can relate to the anxiety and depression that often accompany a diagnosis but can also be the result of psychological or physical damage following certain treatments, disfiguring surgery, and the side effects of chemotherapy and hormone treatment. It is often difficult to separate the emotional aspects of cancer and its recurrence from the side effects of treatment.

Rheumatoid Arthritis This is a chronic condition that can cause major disability over one's lifetime. This type of arthritis is systemic, meaning that it is a problem that affects the body systems in general rather than a specific joint. It causes pain and swelling in the synovial membranes, or linings of the joints. This often causes enlarged red areas around the joints, causing pain and swelling. Although any joint can be affected, those most likely to be involved are the wrists, knuckles, knees, and the joints of the ball of the foot. The infection is typically symmetrical; if it affects a joint on the left side, it affects the same joint on the right side. This disease generally begins in midlife but can be acquired at any age, including in children as young as 5 or 6 (juvenile arthritis). Three quarters of those affected are women, and the cause of the disease is not known. Individuals go through cycles in which the disease goes into remission and they feel better; however, the symptoms come back, often without warning (Mackelprang & Salsgiver, 1999).

HIV-AIDS Human immunodeficiency virus (HIV) gradually destroys the immune system and results in infections that the body is unable to fight. HIV is transmitted through exchange of certain bodily fluids such as blood, semen, vaginal secretions, and breast milk. To produce an infection, the virus must pass through the skin or mucous membranes of the body. Once considered a fatal disease, HIV is now considered a chronic illness, although given the young ages at which people generally become infected, it is hard to predict how long the life span will be. HIV infection occurs in all age groups, and 25% of babies born to untreated mothers infected with HIV develop HIV infection. HIV progresses in stages that are based on symptoms and the amount of virus in the affected individual's blood. Within 3 to 6 weeks of becoming infected, flulike symptoms often appear, and these may include fever, headache, skin rash, sore throat, muscle aches and joint pain, and enlarged lymph nodes in the neck, armpits, and groin. These initial symptoms can range from mild to severe but usually disappear in 2 to 3 weeks. After the initial infection, it is possible for individuals to live many years without any other visible sign of illness. Some reoccurring symptoms at this stage may include confusion, diarrhea, dry cough, fatigue, mouth sores, night sweats, swollen lymph nodes in the neck, armpits, and groin, tingling, numbness and weakness in the limbs, and recurrent outbreaks of herpes simplex. Additional symptoms in women may include more than three vaginal yeast infections in a year that are not related to the use of antibiotics, recurrent pelvic inflammatory disease, and an abnormal PAP test or cervical cancer. Children infected with HIV may exhibit various symptoms, including delayed growth or an enlarged spleen. Treatment for HIV includes potent antiretroviral therapy. If left untreated, HIV generally progresses to *acquired immunodeficiency syndrome (AIDS),* the final and most serious stage of this disease, 12 to 13 years after the initial infection. A small number of people who are infected with HIV develop AIDS within about 3 to 4 years, but the reason why the infection progresses so quickly in these individuals is not known. They may have had a problem with their immune system and are therefore at higher risk. Treatment for HIV may delay or prevent its progression to AIDS; thus testing is very important. AIDS is the leading cause of death among people between the ages of 25 and 44. This is an infectious disease that has wiped out nearly whole generations of people in sub-Saharan countries (Auerbach & Coates, 2000, p. 1031). The symptoms of AIDS include fatigue, weight loss, diarrhea, fever, night sweats, infection in the mouth (thrush), and opportunistic infections. *Opportunistic infections* occur when a person's immune system has been weakened and can include serious life-threatening diseases, including pneumonia, tuberculosis, and certain kinds of cancer such as Kaposi's sarcoma, lymphoma, and cancer of the cervix. The risk of developing AIDS is increased when individuals engage in intravenous drug use; oral, anal, or vaginal sex without condoms; an increased number of sexual partners; substance abuse; tattoos, and body piercing with unsterile needles or instruments. It is important to counsel HIV-infected individuals about how to prevent transmission of the virus to other people: practicing safer sex; using a new, sterile syringe each time she or he injects; never sharing injection equipment; proper cleaning of infection equipment with bleach; and proper cleaning of injection sites. It is also important for infected individuals to be counseled about the dangers of having unprotected sex with other HIV-positive individuals who are on antiviral therapy. This behavior incurs multiple risks, including the possibility of becoming infected with a more virulent strain of HIV (Centers for Disease Control, 2004; Department of Health and Human Services, 2004).

Racial and ethnic minority groups are more vulnerable to HIV and AIDS than whites, with blacks accounting for more than half of all new HIV and AIDS cases diagnosed in the United States between 2000 and 2006 (Centers for Disease Control, 2004; 2008). Black males are at highest risk (seven times at greater risk than whites); black women are at lower risk than black men but still 18 times more likely than white women to have HIV. Latino men and women (9.5) have rates of infection three times higher than white men and women (Diaz et al., 2001; Timmins 2002).

These groups remain vulnerable to the impact of HIV-AIDS due to their concentration in high-density urban communities affected by poverty, drugs, violence, racism, and oppression (see Chapter 4 on identity development and Chapter 12 on adolescence; Paradis, 1997; Zierler and Krieger, 1997). Herdt (2001, p. 141 references Diaz, 1998) who writes: "If we . . . imagine those places in which AIDS has had the most impact, then we begin to understand how discrimination, stigma, and the tenuous structures of civil society have influenced rates of HIV infectivity; whether by color, gender, sexual orientation, etc. People in these vulnerable populations do not hold the same ability or have at their disposal the same resources to protect themselves."

According to the *National Health Guide*, there are important benefits to being tested for HIV. They include the availability of medications that prevent or delay AIDS and other serious infections. Test results can also help people to make choices about contraception and pregnancy and thus halt the spread of the virus to unaffected groups, including infants. Individuals diagnosed with HIV often suffer from psychological trauma, which stems from the difficulty of reconciling two contradictory life orientations: life with possibilities and a possible premature death if the illness progresses. However due to the stigma associated with this disease initially diagnosed in gay men and intravenous drug users, some people are afraid that their test results will cause them to be discriminated against. They fear confidentiality breaches that could lead to social reprisals based on moral judgments such as those that occurred in the early days of AIDS detection when it was referred to as the "gay plague." Herdt (2001, p 147) concurs and writes, "Basic social inequalities in local cultures contain the force to marginalize people and set up processes of AIDS stigmatizing or superstigmatizing of marginalized people who are suspected carriers of HIV." Anonymous HIV testing is available, but due to the continuing stigma associated with this illness (despite public education and progress in this area) this provides little comfort to many people who remain skeptical that their confidentiality will be protected. Copenhaver and Fisher (2006), in writing about the current HIV epidemic in the United States, highlight the "subepidemics" among groups at risk: injection drug users (IDU), men who have sex with men (MSM), and heterosexuals (p. 105). They underscore that some of these new infections are directly related to risk behavior among HIV-positive MSM and IDUs. These authors make the point that despite tremendous gains in the medical treatment of HIV-positive persons, little progress has been made in reducing the rate of new HIV infections. In a study they conducted using a behavioral orientation to HIV prevention, the authors collected information about behaviors thought to have affected the HIV epidemic as well as behaviors that might improve the HIV epidemic. Although a detailed discussion of their study is beyond the scope of this chapter (see Copenhaver & Fisher, 2006), their results highlighted the need for "empirically or theoretically based interventions that are more sensitively tailored to the characteristics of target populations" (p. 108). Another significant finding was concern about the lack of funding and resources devoted to HIV prevention relative to the high risk levels among certain populations. Multiple risk factor reasons such as drug use, physical and mental abuse, racism, depression, and other mental health issues often lead to risk taking.

Constant or Permanent Conditions

Deafness Foster (1996) described three different models of understanding deafness. The *medical model* defines deafness as the failure of a critical sensory system, resulting in hearing deficit(s). There are several types and causes of deafness such as middle ear infections, injury to the small bones of the middle ear, and certain genetic conditions, among others. The *sociocultural model* emphasizes that the barriers experienced by deaf persons result from social, language, and cultural differences. The *political model* expands on the social model and emphasizes the power differences between hearing and deaf persons. In other words, hearing persons (who form the majority group) impose their definitions of the meaning of deafness on deaf persons, who are considered a cultural or linguistic minority. Congruent with this view is the fact that many deaf people feel they constitute a deaf culture. "Deaf culture" refers to people who "behave as Deaf persons do, use the language of Deaf people, and share the beliefs of Deaf people toward themselves and other people who are not deaf" (Padden, 1989, p. 5).

Language presents an area of controversy for deaf people. At least some of this has to do with the age of onset of the hearing loss, which is significant with regard to language development. *Prelingual deafness* occurs prior to age 3, and these children do not become fluent in auditory language prior to their deafness. Their first or native language is generally *American Sign Language* (*ASL*), a visual and manual language. *Postlingual deafness* occurs after acquiring spoken language, usually at 3 years of age or later. Spoken language, therefore, is the first language for most persons with postlingual deafness. American Sign Language, learned after the onset of deafness, becomes a second language. Proponents of *oral language acquisition,* where the primary language to be learned is lip reading and speech, feel that deaf people need to function in a hearing world and need to learn the language of the hearing population. Unfortunately, deaf people who rely on oral language can have problems becoming fluent with the primary language because they are difficult to understand. American Sign Language (ASL) is the language of first choice and an influential component of deaf culture and a deaf worldview (Bonvillian & Folven, 1993; Foster, 1996; Mackelprang & Salsgiver, 1999). Humphries, Martin, & Coye (1989) suggested that a bilingual, bicultural approach to teaching English to deaf people may be the most helpful. For example, some language methods, such as *cued speech,* combine English-based oral language and facilitative signing. We need to honor an individual's culture while acknowledging the intersections with the larger society. Ahmad (2000) raised the important concern of the shortage of sign language interpreters who are from minority, immigrant, and ethnic communities and fluent in languages other than English. He underscored the important point that there are differences in the use of sign language between ethnic, social, and age groups. For example, signs and cultural signifiers for Asian people and cultures are not always picked up by white interpreters. Even when interpreters and deaf people from minority ethnic communities do not share a common culture or language, there may be a shared experience of minority status within a dominant white culture, which contributes to rapport and trust (Aguyo, 2001).

Blindness and Visual Impairment There are several functional categories of visual impairment. Category one encompasses *total blindness* (in other words, the individual does not perceive any light at all). Category two centers on the ability to perceive whether or not the light is present. Category three, *economic blindness* (considered *legally blind*), establishes that the individual cannot do any kind of work for which sight is essential. The fourth category, *vocational blindness,* includes those who are not able to do the work for which they have been trained. Category five, *educational blindness,* is a level of impairment that would make it difficult, if not impossible, to learn by usual and traditional methods of education. With reasonable accommodations, most vocational and educational activities can be mastered by a person with limited vision. The most common causes of blindness are glaucoma, cataracts, and diabetic retinopathy. Gonorrhea, retinitis pigmentosa, syphilis, trachoma, smallpox, and rubella are diseases that may also cause blindness. Others may lose their sight through accident or physical abuse or injury. Many older people lose their eyesight through macular degeneration. Less than 2% of blindness is congenital or develops in early childhood. Many people who are blind or visually impaired use canes for mobility. Some people use guide dogs specifically trained to move around obstacles, go through doorways, and stop at curbs and stairs. Persons who are blind use a variety of cues to help them locate specific places and addresses. Most people who are blind learn to read by using transcribed books on audiotape or by using Braille. *Braille* is read by feeling a numbered set of dots and different combinations of dots in relationship to the letter, number, or note they stand for. Technological advances make accommodation easier than in the past, and with training and assistive equipment, people who are blind have the same range of abilities as people who are not (Mackelprang & Salsgiver, l999; Rothman, 2003).

Relapsing or Episodic Conditions

Multiple Sclerosis (MS) This is a progressive, neurological disease that typically has its onset between the ages of 20 to 40. More women than men (60% vs. 40%) are affected. The early symptoms include complaints of fatigue, clumsiness, visual disturbance, weakness of limbs, and numbness or tingling in parts of the body. There is a gradual onset of this disease, but as it progresses, more pronounced symptoms such as loss of vision, loss of bowel and bladder control, and paralysis may occur. The mean survival time is estimated at 30 years from time of onset.

Systemic Lupus Lupus is an autoimmune disorder of unknown cause in which the body's immune system attacks the body itself. It is considered a musculoskeletal disease because it also affects the nervous system, the skin, the kidneys, the lungs, the heart, and the pancreas. The symptoms of lupus include fever, weakness, and loss of hair. Individuals can develop a symmetrical (the same occurring on both sides of the body) skin rash on their face, neck, and arms. It includes pain in motor joints, including hands, wrists, elbows, knees, and ankles, as well as general muscle aches, and sometimes nausea and vomiting that can lead to loss of appetite and substantial weight loss. It is eight times as common in women as in men. This condition occurs more often in blacks, Asians, and Native Americans than in white people. Lupus can go into remission without treatment.

Fibrositis or Fibromyalgia This condition is associated with specific tender joints. Pain appears to come from the muscles themselves or from the points at which ligaments attach muscles to bones. However, the condition shows no identifiable damage to joints, ligaments, or tendons. The most common symptom is pain. There is aching, stiffness, and tenderness near the joints or muscles. Those with the condition experience sleep abnormalities; however it is unclear whether sleep disturbance is the cause or the result of the condition. Individuals with this condition are often depressed because they are in a constant state of pain and discomfort.

Chronic Pain Pain can be defined as the "unpleasant experience that accompanies both sensory and emotional modalities; may or may not be accompanied by identifiable tissue damage; and is influenced by multiple factors, including cognitive, affective, and environmental" (Turk & Okifuji, 2001). A distinction must be made between acute pain and chronic pain. *Acute pain* is typically associated with an active disease state or a traumatic injury. When the damaged area heals, the pain typically goes away. There are three types of *chronic pain:* (a) pain that lasts after the normal feeling of a disease or injury, (b) pain associated with a chronic medical condition, and (c) pain that develops and persists in the absence of identifiable organic problems. There are three important components to pain responses: sensory responses, psychological responses, and pain behaviors.

Sensory Physiology of Pain The process of receiving sensory information is called *nociception.* Sensory stimulation activates nerve endings within the skin, the underlying tissue, or the viscera. These signals are conducted to the dorsal horn of the spinal cord, where they are directed to appropriate centers in the brain. Axons of nociceptive neurons terminate in several different centers to the brain stem and thalamus. Within the brain, nociceptive stimulation is received and acted on. In addition, there are descending pain pathways in which messages from the central nervous system are conveyed back to the originating tissues. Neurochemical events can modulate nociceptive stimulation along these pathways. A variety of medicines can be used to block nociceptive stimulation and may affect either the brain itself or the communication of information along these pathways. A variety of different receptors receive sensory information. There is great variability in the treatment of chronic pain, perhaps more so than any other medical condition. Medications are available that alleviate pain, but most have serious side effects. In addition, people can develop dependency on these medications, and addiction to prescription pain medication is a large problem.

Psychological Response to Pain Pain is the perception of sensation arising from nociception; it does not necessarily correspond with the amount of tissue damage. These connections are not always clear. For example, phantom limb syndrome is a condition in which patients with limb amputations report pain arising from the amputated arm or leg. Suffering is an emotional response. It is sometimes triggered by nociception, but not always. Melzack and Wall (1965) and Melzack (1982) put forth a "gate control theory of pain." This proposed that the brain plays a dynamic role in pain perception. A gating mechanism in the spinal cord can widen or narrow as a result of descending signals from the brain, allowing more, or fewer, pain signals to reach the brain. Psychological factors can inhibit or enhance the sensory flow of pain signals, influencing the way the brain ultimately responds to painful stimulation. This important research paved the way for pain integration of psychological methods of pain management with medical management (Thorn, 2004, p. 6).

Pain Behaviors There are "verbal or nonverbal actions that communicate discomfort (sighing, grimacing) or are used in an attempt to ameliorate pain (rubbing, prosthetic devices" (Thorn, 2004, p. 7). There may be an association between the experience of chronic pain and "learned helplessness." One of the main consequences of learned helplessness is depression. Helplessness may also be a function of the disease and pain itself and therefore result in depression. Depression can be predicted based on the amount of pain and the coping strategies used by the person experiencing the pain. The *stress-appraisal-coping model* of pain suggests that individuals' cognitions have a direct impact on their adjustment to chronic pain through appraisal of the pain and related stressors, their beliefs about their ability to exert control over the pain situation, and their choice of coping options (Thorn, 2004, p. 8; also see Chapter 3 for discussion of cognitive therapy).

Chronic Pain and Posttraumatic Stress Disorder

Otis, Keane, and Kerns (2003) examined the relationship between chronic pain and posttraumatic stress disorder (PTSD; see Chapter 16, "Trauma and Development") in a series of models described next.

Mutual Maintenance Model Attentional biases may be present in chronic pain and PTSD patients, causing them to attend to threatening or painful stimuli. Anxiety sensitivity may contribute toward a vulnerability to catastrophize. Pain may be a reminder of the traumatic event, triggering an arousal response, avoidance of the cause of pain, and any memories of the trauma. In both disorders (attentional biases and anxiety sensitivity) avoidance may be adopted as a means to minimize pain and disturbing thoughts. Fatigue and lethargy associated with depression and general anxiety may contribute to both disorders. Finally, the cognitive demands from the symptoms of pain and PTSD may limit the use of adaptive coping strategies.

Shared Vulnerability Model Anxiety sensitivity is a predisposing factor that contributes to the development of both chronic pain and PTSD. A person with high levels of anxiety will become fearful in response to physical sensations such as heart pounding and breathlessness, thinking that these symptoms may signal impending doom. The tendency to respond with fear to the physical symptoms of anxiety may be a *shared vulnerability* contributing to the development of either chronic pain or PTSD. In the case of PTSD, the degree of alarm caused by the stressor is combined with the alarm of physiological sensations to further exacerbate the emotional reaction, thereby increasing the risk of developing PTSD. Anxiety sensitivity heightens fear and avoidance of activities that may induce pain, which further increases the chances that pain will be maintained over time.

Fear Avoidance Model This model emphasizes the contributions of physiological symptoms and arousal. These symptoms may directly increase pain sensations and reinforce fears and negative beliefs that activities will be painful. When these are confirmed, avoidance behaviors increase. Physiological arousal may produce bodily sensations such as muscle tension, which could be misinterpreted as being pain related. The misinterpretations are thought to be influenced by an individual's tendency to respond with fear to sensations that are anxiety provoking.

Triple Vulnerability Model An integrated set of triple vulnerabilities needs to be present for developing an anxiety disorder: a generalized biological vulnerability, a generalized psychological vulnerability based on early experiences of control over salient events, and a more specific psychological vulnerability in which one learns to focus anxiety on specific situations. It is possible that for many people to develop a chronic pain condition, they must also develop a belief that the pain is preceding in an unpredictable and uncontrollable manner. A feeling of low efficacy may then develop along with negative affect, fear, and avoidance of situations in which pain may occur. This further fuels the negative affect and feelings of uncontrollability and low self-efficacy. Chronic pain and PTSD are always moderated by social support and coping skills.

Psychiatric Disabilities

Psychiatric disorders include a wide range of conditions that are listed in the *Diagnostic and Statistical Manual of Mental Disorders* (*DSM-IV TR;* American Psychiatric Association, 2000). Included among these are schizophrenia and other psychotic disorders, mood disorders (such as bipolar disorder), dissociative disorders, eating disorders (anorexia nervosa and bulimia nervosa), and anxiety disorders (such as obsessive compulsive disorder). Only a small percentage of people diagnosed with a major mental disorder experience ongoing psychotic symptoms (including hallucinations, delusions, and disorganized or disordered thinking); most have psychotic episodes. These episodes may be unpredictable and variable in frequency and may occur anywhere from once or twice to multiple times in a year. Hallucinations may include hearing voices, feeling tactile sensations, seeing visual images, or sensing tastes, all of which originate from within the person's brain but are experienced as real. A disturbed perception of the self and the world is the essence of psychosis in mental illness that causes people a great deal of stress because they cannot accommodate to the two realities of their inner world and the world as experienced by other people. *Psychotropic medications* have been effective in ceasing or reducing psychotic symptoms; however, they often have unpleasant side effects (Wedenoja, 1999).

Legislation and services for people with psychiatric disabilities have traditionally been separated from those for people with physical disabilities, despite evidence that those with psychiatric impairments also experience difficulties in functioning at home and work. They are often subject to discrimination. A societal challenge that often arises with regard to psychiatric disabilities is the boundary between an individual's right to self-determination and the public's obligations to ensure safety. The National Alliance for the Mentally Ill (NAMI) is a nonprofit, self-help organization of consumers (persons with mental illness) and their families and friends who work to improve public understanding of the biological causes of mental illness. They also advocate for government resources needed for treatment and ongoing research (Kurtz, 2004). The elements of self-help that this organization provides—emotional support and education—are important resources, especially because persons with psychiatric disabilities are often not included in the wider discourse on persons with disabilities. This is at least partially due to the fact that the nature of their illnesses may not make them the most articulate or reliable reporters. It also has to do with the stigma about mental illness in our society (Roos, 2005). Thomas Szasz (1970) called mental illness a "myth." He felt that society imposes this label on individuals when their behavior breaks the social rules; in other words, when their personal conduct violates certain ethical, political, and social norms. Similar to contemporary disability discourse, Szasz felt that diagnoses of psychiatric disorders were socially constructed and varied from culture to culture. Although neurobiological advances (see Chapter 2) may make the argument presented by Szasz seem outdated, we must also remember that "homosexuality" was once included in the *DSM-IV TR*. The American Psychiatric Association (APA) and the World Health Organization (WHO) voted in 1973 to exclude homosexuality as a mental illness (Longress, 1995). A listing in the current *DSM-IV TR* (2000) that is considered by many to be another socially constructed and discriminatory label is *gender identity disorder*. The point being made here is that although Szasz may have gone too far in postulating that mental illness was *solely* the construction of society, there is credence to the argument that social trends change with the development of knowledge, with change in attitude, and with legislation.

Disability across the Life Cycle

Crate (1965) outlined five stages of adaptation to a disability:

- *Disbelief:* The person denies the disability or minimizes its effects.
- *Developing awareness:* The denial cannot be maintained.
- *Reorganization:* The person accepts limitations imposed by the disability and begins to modify lifestyle and/or relationships.
- *Resolution:* The individual comes to grips with loss of function, grieves, and begins to identify with others with the same or a similar disability.
- *Identity change:* The person accepts the disability and modifies behavior accordingly.

Although it is helpful to consider these stages, the disability and chronic illness narrative is complex. The way one views disability or illness becomes part of the wider process of development, coping strategies, the everyday experience of living with a chronic illness or disability, and the support of family and community relationships (Seltzer & Heller, 1997). Rolland (1988) wrote that the time of *onset* in the life cycle, the *course* of the condition (whether constant, progressive, or episodic, as previously discussed), the *outcome* (pain and other quality-of-life issues and projected life span), and the *severity of impairment* (degree of incapacitation) can affect whether and how someone experiences disabling consequences. Appleby, Colon, and Hamilton suggested eight variables to consider when assessing a person's experiences with disability: (a) the specific nature of the disability, (b) the age at onset, (c) the person's character and personality, (d) family characteristics, (e) the characteristics of the person's community, (f) socioeconomic status, (g) ethnic group, and (h) cultural and societal interactions (2001, p. 183, cited in Rothman, 2003, p. 197). The following section presents some of the themes to consider regarding the impact of disability and chronic illness at different stages of life. Although not meant to be inclusive of all issues or persons, they provide some important insights and considerations for social work practice (Mackelprang & Salsgiver, 1999).

Birth to Age 3 About 3 of every 100 babies are born some with anomaly at birth. These include congenital heart defects, neural tube defects (such as spina bifida), hydrocephalus, and chromosomal abnormalities such as Down syndrome. Many prenatal tests allow genetic screening during pregnancy. These technological advances present prospective parents and medical and human service providers with ethical dilemmas. Parents who find out they are carrying a fetus with a major birth defect may choose to have an abortion. Other parents are filing "wrongful life" and "wrongful death" lawsuits against doctors and hospitals who either failed to recommend prenatal testing that could have detected a genetic abnormality or even, in some cases, when the infant is born with a birth defect that may not have been detected with screening. Parents faced with the issue of whether to abort a fetus might consider several factors regarding genetic conditions: onset, course, outcome, incapacitation, and uncertainty (Nelson, 1998). Children who acquire disabilities early experience life differently from those who acquire a disability later. The disability is present before the child has the cognitive skills to be aware of the disability. Their first experiences are, therefore, from a disability perspective. These children may experience more protectiveness and increased contact with parents and caregivers. We need to consider the impact of separations from caregivers due to hospitalizations and the nature of the attachment relationships that develop. Children with disabilities are at greater risk for abuse than children without disabilities. The less satisfied the caregivers are with their child, and the more they perceive parenting as less enjoyable and more difficult, the greater the risk of maltreating their infant or toddler (Scanapieco & Connell-Carrick, 2005; Rothman, 2003).

3 to 6 Years of Age Disabilities can significantly affect this time of childhood. Language development, for example, is often different for children with learning disabilities, children with hearing loss, and children who are visually impaired because each of these conditions affects the symbolic scheme development of children. Language and communication are critical to help children develop at this stage. Children need supports to begin to expand their social environments. Playing and interacting with other children with and without disabilities are crucial. These relationships may give children their first experiences in being "different," and children may require the support of parents, caretakers, and teachers during this time (Rothman, 2003).

6 to 12 Years of Age As children enter the school setting, they become students and learners. This is a time for opportunity as well as increased problems. Maas's (1984) concept of the "supportive environment" is particularly important as educators struggle to establish the need for integration with other students without sacrificing the educational needs of the child with the disability. Meaningful contact with peers with disabilities—particularly those similar to the child's—is important at this age. Compliance with medications begins to present problems because the medication is an acknowledgment that the child has the illness or the problem. Noncompliance often represents a symbolic attempt at normality within the broader context of growing up. Children may find the regular need for medication and precautions restrictive and disruptive, preventing them from following pursuits that would help them emphasize their normality and similarity with peers. Children at the older end of this life stage can also begin to feel that they are somehow letting their parents down. This can contribute to feelings of low self-esteem and guilt that their illness or disability may be causing problems for their parents. Children's views about reward and punishment also become evident during these ages; for example, they may feel if they are "good" they would not have a flare-up or a crisis. Sadness about illness or disability can emerge during these years and is greater during some periods than at other times. Children under 12 are likely to follow most precautions as they usually abide by the limits set by their parents. Few question the need for precautions or parental involvement. As children grow older and attempt to assert their independence, they are more likely to challenge parental and professional definitions of their needs. If the onset of the disability occurs during this time of life, it can be especially confusing. Grief and mourning can also be experienced by the child as she or he adjusts to life with the disability, such as a new body image (Rothman, 2003).

12 to 18 Years of Age Individuals who acquire disabilities during adolescence face greater challenges than those who had them earlier. As they seek to develop their own identities, adolescents may reject their parents' or professionals' definitions of what is in their best interests. Compliance tends to feel imposed rather than negotiated, and the parent–child relationship becomes fundamental in negotiating responsibility for compliance. Adolescents with disability and chronic illness have the same desire for independence and opportunity as all other adolescents. However, they may believe that their peers do not have to tolerate the same degree of parental interference. Adolescents may feel that their parents are being overprotective and preventing them from pursuing normal activities. On the other hand, acknowledgment of parental concerns coupled with the need to establish their own sense of autonomy contributes to confusion and guilt. Adolescents may also take out their frustrations on their parents, a key feature of growing up with a chronic illness or disability. There is a conflict between overprotectiveness and the promotion of autonomy faced by the parents of these teens. Ambivalence and conflict can be heightened between adolescents and parents when the adolescent needs the parent to assist with activities of daily living but resents the need for parents to provide such intimate care. Technological and caregiving aids may therefore be preferable at this age. Adolescents with disabilities need to develop disability-affirming self-images and reject shame-based identities. Positive self-identity can help these adolescents recognize injustices rather than accept socially imposed *ableism*. However, the desire for normalcy rather than a desire for recognition and celebration of differences in this population is more often their response to discrimination and limited opportunity. Other challenges include limited social opportunities at a time when the need for a social group is most important. Adolescents with disabilities are more susceptible to sexual abuse when intimate care is provided by caregivers and/or family members. Another issue to consider is the objectification of their body by others (even in routine care that is not sexually abusive), leading adolescents to view themselves as asexual. Making the transition into educational and/or occupational roles that provide recognition and income is important for the development of independence and autonomy in adulthood (Rothman, 2003).

Young Adulthood/Adulthood The way in which young adults with disabilities meet the challenges of this life stage can depend on how well families have prepared them to launch independent lives. Adolescents are often faced with fragmented and waning services when they leave high school. Adolescents in rural areas face even greater obstacles, including limited transportation, access difficulties, and scarce financial resources, although this may sometimes be balanced by the unique aspects of rural life such as community cohesion and safety. Twenty percent of adolescents with disabilities have not completed high school, compared with 9% for those without disabilities. At this time of life, people look for intimacy with others. The barriers to intimacy must therefore be removed. Jobs, educational opportunities, and access to transportation are especially important for this group. Deprofessionalizing services and redirecting resources to the control of individuals allow people who use attendants to hire and direct their personal attendants rather than being dependent on others to control how and from whom they receive care. There is a need for young adults to have the opportunities for higher education, job and social opportunities, independence, and home ownership that are enjoyed by their peers (Bricout & Bentley, 2000; DePoy, Gilmer, & Haslen, 2000; Sands and Weymeyer, 1996). Unemployment among disabled young women in all societies is 50% higher than among comparably educated young men which is double that of their non-disabled peers (Groce, 2004) People who become disabled during their young adulthood face major challenges to their identity and self-image. Relationships forged prior to becoming disabled become compromised or lost, and young people need a lot of support and encouragement to develop new identities and relationships that encourage self-worth (Rothman, 2003).

Middle Adulthood People in their middle years can receive personal satisfaction by acting as role models for future generations, as well as effecting change on the local, state, and national levels for generations that follow. For example, this age cohort has provided the leadership in defining and expanding the disability culture (see following description). People in their middle years of life have been leaders in expanding a disability culture and in changing the political, social, and legal landscape for the generations that follow. People in midlife also contribute to positive ideas about persons with disabilities. (Franklin Delano Roosevelt was a famous man with a disability from polio who used a wheelchair. He became president of the United States during his middle years of adulthood and led the United States through the Great Depression and World War II.) They may, however, feel compromised in their ability to care for their own aging parents. There may be challenges with adolescents who may resist following parental rules, especially if they are expected to assist with caregiving or additional household chores. People may also acquire disabilities at this stage of life. Those who do may have to forge new identities and mourn the loss of earlier identities and abilities. Many of these individuals do not identify with the culture of disability and may not therefore benefit from some of the supports it can provide. Predisability friendships may be strengthened or may wane and there could be limited energy to form new friendships. Nonetheless, this can also be a time when people have the maturity and inner resourcefulness to adapt and find meaning in less-ambitious pursuits, interests, and hobbies.

Older Adulthood A common phrase in the disability community is *temporarily able-bodied* (TAB), meaning that with age, most people acquire disabilities from a variety of conditions. Visual, hearing, and physical disabilities, for example, become more common as people grow older. Arthritis is the main cause of disability for people ages 65 and older. Strokes are another cause of disability in later life. Persons who have lived their entire lives with disabilities can be better prepared for some of the problems as well as the available social supports to help them. They may, however, also be susceptible to many problems that are related to living with disability. For example, people who have used wheelchairs most of their lives may experience shoulder deterioration due to long-term wear and tear of pushing their chairs (Maas, 1984).

Disability Culture

A "disability culture" has evolved over the years that provides a sense of cohesion for persons with disabilities and helps to explain their identity and place in the world. The term refers to "the social, civil rights, or minority model of disability; disability as socially constructed, with an emphasis on its social meaning and on social obstacles as the primary problem for people with disabilities and their families" (Schriver, 2004, p. 366). Gill (1995) defined the disability culture as including a unified worldview, art, and a historical legacy, as well as symbols, beliefs, values, and strategies for using. A shared language (including terms such as *handiabled, differently abled, physically challenged,* and *able-disabled,* among others) emerges from within the disability community to create bonds to counter derogatory and oppressive language used by those external to the community (Gilson & DePoy, 2000). The "disability culture" has led to the development of a "*disability discourse*"—the public dialogue among different disability stakeholder groups (Barnartt, 1996). The first coalition for disability rights—the American Coalition of Citizens with Disabilities (ACCD; P.L. 101–336)—referred to as the "Emancipation Proclamation" for people with disabilities—is the most significant piece of federal legislation that prohibits discrimination against people with disabilities in both the public and private sectors (Pardeck, 2002a, 2002b). Jones and Kilpatrick (1996) apply *wellness theory*—a recognition that the development of the wellness state is an ongoing, lifelong process in which quality of life, rather than length of life, is the primary concern. A wellness perspective on disability insists on separating the individual from the disability and concentrates on reducing the barriers to life with disability (Schriver, 2004).

Piastro writes that disability discourse is different from individual experiences with disability, sharing her own experience with becoming disabled at age 34 (1999, p. 43). She describes her personal struggle to accept herself when her abilities changed. She raises the important question of how persons with disabilities can "get society to accept us if we cannot accept ourselves when our abilities change and we are different." Courvant talks about her struggles with coming to terms with increasing impairment caused by a neuromuscular disease that caused chronic pain: "Perhaps that was the worst aspect of my pain, that no one could see it. A cane would be my pain made visible . . . if I carried a cane, was I disabled? Would people offer to me the seats in the front of the bus? . . . but coming to work able one day, disabled the next? Did that require being hit by a car or run over by a train? Where was the line between ability and disability in my own life? The longer I held onto my job through the pain, the more I believed that I could keep it indefinitely. Is inability to make money the real disability?" (1999, pp. 102–103). Frank (1995) writes about the need of people who are ill or disabled to tell their stories to develop new perceptions of their relationship to the world.

Disability and Diversity

Some authors (Fleischer & Zames, 1998; Groce & Zola, 1993) describe the disability culture and the disability rights movement as representative of white, middle-class concerns rather than those of the diverse ethnic and racial populations of people with disabilities throughout our country. An example of this is the well-intentioned argument of some disability rights advocates for increased "self-determination" in treatment and care plans because it is the person with the disability who has the most knowledge about her or his disability (Groce & Zola, 1993). Many people, however, live in communities where lines may be drawn between members of society based on education and wealth. Professionals such as physicians, nurses, teachers, and social workers are often at the upper end of the hierarchy and consequently their word may carry great weight. Groce and Zola wrote: "In such environments a professional asking a patient whether a particular course of action is acceptable will be met with confusion . . . such a question may be virtually meaningless within their frame of reference" (p. 1052).

Professionals are expected to know the best way to proceed, and asking for involvement by the person with the disability may indicate a lack of knowledge or training. Devlieger and Albrecht (2000) wrote about the experiences of four Chicago inner-city African-American individuals with disabilities. They did not embrace the idea of a "disability culture" but felt more affected by what they described as a "culture of persecution" defined by poverty, racism, drug use, unemployment, and poor medical services. This is particularly significant because blacks have a higher percentage of disability than whites (for example, in the 15- to 64-year-old range, 20.8% compared to 17.7% for whites and 16.9% for Latinos). The group of blacks with a severe disability is almost double that of whites (16% compared to 9%), and the impact of disability on blacks is felt most keenly in the inner city and is highest for low-income blacks living in single-parent households. The people interviewed by these authors/researchers did not consider people with disabilities to be like them or their people. Church and family kinship systems are important support structures in the African-American communities where distinctions are sometimes made between "white disabilities" and "black disabilities." For example, diabetes or "having sugar" is a black disability, and the resulting disabling effects seem known and manageable within the black community (Belgrave & Bowe, 2000). Multiple sclerosis is a "white disease" and can be threatening to one's identity (p. 59). Many African Americans are knowledgeable and realistic about disability; however social class, poverty, race and ethnicity, gender, age, and generational differences play a role in shaping the meaning of the experience for the individual. Other authors have written about people of color who have disabilities. The term "double discrimination" (McDonald & Oxford, 1999) combines institutional racism with disablism. Another concept introduced by Stuart (1992) is "simultaneous oppression" (disability and racism) based on the work of Carby (1982) to describe the feelings of oppression faced by black women in contrast to their white peers. Diversification based on race, ethnicity, and class will expand the voices being heard and broaden the political clout of the disability rights movement and help individuals who do not have disabilities to understand and join the ongoing struggle for civil rights for persons with disabilities (Devlieger & Albrecht, 2000).

Family Adjustment to Disability

The ability of an individual—especially a child—to adapt and cope with a chronic illness or disability is often dependent on the family—including the reactions of parents, siblings, and other family members. Family reactions are affected by racial, ethnic, and cultural factors, religious and spiritual beliefs, and socioeconomic factors. The reaction of the wider community—including peers, neighbors, and friends—is also a contributing factor. Any understanding or assessment of an individual with a disabling condition must take account of the family system, including the challenges the disability presents and the resources that the family (and each individual member within it) has to cope (Rothman, 2003). Rolland

(1988, 1989, 1994) discusses three time phases to which individuals and families must adjust when a member is born with or acquires a disability or chronic illness: the *initial crisis phase,* the *chronic phase,* and the *terminal phase.* Freeman (2005) writes about the anticipatory grief that may accompany a chronic or prolonged illness in which the survivors may begin the process of grieving in advance of losses. He writes: "Anticipating a specific loss may allow time to prepare psychological and/or physical coping mechanisms than can aid in the post-loss adjustment" (p. 59). Roos (2002) writes about the "chronic sorrow" that may be a parental response to the long-term mental and physical effects of birth defects, sudden injury, or chronic illness in a child. She describes the loss that the parents may experience at every developmental milestone not achieved by their child. In addition, the demands of the child may go beyond the life span of the parent's ability to provide physical, emotional, and financial care. This certainly is not the experience of all parents with a child living with a disability. However, it helps us appreciate that even in the face of such sorrow, we must look at families coping with disability through a normative lens and not be quick to pathologize feelings or behaviors.

The Family Systems Illness Model

Developed by Rolland (1994), this model emphasizes multigenerational life-cycle issues and belief systems. He discussed the significance of the following family organizational patterns and communication processes with regard to chronic conditions.

- *Constellation.* This includes all members of the current household, the extended family system, and key people who function as family insiders. Professionals who become involved in the care of an ill or disabled family member's care become part of the "health related family unit" (p. 65).
- *Adaptability.* This is one of the key requisites for well-functioning family systems and refers to the ability of the family to adapt to changing circumstances or life-cycle developmental tasks, balanced by the family's need for enduring values or traditions and predictable family rules. Internally, the family must reorganize in response to the developmental imperatives brought on by progressive illness. Major illnesses cause the family sufficient stress, and there must be adaptational shifts in family rules to ensure continuity of family life.
- *Cohesion.* Families must balance closeness and connectedness with respect for separateness and individual differences. Consider how the condition may have affected the family members' ability to talk directly and openly with one another. For example, is the illness or disability expressed openly? How has the family mood been affected by this disorder? Which relationships have become closer and which more distant?
- *Generational Boundaries.* Patterns of enmeshment and disengagement can be risk factors for families' ability to cope and adapt. The rules differentiating parent and child roles, rights, and obligations maintain the hierarchical

organization of families. An effective parental/marital coalition, for example, is imperative with chronic disorders in childhood. On the other hand, a child caring for an ill parent might breach the age-appropriate developmental needs and boundaries for that child.

- *Family-Community Boundaries.* Families can become isolated and may need social networks for support and remaining connected to the community.

There are cultural and social reasons why individuals and families act certain ways or make certain decisions about a disability or illness. Among these are beliefs about why the disability or illness occurred, the expectations for survival, and how that may affect both the immediate care and planning for future care, and the social roles that are considered appropriate for children and adults who are disabled or chronically ill (Seltzer & Heller, 1997; Stone, 2005). Belgrave and Bowe (2000) wrote that the Afrocentric worldview may facilitate functioning among African Americans with disabilities. Atkins discusses cultural values such as spirituality and communalism and wrote, "Asset orientation reflects a belief that positive outcomes originate from shaping strengths and failure results from a concentration on limitations, fears, and negatives" (1998, p. 45). Fadiman (1998) wrote a poignant account of the clash between the medical establishment in one U.S. hospital and immigrant Hmong parents around the conceptualization and treatment of their daughter's seizure disorder: "Neil and Peggy were excellent physicians . . . but . . . a concern for the psychosocial and cultural factors that give illness context and meaning—they were, at least during their early years with Lia, imperfect healers" (1997, p. 265). In an exploratory study that examined the environment of 10 families, each with an adolescent with a physical disability Nelson et al. (1992) found that the families viewed themselves as "normal" and, although they experienced stress, believed that raising a disabled child had brought them closer together. Warfield (2001) studied the influence of employment on the well-being of mothers with children with disabilities. She found that the limited availability of child care, the inability or unwillingness of day-care providers to accept children with special needs, the lack of structurally accessible child-care facilities, and the lack of child-care workers experienced in caring for children with disabilities and behavioral problems adversely caused greater absenteeism and problems in work and career development for these women (Fujiura & Yamaki, 2000; Park, Turnbull, & Turnbull, 2002).

We would like to give some attention in this section to parents with physical and cognitive disabilities and the impact this has on their children and the family. This group continues to require attention particularly because parents with cognitive disabilities often are unable to advocate for themselves or their children. Parentification of children is often an issue for parents with cognitive disabilities. This was poignantly illustrated in the movie *I Am Sam* about a cognitively impaired single father raising a daughter. Like Sam, many of these parents face the threat of having their children taken away from them, especially in the face of inadequate child-care assistance and support. There are myriad other challenges these parents face: transportation, housing, recreational access, personal assistance with child care, adaptive techniques and equipment to foster attachment between mothers and infants, and barriers to child care. Schriver talks about the concept of *distributed competence,* underscoring the fact that parenting is a shared activity and acknowledging the interdependencies that comprise the parenting task (2004, p. 376). This is consistent with the disability culture's contextual view of parenting that focuses on the supportive, compensatory, and nurturing elements in the social environment (versus those that are undermining and stressful). Penn (2001) uses the phrase "relational trauma" to describe the relationally traumatizing effects of an illness on members of the family as well as the person with the illness. She writes about breaking the silence that develops in these families and the importance of opening conversations with and among these family members about the impact of the illness. Whether the caregiver is a parent with a disability caring for a young child, or an adolescent with a chronic illness being cared for by a parent, or an elder caring for an aging spouse, it is important to adequately assess the needs of caregivers and family members (Rothman, 2003).

Disabilities and Abuse of Women

Women with disabilities are at risk for personal abuse. The abusers are usually men who are known to them, and most assaults occur within the home or place of residence. Women with disabilities are also vulnerable to abuse from personal care assistance providers, health and social service providers, and persons essential to their independence such as transportation providers. There is a lack of research on this population contributing to their invisibility. Women with disabilities who are abused are also likely to suffer from secondary injury, exacerbation of their disability, or both. Withholding medication, for example, can result in a seizure. The environmental and cultural factors that contribute to abuse of this population include pervasive stigma and marginalization, devaluation by society, and stereotyping. Feminist disability theorists have identified the intersection of gender and disability as a position of compounded vulnerability for women with disabilities (Thomas, 1999). Women with disabilities are stereotyped as passive, asexual, and dependent. They have often been stripped of traditional female roles such as caregiver, wife, and mother. Traditional male roles—provider, worker, independent thinker—have also been deemed as off limits. This systematic rolelessness places women at a disadvantage psychologically, socially, and economically. Health-care systems often contribute further to their disability. Many women with disabilities are reluctant to report abuse, especially if the abusers are their caregivers, as they often feel they must choose between having essential health care and their personal needs met or experiencing abuse. These women are at risk from two types of caregivers: those with and without an attachment to them. Personal assistants who promote dependency rather than enhancement of abilities—even when not abusive—are not the best caregivers. Women of color with disabilities are among the most impoverished and socially isolated of all minority groups (Krotoski, Nosek, & Turk, 1996, p. 10). Another area of major concern for women with disabilities is sexuality and reproductive health. There are many stories about women with disabilities who have had their babies taken away from them on the basis of their disability. Personal stories of different women with disabilities underscore how stressful it is to be socially devalued. It is even more stressful to feel invisible. The message is not only that you are inferior, but it also doesn't matter that you are because you don't matter. Osgood and Eisenhandler (1994) wrote about women who are so depressed and hopeless that they come to believe they should die because they are socially denied a meaningful role in life. They are left without economic or social support and are bombarded with messages that they fall far short of society's standards for womanhood. These authors called this *"acquiescent suicide,"* which happens not because the woman has a disability but because of the way in which she is treated as a woman with a disability (Curry, Hassouneh-Phillips, & Johnston-Silverberg, 2001; Fawcett, 2000).

Sociological Aspects of Chronic Illness and Disability

Access to good medical care is the first priority of persons diagnosed with a disability or chronic illness, followed by finances and transportation to access health care. The nation's prevention agenda—*Healthy People 2010*—has a primary goal of eliminating health disparities.

Researchers are seeking a better understanding of how a person's health is affected by socioeconomic status, including income, education, occupation, and neighborhood and community characteristics. People are economically segregated in our society. The quality of schools is partially determined by community resources; people in poor communities often get poor quality education. They then have fewer opportunities for good jobs and incomes. These individuals—particularly children—may also suffer from nutritional deficits and family pressures. They also face the effects of lowered expectations; for example, women with less education often lack information about reproductive health. Poor people live in resource-poor neighborhoods with limited health-care facilities and where escaping from low-paying service jobs is difficult. They experience transportation problems, high crime rates, a pervasive sense of insecurity, and less control over their environments. Income segregation is further compounded by racial segregation (that is why black poverty is different from white poverty). Residential inequalities make it difficult for many members of racial minorities to improve their living conditions. Public health officials must capture the contextual realities of racial and ethnic communities. For example, the rate of diabetes among African Americans is 70% higher than among whites. The rate of low birth weight among infants is more than double. Illness and death from asthma are particularly high among poor, African-American, inner-city residents. Although asthma is only slightly more prevalent among minority children than among whites, it accounts for three times the number of deaths. The financial burden of these illnesses adds to the economic strain on families. For African Americans and other persons of color, such economic burdens are often compounded by the inherited disadvantages of institutionalized racism.

Health is produced not merely by having access to medical prevention and treatment, but also to a measurably greater extent by the cumulative experience of social conditions over the course of one's life. A large percentage of people on disability have no health insurance or limited health insurance. The condition that is the source of disability is often excluded from coverage due to a preexisting condition. The cost of insurance is very high when expenditures for deductibles and copayments are considered. Health insurance may cover the cost of acute care, but not necessarily the expenditures necessary for the maintenance of functioning with a chronic condition (especially assistive devices). Disparities of adequate insurance and local health care affect racial and ethnic minorities more than whites. The broader issues of social inequality must be addressed before the puzzle of health disparities can be resolved (Charlton, 1998; Prohanska, Peters, & Warren, 2000; Smedley, Stith, & Nelson, 2002).

A final point to be made about the structure of the health-care system is that it often pushes people who require assistance with activities of daily living into nursing homes because attendant services are not covered. The independent living model supports persons with disabilities who wish to live independently in the community. Some of the principles of this model follow.

- People with disabilities are viewed as active, responsible consumers, not patients or clients.
- Traditional treatment approaches are considered offensive and disenfranchising.
- Personal responsibility to hire and fire personal care assistants should be retained (rather than allowing formal structures to provide and control the caregivers).
- Attendants who are trained by the individual with disabilities themselves are preferred.
- Empowerment is self-developed and not bestowed by professionals
- The greatest constraints on persons with disabilities are environmental and social.
- A philosophy that advocates natural support systems under the direction of the consumer is significant (Schriver, 2004, p. 526).

A primary source of social support for persons with disabilities who face these challenges is the disability-specific organization that provides special services. These groups provide information, support, and opportunities for socialization. Some of them include the AIDS Foundation, American Cancer Society, Arthritis Foundation, Lupus Foundation, Multiple Sclerosis Society, and the American Epilepsy Society (Rothman, 2003, p. 260). If society, the helping professions, and the general public were to truly embrace the idea that it is acceptable to be disabled, then people without disability must partner with those who have a disability to concentrate on reducing the barriers to life with disability (Folkman & Greer, 2000). See Practice Example 17.1.

PRACTICE EXAMPLE 17.1

Illustrative Reading—Chronic Illness and Disability

Steve Bogatz

Social workers in assorted environments help patients with acute and chronic mental and physical illnesses. The variety of this type of practice is as varied as the setting (Holosko & Taylor, 1994). Numerous chronic illnesses can linger for years or even decades, and the task becomes maximizing the patient's quality of life within the context of the health challenges faced.

According to the National Kidney Foundation (2005), kidney disease affects 20 million Americans or 1 in 9 U.S. adults. End-stage renal disease, now called chronic kidney disease, stage 5, affects over 500,000 people in the United States who require either repeated dialysis or a transplant to live (U.S. Renal Data System, 2004). Much has been written (Faber & Wilde, 1993; Faris, 1994; Levy, 1981; Phillips, 1987) about the fear, anxiety, and reactive depression that people starting dialysis treatment may face as well as the resulting diet and fluid restrictions and fatigue. Like all chronic challenges, some patients are able to adjust better than others. This ability likely depends on a combination of self-fortitude and outside support, commonly called nature and nurture. Two other factors that may affect adjustment are locus of control (internal = I change the world; external = the world changes me; Cvenros, Christensen & Lawton, 2005) and the ability to self-organize (be believed, access resources, take action and responsibility; Monsivais, 2005). At their best, and perhaps with help, the mind and spirit can transcend chronic illness and pain to reach a person's true potential—what Maslow describes as self-actualization. One such rewarding case is described here.

"Larry" (not his real name) was born in the autumn of 1960. He is the youngest of five African-American children. The oldest brother is a minister and started dialysis about 8 years after Larry. The next oldest brother was born deaf and mute; he learned sign language, played football in high school, and earned a GED. The third brother contracted tetanus at the tender age of four and passed away. Larry's only sister died when she was 36 from cirrhosis of the liver due to alcoholism. Larry and his wife, "Lucy," became the guardians of his sister's two children and raised them as their own. "Chanda" was 13 and "Tara" was 10 when Larry and Lucy became their de facto parents. They also had a son, "Deen" together, who was about 10 at the time. Sadly, Chanda perished in a car accident in 1995 when she was 20.

Larry had been a successful high-school athlete participating in football, softball, and track. After graduating, he worked for 17 years as a machinist for a national defense contractor. He went on disability and stopped working in 1995 when he began dialysis. The etiology of his kidney disease remains ambiguous, but may be related to the treatment for HIV, which he contracted in 1989 at the age of 29. Faithful in marriage, Larry was apparently infected by his unsuspecting wife after she had been exposed to tainted blood for the treatment of a ruptured appendix. The cocktail of medicines that Larry takes for his HIV has controlled it well, and his T-cell count remains high.

When I met Larry in the summer of 1996, he had been successfully performing peritoneal dialysis at home for about a year. Young, intelligent, and independent with his ADLs, Larry appreciated the autonomy that this modality afforded him in living his life. Peritoneal dialysis stopped working in 1997, and Larry had to switch to in-center hemodialysis, three times a week, 4-and-a-half hours a treatment to sustain life.

As a younger, white, newly graduated MSW, I was cognizant of the fact that my predecessor had been a competent, attractive African-American female with whom the patient had a strong rapport. Larry initially presented as

(Continued)

reticent to talk, very serious, almost stoic during our monthly interdisciplinary care meetings when the physician, nurse, dietician, and I conferred with him. However, during my one-on-one psychosocial assessment as I gently probed and uncovered the salient aspects of his life and environment, a relationship of mutual trust began to evolve. I learned that Larry was very involved in community and neighborhood organizations that aimed to make his urban community a better place. He took pride in being a homeowner, helped organize an annual summer block party, attended town hall meetings, and wrote letters to the editor of the local newspaper when he perceived that citizens were getting a poor deal from town local government. Impressed by his energy and accomplishments, I asked Larry for permission to write an article about him in a newsletter I created for our patient and staff community. I also solicited Larry's participation in a Patient Advocacy task-oriented group that would meet with our unit's management and myself about every 2 months to discuss concerns, compliments, and ideas to make the treatment area a better place. And I relied on Larry's willingness to grill food for approximately 100 people and help set up the furniture for an annual summer picnic of our dialysis community.

Larry's youth and vitality, despite the chronic nature of his medical challenges, distinguish him from a majority of our patients in their 70s and 80s, who use wheelchairs, stretchers, or prosthetic limbs to move. The dissimilarity is not lost on Larry, who I quickly learned displayed a fondness for many of the patients and staff he interacts with 3 days a week, 52 weeks a year. His introspection does help him to see good and bad in others' situations and compare theirs to his own in a self-therapeutic way.

The "Achilles' heel" of the dialysis process is how the machine accesses the body. Our veins and arteries simply were not designed for repeated punctures. Modern medical technology offers external catheters, internal grafts, or fistulas (vein sewn to an artery), but each has its own problems, and their permanence (when they work) is not always measured in years, but rather months and sometimes weeks or days. The insertion of an access requires outpatient surgery. New grafts and fistulas involve some swelling, pain, and sometimes permanent disfigurement due to bumps from the surgical results under the skin. Although he did peritoneal dialysis, Larry needed a succession of three catheters in his belly. For the subsequent hemodialysis, he has endured 11 accesses in 7 years: a left forearm fistula, a right forearm fistula, a left forearm graft, a catheter on the left side, a catheter on the right, a left upper arm fistula, a right forearm graft, two catheters, a right-side lumbar catheter, and a left-thigh graft that continues to work. Handsome and fitness conscious as a younger man, Larry's initial dread of the bumpy disfigurement was soon replaced by an awareness of the devices' importance. Each access failure was understandably met with disappointment and grieving before Larry could bolster himself to try again. The poet Andrew Marvell, lamenting mortality, wrote aptly in *A Dialogue between the Soul and Body* "Constrain'd not only to endure\ Diseases, but, what's worse the cure."

Because Larry was physically active, relatively young, and a dynamic parent, transplant had been on his mind. Yet conventional wisdom stated that patients with the HIV virus were poor candidates for fear of dangerous side-effects via immunosuppression. The two transplant centers in our New England state plainly stated they would not attempt a transplant with an HIV patient, citing a lack of precedence and data. But as Larry went though a succession of failed accesses, he began to look for alternatives that could extend his life. I and my MSW intern conducted Internet and telephone research and discovered that two states away, less than a 4-hour drive, a respected transplant center was starting up a kidney transplant program for HIV patients. Larry made an appointment for an interview and, in his words, "weighed the pros and cons of being a guinea pig to running out of accesses." After some soul-searching, he decided to try. To qualify, he underwent many tests, including a successful heart bypass.

Larry' new kidney, from a donor who perished in a car accident, lasted only 6 months, from the beginning of November 2004 to the middle of March 2005, when the rejection became untreatable. He and we were exceptionally disappointed. He needed to return to dialysis after a hospitalization, and we were back to using the thigh graft. When I debriefed him after he returned, he stated adamantly that he was glad that he had tried the transplant and had generated data for the researchers to use. But he now accurately viewed dialysis as his sole passport to living.

Throughout his chronic illnesses and treatments, Larry has been able to successfully integrate those experiences into an evolving sense of self. Whereas he may have used repression and denial early on and still occasionally as medical events unfold, he has self-organized and achieved sublimation. Living through the positive and negative events of his siblings and niece, valuing his role as a parent and husband, believing strongly in a higher power, and witnessing how his volunteerism positively affects others, Larry remains mentally healthy and in control of his life through trying times. We call these qualities grace and fortitude. No doubt, the internal peace he has been able to achieve has not been without concessions, most notably his acceptance that he will probably have less time on earth. Certainly the marching of time toward our physical end, when accelerated in the chronically sick, may lead to depression, anxiety, and a paralysis in living. It is therefore to Larry's credit that his engagement in life remains vibrant and motivating to those around him.

References

Cvenros J. A., Christensen A. J., & Lawton W. J. (2005). Health locus of control and depression in chronic kidney disease: a dynamic perspective. *Journal of Health Psychology, 10*(5), 677–686.

Faber, R. L., & Wilde S. W. (Eds.). (1993). *The KT/DA kidney patient handbook.* Boston: Kidney Transplant/Dialysis Association.

Faris M. H. (1994). *When your kidneys fail: A handbook for patients and their families* (3d ed.). Los Angeles: National Kidney Foundation of Southern California.

Holosko, M. J., & Taylor, P. A. (Eds.). (1994). *Social work practice in health care settings.* Toronto: Canadian Scholars Press.

Levy, N. B. (Ed.). (1981). *Psychonephrology 1: Psychological factors in hemodialysis and transplantation.* New York: Plenum Medical.

Monsivais, D. (2005). Self-organization in chronic pain: A concept analysis. *Rehabilitation Nursing 30*(4), 147–151.

National Kidney Foundation. (2005). *The facts about chronic kidney disease.* Retrieved September 24, 2005, from htpp://www.kidney.org/kidneyDisease

Phillips R. H. (1987). *Coping with kidney failure.* Garden City Park, NY: Avery.

U.S. Renal Data System. (2004). *Annual data report: Atlas of end-stage renal disease in the United States.* Bethesda, MD: National Institutes of Health, National Institute of Diabetes and Digestive and Kidney Diseases.

Summary

There are many ways in which social workers can provide assistance to persons with disabilities and chronic illness. These include political and social advocacy; individual, group, and family counseling; knowledge of population and disease-specific entitlements; case management; brief interventions and qualitative assessments to document effectiveness; and ethical decision making (Galambos, 2004; Volland, Berkman, Phillips, & Stein, 2003). Rothman (2003) reminds us to remain mindful of our commitment to a sound biopsychosocial assessment in addressing the needs of individuals with chronic illnesses and disabilities. A cultural and spiritual assessment (see Chapter 8) may be particularly relevant in providing an understanding of how a person's worldview may be contributing to either the understanding or adaptation to disability. We ended this chapter with a contribution by a Caucasian male social worker based on his experience with an African-American man who suffered from kidney disease related to treatment for HIV that he contracted 12 years earlier at the age of 29. This example illustrates several important practice principles highlighted by Mackelprang and Salsgiver (1999) and that we recommend for social work practitioners.

- Assume that people are capable or potentially capable.
- Reject pathological interpretations of disability or the *assumption* that disability requires grief and mourning.
- Consider that disability is a social construct and that persons with disabilities and practice must include attention to eliminating environmental, attitudinal, and policy barriers to their full participation in society.
- Appreciate the history of oppression that persons with disabilities have faced and become familiar with disability history and culture.
- View disability as different but not dysfunctional and in so doing work toward helping persons adopt disability-affirming identities.
- Respect the right to self-determination that persons with disabilities have and provide counseling and consultation, but not control.

18 Social Policy Through the Life Cycle

Joyce E. Everett, PhD
Professor, Smith College School for Social Work

Introduction

Social work practice irrespective of setting, modality, or client group is shaped by social welfare policy. Social welfare policy is important because social workers implement policy; help to create these policies; and rely on the resource allocations authorized in social welfare policies to help individuals, families, groups, and communities. Social welfare policy authorizes social work practice with a variety of client systems and lends creditability, legitimacy, and respect for social work services. Through these policies and those of agencies, the goals of services are specified, as are the characteristics of the clientele eligible to receive services and any restrictions on what services may or may not be offered. As a profession, social work is regulated by social welfare policies that grant licensure to social work practitioners. Thus, the study of social welfare policy is directly relevant for practice.

Social welfare is a broad and elusive concept, making it difficult to offer a universal definition of its meaning. Throughout American history we have seen the scope and function of social welfare policy constantly changing in response to societal values, human need, and technological advances. Many of the activities associated with social welfare policy overlap with the activities of other institutions. For example, child-care tax credits are usually associated with the economy, but they function as a social welfare activity just as much as child-care vouchers to welfare recipients do. For these reasons arriving at a definition of the term that fits no other activity (exclusively) and encompasses every social welfare activity (inclusively) is not easy.

This chapter uses systems theory to define the context for social welfare activities, provides an overview of the functions and scope of social welfare, describes the major income support programs used by clients and, by using a life-cycle perspective, identifies and summarizes the social welfare programs and services commonly offered during infancy, early and middle childhood, adolescence, young adulthood, midlife, and older adulthood. Describing social welfare programs and services that are associated with different life stages may enable students to integrate theory, practice, and policy in ways that help to differentiate what is provided from what is not provided and to whom during these critical life stages. Rather than presenting a comprehensive definition of the term, this chapter begins by using systems theory to describe the institutional functions of social welfare.

The Functions of Social Welfare: A Systems Perspective

The essential activities of community life in all human societies are organized through interrelated and interlocking structures. These structures or institutions have primary responsibility for carrying out societal functions that are central to community life, such as childrearing; the production, consumption, and distribution of goods and services; spiritual development; social protection; and so forth (Gilbert & Terrell, 2005). Each of these institutions represents a distinct system, with its own distinct identity. As described in Chapter 1, a system is a complex whole comprised of component parts that work together in orderly ways, over an extended period of time, toward the achievement of a common goal. Each institution is interconnected with the other. Although each of these institutions has primary responsibility for carrying out an essential function, other institutions play a role as well. For example, although religious institutions have primary responsibility for the spiritual development of societal members, the family also influences the spiritual development of its members. Each institution is interconnected or interlocked with the other.

Five fundamental institutions including the *family or kinship group, religion, the economy, the polity,* and *social welfare* (Day, 1989) carry out the essential societal functions. Early in our country's history, the extended *family* fulfilled all these societal functions; however, as the society shifted from an agrarian to a more industrial economy and families became more mobile, creating larger communities, social institutions were created to fulfill these societal functions. The family, whether extended or nuclear, is primarily responsible for the socialization of generations of its members by transmitting values, norms, and behavior patterns from one generation to another. It also plays a role in the social integration of its members into the larger society.

Organized and unorganized religious institutions fulfill the important function of guiding the spiritual and moral development of societal members. Through *religious institutions* the traditional ceremonies and observances of systems of worship are maintained and flourish (Gilbert & Terrell, 2005). Religious institutions along with the family help to clarify how each of us fits into the larger society. In today's world, the influence of religious organizations in our everyday lives and in the political sphere has become much more evident. All aspects of the production, distribution, and consumption of goods and services are encompassed by the *economy.* A major part of the economy is the market economy—the system through which we buy and sell goods and services—as well as tax transfers in the form of subsidies to farmers, businesses, and individuals through vouchers, direct payments, and credits. The organization of the workforce, employment, and unemployment are all intricate components of the economy. Without the workforce it would be difficult to manage the production, distribution, and consumption of goods and services. Institutions that constitute the *polity* exercise power within society, generally through national, state, and local governments based on legal statutes, regulations, judicial decisions, executive order, or budgetary decisions. These institutions can enforce, impose, monitor, or prevent certain behaviors.

Mutual aid, or mutual support, is the primary function of social welfare institutions. Social welfare activities usually take place outside the market system and only come into play when human needs are not being met through the family, religious institutions, the economy, or the polity (Gilbert & Specht, 1974). Although each of these systems—the family, religious institutions, the economy, polity, and social welfare—constitute an interlocking network and provide

FIGURE 18.1

Systems Interlocking Model

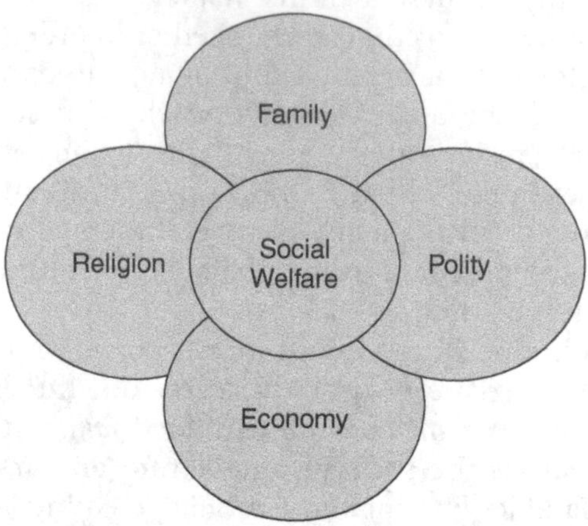

Source: Adapted from N. Gilbert, H. Specht, & P. Terrell, *Dimensions of Social Welfare Policy*, published by Allyn & Bacon, Boston, MA. Copyright © 1974 by Pearson Education. Reprinted by permission of the publisher.

mutual assistance, social welfare is most explicitly focused on mutual aid. For example, through the workplace individuals receive fringe benefits, such as health care, retirement, and disability benefits along with regular paychecks; religious institutions sponsor food production and distribution services, social services, and counseling; and private firms are increasingly offering child-care services to employees. However, through social welfare activities society acknowledges the interdependence among its members and "the desire to assist the less fortunate" (Gilbert & Terrell, 2005, p. 10). Social welfare, according to Popple and Leighninger (2001), deals with dependency. When there is a disruption or change in the ability of the family, religious institutions, the economy, or the polity to carry out their specific functions, it affects the other parts of the network causing disequilibria. Figure 18.1 illustrates the relationship among these systems. To counterbalance this disequilibria, the institution of social welfare steps in to supplement, substitute, or augment the essential societal functions the other institutions are no longer able to provide. Social welfare acts as a safety net.

The Enduring Debate about Social Welfare

One of the inherent debates regarding social welfare activities places individual versus collective values at odds with each other. Since the 1970s the nature of this debate has focused on whether dependency is a *personal responsibility* versus a *societal responsibility*. From an *individualist perspective*, social problems reflect bad choices, personal dysfunction, personal inadequacy, flawed or immoral characters, and a culture of poverty. Reliance on public aid undermines the exercise of personal responsibility, resulting in excessively high governmental budgets increasing the size of government and its role in controlling individual interests. In the late 1990s dependency was defined as a social problem that could be ameliorated by programmatic efforts to transition those in need from welfare to low-wage work, marriage, and limited access to income supports.

A *collective perspective* attributes social problems to "fundamental socioeconomic circumstances, barriers to access, lack of opportunities" (Gilbert & Terrell, 2005, p. 18) and inequality. Dependency is not a phenomenon exclusively relegated to the poor or the disadvantaged. Rather dependency may affect us all at different times and places. For example, the devastating effects of hurricanes Katrina and Rita in New Orleans, the Mississippi Gulf Coast, and Texas in September 2005 were not limited to poor, disadvantaged minorities. Instead, these hurricanes affected all socioeconomic classes, though the disadvantaged felt its devastating effects more. The public's response to this catastrophe was a collective response to ensure the safety and well-being of all those who were affected. Resolving the problems of homelessness, economic disaster, and displacement from a collective perspective requires governmental interventions large enough to advance the social welfare aims of reducing inequalities. This debate may never be completely resolved, but the basic tenets of the individualist and collective perspective have been constantly reframed irrespective of the context throughout American history.

Scope of Social Welfare: Problem versus Population Focus

Social welfare activities affect all aspects of our life throughout the life span beginning with birth and ending with death. Different methods have been used to categorize social welfare programs and services. Day (1989) describes the field of social services in terms of life necessity activities; educational, recreational, or rehabilitative services; protective and/or custodial services; and personal social services. Even within these general fields social welfare services may be directed toward specific problems such as juvenile delinquency, teen pregnancy, child care, drug addiction, housing or malnutrition, or specific populations such as the disabled, the elderly, immigrants, unemployed, or school-aged children. Contrast this approach with another that categorizes social welfare programs in terms of universal and selective services. *Universal* services are provided to a class of individuals, such as the elderly, unemployed workers or children in need of medical care, whereas *selective* services are given on the basis of a means test. For example, food stamps, school food programs, and some disability services are means-tested, whereas Social Security is provided to all elderly persons who worked and contributed to the program. Still another way to categorize social welfare activities is by specifying the forms of assistance offered. Social assistance or social welfare may be offered in the form of cash support, vouchers, in-kind goods (i.e., direct provision of necessities), services, tax credits, and opportunities. In almost all cases social welfare services are more readily available for individual members of a population or individuals afflicted by the specific problem, instead of groups such as families. However, individuals are not the only ones affected by a problem. The entire family may also be affected in ways that increase their dependency. For example, elderly parents living with their adult children may receive financial assistance, social services, health care, and other services while their adult caregivers frequently feel the emotional strain of caregiving and the financial burdens associated with leaving the labor force to provide care, receive little or no assistance through the social welfare system.

Social welfare services and programs are authorized through federal or state legislation, legislative regulations, judicial rulings, budgetary allocations, administrative manuals, or some combination of these sources. For example, President Bush's Faith Based Initiative is not authorized through federal or state legislation but instead is authorized through executive order and budgetary allocations. Whether authorized by legislation, judicial ruling, or administrative manuals, the delivery of social welfare services can be quite cumbersome, confusing, and at the very least complex, involving a mixture of federal, state, or county public, private nonprofit, and for-profit agencies. For example, child neglect or abuse is reported to a state public agency that investigates and substantiates allegations. The removal of children from their birth parents or guardians is handled by a state public child welfare agency, however, through purchase of service contracts with the state's child welfare agency; private nonprofit or for-profit agencies place children in foster care, adoptive homes, or residential facilities. Medical care for the child may be provided through a public or private hospital, and private for-profit or nonprofit agencies might offer counseling, parent education, or family reunification services to the parents. For birth parents, guardians, and children the service delivery system is indeed complex, confusing, and cumbersome.

Income Support Programs According to Maslow's (1970) hierarchy of human needs, physiological or deficiency needs must be met before moving on to a higher level of need. Physiological needs are biological needs consisting of the need for oxygen, water, and food and are the strongest, most basic human needs that control behavior and thought. Many social welfare programs provide for the basic necessities of life that correspond to Maslow's (1970) hierarchy of human needs. The major income support and health care programs designed to meet basic human needs are briefly described next.

The foundation of federal income support for the poor was established in the Social Security Act of 1935. Although the act has been amended quite frequently since then, it outlines a basic framework for cash assistance consisting of two types of aid: (a) social insurance, including Old Age Survivors Disability Insurance (OASDI) and Unemployment Insurance and (b) public assistance for the elderly, blind, the disabled, and families with dependent children. Social insurance programs distribute payments based on prior earnings, while the public assistance programs distribute payments on the basis of need; they are means-tested programs (Levitan, Mangum, & Mangum, 1998). Besides variations in how these programs are funded, programs differ in terms of whether they are state or federally administered and in terms of benefit levels.

Insurance Programs Old Age Survivors Disability Insurance (OASDI), established in 1935, is by far the largest cash assistance program in the United States, providing benefits to some 48 million people and covering more than 154 million workers (Blau, 2007). It is funded through a payroll tax on employers and employees of 6.2% of the worker's salary. These funds are then deposited into the Social Security Trust Fund. Unlike other types of trust funds, the monies deposited into the fund by current workers pay for the benefits of current retirees. Social Security is a pay-as-you-go program. This is not a means-tested program; to be eligible to receive OASDI benefits, workers must have contributed into the fund for a minimum of 40 quarters (10 years). The average monthly Social Security benefit for all retired workers was $1002 a month in 2006. Approximately 40 million retirees are recipients of the program.

Congress added the Disability Insurance component to Old Age Survivors Insurance in 1956. Disability Insurance is financed through an employee payroll tax, as is Old Age Survivors Insurance. Workers below the age of 50 are eligible for cash assistance if they have a total of 20 quarters of coverage (5 years) in the preceding 40 quarters (10 years) and meet disability standards. According to law, disability is defined "as an inability to engage in 'substantial gainful activity' due to a physical or mental impairment that has lasted five months and is expected to last for at least 12 months or result in death" (Blau, 2004, p. 290). Average benefits under this program were $1064 monthly in 2006. Some 7 million individuals are recipients of this program.

Unemployment Insurance (UI), established in 1935, was designed to help tide workers over during spells of unemployment (Levitan, Mangum, & Mangum, 1998). The program is financed through a payroll tax on employers. Currently, the tax rate is 6.2% of the first $7,000 of an employee's annual earnings, 87% of which is returned to the states to fund state unemployment insurance benefits, while the remainder, the federal portion, is earmarked to cover the administrative costs of the program. States establish eligibility criteria and determine the duration and amount of benefits, which results in wide variations in benefit levels across states. Depending on economic conditions between 7 and 10 millions individuals receive unemployment insurance benefits annually.

Workers Compensation, established in 1908, is a state-administered program, providing cash, medical, and rehabilitation benefits to those employees whose labor force participation has been interrupted due to workplace accidents or disease. As with unemployment insurance, states have broad discretion in the administration of worker's compensation. States determine the duration, amount, and extent of compensation awarded to individual workers; however, the program is not means-tested. Thus there are wide variations in the type, amount, and length of compensation. About 126 million workers are covered by workers compensation. Though not described in this chapter, similar types of income support in the form of compensation and pension programs have been provided to veterans, their dependents, and survivors since the Revolutionary War.

Although these social insurance programs provide assistance to workers due to retirement, unemployment, disability, or workplace injury and are financed through employee and/or employer taxes, public assistance programs are primarily funded from general revenues. These programs are described next.

Public Assistance In 1972 Congress revamped the Old Age Assistance, Disability Assistance, and Aid to the Blind state-run programs with a federal program now known as the Supplemental Security Income (SSI) program that assists poor people who are age 65 or older, blind, or disabled (Levitan, Mangum, & Mangum,

1998). SSI is a means-tested program that places stringent resource limitations on its recipients. Individuals may not have more than $2,000 in resources (couples no more than $3,000), such as savings, investments, and so forth; must be U.S. citizens, or have legal resident status attained by August 1996 (the date the welfare reform bill was passed); and monthly incomes less than the SSI payment (Blau, 2004, p. 291). In 2006, SSI benefit levels for individuals were $603 a month and $904 a month for couples. About 6.5 million people were beneficiaries of SSI in 2005.

Amid cries for welfare reform during the Clinton administration, Congressional actions in 1996 replaced the Aid to Families with Dependent Children program (AFDC), a federal guarantee of assistance to women with children, with the Temporary Assistance for Needy Families program (TANF). Passage of the Personal Responsibility and Work Opportunity Reconciliation Act of 1996 that created the TANF program emerged from an individualistic perspective of welfare dependency, where reliance on AFDC undermined the exercise of personal responsibility. The law was intended to help heads of poor families to transition from cash assistance to low-wage work. TANF "provides block grants to the states for cash assistance, but conditions those grants on state policies which establish strict time limits on assistance and require mothers to work in exchange for their benefits" (Fox Piven, 2003, p. 2). TANF is a means-tested program that ties the receipt of cash benefits to work. As a block grant program, states have more control over eligibility criteria, benefit levels, and benefit duration. TANF cash benefits are restricted to a 5-year lifetime limit. States may also impose other limits on recipients such as a family cap "designed to discourage welfare families from having additional children" (Gilbert & Terrell, 2005, p. 263), discouraging teen pregnancy by restricting benefits to unwed teen parents who are under the age of 18 and do not live with their parents or guardians and do not attend school. Legal immigrants who entered the United States after August 22, 1996 are also barred from receiving assistance under the TANF program. Approximately 5.4 million individuals received TANF benefits in 2002.

One additional program should be mentioned here, the Earned Income Tax Credit (EITC). Created in 1975 and expanded in 1986, 1990, 1993 and 2001, the Earned Income Tax Credit provides a tax refund to supplement the earnings of the working poor. Meyers and Lee (2003) defined the working poor as persons with poverty-level incomes and earned income from employment for at least half a year. To receive the refund requires participation in the labor market and minimum earnings for three categories of recipients: taxpayers with no children, taxpayers with one child, and taxpayers with two or more children (Mendenhall, 2006). Benefits under EITC taper off as the income of workers increases. Thus the program provides more help to those families that earn between $10,000 and $15,000 annually. The value of the tax refund ranged from $412 for married workers without children to $4,536 for workers with two children in 2006 (Blau, 2007).

Health Care Programs Along with these basic income support programs, Medicaid, Medicare, and the Children's Health Insurance Program of 1997 (CHIPS) constitute the primary health-care programs for the poor, elderly, disabled, and medically underserved children. Medicaid, a federal–state program, authorized under Title XIX of the Social Security Act in 1965, provides medical assistance to low-income people, specifically the aged, blind, disabled, and families with dependent children. Amendments to the original bill in 1967 created the Early Periodic Screening, Diagnosis and Treatment Program within Medicaid. These amendments were particularly significant for children because they extended Medicaid's role in "assuring that children receive comprehensive preventive care and follow-up for health problems" (Mann, Rowland, & Garfield, 2003, p. 33). With the addition of this program children became eligible for basic Medicaid services (for example, hospital, physician, laboratory, and nursing home services), and the states were required to provide health screenings at regular intervals.

Medicaid provides in-kind medical services and is financed through federal and state general tax revenues. Patients receive services from physicians or other health-care providers, and the government reimburses the providers directly (DiNitto, 2005, p. 307). "Because each state designs and administers its own program following federal guidelines, the coverage, benefits, and amount of payment for services all vary" (Blau, 2004, p. 380). States must, under federal guidelines, offer inpatient and outpatient hospital services, laboratory and x-ray services, nursing facility care for those over 21 years of age, home health services for those entitled to nursing care, early and periodic screening, diagnosis and treatment (EPSDT) services for those under age 21, family planning services and supplies, and physician and nurse–midwife services, family and pediatric nurse practitioner services, dental surgery, and pregnancy and postpartum services (DiNitto, 2005). Only 32 states cover drugs for the medically needy. Thirty-six million people in 2001 received Medicaid services; however, legal immigrants admitted into the country after August 22, 1996 cannot receive Medicaid for 5 years.

Medicare, established in 1965 under Title XVIII of the Social Security Act, parallels Medicaid, except that it is a national insurance program for nearly 40 million elderly and disabled people. Like the other social insurance programs described earlier, Medicare is financed through employer and employee payroll taxes. Medicare coverage comes in two parts: basic hospital insurance (Part A) and optional supplementary medical insurance (Part B). Part A pays a major part of inpatient hospital services and posthospital extended care, home health services, and hospice care for all Social Security recipients, employees of federal and state governments, and some people who are permanently disabled (Levitan, Mangum, & Mangum, 1998). Beneficiaries of Part A Medicare must pay a deductible ($876 in 2004) for each hospital stay, after which Medicare pays the remainder of the costs for the first 60 days of hospitalization and a portion of any additional days.

Part B is an optional program available to all Part A eligible Medicare recipients that helps pay the cost of physician fees, diagnostic tests, medical supplies, and prescription drugs. Medicare Part A beneficiaries who opt to participate in Part B are assessed a small premium (in 2004 the monthly Part B premium was $66.60). Although Part B beneficiaries must pay the first $100 of services each year, Medicare pays 80% of most services. Though Medicare pays for a significant amount of the health-care costs of the elderly and disabled, benefits are still inadequate. Medicare does not pay for most dental care, custodial nursing home care, eyeglasses and eye examinations, hearing tests, and hearing devices. Beneficiaries have been encouraged to acquire supplemental insurance through Medigap policies from private insurance companies. A drug prescription plan, Plan D, was enacted in 2006 under the Bush administration. Under Plan D participants pay a monthly premium that varies by the number and costs of drugs. After paying an initial deductible of $250, Medicare covers 75% of drug costs up to $2,250. Medicare provides no coverage for prescription costs between $2,251 and $5,100 annually. "For catastrophic coverage in excess of $5,100 Medicare pays 95%" (Blau, 2007, p. 396).

Skyrocketing costs of health care have led the states and the federal government to experiment with private-sector solutions, including the use of managed care plans that, simply put, are different methods for health-care financing and service delivery. Three kinds of managed care include health maintenance organizations (HMOs), preferred provider organizations (PPOs), and a point-of-service (POS) plan. HMOs are membership organizations consisting of dues-paying members who are guaranteed a range of health care services for a fixed monthly fee. HMOs typically hire doctors and other health professionals at fixed salaries to offer services to its members. Insurance companies generally run HMOs. "Under PPOs, employers or their insurance carriers reimburse a higher percentage of services if employees use designated hospitals or other providers" (DiNitto, 2005, p. 329). POSs tend to combine features of the HMO and PPO models and are typically run by medical providers rather than insurance companies. Under a POS the primary care physician acts as a gatekeeper, controlling access to specialists and other health-care providers. Each of these managed care plans is supposed to reduce unnecessary and inappropriate care by controlling access to expensive medical care. Patients who venture outside the network of health-care providers offered through HMO, PPO, or PSO models must pay a greater share of the costs.

More recently the State Children's Health Insurance Program (SCHIP), enacted as part of the 1997 Balanced Budget Act, was designed as a state and federal partnership to help children without health insurance, many of whom come from working families with incomes too high to qualify for Medicaid, but too low to afford private health insurance. Children under the age of 19 qualify for SCHIP if they are not eligible for services to children in families who are not eligible for Medicaid, are not covered by other health insurance, and live in low-income families. Although benefits vary from state to state, children are generally eligible for the following services: regular checkups, immunizations, eyeglasses, doctor visits, prescription drug coverage, dental care, and hospital care (www.childrensdefense.org/childhealth/chip). SCHIP is a state-administered program, and each state sets its own guidelines regarding eligibility and services (www.cms.hhs.gov/schip/consumers).

Although SCHIP is closely related to Medicaid, its structure varies by state. In some states, SCHIP is simply an expansion of the Medicaid program that allows children of parents with higher incomes than in the past to participate and receive health insurance through Medicaid. In other states, SCHIP is a separate program from Medicaid and covers children with parents whose incomes are higher than the state's Medicaid eligibility levels. As of July 2002, 16 states had elected to develop separate SCHIP programs with no Medicaid expansion, 16 states (including the District of Columbia) relied on Medicaid to expand coverage, and 19 states used a combination approach (Mann, Rowland, & Garfield, 2003, p. 38).

SCHIP is administered as a block grant to the states and financed by an increase in the tobacco tax. Funds are allocated based on number of uninsured children in the state. In 2001, 4.7 million of the estimated 9 million uninsured children were covered under SCHIP. Besides these three major health-care programs, several other important federally funded programs deserve to be mentioned, though not fully described. The Department of Veterans Affairs offers health care for those who once served in the armed forces, and through the Defense Department's TRICARE program, health-care services are offered to active-duty military and their dependents and military retirees and their dependents. Members of many Native American tribes in the United States receive health-care services through the federally funded Indian Health Services Program.

This brief overview of income support and health-care programs summarizes some aspects of our social welfare system. Many other aspects of the social welfare system have been omitted, including housing and food programs and benefits for certain populations such as veterans, migrant and seasonal workers, and immigrants. Nevertheless, the provisions for income, health care, and other services were designed to meet some of the basic physiological and biological needs of families and children. As social workers in training, you will likely work with many of the recipients of these programs and/or refer your clients to these programs for assistance.

Social Welfare Programs across the Life Cycle

As mentioned earlier, there are many different ways to categorize social welfare policies and programs. In this chapter, some of those policies and programs that coincide with specific life-cycle stages are described. However, not all social welfare programs can be organized in this way. Some programs are not included in this section, and others may cut across life-cycle stages. For example, job-training programs may be offered to adolescents and young adults. Despite these omissions this review begins with a summary of those programs that address the needs of infants, toddlers, and middle-aged children.

Infancy, Early and Middle Childhood

Infancy is a critical period in a child's development. In the early months, the infant's behavior is innate and instinctual, motivated primarily toward pleasure and survival. However, the special relationship between the infant and caregiver has a long-lasting impact and determines how the child explores and responds to the environment. In the first 2 years of an infant's life, significant changes in psychomotor, cognitive, and language development can occur within a nurturing environment. Several social welfare policies and programs are particularly supportive of infant development. For example, the Family Medical Leave Act (FMLA) of 1993 requires all employers with 50 or more permanent employees to allow employees of either sex up to 12 weeks of unpaid leave in a 12-month period for the birth or adoption of a child, care of an immediate family member with a serious health condition, or for the employee's own serious health condition. Such a policy enables many new parents the opportunity to develop the kind of nurturing relationship or bond with a newborn that is essential for healthy growth. The major drawback of the law is the absence of a provision allowing employees to continue to receive a salary during the leave.

One of several nutrition programs that support the healthy development of infants is the Women, Infants, and Children's Program (WIC). WIC is a federally supported program for low-income pregnant or postpartum women, infants, and children up to age 5 who are at risk of poor nutrition. Risks for poor nutrition include inadequate diet, certain medical conditions such as anemia or a history of pregnancy complications. Besides nutrition education and access to health care for low-income women, infants, and children, WIC participants receive checks or vouchers to purchase specific food items containing high protein, calcium, iron, and vitamins A and C. Typically these food items include infant cereal, iron-fortified adult cereal, fruit or vegetable juice, eggs, milk, cheese, peanut butter, dried beans/peas, tuna fish, and carrots. All 7.5 million recipients of WIC in 2002 had to meet the state's income eligibility standards. The effectiveness of the program has been demonstrated in studies that indicate that women in the program had longer pregnancies, lower levels of fetal mortality, fewer premature births, and larger babies (Blau, 2004).

Gradual physical, emotional and cognitive growth occurs in early and middle childhood, enabling a greater sense of coordination, endurance, and ability. Children in this phase of life are increasingly aware of their ability to retain and forget experiences; prepare cognitively, emotionally, and socially to learn in a group; and to use language to reflect and manipulate thought and actions. Several nutrition-based programs have been established for children. The National School Lunch program and National School Breakfast program provide nutritionally balanced, low-cost, or free lunches to children in nearly 100,000 public and private nonprofit schools and residential child-care institutions each school day. These institutions receive cash subsidies, and U.S. Department of Agriculture (USDA) donates commodities to provide meals that meet official dietary guidelines. Although public criticism of the quality of the foods served in schools has increased lately, especially now that the rate of childhood obesity has increased, providing school breakfasts and lunches has helped to improve attentiveness, academic performance, and attendance in school.

Children during infancy, early, and middle childhood require stability and constancy in caregiving. As the number of women in the labor force has increased, so too has the demand for quality child care. Child care represents a significant portion of family expenditures. Full-time child care can cost as much as $10,000 per year (child-care costs can range from $4,000 to $10,000 annually). Although the cost of child care does not seem to affect women's employment, it does affect the child-care arrangement women choose, in that some women are forced to rely on unsafe or inadequate child-care arrangements to the detriment of their children

(Burman, Maag, & Rohaly, 2005). As a consequence, young children may miss opportunities to develop healthy intellectual and social capabilities.

The governmental response to the need for child care has been relatively slow and specifically targeted to low-income women and their children. The Child Care and Development Block Grant (CCDBG) is the primary federal child care program. Created in 1990, the program was substantially expanded as part of the 1996 welfare reform law. CCDBG money is provided to states through the Department of Health and Human Services and helps low-income families receive appropriate child care. Subsidized child-care services are available to eligible families through certificates (vouchers) or contracts with providers. Parents may select any legally operating child-care provider who meets basic health and safety requirements set by states and tribes. These requirements must address prevention and control of infectious diseases, including immunizations; building and physical premises safety; and minimum health and safety training. Families pay a monthly copayment based on factors such as income, family size, and the number of children in care. The child-care subsidy is typically paid directly to the provider. Federal regulations require that the states target 70% of their entitlement funding to welfare recipients working toward self-sufficiency or families at risk of becoming dependent on federal aid. The rest of the entitlement and discretionary funds may be used for low-income, nonwelfare working families. Finally, states must establish their own child-care licensing standards to receive CCDBG funding.

Some relief of child-care expenses can also be found in the U.S. tax code. The Child and Dependent Care Tax Credit (CDCTC) is the second largest source of federal child-care assistance for which families at all income levels are eligible. However, this tax subsidy helps only those families with income tax liability (if the family paid no income taxes, they would not be eligible for this tax credit). The credit is available to individuals and married couples who, while working or looking for work, paid for child care services for dependents under the age of 13. The tax credit offsets up to 35% of child-care costs up to $3,000 for one child and $6,000 for two or more children. Using the tax system to subsidize child care is administratively simple because most households file annual income tax returns. Its drawback is that for "many low-income households the tax credit may come too late to help pay for childcare" (Burman, Maag, & Rohaly, 2005, p. 2).

All children, regardless of age, need to feel safe, secure, and protected from abuse. At the heart of governmental actions designed to protect children is the doctrine of parens patriae, which means that the state has the right and the duty to protect (Samantrai, 2004). Historically, the problem of child abuse and neglect was associated with poverty until 1962, when C. Henry Kempe, then Chief of Pediatrics at the University of Colorado Medical School, and his colleagues (1997) wrote "The Battered Child Syndrome," indicating that the abuse existed in the middle and upper classes but was not being reported due to weak reporting laws (Samantrai, 2004). Subsequently, models of state reporting laws were proposed. Eventually, in 1974 federal legislation, the Child Abuse Prevention and Treatment Act (CAPTA), was passed. This act has been amended several times since 1974: first with the Child Abuse Prevention, Adoption and Family Services Act of 1988 (P.L. 100–294) and more recently by the Keeping Children and Families Safe Act of 2003 (P.L. 108–36).

These acts authorize federal funding to the states for programs for preventing, assessing, investigating, prosecuting, and treating child abuse and neglect. The act established the National Clearinghouse on Child Abuse and Neglect (NCCAN), a national resource for professionals seeking information on the prevention, identification, and treatment of child abuse and neglect. NCCAN compiles, analyzes, publishes, and conducts research on child abuse and neglect and provides training materials for personnel who are engaged in the prevention, identification, and treatment of child abuse and neglect. Since its enactment, CAPTA has clarified the definition of child abuse and neglect, expanded its scope, established national reporting laws, and made more research/demonstration monies available for public and not-for-profit organizations (Samantrai, 2004). The most recent amendments contain provisions for the training of guardians *ad litem* (advocates for children), child protection service workers and their supervisors, and procedures for criminal record checks for prospective foster and adoption parents.

The CAPTA legislation is only one of several laws that make up the public child welfare system. Other laws in this area include Title IV-A and Title IV-B of the Social Security Act that provide federal matching funds to the states for foster care maintenance payments and social services. The Adoption Assistance and Child Welfare Act of 1980 (P.L. 96–272), later replaced by the Adoption and Safe Families Act of 1997 (P.L. 105–89), lays out the goals for child welfare service. The former established the doctrine of permanence for children removed from their homes, whereas the latter law clarifies the importance of the child's health and safety in case planning for children in foster care and promotes and facilitates adoption by changing the time frames for making decisions regarding permanent placement and the termination of parental rights (Samantrai, 2004).

Corresponding laws authorize funding for family preservation services (i.e., the Family Preservation and Support Services provisions of the Omnibus Budget Reconciliation Act of 1993 that was renamed the Safe and Stable Families Program), including preplacement prevention, reunificiation, and adoption and follow-up services. Adolescents who are aging out of the foster care system receive special assistance toward independent living through funds authorized by the Independent Living Initiative (P.L. 99–272) of 1986 and the John H. Chafee Foster Care Independence Program, Title I of the Foster Care Independence Act of 1999 (P.L. 106–169). On September 17, 2008, Congress passed the Fostering Connections to Success and Increasing Adoption Act, which extends federal foster care payments up to 21 years of age, continues federal assistance to relatives who assume legal guardianship to eligible children in their care, and improves the oversight of health and education needs of children in foster care. As described in Chapter 15, these laws in combination allow state public agencies to investigate and substantiate allegations of child abuse and neglect, remove children from unsafe home environments and place them in temporary foster homes; work toward the reunification of families, and when reunification is not possible to work toward securing permanent homes for children through adoption, long-term foster care, or placement with relatives; and "to assist adolescent children prepare for independent living as they phase out of the foster care system" (Samantrai, 2004, p. 14).

Besides ensuring the safety and protection of children, ensuring that disadvantaged children and those with disabilities are adequately prepared and supported in public schools has also been a national issue. Head Start and Early Head Start programs as well as other preschool programs have been fairly popular since the 1960s. These programs were authorized in the Economic Opportunity Act of 1965 to help prepare disadvantaged children for school. Head Start and Early Head Start are comprehensive child development programs that serve children from birth to age 5, pregnant women, and their families. They are child-focused programs and have the overall goal of increasing the school readiness of young children in low-income families. Head Start funds are awarded directly by the federal government to local agencies or school systems. The basic premise of these programs is that preschool education will have long-lasting effects that improve cognitive and affective development of children. More than 22 million children have enrolled in the Head Start program since it began in 1965.

Children, especially those with disabilities, became a national priority in 1975 with the passage of federal legislation originally known as the Education for All Handicapped Children Act (P.L. 94–142). The law is best known for mandating the handicapped child's right to receive special education and related services to meet their individual needs, affording children with disabilities the right to have a free and appropriate public education in the least-restrictive environment and providing funds to assist states in educating these children (Altshuler & Kopels, 2003). Procedures for protecting children with disabilities from inappropriate placements were outlined in the law, including the legal requirement that schools create and annually review individualized education programs (IEPs) developed by multidisciplinary teams describing the special education and related services to be provided to the child. Subsequent reauthorizations of the Individuals with Disabilities Education Act (IDEA; P.L. 101–476) in 1990 and 1997 expand the federal classification of recognized educational disabilities to include autism and traumatic brain injury, expands the membership of the multidisciplinary teams developing IEPs to include the child's regular education teachers, strengthens the parents' participation in the child's education, delineates the circumstances under which the state is held responsible for reimbursing parents for tuition expenses for those children with disabilities placed in private schools, and recognizes social work services among the related services offered to handicapped children.

Two special programs under the IDEA are designed to address the needs of young children with disabilities: the Handicapped Infant and Toddlers Program and the Preschool Grants program. The Handicapped Infant and Toddlers Program provides for an interdisciplinary system of early intervention services for infants and toddlers who have disabilities. Though early intervention services must be tailored to meet the unique needs of the disabled infant or toddler, the range of early intervention services might include family training, counseling and home visits, special instruction, speech–language pathology and audiology services, occupational therapy, physical therapy, psychological services, vision services, assistive technology devices, and technology services. The Preschool Grants program ensures that all children, ages 3 to 5, with or at risk for disabilities, receive a free appropriate public education.

Meeting the needs of limited-English-speaking (LEP) children who enter the public school systems across the country has a long and controversial history. Civil rights laws, including the Civil Rights Act of 1964 and the Equal Educational Opportunities Act, protect LEP students in circumstances that are not covered elsewhere. Both acts have been used in interpretations of Supreme Court decisions regarding discrimination against limited-English-speaking students. On the federal level, several laws provide funding for programs serving LEP students. Title I Part A of the Elementary and Secondary Education Act of 1965 and the 1994 Improving America's Schools Act contained provisions for "special programs to help immigrant, migrant and refugee school children who do not speak English when they enter U.S. schools" (Porter, 1997). The Office of English Language Acquisition within the Department of Education offers state matching funds for Foreign Language Assistance programs and Elementary School Foreign Language Incentive programs. The services offered under Title I may have addressed the special language needs of LEP students or other academic deficiencies not related to their LEP needs. Studies show that a fairly high proportion of LEP students receive assistance through these programs. The Bilingual Education Act (BEA) of 1968 was passed and subsequently reauthorized in the Improving America's Schools Act in 1994 (P.L. 103–382) to assist local school districts to teach students who did not know English. Most states followed the lead of the federal government, enacting bilingual education laws of their own (www.rethinkingschools.org/archive). The BEA offers grant funding in three specific areas: instructional services, support services, and professional development. The No Child Left Behind Act of 2002 promotes greater flexibility in state funding for bilingual education.

The controversy over bilingual education has more to do with the instructional models on which they are based (i.e., transitional bilingual education, English as a Second Language, structured immersion, two-way dual immersion, or developmental bilingual programs). According to O'Dea (2001), these models may be differentiated by the role of the child's native language. At one end of the continuum are programs that use the student's native language for English acquisition and academic learning in all subjects. Other programs at the other end of the continuum such as English as a Second Language and structured immersion programs expect a relatively rapid grasp of English while placing relatively little emphasis on the student's native language. Submersion programs on the other hand place LEP students in English-only classes without any other accommodations. There is no federal mandate regarding which of these models is most effective, though some states have recently favored one approach over the other. The available research is inconclusive as to the best way to educate LEP students. There are no superior methods for teaching every individual LEP student. Age and the educational background of the student as well as the training of the staff and the quality of the teaching materials may affect the effectiveness of the instructional approach (O'Dea, 2001).

Adolescence

Turbulence is the phrase commonly used to describe adolescence. "The tasks for adolescents include moving from dependence on families or caregivers to independence, facing major decisions about the future, and trying to establish an individual identity" (Austrain, 2008, p. 135). Among the decisions encountered during adolescence are those regarding "whether to engage in sexual activity and to arrive at a sexual identity, whether to use alcohol and drugs, and how to integrate relationships with work" (Austrain, 2008, p. 135). A supportive environment is especially important given these tasks; however, for some the environment may be unsupportive or destructive. The societal context in which an individual is raised affects this life-cycle stage. Studies seem to show increased conflict in parent–child relationships during adolescence. Among early adolescents there is the perception that parents are less supportive (Nickerson & Nagle, 2005). Conversely, peers are perceived as a greater source of support. Relationships with peers are an important aspect of the quest for autonomy, and adolescent friendships become the foundation for later intimate relationships. Supportive friendships with peers are positively correlated, particularly among girls, with school achievement, self-esteem, and psychosocial adjustment and negatively correlated with school problems, identity problems, and depression (Nickerson & Nagle, 2005).

Because adolescence is a period in which conflict and rebellion are common, the range of problem behaviors likely to emerge include academic failure, substance abuse, tobacco use, delinquent behaviors, sexually transmitted diseases, and teen pregnancy. Although there are many government programs designed to address these problems after their occurrence, in the last three decades prevention approaches that emphasize promoting positive youth development have been advocated (Catalano et al., 2004). Programs emphasizing positive youth development seek to promote emotional attachment and commitment to social relationships; resilience; social, emotional, cognitive, behavioral, and moral competencies; self-determination; spirituality; self-efficacy; positive identity; a belief in the future; recognition for positive behavior; opportunities for prosocial involvement; and prosocial norms (Catalano et al., 2004, pp. 101–102). The more common interventions used in these programs include skill and competence-based curriculum, mentoring programs, health-promotion-focused interventions, parent training or education, parent involvement in program implementation, home visits, and linkages with community assets and resources. Big Brothers/Big Sisters, Success for All, and Adolescent Transitions are illustrations of positive youth development programs. Many of these programs take place in school-based settings or not-for-profit agencies and receive funding from a variety of government sources.

The Office of Safe and Drug Free Schools in the Department of Education administers programs that promote the health and well-being of students and families. These programs, outlined by Title IV and V of the Elementary and Secondary Education Act of 1965 and authorized by the American Schools Act of 1994, provide financial assistance to the states for local drug and violence prevention activities in elementary and secondary schools. The range of programs funded through this office includes student drug-testing programs, mentoring programs, school emergency response to violence programs, gun-free school programs, safe schools/healthy students activities, and programs to expand counseling programs in K through 12 schools.

The major federal law governing the juvenile justice system is the Juvenile Justice and Delinquency Prevention Act (P.L. 107–273), which provides financial assistance to the states for comprehensive juvenile justice and delinquency prevention and intervention programs. Two fairly innovative programs funded through the Office of Juvenile Justice and Delinquency Prevention are the Gang Reduction Program and juvenile drug courts. The Gang Reduction Program is being funded in four targeted communities in East Los Angeles, California, Milwaukee, Wisconsin, North Miami Beach, Florida, and Richmond, Virginia. These communities are characterized by high rates of crime and gang activity, strong citizen involvement, and program investment. The program is designed to address a range of personal, family, and community factors that contribute to gang activity and to provide interventions that prevent and, in some cases, suppress delinquent and gang activity. "Since 1994, federal and state governments have invested more than a billion dollars in drug courts, specialized programs that supervise substance-abuse treatment for certain nonviolent offenders. The courts give offenders an opportunity to change their behavior and stop using illegal drugs before becoming enmeshed in the legal and penal systems" (www.urban.orgjustice). Juvenile drug courts divert less-serious criminal offenses from the juvenile justice system by offering what some refer to as "soft justice" and treatment. Because the youth typically referred to juvenile drug court have been drinking alcohol and smoking marijuana for a few years and are between 15 and 16 years of age, they are less likely to respond to programs that stress recovery and relapse in adult addiction programs. These youth, according to Butts and Roman (2004), usually respond positively to interventions designed to improve relationships and offer recreational opportunities, job preparation, and family counseling to support them in making positive choices. The effectiveness of these programs is not well known despite their popularity.

Embedded in each of these programs are mental health services for youth. However, only 6% of seriously emotionally disturbed youth have been found to receive services from only one of these systems and 4 out of 10 received services from three systems (Howell et al., 2004). From a positive youth development perspective, programs designed to focus on a single problem behavior are less effective than prevention models aimed at the co-occurrence of problem behaviors. Therefore greater emphasis should be placed on the integration of services offered through the juvenile justice, mental health, and substance abuse, education, and child welfare systems.

A number of policies are directed toward the problems of adolescent sexual behavior and pregnancy. The Family Planning program, authorized under Title X of the Public Health Service Act, is the only federal program devoted solely to the provision of family planning and reproductive health care. The program is designed to provide access to contraceptive supplies and information. Title X-supported clinics also provide a number of preventive health services such as patient education and counseling; breast and pelvic examinations; cervical cancer, STD and HIV screenings; and pregnancy diagnosis and counseling. Additional federal support for family planning services is "channeled through Medicaid, the social services block grant and Maternal and Child Health block grant programs" (Levitan, Mangum, & Mangum, 1998, p. 151). Adolescent health care is also supported through the State Children's Health Insurance Program (SCHIP).

Adolescent sexual activity has provoked two extremes in policy interventions. One view is that sexual activity among those who are not married should be discouraged, and although others agree with this premise, they are as concerned about the negative consequences of sexual activity including sexually transmitted diseases (STDs) and pregnancy. These views are reflected in two different pregnancy prevention approaches. The Adolescent Family Life (AFL) program provides funding for prevention and medical and social services to pregnant or parenting teens. Prevention activities funded through this program offer sex education with or without contraceptives and distribution. The Abstinence Education Program centers on the abstinence-only message and only funds programs that adhere solely to bolstering that message. The Abstinence Education Program, created in 1996 as part of the welfare reform law passed in 1996 (Personal Responsibility and Work Opportunity Reconciliation Act), offers mentoring and counseling to promote abstinence. (The welfare reform legislation also offered incentives to the states to reduce teen pregnancy by restricting benefits to unmarried teen parents and promoting marriage.) These intervention programs can be community based, school based, or linked with schools in clinical and nonclinical settings and are often supplemented by statewide media campaigns. The success of these programs is still under investigation. Concerns about adolescent sexual activity are not limited to heterosexual youth, however. In a society that is avoidant, hostile, and contemptuous of homosexuals, sexual minority youth face significant challenges as they attempt to formulate and consolidate their sexual identities. Differentiating and providing meaning to sexual feelings during adolescence is anxiety provoking and draining. Confused and isolated from family, peers, and professionals, there are fewer resources available to sexual minority youth. School counselors are in the best position to help this group by creating a more hospitable environment for teens questioning their sexual identity (Fontaine, 1996, p. 829). Simple interventions designed to provide information in the schools about gay and lesbian teens and offering training to teachers and administrators on gay and lesbian issues can be effective. Groups with peers are also helpful.

Early and Middle Adulthood

Adulthood, the longest stage of the life cycle, has received the least amount of scholarly attention, though major decisions about almost every aspect of an individual's life are made during this life-cycle stage, including education, training, career choices, sexual orientation, selecting a mate, and childbearing. Self-actualization is the focus for young adults in their 20s. Identifying a career or work life and developing intimacy through relationships is a primary focus during early adulthood. The expectation is that one is able to separate from parents and establish oneself as an independent adult. Young adults are expected to pursue college, job training, or employment. Forming lasting intimate relationships and deciding whether to have children occupies the attention of those in their thirties. Adults in their 40s and 50s are more reflective, less self-critical, and less concerned with external demands (Austrian, 2008); most have achieved seniority in their work world, though physical and cognitive declines may affect decision making about their future lives. Although the federal government has never committed to a comprehensive employment policy, it has funded nearly 125 different employment programs since the 1960s for the economically disadvantaged, out-of-school youth, veterans, Native Americans, and the homeless (Blau, 2004). Many of these programs were costly and often duplicated each other. In 1998 Congress addressed some of these problems by enacting the Workforce Investment Act (WIA; P.L. 105–220). Although WIA retained many of the previously enacted employment programs by maintaining separate funding streams for adults, dislocated workers, and youth, it made the general public eligible for services and establishes a one-stop delivery system as the access point for employment-related and training services.

Three tiers of service are authorized under WIA through such programs as an employment service program that matches employers with job seekers; trade adjustment assistance programs for those workers adversely affected by foreign trade; Job Corps, the largest intervention program for youth; a migrant and seasonal farm workers program; and veterans employment and training programs for disabled veterans. At the core of the service tiers is job search assistance, where staff offers assistance to workers in searching the classified pages and tips on interviewing. The second tier consists of more intensive services to help workers get jobs on their own such as case management and assessment. If all the previous efforts have failed, job training is offered as the third tier of services (Blau, 2004). These services are provided through contracts between the state and public and private employment counseling and job training agencies.

WIA de-emphasizes training by relying on a worker's ability to secure employment on their own through the normal market mechanisms. It encourages increased coordination among programs on the state and local levels through workforce investment boards that match workers needing training with local industries. Critics argue that although WIA is an umbrella program that unifies previously existing programs, job training has had little effect on the employment of workers. Instead critics advocate raising the minimum wage to increase the earnings of the working poor. The minimum wage, established in 1938 in the Fair Labor Standards Act, guarantees "a wage that would sustain a decent standard of living for all workers" (DiNitto, 2005, p. 372). The minimum wage was raised to $7.25 per hour in 2009.

Of course, federal dollars are also available to assist young adults seeking vocational and college education. Most of these programs are need-based. For example, the Federal Pell Grant Program provides need-based grants to low-income undergraduate and certain postbaccalaureate students to promote access to postsecondary education. Grant amounts are dependent on the student's expected family contribution (EFC), the cost of attending the institution, whether the student attends full time or part time, and whether the student attends for a full academic year or less. Students may not receive Federal Pell Grant funds from more than one school at a time. Financial need is determined by the U.S. Department of Education using a standard formula established by Congress. The fundamental elements in this standard formula are the student's and, in the case of dependent students, the parents' income and assets; the family's household size; and the number of family members attending postsecondary institutions. In addition, the Federal Work-Study Program provides funds that are earned through part-time employment to assist students in financing the costs of postsecondary education. Hourly wages under this program must not be less than the federal minimum wage. The Perkins Loan Program provides low-interest loans to help needy students finance the costs of postsecondary education.

Today military employment constitutes another career choice for young men and women. As a volunteer military force, an occupational model dominates rather than the professional brotherhood model of military service. A voluntary military force has resulted in demographic differences among enlisted and active military personnel. More than 81% are between the ages of 20 and 44 years, are better educated, and are married with at least one preschool child. An increasing number of women are in the military, many of whom are single parents or dual-career military couples. About a third of the military are minorities who have found better employment opportunities in the military than in society at large (Knox & Price, 1995). There are approximately 1,168,094 active duty military personnel across all four branches of service (i.e., Army, Navy, Marine Corps, and Air Force), according to the Department of Defense as of November 2008. Deployment to world crisis areas, reunions following deployment, combat stress, and the stress associated with the separation from families are the major stresses of military service. Although the military establishment provides mental health services, seeking assistance for psychosocial problems is perceived to have a negative impact on building a military career. The culture of the military prohibits seeking assistance for psychological problems (Knox & Price, 1995). Military mental health services focus on prevention through psychoeducational and cognitive behavioral interventions provided before and after deployment. In addition, the military family assistance centers and family support groups serve as one-stop multiservice centers for military and civilian personnel. The Veterans Bureau, with more than 232 vet centers, offers readjustment and outreach services to all veterans.

"Mental health in adulthood is characterized by the successful performance of mental function, enabling individuals to cope with adversity and to flourish in their education, vocation, and personal relationships" (www.surgeongeneral.gov/library/mentalhealth). These are the areas of functioning most widely recognized in the mental health field. Federal support for public mental health services has a long history dating back to the 1960s when the Community Mental Health Act of 1963 mandated that community mental health centers provide five essential services: inpatient care, outpatient care, emergency services, partial hospitalization (day care), and consultation and education. Other essential services such as special programs for children and the elderly and aftercare and halfway housing for patients discharged from mental hospitals were added in 1975. In 1980 a Mental Health Systems Act was enacted that included provisions for people with serious mental illness and severely disturbed children and adolescents. However, 1 year later, under the Reagan administration, the act was rescinded (in 1981), federal funds were channeled through block grants to the states for mental health services (previously federal funds were made directly to community mental health centers), and states were required to develop State Comprehensive Mental Health Services Plans. Federal funding for mental health services shrank as a result (DiNitto, 2005). Subsequently, Medicaid and Medicare expanded public mental health services beyond community mental health centers to other mental health providers, many in private practice, who accepted public payments (DiNitto, 2005). Today, Medicaid is the largest payer of mental health services. Along with the expansion of services under Medicaid and Medicare, provisions in the 1973 HMO Act require HMO programs to offer treatment for physical disorders as well as crisis intervention mental health services. Consequently, within HMOs coverage for counseling and psychotherapy has been rationed.

Faced with increasing demands for mental health services, President George W. Bush established the New Freedom Commission on Mental Health in 2002 to advise the president on methods of improving the system and to conduct a comprehensive study of the U.S. mental health service delivery system, including public- and private-sector providers. After a year of study, the commission issued its report in 2003, concluding that "the system is not oriented toward recovery" (DiNitto, 2005, p. 395). Moreover, the commission noted that multiple programs with disparate objectives and requirements finance mental health services "creating an approach that is complex, fragmented, and inconsistent in its coverage" (New Freedom Commission on Mental Health, 2003, p. 21). The commission recommended a transformation of the public mental health system based on two general principles; namely, that services and treatment be patient and family centered, giving consumers real and meaningful choices about treatment options and providers and focusing care on increasing consumers' ability to successfully cope with life's challenges. How and when the transformation occurs are still unclear. A Mental Health Parity Bill was signed into law under the Bush administration in 2008. Under the bill, employers who provide coverage for mental health care are required to equalize annual and lifetime spending limits for mental and physical illness. Prior to the enactment of this bill, many health insurance plans would restrict mental health care coverage. For example 31% of full-time employees working in medium and large private firms with mental health benefits had separate inpatient day limits, and 19% had separate outpatient visit limits (Barry, 2006). Parity legislation requires health plans to provide an equivalent level of coverage for mental health and general health care.

Life stressors in young adulthood and midlife such as unemployment, death of a parent, family illness, and financial strains can negatively affect personal relationships, especially marital relationships, resulting in domestic abuse or divorce. Domestic violence prior to the 1970s was seldom acknowledged as a public issue. According to Cowan and Schwarz, before the 1970s police departments used "stitch rules" when responding to cases of domestic assault—"a wife who was abused had to require a certain number of surgical sutures before a husband could be arrested for assault and battery" (2004, p. 1068). Men who were convicted of domestic violence were more likely to receive relatively light prison sentences, if they were prosecuted at all. Women were also unable to obtain restraining orders unless they filed for divorce at the same time. However a series of factors led to a change in these policies by the 1990s, including the political pressure from organized women's groups advocating for equal protection for battered women, a series of class-action suits against local police departments and district attorney offices, and the passage of state legislation providing for protection orders in cases of domestic violence (the Pennsylvania Protection from Abuse Act of 1976 was the first to be passed).

The Violence Against Women Act (VAWA), enacted as federal legislation in 1994, reauthorized in 2000 and 2005, provides funding to hire more prosecutors and improve domestic violence training among prosecutors, police officers, and health and social services professionals. It also provided for more shelters, counseling services, and research into causes of violence and effective community campaigns to reduce violence against women. The VAWA also addressed the key problems in enforcement of protection orders by setting new federal penalties for those who cross state lines to continue abusing a spouse or partner (Cowan & Schwartz, 2004). The bill in effect made interstate domestic abuse and harassment a federal offense and requires states to honor protective orders issued in other states. The 2005 reauthorization bill included funding provisions for direct services for children exposed to violence, sexual assault victims, victims of trafficking, victims from communities of color, and immigrant and tribal victims. This law offers much-needed resources for victims of domestic violence across multiple settings.

Marital stressors including incompatibility often lead to the disruption of marriages. Divorce is a highly emotional and stressful event in the lives of spouses and their children. Numerous studies have shown that the consequences of divorce are devastating for women and their children's economic, social, and psychological adjustment (Wallerstein, 1985). State laws that vary considerably regulate divorce and child custody. Many states have enacted no-fault divorce statutes that allow for the dissolution of a marriage based on a finding that the relationship is no longer viable. Whether the enactment of these statutes is the cause or the effect of the rise in the divorce rates observed over the last two decades is difficult to determine. Far too often divorcing couples have concerns about the custody of their children. States laws authorize the courts to make decisions about which parent has the right and duty to care for a child on a day-to-day basis and to make decisions about the child. However, according to the American Bar Association, most divorcing parents have reached an agreement about the child's custody before they go to court. There are three types of custody arrangements. In sole custody arrangements, the child resides with one parent (the custodial parent) most of the time, and that parent also makes decisions about the child's education, health care, and religious training. The noncustodial parent usually has a right to visitation. Joint legal custody arrangements allow both parents to share in making decisions affecting the child's care. In joint physical custody arrangements, the child resides with each parent for a substantial amount of time. Whether any one or more of these child custody arrangements affects the child's postdivorce adjustment has become the subject of considerable research.

Besides child custody decisions, state courts also award child support orders (i.e., cash payments from birth parents). The courts consider the income of the parents, the number of children, and other factors when awarding child support. From 1950 to 1975 the federal government's role in enforcing child support orders was limited to only those children receiving public assistance. Amendments to the Social Security Act in 1975 provided federal matching funds to the states to establish child support enforcement agencies (CSE) authorized to collect child support and establish paternity for children receiving welfare assistance. More than 10 years later, during the Reagan administration, the Child Support Enforcement Amendments of 1984 (P.L. 98–378) were enacted. These amendments "toughened the methods states could use to collect overdue support payments and required states to pursue medical support awards to ensure that children of single parents have access to healthcare" (DiNitto, 2005, p. 208). Under these amendments families not receiving welfare could avail themselves of CSE services. The amendments allowed CSE agencies to garnish wages, intercept federal and state income tax refunds, seize and sell property, tap unemployment checks, and file civil and criminal charges against parents whose payments were in arrears. The use of these enforcement methods certainly increased the amount of child support being collected, but collections still fell below what was owed. The 1996 Personal Responsibility and Work Opportunity Reconciliation Act provided funding to the states to create automated databases for locating parents and for tracking and monitoring cases. In addition, to increase the establishment and enforcement of child support orders for noncustodial parents living in a different state than their children, all states were required to adopt the model Uniform Interstate Family Support Act. The Uniform Interstate Family Support Act (UIFSA) is a law that regulates the processing of all cases in which parties are located in more than one state. The 1996 law also established a National Directory of New Hires that is used by CSE agencies to determine if individuals are in arrears on child support. The directory is compiled on the basis of the names employers submit of newly employed workers. Subsequent legislation in 1998 offered more help to the states to increase the effectiveness and efficiency of their CSE offices.

The legal rights for same-gender couples and their families remain uncertain but may be the greatest civil rights battle facing the country in this century (Avery, Chase, Johansson, Litvak, Monteo, & Wydra, 2007). Massachusetts was the first state issuing marriage licenses to same-gender couples in May 2004 and in 2008 Connecticut's Supreme Court ruled that same-sex couples have a constitutional right to marry. Vermont, New Hampshire, Iowa, and New Jersey have legalized civil unions for same-sex couples, whereas Maine, Washington, Oregon, the District of Columbia, and Hawaii have registered domestic partnerships for same-gender couples. These gains were, however, overshadowed by a California majority vote on a proposition banning same-sex marriage in 2008. Same-gender couples seek the same benefits (i.e., inheritance, retirement, and Social Security benefits), protections and responsibilities that married heterosexual couples receive under law. Civil unions and domestic partnerships do not grant the same rights, protections, and responsibilities as legal marriage. Opponents to same-gender marriage argue that marriage is exclusively a right for heterosexual men and women and that the purpose of marriage is procreation. Opponents view the legalization of same-gender marriages as a violation of the sanctity of the institution of marriage. Though some have called for federal legislation to ban same-gender marriage, state laws govern the terms and conditions for marriage and vary considerably.

Older Adulthood

Older adulthood is the final transitional stage of development. Indicators of older adulthood differ in terms of chronological age, functional capacity, and life stage. Chronological age is often used to arbitrarily identify the time when older adulthood begins and to divide older adults into categories of "young-old" and "old-old" (Kolb, 2008, p. 286). Functional capacity refers to the functional capacity of the elderly, including physical appearance, strength, coordination, mobility, and mental capacity—all of which are used to assign people to age categories. Definitions of life stage include later adulthood and old age. Later adulthood is associated with major shifts such as retirement, deaths of friends and family, widowhood, and caregiving of parents. The "old life stage" is defined in terms of physical and mental frailties that occur in the late 70s and early 80s. Individuals do not always show all the signs typically associated with later adulthood or old age, however. Older adults are in a better position to reflect on and accept the total shape of their lives and take pride in what they created (i.e., children, career, friendships). Older adults are independent, willing to dare new things, and continue to learn and contribute to society based on the wisdom gained over the life cycle. Today the percentage of older adults in the United States is expected to double between now and 2030. Older adults are not just greater in number, but they are also living much longer. The population of older adults age 85 and over has grown 31 times larger since the turn of the century (Takamura, 1999). Many stressful life events such as declining health, changing financial status, and/or the loss of mates, family members, or friends increase with age. Over time older adults become physically and emotionally frail. Some are extremely vulnerable due to depression and dementia. Housing constitutes another problem for the older adult, many of whom are no longer able to afford or want to maintain their existing homes. Although the Department of Housing and Urban Development offers seniors public housing programs, the Bush administration cut the department's budget in 2007. Protecting the integrity, health, and welfare of older adults began in 1935 with the passage of the Social Security Act and continued in 1965 with the enactment of the Medicare and Medicaid programs and the Older Americans Act (P.L. 89–73).

The Older Americans Act (OAA) authorized grants to states for community planning and service programs, research, demonstration, and training projects in the field of aging. The act created a "nationwide aging network composed of 57 state and 655 local agencies on aging, 225 Native American Indian tribal organizations representing more than 300 tribes, more than 2,000 senior centers, and 27,000 providers of services" (Takamura, 1999, p. 234) through which older people and their families are served. Although the legislation prohibits state and local agencies on aging from providing services directly, they usually contract with local agencies to deliver such services as nutrition programs, senior centers, information and referral, transportation, legal counseling, escort services, home repair and renovation, homemaker and chore services, home health aid, visitation, shopping assistance, and telephone assurance (i.e., phone calls to the elderly to check on their needs).

As previously mentioned in this chapter, family caregivers are seldom offered assistance by federal or state agencies; however, "the 2000 reauthorization of OAA makes $125 million available to establish the National Family Caregiver Support Program" (DiNitto, 2005, p. 430). Through this program, family caregivers of the elderly working with local area offices on aging have access to information, education, counseling, support groups, daytime and overnight respite services through adult day care, residential care, and other options. Title VII, Vulnerable Elder Rights Protection, of OAA addresses the concerns of elderly residents of long-term care facilities. Although most elders living in these facilities fare well, many are neglected or experience other unfortunate incidents of psychological or physical abuse. Through the long-term-care ombudsmen programs, 1,000 paid and 14,000 volunteer staff regularly visit long-term care facilities (i.e., nursing homes, board and care homes, assisted-living facilities, and similar adult care facilities) to advocate for elderly residents, provide information about the long-term-care system to residents and families, and monitor the care and conditions of long-term care facilities. In 2001, ombudsmen investigated 264,269 complaints made by or on behalf of residents of nursing homes and other adult care facilities. The lack of resident care due to inadequate staffing was the most frequent complaint.

Title VII of the OAA also authorizes funding for the National Center on Elder Abuse, elder abuse training, and coordination of activities in states and local communities. It does not, however, fund adult protective services or shelters for abused older persons. All 50 states have enacted legislation regarding elder abuse prevention and have set up reporting systems. As might be expected, there is considerable variation among these laws and the definitions of elder abuse. Elder abuse is generally described as the willful infliction of physical pain or injury, sexual abuse, the infliction of mental or emotional anguish, financial or material exploitation, neglect on the part of a caregiver, or behavior of an elder that threatens his/her own health or safety (self-neglect; www.aoa.gov/eldfam). Adult protective service (APS) agencies receive and screen reports of suspected elder abuse and assign a case worker to conduct an investigation of the report to substantiate the allegation. If the allegations are substantiated and the elder agrees or has not been declared incapacitated by the court and a guardian has been appointed, APS works with community agencies to provide services that ensure the safety and health of the elder. A 1998 National Elder Abuse Incidence Study funded by AOA found that 551,011 persons aged 60 and over experienced abuse, neglect, and/or self-neglect in a 1-year period and that in 90% of the cases the perpetrator was a family member (www.aoa.gov/edlfam). Mental health coverage for the elderly and disabled is inadequate, partly because of the costs associated with copayments. To address the problem the Stop Senior Suicide Act is being considered in Congress. The Act would create grants for public and private organizations to plan and implement elderly suicide early intervention and prevention strategies on the state and local level. Though the law has not been passed, it represents one solution to the problem of senior suicide and mental health treatment.

Summary

Though far from being exhaustive, this review of significant social welfare policies affecting individuals across the life cycle offers a glimpse of the range of needs to be met in ensuring the health, welfare, and safety of various members of our population. Other programs in the areas of housing, criminal law enforcement, employment, occupational safety, agriculture, and even tax policy might also be added to the list of programs assisting the public. The federal government's involvement in meeting social welfare needs is enormous, and without it, state and local governments would be hard pressed to respond. Evaluations of the effectiveness and efficiency of these and other programs is sparse. There is a tremendous need for process and outcome evaluations of social welfare programs: Without such evaluations, it is difficult to determine the extent to which they meet their intended goals and objectives as well as the unintended consequences of policy initiatives. For every program or policy enacted by Congress there are the unexpected, unanticipated consequences that later legislative action is intended to address. Program evaluation is one mechanism that legislative and administrative offices use to monitor the success or failure of policy.

Yet program evaluation cannot address the fragmentation in program design or the duplication of services across program areas. For example, adolescents who enter the juvenile justice system are frequently the same adolescents served by the child welfare, education, and mental health systems. Funding restrictions and inflexible administrative rules and regulations frequently make it difficult to offer holistic services to these adolescents. Many policy makers and administrators are presently working toward the development of "systems of care." The systems of care approach focuses on building infrastructures through interagency collaboration, individualized, strengths-based care practices, cultural competence, and community-based services to ensure positive outcomes for children and families. A systems of care approach attempts to create linkages across all program areas related to a specific child's or family's needs. Making these systems of care work requires more flexibility in funding streams and administrative layers. Whether this approach enhances service delivery is unclear.

In reviewing the aforementioned programs and policies, two central questions that should come to mind are, Who does not benefit? What is not provided? Most of these programs are intended to serve the least-advantaged members of society. But among this group there are subgroups who are ineligible for service and even more advantaged groups who might benefit. Child support enforcement legislation was initially intended to help child recipients of public assistance programs, but it has now become a service offered to all children. In this instance, we have witnessed the blurring of the line between traditionally targeted and more universally oriented programs (Crowley, 2003). By the same token, there is growing concern about what is not provided in these programs, calling attention to the adequacy of services in such areas as health and mental health care. From the description of the programs in these areas, there is little doubt that additional funding will be required to meet the mental health and health care needs of society. Examining social welfare policies across the life span highlights some of the deficiencies in programming.

Appendix A

Genogram

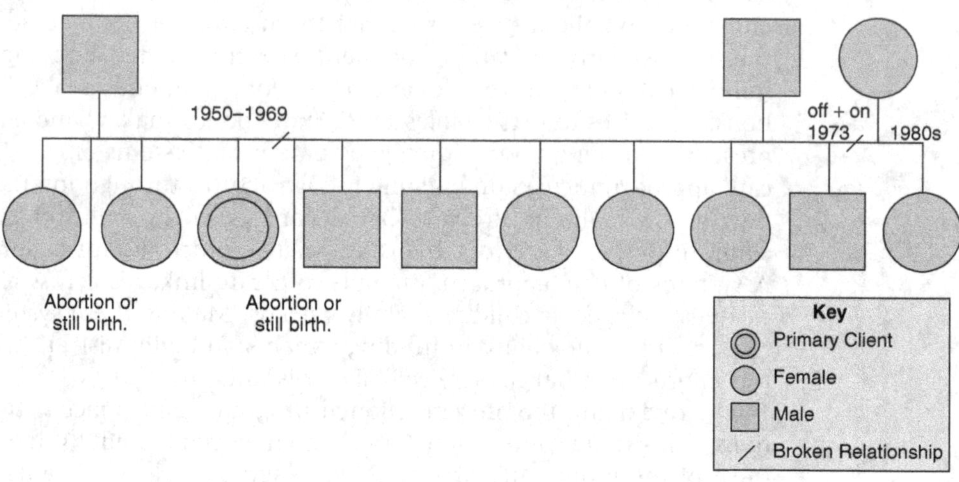

Appendix B

Eco-Maps

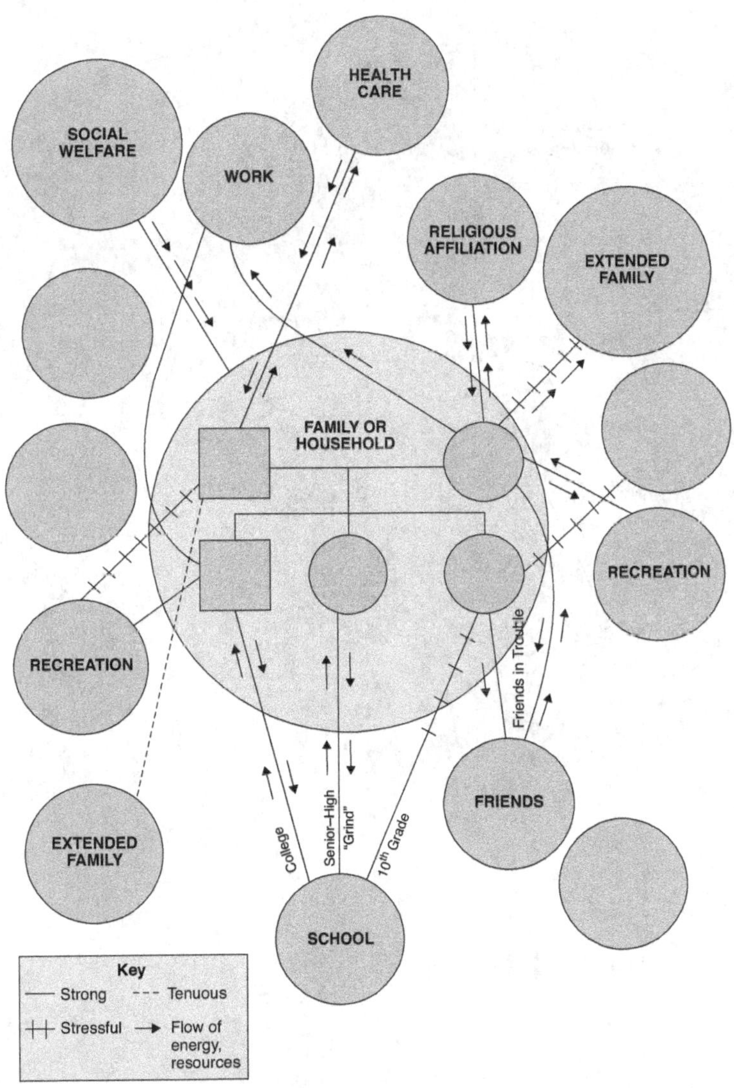

Source: A. Hartman, 1978, "Diagrammatic Assessment of Family Relationships" (Figure 3, "An eco-map"), *Social Casework* 59(8), p. 470. Reprinted with permission from *Families in Society* (www.familiesinsociety.org), published by the Alliance for Children and Families.

Appendix C

Social Network Map

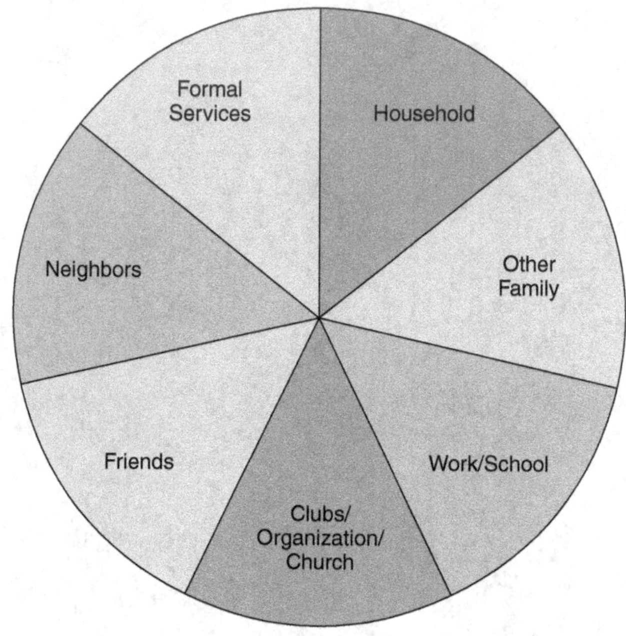

Source: E. M. Tracy and J. K. Whittaker, 1990, "The Social Network Map: Assessing Social Support in Clinical Social Work Practice," *Families in Society* 71(8), pp. 461–470. Reprinted by permission of the authors.

Appendix D

Culturagram

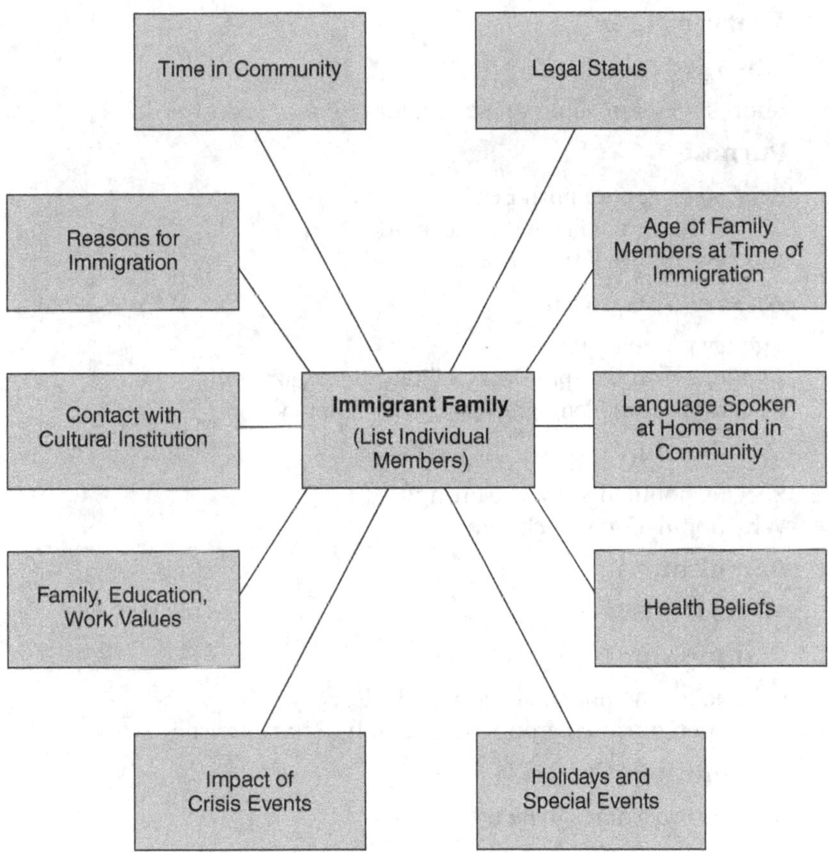

Source: E. P. Congress, 1994, The Use of Culturagrams to Assess and Empower Culturally Diverse Families (Figure 1,"Culturagram"), *Families in Society* 75(9), p.532. Reprinted with permission from *Families in Society* (www.familiesinsociety.org), published by the Alliance for Children and Families.

Appendix E

Outline for a Group Proposal

Treatment/Task

Abstract

Short statement summarizing major points of group

Purpose

Brief statement of purpose
How the group will conduct its work
Job description of the worker

Agency Sponsorship

Agency name and mission
Agency resources (physical facilities, financial, staff)
Geographic and demographic data on agency

Membership

Specific population for the group
Why population was chosen

Recruitment

Methods to be used

Composition

Criteria for member inclusion/exclusion
Size, open or closed group, demographic characteristics

Orientation

Specific procedures to be used

Contract

Number, frequency, length, and time of meeting

Environment

Physical arrangements (room, space, materials)
Financial arrangements (budget, expense, income)
Special arrangements (child care, transportation)

Source: Ronald W. Toseland and Robert F. Rivas, *An Introduction to Group Work Practice* (4th ed.). Published by Allyn & Bacon, Boston, MA.

Appendix F

Standards for Social Work Practice in Groups

I. Core Knowledge and Values

A. Familial. Social, political, cultural context of member identity, interactional style and concern
Members are viewed as citizens.
Members are capable of change and capable of helping one another.

B. Attention to the whole person
Systems perspective used in assessment and intervention person and environment
Bio-psycho-social perspective
Member in group
Group-in-community

C. Competency-based assessment
Emphasis on member strengths as well as concerns

D. Mutual aid function
Group consists of multiple helping relationships.
Worker's primary role is one of helping members to help one another.

E. Groups characterized by democratic process.
Members are helped to own the group.
Equal worth of members and worker.
Worker is not all-powerful "expert."
Worker-to-group and worker-to-members relationships characterized by egalitarianism and reciprocity.

F. Emphasis on empowerment
Group goals emphasize individual member growth and social change.
Group work promotes individual and group autonomy.

G. Worker's assessment and interventions characterized by flexibility and eclecticism.

H. Small group behavior
Group as an entity separate and distinct from individual members.
Phases of group development foster change throughout the life of a group.
Recognition of how group process changes and influences individual member behavior.

I. Groups formed for the different purposes and goals.
Group type (e.g., education, problem-solving, social action) influences what worker does and how group accomplishes its goals.
J. Monitoring and evaluation of success of group in accomplishing its objectives through observation and measurement of outcomes and/or processes.

II. Group Work in the Pregroup Phase

A. Identify common needs of potential group members.
B. Plan and conduct outreach, recruitment of members.
C. Secure organizational support and sanction for group, if needed.
D. Address organizational resistance to groups, if needed.
E. Screen and prepare members for group, when appropriate.
F. Secure permission for members' participation, when needed.
G. Develop compositional balance, if appropriate.
H. Select appropriate group type, structure, and size.
I. Establish meeting place, time, etc. that promotes member comfort and cohesion.
J. Develop and articulate verbally and/or in writing a clear statement of group purpose that reflects member needs and, where appropriate, agency mission.
K. Develop and articulate clear statement of worker role that reflects the group's purpose.
L. Use preparatory empathy to tune into members' feelings and reactions to group's beginning.

Knowledge Needed

A. Organization's mission and function and how this influences nature of group work service.
B. Social and institutional barriers that may affect the development of group work service.
C. Issues associated with group compensation.
D. Human life cycle and its relationship to potential members' needs.
E. Cultural factors and their influence on potential members' lives and their ability to engage in group and relate to others.
F. Types of groups and their relationship to member needs.
G. Specific types of individual and social problems that lead to a need for group.

III. Group Work in Beginning Phase

Tasks

A. Provide clear statement of group (and if necessary, agency) purpose and worker role.
B. Elicit members feedback regarding perception of needs, interests, and problems.
C. Encourage members to share concerns and strengths with one another.
D. Facilitate connections between members and members and workers.
E. Encourage awareness and expression of commonalities among members.
F. Monitor group for manifestations of authority theme and, when needed, respond directly.

G. Assess impact of cultural differences between members and between members and workers and address directly when needed.
H. Assess group in establishing rules and norms and promote change and growth.
I. Use of self to develop cohesion among members and comfort with worker.
J. Assist members in establishing individual and group goals.
K. Clarify link between individual and group goals.
L. Help members to establish a beginning contract that provides clarity and direction to their work together.
M. Promote individual autonomy and empowerment of member.
N. Create and maintain environment of sociocultural safety.

Knowledge Needed

A. Group dynamics in beginning stage of group.
B. Causes/manifestations of resistance to change among members and in external environment.

IV. Group Work in the Middle Phase

Tasks

A. Point out commodities among members.
B. Reinforce connection between individual needs/problems and group goals.
C. Encourage and model supportive honest feedback between members and between members and workers.
D. Use here and now/process illumination to further group's work.
E. Help members use role playing, behavioral rehearsal, and other verbal and nonverbal activities to accomplish individual and group tasks.
F. Monitor norms that govern group's work.
G. Assess group' progress toward its goals.
H. Recontract with members, if needed, to assist them in achieving individual and group goals.
I. Identify obstacles to work within and outside group's boundaries and deal with them directly.
J. Clarify and interpret communication patterns between members, between members and the worker, and between the group and others external to the group.
K. Identify and highlight member conflict, when needed, and facilitate resolution.
L. Summarize sessions.

Knowledge Needed

A. Group dynamics in the middle phase.
B. Role theory and its application to members' relationships with one another and with worker.
C. Communication theory and its application to verbal and nonverbal interactions within group and between group and others external to group.
D. Member interactions as manifestations of sociocultural forces of race, class, gender, sexual orientation.

E. Member interactions as manifestations of psychodynamic factors.
F. Purposeful use of verbal and nonverbal activities.

V. Group Work in the Ending Phase

Tasks

A. Identify and point out direct and indirect signs of members' reactions to ending.
B. Share worker's endings feelings with members.
C. Assist members in sharing their feelings about endings with one another.

AASWG, Inc.
c/o University of Akron
Akron. OH 44325-8050
jhramey/commatuakron.edu, www.aaswg.org

Web Sites

Chapter 1

Council on Social Work Education (CSWE): www.cswe.org
National Association of Social Workers (NASW): www.socialworkers.org
National Association of Black Social Workers: www.nabsw.org
International Council on Social Welfare: www.icsw.org
International Federation of Social Workers: www.ifsw.org
Latino Social Workers Organization: www.whittier.cps.k12.il.us/Community/PrOrg/LSWO.html

Chapter 2

Children's Neurobiological Solutions Foundation: www.cnsfoundation.org
Autism Society of America: www.autismsociety.org
Children and Adults with Attention Deficit Disorder: www.chadd.org
The Dana Foundation: www.dana.org
The Bipolar Information Network: www.moodswing.org/index.shtm;
Epilepsy Foundation of America: www.efa.org.
Learning Disabilities Association of America: www.ldanatl.org.
National Downs Syndrome Society: www.downsyndrom.com
National Federation of the Blind: www.nfb.org
Stuttering Foundation of America: www.stutterfa.org
Tourtette Syndrom Association: www.tsa.org

Chapter 3

Association for Play Therapy: www:A4PT.org
Clinical Social Workers Association: www.clinicalsocialworkassociation.org
International Association of Cognitive Psychotherapy: www.theiac.com
International Association for Self Psychology: www.psychologyoftheself.com
Society for the Exploration of Psychotherapy Integration: www.cyberpsych.org/sepil/

Chapter 4

Center for Identity Development: www.centeridentity.apg.com
International Foundation for Gender Education: www.ifge.org
National Gay and Lesbian Task Force: www.ngltf.og
National Center for Transgender Equality: www.nctequality.org

Chapter 5

American Association for Marriage and Family Therapy: www.aamft.org
Center on Contemporary Families: www.contemporaryfamilies.org
National Military Family Association (NMFA): www.nmfa.org/
Allyn and Bacon Family Therapy Website: www.abacon.com/famtherapy/index.html

Chapter 6

Association for the Advancement of Social Work with Groups: www.aaswg.org
Association for Specialists in Group work: www.asgw.org
Support-Group.com: www.support-group.com/

Chapter 7

Association of Community Organizations for Reform Now (ACORN): http://www.acorn.org/
Community Workforce Diversity: www.workforcediversitynetwork.com
The Association for community Organization and Social Administration: www.acosa.org
The International Federation of Social Workers: www.ifsw.org
Story Corps: www.storycorps.org
The Institute on Community Integration ici.umn.edu

Chapter 8

The Society for Spirituality and Social Work: www.ssw.asu.edu/spirituality/sssw/

Chapter 9

Boston Institute for the Development of Infants and Parents http://www.bidip.org/
Center on Infant Mental Health and Development http://www.cimhd.org/
Texas Association for Infant Mental Health http://www.taimh.org/
American Academy of Pediatrics: www.aap.org

Chapter 10

Office of Child Development and Early Learning http://www.dpw.state.pa.us/About/OCDEL/
American Academy of Pediatrics http://www.aap.org/
Encyclopedia on Early Childhood Development http://www.child-encyclopedia.com/en-ca/home.html

Center for Early Education and Development http://www.cehd.umn.edu/ceed/

The Child Welfare League of America: www.cwla.org

Children's Defense Fund: www.childrensdefense.org

National Association for Child Development: www.nacd.org

Chapter 11

American Academy of Child and Adolescent Psychiatray: www.aacap.org

Child Development Institute: www.childdevelopmentinfor.com

School Social Work Association of America: www.members.aol.com/SSWAAWEB/SSWAA1.htm

Society of Clinical Child and Adolescent Psychology: www.sccap.tamu.edu

Chapter 12

European Association for Research of Adolescents: www.earonline.org

International Association for Adolescent Health: www.iaah.org

Chapter 13

Alcoholics Anonymous: www.aa.org

Al-Anon and Ala-teen: www.al-anon.alateen.org

Narcotics Anonymous: na.org

Society for the Study of Emerging Aduthood: www.ssea.org

Chapter 14

Coaching4Midlife: www.coachingformidlife.com

Grandparentsraisinggrandchildren: www.raisingyourgrandchildren.com

Chapter 15

Alzheimer's Association: www.alz.org

American Association for Geriatric Psychiatry: www.aagponline.org

American Geriatrics Society: www.americangeriatrics.org

American Society on Aging USA: www.asaging.org

Council on Social Work Education – Gero Ed Center: www.CSWE.org/CenterInitiatives/GeroEdCenter.asx

Gerontological Society of America: www.geron.org

National Committee for the Prevention of Elder Abuse: www.preventelderabuse.org

Chapter 16

American Red Cross: www.redcross.org

Gateway to Post Traumatic Stress Disorder Information: www.ptsdinfo.org

National Center for PTSD: www.ptsd.va.gov.

National Institute for Trauma and Loss in Children: www.starraining.org

Veterans Affairs: www.va.gov/

Chapter 17

The American Association of the Deaf-Blind: www.aadbiorg

American Cancer Society: www.cancer.org

Association of Oncology Social Workers (AOSW): www.biostat.wisc.edu/aosw/aoswhello.html.

Cancer Care: www.cancercareinc.org

Disability Rights Activist: www.teleport.com/-abarhydt/

National Federation of the Blind: www.nfb.org

Epilepsy Foundation of America: www.efa.org

The Institute of Community Integration: www.ici.umn.edu

Muscular Dystrophy Association: www.mdausa.org

National Alliance for the Mentally Ill: www.nami.org

National Information Center for Children and Youth with Disabilities (NICHCY): www.nichy.org

Society for Social Work Leadership in Health Care: www.ssw/hc.org

United Cerebral Palsy: www.ucpa.org

Chapter 18

The Brookings Institute: www.brook.edu

US Department of Health and Human Services: www.hhs.gov Administration on Aging www.aoa.gov www.urban.org the urban institute

US Education Department www.ed.gov www.childtrends.org child trends

The Child Welfare League of America www.cwla.org

Glossary

Able-disabled See *Differently abled.*

Accelerated aging A problematic self-image developed when one has a negative view of aging, or places great importance on one's youthful attractiveness. Considered of particular concern for older gay men.

Acculturation The process of adapting to a new culture, involving an understanding of its values, beliefs, and behavioral patterns.

Acetylcholine A *neurotransmitter* that has an important role in memory and learning and that appears greatly diminished in people with *Alzheimer's disease.*

Achieving stage Stage of cognitive development in early adulthood during which individuals apply their intelligence to accomplishing personal, family, career, and social goals.

Action knowledge Form of traumatic memory in which knowing becomes consciously sequential and determines subsequent action.

Activity theory The idea that people can have successful and satisfying older adulthood by remaining engaged and involved in social activities.

Acts of others toward the self Category of the cyclical maladaptive pattern that focuses on the actual behaviors of the other people as observed and interpreted by the patient.

Acts of the self Category of the cyclical maladaptive pattern that includes the interpersonal thoughts, feelings, motives, perception, and behavior of the patient.

Acts of the self toward the self Category of the cyclical maladaptive pattern that includes all the patient's behaviors or attitudes toward her- and himself.

Acute pain Pain associated with an active disease state or a traumatic injury that goes away when the damage heals.

Acute stress disorder Severe emotional condition caused by exposure to a traumatic event in which both of the following conditions are present: threatened death or serious injury to the self or others; and the individual's response involved fear, helplessness, or horror.

Adaptability In the *family systems illness model,* the ability of the family to reorganize in response to the developmental imperatives brought on by progressive illness.

Adaptive social behavior Behavior that enables an individual to successfully adjust to the current social environment, such as bonding and teamwork.

Adrenalin A hormone produced by the adrenal gland that stimulates the heart, blood vessels and respiratory system and has a role in readying the body for acting under physical or mental stress.

Alexithymia A condition in which an individual experiences an emotional reaction but is unable to articulate the reason for the reaction.

Alter ego selfobject One of Kohut's three relationships between the self and its objects, the alter ego selfobject provides a sense of sameness with the *selfobject* that is essential to psychic growth and a sense of competence. Also called twinship or partnering selfobject.

Alzheimer's disease Progressive, severe dementia and memory loss caused by the degeneration of brain cells.

Amygdala A part of the *limbic system* of the brain that affects the emotions and defensive behavior.

Anal (developmental stage) Second stage of psychosexual development in which the main gratification is on expelling or retaining feces. This stage represents a child's ability to control his or her environment.

Anterior cingulate A part of the brain's *limbic system* that plays a role in decision making and emotion, as well as regulating autonomic functions such as heart rate and blood pressure.

Anterior commissure A part of the brain's *limbic system* made up of nerve fibers that connect the cerebral hemispheres.

Arousal A state of readiness or alertness.

Assertiveness training A behavior therapy technique used to teach individuals how to communicate their feelings and desires at an appropriate level of assertiveness without being confrontational or aggressive.

Asset building Referring to the development of tangible *community assets* such as housing, small businesses, and financial investments.

Asset claiming A community-building strategy involving helping people to identify and obtain public resources to which they are entitled.

Asset identifying and mobilizing Identification, nurturing, and use of underused social capital within communities.

Assisted living A housing facility for the elderly or disabled that provides the level of day-to-day care needed by the individuals in residence.

Attachment relationship The relationship between a child and the child's attachment figures that forms the basis for the views that the child develops of him- or herself.

Attention deficit hyperactivity disorder (ADHD/ADD) A developmental and behavioral disorder, most often associated with children, marked by inability to concentrate, distractibility, and excessive activity.

Autism A pervasive developmental disorder involving a variety of symptoms, including impaired language and social communication skills, inability to form relationships with others, or respond appropriately to the outside world.

Autonomic anxiety Neurobiologic distress invoked by social separation.

Autonomic nervous system Part of the nervous system responsible for internal, involuntary bodily functions, such as breathing, digestion, and circulation.

Autopoiesis In constructivism, the process whereby an organization produces itself.

Basal ganglia A part of the forebrain that controls involuntary motor movement.

Behavior Actions and reactions in response to the outside environment or internal stimuli.

Behavioral play therapy See *Cognitive-behavioral play therapy*.

Behaviorally inhibited Classification of children who seem cautious and shy and tend to withdraw emotionally in response to the stress of a new situation.

Biopsychosocial framework A social model used within the health-care community that stresses collaboration between family, environment, and practitioners in developing an effective health-care system.

Bipolar disorder Condition in which the individual experiences alternating periods of severe depression and mania.

Blended family A family in which both parents were previously divorced, and which includes a child or children from each of the previous marriages.

Boundary physical or conceptual borders or lines of separation that distinguish the system from the rest of its environment.

Brief treatment Short-term therapy.

Bureaucracy A hierarchical system of government characterized by complex, stringent rules and procedures.

Capability The physical or intellectual ability of an individual to perform tasks and to complete projects.

Capital See *Community assets*.

Castration anxiety In Freud's stages of psychosexual development, the fear experienced by a male in the phallic stage that his father will castrate him for having sexual desire for his mother.

Catecholamines A group of chemical *neurotransmitters* produced by the adrenal glands that act on the nervous system, triggering increased heart rate and blood pressure.

Caudate nucleur A part of a cluster of nuclei in the brain that control tic movement.

Cerebellum Part of the brain that controls balance and muscle coordination.

Chronic brain syndrome The progressive and lengthy occurrence of abnormal behaviors resulting from brain disease.

Chronic illness An unremitting illness with progressively severe symptoms that causes gradual physical deterioration and, eventually, *disability*.

Chronic pain Unremitting pain that usually falls into one of three categories: pain lasting after the normal feeling of a disease or injury; pain associated with a chronic medical condition; or pain that develops and persists in the absence of an identifiable organic problem.

Circularity The idea that all behavior is sustained by cycles of interaction between and among people.

Classical conditioning Learning mode in behavioral theory that makes a direct link between stimulus and response.

Cognitive Relating to all types of conscious intellectual activity.

Cognitive behavioral therapy A form of therapy that emphasizes the role of negative thought patterns and beliefs in shaping people's emotional responses to the outside world.

Cognitive distortions Negative cognitive biases in individuals that may contribute to detrimental feelings such as depression and anxiety.

Cognitive specificity hypothesis Theory that presumes emotional states can be distinguished by their specific cognitive contents and processes.

Cognitive therapy An approach to the treatment of depression based on the theory that the symptoms are caused by pessimistic thinking and can be alleviated by challenging and altering negative cognitive patterns.

Cognitive-behavioral play therapy Method of child play therapy that focuses on identifying and changing the patterns of reinforcements, consequences, and cognitions that contribute to the child's developmentally inappropriate behavior.

Cohesion In the *family systems illness model*, the ability of the family to balance closeness and connectedness with respect for separateness and individual differences.

Collaborative empiricism One of the three fundamental constructs of cognitive theory in which the therapist and the patient are coinvestigators who examine the evidence to support or refute the patient's cognitions.

Communicative-interactive approach In family therapy, the idea that all behavior, verbal and nonverbal, has communication value and conveys multilayered messages between individuals.

Community A group of people who share a particular interest or locality or who depend on each other for survival.

Community assets The strengths and resources that are available to empower a community, including things both tangible (money, housing) and intangible (spirituality, civic engagement).

Community capability The ability of the members of a community to do things together as a community.

Community cohesion The strength and togetherness of a community fostered by the engaged participation of its members in the community's institutions and social life.

Community competence The ability of a community to act effectively on its own behalf.

Community of interest A group of people bound together by a common identity or interest.

Compartmentalization A defense mechanism through which troubling thoughts and memories are isolated and placed in unreachable areas of the psyche.

Complementarity A state in which people in relationships engage in interactional patterns over time that are mutually sustaining.

Componential intelligence One of Sternberg's three elements of intelligence, comprising the ability to analyze data, solve problems, and use information to develop problem-solving strategies.

Compression of morbidity A much-debated theory in gerontology positing that longer lives due to healthier lifestyles can result in compressing old age illness to a shorter period of time at the end of life.

Conditioning Behavioral therapy based on a direct link between stimulus and response. When a response to a stimulus is learned, behaviors are conditioned or associated with a stimulus that does not naturally produce the response.

Conscience The awareness of the moral consequences of one's actions.

Conscious The part of the mind that the individual is fully aware of at all times.

Constant (disability) See *Progressive disability.*

Constellation Component of the *family systems illness model* that includes all members of the household, extended family, and key people who function as family insiders.

Contextual intelligence One of Sternberg's three elements of intelligence, referring to the ability of an individual to meet the challenges of everyday life successfully.

Contextualized Shaped in a way that conforms to the prevailing situation or environment.

Continuity theory The viewpoint that individuals tend to use the same coping styles from middle adulthood on, and those patterns determine how they adapt to the changes and challenges faced in old age.

Corpus callosum A nerve fiber bundle in the brain that connects the two cerebral hemispheres.

Cortex The layer of nerve cells that covers the brain.

Countertransference The therapist's unrealistic and inappropriate reactions to the client as a result of the client's own unconscious conflicts or developmental obstructions.

Couple subsystem A family *subsystem* comprised of an adult couple whose functions include providing a haven from the external demands and stressors of life and serving as a source of contact with other social systems.

Crystallized intelligence An individual's accumulated knowledge.

Cultural countertransference The total of the therapist's conscious and subconscious emotional and cognitive reactions to and fantasies about the client's history and background within a social and historical context.

Culture The accumulated knowledge, values, beliefs, and attitudes developed and passed on by a social group.

Cumulative disadvantage Referring to the way in which limited resources and opportunities as a result of socioeconomic conditions or discrimination tend to compound, rather than improve, over the life course, resulting in inequality of income and access to resources reaching into old age.

Curanderismo Alternative system of health care among Mexican-American people that focuses on the social, spiritual, and psychological reasons behind illness. Herbal medicines, symbols, prayers, and rituals are used in the treatment of ailments under this system.

Cyclothymia A persistent disorder marked by irregular, short cycles of depression and *hypomania.*

Deaf culture The shared culture, including language, beliefs, and self-image held by deaf people, that rejects the definitions and meanings of deafness imposed by hearing persons.

Deconditioning In trauma therapy, the anxiety, fear, and other learned responses to traumatic events and memory are "unlearned."

Decontextualized Formed in a way that is flexible to changing trends and not narrowed by the prevailing situation or environment.

Defense mechanisms Unconscious reactions that protect an individual from unwanted emotions that threaten the ego, such as anxiety and guilt.

Denial A defense mechanism consisting of an unconscious inability to acknowledge things, or actions on the part of others, that are unpleasant or intolerable.

Depersonalization Feelings of unreality associated with the internal world and the self.

Derealization The feeling that the external world is unreal.

Deskill To downgrade a job's classification and/or pay rate from skilled to unskilled, due to advances in technology.

Detachment The condition of emotionally insulating oneself from the world in response to severe trauma.

Developing awareness The second of Crate's five stages of adaptation to disability in which the individual's denial of the condition cannot be maintained.

Developmental conflict The turning point in a developmental stage during which an individual must move forward. Inability to resolve a developmental conflict results in either *fixation* or regression.

Developmental play therapy Method of child play therapy that emphasizes the role of a child's interactions with caregivers as essential to healthy development.

Dialectical behavioral therapy (DBT) A form of treatment that teaches various mindfulness and emotion regulation skills to counteract self-injurious behaviors.

Differentiation Behaviors designed to enable a person to resist the urge to automatically comply with family preferences, thereby gaining freedom to be different and separate from other family members.

Differently abled An alternative term for disability created within the disability culture to counter derogatory and oppressive terms used by those outside of the community.

Disability The inability to perform activities due to *impairment*.

Disability discourse The public dialogue among different disability stakeholder groups.

Disbelief The first of Crate's five stages of adaptation to disability in which the individual denies the disability or minimizes its effects.

Disengaged family A family whose members have little to no interaction and are separated emotionally from each other to the extent that little to no family feeling exists.

Disengagement theory In gerontology, a theory that the gradual disengagement of older people from work and society is a natural and unavoidable circumstance.

Disinhibition Inability to restrain inappropriate behaviors and emotions.

Displacement In children, the act of redirecting feelings and impulses from an object that is powerful to a safer, less-threatening one.

Dissociation A defense mechanism against trauma in which one disengages from the external environment and retreats to the inner world of the psyche.

Diversity Recognition of the multiplicity of cultural, ethnic, race, class, religious, and sexual orientation differences that exist between and within societal groups.

Domestic violence Violent acts perpetrated on a partner in a relationship in the presumed safety and privacy of the home.

Donepezil A prescription drug prescribed to treat Alzheimer's disease by increasing cortical *acetylcholine*.

Dopamine A *catecholamine* neurotransmitter that is essential to movement and muscle control.

Dopaminergic cells Nerve cells that use dopamine as a neurotransmitter, the reduction of which can result in Parkinson's disease.

Drifters People who wander from place to place with no fixed residence (Viswanath et al.). People who have lived in a neighborhood for less than 5 years and are very likely to move away.

Drive theory One of the four major theories of psychodynamic psychotherapy that focuses on inner urges that cause or inhibit action.

Dual-earner family Family in which both parents work outside the home.

Durable power of attorney for health care A legal document that assigns a close relative or friend to act on one's behalf should one become medically incapacitated.

Dyslexia Learning disability typified by reading difficulty and a tendency to reverse letters when writing.

Ecological (model of domestic violence) An integrative model of the causes of domestic violence that takes all models into consideration to construct an effective intervention.

Ecological perspective a perspective on human behavior that explores the nature of the relationship between the individual and the environment, and examines the ways in which human potentials are either nurtured and supported, or impeded by the physical and social environment.

Economic limitation Definition of disability that concerns whether an individual is able to function in a paid-for-work capacity.

Effortful control The ability to adapt one's responses appropriately as a situation demands. This is considered an important step in a child's development.

Ego One of the three main divisions of the mind in psychoanalytic theory, the ego maintains a balance between impulse and conscience.

Ego adaptation Concept of ego psychology that the ego develops secondary autonomy and serves adaptive purposes when neutralized and divested of conflict.

Ego autonomy Concept of ego psychology that certain ego functions, such as cognition, reality testing, and judgment, are innate and autonomous and independent of instinctual drives.

Ego functions In ego psychology, the roles of the ego that are reality based and center on self-awareness and perception of the external world.

Ego ideal The part of the ego that contains values and ethics instilled by a person's parents.

Ego mastery and adaptation See *Ego adaptation* and *Ego autonomy*.

Ego psychology One of the four major theories of psychodynamic psychotherapy that concentrates on the ego and its role in impulse control and navigating the external world.

Ego strength The internal psychological equipment that an individual brings to interactions with others and with the social environment.

Ego weakness Ego function that reflects deficiencies in an individual's internal equipment that may lead to maladaptive transactions with the social environment.

Electroconvulsive therapy A treatment, used primarily to relieve cases of severe depression, in which an electric current is passed through the brain causing a convulsion or seizure.

Emotional competence The ability to express one's feelings appropriately, to recognize one's own and others' feelings, and to consciously control one's emotions.

Emotional suppression When a parent attempts to regulate a child's behavior by controlling the child's emotions, resulting in the child suppressing those emotions altogether.

Empathic-introspective model Kohut's model of psychological investigation that uses empathy, or "vicarious introspection" to gather information, make interpretations, and evaluate the outcome of treatment interventions.

Empty nest syndrome The feeling of sadness experienced by women whose primary career was that of wife and mother, when the youngest child leaves home.

Endocrine system The series of glands, including the pituitary, adrenal, and pancreas, that secrete hormones into the bloodstream.

Endorphins Neurochemicals produced by the brain that can block pain and improve mood.

Enmeshed family A family whose members are tightly bonded to the extent that individual and subsystem boundaries are too porous and open, and behaviors by individuals affect every other member of the family excessively.

Episodic syndrome Permanent disabilities whose symptoms are unpredictable and consist of interludes of relief and activity interspersed with periods of disability.

Estrogen Term used for the female hormone that induces menstruation in women and stimulates the development of secondary sexual characteristics.

Estrogen replacement therapy The use of synthetic estrogen to alleviate the physical and emotional symptoms of menopause.

Ethnomethodology A sociological discipline focusing on the role of personal experiences and interactions in an individual's understanding of the social world.

Excitatory neurotransmitters Chemicals that transmit impulses between nerve cells and trigger, rather than inhibit, bodily processes and emotional responses.

Executive functions Higher activities of the mind that are needed for day-to-day functioning, such as reasoning, planning, strategizing, and problem solving.

Executive stage Stage of cognitive development in advanced middle adulthood in which an individual's attention is focused beyond the personal and toward an interest in societal institutions.

Expectations of others' reactions Category of the cyclical maladaptive pattern that focuses on how the individual imagines others will react in response to his or her interpersonal behavior.

Experience A term used to describe firsthand knowledge obtained in living through a situation, event, or feeling.

Experiential intelligence One of Sternberg's three elements of intelligence, involving an individual's ability to apply knowledge acquired through past experience in solving current problems.

Explicit memory Conscious, long-term memory that stores facts explicit to the self.

Expressive roles Role or function within a family that performs emotional tasks such as mediation, rebellion, and obedience.

External Emanating from a source outside the individual, not from within.

Extinguish The process by which the therapist extinguishes the frequency of a behavior either by administering punishment or withholding reinforcement.

Extrinsic motivation The external factors that contribute to the satisfaction associated with *work*, such as salary, status, and prospect for advancement.

Eye movement desensitization and reprocessing (EMDR) Form of therapy used for posttraumatic stress disorder in which the patient visualizes the traumatic event while performing side-to-side eye movements.

Family narratives Explanations constructed by families to organize and make sense of their experiences.

Family roles The different functions taken on by members of a family based on their status in the family, cultural expectations, and personal and family characteristics and needs.

Family rules Explicit and implicit rules established among family members that guide behavior and regulate interactions within the family group and with the outside world.

Family structure The predictable, established patterns of relationships and interactions within a family that occur over time.

Family systems illness model Disability adjustment model, developed by Rolland, that emphasizes the significance of family organizational patterns and communication processes with regard to chronic conditions.

Family systems theory A concept of the family as a social system that adheres to most of the behavioral rules and assumptions that apply to all social systems, and that shares properties similar to those of other social systems.

Family-community boundaries In the *family systems illness model*, the necessity of creating social networks for support and remaining connected to the community.

Fear responsiveness The ability to exhibit effective behaviors despite fear.

Feedback The process by which a system gets information about its performance.

Fictive kin Close friends of a family that come to be considered as family members and are often referred to in familial terms, such as "aunt" or "uncle."

Filial anxiety The emotions experienced during the *filial crisis*.

Filial comprehending The understanding of one's parents as persons with their own needs.

Filial crisis The initial stage during which adult children work through the change in perspective needed to care for aging parents.

Filial distancing The process of becoming emotionally independent of one's parents.

Filial maturity (Blenkner) The change in perspective that allows the adult caring for an aging parent to meet caregiving needs in a reciprocal relationship between adults.

Filial therapy A method for treating children that focuses on training the parent or caregiver to become the child's primary therapeutic agent.

Fixation Inability to proceed to the next stage of psychosexual development due to excessive gratification or frustration experienced during the current stage.

Fluid intelligence An individual's ability to reason abstractly.

Formal organization Group that is deliberately created to accomplish a specific purpose within a community.

Formality The level of structure or system within an organization.

Formalization The process of creating structure within an organization through establishing a hierarchy and creating rules and regulations.

Forms of memory Categories of traumatic memory, developed by Auerhahn and Laub, based on the psychological distance from the traumatic experience.

Fragmentation A defense mechanism through which the memory of traumatic events is fragmented in the mind and thus cannot be recalled coherently.

Free association Technique of psychotherapy in which the client is asked to speak everything that comes to mind without censorship.

Free radicals Oxygen atoms with one impaired electron that are a normal by-product of metabolism, but can damage other cells, causing signs of aging, and sometimes leading to degenerative diseases.

Frontal cortex The frontal region of the cerebral cortex involved in complex cognitive functions.

Frontal lobe The front portion of the brain associated with motor functions, reasoning, and emotion.

Fugue states Form of traumatic memory in which severely traumatic events are relived in an altered state of consciousness.

Fusion (Friedman) Behavior involving actions, thoughts, and language that conform to a family's preferred behavioral patterns, encouraging closeness.

Gender identity disorder A psychosexual condition that consists of the rejection of one's anatomic sexuality and expected gender roles, and the desire to become a person of the opposite gender.

Gender typed When differences in behaviors, preferences, and self-concepts between the sexes are acknowledged by the individual, and gender becomes part of one's self-concept.

Gene A segment of DNA that contains information on biological hereditary characteristics and carries that information from one generation to the next.

Gene expression The translation of a gene's coded information into a protein or RNA sequence that determines an organism's characteristics.

Generational boundaries In the *family systems illness model*, the necessity of the family to maintain appropriate roles and hierarchies when dealing with chronic illness within the family.

Generative script The inner narration of the adult's own awareness of where efforts to be generative fit into one's personal history, contemporary society, and the social world.

Generativity The concern for and commitment to integrity and moral principles that serve as a guide for future generations. Moral action is a fundamental part of a moral exemplar's ideological belief system.

Genital (developmental stage) Final stage of psychosexual development in which a mature pattern of behavior is developed, including adult desires and the urge to satisfy them.

Glutamate The primary excitatory neurotransmitter in the brain, comprised of glutamic acid.

Goal displacement Tendency that develops over time in some organizations to place the implementation of rules and procedures ahead of performing the primary purpose of the organization.

Group therapy Form of therapy that involves more than one patient working out behavioral problems with a therapist.

Guided discovery One of the three fundamental constructs of cognitive theory in which the therapist encourages the patient to use facts, probabilities, and behavioral experiments to modify maladaptive cognitive beliefs.

Handi-abled See *Differently abled*.

Handicap The disadvantage one confronts in social settings due to a *disability*.

Hedonia The experience of pleasure or enjoyment.

Hesitant expression A form of traumatic memory in which the individual partially expresses the traumatic event as an overpowering narrative.

Hierarchy The organization of a family in which the parental *subsystem* has the most authority, provides guidance, and has the decision-making role. Families that lack hierarchy are often dysfunctional.

Hippocampal memory functions The functions of the hippocampus, which is the area of the *limbic system* of the brain that is associated with memory and emotion.

Hippocampus A part of the *limbic system* of the brain associated with memory and emotional functions.

Horizontal Line or plane running side to side, parallel to the horizon. In Warren's linkages work, referring to relationships with systems within a community.

Hormonal release Process whereby the endocrine system provides stability to the body's internal environment through the release of *hormones*.

Hormones A variety of chemical substances created in the body that, when released into the bloodstream, regulate, trigger, or suppress the functions of tissues and cells.

Hospice movement Form of end-of-life care that stresses comfort and pain relief and seeks to address the needs of both the dying person and the grieving family members.

HPA neuroendocrine axis A part of the neuroendocrine system that regulates the body's responses to stress by coordinating interactions between hormones, glands, and parts of the midbrain.

Hyperactivity A condition characterized by restless, overactive movement and behavior.

Hyperthyroidism See *Hypothyroidism*.

Hypomania A mild form of mania characterized by elevated mood, talkativeness, and a feeling of higher creativity.

Hypothalamus In the brain, a grouping of small nuclei forming part of the diencephalon and generally lying at the junction of the midbrain and thalamus.

Hypothyroidism A pathological condition resulting from insufficient production of the internal secretion of the thyroid gland.

Id One of the three main divisions of the mind in psychoanalytic theory consisting of instincts and impulses geared toward one's own gratification.

Idealizing selfobject One of Kohut's three relationships between the self and its objects, the idealizing selfobject links a child with admired caretakers.

Identity change The final of Crate's five stages of adaptation to disability in which the individual accepts the disability and modifies behavior accordingly.

Idiosyncratic Category of midlife developmental experience (Franz) that is unique to each individual.

Imagery-based techniques The use of positive mental images in therapy to reduce anxiety.

Imitation Imitation behavior whereby an individual observes and replicates another's. A process by which an individual observes and duplicates another's behavior.

Immune system Complex system of the body that includes organs such as the thymus, spleen, lymph nodes, and skin, involved in defending against illness-producing agents.

Impairment A physiological loss that occurs to the body as a result of disease, injury, or accident.

Implicit memory Memory of which the individual is not immediately aware but which can unconsciously surface to influence behavior or learning.

Impulsivity A tendency to act or speak too quickly without considering the consequences.

Individual (model of domestic violence) The attribution of domestic violence to personal characteristics of the abuser and/or the victim.

Individuation The developmental process of forming one's own unique and individual personality.

Infertility The inability to conceive a child after a year of regular intercourse.

Initiative (Erikson) The urge to actively investigate and understand the environment on a conceptual level.

Instinct theory Theory of psychotherapy that concerns the innate biological aggressive and libidinal drives.

Institutional A view of the social welfare system as an institution to provide ongoing, preventative aid to citizens when other social institutions are unable to do so. Contrasted with *Residual* approach.

Instrumental role Role or function within a family that performs socioeconomic tasks such as caregiving, wage earning, and household management.

Integrality (Erikson) The ability to maintain a sense of wholeness in the face of bodily and sometimes mental and physical deterioration.

Intelligence quotient (IQ) test A standardized test that measures a person's level of intelligence based on an index that determines the percentage of the subject's mental age in relation to his or her chronological age.

Internalization The mental process by which an individual transforms the regulatory characteristics of the environment into internal regulations and characteristics.

Internalization of speech A reasoning process in which a person conducts a silent, inward conversation when considering a plan of action, determining moral behavior, or attempting to comfort oneself in a troubling situation, among other things.

Interpersonal trauma Physical or emotional harm inflicted by a caregiver or other trusted person that can lead to a pathological delay in the developmental process.

Interpretation The process of causing something unconscious to become conscious by naming it.

Intrinsic motivation The internal factors contributing to the satisfaction associated with *work*, including feelings of competence and achievement, challenge, and continued interest in the occupation.

Knowing (states of) See *Forms of memory*.

Latency period The stage of psychosexual development when sexual energy decreases, normally from the age of 5 or 6 to the onset of adolescence.

Lavender ceiling Term denoting the limitations for advancement in the workplace due to oppression of gays and lesbians.

Learned helplessness State of passivity induced by the perception that one is unable to exert effective control over one's experience. In situations of domestic violence, this state may develop over time after repeated experience of abuse, rendering the victim unable or unwilling to escape the situation.

Learning disability A term denoting a variety of learning disorders marked by deficiencies in scholastic abilities. These deficiencies include language-based learning disabilities, language-reception problems such as dyslexia, central auditory processing difficulties, and expressive language problems, both verbal and written.

Learning disorder The inability to learn at a rate that is considered normal for one's age group.

Left hemisphere The left side of the brain responsible for verbal, conscious functions, and sequential analysis such as logical interpretation of information, interpretation and production of symbolic information, language, mathematics, abstraction, and reasoning.

Life course The process of human development through the various developmental milestones into old age.

Life review A personal effort, usually in old age, to reinterpret and come to terms with one's life experiences to give it meaning and significance.

Limbic system The term used for the portions of the brain, including the hippocampus, and amygdala, that are involved in the regulating memory, learning, and emotion.

Liminality A period of transition during which one lacks a defined social or cultural role.

Livelihood The means by which a person acquires what is needed for self-sustenance, usually a paid occupation.

Living will A legal document stating the extent to which an individual wishes to have his or her life extended through technology.

Locus noradrenaline A part of the brainstem that acts as one of the brain's many *catecholamine* receptors.

Love One of the two overarching themes of adulthood (with *work* being the other) denoting intimate relationships, including romantic partners, family members, and other relationships that provide a sense of belonging or security.

Macro Consisting of a wide scope of vision or capability.

Male menopause A term used to denote anxiety experienced by men over the age of 50 undergoing reduced sexual potency due to a drop in male hormone levels.

Mandate A description of what an organization is required to do according to its charter, articles of incorporation, or by law.

Manic-depressive disorder See *Bipolar disorder*.

Medial temporal lobe The middle part of the temporal or lateral region of the brain.

Medicaid Benefits program funded by the federal government, and administered by the states, that pays for health care for low-income citizens.

Medical (model of disability) A definition of disability from a functional limitations perspective, which focuses on a physical, behavioral, psychological, cognitive, or sensory difficulty situated within the person.

Medicare A federal health insurance plan for people aged 65 and older.

Menopause A period in the female reproductive cycle, normally between ages 45 and 55, during which menstruation ceases.

Mental activity See *Mental processes*.

Mental processes Cognitive activities that affect the contents of the mind, such as perceiving, imagining, and reasoning, among others.

Metaphor The comparison of two unrelated things or concepts in an attempt to give a clearer meaning or description.

Metapsychological approach A model of psychotherapy that combines dynamic, economic, topographical, structural, interpersonal, and cultural points of view into a theory of personality.

Midlife The period of life, between age 40 and 60, during which development is less affected by biological maturation than by personal and social factors.

Midlife crisis The impulse on the part of some adults over 40, fed by the negative perception of older age, that they need to act out and experience feelings and emotions similar to those they felt when younger.

Midlife transition A period in middle adulthood during which an individual reevaluates life choices and decides whether or not to change course.

Mirroring selfobject One of Kohut's three relationships between the self and its objects, the mirroring selfobject recognizes a child's unique capabilities and talents.

Mission statement A short statement outlining an organization's reason for existence.

Model minority The term used to denote an ethnic, racial, or religious group that is considered by the members of the country in which they reside to be able to regularly achieve success in areas such as education and business.

Monoamine oxidase An enzyme in the brain that breaks down neurotransmitters.

Motivation Inner forces and needs that drive the individual to act toward a particular goal.

Motor cortex Area of the cerebral cortex of the brain that controls bodily movements.

Multicultural counseling Counseling model concerned with helping clients "live with intentionality" within their own cultural frameworks and with respect for other's.

Multicultural theory A conceptual framework that guides the practitioner in selecting and using the theoretical approach most consistent with the life experiences and cultural perspective of the client.

Mutual accommodation The state in which a couple accepts a state of mutual interdependence in which some degree of individual separateness is relinquished in favor of a sense of belonging.

Mutual empathy In self-in-relation theory, the interactive process that is the basis for creating and being in a growth-enhancing relationship.

Mutuality Interdependence of the various members and groups within a society which fosters cooperative and reciprocal relationships between those members and groups.

Narrative constructivism Through therapeutic dialog or conversation, the therapist and client use the metaphor of story to construct a narrative about the person's life.

Native People who are indigenous to a particular area (Viswanath et al.); those who have lived in a community for over 5 years and who are unlikely to move away.

Nature Referring to inborn behavior that is not learned from or affected by the environment. Often contrasted with *nurture*.

Neocortex A part of the cerebral cortex assumed to be the most recent evolutionary stage of brain development.

Neural substrate The specialized circuitry of the brain that brings about mental processes and behaviors.

Neuroendocrine activity Referring to chemical messengers that travel through the bloodstream to transmit information from one part of the body to another, having a specific regulatory effect on the activity of certain organs. The brain is often either the source or the target of these messengers.

Neuroglia Cells of the central nervous system that provide the *neurons* with nourishment, protection, and structural support. Neuroglia also have a primary role in the response of the nervous system to injury and infection.

Neurons Cells of the nervous system that carry out the brain's functions of sending and receiving signal impulses controlling behavior and body functions.

Neurotonin Anticonvulsant drug used for treating epilepsy and also used to treat pain. Also known as Gabapentin.

Neurotransmitters Chemical messengers released by nerve cells that transmit messages to other nerve cells.

Nonnormative (family demands) Stressful events and experiences that are unexpected in the development of a family such as unemployment, illness, or substance abuse.

Noradrenaline See *Norepinephrine*.

Norepinephrine A *neurotransmitter* found in parts of the brain responsible for regulating heart rate and blood pressure that affects concentration, attentiveness, and other components of the "fight-or-flight" response.

Normative (Franz) Category of midlife developmental experience that describes typical changes in response to life events.

Normative (family demands) Events and experiences that are normal and usual in the development of a family, such as the birth of a child.

Not knowing Form of traumatic memory in which one has no conscious awareness of the traumatic event.

Nurturant A tendency to look after the physical and emotional well-being of others.

Nurture The process of passing on learned information and behavior from a person or cultural environment to another person. Often contrasted with *Nature.*

Object The significant person or thing that is the target or "object" of another's feelings or drives.

Object relations theory One of the four major theories of psychodynamic psychotherapy that emphasizes a person's relations with other people or things that function as sources of gratification.

Objectlessness A condition caused by trauma in which there is a complete absence of object representation that leads to a void and a rupture of the self.

Obsessive compulsive disorder An anxiety disorder in which an individual experiences recurrent unpleasant thoughts and unstoppable urges to perform repetitive acts.

Operant conditioning Learning mode in behavioral theory that focuses on the individual's ability to change or modify a behavior by changing the consequences of that behavior.

Optimism A character trait typified by cheerfulness and looking at most situations and things as good.

Oral (developmental stage) The first stage of psychosexual development during which the primary sexual focus is on the mouth through sucking and biting.

Organizational culture The pattern of assumptions, values, rules, and norms developed by an organization's members that guide their behavior within the organization and with external systems.

Osteoporosis A condition that occurs particularly in women following menopause, characterized by diminished bone mass and density, and which can result in curvature of the spine.

Parental maturity The stage at which parents are able to distance themselves from their children so that they can encourage them to become independent adults.

Partnering selfobject See *Alter ego selfobject.*

Permanent disability A disability, such as spinal cord injury, blindness, deafness, whose symptoms are incessant and, in some cases, progressive.

Personal responsibility The individualist perspective on social welfare that attributes social problems to a person's own bad choices and inadequacies.

Pervasive developmental disorders Neurological disorders normally discovered in early childhood that are characterized by severe impairment in social interaction and communication abilities.

Phallic (developmental stage) The stage of psychosexual development during which the primary sexual focus is on the genitals.

Phantom memory A memory of a traumatic event "inherited" by a child from a parent who actually experienced the trauma. Phantom memories are accompanied by many of the symptoms of trauma experienced by the parent.

Phantom transmission When a parent who is a survivor of a traumatic event imperceptibly passes on the memory of that traumatic event to the child.

Phenomenology The idea that understanding of human behavior should be based primarily on the study of continuing interactions and experiences, rather than analysis.

Physically challenged See *Differently abled.*

Physiological Relating to the normal functions of the body.

Pituitary Gland located in the base of the brain that produces a number of hormones involved in growth and development.

Postformal thought Cognitive changes that occur after adolescence, the Piagetian end point of formal cognitive development. Postformal thought is characterized by the integration of logical processes associated with formal operational thought with more flexible, interpretative ones.

Postmodern perspective In constructivism, the position that knowledge is not imparted to the human mind from an external, objective world but is a function of experience and the basic nature of the human mind.

Posttraumatic Stress Disorder (PTSD) Severe emotional reaction to a traumatic event, similar to *acute stress disorder*, but the symptoms of which last longer than 1 month.

Practical intelligence See *Contextual intelligence*.

Preconscious In psychoanalytic theory, thoughts, feelings, and impulses of which the individual is not currently aware, but which can be brought quickly into consciousness.

Premature aging See *Accelerated aging*.

Premenopause The period preceding *menopause* during which the menstrual cycle may become irregular, monthly flow decreases, and premenstrual symptoms may increase.

Premotor cortex Area of the brain, located in the frontal lobes, involved in the movement of the limbs.

Primary process thinking In Freudian theory, the original (or primary) way in which the psychic apparatus functions.

Private, for-profit organization Privately owned group whose primary goal is to make a profit through the provision of services.

Professional obsolescence The use of information, theories, and technology that are less useful in performing tasks than what is currently available in one's field of practice.

Progesterone Female hormone secreted by the ovaries that facilitates conception.

Progressive, permanent disability A condition, such as diabetes, arthritis, or Parkinson's disease, whose symptoms are continual and can become progressively more debilitating with time.

Projection Developmental stage in infants during which they attribute their own impulses to objects.

Psychic determinism The basic underlying principle of psychodynamic theory meaning that in mental functioning nothing happens by chance, and every action has a psychological motive.

Psychoanalytic play therapy Technique of child play therapy through which the process of play is used to help the child work through unconscious conflicts.

Psychoanalytic theory A psychiatric treatment theory that relies on discovering and interpreting the unconscious motivations behind human behavior.

Psychodynamic psychotherapy A perspective of psychotherapy that focuses on an individual's inner causes and drives and emphasizes developmental processes.

Psychodynamic theory A theory of psychotherapy emphasizing causes and drives within the individual.

Psychoeducation A treatment that involves teaching people about their problem, how to treat it, and how to recognize signs of relapse so that further treatment can be sought.

Psychopharmacology The study of how drugs can affect psychological and behavioral functions and treat psychiatric disorders.

Psychosexual development In psychoanalytic theory, the development of personality as the individual moves through the main stages of sexual development.

Public organizations Formal group established and run by federal, state, or local governments.

Putamen A structure in the middle of the brain that forms part of the basal ganglia and has a role in learning.

Rating scales Symptom-focused, empirically tested rating scales used in cognitive therapy.

Reattachment Referring to the phase of recovery from trauma when individuals begin to feel safe enough to engage in interpersonal relationships with other people. Also called *Reconnection*.

Receptor A molecule on the surface of a cell that receives *neurotransmitters* specific to the functioning of that cell.

Reciprocal causality See *Circularity*.

Reconnection See *Reattachment*.

Reconstituted family A family in which both parents were previously divorced, and which includes a child or children from one or both of the previous marriages.

Reconstitution A process by which an individual analyzes a task to organize and make sense of that task.

Red tape Derogatory term denoting excessive rules and regulations that render an organization ineffective.

Redlining The discriminatory practice of banks and other lending institutions to deny loans to those deemed "high risk" due to their race or ethnicity.

Refractory period A recovery phase after the firing of a muscle cell or nerve fiber during which it is unresponsive to stimulation.

Regression The act of retreating to earlier developmental levels of behavior, normally used by children as a defense mechanism.

Reinforcement The use of positive consequences in behavioral therapy to change maladaptive or undesirable behaviors.

Reintegrative stage (Schaie) Stage of cognitive development in later adulthood when an individual's attention is focused on personal concerns.

Relapsing syndrome See *Episodic syndrome*.

Relational play therapy A method of child play therapy in which the mutual creativity of the child and the therapist creates a newly developed self or self-and-other experience for the child.

Relationship authenticity In self-in-relation theory, the ongoing challenge to feel emotionally real, connected, vital, clear, and purposeful in a relationship.

Relationship differentiation In self-in-relation theory, the process of increasing levels of complexity in a relationship within which individual development occurs.

Relationship seeking Object relations theory that emphasizes the influence of external objects to build internal psychic organization.

Relaxation training A therapy aimed at using relaxation to reduce anxiety and to promote physical and mental well-being.

Relocators People who have lived in a neighborhood for 5 years, but are likely to move somewhere else.

Reminiscence groups Form of group therapy in which members are encouraged to remember and discuss their life histories. Most often used to encourage socialization, create a sense of well-being, and to improve cognitive function in older people.

Reorganization The third of Crate's five stages of adaptation to disability in which the individual accepts the limitations imposed by the disability and begins to modify lifestyle and relationships.

Residual A view of the social welfare system that views it as a backup system or safety net to provide temporary aid to dependent people when other social institutions cannot. Contrasted with *Institutional* approach.

Resistance The term used to describe any behavior on the client's part that impedes the course of free association and the therapeutic work.

Resolution The fourth of Crate's five stages of adaptation to disability in which the individual comes to grips with loss of function, grieves, and begins to identify with others with the same or similar disability.

Respondent (learning mode) See *Classical conditioning*.

Responsible stage (Schaie) Stage of cognitive development in middle adulthood during which individuals concentrate primarily on their family and career.

Restrictive covenants Legal obligation agreed to by the buyer of real estate that restricts or prohibits certain usage of the property, sometimes used in the early-to mid-twentieth century to prevent property from being sold to racial minorities, thus contributing to housing segregation.

Restructuring The process of adjusting one's psychological image of a thing or a situation in an effort to adapt to change.

Reuptake The process by which a *neurotransmitter* is taken back in by the neuron that originally released it to be reused or destroyed.

Right hemisphere The half of the brain that is responsible for nonverbal functioning such as the processing of multisensory input, visual-spatial functions, and memory, stored in auditory, visual, and spatial modalities.

Sandwich generation Term denoting adults in their middle years who are simultaneously caring for children and aging parents.

Schemata In cognitive theory, generalizations stored in memory that influence the cognitive processes of attention, encoding, retrieval, and inference.

Scientific management A form of organizational management that strives to get the most accomplished with the smallest amount of input. Viewed as a way to increase efficiency.

Screen memories Form of traumatic memory in which an individual substitutes true but less disturbing memories for those memories too traumatic to be brought to mind.

Secondary process thinking Thought process, developed gradually during the first years of life, which is based on realistic approaches to problem solving.

Self-empathy In self-in-relation theory, the idea that one's internalized self-representations must undergo a change so that women can direct the empathy they bring to their relationships toward themselves.

Selfobject Term used to describe three distinct relationships that take place between the self and its objects: the *mirroring, idealizing,* and *alter ego* selfobject relationships.

Self-psychology One of the four major theories of psychodynamic psychotherapy that explores how early relationships form the self and the structures of the self.

Self-regulation of affect An *executive function* by which an individual is able to consider emotional responses and thereby respond to situations appropriately.

Senile dementia Chronic, irreversible brain disorder caused by the deterioration of blood vessels in the brain, resulting in loss of memory and cognitive function and adverse changes in behavior and personality.

Sensory integration disorders A disorder in children in which the senses do not integrate properly, causing, among other symptoms, an unusual sensitivity to sound, light, and touch, and delays in speech and motor activity.

Separation-individuation process A multistage process by which an infant separates self from the primary caregiver and achieves autonomy.

Serial monogamy The tendency to form monogamous relationships without a commitment to a shared future or marriage.

Serotonin A neurotransmitter that is responsible for mood elevation and appetite. Depression is linked to a lack of serotonin in the brain.

Serotonin reuptake inhibitors Antidepressant drugs used to treat depression and anxiety disorders. These drugs increase the amount of *serotonin* within the brain by slowing its *reuptake*.

Settlers People who move to and stay in a new location by choice; people who have lived in a neighborhood for less than 5 years and plan to stay.

Social Referring to the relationships and interactions between people within human society.

Social construction of aging A theory that posits that aging is a socially constructed phenomenon whereby the individual's self-conceptions about aging arise through interaction with the social environment.

Social control A set of rules, customs, and behaviors established by a community in an attempt to maintain order.

Social death The prevailing sense of despair, often equated with being "dead already," in older people who have become disengaged and isolated from society.

Social extrusion Expulsion of an individual from the community to which the individual belongs due to personality traits or behavior that are considered unfit for the community.

Social learning In behavioral theory, a learning mode that demonstrates that behaviors are learned through imitation, modeling, and observation.

Social participation The engaged involvement of individuals in the social life and institutions of a community.

Social phobia A type of anxiety disorder characterized by a powerful fear or anxiety of social or performance situations.

Social skills training A technique used to correct a variety of socially unacceptable behaviors in children and adults.

Socialization The process by which individuals learn the culture, beliefs, and behavioral norms of their social group.

Societal responsibility The collective perspective on social welfare maintaining that social problems are a result of certain socioeconomic circumstances, such as barriers to access, lack of opportunities, and inequality.

Sociological (model of domestic violence) Associates domestic violence with social factors, including family structure, stresses on the family, and intergenerational transmission of violent tendencies.

Sociopolitical (definition of disability) The conceptualization of disability as the function of social, economic, and political forces working together against the individual with the disability.

Sociostructural (model of domestic violence) A feminist theory of domestic violence that focuses on gender inequality and social acceptance of patriarchy and violence as root causes.

Socratic dialogue One of the three fundamental constructs of cognitive theory in which the therapist poses a number of questions designed to help the patient arrive at logical conclusions.

Speechless terror An experience of terror so severe that the individual is unable to describe the event in words.

Spirituality of work The extent to which the workplace contributes to one's sense of spirituality, self-worth, and well-being.

Strengths' perspective Model of therapy in social work that emphasizes uncovering and drawing on one's own strengths, abilities, interests, and knowledge to cope with life's adversities.

Stress-appraisal-coping model Cognitive behavioral model of pain behavior suggesting that the individual's cognitions have a direct impact on the adjustment to chronic pain.

Striatum See *Caudate nucleur*.

Structural coupling The principle of constructivism that allows *autopoietic* individuals to interact with entities other than themselves and their own nervous systems.

Structural determinism A principle of constructivism that the elements comprising a human experience are characterized primarily by the forming of information from within.

Structural theory Freud's theory of personality that the psyche is comprised of the *id*, the *ego*, and the *superego*.

Subordinates Individuals or subsystems that have less power or authority in interactions with other individuals or subsystems

Substantia nigra A part of the *basal ganglia* that produces dopamine.

Subsystem A subgroup of a larger system that has systemic properties and performs functions for the larger system

Superego In psychoanalytic theory, the division of the mind that represents the conscience.

Symbolic interactionism Sociological perspective that humans are active participants in the shaping of their social world, rather than passive conformists to the world that exists around them.

Synapse The gap between nerve cells into which *neurotransmitters* are released and impulses are passed from a *neuron* to another cell.

Systematic desensitization A therapy in which a client in a relaxed state is exposed to increasingly unpleasant stimuli with the purpose of eventually reducing anxiety or fear associated with the stimuli.

Target behavior Behavior focused on by the therapist that needs to be altered, encouraged, or eliminated.

Testosterone Male sex hormone that stimulates blood flow and tissue growth and triggers secondary sexual characteristics in men.

Thalamus An area deep inside the brain that acts as a relay center for sensory information and is responsible for the body's motor control.

Theraplay A method of developmental play therapy that focuses on problems of attachment in young children.

Third separation individuation The stage of separation in which an adult child in the course of caring for an aging parent can work on internal issues and develop more realistic internalizations of oneself and the parent.

Time-limited dynamic psychotherapy Psychotherapy that is restricted to a fixed number of sessions.

Transcendence Term describing the integration of the various components of the self resulting in a state of completeness.

Transference The experience of feelings, drives, attitudes, fantasies, and defenses toward a person in the present that are a repetition of reactions originating in regard to significant persons of early childhood, unconsciously displaced onto figures in the present.

Transference phenomena A form of traumatic memory in which one believes that the traumatic legacy is lived out as one's inevitable fate.

Transmuting internalization The process of internalizing selfobject functions early in life to develop the ability to choose selfobjects in adulthood that are not based on unmet childhood needs.

Trauma An event or events that are so extreme, severe, powerful, harmful, or threatening to the individual that they demand extraordinary coping efforts.

Traumatic memory Memory of a severely traumatic event that causes extreme stress when the event is recalled.

Treatment agenda Specific list of items, such as discussion topics, self-report scale reviews, and homework, that give therapy sessions structure.

Triangle The formation of a three-person *subsystem* in which one member is emotionally excluded.

Triangle of conflict (Malan) Area of conflict that includes the impulse or feelings, the defense erected against it, and the symptom or anxiety that results when the defense fails.

Triangle of person (Malan) Area of conflict that concerns the objects toward whom an impulse is felt.

Twinship See *Alter ego selfobject.*

Unconscious In psychoanalytic theory, thoughts, feelings, and desires that the individual is not aware of but that exert powerful influence on behavior.

Universalistic (Franz) Category of midlife developmental experience that is age- or stage-related.

Upper auditory cortex The region of the brain thought to be concerned with integrating stimuli from several sources.

Vertical An "up-and down" orientation, the opposite of *horizontal.* In Warren's linkages work, referring to relationships between a community and the outside world.

Voluntary nonprofit organization Group that is legally incorporated as a not-for-profit organization, whose earnings are used for the public good and do not benefit any member of the organization.

War on Poverty Term introduced by President Lyndon Johnson in 1964 to define his administration's program of legislation, jobs programs, and educational initiatives aimed at reducing poverty in the United States.

Wisdom Ability to use correct judgment, particularly in practical matters and social conduct.

Witnessed narrative Form of traumatic memory in which the individual organizes events in a narrative structure.

Work One of the two overarching themes of adulthood (*love* being the other) representing activities in which people engage in an effort to be purposeful, gain mastery, and create order within their world. Work can include *paid* employment as well as unpaid activities undertaken for the common good.

Work limitation See *Economic limitation.*

Working memory A memory for temporarily storing information while working on a particular task; more commonly known as "short-term memory."

Zone of proximal development In play therapy, when a child is encouraged in a pretend setting to practice skills not yet mastered in real life.

References

Aaron, L. (1996). *Meeting of minds: Mutuality in psychoanalysis*. Hillsdale, NJ: Analytic Press.

AARP Home Depot link. (2004, December 2). *The Republican*.

Aarts, P. G., & Op den Velde, W. (1996). Prior traumatization and the process of aging: Theory and clinical implications. In B. van der Kolk, A. McFarlane, & L. Weisaeth (Eds.), *Traumatic stress: The effects of overwhelming experience on mind, body, and society* (pp. 359–377). New York: Guilford Press.

AASWG (Association for the Advancement of Social Work with Groups). (2004). *Social work with groups*. Newsletter. Akron, OH: Author.

AASWG (Association for the Advancement of Social Work with Groups). (2006). *Standards for social work practice with groups* (2nd ed.). Akron, OH: Author.

Aber, J. L., & Allen, J. P. (1987). Effects of maltreatment on young children's socioemotional development: An attachment theory perspective. *Developmental Psychology, 23*, 406–414.

Abikoff, H. (1985). Efficacy of cognitive training intervention in hyperactive children: A critical review. *Clinical Psychology Review, 5*, 479–512.

Abrahams, L. S., & Gordon, A. L. (2003). Self-harm narratives of urban and suburban young women. *Affilia, 18*(4), 429–444.

Abram, J. (1997). *The language of Winnicott*. Northvale, NJ: Jason Aronson.

Abrams, D. B., & Clayton, R. R. (2001). Trans-disciplinary research to improve brief interventions for addictive behaviors. In P. M. Monti, S. M. Colby, & T. A. O'Leary (Eds.), *Adolescents, alcohol and substance abuse: Reaching teens through brief intervention* (pp. 321–341). New York: Guilford Press.

Access Unlimited. (1999). Disability services: Disability categories. Retrieved from http://www.uncwil .edu/stuaff/DISABILITY

Achenback, T., Dumenci, L., and Rescorla, L. (2003). Are American Children's Problems still Getting Worse? A 23-year Comparison, *Journal of Abnormal Child Psychology, 31*, 1–11.

Adams, P., & Krauth, K. (Eds.). *Reinventing human services: Community and family-centered practice* (pp 87–109). Hawthorne, NY: Aldine de Gruyter.

Addams, J. (1910) *Twenty years at Hull House*. New York: Macmillan

Administration on Aging. (2005). Addressing diversity. Department of Health and Human Services. Retrieved June 30, 2005, from http://www.aoa.gov/prof/adddiv/healthy/addiv_healthy.asp

Aguyo, M. (2001). The experience of deafened adults: Implications for rehabilitative services. *Health and Social Work, 26*(4), 269–276.

Ahmad, W. I. U. (Ed.). (2000). *Ethnicity, illness and chronic illness*. Philadelphia: Open University Press.

Ainslie, J., & Feltey, K. M. (1991). Definitions and dynamics of motherhood and family in lesbian communities. In T. D. Marciano & M. B. Sussman (Eds.), *Wider families: New traditional family forms*. New York: Haworth Press.

Ainsworth, M. D. S. (1963). The development of infant–mother interaction among the Ganda. In B. M. Foss (Ed.), *Determinants of infant behavior* (Vol. 2, pp. 67–112). New York: Wiley.

Ainsworth, M. D. S. (1967). *Infancy in Uganda: Infant care and the growth of love*. Baltimore: Johns Hopkins University Press.

Ainsworth, M. D. S. (1969). Object relations, dependency, and attachment: A theoretical review of the infant–mother relationship. *Child Development, 40*, 969–1025.

Ainsworth, M. D. S. (1973). The development of mother–infant attachment. In B. Caldwell & H. Ricciuti (Eds.), *Review of child development research* (Vol. 3, pp. 1–94). Chicago: University of Chicago Press.

Ainsworth, M. D. S., Blehar, M. C., Waters, E., & Wall, S. (1978). *Patterns of attachment: A psychological study of the strange situation*. Hillsdale, NJ: Erlbaum.

Albano, A. M. (2003). Treatment of social anxiety disorder. In M. A. Reineck, F. M. Dattilio, & A. Freeman (Eds.), *Cognitive therapy with children and adolescents: A casebook for clinical practice* (2d ed., pp. 128–162). New York: Guilford Press.

Aldarono, D. (2001). Racial and ethnic identity models and their application: Counseling biracial individuals. *Journal of Mental Health Counseling, 23*(13), 238–255.

Alday, R. S., & Kuzuhara, L. W. (2005) *Mastering management skills*. Mason, OH: South-Western.

Alessandri, S. M. (1992). Attention, play, and social behavior in ADHD preschoolers. *Child Psychology, 20,* 289–302.

Alexander, D. (1998). Prevention of mental retardation: Four decades of research. *Mental Retardation & Developmental Disabilities Research Reviews, 4,* 50–58.

Alexander, J. C. (2004). Toward theory of cultural trauma. In J. C. Alexander, R. Eyerman, B. Giesen, N. J. Smelser, & P. Sztompka (Eds.), *Cultural trauma and collective identity* (pp. 1–29). Berkeley: University of California Press.

Alexander, J. C., Eyerman, R., Giesen, R. B., Smelser, N. J., & Sztompka, P. (2004). *Cultural trauma and collective identity*. Berkeley: University of California Press.

Alford, S., Huberman, B., & Moss, T. (2003). *Science and success: Sex education and other programs that work to prevent teen pregnancy, HIV and sexually transmitted infections.* Washington, DC: Advocates for Youth. Retrieved November 23, 2005, from http://www.advocatesforyouth.org/programsthatwork/index/htm

Allen, A. K., & Demo, D. H. (1995). The families of lesbians and gay men: A new frontier in family research, *Journal of Marriage and the Family, 57,* 111–127.

Allen, I. M. (1996). PTSD among African Americans. In A. J. Marsella, M. J. Friedman, E. T. Gerrity, & R. M. Scurfield (Eds.), *Ethnocultural aspects of posttraumatic stress disorder* (pp. 209–239). Washington, DC: American Psychological Association.

Allen, J. G. (1995). *Coping with trauma: A guide to self-understanding*. Washington DC: American Psychiatric Press.

Allen, J. G. (2001). *Traumatic relationships and serious mental disorders*. New York: Wiley.

Allen, J. P., & Land, D. (1999). Attachment in adolescence. In J. Cassidy & P. R. Shaver (Eds.), *Handbook of attachment: Theory, research and clinical applications* (pp. 319–335). New York: Guilford Press.

Alter, K. (2000). Inter-Organizational Collaboration in the Task Environment. In R. Patti (Ed.), *The handbook of social welfare management*. Thousand Oaks, CA: Sage

Alter, K., & Hague, J. (1993). *Organizations working together*. Newbury Park: Sage Publications.

Altman, B. (2001). Disability definitions models, classification schemes and applications. In G. L. Albrecht, K. D. Seelman, & M. Biery (Eds.), *Handbook of disability studies* (pp. 97–122). Thousand Oaks, CA: Sage.

Altman, N., Briggs, R., Frankel, J., Gensler, D., & Pantone, P. (2002). *Relational child psychotherapy.* New York: Other Press.

Altshuler, S., & Kopels, S. (2003). Advocating in schools for children with disabilities: What's new with IDEA? *Social Work, 48*(3), 320–329.

Alzheimer's Association. (2005a). *New research reveals lifestyle habits linked to risk of getting Alzheimer's.* Alzheimer's Association International Conference on the Prevention of Dementia (June 18–21, Washington, DC). Retrieved June 28, 2005, from http://www.alz.org/preventionconference/pc2005/061905lifestyleHabits.asp

Alzheimer's Association. (2005b). *Behavioral and psychiatric symptoms.* Retrieved June 28, 2005, from http://www.alz.org/Health/Treating/agitation.asp

Alzheimer's Association. (2005c). *Treating cognitive symptoms.* Retrieved June 28, 2005, from http://www.alz.org/Health/Treating/symptoms.asp

Alzheimer's Association. (2005d). *News from the Alzheimer's prevention conference: New research, cost of care and how to "maintain your brain" as you get older.* Retrieved June 28, 2005, from http://www.radionewz.com/pages/news.html

Amaro, H., & Raj, A. (2000). On the margin: Power and women's HIV risk reduction strategies. *Sex Roles, 42,* 723–750.

Amato, P. R. (2001). Children of divorce in the 1990's: An update of the Amato and Keith (1991) meta-analysis. *Journal of Family Psychology, 15,* 355–370.

Amato, P. R., & Booth, A. (1996). A prospective study of divorce and parent–child relationships. *Journal of Marriage and the Family, 58,* 356–365.

Amato, P. R., & Booth, A. (2000). *A generation at risk: Growing up in an era of family upheaval.* Cambridge, MA: Harvard University Press.

Ambert, A.-M. (2003). *Same-sex couples and same-sex-parent families: Relationships, parenting and issues of marriage*. Ottawa, Canada: Vanier Institute of the Family. Retrieved January 10, 2006, from http://www.vifamily.ca

American Academy of Pediatrics. (1998). Guidance for effective discipline. *Pediatrics, 101*(4), 723.

American Association on Mental Retardation. (2002). *Mental retardation: Definition, classification, and systems of supports* (10th ed.). Washington, DC: Author.

American Health Assistance Foundation. (2004). Anatomy-Brain. Retrieved August 21, 2004, from http://www.ahaf.org/alzdis/about/AnatomyBrain.htm

American Psychiatric Association. (2000a). *Diagnostic and statistical manual of mental disorders* (4th ed.). Washington, DC: Author.

American Psychiatric Association. (2000b). *Diagnostic and statistical manual of mental disorders (DSM-IV-TR)* (4th ed., rev.). Washington, DC: Author.

Americans with Disabilities Act of 1990 (P.L. 101–336).

Andersen, B. F. (1998). Therapeutic issues in working with transgendered clients. In D. Denny (Ed.), *Current concepts of transgendered identity* (pp. 215–226). New York: Garland.

Anderson, M. L. (2005). "Your blues ain't like my blues": Race, ethnicity, and social inequality. *American Contemporary Sociology, 29*(6), 796–805.

Anderson, R. E., & Carter, I. (1990). *Human behavior in the social environment: An ecological view* (4th ed.). New York: Aldine De Gruyter.

Anthias, F. (1998). Rethinking social divisions: Some notes towards a theoretical framework. *Sociological Review, 46*(3), 506–535.

Anthias, F. (2001). The material and the symbolic in theorizing social stratification: Issues of gender, ethnicity and class. *British Journal of Sociology, 52*(3), 367–390.

Applebaum, R. A., Mehdizadeh, S. A., & Straker, J. K. (2004). The changing world of long-term care: A state perspective. *Journal of Aging and Social Policy, 16*(1), 1–19.

Appleby, G. A., Colon, E., & Hamilton, J. (2001). *Diversity, oppression, and social functioning: Person-in-environment assessment of intervention*. Boston: Allyn & Bacon.

Applegate, J. S., & Bonovitz, J. M. (1995). *The facilitating partnership: A Winnicottian approach for social workers and other helping professionals*. Northvale, NJ: Jason Aronson.

Aron, E. (1996). *The highly sensitive person*. New York: Broadway Books.

Arredondo, P., & McDavis, P. (1992). Multicultural counseling competencies and standards. *Journal of Counseling and Development, 70*, 447–486.

Artman, L., & Cahan, S. (1993). Schooling and the development of transitive inference. *Developmental Psychology, 29*, 753–759.

Asch, A., & Abelson, P. (1993). Serving workers through managed mental health care: The social work role. In P. A. Kurzman & S. H. Akabas (Eds.), *Work and well-being: The occupational social work advantage* (pp. 123–137). Washington, DC: National Association of Social Workers.

Ashford, J. B., & LeCroy, C. W. (2010). *Human behavior in the social environment: A multidimensional perspective* (4th ed.). Belmont, CA: Brooks/Cole.

Ashford, J. B., LeCroy, C., & Lortie, K. (2001). *Human behavior in the social environment* (2nd ed.). Belmont, CA: Wadsworth.

Ashford, J. B., LeCroy, C. W., & Lortie, K. L. (2006). *Human behavior in the social environment: A multidimensional perspective* (3rd ed.). Belmont, CA: Wadsworth.

Asperger, H. (1991). "Autistic psychopathy" in childhood (U. Frith, Trans.). In U. Frith (Ed.), *Autism and Asperger syndrome* (pp. 37–92). Cambridge: Cambridge University Press.

Association for Play Therapy. (1997). A definition of play therapy. *Association for Play Therapy Newsletter, 16*(1), 7.

Association for Play Therapy. (2000). *Standards of practice*. Fresno, CA: Author.

Atchley, R. C. (1985). *Social forces and aging: An introduction to social gerontology*. Belmont, CA: Wadsworth.

Athol, S., & Golensky, M. (2004). Counseling, support and advocacy for clients who stutter. *Health and Social Work, 29*(3), 197–205.

Atkins, B. (1998). An asset oriented approach to cross cultural issues: Blacks in rehabilitation. *Journal of Applied Rehabilitation Counseling, 19*, 45–49.

Atkinson, D. R., Morten, G., & Sue, D. W. (1979). *Counseling American minorities: A cross cultural perspective*. Dubuque, IA: Wm. C. Brown.

Atkinson, D. R., Morten, G., & Sue, D. W. (1989). A minority identity development model. In D. R. Atkinson, G. Morten, & D.W. Sue (Eds.), *Counseling American minorities* (pp. 35–52). Dubuque, IA: Wm.C. Brown.

Atkinson, D. R., Morten, G., & Sue, D. W. (1998). Addressing the Mental Health Needs of Racial/Ethnic Minorities. In D. R. Atkinson, G. Morten and D. W. Sue (Eds.). *Counseling American Minorities* (pp. 51–80). Boston: McGraw-Hill.

Atwood, G. E., & Stolorow, R. D. (1984). *Structures of subjectivity: Explorations in psychoanalytic phenomenology*. Hillsdale, NJ: The Analytic Press.

Au, W. (1989). *By way of the heart: Toward a holistic Christian spirituality*. New York: Paulist Press.

Auerbach, J. D., & Coates, P. J. (2000). HIV prevention research: Accomplishments and challenges for the third decade of AIDS. *American Journal of Public Health, 90*(7), 1029–1032).

Auerhahn, N. C., & Laub, D. (1998). Intergenerational memory of the Holocaust. In Y. Danieli (Ed.), *Intergenerational handbook of multigenerational legacies of trauma* (pp. 21–41). New York: Plenum Press.

Aunola, K., Stattin, H., & Nurmi, J. E. (2000). Parenting styles and adolescents: Achievement strategies. *Journal of Adolescence, 23,* 205–222.

Austrain, S. (Ed). (2008). *Developmental theories through the life cycle* (2nd ed.). New York: Columbia University Press.

Australian Bureau of Statistics. (2003). *Divorce rates.* Retrieved January 10, 2006, from http://www.abus.gov.au

Avery, A., Chase, J., Johansson, L., Litvak, S., Montero, D., & Wydra, M. (2007). America's changing attitudes toward homosexuality, civil unions, and same-gender marriage: 1977–2004. *Social Work, 52*(1), 71–79.

Aytac, A., Arayo, A. B., Johannes, C. B., Kleinman, K. P., & McKinlay, J. B. (2000). Socioeconomic factors and incidence of erectile dysfunction: Findings of the Longitudinal Massachusetts Male Aging Study. *Journal of Social Science and Medicine, 51,* 771–778.

Azar, S. T., & Rohrbeck, C. A. (1986). Child abuse and unrealistic expectations: Further validation of the Patient Opinion Questionnaire. *Journal of Consulting & Clinical Psychology, 54,* 867–868.

Bacal, H. A., & Newman, K. M. (1990). *Theories of object relation: Bridges to self psychology.* New York: Columbia University Press.

Baer, J. S., & Peterson, P. L. (2002). Motivational interviewing with adolescents and young adults. In W. R. Miller & S. Rollnick (Eds.), *Motivational interviewing: Preparing people for change* (2nd ed., pp. 320–333). New York: Guilford Press.

Bagilishya, D. (2000). Mourning and recovery from trauma: In Rwanda tears flow from within. *Transcultural Psychiatry, 37*(3), 337–353.

Baker, B., Brightman, A., Balacher, J., Heifetz, L., Hinshaw, S., & Murphy, D. (2004). *Steps to independence: Teaching everyday skills to children with special needs* (4th ed.). Baltimore: Paul H. Brookes.

Baldwin, A., Baldwin, C., & Cole, R. E. (1990). Stress-resistant families and stress-resistant children. In J. E. Rolf, A. S. Masten, D. Cicchetti, K. N. Wechterlein, & S. Weintraub (Eds.), *Risk and protective factors in the development of psychopathology* (pp. 257–280). New York: Cambridge University Press.

Balint, M., Ornstein, P. H., & Balint, E. (1972). *Focal psychotherapy: An example of applied psychoanalysis.* London: Tavistock.

Ball, D. W. (1974, Winter). The family as a sociological problem: Conceptualization of the taken for granted as prologue to social problems analysis. *Social Problems, 19,* 295–305.

Bandura, A. (1969). Social learning theory of identificatory processes. In D. A. Goslin (Ed.), *Handbook of socialization theory and research.* Chicago: Rand McNally.

Bandura, A. (1977). *Social learning theory.* Englewood Cliffs, NJ: Prentice Hall.

Bandura, A. (1980). Gauging the relationship between self-efficacy judgment and action. *Cognitive Therapy and Research, 4,* 263–268.

Bandura, A. (1986). *Social foundation of thought and action: A social cognitive theory.* Englewood Cliffs, NJ: Prentice Hall.

Banister, R. (1999). Evolving reflexivity: Negotiating meaning of women's midlife experience. *Qualitative Inquiry, 5*(1), 3–23.

Barber, B. K., & Olsen, J. A. (1997). Socialization in context: Connection, regulation, and autonomy in the family, school, and neighborhood, and with peers. *Journal of Adolescent Research, 12,* 287–315.

Barkley, R. A. (1996). Attention-deficit hyperactivity disorder. In E. J. Mash & R. A. Barkley (Eds.), *Child psychopathology* (pp. 63–107). New York: Guilford Press.

Barkley, R. A. (1997a). *ADHD and the nature of self control.* New York: Guilford Press.

Barkley, R. A. (1997b). *Defiant children: A clinician's manual for assessment and parent training* (2nd ed.). New York: Guilford Press.

Barkley, R. A. (1998). *Attention deficit hyperactivity dis-order: A handbook for diagnosis and treatment* (2nd ed.). New York: Guilford Press.

Barkley, R. A. (2000). Genetics of childhood disorders: XVII, ADHD, Part 1: The executive function of ADHD. *Journal of the American Academy of Child and Adolescent Psychiatry, 39*(8), 1064–1068.

Barkley, R. A. (2003). Attention deficit/hyperactivity disorder. In E. J. Mash & R. A. Barkley (Eds.), *Child psychopathology* (2nd ed., pp. 75–143). New York: Guilford Press.

Barkley, R. A., Murphy, K. R., & Fisher, M. (2008). *ADHD in adults: What the science says.* NY: Guilford.

Barlow, D. E. (Ed.). (2001). *Clinical handbook of psychological disorders* (3rd ed.). New York: Guilford Press.

Barlow, D. H. (2002). *Anxiety and its disorders: The nature and treatment of anxiety and panic* (2nd ed.). New York: Guilford Press.

Barnartt, S. (1996). Disability culture or disability consciousness? *Journal of Disability Policy Studies, 7*(2), 2–19.

Baron-Cohen, S. (2001). Theory of mind and autism: A review. In L. M. Glidden (Ed.), *International review of research in mental retardation: Autism* (Vol. 23, pp. 169–184). San Diego, CA: Academic Press.

Barouh, G. (1992). *Support groups: The human face of the HIV/AIDS epidemic.* Huntington Station, NY: Long Island Association for AIDS Care.

Barrett, P. M., & Shortt, A. L. (2003). Parental involvement in the treatment of anxious children.

In A. E. Kazdin & J. R. Weisz (Eds.), *Evidence-based psychotherapies for children and adolescents* (pp. 101–120). New York: Guilford Press.

Barry, C. (2006). The political evolution of mental health parity. *Harvard Review of Psychiatry, 14,* 185–194.

Basham, K. (2004). Weaving a tapestry: Anti-racism and the pedagogy of clinical social work. *Smith College Studies in Social Work, 74*(2), 289–311.

Baskin, T. W., & Enright, R. D. (2004). Intervention studies of forgiveness: A meta-analysis. *Journal of Counseling and Development, 82,* 79–90.

Bass, A. (2002). Historical unconscious trauma: Racism and psychoanalysis. *Constellations: An International Journal of Critical and Democratic Theory, 9*(2), 274–275.

Bateson, G. (1951). Information and codification: A philosophical approach. In J. Ruesch & G. Bateson (Eds.), *Communication: The social matrix of psychiatry.* New York: Norton.

Bateson, G., Jackson, D. D., Haley, J., & Weakland, J. (1956). Toward a theory of schizophrenia. *Behavioral Sciences, 1,* 251–264.

Battin-Pearson, S., Newcomb, M. D., Abbott, R. D., Hill, K. G., Catalano, R. F., & Hawkins, J. D. (2000). Predictors of early high school dropout: A test of five theories. *Journal of Educational Psychology, 92*(3), 568–585.

Baumrind, D. (1967). Child care practices anteceding three patterns of preschool behavior. *Genetic Psychology Monographs, 75,* 43–48.

Baumrind, D. (1971). Current patterns of parental authority. *Developmental Psychology Monograph, 4*(No.1, Pt. 2).

Baumrind, D., & Black, A. E (1967). Socialization practices associated with dimension of competence in preschool boys and girls. *Child Development, 38,* 291–327.

Bauserman, R. (2002). Child adjustment in joint-custody versus sole-custody arrangement: A meta-analytic view. *Journal of Family Psychology, 16,* 91–102.

Baxter, L. A., & Montgomery, B. M. (1996). Relating: Dialogues and dialects. In R. Y. Hirokawa & M. S. Poole (Eds.), *Communication and group decision making.* Thousand Oaks, CA: Sage.

Beaver, M. L., & Miller, D. A. (1992). *Clinical social work practice with the elderly: Primary, secondary, and tertiary intervention.* Belmont, CA: Wadsworth.

Beck, A. T. (1963). Thinking and depression: Idiosyncratic content and cognitive distortions. *Archives of General Psychiatry, 9,* 324–333.

Beck, A. T., Emery, G., & Greenberg, R. L. (1985). *Anxiety disorders and phobias.* New York: Basic Books.

Beck, A. T., Epstein, N., Brown, & Steer, R. A. (1988). An inventory for measuring clinical anxiety: Psychometric properties. *Journal of Consulting and Clinical Psychology, 56,* 893–897.

Beck, A. T., Ward, C. H., Mendelson, H., Mock, J. E., & Erbaugh, J. K. (1961). An inventory for measuring depression. *Archives of General Psychiatry, 4,* 561–571.

Beck, A. T., & Weishaar, M. E. (1989). Cognitive therapy. In A. Freeman, K. M. Simon, L. Beutler, & H. Arkowitz (Eds.), *Comprehensive handbook of cognitive therapy* (pp. 21–36). New York: Plenum.

Beck, J. (1995). *Cognitive therapy: Basics and beyond.* New York: Guilford Press.

Beidel, D., & Morris, T. (1995). Social phobia. In J. S. March (Ed.), *Anxiety disorders in children and adolescents* (pp. 181–211). New York: Guilford Press.

Belgrave, F. X., & Bowe, F. (2000). Psychosocial aspects of chronic illness and disability among African Americans. *Contemporary Psychology, 45*(2), 164.

Bellak, L., Hurvich, M., & Gediman, H. (1973). *Ego functions in schizophrenics, neurotics and normals.* New York: Wiley.

Bem, L. L. (1981). Gender schema theory: A cognitive account of sex typing. *Psychological Review, 88,* 354–364.

Benenson, J. F. (1993). Greater preference among females than males for dyadic interaction in early childhood. *Child Development, 64,* 544–555.

Benjamin, J. (1988). *The bonds of love.* New York: Pantheon Books.

Benson, H. (1975). *The relaxation response.* New York: Morrow.

Benson, P. (1997). *All kids are our kids: What communities must do to raise caring and responsible children and adolescents.* San Francisco: Jossey-Bass.

Benson, P., & Roehlkepartain, E. C. (1993, July). *Youth in single-parent families: Risk and resiliency.* Search Institute Background Paper. Minneapolis, MN: Search Institute.

Berger, B. M. (1998). Disenchanting the concept of community. *Society, 35*(2), 324–327.

Berger, R. L., & Federico, R. C. (1982). *Human behavior: A social work perspective.* New York: Longman.

Berger, R. L., McBreen, J. T., & Rifkin, M. J. (1996). *Human behavior: A perspective for the helping professions.* White Plains, NY: Longman.

Bergeron, L. R., & Gray, B. (2003). Ethical dilemmas of reporting suspected elder abuse. *Social Work, 48*(1), 96–105.

Berk, L. E. (1999a). *Child development* (5th ed.). Boston: Allyn & Bacon.

Berk, L. E. (1999b). *Infants and children: Prenatal through middle childhood* (3d ed.). Boston: Allyn & Bacon.

Berk, L. E. (2003). *Child development* (6th ed.). Boston: Allyn & Bacon.

Berk, L. E. (2005). *Infants and children: Prenatal through middle childhood* (5th ed.). Boston: Pearson.

Berkman, B., & Harootyan, L. (2003). *Social work and health care in an aging society: Education, policy, practice, and research.* New York: Springer.

Berkman, L. F., & Syme, S. L. (1979, February). Social networks, host resistance and mortality. A nine-year follow-up study of Alameda county residents. *American Journal of Epidemiology, 109,* 186–204.

Berman, S., & Rappaport, M. B. (1985). Social work and Alzheimer's disease: Psychosocial management in the absence of medical cure. *Social Work in Health Care, 10*(2), 53–70.

Bernstein, P. (1997). *American work values: Their origin and development.* Albany: State University of New York Press.

Bertalanffy, L. (1962). General systems theory: A critical review. *General Systems Yearbook, 7,* 1–20.

Bertenthal, B. I., & Clifton, R. K. (1998). Perception and action. In W. Damon, D. Kuhn, & R. S. Siegler (Eds.), *Handbook of child psychology: Vol. 2. Cognition, perception, and language* (5th ed., pp. 51–102). New York: Wiley.

Berzoff, J., Flanagan, L. M., & Hertz, P. (1996). *Inside out and outside in: Psychodynamic clinical theory and practice in contemporary multicultural contexts.* Northvale, NJ: Jason Aronson Press.

Bessell, A. G. (2001). Children surviving cancer: Psychosocial adjustment, quality of life, and school experiences. *Exceptional Children, 67*(3), 345–359.

Bettleheim, B. (1954). *Symbolic wounds, puberty rites and the envious male.* Glencoe, IL: Free Press.

Bialystock, E. (2001). *Bilingualism in development: Language, literacy, and cognition.* New York: Cambridge University Press.

Bialystock, E., & Hakuta, K. (1999). Confounded age: Linguistic and cognitive factors in age differences in second language acquisition. In D. Birdsong (Ed.), *Second language acquisition and the critical period hypothesis* (pp. 161–181). Mahwah, NJ: Erlbaum.

Biederman, J., Mick, E., Faraone, S. V., Spencer, T., Wilens, T. E., & Wozniak, J. (2000). Pediatric mania: A developmental subtype of bipolar disorder? *Biological Psychiatry, 48,* 458–466.

Billingsly, A., & Morrison-Rodriguez, B. (1998). The black family in the 21st century and the church as action system: A macro perspective. In *Journal of Human Behavior and the Social Environment 1*(2/3), 31–47. The Haworth Press.

Blackman, J. A., Westervelt, V. D., Stevenson, R., & Welch, A. (1991). Management of preschool children with attention deficit-hyperactivity disorder. *Topics in Early Childhood Special Education, 11,* 91–104.

Blakeslee, S. (1995, August 29). In brain's early growth, timetable may be crucial. *New York Times,* Section C, p. 1.

Blau, J. (2004). *The dynamics of social welfare policy.* New York: Oxford Press.

Blau, J. with Abramovitz, M. (2007). *The dynamics of social welfare policy* (2nd ed.). New York: Oxford University Press.

Blau, P. M. (1964). *Exchange and power in social life.* New York: Wiley.

Blenkner, M. (1965). Social work and family relationships in later life with some thoughts on filial maturity. In E. Shanas & G. Streib (Eds.), *Social structure and the family: Generational relations* (pp. 46–59). Englewood Cliffs, NJ: Prentice Hall.

Blieszner, R., Mancini, J. A., & Marek, L. I. (1996). Looking back and looking ahead: Life-course unfolding of parenthood. In C. D. Ryff & M. M. Seltzer (Eds.), *The parental experience in midlife* (pp. 607–641). Chicago: University of Chicago Press.

Bloom, B. L. (1997). *Planned short term psychotherapy: A clinical handbook.* Boston: Allyn & Bacon.

Bloom, L. (1998). Language acquisition in its developmental context. In W. Damon, D. Kuhn, & R. S. Siegler (Eds.), *Handbook of child psychology: Vol. 2. Cognition, perception, and language* (5th ed., pp. 309–370). New York: Wiley.

Blos, P. (1975). The second individuation process of adolescence. In A. Esman (Ed.), *The psychology of adolescence: Essential readings* (pp. 156–178). New York: International Universities Press.

Blow, F. (1998). *Substance abuse among older adults.* U.S. Department of Health and Human Services, Public Health Service, Substance Abuse and Mental Health Services Administration, Center for Substance Abuse Treatment Improvement Protocol (TIP) Series No. 26. Retrieved December 29, 2008, from http://www.ncbi.nlm.nih.gov/books/bv.fcgi?rid=hstat5.chapter.48302

Bondy, A., & Frost, L. (2002). *A picture's worth: PECS and other visual communication strategies in autism.* Bethesda, MD: Woodbine House.

Bonvillian, J. D., & Folven, R. J. (1993). Sign language acquisition: Developmental aspects. In M. Marschark & M. D. Clark (Eds.), *Psychological perspectives on deafness* (pp. 27–48). Hillsdale, NJ: Erlbaum.

Bornstein, B. (1951). On latency. *Psychoanalytic Study of the Child, 6,* 279–285.

Bornstein, M. H. (1995). Parenting infants. In M. H. Bornstein (Ed.), *Handbook of parenting: Vol. 1. Children and parenting* (pp. 3–39). Mahwah, NJ: Erlbaum.

Borthwick-Duffy, S. (1994). Epidemiology and prevalence of psychopathology in people with mental retardation. *Journal of Consulting & Clinical Psychology, 62*, 17–27.

Boul, L. A. (2003). Men's health and middle age. *Sexualities, Evolution and Gender, 5*(1), 5–22.

Bowen, M. (1966). The use of family theory in clinical practice. *Comprehensive Psychiatry, 7*, 345–74.

Bowen, M. (1974). Toward the differentiation of self in one's family of origin. In F. Andre & J. Lorio (Eds.), *Georgetown Family Symposium* (Vol. 1). Washington, DC: Department of Psychiatry, Georgetown University Medical Center.

Bowers, W. A., Evans, K., LeGrange, D., & Andersen, A. E. (2003). Treatment of adolescent eating disorders. In M. A. Reinecke, F. M. Dattilo, & Freeman (Eds.), *Cognitive therapy with children and adolescents: A casebook for clinical practice* (2d ed., pp. 247–281). New York: Guilford Press.

Bowes, J. (1996). Out of the closet and into the marketplace: Meeting basic needs in the gay community. *Journal of Homosexuality, 31*(1/2), 219–244.

Bowlby, J. (1958). The nature of the child's tie to his mother. *International Journal of Psychoanalysis, 39*, 350–373.

Bowlby, J. (1969/1982). *Attachment and loss: Vol. 1. Attachment*. New York: Basic Books.

Bowlby J. (1980). *Attachment and loss: Vol. 3. Loss*. New York: Basic Books.

Bowlby, J. (1984). Caring for the young: Influences on development. In R. S. Cohen, B. J. Cohler, & S. H. Weissman (Eds.), *Parenthood: A psychodynamic perspective* (pp. 269–284). New York: Guilford Press.

Bowlby, J. (1988a). *A secure base: Clinical applications of attachment theory*. London: Tavistock/Routledge.

Bowlby, J. (1988b). A secure base: Parent-child attachment and healthy human development (p. 136). New York: Basic Books. Quoted in D. Davies, *Child development: A practitioner's guide* (p. 6). New York: Guilford Press, 2004.

Brabender, V. (2002). *Introduction to group therapy*. New York: Wiley.

Bradley, S. J. (2000). *Affect regulation and the development of psychopathology*. New York: Guilford Press.

Brandler, S., & Roman, C. (1999). *Group work: Skills and strategies for effective interventions* (2d ed.). New York: Haworth Press.

Braswell, L., & Kendall, P. (1987). Treating impulsive children via cognitive behavioral therapy. In N. Jacobson (Ed.), *From psychotherapist in clinical practice: Cognitive and behavioral perspectives* (pp. 153–189). New York: Guilford Press.

Brendt, T. J., Cheung, P. C., Lau, S., Hau, K.-T., & Lew, W. J. F. (1993). Perceptions of parenting in mainland China, Taiwan, and Hong Kong: Sex differences and societal differences. *Developmental Psychology, 29*, 156–164.

Brennan, K. A., & Morris, K. A. (1997). Attachment styles, self-esteem, and patterns of seeking feedback from romantic partners. *Personality and Social Psychology Bulletin, 23*, 23–31.

Brennan, K. A., & Shaver, P. R. (1995). Dimensions of adult attachment, affect regulation, and romantic relationship functioning. *Personality and Social Psychology Bulletin, 21*, 267–283.

Brenner, C. (1974). *An elementary textbook of psychoanalysis*. Garden City, NY: Anchor Books.

Bretherton, I., & Munholland, K. A. (1999). Internal working models in attachment relationships: A construct revisited. In J. Cassidy & P. R. Shaver (Eds.), *Handbook of attachment: Theory, research, and clinical applications* (pp. 89–114). New York: Guilford Press.

Brice, C. (Ed.). (2003). *Age ain't nothing but a number: Black women explore midlife*. New York: Beacon Press.

Bricker, D., Young, J., & Flanagan, C. (1993). Schema focused cognitive therapy: A comprehensive framework for characterological problems. In K. T. Kuehlwein & H. Rosen (Eds.), *Cognitive therapies in action: Evolving innovative practice* (pp. 88–125). San Francisco: Jossey-Bass.

Bricout, J. C., & Bentley, K. J. (2000). Disability status and perceptions of employability by employers. *Social Work Research, 24*(2), 87–95.

Bride, B. E. (2007). Prevalence of secondary traumatic stress among social workers. *Social Work, 52*(1), 63–70.

Brim, O. V., Ryff, C. D., & Kessler, R. C. (Eds.). (2004). *How healthy are we? A national study of well-being at midlife*. Chicago: University of Chicago Press.

Brody, L. (1999). *Gender, emotion, and the family*. Cambridge, MA: Harvard University Press.

Brohl, K. (1996). *Working with traumatized children: A handbook for healing*. Washington, DC: CWLA Press.

Brooks, D., & Barth, R. P. (1999). Adult transracial and in racial adoptees: Effects of race, gender, adoptive family structure, and placement history on adjustment outcomes. *American Journal of Orthopsychiatry, 69*, 87–99.

Brown, J., & Isaacs, D. (1994). Merging the best of two worlds: The core processes of organizations as communities. In P. Senge, A. Kleiner, C. Roberts, R. Ross, & B. Smith (Eds.), *The fifth discipline fieldbook* (pp. 508–517). New York: Doubleday.

Brown, L. B., Cook, T., Sarosy, S., & Quartro, G. (1997). *Gay men and aging*. New York: Garland.

Brown, L. M. (1991). *Groups for growth and change*. New York: Longman.

Brown, L. M., & C. Gilligan. (1992). *Meeting at the crossroads: Women's psychology and girl's development.* New York: Ballantine Books.

Brown, L. S. (2008). *Cultural competence in trauma therapy: Beyond the flashback.* Washington DC: American Psychological Association.

Brown, R. T., Freeman, W. S., Perrin, J. M., Stein, M. T., Amler, R. W., Feldman, H. M., et al. (2001). Prevalence and assessment of attention-deficit/hyperactivity disorder in primary care settings. *Pediatrics, 107,* E43.

Brown, T. E. (2000a). *Attention-deficit disorders and co-morbidities in children, adolescents, and adults.* Washington, DC: American Psychiatric Press.

Brown, T. E. (2000b). Emerging understanding of attention-deficit disorders and co-morbidities. In T. E. Brown (Ed.), *Attention-deficit disorders and co-morbidities in children, adolescents and adults* (pp. 3–55). Washington, DC: American Psychiatric Press.

Bruner, J. S. (1985). Vygotsky: A historical and conceptual perspective. In J. V. Wertsch (Ed.), *Culture, cognition and communication. Vygotskian perspectives* (pp. 21–34). New York: Cambridge University Press.

Bruner, J. S., & Lucariello, J. (1989). Monologue as narrative recreation of the world. In K. Nelson (Ed.), *Narratives from the crib* (pp. 73–97). Cambridge, MA: Harvard University Press.

Bryson, J. M. (1989). *Strategic planning for public and nonprofit organizations.* San Francisco: Jossey-Bass.

Brzuzy, S. (1999). Deconstructing disability: The impact of definition. *Journal of Poverty, 1*(1), 81–91.

Bubolz, M. M. (2001). Family as source, user, and builder of social capital. *Journal of Socio-Economics, 30,* 129–131.

Buchanan, M., Dzelme, K., Harris, D., & Hecker, L. (2001). Challenge of being simultaneously gay or lesbian and spiritual and/or religious: A narrative perspective. *American Journal of Family Therapy, 29,* 435–449.

Buckley, W. (1967). Systems and entities. In W. Buckley (Ed.), *Sociology and modern systems theory* (pp. 42–66). New York: Aldine.

Bullis, R. (1996). *Spirituality in social work practice.* Washington, DC: Taylor & Francis.

Burke, B. L., Vassilev, G., Kantchelov, A., & Zweben, A. (2002). Motivational interviewing with couples. In W. R. Miller & S. Rollnick (Eds.), *Motivational interviewing: Preparing people for change* (2nd ed., pp. 347–361). New York: Guilford Press.

Burman, L., Maag, E., & Rohaly, J. (2005, July). Tax credits to help low-income families pay for child care. *Tax policy: Issues and options.* Washington, DC: Urban-Brookings Tax Policy Center.

Burnette, D., & Kang, S.-Y., (2003). Self-health care by urban, African American elders. In B. Berkman & L. Harootyan (Eds.), *Social work and health care in an aging society: Education, policy, practice, and research* (pp. 123–147). New York: Springer.

Bus, A. G., Leseman, P. P. M., & Keultjes, P. (2000). Joint bookreading across cultures: A comparison of Surinamese-Dutch, Turkish-Dutch, and Dutch parent–child dyads. *Journal of Literacy Research, 32,* 1, 53–76

Buss, A. H., & Plomin, R. (1984). *Temperament: Early developing personality traits.* Hillsdale, NJ: Erlbaum.

Butler, J. (2006). *Gender trouble: Feminism and the subversion of identity.* New York: Routledge Classics.

Butler, R. (1963). The life review: An interpretation of reminiscence in the aged. *Psychiatry, 26,* 65–76.

Butts, J., & Roman, J. (Eds.). (2004). *Juvenile drug courts and teen substance abuse.* Washington, DC: Urban Institute Press.

Cain, R. (1991). Relational contexts and information management among gay men. *Families in Society, 72*(6), 344–352.

Calhoun, C. (2000). *Feminism, the family and the politics of the closet: Lesbian and gay displacement.* New York: Oxford University Press.

Calkins, S. D., Fox, N. A., & Marshall, T. R. (1996). Behavioral and physiological antecedents of inhibited and uninhibited behavior. *Child Development, 67,* 523–540.

Call, K. T. (2001). *Arenas of comfort in adolescence: A study of adjustment in context.* Mahwah, NJ: Erlbaum.

Campbell, F. A., & Ramey, C. T. (1994). Effects of early intervention on intellectual and academic achievement: A follow up study of children for low-income families. *Child Development, 65,* 684–698.

Campbell, S. B. (1990). *Behavior problems in preschool children: Clinical and developmental issues.* New York: Guilford Press.

Campo, A. T., & Rohner, R. P. (1992). Relationships between perceived parental acceptance-rejection, psychological adjustment, and substance abuse among young adults. *Child Abuse and Neglect, 16,* 429–440.

Canabal, I. (1995). *Latino group identity and collective self esteem.* PhD dissertation, University of Maryland, College Park.

Canda, E. (1988). Spirituality, religious diversity and social work practice. *Social Casework, 69,* 238–247.

Canda, E., & Furman, L. (1999). *Spiritual diversity in social work practice: The heart of helping.* New York: Free Press.

Carby, H. (1982). "White women listen!" Black feminism and the boundaries of Sisterhood. In Centre for Contemporary Studies, Cultural (Eds.), *The empire strikes back* (pp. 23–33). London: Hutchinson.

Carlson, G. A. (2002). Bipolar disorder in children and adolescents: A critical review. In D. Shaffer & B. Waslick (Eds.), *The many faces of depression in children and adolescents* (Vol. 21, pp. 105–128). Washington, DC: APPI Press.

Carlton-LaNey, I. B. (1997). Social workers as advocates for elders. In M. Reisch, & E. Gambrill (Eds.), *Social work in the 21st century*. Thousand Oaks, CA: Pine Forge Press.

Carlton-LaNey, I. B. (2000). Women and interracial cooperation in establishing the Good Samaritan Hospital. *Affilia, 15*, 65–81.

Carlton-LaNey, I. B., (Ed.). (2001). *African American leadership: An empowerment tradition in social welfare history*. Washington, DC: NASW Press.

Carnegie Council on Adolescent Development. (1989). *Turning points: Preparing American youth for the 21st century*. Washington, DC: Carnegie Corporation of New York.

Carpenter, D. (1996). Constructivism and social work treatment. In F. J. Turner (Ed.), *Social work treatment: Interlocking theoretical approaches* (4th ed., pp. 146–168). New York: The Free Press.

Carter, B., & McGoldrick, M. (1989). *The changing family life cycle: A framework for family therapy* (2nd ed.). Boston: Allyn & Bacon.

Carter, B., & McGoldrick, M. (Eds.). (1999). *The expanded family life cycle* (3d ed.). Boston: Allyn and Bacon.

Carter, R. (1999). *Mapping the mind*. Berkeley and Los Angeles: University of California Press.

Carver, P. R., Yunger, J. L., & Perry, D. G. (2003). Gender identity and adjustment in middle childhood. *Sex Roles, 49*(3/4), 95–109.

Casas, J. M., Wagenheim, B. R., Banchero, R., & Mendoza-Romero, J. (1994). Hispanic masculinity: Myth or psychological schema meriting clinical consideration. *Hispanic Journal of Behavioral Sciences, 16*, 315–331.

Cass V. (1979). Homosexual identity formation: A theoretical model. *Journal of Homosexuality, 4*, 219–235.

Cass, V. (1984). Homosexual identity formation: Testing a theoretical model. *Journal of Sex Research, 20*, 143–167.

Cass, V. (1990). The implications of homosexual identity formation for the Kinsey model and scale of sexual preference. In D. McWhirter, S. Sanders, & J. Reinish (Eds.), *Homosexuality/heterosexuality: Concepts of sexual orientation* (pp. 23–66). New York: Oxford University Press.

Cassidy, J. (1999). The nature of the child's ties. In J. Cassidy & P. R. Shaver (Eds.), *Handbook of attachment* (pp. 3–20). New York: Guilford Press.

Castilli, R. J. (1995). Culture, trance, and the mind–brain. *Anthropology of Consciousness, 6*, 17–34.

Castillo, R. J. (1997). Culture and Mental Illness: A Client-Centered Approach. Pacific Grove, AA: Brooks-Cole.

Castle, J., Groothues, C., Bredenkamp, D., Beckett, D., O'Connor, T., Rutter, M., & the E.R.A. Study Team. (1999). Effects of qualities of early institutional care on cognitive attainments. *American Journal of Orthopsychiatry, 69*, 424–437.

Catalano, R., Berglund, M., Ryan, J., Lonczak, H., & Hawkins, J. (2004). Positive youth development in the United States: Research findings on evaluation of positive youth development programs. *Annals of the American Academy of Political and Social Sciences, 591*, 98–124.

Cattan, P. (1991). Child care problems: An obstacle to work. *Monthly Labor Review, 114* (10), 3–9.

Ceci, S. J., & Roazzi, A. (1994). The effects of context on cognition: Postcards from Brazil. In R. J. Sternberg (Ed.), *Mind in context* (pp. 74–101). New York: Cambridge University Press.

Centers for Disease Control and Prevention (CDC). (1995a). *Adolescent health: State of the nation—pregnancy, sexually transmitted diseases, and related risk behaviors among U.S. adolescents*. Monograph Series No. 2, DHHS Publication No. CDC 099–4630. Atlanta, GA: Author.

Centers for Disease Control and Prevention (CDC). (1995b). Trends in sexual risk behavior among high school students—United States, 1990, 1991, and 1993. *Morbidity and Mortality Weekly Reports, 44*(7), 124–133.

Centers for Disease Control and Prevention (CDC). (1999a). *Prevention of genital HPV infection and sequelae: Report of an external consultant's meeting*. Atlanta, GA: Author.

Centers for Disease Control and Prevention (CDC). (1999b). *CDC surveillance summaries*. MMWR. Atlanta, GA: Author.

Centers for Disease Control and Prevention (CDC). (1999c). *CDC HIV/AIDS prevention research project compendium of HIV prevention interventions with evidence of effectiveness*. Atlanta, GA: Author.

Centers for Disease Control and Prevention (CDC). (2000). *A glance at the HIV epidemic*. Atlanta, GA: Author.

Center for Disease Control and Prevention (CDC). (2003). *AIDS cases in adolescents and adults by age—United States, 1994–2000*. HIV/AIDS Surveillance Supplemental Report, *9*(1). Retrieved December 28, 2008, from http://www.cdc.gov/hiv/stats/hasrsuppVol9No1.htm

Centers for Disease Control and Prevention (CDC). (2004). www.cdc.gov/aboutcdc.htm. Retrieved November 7, 2005.

Centers for Disease Control and Prevention (CDC) (2008). *HIV/AIDS surveillance report, Vol. 18*. Atlanta: U.S. Department of Health and Human Services.

Center for Substance Abuse Treatment (CSAP). (1998). *Treatment improvement protocol No 26: Substance abuse among older adults*. Substance Abuse and Mental Health Services Administration. DHHS No. (SMA) 98-3179. Retrieved December 29, 2008, from http://www.ncbi.nlm.nih.gov/books/bv.fcgi?rid=hstat5.section.48698

Center for Substance Abuse Treatment (CSAP). (1999). *Treatment improvement protocol No. 34: Brief alcohol interventions and therapies in substance abuse treatment*. Substance Abuse and Mental Health Services Administration. DHHS No. (SMA) 99-3353. Retrieved December 29, 2008, from http://www.ncbi.nlm.nih.gov/books/bv.fcgi?rid= hstat5.section.59497

Chadiha, L. A., & Adams, P. (2003). Physical health and economic well-being of older African American women: Toward strategies of empowerment. In B. Berkman & L. Harootyan (Eds.), *Social work and health care in an aging society: Education, policy, practice, and research* (pp. 149–176). New York: Springer.

Chao, R. K. (1994). Beyond parental control and authoritarian parenting style: Understanding Chinese parenting through the cultural notion of training. *Child Development, 65*, 1111–1119.

Charlton, J. I. (1998). *Nothing about us without us: Disability oppression and empowerment*. Berkeley and Los Angeles: University of California Press.

Charman, T., Swettenham, J., Baron-Cohen, S., Cox, A., Baird, G., & Drew, A. (1997). Infants with autism: An investigation of empathy, pretend play, joint attention, and imitation. *Developmental Psychology, 33*, 781–789.

Charney, D. S. (2004, February). Psychobiological mechanisms of resilience and vulnerability: Implications for successful adaptation to extreme stress. *American Journal of Psychiatry, 161*(2), 195–216.

Chaskin, R. J., Brown, R. J., Venkatesh, S., & Vidal, A. (2001). *Building community capacity*. New York: Aldine de Gruyter.

Chaskin, R. J., Joseph, M. L., & Chipenda-Dansokho, S. (1997). Implementing comprehensive community development: Possibilities and limitations. *Social Work, 42*(5), 435–444.

Chattergee P., & Koleski, R. E. (1970). The concept of community and community organization: A review. *Social Work, 15*(3): 82–92.

Chavez, A. F., & Guido-DiBrito, F. (1999). Racial and ethnic identity and development. *New Directions for Adult and Continuing Education, 84*, 39–47.

Checkoway, B. (1997). Core concepts for community change. *Journal of Community Practice, 4*(1), 11–29.

Chen, X., Hastings, P. D., Rubin, K. H., Chen, H., Cen, G., & Stewart, S. L. (1998). Child-rearing attitudes and behavioral inhibition in Chinese and Canadian toddlers: A cross cultural study. *Developmental Psychology, 34*, 677–686.

Chen X., Rubin, K. H., & Li, Z. (1995). Social functioning and adjustment in Chinese children: A longitudinal study. *Developmental Psychology, 31*, 531–539.

Cheour, M., Ceponiene, R., Lehtokoski, A., Luuk, A., Allik, J., Alho, K., & Naatanen, R. (1998). Development of language-specific phoneme representations in the infant brain. *Nature Neuroscience, 1*, 351–353.

Cherlin, A., & Furstenberg, F. F. (1992). *The new American grandparent*. New York: Basic Books.

Chi, M. T. H., Glaser, R., & Rees, E. (1982). Expertise in problem solving. In R. J. Sternberg (Ed.), *Advances in the psychology of human intelligence* (Vol. 1). Hillsdale, NJ: Erlbaum.

Chiao, S. (2001). *Women of color bridging the gap: Conversation with pioneering women working in the overlap between feminist and multicultural psychology*. PhD dissertation, California School of Professional Psychology, Berkeley.

Chilcoat, H. D., & Menard, C. (2007). Comorbidity of PTSD and substance use disorder. In P. Ouimette & P. J. Brown (Eds.), *Trauma and substance abuse: Causes, consequences and treatment of comorbid disorders* (pp. 9–28). Washington, DC: American Psychological Association.

Children's Defense Fund. (2002). *The state of children in America's union: A 2002 action guide to leave no child behind*. Washington, DC: Author.

Children's Defense Fund. (2005). Retrieved October 11, 2005, from www.childrensdefense.org/childhealth/chip.

Children's Defense Fund (2008). *The state of America's children 2008*. Washington DC: Author

Chodorow, N. (1973). *The reproduction of mothering*. Berkeley and Los Angeles: University of California Press.

Chodorow, N. (1978). *The reproduction of mothering*. Berkeley and Los Angeles: University of California Press.

Chou, K. L. & Chi, I. (2005). Prevalence and correlates of depression in Chinese oldest-old. *International Journal of Geriatric Psychiatry, 20*(1), 41–50.

Cicchetti, D. (1984). The emergence of developmental psychology. *Child Development, 55,* 1–7.

Cicchetti, D. (1994). Advances and challenges in the study of the sequelae of child maltreatment. *Development and Psychopathology, 6,* 1–247.

Cicchetti, D., & Tucker, D. (1994). Development and self-regulatory structures of the mind. *Development and Psychopathology, 6,* 533–550.

Ciricelli, V. G. (1983). Adult children and their elderly parents. In T. Brubaker (Ed.), *Family relationships in later life.* Beverly Hills, CA: Sage.

Clark, D. A., Beck, A. T., & Alford, B. A. (1999). *Scientific foundations of cognitive theory and therapy of depression.* New York: Wiley.

Clark, D. B. (1993, March). *Assessment of social anxiety in adolescent alcohol abusers.* Paper presented at the Anxiety Disorders Association of American Annual Convention, Charleston, SC.

Clark, S. H., & Chwiebert, V. L. (2001). Penelope's loom: A metaphor of women's development in midlife. *Canadian Review of Sociology and Anthropology, 38,* 441–464.

Clausen, J. A. (1986). *The life course: A sociological perspective.* Englewood Cliffs, NJ: Prentice Hall.

CNN/*USA Today*/Gallup. (2005). *Make wealthy pay for Social Security.* Retrieved February 9, 2005, from http://www.money.cnn.com/2005/02/08/retirement/pollandlowbar;socsec/index.htm? cnn=yes

Cohen, A. B., & Koenig, H. G. (2003). Religion, religiosity and spirituality in the biopsychosocial model of health and ageing. *Ageing International, 28*(3), 215–241.

Cohen, A. P. (1985). *The symbolic construction of community.* New York: Tavistock Publication and Ellis Horwood Limited.

Cohen, D. J., & Volkmar, F. R. (Eds.). (1997). *Handbook of autism and pervasive developmental disorders.* New York: Wiley.

Cohen, K. M., & Savin-Williams, R. C. (1996). Developmental perspectives on coming out to self and others. In R. C. Savin-Williams & K. M. Cohen (Eds.), *The lives of lesbians, gays and bisexuals* (pp. 113–151). Orlando, FL: Harcourt Brace.

Cohler, B. J., & Hammack, P. L. (2007). The psychological world of the gay teenager: Social change, narrative and "normality." *Journal of Youth and Adolescence, 36,* 47–50.

Cole, M., & Cole, S. R. (1996). *Development of children* (3rd ed.). New York: W. H. Freeman.

Cole, S. S., & Cole, T. M. (1999). Sexuality, disability, and reproductive issues through the lifespan. In R. P. Marinelli, & A. E. Dell Orto (Eds.), *The psychological and social impact of disability* (pp. 241–254). New York: Springer.

Coleman, D. (1986, December 1). Major personality study finds that traits are mostly inherited. *The New York Times,* Section C, pp. C1–C2.

Coleman, E. (1982). Developmental stages in the coming out process. In W. Paul, J. D. Weinrich, J. C. Gonsiorek, & M. E. Hotvedt (Eds.), *Homosexuality: Social, psychological and biological issues* (pp. 149–159). Beverly Hills, CA: Sage.

Coleman, J. C. (1980). *The nature of adolescence.* New York: Methuen.

Coleman, J. C. (1990). *The nature of adolescence* (2nd ed.). New York: Routledge.

Coll, C. G. (1992). Cultural diversity: Implications for theory and practice. *Work in Progress,* No. 59, Wellesley, MA: Stone Center Working Paper Series.

Coll, C. G., Cook-Nobles, R., & Surrey, J. L. (1995). Diversity at the core: Implications for relational theory. *Work in Progress,* No. 75. Wellesley, MA: Stone Center Working Paper Series.

Colon, F. (1980). The family life cycle of the multi-problem poor family. In B. Carter & M. McGoldrick (Eds.), *Family life cycle* (pp. 343–81). New York: Gardner Press.

Comas-Diaz, L. (1994). An integrative approach. In L. Comas-Diaz & B. Greene (Eds.), *Women of color. Integrating ethnic and gender identities in psychotherapy* (pp. 287–318). New York: Guilford Press.

Congress, E. (1994). The use of culturagrams to assess and empower culturally diverse families. *Families in Society, 75*(9), 531–540.

Conner, K. A. (2000). *Continuing to care: Older Americans and their families.* New York: Palmer Press.

Constable, R. (1990). Spirituality and social work: Issues to be addressed. *Spirituality and Social Work Communicator, 1*(1), 4–6.

Cook, D. A. (1993) Research in African American churches: A mental health counseling imperative. *Journal of Mental Health Counseling, 15,* (pp. 320–333).

Cooney, T. M., Pedersen, F. A., Indelicato, S., & Palkovitz, R. (1993). Timing of fatherhood: Is "on-time" optimal? *Journal of Marriage and the Family, 55,* 205–215.

Cooper, M. G., & Lesser, J. G. (2005). *Clinical social work practice: An integrated approach.* Boston: Allyn & Bacon.

Cooper, M., Todd, G., & Wells, A. (2000). *Bulimia nervosa: A cognitive therapy program for clients.* Philadelphia: Jessica Kingsley.

Cooper, T. (1999). Practice with transgendered youth and their families. *Journal of Gay and Lesbian Social Services, 10,* 111–129.

Cooper, Z., Fairburn, C. G., & Hawker, D. M. (2004). *Cognitive-behavioral treatment of obesity: A clinician's guide.* New York: Guilford Press.

Copenhaver, M. M., & Fisher, J. D. (2006). Experts outline ways to decrease the decade-long yearly rate of 40,000 new HIV infections in the US. *AIDs and Behavior, 10*(1), 105–114.

Corbin, J. (2006). School-based clinical practice and school reform. In A. Lightburn, & P. Sessions (Eds.), *Handbook of community-based clinical practice* (pp. 322–336). New York: Oxford University Press.

Cornett, C. (1998). *The soul of psychotherapy: Recapturing the spiritual dimension in the therapeutic encounter.* New York: Simon & Schuster.

Corwin, M. (2006) Culturally competent community-based clinical practice: a critical review. In A. Lightburn & P. Sessions (Eds.). *Handbook of community-based clinical practice* (pp. 99–110). New York: Oxford University Press

Costanzo, P., Miller-Johnson, S., & Wencel, H. (1995). Social development. In J. March (Ed.), *Anxiety disorders in children and adolescents* (pp. 82–109). New York: Guilford Press.

Cottrell, L. (1976). The competent community. In B. H. Kaplan, R. N. Wilson, & A. H. Leighton (Eds.), *Further explorations in social psychiatry* (pp. 195–209). New York: Basic Books.

Council on Social Work Education. (2003). Program objectives. In *Handbook of accreditation standards* (5th ed. 33–34). Alexandria, VA: Author.

Council on Social Work Education. (2009). *Boom of gay seniors present challenge to service sector.* West End Word, 11/26/08, by Kara Krekeler, Retrieved January 5, 2009, from http://www.westendword.com/print_edition.php?id=1144

Courvant, D. (1999). Coming out disabled: A transsexual woman considers queer contributions to living with disability. *Journal of Gay, Lesbian, and Bisexual Identity, 4*(1), 97–105.

Cousins, L. (2003). Culture. In E. D. Hutchinson (Ed.), *Dimensions of human behavior: Person and environment* (3rd ed., pp. 261–295). Thousand Oaks: CA: Sage.

Cowan, A., & Schwartz, I. (2004). Violence in the family: Policy and practice disparities in the treatment of children. *Children and Youth Services Review, 26,* 1067–1080.

Cowen, E. L., Hightower, A. D., Pedro-Carroll, J. P., Work, W. C., Wyman, P. A., & Haffey, W. G. (1996). *School-based prevention for children at risk: The primary mental health project.* Washington, DC: American Psychological Association.

Cox, S., & Gallois, C. (1996). Gay and lesbian identity development: A social identity perspective. *Journal of Homosexuality, 30*(4), 1–30.

Coyle, G. L. (1930). *Social process in organized groups.* New York: Richard R. Smith.

Coyne, J. C., & Kazarus, R. S. (1980). Cognitive style, stress, perception and coping. In I. L. Kutash & L. B. Schlesinger (Eds.), *Handbook on stress and anxiety* (pp. 144–58). San Francisco: Jossey-Bass.

Cozolino, L. (2002). *The neuroscience of psychotherapy: Building and rebuilding the human mind.* New York: Norton.

Craig, G. J. (1999). *Human development* (8th ed.). Upper Saddle River, NJ: Prentice Hall.

Craig-Bray, L., Adams, G. R., & Dobson, W. R. (1988). Identity formation and social relations during late adolescence. *Journal of Youth and Adolescence, 17,* 173–188.

Crate, M. A. (1965). Adaptation to chronic illness. *American Journal of Nursing, 65,* 73–76.

Crawford, N. (2002). New ways to stop bullying. *Monitor on Psychology, 33,* 64.

Crawford-Brown, C. (1997). The impact of parent–child socialization on the development of conduct disorder in Jamaica male adolescents. In J. L. Rooparine & J. Brown (Eds.), *Caribbean families: Diversity among ethnic groups* (pp. 205–222). Greenwich, CT: Ablex.

Crawford-Brown, C. (1999). The impact of parenting on conduct disorder in Jamaican male adolescents. *Adolescence, 34,* 417–436.

Crick, N. R., Casas, J. F., & Nelson, D. A. (2002). Toward a more comprehensive understanding of peer maltreatment: Studies of relational victimization. *Current Directions in Psychological Science, 11,* 98–101.

Crosbie-Burnett, M., & Helmbrecht, L. (1993). A descriptive empirical study of gay male stepfamilies. *Family Relations, 42,* 256–62.

Cross, W. E. (1971). Toward a psychology of Black liberation: The Negro to Black convergence experience. *Black World, 29*(9), 13–27.

Cross, W. E. (1991). *Shades of black.* Philadelphia: Temple University Press.

Cross, W. E. (1995). The psychology of Niegrscence: Revising the Cross model. In J. Ponterotto, J. M. Casas, L. A. Suzuki, & C. M. Alexander (Eds.), *Handbook of multicultural counseling* (pp. 93–122). Thousand Oaks, CA: Sage.

Crowley, J. (2003). The gentrification of child support enforcement services, 1950–1984. *Social Services Review, 77*(4), 585–604.

Cumming, E., & Henry, W. E. (1961). *Growing old: The process of disengagement.* New York: Basic Books.

Cummings, E. M., Hennessy, K., Rabideau, G., & Cicchetti, D. (1994). Responses of physically abused boys to interadult anger involving their mothers. *Development & Psychopathology, 6,* 31–42.

Curry, J. E., & Reinecke, M. A. (2003). Modular therapy for adolescents with major depression. In M. A. Reinecke, F. M. Dattilio, & A. Freeman (Eds.), *Cognitive therapy with children and adolescents: A casebook for clinical practice* (pp. 95–128). New York: Guilford Press.

Curry, M. A., Hassouneh-Phillips, D., & Johnston-Silverberg, A. (2001). Abuse of women with disabilities: An ecological model and review. *Violence against Women, 7*(1), 60–79.

Cutler, N. E. (1997). The financial gerontology birthdays of 1995–1996: Social security at 60 and the "baby" boom at 50. In M. Reisch, & E. Gambrill (Eds.), *Social work in the 21st century* (pp. 143–151). Thousand Oaks, CA: Pine Forge Press.

Daft, R. L. (2008). *Management* (8th ed.) Mason, OH: South-Western

Damon, W., & Hart, D. (1988). *Self-understanding in childhood and adolescence.* New York: Cambridge University Press.

Dana, R. H., Behn, J. D., & Gonwa, T. (1992). A checklist for the examination of cultural competence in social service agencies. *Research on Social Work Practice, Vol. 2, No. 2,* April, 220–233.

Daniels, J. A. (2001). Conceptualizing a case of indirect racism using the White Identity Development Model. *Journal of Mental Health Counseling, 23*(3), 256–268.

Dannefer, D., & Perlmutter, M. (1990). Development as a multidimensional process: Individual and social constituents. *Human Development, 33,* 108–137.

D'Augelli, A. R., Hershberger, S. L., & Pilkington, N. W. (1998). Lesbian, gay and bisexual youth and their families: Disclosure of sexual orientation and its consequences. *American Journal of Orthopsychiatry, 68,* 361–371.

D'Augelli, P., & Patterson, C. (Eds.). (1995). *Lesbian, gay and bisexual identities over the lifespan.* New York: Oxford University Press.

Davies, D. (2004). *Child development: A practitioner's guide* (2nd ed.). New York: Guilford Press.

Davis, E. (1995, March). *Untitled presentation to Mimi.* White house conference on grandparents raising grandchildren. University College, University of Maryland, College Park, Maryland.

Dawson, P., & Guare, R. (2004). *Executive skills in children and adolescents.* New York: Guilford Press.

Day, P. (1989). *A new history of social welfare.* Englewood Cliffs, NJ: Prentice Hall.

DeAngelis, T. (1997, November). Menopause symptoms vary among ethnic groups. *APA Monitor,* 16–17.

Deaux, K., Reid, A., Mizrahi, K., & Cotting, D. (1999). Connecting the person to the social: The function of social identification. In T.R. Tyler, R. M. Kramer, & O. P. John (Eds.), *The psychology of the social self* (pp. 91–113). Mahwah, NJ: Erlbaum.

DeBellis, M. D., Keshavan, M. S., Clark, D. B., Casey, B. J., Giedd, J. N., Boring, A. M., Frustaci, K., & Ryan, N. D. (1999). A. E. Bennett Research Award. Developmental traumatology. Part II, Brain development. *Biological Psychiatry, 45,* 1271–1284.

DeCasper, A. J., & Spence, M. J. (1986). Prenatal maternal speech influences newborns: Perceptions of speech sounds. *Infant Behavior and Development, 9,* 133–150.

DeFries, J. C., Plomin, R., & Fulker, D. W. (1994). *Nature and nurture during middle childhood.* Cambridge, MA: Blackwell.

DeGangi, G. (2000). *Pediatric disorders of regulation in affect and behavior: A therapist's guide to assessment and treatment.* San Diego, CA: Academic Press.

Degges-White, S., Rice, B., & Myers, J. E. (2000). Revisiting Cass' theory of sexual identity formation: A study of lesbian development. *Journal of Mental Health Counseling, 22*(4), 318–333.

DeHoyos, G., & Jensen, C. (1985). The systems approach in American social work. *Social Case-work: The Journal of Contemporary Social Work, 66*(8), 490–497.

Delgado, M. (1997). Role of Latina-owned beauty shops in a Latino community. *Social Work, 42*(5), 445–453.

Delgado, M. (1998). *Social work practice in non-traditional urban settings.* New York: Oxford University Press.

Delgado, M. (1998). Social services in Latino Communities: Research and Strategies. Binghampton, NY: Haworth.

Deming, W. E. (1986). *Out of the crisis.* New York: Random House.

Demo, D. H., & Allen, K. R. (1996). Diversity within lesbian and gay families: Challenges and implications for family theory and research. *Journal of Social and Personal Relationships, 13*(3), 415–434.

Denby, R. (1996). Resiliency and the African American community. In S. Logan (Ed.), *The Black Family* (pp. 144–163). Boulder, CO: Westview Press.

Denham, S. A., Blair, K. A., DeMulder, E., Levitas, J., Sawyer, K., Auerbach-Major, S., et al. (2003). Preschool emotional competence: pathway to social competence? *Child Development, 73,* 621–635.

Denny, D., (Ed.). (1998). *Current concepts in transgender identity.* New York: Garland.

Dentinger, E., & Clarkberg, M. (2002). Informal caregiving and retirement timing among men and women. *Journal of Family Issues, 23*(7), 857–879.

Department of Health and Human Services. (2004). www.aidsinfor.nih.gov/. Retrieved January 15, 2006.

Department of Health and Human Services. Administration on Aging. (2004, September). *For care-givers*. Retrieved October 21, 2005, from http://www.aoa.gov/eldfam

Department of Health and Human Services, Administration on Children and Families. (2005, July). *Child care and development fund*. Retrieved October 19, 2005, from http://www.acf.hhs.gov/programs/ccb/gen-info/ccdfdesc.htm

Department of Health and Human Services, Centers for Medicaid and Medicare Services. Retrieved October 13, 2005, from www.cms.hhs.gov/schip/ consumers.

DePoy, E., Gilmer, D., & Haslen, D. (2000, Spring). Adolescents with disabilities and chronic illness in transition: A community action needs assessment. *Disability Studies*, 17–25.

Derryberry, D., & Rothbart, M. K. (1997). Reactive and effortful processes in the organization of temperament. *Development and Psychopathology, 9*, 633–652.

Desai, L. (1999). Relational theory in a South Asian context: An example of the dynamics of identity development. *Work in Progress*, 86. Wellesley, MA: Stone Center Working Paper Series.

Devlieger, P. J., & Albrecht, G. L. (2000). Your experience is not my experience. *Journal of Disability Policy Studies, 11*(1), 51–60.

Devor, H. (2002). Who are "we"? Where sexual orientation meets gender identity. *Journal of Gay and Lesbian Psychotherapy, 6*(2), 5–19.

DeVries, M. (1996). Trauma in cultural perspective. In B. van der Kolk, A. McFarlane, & L. Weisaeth (Eds.), *Traumatic stress: The effects of overwhelming experience on mind, body and society* (pp. 398–416). New York: Guilford Press.

DeYoung, M., & Lowry, J. A. (l992). Traumatic bonding: Clinical implications in incest. *Child Welfare, 71*, 165.

Diaz, R. M. (1998). *Latino gay men and HIV*. New York: Routledge

Diaz, R. M., Ayala, G., Bein, E., Henne, J., & Marin, B. V. (2001). The impact of gay and bisexual Latino men: Findings from three U.S. cities. *American Journal of Public Health, 91*(6), 927–932.

DiClemente, C. C., & Velasquez, M. M. (2002). Motivational interviewing and the stages of change. In W. R. Rollnick & S. Rollnick (Eds.), Motivational interviewing: Preparing people for change (2nd ed.). New York: Guilford Press.

DiClemente, R. J. (1992). Epidemiology of AIDS, HIV prevalence, and HIV incidence among adolescents. *Journal of School Health, 62*(7), 325–330.

DiNitto, D. (2005). *Social welfare: Politics and public policy* (6th ed.). Boston: Pearson.

Dinnerstein, D. (1977). *The mermaid and the minotaur*. New York: Harper.

Disability Statistics Research Center. (1992). *United States National Health Interview Survey*. Retrieved November 24, 2005, from http://www.dsc.ucsf.edu

Diller, J. V. (1999). *Cultural diversity: A primer for the human services*. Belmont, CA: Brooks/Cole-Wadsworth.

Diwan, R. (2000). Relational wealth and the quality of life. *Journal of Socio-Economics, 29*, 305–340.

Doka, K. J., with Morgan, J. D. (1993). *Death and spirituality*. New York: Baywood.

Dokecki, P. R., Newbrough, J. R., & O'Gorman, R. T. (2001). Toward a community-oriented action research framework for spirituality: Community psychological and theological perspectives. *Journal of Community Psychology, 29*(5), 497–518.

Dombeck, M., & Karl, J. (1987). Spiritual issues in mental healthcare. *Journal of Religion and Health, 26*(3), 183–197.

Donner, S., & Miller, J. (2006). *The Road to Becoming an Anti-Racism Organization*. In A. Lightburn and P. Sessions (Eds) Community-Based Clinical Practice. Oxford, NY: Oxford University Press.

Downey, T. (1995, March). *Untitled presentation to Mimi*. White House Conference on grandparents raising grandchildren. University College, University of Maryland, College Park, MD.

DuBois, D. L., Felner, R. D., Lockerd, E. M., Parra, G. R., & Lopez, C. (2003). The quadripartite model revisited: Promoting positive mental health in children and adolescents. In M. A. Reinecke, F. M. Dattilio, & A. Freeman (Eds.), *Cognitive therapy with children and adolescents* (2nd ed., pp. 402–434). New York: Guilford Press.

Dudley-Marling, C. (2004). The social construction of learning disabilities. *Journal of Learning Disabilities, 37*(6), 482–489.

Duncan, G., Brooks-Gunn, J., & Klebanov, P. (1994). Economic deprivation and early development. *Child Development, 65*, 296–318.

Dunn, A. B., & Dawes, S. J. (1999). Spirituality-focused genograms: Keys to uncovering spiritual resources in African American families. *Journal of Multicultural Counseling & Development, 27*(4), 240–254.

Dunn, J., Cutting, A. L., & Fisher, N. (2002). Old friends, new friends: Predictors of children's perspective on their friends at school. *Child Development, 72*, 491–505.

Durand, V. M., & Mapstone, E. (1999). Pervasive developmental disorders. In W. K. Silverman & T. H. Ollendick (Eds.), *Developmental issues in the clinical treatment of children* (pp. 307–317). Boston: Allyn & Bacon.

Dutton, D., & S. L. Paintere. (1981). Trauma bonding. *Victimology: An International Journal, 6*(1–4), 139–155.

Dutton, D. G., & Painter, S. (1993). Battered women syndrome: Effects of severity and intermittency of abuse. *American Journal of Orthopsychiatry, 63*, 614–27.

Dwyer, D. C., Smokowski, P. R., Bricout, J. C., & Wodarski, J. S. (1996). Domestic violence and woman battering: Theories and practice. In A. R. Roberts (Ed.), *Helping battered women: New perspectives and remedies*. New York: Oxford University Press.

Dziegielewski, S. F., Heyman, C., Green, C., & Gichia, J. E. (2002). Midlife changes: Utilizing a social work perspective. *Journal of Human Behavior in the Social Environment, 6*(4), 6–86.

Easterbrooks, M. A., & Goldberg, W. A. (1990). Security of toddler–parent attachment: Relation to children's sociopersonality functioning during kindergarten. In M. T. Greenberg, D. Cicchetti, & E. M. Cummings (Eds.), *Attachment in the preschool years: Theory, research and intervention* (pp. 221–224). Chicago: University of Chicago Press.

Eckert, J. W., & Shulman, S. C. (1996). Daughters caring for their aging mothers: A midlife developmental process. *Journal of Gerontological Social Work, 25*(3/4), 17–32.

Eckert, T. L., McGoey, K. M., & DuPaul, G. J. (1996). *Preschool-aged children at risk for ADHD: A needs assessment*. Paper presented at the annual meeting of the Association for the Advancement of Behavior Therapy, New York.

Eifert, G. H., & Forsyth, J. P. (Eds.). (2005). *Acceptance and commitment therapy for anxiety disorders: A practitioner's treatment guide to using mindfulness, acceptance, and values-based change strategies*. Oakland, CA: New Harbinger Publications.

Eisenberg, J. F. (1966). The social organization of mammals. *Handbuch Zoologie, 8*, 1–92.

Eisenberg, N., & Fabes, R. A. (1998). Prosocial development. In N. Eisenberg (Ed.), *Handbook of child psychology. Vol. 3. Social, emotional, and personality development* (5th ed., pp. 701–778). New York: Wiley.

Eisenbruch, M. (1991). From posttraumatic stress disorder to cultural bereavement: Diagnosis of Southeast Asian refugees. *Social Science and Medicine, 33*(6), 673–680.

Elbaum, B., & Vaughn, S. (2003). Self concept and students with learning disabilities. In H. L. Swanson, K. R. Harris, & S. Graham (Eds.), *Handbook of learning disabilities* (pp. 229–241). New York: Guilford Press.

Elder, S. H. (1992). The life course. In E. Borgatta & M. Borgatta (Eds.), *Encyclopedia of sociology*. New York: Macmillan.

Elder, S. H. (1996). *Children of the great depression: Social change in life experience* (Rev. ed.). Boulder, CO: Westview.

Eliason, M. J. (1996). Identity formation for lesbian, bisexual, and gay persons: Beyond a "minoritizing" view. *Journal of Homosexuality, 30*(3), 31–58.

Eli Lilly & Company. (2004). *Bipolar help center*. Retrieved August 21, 2004, from http://www.bipolardisorders.com

Elkind, D. (1971). The development of religious understanding in children and adolescents. In M. P. Strommen (Ed.), *Research on religious development: A comprehensive handbook* (pp. 655–685). New York: Hawthorn Books.

Elkins, D. N., Hedstrom, L. J., Hughes, L. L., Leaf, J. A., & Saunders, C. (1988). Toward a humanistic-phenomenological spirituality: Definition, description and measurement. *Journal of Humanistic Psychology, 28*(4), 5–18.

Ellenberg, L. (1999). Executive functions in children with learning disabilities and attention deficit disorder. In J. A. Incorvaia, B. S. Mark-Goldstein, & D. Tessmer (Eds.), *Understanding, diagnosing and treating AD/HD in children and adolescents: An integrative approach* (pp. 197–219). Northvale, NJ: Jason Aronson.

Ellis, S. J. (2000). Ego-identity development and the well-adjusted lesbian: Reclaiming Marcia's identity status model. *Feminism & Psychology, 10*(1), 147–151.

Elman, C., & O'Rand, A. M. (1998). Midlife work pathways and educational reentry. *Research on Aging, 20*(4), 475–506.

Elson, M. (1986). *Self psychology in clinical social work*. New York: Norton.

Emde, R. N., & Buchsbaum, H. K. (1990). "Didn't you hear my mommy?" Autonomy with connectedness in moral self-emergence. In D. Cicchetti, & M. Beeghly (Eds.), *Development of the self through transition* (pp. 35–60). Chicago: University of Chicago Press.

Emerson, R. (1962). Power–dependence relations. *American Sociological Review, 17*(27), 31–41.

Enright, R. D. (2001). *Forgiveness is a choice: A step-by-step process for resolving anger and restoring hope*. Washington, DC: American Psychological Association.

Epstein, M. (1995). *Thoughts without a thinker*. New York: Basic Books.

Epstein, S. (1994). An integration of the cognitive and the psychodynamic unconscious. *American Psychologist, 49*, 709–724.

Epstein, S., & Meier, P. (1989). Constructive thinking: A broad coping variable with specific components. *Journal of Personality and Social Psychology, 57*, 332–350.

Erikson, E. H. (1950). *Childhood and society* (2nd ed.). New York: Norton.

Erikson, E. H. (1951). *Childhood and society*. London: Imago.

Erikson, E. H. (1956). The problem of ego identity. *Journal of the American Psychoanalytic Association, 4*(56), 121.

Erikson, E. H. (1958). *Young man Luther*. New York: Norton.

Erikson, E. H. (1959/1980). *Identity and the life cycle*. New York: Norton.

Erikson, E. H. (1963). *Childhood and society* (2nd ed.). New York: Norton.

Erikson, E. H. (1968a). *Identity, youth and crisis*. New York: Norton.

Erikson, E. H. (1968b). Life cycle. In D. L. Sills (Ed.), *International encyclopedia of the social sciences* (Vol. 9). New York: Crowell, Collier.

Erikson, E. H. (1972). Play and actuality. In M. W. Piers (Ed.), *Play and development* (pp. 127–167). New York: Norton.

Erikson, E. H. (1975). *Life history and the historical moment*. New York: Norton.

Erlichman, K. L. (2001). Together we build a mishkan: Integrating Jewish spirituality into feminist social work practice. Co-published simultaneously in *Women and Therapy, 24*(3/4), 35–53, and in E. Kaschak (Ed.), *The Invisible Alliance: Psyche and Spirit in Feminist Therapy* (pp. 35–53). Hawthorne, New York: Haworth Press.

Eth, S., & Pynoos, E. (Eds.). (1985). *Post traumatic stress disorder in children*. Washington, DC: American Psychiatric Press.

Evans, G. (2004). The Environment of Childhood Poverty. *American Psychologist 59*, 77–92.

Evans, N. J., & D'Augelli, A. R. (1996). Lesbians, gay men, and bisexual people in college. In R. C. Savin-Williams & K. M. Cohen (Eds.), *The lives of lesbians, gays and bisexuals* (pp. 201–226). Orlando, FL: Harcourt Brace.

Eyerman, R. (2003). *Cultural trauma, slavery, and the formation of African American identity*. Cambridge: Cambridge University Press.

Fadiman, A. (1997). *The spirit catches you and you fall down: A Hmong child, her American doctors, and the collusion of two cultures*. New York: Farrar, Straus, & Giroux.

Fagot, B., & Leinbach, M. (1986). Gender identity: Some thoughts on an old concept. *Journal of American Academy of Child Psychiatry, 24*, 684–688.

Fagot, B., & Leinbach, M. (1989). The young child's gender schema: Environmental input, internal organization. *Child Development, 60*, 663–672.

Fagot, B., Leinback, M., & Hagan, R. (1986). Gender labeling and the adoption of sex-typed behaviors. *Developmental Psychology, 22*, 440–443.

Fairbairn, W. R. D. (1952). *An object relations theory of the personality*. New York: Basic Books.

Fairburn, C., & Brownell, K. (Eds.). (2002). *Eating disorders and obesity: A comprehensive handbook* (2nd ed.). New York: Guilford Press.

Fairburn, C., & Wilson, G. (Eds.). (1996). *Binge eating: Nature, assessment, and treatment*. New York: Guilford Press.

Fawcett, B. (2000). *Feminist perspectives on disability*. Essex, UK: Pearson Education.

Federal Bureau of Investigation (FBI). (2000). *Uniform crime reports*. Retrieved November 24, 2005, from http://www.fbi.gov/ucr/00cius.htm

Feeney, J. A. (1999). Adult romantic attachment and couple relationships. In J. Cassidy & P. R. Shaver (Eds.), *Handbook of attachment: Theory, research, and clinical applications*. New York: Guilford Press.

Feeney, J. A., & Noller, P. (1990). Attachment style as a predictor of adult romantic relationships. *Journal of Personality and Social Psychology, 58*, 281–291.

Feeney, J. A., Noller, P., & Callan, V. J. (1994). Attachment style, communication and satisfaction in the early years of marriage. In K. Bartholomew & D. Perlman (Eds.), *Advances in personal relationships: Vol. 5. Attachment processes in adulthood* (pp. 269–308). London: Jessica Kingsley.

Feifel, H. (1990). Psychology and death: Meaningful rediscovery. *American Psychologist, 45*, 537–43.

Feingold, A. (1994). Gender differences in personality: A meta-analysis. *Psychological Bulletin, 116*, 429–456.

Feldman, R. F. (1997). *Development across the lifespan*. Upper Saddle River, NJ: Prentice Hall.

Fellin, P. (2001). *The community and the social worker* (3d ed.). Itasca, IL: F.E. Peacock.

Fiedler, R. (1967). *A theory of leadership effectiveness*. New York: McGraw-Hill.

Fiering, C., Taska, L., & Lewis, M. (1998). The role of shame and attributional style in children's and adolescent's adaptation to sexual abuse. *Child Maltreatment, 3*, 129–142.

Figley, C. R. (Ed.). (2002). *Treating compassion fatigue*. New York: Brunner-Routledge.

Figley, C. R. (1999). Compassion fatigue as secondary traumatic stress disorder: An overview. In C. R. Figley (Ed.), *Compassion fatigue: Coping with secondary traumatic stress disorder in those who treat the traumatized* (pp. 1–20), New York: Brunner/Mazel.

Figley, C. R. (1995). *Compassion fatigue: Coping with secondary traumatic stress disorder in those who treat the traumatized.* Levittown, PA: Brunner/Mazel.

Finkel, M. (2000). Initial medical management of the sexually abused child. In R. Reece (Ed.), *Treatment of child abuse: Common ground for mental health, medical and legal practitioners* (pp. 3–13). Baltimore: Johns Hopkins University Press.

Finkelhor, D. (1995). The victimization of children: A developmental perspective. *American Journal of Orthopsychiatry, 65,* 177–193.

Finley, G. E. (1999). Children of adoptive families. In W. K. Silverman & T. H. Ollendick (Eds.), *Developmental Issues in the clinical treatment of children.* Boston: Allyn & Bacon

Fiori, K. L., Hays, J. C., & Meador, K. G. (2004). Spiritual turning points and perceived control over the life course. *International Journal of Aging and Human Development, 59*(4), 391–420.

Fisher, R., & Karger, H. J. (1997). *Social work and community in a private world.* New York: Longman.

Flanigan, H. (1992). *Forgiving the unforgivable.* New York: Macmillan.

Flavell, J. H. (2000). Development of children's knowledge about the mental world. *International Journal of Behavioral Development, 24,* 15–23.

Fleischer, D. Z., & Zames, Z. (1998, Spring). Disability rights. *Social Policy,* 52–55.

Foa, E. B., Keane, T. M., & Friedman, M. J. (2004). *Effective treatments for PTSD: Practice guidelines from the International Society for Traumatic Stress Studies.* New York: Guilford Press.

Folkman, S., & Greer, S. (2000). Promoting psychological well being in the face of serious illness: When theory, research and practice inform each other. *PsychoOncology, 9,* 11–19.

Follette, V., Ruzek, J., & Abueg, F. (Eds.). (1998). *Cognitive-behavioral therapies for trauma.* New York: Guilford Press.

Fonagy, P., & Target, M. (2003). *Psychoanalytic theories: Perspectives from developmental psychology.* NY: Routledge.

Fontaine, J. H. (1996). Counseling issues with gay and lesbian adolescents. *Adolescence, 31*(124), 817–830.

Fontaine, J. H., & Hammond, N. L. (1996). Counseling issues with gay and lesbian adolescents. *Adolescence, 31,* 817–830.

Ford, A. B. (1999). Physical and functional health. In M. L. Wykle & A. B. Ford (Eds.), *Serving minority elders in the 21st century.* New York: Springer.

Forsyth, D. (1999). *Group dynamics* (3rd ed.). Belmont, CA: Wadsworth.

Foster, S. (1996). Doing research in deafness: Some considerations and strategies. In P. C. Higgins & J. Nash (Eds.), *Understanding deafness socially: Continuities in research and theories.* Springfield, IL: Charles C. Thomas.

Fouad, N. A., & Brown, M. T. (2000). Role of race and social class in development: Implications for counseling psychology. In S. D. Brown & R. W. Lent (Eds.), *Handbook of counseling psychology* (3rd ed., pp. 379–408). New York: Wiley.

Fowler, J. W. (1981). *Stages of faith: The psychology of human development and the quest for meaning.* San Francisco: Harper & Row.

Fowler, J. W. (1991). Stages in faith consciousness. In F. K. Oser & W. G. Scarlett (Eds.), *Religious development in childhood and adolescence* (pp. 27–45). San Francisco: Jossey-Bass.

Fowles, D. C., & Kochanska, G. (2000). Temperament as a moderator of pathways to conscience in children: The contribution of electrodermal activity. *Psychophysiology, 37,* 788–795.

Fox, M. (1994). *The reinvention of work: A new vision of livelihood for our time.* San Francisco: Harper-San Francisco.

Fox, N. A., Bell, M. A., & Jones, N. A. (1992). Individual differences in response to stress and cerebral asymmetry. *Developmental Neuropsychology, 8,* 161–184.

Fox, N. A., Calkins, S. D., & Bell, M. A. (1994). Neural plasticity and development in the first two years of life: Evidence from cognitive and socioemotional domains of research. *Development and Psychopathology, 6,* 677–696.

Fox, R. (1995). Bisexual identities. In C. J. Patterson & A. R. D'Augelli (Eds.), *Lesbian, gay and bisexual identities in families: Psychological perspectives.* New York: Oxford University Press.

Fox, Piven, F. (2003). Plenary remarks at rediscovering the other America: A national forum on poverty and inequality. *Journal of Poverty,* 7(3), 1–11.

Frable, D. E. S. (1989). Sex typing and gender ideology: Two facets of the individual's gender psychology that go together. *Journal of Personality & Social Psychology, 56,* 95–108.

Frable, D. E. S. (1997). Gender, racial, ethnic, sexual and class identities. *Annual Review of Psychology, 48,* 139–162.

Fracasso, M. P., & Busch-Rossnagel, N. A. (1992). Parents and children of Hispanic origin. In M. E. Procidano, & C. B. Fisher (Eds.), *Contemporary families* (pp. 83–98). New York: Teachers College Press.

Frame, M. W., Williams, C. B., & Green, E., (1999). Balm in Gilead: Spiritual dimensions in counseling African American women. *Journal of Multicultural Counseling and Development, 27* (pp. 182–192).

Frank, A. (1995). *The wounded storyteller*. Chicago: University of Chicago Press.

Franklin, C., & Corcoran, J. (2000). Preventing adolescent pregnancy: A review of programs and practices. *Social Work, 45*, 40–52.

Franz, C. E. (1997). Stability and change in the transition to midlife: A longitudinal study of midlife adults. In M. Lahman, & J. B. James (Eds.), *Multiple paths of midlife development* (pp. 45–66). Chicago: University of Chicago Press.

Fraser, M. W., & Galinsky, M. J. (2004). Risk and resilience in childhood: Toward an evidence-based model of practice. In M. Fraser (Ed.), *Risk and resilience in childhood: An ecological perspective* (pp. 385–402). Washington, DC: NASW Press.

Fraser, M. W., Kirby, L. D., & Smokowski, P. R. (2004). Risk and resilience in childhood: An ecological perspective. In M. W. Fraser, L. D. Kirby, & P. R. Smokowski (Eds.), *Risk and resilience in childhood: An ecological perspective* (pp. 13–66). Washington DC: NASW Press.

Frazier, E. F. (1924a). Discussion. *Opportunity, 2*, 239.

Frazier, E. F. (1924b). A Negro industrial group. *The Howard University Review, 1*, 196–232.

Frazier, E. F. (1924c). A note on Negro education. *Opportunity, 2*, 144.

Frazier, E. F. (1924d). Social work in race relations. *Crisis, 27*, 252–254.

Frazier, E. F. (1926). Family life of the Negro in the small town. *Proceedings of the National Conference of Social Work* (pp. 384–388).

Frazier, E. F. (1927). The pathology of race prejudice. *Forum, 70*, 856–861.

Freeman, A., & M. Reinecke. (1995). Cognitive therapy. In A. Gurman & S. Messer (Eds.), *Essential psychotherapies: Theory and practice* (pp. 182–115). New York: Guilford Press.

French, J. R. P., & Raven, B. (1959). The bases of social power. In D. Cartwright & A. Zander (Eds.), *Group dynamics. Research and theory* (3rd ed., pp. 259–269). New York: Elmsford, Row, Peterson and Co.

Freud, A. (1936a). *The ego and the mechanisms of defense*. New York: International Universities Press, 1966.

Freud, A. (1936b). Instinctual anxiety during puberty. In A. Esman (Ed.), *The psychology of adolescence* (pp. 109–121). New York: International Universities Press.

Freud, S. (1895/1966). Project for a scientific psychology. In J. Strachey (Ed. & Trans.), *The standard edition of the complete psychological works of Sigmund Freud* (Vol. 1, pp. 281–397). London: Hogarth Press. (Original work published 1895)

Freud, S. (1905). *Three essays on the theory of sexuality*. Standard ed. (Vol. 7, pp. 125–245). London: Hogarth Press.

Freud, S. (1911). *Formulations on the two principles of mental functioning*. Standard ed. (Vol. 12, pp. 218–226). London: Hogarth Press.

Freud, S. (1912–1913). *Totem and taboo*. Standard ed. (Vol. 13, pp. 1–162). London: Hogarth Press.

Freud, S. (1915). *Instincts and their vicissitudes*. Standard ed. (Vol. 14, pp. 117–140). London: Hogarth Press.

Freud, S. (1920). *Beyond the pleasure principle*. Standard ed. (Vol. 18, pp. 3–64). London: Hogarth Press.

Freud, S. (1921/1949). Group psychology and the analysis of the ego. *Standard Edition of the complete works of Sigmund Freud* (Vol. 18, pp. 65–143). London: Hogarth Press, 1953–1974.

Freud, S. (1923). The ego and the id. *Standard edition of the complete psychological works of Sigmund Freud* (Vol. 19, pp. 1–66). London: Hogarth Press, 1953–1974.

Freud, S. (1925/1961). Some psychical consequences of the anatomical differences between the sexes. In J. Strachey (Ed. & Trans.), *Standard edition of the complete works of Sigmund Freud* (Vol. 19, pp. 241–248). London: Hogarth Press.

Freud, S. (1926). *Inhibitions, symptoms and anxiety*. Standard ed. (Vol. 20, pp. 75–175). London: Hogarth Press.

Freud, S. (1929/1955). Three essays on the theory of sexuality. In J. Strachey (Ed.), *The standard edition of the complete psychological works of Sigmund Freud* (Vol. 7). London: Hogarth Press.

Freud, S. (1930). *Civilization and its discontents*. Standard ed. (Vol. 21, pp. 59–145). London: Hogarth Press.

Freud, S. (1933/1964). New introductory letters in psychoanalysis. In J. Strachey (Ed. & Trans.), *Standard edition of the complete works of Sigmund Freud* (Vol. 22, pp. 1–182). London: Hogarth Press.

Freud, S. (1939). *An outline of psychoanalysis*. Standard ed. London: Hogarth Press.

Frey, V., & Ruble, D. (1992). Gender constancy and the "cost" of sex-typed behavior: A conflict hypotheses. *Developmental Psychology, 28*, 714–21.

Frey, W. (1990). Metropolitan America: Beyond the transition. *Population Bulletin, 45*(2), 3–42.

Friedberg, R. D., & McClure, J. M. (2002). *Clinical practice of cognitive therapy with children and adolescents: The nuts and bolts*. New York: Guilford Press.

Friedman, D., Berman, S., & Hamberger, M. (1993). Recognition memory and ERPs: Age-related changes in young, middle-aged, and elderly adults. *Journal of Psychophysiology, 17*, 181–201.

Friedman, E. H. (1971). Ethnic identity as extended family in Jewish-Christian marriage. In J. O. Bradt &

C. J. Moynihan (Eds.), *Systems therapy*. Washington, DC: Bradt and Moynihan.

Friedman, M. L., Friedlander, M. L., & Bluestein, D. L. (2005). Toward an understanding of Jewish identity: A phenomenological study. *Journal of Counseling Psychology, 52*(1), 17–83.

Friedman, N. (2006). Posttraumatic stress disorder among military returnees from Afghanistan and Iraq. *American Journal of Psychiatry, 163,*(4), 586–593.

Friend, R. A. (1990). Older lesbian and gay people: Responding to homophobia. *Marriage and Family Review, 14,* 241–263.

Friend, R. A. (1991). Older lesbian and gay people: A theory of successful aging. *Journal of Homosexuality,* 20, 99–118.

Friend, R. A. (1998). Heterosexism, homophobia, and the culture of schooling. In S. Books (Ed.), *Invisible children in the society and its schools* (pp. 137–166). Mahwah, NJ: Erlbaum.

Fries, J. F. (1990). The sunny side of aging. In H. R. Moody (Ed.), *Aging: Concepts and controversies* (4th ed., pp. 344–347). Thousands Oaks, CA: Pine Forge Press.

Frombonne, L. (2002). Prevalence of childhood disintegrative disorder. *Autism, 6*(2), 149–157.

Frumkin, P. Andre-Clarke, A. (2000). When missions, markers and politics collide: Values and strategy in the non-profit human services. *Non-profit and Voluntary Sector Quarterly, 29*(1), 141–163.

Fujiura, G. T., & Yamaki, K. (2000). Trends in demography of childhood poverty and disability. *Exceptional Children, 66,* 187–199.

Fuller-Thompson, E., & Minkler, A. (2002). African American grandparents raising grandchildren: A national profile of demographic and health characteristics. *Health and Social Work, 25*(2), 109–118.

Furman, R., & Negi, N. J. (2007). Social work practice with transnational Latino populations. *International Social Work, 50*(1), 107–112

Gagne, P., & Tewksbury, R. (1996). No man's land: Transgenderism and the stigma of the feminine man. In M. J. Segal & V. Demos (Eds.), *Advances in gender research*. Greenwich, CT: JAI Press.

Gagne, P., Tewksbury, R., & McGaughey, D. (1997). Coming out and crossing over: Identity formation and proclamation in a transgender community. *Gender and Society, 11*(4), 478–508.

Galambos, C. M. (2004). Social work practice with people with disabilities: Are we doing enough? *Health and Social Work, 29*(3).

Gallo-Lopez, L. (2000). A creative play therapy approach to the group treatment of young sexually abused children. In H. G. Kaduson & C. E. Schaefer (Eds.), *Short-term play therapy for children* (pp. 269–296). New York: Guilford Press.

Gannon, S., & Korn, S. J. (1983). Temperament, cultural variation, and behavior disorder in preschool children. *Child Psychiatry and Human Development, 13,* 203–212.

Ganzer, C., & Ornstein, E. D. (2002). A sea of trouble: A relational approach to the culturally sensitive treatment of a severely disturbed client. *Clinical Social Work Journal, 30*(2), 127–144.

Garbarino, J. (1999). *Lost boys: Why our sons turn violent and how we can save them.* New York: Free Press.

Garden, S. E., Phillips, L. H., & MacPherson, S. E. (2001). Midlife aging, open-ended planning, and laboratory measures of executive function. *Neuropsychology, 15*(4), 472–482.

Gardner, H. (1983). *Frames of mind: The theory of multiple intelligences*. New York: Basic Books.

Gardner, H. (1993). *Multiple intelligences: The theory in practice*. New York: Basic Books.

Gardner, J. R. (1999). Using self psychology in brief psychotherapy. *Psychoanalytic Social Work, 6*(3/4), 43–85.

Garland, J. A., Jones, H. E., & Kolodny, R. L. (1973). A model for stages of development in social work groups. In S. Bernstein (Ed.), *Explorations in group work* (pp. 17–71). Boston: Milford House.

Garner, D. M., & Garfinkel, P. E. (Eds.). (1997). *Handbook of treatment for eating disorders* (2nd ed.). New York: Guilford Press.

Garrison, V. (1978). Support systems of schizophrenic and non-schizophrenic Puerto Rican women in New York City. *Schizophrenia Bulletin, 4,* 561–596.

Gastil, J. (1994). A definition and illustration of democratic leadership. *Human Relations, 47*(8), 953–975.

Gatson, M., & Porter, G. K. (2001). *Primetime: The African American women's complete guide to midlife health and wellness.* New York: Ballantine.

Geary, D. C. (1998). *Male, female: The evolution of human sex differences*. Washington, DC: American.

General Accounting Office (2004). Defense of Marriage Act: Update prior to report, GAO-04-353R. Retrieved October 23, 2004 from http://www.goa.gov/n.items/dp4353r.pdf

George, C., & Solomon, J. (1999). Attachment and caregiving: The caregiving behavioral system. In J. Cassidy & P. R. Shaver (Eds.), *Handbook of attachment* (pp. 3–20). New York: Guilford Press.

Germain, C. (1979a). *General system theory and ego psychology, an ecological perspective*. New York: Columbia University Press.

Germain, C. (1979b). *Social work practice: People and environments, an ecological perspective*. New York: Columbia University Press.

Germain, C. (1979c). Space, an ecological variable in social work practice. *Social Work, 59*, 515–522.

Germain, C. (1981). The ecological approach to people environment transactions. *Social Casework, 62*, 323–331.

Germain, C. (1987). Ecological perspective. In *Encyclopedia of social work* (18th ed., Vol. 1). Silver Spring, MD: National Association of Social Workers.

Germain, C. (1991). *Human behavior in the social environment: An ecological view*. New York: Columbia University Press.

Germain, C. B., & Bloom, M. (1999). *Human behavior in the social environment*. New York: Columbia University Press.

Germain, C. B., & Gitterman, A. (1979). The Life Model of Social Work Practice. In F. Turner (Ed.), *Social Work Treatment*. New York; Free Press

Germain, C. B., & Gitterman, A. (1980). *The life model of social work practice*. New York: Columbia University Press

Germer, C. K. (2009). The mindful path to self compassion: Freeing yourself from destructive thoughts and emotions. New York: Guilford Press.

Germer, C. K., Siegel, R. D., & Fulton, P. R. (2005). *Mindfulness and psychotherapy*. New York: The Guilford Press.

Gfroerer, J. C. (2002). Substance abuse treatment need among older adults in 2020: The impact of the aging baby-boom cohort. *Drug and Alcohol Dependence, 69*(2), 127–135. Retrieved January 1, 2009, from http://linkinghub.elsevier.com/retrieve/pii/S0376871602003071

Gfroerer, J. C., Greenblatt, J. C., & Wright, D. A. (1997). Substance use in the U.S. college-age population: Differences according to educational status and living arrangement. *American Journal of Public Health, 87*, 62–65.

Giannino, A., & Tronick, E. Z. (1986). Interactive mismatch and repair: Challenges to the coping infant: Zero to three. *Bulletin of the Center for Clinical Infant Programs, 6*(3), 1–6.

Giannino, A., & Tronick, E. Z. (1998). The mutual regulation model: The infant's self and interactive regulation and coping and defensive capacities. In T. Field et al. (Eds.), *Stress and coping across development* (pp. 47–68). Hillsdale, NJ: Erlbaum.

Gibbs, J. T. (2003). *Children of color: Psychological interventions with culturally diverse youth*. San Francisco: Jossey-Bass.

Gibbs, P., Locke, B. L., & Lohmann, R. (1990). Paradigm for the generalist-advanced generalist continuum. *Journal of Social Work Education, 26*(3), 323–343.

Gibelman, M., & Demone, H. W., Jr. (Eds.). (1998). *The privatization of human services*. New York: Springer.

Gibelman, M., & Demone, H, Jr. (2002). The commercialization of health and human services: national phenomena or cause for concern? *Families in Society, 83*(4), 387–397.

Gibelman, M., & Furman, R. (2008). Navigating Human Services Organizations (2nd Ed.). Chicago, Ill.: Lyceum Books, Inc.

Gil, E. (1991). *The healing power of play*. New York: Guilford Press.

Gil, E., & Drewes, A. A. (Eds.). (2005). *Cultural issues in play therapy*. New York: Guilford Press.

Gilbert, N., & Specht, H. (1974). *Dimensions of social welfare policy*. Englewood Cliffs, NJ: Prentice Hall.

Gilbert, N., & Terrell, P. (2005). *Dimensions of social welfare policy* (6th ed.). Boston: Pearson.

Gill, C. J. (1995). A psychological view of disability culture. *Disability Studies Quarterly, 15*(4), 16–19.

Gilligan, C. (1982a). Adult development and women's development: Arrangements for a marriage. In J. Gield (Ed.), *Women in the middle years*. New York: Wiley.

Gilligan, C. (1982b). *In a different voice: Psychological theory and women's development*. Cambridge, MA: Harvard University Press.

Gilligan, C. (1990). Joining the resistance: Psychology, politics, girls, and women. *Michigan Quarterly Review, 29*(4), 501–531.

Gilligan, C. (1991). Women's psychological development: Implications for psychotherapy. In C. Gilligan, A. Rogers, & D. L. Tolman (Eds.), *Women, girls, and psychotherapy: Reframing resistance*. Binghamton, NY: Harrington Park Press.

Gilligan, C. (1996). The centrality of relationships in human development: A puzzle, some evidence and a theory. In G. D. Noam & K. W. Fischer (Eds.), *Development and vulnerability in close relationship* (pp. 237–261). Mahwah, NJ: Erlbaum.

Gilson, S. F., & DePoy, E. (2000). Multiculturalism and disability: A critical perspective. *Disability and Society, 15*(2), 207–218.

Ginsberg, J. I. D., Mann, R. E., Rotgers, F., & Weekes, J. R. (2002). Motivational interviewing with criminal justice populations. In W. R. Miller & S. Rollnick (Eds.), *Motivational interviewing: Preparing people for change* (2nd ed., pp. 333–346). New York: Guilford Press.

Ginsberg, L., Nackerud, L., & Larrison, C. R. (2004). *Human biology for social workers: Development, ecology, genetics and health*. Boston: Allyn & Bacon.

Gitterman, A. (2004). The mutual aid model. In C. D. Garvin, L. M. Gutierrez, & M. J. Galinsky (Eds.), *Handbook of social work with groups*. New York: Guilford Press.

Glaxo Smith Kline. (n.d.). www.depression.com/types_of_depression.html

Goldberg, E. (2001). *The executive brain: Frontal lobes and the civilized mind*. New York: Oxford University Press.

Goldberg, R. (1973). A psychotherapy of narcissistic injuries. *Archives of General Psychiatry, 28*, 722–726.

Golden, C. (1994). Our politics and choices: The feminist movement and sexual orientation. In B. Greene & G. Herek (Eds.), *Lesbian and gay psychology: Theory, research and clinical applications* (pp. 54–70). Newbury Park, CA: Sage.

Goldstein, E. (1984). *Ego psychology and social work practice*. New York: Free Press.

Goldstein, E. (1996). Ego psychology theory. In F. Turner (Ed.), *Social work treatment: Interlocking theoretical approaches* (4th ed., pp. 168–191). New York: Free Press.

Golembiewski, R. T. (1995). Managing Diversity in Organizations. Tuscaloosa: University of Alabama Press.

Golumbok, S., Cook, R., Bish, A., & Murray, C. (1995). Families created by the new reproductive technologies: Quality of parenting and social and emotional development of the children. *Child Development, 66*, 285–298.

Gondolph, E. W., & Fisher, E. R. (1988). *Battered women as survivors: Alternatives to treating learned helplessness*. Lexington, MA: Lexington Books.

Gorman, C. (2000, July 17). Advice for caregivers: Three states of Alzheimer's. *Time*, pp. 44–45.

Gottfried, A. E., Fleming, J. S., & Gottfried, A. W. (1998). Role of cognitively stimulating home environment in children's academic intrinsic motivation: A longitudinal study. *Child Development, 69*(5), 1448–1460.

Gray, B. (1989). *Collaborating: Finding common ground for multiparty problems*. San Francisco: Jossey-Bass.

Gray, J. (1998). *False down: The delusion of global capitalism*. London: Granta Books.

Gray, M. R., & Steinberg, L. (1999). Unpacking authoritative parenting: Reassessing a multidimensional construct. *Journal of Marriage and the Family, 61*, 574–587.

Green, J. W. (1999). *Cultural Awareness in Human Services: A Multi-Ethnic Approach* (3rd Ed). Needham Hts. MA: Allyn and Bacon.

Green, R. J. (2007). Gay and Lesbian Couples in Therapy: a Social Justice Perspective. In *Advancing Social Justice through Clinical Practice*. Etiony Aldarondo (Ed.). Mahwah NJ: Lawrence Erlbaum Associates.

Green, M. C., & Luce, S. C. (Eds.). (1996). *Behavioral intervention for young children with autism: A manual for parents and professionals*. Austin, TX: Pro-Ed.

Greenberg, J., & Cheselka, O. (1995). Relational approaches to psychoanalytic psychotherapy. In A. S. Gurman & S. B. Messer (Eds.), *Essential psychotherapies: Theory and practice* (pp. 55–85). New York: Guilford Press.

Greenberg, J., & Mitchell, L. (1983). *Object relations in psychoanalytic theory*. Cambridge, MA: Harvard University Press.

Greenberg, S. (1994). Mutuality in families: A framework for continued growth in late life. *Journal of Geriatric Psychiatry, 26*(1), 79–96

Greene, B. (Ed.) (1997). *Ethnic and cultural diversity among lesbians and gay men*. Thousand Oaks, CA: Sage.

Greene, R. R. (1991a). General systems theory. In R. R. Greene & P. H. Ephross (Eds.), *Human behavior theory and social work practice*. New York: Aldine de Gruyter.

Greene, R. R. (1991b). Human behavior theory and professional social work practice. In R. R. Greene & P. H. Ephross (Eds.), *Human behavior theory and social work practice*. New York: Aldine de Gruyter.

Greene, R. R., & Ephross, P. H. (1991). *Human behavior theory and social work practice*. New York: Aldine de Gruyter.

Greene, T. P. (2001). *Psychotherapy and social class: Contradictions in providing patient care within the structures of capitalism*. PhD dissertation, Wright Institute Graduate School of Psychology, Berkeley, CA.

Greer, S. (1995). The psychological toll of cancer. In A. Horwich (Ed.), *Oncology* (pp. 189–198). London: Chapman & Hall.

Griffith, J. L., & Griffith, M. E. (2002). *Encountering the sacred in psychotherapy*. New York: Guilford Press.

Groce, N. E. (2004). Adolescents and youth with disability: Issues and challenges. *Asia Pacific Disability Rehabilitation Journal, 15*(2), 1–32.

Groce, N. E., & Zola, I. K. (1993). Multiculturalism, chronic illness, & disability. *Pediatrics, 91*(5), 1048–1055.

Grodstein, F., Manson, J. E., Colditz, G. A. , Willet, W. C., Speizer, E. E., & Stampfer, M. J. (2000). A prospective observational study of post-menopausal hormone therapy and primary prevention of cardiovascular disease. *Annals of Internal Medicine, 133*, 933–941.

Gross, J. (2005). Grandma helps to fill the void left by September 11 (February 1, 2002). *Themes of the Times for human behavior in the social environment*. Boston: Allyn & Bacon.

Grossman, A. H., D'Augelli, A. R., & Dragowski, E. A. (2007). Caregiving and care receiving among older lesbian, gay, and bisexual adults. *Journal of Gay & Lesbian Services, 18*(3/4), 15–38.

Grotevant, H. D., Miller Wrobel, G., van Dulmen, M. H., & McRoy, R. G. (2001, September). The emergence of psychosocial engagement in adopted adolescents: The family as context over time. *Journal of Adolescent Research, 16*(5), 469–490.

Guarente, L. (2004, January 9). Longevity: Immortality in a pill? *The Republican*, p. E01.

Guerney, B. G., Jr. (1969). Filial therapy: Description and rationale. In B. G. Guerney, Jr. (Ed.), *Psychotherapeutic agents: New roles for nonprofessionals, parents and teachers* (pp. 450–460). New York: Holt, Rinehart & Winston.

Guerney, B. G., Jr., Guerney, L., & Andronico, M. (1999). Filial therapy. In C. Schaefer (Ed.), *The therapeutic use of child's play* (pp. 553–566). Northvale, NJ: Jason Aronson.

Guerney, L. F. (1990). *Parenting adolescents: A supplement to parenting, a skills training program.* Silver Spring, MD: Ideals.

Guerra, N. G. (1993). Cognitive development. In P. H. Tolan, & B. J. Cohler (Eds.), *Handbook of clinical research and practice with adolescents* (pp. 45–62). New York: Wiley.

Gunnar, M. R., Bruce, J., & Grotevant, H. D. (2000). International adoption of institutionally reared children: Research and policy. *Development and Psychopathology, 12*, 677–693.

Gunnar, M. R., & Nelson, C. A. (1994). Event-related potentials in year-old infants: Relations with emotionality and cortisol. *Child Development, 65*, 80–94.

Guntrip, H. (1969). *Schizoid phenomena, object relations and the self.* New York: International Universities Press.

Guralnik, O., & Simeon, D. (2001). Psychodynamic theory and treatment of impulsive self-injurious behaviors. In D. Simeon & E. Hollander (Eds.), *Self injurious behaviors* (pp. 175–197). Washington DC: American Psychological Association.

Gusfield, J. R. (1975). *Community: A critical response.* New York: Harper and Row.

Gusman, F. D., Stewart, J., Young, B. H., Riney, J., Abueg, F. R., & Blake, D. D. (1996). A multicultural developmental approach for treating trauma. In A. J. Marsella, M. J. Friedman, E. T. Gerrity, & R. M. Scurfield (Eds.), *Ethnocultural aspects of post-traumatic stress disorder: Issues, research and clinical applications* (pp. 439–459). Washington, DC: American Psychological Association.

Hahn, H. (1981). The social component of sexuality and disability: Some problems and proposals. *Sexuality and Disability, 4*(4), 220–234.

Hahn, T. N. (1992). *Peace is every step.* New York: Bantam.

Hall, L. K. (2008) *Counseling Military Families: What Mental Health Professionals Need to Know.* New York: Routledge/Taylor and Francis Group.

Halpern, R. (1993). Poverty and infant development. In C. H. Zeanah, Jr. (Ed.), *Handbook of infant mental health* (pp. 73–86). New York: Guilford Press

Hamilton, B. E., Ventura, S. J., Martin, J. A., & Sutton, P. D. (2005). *Preliminary births for 2004.* Tables 1 and 2. National Center for Health Statistics, Hyattsville, Maryland. Retrieved December 1, 2005, from www.childtrendsdatabank.or/indicators79Birthrates.cf

Hamilton, C. E. (2000). Continuity and discontinuity of attachment from infancy through adolescence. *Child Development, 71*, 690–694.

Hammer, T., & Turner, P. (2001). *Parenting in contemporary society.* Boston: Allyn & Bacon.

Handmaker, N., Packard, M., & Conforti, K. (2002). Motivational interviewing in the treatment of dual disorders. In W. R. Miller & S. Rollnick (Eds.), *Motivational interviewing: Preparing people for change* (2nd ed., pp. 362–376). New York: The Guilford Press.

Hanna, F. J., Talley, W. B., & Guindon, M. H. (2000). The power of perception: Toward a model of cultural oppression and liberation. *Journal of Counseling and Development, 78*, 430–446.

Hardaway, T. G. (2000). Family play therapy and child psychiatry in an era of managed care. In H. G. Kaduson & C. E. Schaefer (Eds.), *Short-term play therapy for children* (pp. 256–269). New York: Guilford Press.

Hardcastle, D. A., & Powers, P. R. with Wenocur, S. (2004). *Community practice: Theories and skills for social workers* (2nd ed.). New York: Oxford University Press.

Hardcastle, D. A., Wenocur, S., & Powers, P. (1997). *Community practice: Theories and skills for social workers.* New York: Oxford University Press.

Harkness, S., & Super, C. M. (1990). Culture and Psychopathology. In M. Lewis and S. M. Miller (Eds.). *Handbook of Developmental Psychopathology* (pp. 41–52). New York: Plenum Press.

Harley, D. A., Jolivette, K., McCormick, K., & Tice, K. (2002). Race, class and gender: A constellation of positionalities with implications for counseling. *Journal of Multicultural Counseling & Development, 30*, 216–238.

Harrison, A. O., Wilson, M. N., Pine, C. J., Chan, S. Q., & Buriel, R (1994). Family ecologies of ethnic minority children. In G. Handel, & G. G. Whitchurch (Eds.), *The psychosocial interior of the family* (pp. 187–210). New York: Aldine de Gruyter.

Hart, C. H., Ladd, G. W., & Burleson, B. R. (1990). Children's expectations of the outcomes of social strategies: Relations with sociometric status and maternal disciplinary styles. *Child Development, 61,* 127–137.

Hart, C. H., Newell, L. D., & Olsen, S. F. (2002). Parenting skills and social/communicative competence in childhood. In J. O. Greene, & B. R. Burleson (Eds.), *Handbook of communication and social interaction skill.* Hillsdale, NJ: Erlbaum.

Hart, E. L., Lahey, B. B., Loeber, R., Applegate, B., & Frick, P. J. (1995). Developmental change in attention-deficit hyperactivity disorder in boys: A four-year longitudinal study. *Journal of Abnormal Child Psychology, 23,* 729–750.

Hart, N. (1994). The NEW! IMPROVED! Classless society. In J. Penelope (Ed.), *Out of the class closet: Lesbians speak* (pp. 384–389). Freedom, CA: Crossing Press.

Hartman, A. (1978). Diagrammatic assessment of family relationships. *Social Casework, 59,* 465–476.

Hartman, A., & Laird, J. (1983). *Family-centered social work practice.* New York: Free Press.

Hartman, H. (1939). *Ego psychology and the problem of adaptation.* New York: International Universities Press.

Hasenfeld, Y. (1983). *Human Service Organizations.* Englewood Cliffs, NJ: Prentice Hall.

Haug, H. (1991). Aging of the brain. In F. C. Ludwig (Ed.), *Life span extension: Consequences, intimacy and close relationships.* New York: Springer.

Havighurst, R. J. (1968). Personality and pattern of aging. *The Gerontologist, 8,* 20–23.

Havighurst, R. J. (1973). History of developmental psychology: Socialization and personality development. In P. B. Baltes & K. W. Schaie (Eds.), *Life-span developmental psychology* (pp. 3–24). New York: Academic Press.

Hayes, P. A. (2008). *Addressing cultural complexities in practice: Assessment, diagnosis and treatment* (2nd ed.). Washington, D.C.: American Psychological Association.

Hayes, S. C., Follette, V. M., & Linehan, M. (Eds.). (2004). *Mindfulness and acceptance: Expanding the cognitive-behavioral tradition.* New York: Guilford Press.

Hayghe, H. V. (1988). Employers and child care: What roles do they play? *Monthly Labor Review, 111*(9), 38–44.

Hayslip, B., & Kaminski, P. (2005). Grandparents raising their grandchildren: A review of the literature. *The Gerontologist, 45,* 262–269.

Hayward, M. D., Crimmins, E. M., & Saito, Y. (1998). Cause of death and active life expectancy in the older population of the United States. *Journal of Aging and Health, 10*(2), 192–213.

Hazan, C., & Shaver, P. R. (1987). Attachment as an organizational framework for research on close relationships. *Psychological Inquiry, 65,* 1–22.

Hedrick, S., Guihan, M., Chapko, M., Manheim, L., Sullivan, J., Thomas, M., Barry, S., & Zhou, A. (2007). Characteristics of residents and providers in the assisted living pilot program. *The Gerontologist, 47*(3), 365–377.

Hellreigel, D. and Slocum Jr., J. W. (2007). *Organizational behavior* (11th ed.). Mason, OH: South-western.

Helms, J. E. (1984). Toward a theoretical model of the effects of race on counseling: A black and white model. *Counseling Psychologist, 12,* 153–165.

Helms, J. E. (1990). *Black and white racial identity: Theory, research and practice.* Westport, CT: Greenwood Press.

Helms, J. E. (1995). An update of Helm's white and people of color racial identity models. In J. G. Ponterotto, J. M. Casas, L. A. Suzuki, & C. M. Alexander (Eds.), *Handbook of multicultural counseling* (pp. 181–198). Thousand Oaks, CA: Sage.

Hemingway, T. (1980). Prelude to change: Black Carolinas in the war years, 1914–1920. *Journal of Negro History, 65,* 212–227.

Henriksen, R. C., Jr. (2000). *Black/white biracial identity development: A grounded theory study.* PhD dissertation, Commerce Texas A & M University–Commerce.

Henriksen, R. C., Jr., & Trusty, J. (2004). Understanding and assisting black/white biracial women in their identity development. *Women & Therapy, 27*(1/2), 65–83.

Henry, B. (1993). *Black grandmotherhood: As it relates to infants of adolescent mothers.* PhD dissertation. Temple University, Philadelphia.

Hepworth, D. H., Rooney, R. H., & Larsen, J. (1997). *Direct social work practice: Theory and skills* (5th ed.). Pacific Grove, CA: Brooks/Cole.

Herdt, G. H. (2001). Stigma and the ethnographic study of HIV: Problems and prospects. *AIDS and Behavior, 5*(2), 141–148.

Herdt, G. H., Beeler, J., & Rawls, T. W. (1997). Life course diversity among older lesbians and gay men: A study in Chicago. *Journal of Gay, Lesbian, and Bisexual Identity, 2,* 231–246.

Herman, J. (1992). *Trauma and recovery.* New York: Basic Books.

Herman, M. R., Dornbusch, S. M., Herron, M. C., & Herting, J. R. (1997). The influence of family regulation, connection, and psychological autonomy on six measures of adolescent functioning. *Journal of Adolescent Research, 12,* 34–67.

Hernandez, M., & McGoldrick, M. (2005). Migration and the Family Life Cycle. In B. Carter & M. McGoldrick (Eds.). *The Expanded Family Life Cycle: Individual, Family and Social Perspectives* (3rd Ed). Boston, MA: Pearson/Allyn and Bacon.

Herrenkohl, T. I., Maguin, E., Hill, K. G., Hawkins, J. D., Abbott, R. D., & Catalano, R. F. (2000). Developmental risk factors for youth violence. *Journal of Adolescent Health, 26*(3), 176–186.

Hersov, L. (1994). Adoption. In M. Rutter, E. Taylor, & L. Hersov (Eds.), *Child and adolescent psychiatry: Modern approaches* (3rd ed., pp. 267–282). Oxford: Blackwell Scientific.

Hetherington, E. M., & Kelly, J. (2003). *For better or worse: Divorce reconsidered.* New York: Norton.

Hetherington, E. M., & Stanley-Hagan, M. (2000). Diversity among step-families. In D. H. Demo, K. R. Allen, & M. A. Fine (Eds.), *Handbook of family diversity* (pp. 173–196). New York: Oxford University Press.

Heuber, A. J., & Mancini, J. A. (2005). *Final report to the Military Family Research Institute and Department of Defense Qualify of Life Office.* Blacksburg, VA: Virginia Polytechnic Institute and State University, Department of Human Development.

Hick, S. F. (2008). Cultivating therapeutic relationships: The role of mindfulness. In S. F. Hick & T. Bien (Eds.), *Mindfulness and the therapeutic relationship* (pp. 3–19). New York: Guilford Press.

Higgins, P. C. (1992). *Making disability: Exploring the social transformation of human variation.* Springfield, IL: Charles C. Thomas.

Hill, R. (1998). Enhancing the resilience of African American families. *Journal of Human Behavior and the Social Environment, 1*(2/3), 49–61.

Hill, R., Billingsley, A., Engram, E., Malson, M., Rubin, R., Stack, C., Stewart, J., & Teele, F. (1993). *Research on the African American family.* Westport, CT: Auburn House.

Hill, S. W. (l995). *Theraplay: An overview.* Retrieved January 12, 2006, from www.angelfire.com/oh/avalancheDiode/THERAPLAY.html

Hillery, G. (1955). Definitions of community: Areas of agreement. *Rural Sociology, 20,* 111–123.

Hines, P. M. (2005). The Family Life Cycle of African American Families Living in Poverty. In B. Carter & M. McGoldrick (Eds.). *The Expanded Family Life Cycle: Individual, Family, and Social Perspectives* (3rd Ed.). Boston, MA: Pearson/Allyn and Bacon.

Hines, P. M. (1989). The family life cycle of poor black families. In B. Carter & M. McGoldrick (Eds.), *The changing family life cycle: A framework for family therapy* (2nd ed.). Boston: Allyn & Bacon.

Hines, P. M., & Boyd-Franklin, N. (1996). African American families. In M. McGoldrick, J. Giordano, & J. Pearce (Eds.), *Ethnicity and family therapy* (2nd ed., pp. 66–84). New York: Guilford Press.

Hinshaw, S. P. (1994). *Attention deficits and hyperactivity in children.* Thousand Oaks, CA: Sage.

Ho, M. K. (1987). *Family therapy with ethnic minorities* (pp. 123–177). Beverly Hills, CA: Sage.

Hoare, K. H. (2002). *Erikson on development in adulthood: New insights from the unpublished papers.* New York: Oxford University Press.

Hochschild, A., & Machung, A. (1990). *The second shift.* New York: Avon.

Hodge, D. R. (2001). Spiritual genograms: A generational approach to assessing spirituality. *Families in Society, 82*(1), 35–48.

Hodge, D. R. (2003a). The challenge of spiritual diversity: Can social work facilitate an inclusive environment? *Families in Society: The Journal of Contemporary Human Services, 84*(3), 348–358.

Hodge, D. R. (2003b). *Spiritual assessment: A handbook for helping professionals.* Botsford, CT: North American Association of Christians in Social Work.

Hodge, D. R. (2004). Spirituality and people with mental illness: Developing spiritual competency in assessment and intervention. *Families in Society: The Journal of Contemporary Human Services, 85*(1), 36–44.

Hodges, J., & Tizard, B. (1989). Social and family relationships of ex-institutional adolescents. *Journal of Child Psychology and Psychiatry, 30,* 77–97.

Holder, H. D., Salz, R. F., Grube, J. W., Boas, R. B., Gruenwald, R. M., & Treno, A. J. (1997). A community prevention trial to reduce alcohol-involved accidental injury and death: Overview. *Addiction, 92*(Suppl. 2), S155–S172.

Holland, T. P. (1995). Organizations: Context for social service delivery. In R .L. Edwards (Ed. In chief) *Encyclopedia of Social Work* (19th Ed.) (pp. 1787–1794). Washington, DC: NASW Press.

Hollis, F. (1972). *Casework: A psychosocial therapy* (2nd ed.). New York: Random House.

Holmbeck, G. N. (1996). A model of family relational transformations during the transitions to adolescence: Parent–adolescent conflict and adaptation. In J. A. Graber, J. Brooks-Gunn, & C. Petersen (Eds.), *Transitions through adolescence: Interpersonal domains and context* (pp. 167–199). Mahwah, NJ: Erlbaum.

Holmbeck, G. N., Colder, C., Shapera, W., Westhoven, V., Kenealy, L., & Updegrove, A. (2000). Working with adolescents: Guides from developmental psychology. In P. Kendall (Ed.), *Child and adolescent therapy:*

Cognitive-behavioral procedures (2nd ed., pp. 334–385). New York: Guilford Press.

Holmbeck, G. N., & Shapera, C. (1999). Research methods with adolescents. In P. C. Kendall, J. N. Butcher, & G. N. Holmbeck (Eds.), *Handbook of research methods in clinical psychology* (2nd ed., pp. 634–661). New York: Wiley.

Homans, G. C. (1974). *Social behavior: Its elementary forms*. New York: Harcourt Brace Jovanovich.

Hood, R. W., Spilka, B., Hunsberger, B., & Gorsuch, R. (1996). *The psychology of religion*. New York: Guilford Press.

Hooper, S. R., & March, J. S. (1995). Neuropsychology. In J. S. March (Ed.), *Anxiety disorders in children and adolescents* (pp. 35–61). New York: Guilford Press.

Hopcke, R. H. (1992). Midlife, gay men, and the AIDS epidemic. *Quadrant, 35*(1), 101–109.

Hope, S., Power, C., & Rodgers, B. (1999). Does financial hardship account for elevated psychological distress in lone mothers? *Social Science and Medicine, 29,* 381–389.

Horn, J. L. (1994). The rise and fall of human abilities. *Journal of Research and Development in Education, 12,* 59–78.

Horney, K. (1942). *The collected works of Karen Horney* (Vol. II). New York: Norton.

Horowitz, M. (1991). Short term dynamic therapy of stress response syndromes. In P. Crits-Christoph & J. P. Barber (Eds.), *Handbook of short term dynamic psychotherapy* (pp. 166–198). New York: Basic Books.

Hort, B., Leinbach, M., & Fagot, B. (1991). Is there coherence among the cognitive components of gender acquisition? *Sex Roles, 24,* 195–207.

Horwitz, A. V., White, H. R., & Howell-White, M. S. (1996). Becoming married and mental health: A longitudinal study of a cohort of young adults. *Journal of Marriage and the Family, 58,* 895–907.

Howell, E. F. (2005). *The dissociative mind*. Hillsdale, NJ: The Analytic Press.

Howell, J., Kelly, M., Palmer, J., & Mangum, R. (2004). Integrating child welfare, juvenile justice, and other agencies in a continuum of services. *Child Welfare, 83*(2), 143–156.

Howell, L. C., & Beth, A. (2004). Pioneers in our own lives: Grounded theory of lesbians' midlife development. *Journal of Women and Aging, 16*(3/4), 133–147.

Huff, R. G. (2001). *Gangs in America*. Thousand Oaks, CA: Sage.

Huffman, S. B., & Myers, J. E. (1999). Counseling women in midlife: An integrative approach to menopause. *Journal of Counseling and Development, 77,* 258–266.

Hugen, B. (Ed.). (1998). *Christianity and social work*. Botsford, CT: North American Association of Christians in Social Work.

Hughes, C. (1998). Finding your marbles: Does preschoolers' strategic behavior predict later understanding of mind? *Developmental Psychology, 34,* 1326–1339.

Hulko, W. (2009). The time and context contingent nature of intersectionality and interlocking oppressions. Affilia: *Journal of Women and Social Work, 24*(1), 44–55.

Humphries, T., Martin, B., & Coye, T. (1989). A bilingual, bicultural approach to teaching English (how two hearies and a deafie got together to teach English). In S. Wilcox (Ed.), *American deaf culture: An anthology* (pp. 121–143). Burtonsville, MD: Linstock.

Hunter, J., & Mallon, G. P. (2000). Lesbian, gay, and bisexual adolescent development: Dancing with your feet tied together. In B. Greene & G. L. Croom (Eds.), *Education, research, and practice in lesbian, gay, bisexual and transgendered psychology: A resource manual* (pp. 226–243). Thousand Oaks, CA: Sage Publications, Inc.

Hunter, S., & Hickerson, J. C. (2003). *Affirmative practice: Understanding and working with lesbian, gay, bisexual and transgender persons*. Washington, DC: NASW Press.

Hunter, S., Sundel, S. S., & Sundel, M. (2002). *Women at midlife: Life experiences and implications for the helping professions*. Washington, DC: NASW Press.

Hurtado, A., Gurin, P., & Peng, T. (1994). Social identities—a framework for studying the adaptations of immigrants and ethnics: The adaptations of Mexicans in the United States. *Social Problems, 41,* 129–151.

Huston, A. C. (1991a). *Children in poverty: Child development and public policy*. New York: Cambridge University Press.

Huston, A. C. (1991b). Children in poverty: Developmental and policy issues. In A. C. Huston (Ed.), *Children in poverty: Child development and public policy* (pp. 1–22). New York: Cambridge University Press.

Hutchison, E. D. (1999). *Dimensions of human behavior: Person and environment*. Thousand Oaks, CA: Pine Forge Press.

Hutchinson, E. D., & Waldbillig, A. (2003). Social institutions and social structure. In E. D. Hutchinson (Ed.), *Dimensions of human behavior* (2nd ed., pp. 355–433). Thousand Oaks, CA: Sage.

Huttenlocker, P. R., & Dabholkar, A. S. (1997). Regional differences in synaptogenesis in the human cerebral cortex. *Journal of Comparative Neurology, 387,* 167–178.

Hyman, S. E. (1999). Preface. In H. Johnson (Ed.), *Psyche, synapse and substance: The role of neurobiology in emotions, behaviors, thinking, and addiction for non-scientists* (pp. i–iii). Greenfield, MA: Deerfield Valley Publishing.

Ibrahim, F. A. (1984). Cross-Cultural Counseling and Psychotherapy: An Existential-Psychological Perspective. *International Journal for the Advancement of Counseling, 7,* 159–169.

Ibrahim F. A. (1991), Contribution of Cultural Worldview to Generic Counseling and Development. *Journal of Counseling and Development,* 70, (13–19). Theory and Cultural Identity. In J. McFadden (Ed.), *Trans-cultural Counseling* (2nd ed., pp. 23–58). Alexandria, Va: American Counseling Association

Ibrahim, F. A., Roysircar-Sodosky, G., & Ohnishi, H. (2001), Worldview: Recent Developments and Needed Directions. *In Handbook of Multicultural Counseling* (2nd. Ed.) by J. Poderotto, J. Manuel Casas, L. A. Suzuki, C. M. Alexander (Eds.), Thousand Oaks, CA: Sage Publications, Inc.

Inclan J. (1985). Variations in Value Orientation in Mental Health Work with Puerto Ricans, *Psychotherapy, 22,* 324–334.

Istar, A. (Feb 2006). *Transgender emergence: Understanding diverse gender identities and expressions.* Boston: NASW.

Jackson, H. L., & Westmoreland, G. (1992). Therapeutic issues for black children in foster care. In L. A. Vargar, & J. D. Koss-Chioino (Eds.), *Working with culture: Psychotherapeutic interventions with ethnic minority children and adolescents.* San Francisco: Jossey-Bass.

Jacques, E. (1965). Death and the midlife crisis. *International Journal of Psychoanalysis, 46,* 502–514.

Jaeger, P. T., & Bowman, C. A. (2003). *Understanding disability: Inclusion, access, diversity and civil rights.* Westport, CT; Praeger Publishing.

James, B. (1989). *Treating traumatized children: New insights and creative interventions.* New York: Free Press.

James, B. (1994). *Handbook for treatment of attachment trauma problems in children.* New York: Free Press.

Janet, P. (1919/1925). *Psychological healing* (Vols. 1–2). New York: Macmillan. (Original work published, 1919)

Janis, I. L. (1982). *Victims of groupthink.* Boston: Houghton Mifflin.

Jantzen, C., & Harris, O. (1980). *Family treatment in social work practice.* Itasca, IL: F.E. Peacock.

Jenkins, E., & Bell, C. (1997). Exposure and response to community violence among children and adolescents. In J. Osofsky (Ed.). *Children in a violent society* (pp. 9–32). New York: Guilford.

Jenkins, P. L. (2001). A culture of hope. The effects of slavery on contemporary African Americans as communicated in the folklore (stories) of African Americans. *Dissertation Abstracts International.* Section B, *The Sciences and Engineering, 62,* 3-B.

Jenson, J. M. (2005). *Social policy for children and families: A risk and resilience perspective.* New York: Sage.

Jernberg, A. M. (1979). *Theraplay: A new treatment using structured play for problem children and their families.* San Francisco: Jossey-Bass.

Jernberg, A. M., & Booth, P. (1999). *Theraplay: Helping parents and children build better relationships through attachment based play* (2nd ed.). San Francisco: Jossey-Bass.

Jessor, R., Donovan, J. E., & Costa, F. M. (1991). *Beyond adolescence: Problem behavior and young adult development.* New York: Cambridge University Press.

Johnson, D., & Johnson, F. (1991). *Joining together: Group theory and group skills* (4th ed.). Englewood Cliffs, NJ: Prentice Hall.

Johnson, D. E. (2002). Adoption and the effect on children's development. *Early Human Development, 68,* 39–54.

Johnson, G. S., Jr. (2002). About brain injury: A guide to brain anatomy, function and symptoms. Retrieved August 21, 2004, from www.waiting .com/ brainfunction.html

Johnson, H. C. (Ed.). (1999). *Psyche, synapse and substance: The role of neurobiology in emotions, behavior, thinking and addiction for non-scientists.* Greenfield, MA: Deerfield Valley Publishing.

Johnson, J. H., & Sheeber, L. S. (1999). Developmental assessment. In W. K. Silverman & T. H. Ollendick (Eds.), *Developmental issues in the clinical treatment of children* (pp. 44–60). Needham Heights, MA: Allyn & Bacon.

Johnson, M. H. (1998). The neural basis of cognitive development. In W. Damon, D. Kuhn, & R. S. Siegler (Eds.), *Handbook of child psychology: Vol. 2. Cognition, perception, and language* (5th ed., pp. 1–50). New York: Wiley.

Johnson, M. J., Jackson, N. C., Arnette, J. K., & Koffman, S. D. (2005). Gay and lesbian perceptions of discrimination in retirement care facilities. *Journal of Homosexuality, 49*(2), 83–102.

Johnson, R., & Leahy, J. (2004). Psychological treatment of bipolar disorder. NY: Guilford.

Johnson, S. L., & Leahy, R. L. (Eds.). (2005). *Psychological treatment of bipolar disorder.* New York: Guilford Press.

Johnson, S. M., & Denton, W. (2002). Emotionally focused couple therapy: Creating secure connections. In A. S. Gurman & N. S. Jacobson (Eds.), *Clinical handbook of couple therapy* (3rd ed.). New York: Guilford Press.

Johnston, D. C. (2002a, February, 5). Is the human rights era ending? *New York Times,* pp. A13.

Johnston, D. C. (2002b, February 18). U.S. corporations are using Bermuda to slash tax bills: Profits over patriotism. *New York Times,* pp. A1, A12.

Johnston, D. C. (2003, June 26). Very richest's share of wealth grew even bigger, data show. *New York Times,* pp. A1, C2.

Johnston, L. D., O'Malley, P. M., & Bachman, J. G. (Eds.). (1997). *National survey results on drug use from the Monitoring the Future Study, 1975–1995: Vol. 2. College students and young adults* (NH Publication No. 94-3810). Washington, DC: U.S. Government Printing Office.

Johnston, L. D., O'Malley, P. M., & Bachman, J. G. (2005). *National survey results on drug use from the Monitoring the Future Study, 1975–97.* Rockville, MD: National Institute on Drug Abuse.

Jones, E. (1938[1922]). Some problems of adolescence. In *Papers on psychoanalysis* (pp. 500–518). London: Balliere, Tindall and Cox.

Jones, G. C., & Kilpatrick, A. C. (1996). Wellness theory: A discussion and application to clients with disabilities. *Families in Society: The Journal of Contemporary Human Service, 77*(5), 255–267.

Jones, J. T., & Cunningham, J. D. (1996). Attachment styles and other predictors of relationship satisfaction in dating couples. *Personal Relationships, 3,* 387–399.

Jordan, J. V. (1991). *A relational perspective for understanding women's development: Women's growth in diversity.* New York: Guilford Press.

Jordan, J. V. (1994). A relational perspective on self esteem. *Work in Progress, 70.* Wellesley, MA: Stone Center Working Paper Series.

Jordan, J. V. (1997b). A relational perspective for understanding women's development. *Women's Growth in Diversity.* New York: Guilford Press.

Jordan, J. V., Kaplan, A. G., Miller, J. B., Stiver, I. P., & Surrey, J. L. (1991). Women's growth in connection. In *Writings from the Stone Center.* New York: Guilford Press.

Joseph, M. V. (1988). Religion and social work practice. *Social Casework, 69,* 443–452.

Josselson, R. (1994). The theory of identity development and the question of intervention. In S. L. Archer (Ed.), *Interventions for adolescent identity development* (pp. 12–25). Thousand Oaks, CA: Sage.

Jung, C. G. (1930/1983). The stages of life. In A. Storr (Ed.), *The essential Jung* (pp. 72–74). Princeton, NJ: Princeton University Press.

Kabat-Zinn, J. (1990). *Full catastrophe living: Using the wisdom of your body and mind to face stress, pain and illness.* New York: Dell.

Kabat-Zinn, J. (2005). *Coming to our senses: Healing ourselves and the world through mindfulness.* New York: Hyperion.

Kagan, J. (1984). *The nature of the child.* New York: Basic Books.

Kagan, J., Kearseley, R. B., & Zelazo, P. R. (1978). *Infancy: Its place in human development.* Cambridge, MA: Harvard University Press.

Kagan, J., Reznick, J. S., & Snidman, N. (1988). Biological bases of childhood shyness. *Science, 240,* 167–171.

Kalat, L. J. W. (2001). *Biological psychology* (7th ed.). Belmont, CA: Wadsworth.

Kalish, R. A. (1968). Life and death: Dividing the indivisible. *Social Science and Medicine, 2,* 249–259.

Kamsner, S., & McCabe, M. P. (2000). The relationship between adult psychological adjustment and childhood sexual abuse, childhood physical abuse and family of origin characteristics. *Journal of Interpersonal Violence, 15,* 1243–1261.

Kansteiner, W. (2004). Testing the limits of trauma: The long term psychological effects of the Holocaust on individuals and collectives. *History of the Human Sciences, 17*(2/3), 97–123.

Kaplan, J. A. (2004). The "good enough" fit: Psychoanalytic psychotherapy and psychoanalysis as culturally sensitive practice. *Clinical Social Work Journal, 32*(1), 51–59.

Kashani, J. H., & Orvaschel, H. (1990). A community study of anxiety in children and adolescents. *American Journal of Psychiatry, 147,* 313–318.

Kazdin, A. E. (1992). Child and adolescent dysfunction and paths toward maladjustment: Targets for intervention. *Clinical Psychology Review, 12,* 785–817.

Keating, D. P. (1990). Adolescent thinking. In S. S. Feldman & G. R. Elliott (Eds.), *At the threshold: The developing adolescent* (pp. 54–89). Cambridge, MA: Harvard University Press.

Kegan, R. (1982). *The emerging self: Problem and process in human development.* Cambridge, MA: Harvard University Press.

Kelley, P. (1996). Narrative theory and social work treatment. In F. J. Turner (Ed.), *Social work treatment: Interlocking theoretical approaches* (pp. 461–480). New York: Free Press.

Kellman, P. J., & Banks, M. S. (1998). Infant visual perception. In W. Damon, D. Kuhn, & R. S. Siegler (Eds.), *Handbook of child psychology: Vol. 2. Cognition, perception and language* (5th ed., pp. 103–146). New York: Wiley and Banks.

Kelly, M. P. (1992). *Colitis.* London: Routledge.

Kelly, S. (1993). Caregiver stress in grandparents raising grandchildren. *IMAGE: Journal of Nursing Scholarship, 25,* 331–337.

Kempe, H., Silverman, F., Steele, B., Drougmueller, W., & Silver, H. (1962). The battered child syndrome. *Journal of American Medical Association, 181,* 17–24.

Kempler, W. (1973). *Principles of gestalt family therapy*. Oslo, Norway: A-s Joh. Nordahls Trykkeri.

Kendall, P. C. (Ed.). (2000). *Child and adolescent therapy: Cognitive-behavioral procedures* (2nd ed.). New York: Guilford Press.

Kendall, P. C., Aschenbrand, S. G., & Hudson, J. L. (2003). Child-focused treatment of anxiety. In A. E. Kazdin, & J. R. Weisz (Eds.), *Evidence-based psychotherapies for children and adolescents* (pp. 81–101). New York: Guilford Press.

Kendall, P. C., Chu, B. C., Pimentel, S. S., & Choudhury, M. (2000). Treating anxiety disorders in youth. In P. D. Kendall (Ed.), *Child and adolescent therapy: Cognitive-behavioral procedures* (2nd ed., pp. 235–291). New York: Guilford Press.

Kennedy, A. (2004). Emotional Cycle of deployment: Information for civilian counselors about the military family. *Counseling Today, 47*(1), 1, 12, 45.

Kerbo, H. R. (1996). *Social stratification and inequality: Class conflict in historical and comparative perspective*. New York: McGraw-Hill.

Kernberg, O. (1976). *Object relations theory and clinical psychoanalysis*. New York: Jason Aronson.

Kerr, M. E., & Bowen, M. (1988). *Family evaluation*. New York: Norton.

Kerr Chandler, S. (2001). E. Franklin Frazier and social work: Unity and conflict. In I. B. Carlton-LaNey (Ed.), *African American leadership: An empowerment tradition in social welfare history*. Washington DC: NASW Press.

Kertzner, R. M. (2001). The adult life course and homosexual identity in midlife gay men. *Annual Review of Sex Research, XII*, 75–92.

Kertzner, R. M., & Sved, M. (1996). Midlife gay men and lesbians: Adult development and mental health. In R. P. Cabaj, & T. S. Stein (Eds.), *Textbook of homosexuality and mental health* (pp. 289–303). Washington, DC: American Psychiatric Press.

Kerwin, C., & Ponterotto, J. G. (1995). Biracial identity development. In J. G. Ponterotto, J. M. Casas, L. A. Suzuki, & C. A. Alexander (Eds.), *Handbook of multicultural counseling* (pp. 199–217). Thousand Oaks, CA: Sage.

Keyhani, S., Ross, J. S., Herbert, P., Dellenbaugh, C., Penrod, J. D., & Siu, A. L. (2007). Use of preventive care by elderly male veterans receiving care through the veterans' health administration, Medicare fee-for-service, and Medicare HMO plans. *American Journal of Public Health, 97*(12), 2179–2185.

Kidd, S. M. (2002). *The secret life of bees*. New York: Penguin Putnam.

Kilborn, P. T. (2005). An American town, a sky high divorce rate. In *Themes of the times for human behavior and the social environment* (pp. 32–33). Boston: Allyn & Bacon.

Killilea, M. (1982). Interaction of crisis theory, coping strategies, and social support systems. In H. C. Schulberg & M. Killilea (Eds.), *The modern practice of community mental health* (pp. 163–214). San Francisco: Jossey-Bass.

Kilpatrick, A. C., & Holland, T. P. (1990). Spiritual dimensions of practice. *Clinical Supervisor, 8*(2), 125–140.

Kim, W. J. (2002). Benefits and risks of intercountry adoption. *Lancet, 360*, 423–424.

Kimmel, D. C. (1978). Adult development and aging: A gay perspective. *Journal of Social Issues, 34*, 113–130.

Kirby, J. (1995). Single parent families in poverty. *Human Development & Family Life Bulletin, 1*(Spring), Ohio State University.

Kirchoff, S. (1999, November 20). Disability bill's advocates rewrite the book on lobbying. *Congressional Quarterly Weekly, 27*, 62–66.

Kirst-Ashman, K. K., & Hull, Jr., G. H. (2009). *Generalist Practice with Organizations and Communities* (4th Ed.). Belmont, CA: Brooks/Cole Cengage Learning.

Kiselica, M. S. (2003). Anti-Semitism and insensitivity toward Jews by the counseling profession: A gentile's view on the problem and his hope for reconciliation—A response to Weinrach (2000). *Journal of Counseling and Development, 81*, 426–440.

Kivnick, H. (1983). Dimensions of grandparenthood meaning: Deductive conceptualization and empirical derivation. *Journal of Personality and Social Psychology, 44*, 1056–1068.

Klahr, D. (1982). Nonmonotone assessment of monotone development: An information processing analysis. In S. Strauss (Ed.), *U-shaped behavioral growth*. New York: Academic Press.

Klahr, D., & Wallace, J. G. (1976). *Cognitive development: An information processing view*. Hillsdale, NJ: Erlbaum.

Klee, T. (2005). Object relations theory and therapy. University of Adelaide. Retrieved October 23, 2005, from http://www.object-relations.org

Klein, M. (1948). *Contributions to psychoanalysis, 1921–1945*. London: Hogarth Press.

Klein, M. (1952c). *Some theoretical conclusions regarding the emotional life of the infant: Envy and gratitude and other works, 1946–1963*. New York: Delacorte Press.

Kleinberg, L. (1986). Coming home to self: Going home to parents. *Work in Progress*, No. 24. Wellesley, MA: Stone Center Working Papers Series.

Kleinman, A., & Good, B. (Eds.). (1985). *Culture and depression: Studies in anthropology and cross-cultural psychiatry of affect and disorder*. Berkeley and Los Angeles: University of California Press.

Kliman, J., & Madsen, W. (2005). Social Class and the Family Life Cycle. In B. Carter and M. McGoldrick (Eds.). *The Expanded Family Life Cycle: Individual, Family, and Social Perspectives* (3rd Ed.) Boston, MA: Pearson/Allyn and Bacon.

Klin, A., & Volkmar, F. R. (1997). Asperger's syndrome. In D. Cohen & F. R. Volkmar (Eds.), *Handbook of autism and pervasive developmental disorders* (pp. 94–122). New York: Wiley.

Klin, A., Volkmar, F., & Sparrow, S. (Eds.). (2000). *Asperger syndrome*. New York: Guilford Press.

Klinger, L. G., Dawson, G., & Renner, P. (2003). Autistic disorder. In E. J. Mash, & R. A. Barkley (Eds.), *Child psychopathology* (2nd ed., pp. 409–454). New York: Guilford Press.

Knight, J. R., Sherritt, L., Shrier, L. A., Harris, S. K., & Chang, G. (2002). Validity of the CRAFFT substance abuse screening test among adolescent clinic patients. *Archives of Pediatric Adolescent Medicine, 156*, 607–614.

Knopka, G. (1983). *Social group work: A helping process* (3rd ed.). Englewood Cliffs, NJ: Prentice Hall.

Knox, J., & Price, D. (1995). The changing American military family: Opportunities for social work. *Social Service Review, 69*(3), 479–498.

Knox, Virginia W. (1996). "The Effects of Child Support Payments on Developmental Outcomes for Children in Single-Mother Families." *Journal of Human Resources 31*(4):816–840.

Kobak, R. R., & Sceery, A. (1988). Attachment in late adolescence: Working models, affect regulation, and representations of self and others. *Child Development, 59*, 135–146.

Kochanska, G. (1993). Toward a synthesis of parental socialization and child temperament in early development of conscience. *Child Development, 64*, 325–347.

Kochanska, G. (1995). Children's temperament, mother's discipline, and security of attachment: Multiple pathways to emerging internalization. *Child Development, 66*, 597–615.

Kochanska, G. (1997). Multiple pathways to conscience for children with different temperaments: From toddlerhood to age 5. *Developmental Psychology, 33*, 228–240.

Kochanska, G. (2001). Emotional development in children with different attachment histories: The first three years. *Child Development, 72*, 474–490.

Kochanska, G., Aksan, N., & Koenig, A. (1995). A longitudinal study of the roots of preschoolers' conscience: Committed compliance and emerging internalization. *Child Development, 66*, 1752–1769.

Koestler, A. (1967). *The act of creation*. New York: Dell.

Kohlberg, L. (1966). A cognitive-developmental analysis of children's sex role concepts and attitudes. In E. E. Maccoby (Ed.), *The development of sex differences*. Stanford, CA: Stanford University Press.

Kohlberg, L. (1969). Stage and sequence: the cognitive developmental approach to socialization. In E. A. Gossin (Ed.), *Handbook of socialization theory and research*. Chicago: Rand McNally.

Kohlberg, L. (1981). *The philosophy of moral development*. San Francisco: Harper & Row.

Kohlberg, L. (1984). *The psychology of moral development: The nature and validity of moral stages* (Vol. 2). New York: Harper & Row.

Kohut, H. (1959/1978). Introspection, empathy and psychoanalysis: An examination of the relationship between modes of observation and theory. In P. Ornstein (Ed.), *The search for the self* (Vol. 1, pp. 205–223). New York: International Universities Press.

Kohut, H. (1971). *The analysis of the self*. New York: International Universities Press.

Kreppner, J. M., O'Connor, T., Rutter, M., & the English and Romanian Adoptees Study Team. (2001). Can inattention/overactivity be an institutional deprivation syndrome? *Journal of Abnormal Child Psychology, 29*, 513–528.

Kress, F., & Vandenberg, B. (1998). Depression and attribution in abused children and their nonoffending caregivers. *Psychological Reports, 83*, 1285–1286.

Krestan, J., & Bepko, C. (1989). Alcohol problems and the family life cycle. In M. McGoldrick & B. Carter (Eds.), *The changing family life cycle* (2nd ed.). Boston: Allyn and Bacon.

Kroger, J. (2000). *Identity development: Adolescence through adulthood*. Thousand Oaks, CA: Sage.

Krotoski, D., Nosek, M., & Turk, M. (1996). *Women with physical disabilities: Achieving and maintaining health and well-being*. Baltimore: Paul H. Brookes.

Kruger, A. (1994). The midlife transition: Crisis or Chimers? *Psychological Reports, 75*, 1299–1305.

Krystal, H. (1968). *Massive psychic trauma*. New York: International Universities Press.

Kübler-Ross, E. (1969). *On death and dying*. New York: Macmillan.

Kuczynski, L., Zahn-Waxler, C., & Radke-Yarrow, M. (1987). Development and content of imitation in the second and third years of life: A socialization perspective. *Developmental Psychology, 23*, 276–282.

Kuebli, J., Butler, S., & Fivush, R. (1995). Mother–child talk about past emotions: Relations of maternal language and child gender over time. *Cognition and Emotion, 9*, 265–283.

Kuhl, P. K. (1999). The role of experience in early language development: Linguistic experience alters the perception and production of speech. In N. Fox, L. Leavitt, & J. Warhol (Eds.), *The role of early experience in development* (pp. 101–126). Skillman, NJ: Johnson & Johnson.

Kuhl, P. K., & Meltzoff, A. N. (1982, December 10). The bimodal perception of speech in infancy. *Science, 218*, 1138–1141.

Kulkin, H. S., Chauvin, E. A., & Percle, G. (2000). Suicide among gay and lesbian adolescents and young adults: A review of the literature. *Journal of Homosexuality, 40*(1), 1–29.

Kunreuther, F. (1991). The Hetrick-Martin Institute: Services for youth. *Focal Point, 5*, 10–11.

Kupersmith, J. B., & Dodge, K. A. (Eds.). (2004). *Children's peer relations: From development to intervention*. Washington, DC: American Psychological Association.

Kurdek, L. A. (1995). Lesbian and gay couples. In A. R. D'Augelli & C. J. Patterson (Eds.), *Lesbian and gay identities over the lifespan: Psychological perspectives on personal, relational, and community processes*. New York: Oxford University Press.

Kurdek, L. A., & Fine, M. A. (1994). Family acceptance and family control as predictors of adjustment in young adolescents: Linear, curvilinear, or interactive effects? *Child Development, 65*, 1137–1146.

Kurland, R., & R. Salmon. (1998). *Teaching a methods course in social work with groups*. Alexandria, VA: Council on Social Work Education.

Kurtz, L. F. (2004). Support and self-help groups. In C. D. Garvin, L. M. Gutierrez, & M. J. Galinsky (Eds.), *Handbook of social work with groups* (pp. 139–160). New York: Guilford Press.

Labouvie-Vief, G. (1980). Beyond formal operations: Uses and limits of pure logic in life-span development. *Human Development, 23*, 141–161.

Labouvie-Vief, G. (1986). Modes of knowledge and the organization of development. In M. L. Commons, L. Kohlberg, F. Richards, & J. Sinnott (Eds.), *Beyond formal operations: Models and methods in the study of adult and adolescent thought*. New York: Praeger.

Labouvie-Vief, G. (1990). Modes of knowledge and the organization of development. In M. L. Commons, C. Armon, L. Kohlberg, F. A. Richards, et al. (Eds.), *Adult development: Vol. 2. Models and methods in the study of adolescent thought*. New York: Praeger.

Lachman, M. E. (2001). *Handbook of midlife development*. New York: Wiley.

Ladd, E. C. (1989). The 1988 elections: Continuation of the post-New Deal system. *Political Science Quarterly, 704*(1), 1–18.

Ladd, E. C. (1999). Bowling with Tocqueville: Civic engagement and social capital. *The Responsive Community, 9*(2), 11–21.

Ladd, G. W. (1990). Having friends, keeping friends, making friends, and being liked by peers in the classroom: Predictors of children's early school adjustment? *Child Development, 61*, 1081–1100.

Ladd, G. W. (1999). Peer relationships and social competence during early and middle childhood. *Annual Review of Psychology, 50*, 333–359.

Lagercrantz, H., & Slotkin, T. A. (1986). The stress of being born. *Scientific American, 254*, 92–102.

Laird, J. (1993). Lesbian and gay families. In F. Walsh (Ed.), *Normal family processes*. New York: Guilford Press.

Laird, J. (1996). Family-centered practice with lesbian and gay families. *Families in Society: Journal of Contemporary Human Services, 77*, 559–572.

Laird, J. (2000). Gender in lesbian relationships: Cultural, feminist, and constructionist reflections. *Journal of Marital and Family Therapy, 26*, 455–467.

Lambda Legal Defense and Education Fund. (1997–2005). Retrieved January 10, 2006, from http://www.lambdalegal.org

Lambda Legal Defence and Education Fund. (2004, May 12). Retrieved January 10, 2006, from http://www.lambdalegal.org/cgibin/iowa/news/fact.html?record&1490

Lambda Legal Defence and Education Fund. (2009). *In Your State*. Retreived September, 15, 2009 from http//www.lambdalega.org/in your state

Lambert, C. L., Lyubansky, M., & Achenback, T. (1998). Behavioral and emotional problems among the adolescents of Jamaica and the United States: Parent, teacher, and self reports for ages 12 to 18. *Journal of Emotional and Behavioral Disorders, 6*(3), 180–187.

Land, H. (1998). The feminist approach to clinical social work. In R. A. Dorfman (Ed.), *Paradigms of clinical social work* (Vol. 2, pp. 227–257). New York: Brunner/Mazel.

Landon, P. S. (l995). Generalist and advanced generalist practice. In K. L. Edwards (Ed.), *Encyclopedia of social work* (pp. 1101–1108). Silver Spring, MD: National Association of Social Workers.

Landreth, G. L. (1991). *Play therapy: The art of the relationship*. Muncie, IN: Accelerated Development.

Landreth, G. L. (2002). *Play therapy: The art of the relationship* (2nd ed.). New York: Brunner-Routledge.

Langdridge. D. (2008). Are you angry or are you heterosexual? In L. Moon (Ed.), *Feeling queer or queer feelings: Radical approaches to counseling sex, sexualities and genders* (pp. 23–35). New York: Routledge.

Lantz, J. (1996). Cognitive theory and social work treatment. In F. Turner (Ed.), *Social work treatment: Interlocking theoretical approaches* (pp. 94–116). New York: Free Press.

Lappee, F. M., & DuBois, P. M. (1994). *The quickening of America: Rebuilding our nation, remaking our lives.* San Francisco: Jossey-Bass.

Larson, R. (2000). Toward a psychology of positive youth development. *American Psychologist, 55*(1), 170–183.

Laub, D. (1998). The empty circle: Children of survivors and the limits of reconstruction, *Journal of the American Psychoanalytic Association, 46*(2), 507–529.

Lauer, J. C., & Lauer, R. H. (1986). *Til death do us part: How couples stay together.* New York: Haworth Press.

Laursen, B., Coy, K. C., & Collins, W. A. (1998). Reconsidering changes in parent–child conflict across adolescence: A meta-analysis. *Child Development, 69,* 817–832.

Lazarus, L. (1982). Brief psychotherapy of narcisstic disturbances. *Psychotherapy: Theory, Research and Practice, 19*(2), 228–236.

Leaper, C. (1994). Exploring the correlates and consequences of gender segregation: Social relationships in childhood, adolescence and adulthood. In C. Leaper (Ed.), *New directions for child development,* No. 65. (pp. 67–86). San Francisco: Jossey-Bass.

Leaper, C., Tenenbaum, H. R., & Shaffer, T. G. (1999). Communication patterns of African-American girls and boys from low-income, urban backgrounds. *Child Development, 70,* 1489–1503.

Lee, A. (1997). Psychoanalytic play therapy. In K. O'Connor & L. Braverman (Eds.), *Play therapy theory and practice: A comparative presentation* (pp. 46–78). New York: Wiley.

Le Grange, D. (2005). The Maudsley family based treatment for adolescent anorexia nervosa. *World Psychiatry, 4*(3), 142–146.

Lemme, B. H. (1995). *Development in adulthood.* Needham Heights, MA: Allyn & Bacon.

Lemonick, M. D. (1997, December 1). The new revolution in making babies. *Time,* 40–46.

Lepishak, B. (2004). Building community for Toronto's lesbian, gay, bisexual, transsexual and transgender youth. *Journal of Gay and Lesbian Social Services, 16*(3/4), 81–97.

Lerner, R. M. (1999). Revisiting individuals as producers of their development: From dynamic interactions to developmental systems. In J. Brandstadter & R. M. Lerner (Eds.), *Action and self development: Theory and research through the life span* (pp. 3–36). Thousand Oaks, CA: Sage.

Lerner, R. M. (2000). A holistic, integrated model of risk and protection in adolescence: A developmental contextual perspective about research, programs, and policies. In L. Bergman, & R. Cairns (Eds.), *Developmental science and the holistic approach* (pp. 421–443). Mahwah, NJ: Erlbaum.

Lerner, R. M., Villarruel, F. A., & Castellino, D. R. (1999). Adolescence. In W. K. Silverman, & T. H. Ollendick (Eds.), *Developmental issues in the clinical treatment of children* (pp. 125–136). Boston: Allyn & Bacon.

Leseman, P. P. M. (2002). *Early childhood education and care for children from low-income or minority backgrounds.* Paris: Organisation for Economic Co-operation and Development. Workshop, June 6–7.

Leseman, P. P. M., & De Jong, P. F. (1998). Home literacy: Opportunity, instruction, cooperation, and social-emotional quality predicting early reading achievement. *Reading Research Quarterly, 33,* 3, 294–318.

Leseman, P. P. M., & Van den Boom, D. C. (1999). Effects of quantity and quality of home proximal processes on Dutch, Surinamese-Dutch, and Turkish-Dutch preschoolers' cognitive development. *Infant and Child Development, 8,* 19–38.

Lesser, J. G. (1999). When your son becomes your daughter: A mother's adjustment to a transgender child. *Families in Society: The Journal of Contemporary Human Services, 80*(2), 182–190.

Lesser, J. G. (2000). The group as selfobject: Brief psychotherapy with women. *International Journal of Group Psychotherapy, 50*(3), 363–381.

Lesser, J. G., & Eriksen, H. E. (2000). Brief treatment with a Vietnamese adolescent: Integrating self psychological and constructivist model. *Crisis Intervention, 6*(1), 29–39.

Lesser, J. G., O'Neill, M., Burke, K. W., Scanlon, P., Hollis, K., & Miller, R. (2004). Women supporting women: A mutual aid group fosters new connections among women in midlife. *Social Work with Groups, 27*(1), 75–88.

Lester, B. M., LaGasse, L., & Brunner, S. (1997). Data base of studies on prenatal cocaine exposure and child outcome. *Journal of Drug Issues, 27,* 487–499.

Levinson, D. J. (1986). A conception of adult development. *American Psychologist, 41,* 3–13.

Levinson, D. J. (1996). *The seasons of a woman's life.* New York: Knopf.

Levinson, D. J., Darrow, C. N., Klein, E. B., Levinson, M. H., & McKee, B. (1978). *The seasons of a man's life.* New York: Alfred A. Knopf.

Levitan, S., Mangum, G., & Mangum, S. (1998). *Programs in aid of the poor* (7th ed.). Baltimore: Johns Hopkins University Press.

Levy, F. F. (1995). Incomes and income inequality. In R. Farley (Ed.), *State of the union: America in the 1990s: Vol. I. Economic trends* (pp. 1–57). New York: Russell Sage Foundation.

Levy, G. D., & Fivush, R. (1993). Scripts and gender: A new approach for examining gender roles development. *Developmental Review, 13*, 126–146.

Levy, M. B., & Davis, K. E. (1988). Lovestyles and attachment styles compared: Their relations to each other and to various relationship characteristics. *Journal of Social and Personal Relationships, 5*, 439–471.

Levy, R. (2008). Demystifying ADHD: A clinician's perspective. In R. Barkley (Ed.) *The ADHD Reporter, 16*(6), pp. 15–16.

Levy-Schiff, R. (2001). Psychological adjustment of adoptees in adulthood: Family environment and adoption-related correlates. *International Journal of Behavioral Development, 25*, 97–104.

Lewandoski, C. A., & Canda, E. R. (1995). A typological model for the assessment of religious groups. *Social Thought Journal of Religion in the Social Services, 18*(1), 17–38.

Lieberman, A. F., & Pawl, J. H. (1990). Disorders of attachment and secure base behavior in the second year of life: Conceptual issues and clinical interventions. In M. T. Greenberg, D. Cicchetti, & E. M. Cummings (Eds.), *Attachment in the preschool years: Theory, research and intervention* (pp. 375–397). Chicago: University of Chicago Press.

Lifton, R. J. (1967). *Death in life: Survivors of Hiroshima*. New York: Random House.

Lifton, R. J. (1977). The sense of immortality. In H. Feifel (Ed.), *New meanings of death*. New York: McGraw-Hill.

Lifton, R. J. (1979). *The broken connection*. New York: Simon and Schuster.

Lightburn, A., & Sessions, P. (2006). Community-based clinical practice: Re-creating the culture of care. In A. Lightburn & P. Sessions (Eds.), *Handbook of community-based clinical practice* (pp. 19–35). New York: Oxford University Press.

Lin, C. C., & Fu, V. R. (1990). A comparison of child-rearing practices among Chinese immigrant Chinese and Caucasian-American parents. *Child Development, 61*, 429–433.

Lindsay, R. (2002). *Recognizing spirituality: The interface between faith and social work*. Crawley: University of Western Australia Press.

Linehan, M. (1993). *Cognitive-behavioral treatment of borderline personality disorder*. New York: Guilford Press.

Linn, M. C. (1983). Content, context, and process in reasoning. *Journal of Early Adolescence, 3*, 63–82.

Linver, M., Fuligni, A., Hernandez, M., and Brooks-Gunn, J. (2004) Poverty and Child Development: Promising Interventions. In P. Allen-Meares and M. Fraser (Eds.), *Intervention with Children and Adolescents: An Interdisciplinary Approach* (pp. 106–130). Boston, MA: Allyn and Bacon.

Litz, B. T. (2004). *Early intervention for trauma and traumatic stress*. New York: Guilford Press.

Liu, W. M. (2002). The social class related experiences of men: Integrating theory and practice. *Professional Psychology Research and Practice, 33*(4), 355–360.

Liu, W. M., Ali, S. R., Soleck, G., Hopps, J., Dunston, K., & Pickett, T. (2004). Using social class in counseling psychology research. *Journal of Counseling Psychology, 57*(1), 3–18.

Liu, W. M., & Pope-Davis, D. B. (2003). Understanding classism to effect personal change. In T. B. Smith (Ed.), *Practicing multiculturalism: Internalizing and affirming diversity in counseling and psychology* (pp. 294–310). New York: Allyn & Bacon.

Liu, W. M., Soleck, G., Hopps, J., Dunston, K., & Pickett, T. (2001, March). *Understanding social class in counseling psychology*. Paper presented at the fourth National Conference of Division 17, Houston, TX.

Liu, W. M., Soleck, G., Hopps, J., Dunston, K., & Pickett, T. (2004). A new framework to understand social class in counseling: The social class worldview model and modern classism theory. *Journal of Multicultural Counseling & Development, 32*, 95–122.

Lock, J. (2001). Eating disorders: Innovative family-based treatment for anorexia nervosa. *The Brown University Child and Adolescent Behavior Letter, 17*(4). Retrieved November 13, 2008, from http://www.childresearch.net/RESOURCE/NEWS/2001/200104.HTM#1

Locke, J. L. (1993). *The child's path to spoken language*. Cambridge, MA: Harvard University Press.

Loeber, R., & Farrington, D. P. (2000). Young children who commit crime: Epidemiology, develop-mental origins, risk factors, early interventions, and policy implications. *Development and Psychopathology, 12*, 737–762.

Loeber, R., Green, S. M., & Lahey, B. B. (1990). Mental health professionals' perceptions of the utility of children, parents, and teachers as informants on childhood psychopathology. *Journal of Clinical Child Psychology, 19*, 136–143.

Longdridge, D. (2008). Are you angry or are you heterosexual: A queer critique of lesbian and gay models of identity development. In L. Moon (Ed.), *Feeling queer or queer feelings? Radical approaches to counseling sex, sexualities and genders* (pp. 23–35). New York: Routledge.

Longress, J. F. (1995). *Human behavior in the social environment* (2nd ed.). Itasca, IL: F.E. Peacock.

Lonner W. J., & Ibrahim, F. A. (1996). Appraisal and assessment in cross cultural counseling in P. B. Pederen, J. G. Draguns, W. J. Lonner and J. Trimble (Eds.) *Counseling across cultures* (4th Ed.) pp. 293–322. Thousand Oaks, CA: Sage.

Lopata, H. Z., & Barnewolt, D. (1984). *The middle years: Changes and variations in social role commitments*. In G. Baruch & J. Brooks-Gunn (Eds.), *Women in midlife* (pp. 83–108). New York: Plenum.

Lorenz, K. (1943). Die angeboren formen moglichend Erfahrun. *Zeitschrift fur Tierpsychologie, 5*, 233–409.

Lovinger, R. J. (1984). *Working with religious issues in therapy*. New York: Jason Aronson.

Luborsky, L., Mintz, J., Auerback, A., Cristoph, P., Backrach, H., Todd, T., et al. (1980). Predicting the outcome of psychotherapy: Findings of the Penn Psychotherapy Project. *Archives of General Psychiatry, 37*, 471–481.

Lubrano, M. (2004). *Limbo: Blue collar roots, white collar dreams*. New York: Wiley.

Lugaila, T. A. (1998). Marital status and living arrangements: March 1997 (Update). In *Current Population Reports*, U.S. Census Bureau. Washington, DC: U.S. Government Printing Office.

Lukoff, D., Lu, F., & Turner, R. (1992, November). Toward a more culturally sensitive DSM-IV psycho religious and psycho spiritual problems. *Journal of Nervous and Mental Disease, 180*(11), 673–682.

Luster, T., & McAdoo, H. (1996). Family and child influences on educational attainment: A secondary analysis of the High/Scope Perry Preschool data. *Developmental Psychology, 32*, 26–39.

Lyons, J. A. (2007). The returning warrior: Advice for families and friends. In C. R. Figley and W. P. Nash (Eds.), *Combat stress injury: theory, research and management* (pp. 311–324). New York: Routledge: Taylor and Francis Group.

Maas, H. S. (1984). *People in contexts: Social development from birth to old age*. Englewood Cliffs, NJ: Prentice Hall.

MacFarlane, J. (1975). Olfaction in the development of social preferences in the human neonate. In M. Hoffer (Ed.), *Parent–infant interaction*. Amsterdam: Elsevier.

Mackelprang, R., & Salsgiver, R. (1999). *Disability: A diversity model approach in human service practice*. Pacific Grove, CA: Brooks/Cole.

Mackey, K., Arnold, M. K., & Pratt, M. W. (2001). Adolescents: Stories of decision making in more and less authoritative families: Representing the voices of parents in narrative. *Journal of Adolescent Research, 16*, 243–268.

Macoby, E. E. (1998). *The two sexes: Growing up apart, coming together*. Cambridge, MA: Belknap/Harvard University Press.

Macoby, E. E. (2002). Gender and group process: A developmental perspective. *Current Directions in Psychological Science, 11*, 54–58.

Madsen W. (1999). *Collaborative Therapy with Multi-Stressed Families*. New York: The Guilford Press.

Madsen, W. (2007). *Collaborative Therapy with Multi-Stressed Families* (2nd Ed.). New York: The Guilford Press.

Mahler, M. S. (1963).Thoughts about development and individuation. *Psychoanalytic Study of the Child, 18*, 307–324.

Mahler, M. S. (1968). *On human symbiosis and the vicissitudes of individuation*. New York: International Universities Press.

Mahler, M. S., Pine, F., & Bergman, A. (1975). *The psychological birth of the human infant*. New York: Basic Books.

Mahoney, M. (1999). *Constructive psychotherapy: Exploring principles and practical exercises*. New York: Guilford Press.

Main, M., & Solomon, J. (1990). Procedures for identifying infants as disorganized disoriented during the Ainsworth strange situation. In M. T. Greenburg, D. Cicchetti, & E. M. Cummings (Eds.), *Attachment in the preschool years* (pp. 121–160). Chicago: University Chicago Press.

Malan, D. H. (1978a). Evaluation criteria for selection of patients. In H. Davanloo (Ed.), *Basic principles and techniques in short-term dynamic psychotherapy* (pp. 85–97). New York: Spectrum.

Malan, D. H. (1978b). Principles of technique in short-term dynamic psychotherapy. In H. Davanloo (Ed.), *Basic principles and techniques in short-term dynamic psychotherapy* (pp. 332–342). New York: Spectrum.

Malan, D. H. (1979). *Individual psychotherapy and the science of psychodynamics*. London: Butterworth.

Manalansan, M. F., IV. (1996). Double minorities: Latino, black, and Asian men who have sex with men. In R. C. Savin-Williams & K. M. Cohen (Eds.), *The lives of lesbian, gay men and bisexuals: Children to adults* (pp. 393–425). Ft. Worth, TX: Harcourt Brace.

Manlove, J. (1998). The influence of high school drop out and school disengagement on the risk of school age pregnancy. *Journal of Research on Adolescence, 187*, 220–228.

Mann, C., Rowland, D., & Garfield, R. (2003). Historical overview of children's health care coverage. *Future of Children, 13*(1), 31–53.

Maramaldi, P., & Guevara, M. (2003). Cultural considerations in health care and quality of life. In B. Berkman & L. Harootyan (Eds.), *Social work and health care in an aging society: Education, policy, practice, and research* (pp. 297–318). New York: Springer.

March, J. S. (Ed.). (1995). *Anxiety disorders in children and adolescents*. New York: Guilford Press

Marcia, J. E. (1983). Adolescent female identity development. *Sex Roles, 37,* 175–185.

Marks, N. F. (2005). Does it hurt to care? Caregiving, work-family conflict, and midlife well-being. *Journal of Marriage and the Family, 60*(4), 951–966.

Marks, N. F., & Lambert, J. D. (1998). Marital status continuity and change among young and midlife adults. *Journal of Family Issues 19,* 652–868.

Marlatt, A. G., Baer, J. S., Kiviahan, D. R., Dimeff, L. A., Larimer, M. E., et al. (1998). Screening and brief intervention for high risk college student drinkers: Results from a 2 year follow-up assessment. *Journal of Consulting and Clinical Psychology, 66*(4), 604–617.

Marshall, J. (2006). Counseling on the front line: Providing a safe refuge for military personnel to discuss emotional wounds. *Counseling Today, 48*(8), 1, 32–33.

Marshall, V. W. (1986). A sociological perspective on aging and dying. In V. W. Marshall (Ed.), *Later life: The social psychology of aging* (pp. 125–146). Beverly Hills, CA: Sage Publications.

Marshall, V. W. (1990). Aging and dying. In R. Bin-stock & L. George (Eds.), *Handbook of aging and the social sciences* (pp. 245–260). San Diego, CA: Academic Press.

Martin, C. L., & Fabes, R. A. (2001). The stability and consequences of young children's same-sex peer interactions. *Developmental Psychology 37,* 431–446.

Martin, C. L., & Halverson, C. F., Jr. (1987). The role of cognition in sex role acquisition. In D. B. Carter (Ed.), *Current conceptions of sex roles and sex typing: Theory and research* (pp. 123–137). New York: Praeger.

Martin, C. L., Ruble, D. N., & Szkrybalo, J. (2002). Cognitive theories of early gender development. *Psychological Bulletin* 128, 903–933.

Marty, M. E. (2005a). The long and winding road. *Newsweek,* August 29/September 5, 2005, 65.

Marty, M. E. (2005b, August 29/September 5). Where we stand on faith. *Newsweek,* pp. 48–49.

Marvin R. S., & Britner, P. A. (1999). Normative development: The ontogeny of attachment. In J. Cassidy & P. R. Shaver (Eds.), *Handbook of attachment: Theory, research, and clinical applications* (pp. 44–67). New York: Guilford Press.

Maslow, A. H. (1954). *Motivation and personality.* New York: Harper & Row.

Maslow, A. H. (1970). *Motivation and personality* (2nd ed.). New York: Harper & Row.

Massey, D. S. (1994). America's apartheid and the urban underclass. *Social Service Review, 68*(4), 471–487.

Masten, A. S. (1992). Homeless children in the United States: Mark of a nation at risk. *Current Directions in Psychological Science, 1,* 41–44.

Masterson, J. (1972). *Treatment of the borderline adolescent.* New York: Harper & Row.

Masterson, J. (1976). *Treatment of the borderline adult.* New York: Harper & Row.

Matson, J. L., & Smiroldo, B. B. (1999). Intellectual disorders. In W. K. Silverman & T. H. Ollendick (Eds.), *Developmental issues in the clinical treatment of children* (pp. 295–307). Boston: Allyn & Bacon.

Maturana, H., & Varila, F. J. (1987). *The tree of knowledge: The biological roots of human understanding.* Boston: Shambhala Publications.

May, G. G. (1982). *Will and spirit: A contemplative psychology.* New York: Harper & Row.

Mazor, A., Gampel, Y., Enright, R. D., & Orenstein, R. (1990). Holocaust survivors: Coping with post-traumatic memories in childhood and 40 years later. *Journal of Traumatic Stress, 3*(1), 1–13.

McAdams, D. P. (1990). Unity and purpose in human lives: The emergence of identity as a life story. In A. I. Rabin, A. Zucker, R. A. Emmons, & S. Frand (Eds.), *Studying persons and lives* (pp. 148–200). New York: Springer.

McAdams, D. P. (1993). *The stories we live by: Personal myths and the making of the self.* New York: William Morrow.

McAdams, D. P., & De St. Aubin, E. (1992). A theory of generativity and its assessment through self-report, behavioral acts, and narrative themes in autobiography. *Journal of Personality and Social Psychology, 62,* 1003–1015.

McCall, L. (2005). The complexity of intersectionality. *Signs, 30,* 1771–1800.

McClellan, J., & Werry, J. S. (1997, October). Practice parameters for the assessment and treatment of children and adolescents with bipolar disorder. *Journal of the American Academy of Child & Adolescent Psychiatry, 36*(Supplement), 157–176.

McClure, F. H. & Teyber, E. (1996). The multicultural-relational approach. In F. H. McClure & E. Teyber (Eds.), *Child and adolescent therapy: A multicultural-relational approach* (pp. 1–32). New York: Harcourt, Brace & Company.

McCubbin, H. L., & Figley, C. R. (1983). *Stress and the family: Vol. I. Coping with normative transitions*. New York: Brunner Mazel.

McDonald, G., & Oxford, M. (1999). *The history of independent living*. Retrieved November 10, 2005, from http://www.acils.com

McDonald, L., Billingham, S., Conrad, T., Morgan, A., & Payton, E. (1997). Families and Schools Together (FAST): Integrating community development with clinical strategies. *Families in Society, 78*(1), 115–116.

McFarland, P. L., & Sanders, S. (2003). A pilot study about the needs of older gays and lesbians: What social workers need to know. *Journal of Gerontological Social Work, 40*(3), 67–80.

McGinnis, J. M., & Foege, W. H. (1993). Actual cases of death in the United States. *Journal of the American Medical Association, 270*, 2207–2212.

McGoey, K. E., Eckert,, T. L., & DuPaul, G. J. (2002). Early intervention for pre-school aged children with ADHD: A literature review. *Journal of Emotional and Behavioral Disorders, 10*(1), 14–28.

McGoldrick, M., & Gerson, R. (1985). *Genograms in family assessment*. New York: Norton.

McGoldrick, M., Gerson, R., & Shellenberger, S. (1999). *Genograms: Assessment and intervention* (2nd ed.). New York: Norton.

McGoldrick, M., & Giordano, J. (1996). Overview: Ethnicity and family therapy. In M. McGoldrick, J. Giordano, & J. K. Pearce (Eds.), *Ethnicity and family therapy* (pp. 1–27). New York: Guilford Press.

McLoyd, V. C. (1998). Socioeconomic disadvantage and child development. *American Psychologist, 53*, 185–204.

McNeil, C. B., Bahl, A., & Herschell, A. D. (2000). Involving and empowering parents in short-term play therapy for disruptive children. In H. G. Kaduson & C. E. Schaefer (Eds.), *Short-term play therapy for children* (pp. 228–256). New York: Guilford Press.

McPhail, B. A. (2004). Questioning gender and sexual binaries: What queer theorists, transgendered individuals, and sex researchers can teach social work. *Journal of Gay & Lesbian Social Services, 17*(1), 3–21)

McQuaide, S. (1996). Women at midlife. *Social Work, 43*(1), 21–32.

McQuaide, S. (1998). Opening space for alternative images and narratives of midlife women. *Clinical Social Work Journal, 26*(1), 39–53.

McWhirter, J. J., McWhirter, B. T., McWhirter E. H, & McWhirter, R. J. (2004). *At risk youth: A comprehensive response* (3rd Ed.). Pacific Grove, CA: Brooks/Cole.

Mechanic, D. (1974). Social structure and personal adaptation. In G. V. Coelho, D. A. Hamburg & J. E. Adams (Eds.), *Coping and adaptation* (pp. 32–46). New York: Basic Books.

Medicare Official Touts Drug Plan. (2005, July 14). *The Republican*.

Meenaghan, T. M. (1972). What means community? *Social Work, 17*(6), 94–98.

Meichenbaum, D. (1994). *A clinical handbook/practical therapist manual for assessing and treating adults with posttraumatic stress disorder (PTSD)*. Waterloo, Canada: Institute Press.

Meichenbaum, D. (1996). *Mixed anxiety and depression: A cognitive-behavioral approach*. New York: Newbridge Communications.

Meier, A. (2004). Technology-mediated groups. In C. D. Garvin, L. M. Gutierrez, & M. J. Galinsky (Eds.), *Handbook of social work with groups* (pp. 479–503). New York: Guilford Press.

Meisami, E. (1994). Aging of the sensory systems. In P. S. Timiras (Ed.), *Physiological basis of aging and geriatrics* (2nd ed.). Ann Arbor, MI: CRC Press.

Meltzoff, A. N., & Borton, R. W. (1979). Intermodal matching by human neonates. *Nature, 282*, 403–404.

Melzack, R. (1982). *The challenge of pain*. New York: Basic Books.

Melzack, R., & Wall, P. D. (1965). Pain mechanisms: A new theory. *Science, 150*, 971–979.

Mendenhall, A. (2006). A guide to the Earned Income Tax Credit: What everyone should know about the EITC. *Journal of Poverty, 10*(3), 51–68.

Mental Health Advisory Team. (2006, May 29). Operation Iraqi freedom 04-05 report. Office of the Surgeon Multinational Force-Iraq and Office of the Surgeon General United States Army Medical Command. Retreived February 23, 2007 from http://www.armymedicine.army.mil/news/mhat/mhat_iii/MHAT III_Report_29May2006_redacted.pdf

Mesibov, G. B., Shea, V., & Adams, L. W. (2001). *Understanding Asperger's and high functioning autism*. New York: Kluwer Academic/Plenum.

Messer, S. C., & Beidel, D. C. (1994). Psychosocial correlates of childhood anxiety disorders. *Journal of the American Academy of Child and Adolescent Psychiatry, 33*, 975–983.

Messer, S. P., & Warren, C. S. (1995). *Models of brief psychodynamic therapy: A comparative approach*. New York: Guilford Press.

Meyer, M. D. (2003). Looking toward the interSEXions: Examining bisexual and transgender identity formation from a dialectical theoretical perspective. *Journal of Bisexuality, 3*(3), 151–170.

Meyers, M., & Lee, J. (2003). Working but poor: How are families faring? *Children and Youth Services Review, 25*(3), 177–201.

Middleman, R. R., & Goldberg, G. (1987). Social work practice with groups. In A. Minahan et al. (Eds.), *Encyclopedia of social work* (8th ed., pp. 714–729). Silver Spring, MD: National Association of Social Workers.

Middleman, R. R., & Wood, G. G. (1990). *Skills for direct practice in social work.* New York: Columbia University Press.

Miliora, M. T. (2000). Beyond empathic failures: Cultural racism as narcissistic trauma and disenfranchisement of grandiosity. *Clinical Social Work Journal, 28*(1), 43–54.

Miller, B. C., Fan, X., Christensen, M., Grotevant, H. D., & van Dulmen, M. (2000). Comparisons of adopted and non-adopted adolescents in a large, nationally representative sample. *Child Development, 71,* 1458–1473.

Miller, I. M. S., & Lachman, M. E. (2000). Cognitive performance and the role of control beliefs in midlife. *Aging, Neuropsychology, and Cognition,* 7(2), 69–85.

Miller, J. B. (2002). How change happens: Controlling images, mutuality, and power. *Work in Progress,* 96. Wellesley, MA: Stone Center Working Paper Series.

Miller, J. B. (2003). Telling the truth about power. *Work in Progress.* Wellesley, MA: Stone Center Working Paper Series.

Miller, J., & Garran, A. M. (2007). *Racism in the United States: Implications for the helping professions.* Belmont, CA: Thompson/Brooks Cole.

Miller, J., Garran, A., Milville, M. L., & Helms, J. E. (1996). *Exploring relationships of cultural, gender and ego identity among Latinos/as.* Poster presentation at the annual meeting of the American Psychological Association. Toronto, Canada.

Miller, W. R., & Rollnick, S. (2002). *Motivational interviewing: Preparing people for change* (2nd ed.). New York: Guilford Press.

Milville, M. L., Koonce, D., Darlington, P., & Whitlock, B. (2000). Exploring the relationships between racial/cultural identity and ego identity among African Americans and Mexican Americans. *Journal of Multicultural Counseling & Development, 28*(4), 194–207.

Min, J. W. (2005). Cultural competency: A key to effective future social work with racially and ethnically diverse elders. *Families in Society: The Journal of Contemporary Social Services, 86*(3), 347–358.

Miner-Rubino, K., Winter, D. G., & Stewart, A. J. (2004). Gender, social class, and the subjective experience of aging: Self-perceived personality change from early adulthood to late midlife. *Personality and Social Psychology Bulletin, 30*(12), 1599–1610.

Minkler, M. (1992). The physical and emotional health of grandmothers raising grandchildren in the crack cocaine epidemic. *The Gerontologist, 32,* 752–761.

Minkler, M. (1994, March 21). Grandparents as parents: The American experience. *Aging International,* 24–28.

Minkler, M., Driver, D., Roe, K., & Bedeian, K. (1993). Community interventions to support grandparent caregivers. *The Gerontologist, 33*(6), 807–811.

Minors (1996). From Uni-versity to Poly-versity. In *Perspectives on Racism and the Human Services Sector: A Case for Change.* Carl E. James (Ed). Toronto: University of Toronto Press.

Minuchin, S. (1974). *Families and family therapy.* Cambridge, MA: Harvard University Press.

Mischel, W., & Liebert, R. M. (1966). Effects of discrepancies between observed and imposed reward criteria on their acquisition and transmission. *Journal of Personality & Social Psychology, 3,* 45–53.

Mischell, W. (1996). A social learning view of sex differences in behavior. In E. M. Maccoby (Ed.), *The development of sex differences.* Stanford, CA: Stanford University Press.

Mishra, R. (1999). *Globalization and the welfare state.* Northampton, MA: Edward Elga.

Mistretta, C. M., & Bradley, R. M. (1977). Taste in utero: Theoretical considerations. In J. M. Weiffenbach (Ed.), *Taste and development* (pp. 279–291). DHEW publication No. NIH 77-1068. Bethesda, MD: U.S. Department of Health, Education, and Welfare.

Mitchell, S. (1988). *Relational concepts in psychoanalysis: An integration.* New York: Basic Books.

Mitchell, S. (2000). *Relationality: From attachment to intersubjectivity.* Hillsdale, NJ: Analytic Press.

Mitchell, V., Scarlett, M., & Amata, A. (2001, Fall/Winter). Trauma admission to the ICU of the University Hospital of the West Indies, Kingston, Jamaica. *ITACCS,* 86–89.

Moe, R. C. (1987). Exploring the limits of privatization. *Public Administration Review, 47,* 454–460.

Moen, P., Robinson, J., & Fields, V. (1994). Women's work and caregiving roles: A life course approach. *Journal of Gerontology, 49,* S176–S186.

Monti, P. M., Colby, S. M., & O'Leary, T. A. (2001). *Adolescents, alcohol, and substance abuse: Reaching teens through brief interventions.* New York: Guilford Press.

Moody, H. R. (2002). *Aging: Concepts and controversies* (4th ed.). Thousands Oaks, CA: Pine Forge Press.

Moon, A., Lawson, K., Carpiac, M., & Spaziano, E. (2006). Elder abuse and neglect among veterans in greater Los Angeles: Prevalence, types and intervention outcomes. *Journal of Gerontological Social Work, 46*(3/4), 187–204.

Moore, R., & Garland, A. (2000). *Cognitive therapy for chronic and persistent depression.* New York: Wiley.

Moorey, S., & Greer, S. (2002). *Cognitive behavior therapy for people with cancer.* New York: Oxford University Press.

Morales, E. S. (1990). Transgressing sex and gender. Deconstruction zone ahead? *Siecus Report, 28,* 14–21.

Morgan, P. (Ed.). (1995). *Privatization and the welfare state: Implications for consumers and the workforce.* Aldershot, UK: Dartmouth.

Morison, S. J., Ames, E. W., & Chisholm, K. (1995). The development of children adopted from Romanian orphanages. *Merrill-Palmer Quarterly, 41,* 411–430.

Morris, J. F., Balsam, K. F., & Rothblum, E. D. (2001). Lesbian and bisexual mothers and nonmothers: Demographics and the coming-out process. *Journal of Family Psychology, 16,* 144–156.

Morrison, L. L., & L'Heureux, J. (2001, February). Suicide and gay/lesbian/bisexual youth: Implications for clinicians. *Journal of Adolescence, 24*(1), 39–49.

Moses, A. E., & Hawkins, R. O. (1982). *Counseling lesbian women and gay men: A life issues approach.* St. Louis, MO: Mosby.

Moshman, D. (1998). Cognitive development beyond childhood. In D. Kuhn & R. S. Siegler (Eds.), *Handbook of child psychology: Vol. 2. Cognition, perception, and language* (pp. 957–978). New York: Wiley.

Moulton, R. (1971). A survey and re-evaluation of the concept of penis envy. *Journal of Contemporary Psychoanalysis, 7,* 84–104.

Mulroy, E. A. (2004). Theoretical Perspectives on Social Environment to Guide Management and Community Practice: An Organization in Environment Approach. *Administration in Social Work, 28*(1), 77–96.

Mulroy, E., & Shay, S. (1998). Motivation and reward in non profit interorganizational collaboration in low-income neighborhoods. *Administration in Social Work, 22* (4), 1–17.

Munk, M. (2005). Spiritual development. In D. Comstock (Ed.), *Diversity and development: Critical contexts that shape our lives and relationships* (pp. 319–335). Belmont, CA: Thomson, Brooks/Cole.

Murphy, Y., Hunt, V., Zajicek, A. M., Norris, A. N. & Hamilton, L. (2009). *Incorporating intersectionality in social work practice, research, policy and education.* Washington DC: NASW Press.

Myers, D. G. (2001). *Social psychology* (7th ed.). New York: Worth.

Myers, L. J. (1988). *Understanding an Afrocentric Worldview: Introduction to an Optimal Psychology.* Dubuque, IA: Kendall/Hunt

Myers, M. G., Brown, S. A., Tate, S., Abrantes, A., & Tomlinson, K. (2001). Toward brief interventions for adolescents with substance abuse and co-morbid psychiatric problems. In P. Monti, S. Colby, & T. O'Leary (Eds.), *Adolescents, alcohol and substance abuse: Reaching teens through brief interventions* (pp. 275–297). New York: Guilford Press.

Myers, S. (1995). Midlife crisis. *Psychiatry On-Line.* Retrieved November 25, 2005, from http://www.pol-it-org/mbti2.htm

Nagae, N., & Nedate, K. (2001). Comparison of constructive cognitive and rational cognitive psychotherapies for students with social anxiety. *Constructivism, 6,* 41–49.

Nagda, B., & Zuniga, X. (2003). Fostering meaningful racial engagement through intergroup dialogues. *Group Processes and Intergroup Relations, 6*(1), 111–128.

Nagel, J. (1994). Constructing ethnicity: Creating and recreating ethnic identity and culture. *Social Problems, 41,* 152–176.

Nansel, T. R., Overpeck, M., Pula, R. S., Ruan, W. J., Simons-Morton, B., & Scheidt, P. (2001). Bullying among U.S. youth: Prevalence associated with psychosocial adjustment. *Journal of the American Medical Association, 85,* 2094–2100.

Napier, R., & Gershenfeld, M. K. (1985). *Groups, theory and experience* (3rd ed.). Boston: Houghton Mifflin.

National Association of Social Workers (NASW). (July 2005a). Study: Depression treatment lacking. *NASW News, 50*(7), 10.

National Association of Social Workers (NASW). (2005b, March 18). *Social work imperatives for the next decade.* Adopted at Social Work Congress, Washington, DC.

National Association of Social Workers (NASW). (July 2005c). Summit addresses end-of-life care. *NASW News, 50*(7), 6.

National Center for Learning Disabilities. (1994). *What is dyslexia?* Washington, DC: Author.

National Foundation for Depressive Illness, Inc., www.depression.org.

National Health Guide: *Coping with Aids as a chronic long term illness.* Retrieved October 16, 2005, from http://www.grants.nih.gov/grants/guide/pa-files/PA-99–026.html

National Institute of Child Health and Human Development (NICHD). Early Child Care Research (1997). The effects of infant child care on infant–mother attachment security results of the NICHD study of early child care. *Child Development, 68,* 960–879.

National Institute of Child Health and Human Development (NICHD). Early Child Care Research Network.

(1998). The effects of infant child care on infant–mother attachment security results of the NICHD study of early child care. *Child Development, 69,* 1145–1170.

National Institute of Child Health and Human Development (NICID). (2002). Early child care and children's development prior to school entry: Results from the NICHD Early Child Care Research Network study of early child care. *American Educational Research Journal, 39*(1), 133–164.

National Institute of Mental Health. (2008). *Eating disorders.* Bethesda, MD: Author. Retrieved July 24, 2008, from http://www.nimh.nih.gov/health/publications/eating-disorders.

National Institute on Aging (NIA). (2002). *Aging under the microscope: A biological quest.* NIH Publication No.02–2756. Washington, DC: Author.

National Institute on Alcohol Abuse and Alcoholism (NIAAA). (1998, April). *Alcohol alert, alcohol and aging,* 40, 1–6. Retrieved December 20, 2008, from http://pubs.niaaa.nih.gov/publications/aa40 .htm

National Institute on Disability and Rehabilitation Research. (1992). *Disability Statistics Report: Disability in the United States, Prevalence and Causes.* Washington, DC: Author.

National Joint Committee on Learning Disabilities. (1985). Learning disabilities: Issues in the preparation of professional personnel. *American Speech-Language-Hearing Association, 27*(9), 49–51.

National Public Radio. (2005, July 8). Bush ends inquiry into Schiavo's collapse. Retrieved July 9, 2005, from http://www.cnn.com/2005/US/07/08/gov-ernor.schi-avo.ap/index.html

Neck, C. P., & Manz, C. C. (1994). From groupthink to teamthink: Toward the creation of constructive thought patterns in self-managing work teams. *Human Relations, 47*(8), 929–952.

Neistadt, M. E., & Freda, M. (1987). *Choices: A guide to sex counseling with physically disabled adults.* Malabar, FL: Robert E. Krieger.

Nelson, C. A. (2000). The neurobiological basis of early intervention. In J. P. Shonkoff & S. J. Meisels (Eds.), *Handbook of early childhood intervention* (2nd ed., pp. 204–227). Cambridge: Cambridge University Press.

Nelson, D. A., & Crick, R. A. (1999). Rose-colored glasses: Examining the social information-processing of prosocial young adolescents. *Journal of Early Adolescence, 19,* 17–38.

Nelson, H. D., Humphrey, L. L., Nyugren, P., Teutsch, S. M., & Allan, J. D. (2002). Postmenopausal hormone replacement therapy: Scientific review. *Journal of the American Medical Association, 288,* 872–881.

Nelson, J. L. (1998). The meaning of the act: Reflections on the expressive force of reproductive decision making and policies. *Kennedy Institute of Ethics Journal, 8*(2), 165–182.

Nelson, M., Ruch, S., Jackson, Z., Bloom, L., & Part, R. (1992). Towards an understanding of families with physically disabled adolescents. *Social Work in Health Care, 17*(4), 1–25.

Nemoto, T., Operario, D. Keatley, J., Nguyen, B. S., & Sugano, E. (2005). Promoting health for transgender women: Transgender Resources and Neighborhood Space (TRNS) Program in San Francisco. *American Journal of Public Health, 95*(3), 382–384.

Neugarten, B. L. (1968). The awareness of middle age. In B. L. Neugarten (Ed.), *Middle age and aging* (pp. 93–98). Chicago: University of Chicago Press.

Neugarten, B. L., Havighurst, R. J., & Tobin, S. S. (1968). Personality and patterns of aging. In B. L. Neugarten (Ed.), *Middle age and aging.* Chicago: University of Chicago Press.

Newby, I. (1965). *Jim Crow's defense: Anti-Negro thought in America, 1900–1930.* Baton Rouge: Louisiana State University Press.

New Freedom Commission on Mental Health (2003). Achieving the promise: Transforming mental health care in America. *Executive Summary.* Washington, DC.

Newgarten, B. L., & Weinstein, K. K. (1964). The changing American grandparent. *Journal of Marriage and the Family, 26,* 199–204.

Newman, B. M., & Newman, P. R. (1995). *Development through life: A psychosocial approach.* 6th ed. Pacific Grove, CA: Brooks/Cole.

Newman, B. M., & Newman, P. R. (1999). *Development through life: A psychosocial approach* (7th ed.). Belmont, CA: Brooks/Cole.

Newman, B. M., & Newman, P. R. (2002). *Development through life: A psychosocial approach* (8th ed.). Pacific Grove, CA: Brooks/Cole.

Newstetter, W. (1935). What is social group work? *Proceedings, National Conference of Social Work* (pp. 291–299). Chicago: University of Chicago Press.

Nichols, M. P. (with Schwarz, R.C.) (2008). Family Therapy: Concepts and Methods (2008) 8th Ed. Boston, MA: Pearson/Allyn and Bacon.

Nichols, M. P., & Schwartz, R. C. (2005). *Essentials of family therapy* (2nd ed.). Boston and New York: Pearson.

Nickerson, A., & Nagle, R. (2005). Parent and peer attachment in late childhood and early adolescence. *Journal of Early Adolescence, 25*(2), 223–249.

Nisbett, R. E. (2003). *The geography of thought: How Asians and Westerners think differently . . . and why.* New York: Free Press.

Nix, R. L., Pinderhughes, E. E., Dodge, K. A., Bates, J. E., Pettit, G. S., & McFadyen-Ketchum, S. A. (1999). The relation between mothers: Hostile attribution tendencies and children's externalizing behavior problems: The mediating role of mothers' harsh discipline practices. *Child Development, 70,* 896–909.

Nobles, W. (1991). African Philosophy: Foundations for Black Psychology. In R. L. Jones (Ed.). *Black Psychology* (pp. 47–63). Berkeley, CA: Cobb and Henry Publishers.

Northern, R., & Kurland, R. (2001). *Social work with groups* (3rd ed.). New York: Columbia University Press.

Nukolls, K. B., Cassel, J., & Kaplan, B. H. (1972). Psychosocial assets, life crises, and the prognosis of pregnancy. *American Journal of Epidemiology, 95,* 431–441.

Nydegger, C. N. (1991). The development of paternal and filial maturity. In K. Pillemer, & K. McCartney (Eds.), *Parent–child relations throughout life* (pp. 93–112). Hillsdale, NJ: Erlbaum.

O'Connell, P. (1972, June). Developmental tasks of the family. *Smith College Studies in Social Work, 42,* 203–210.

O'Connor, K. J. (2000). *The play therapy primer* (2nd ed.). New York: Wiley.

O'Connor, K. J., & Braverman, L. (1997). *Play therapy theory and practice: A comparative presentation.* New York: Wiley.

O'Connor, K. J., Ewart, K., & Willheim, L. (2001). Psychodynamic psychotherapy with children. In V. Van Hasselt & M. Herson (Eds.), *The clinical psychology handbook* (pp. 543–564). Elmsford, NY: Pergamon Press.

O'Dea, P. O. (2001). Bilingual education: An overview. *CRS Report for Congress.* Washington, DC: Congressional Research Service, The Library of Congress.

Office of the Surgeon General. (n.d.). *Mental health: A report of the surgeon general.* Retrieved September 4, 2005. from http://www.surgeongeneral .gov/library/mental-health/chapter3/sec3.html

Oldenberg, R. (1999). *The great good place.* New York: Marlow & Co.

Olkin, R. (1999). *What Psychotherapists Should Know about Disability.* New York: Guilford.

Olson, S. L., & Hoza, B. (1993). Preschool developmental antecedents of conduct problems in children beginning school. *Journal of Clinical Child Psychology, 22,* 60–67.

O'Neill, R., & Parke, R. D. (1997, March). *Objective and subjective features of children's neighborhoods: Relations to parental regulatory strategies and children's social competence.* Paper presented at the biennial meeting of the Society for Research in Child Development, Washington, DC.

Onyx, J., & Bullen, P. (2000). Measuring social capital in five communities. *Journal of Applied Behavioral Science, 36*(1), 23–42.

Osborn, A. (1963). *Applied imagination: Principles and procedures of creative problem solving* (3rd ed.). New York: Scribner.

Osgood, N. J., & Eisenhandler, S. A. (1994). Gender and assisted and acquiescent suicide: A suicidologist's perspective. *Issues in Law and Medicine, 9,* 361–374.

Osofsky, J. D., & Thompson, M. D. (2000). Adaptive and maladaptive parenting: Perspectives on risk and protective factors. In J. P. Shonkoff & S. J. Meisels (Eds.), *Handbook of early intervention* (2nd ed., pp. 54–75a). New York: Cambridge University Press.

Otis, J. D., Keane, T. M., & Kerns, R. D. (2003). An examination of the relationship between chronic pain and posttraumatic stress disorder. *Journal of Rehabilitation Research and Development, 40,* 397–406.

Owens, E. B. (2001). Attachment stability and emotional and behavioral regulation from infancy to preschool age. *Development & Psychopathology, 13,* 13–33.

Owens, G. P., Baker, D. G., Kasckow, J., Ciesla, J. A., & Mohamed, S. (2005). Review of assessment and treatment of PTSD among elderly American armed forces veterans. *International Journal of Geriatric Psychiatry, 20,* 1118–1130.

Oxford, M. L., Harachi, T. W., Catalano, R. F., & Abbot, R. D. (2001). Preadolescent predictors of substance initiation: A test of both the direct and mediated effect of family social control factors on deviant peer associations and substance initiation. *American Journal of Drug and Alcohol Abuse, 27*(4): 599–616.

Padden, R. (1989). The deaf community and the culture of deaf people. In S. Wilcox (Ed.), *American deaf culture* (pp. 1–16). Burtonsville, MD: Linstock.

Paikoff, R. L., & Brooks-Gunn, J. (1991). Do parent–child relationships change during puberty? *Psychological Bulletin, 110,* 47–66.

Palmer, P. (1996). Pain and possibilities: What therapists need to know about working class women's issues. *Feminism & Psychology, 6*(3), 457–462.

Palombo, J. P. (2001a). *Learning disorders and disorders of the self in children and adolescents.* New York: Guilford Press.

Palombo, J. P. (2001b). The therapeutic process with children with learning disorders. In J. R. Brandell (Ed.), *Psychoanalytic approaches to the treatment of children and adolescents* (pp. 143–169). Binghamton, NY: Haworth Press.

Palombo, J. P. (2001). *Learning disorders and disorders of the self.* New York: Norton.

Papageorgiou, C., & Wells, A. (Eds.). (2003). *Depressive rumination: Nature, theory and treatment.* New York: Wiley.

Papolos, D., & Papolos, J. (1999). *The bipolar child.* New York: Broadway Books.

Paradis, B. A. (1997). Multicultural identity and gay men in the era of AIDS. *American Journal of Orthopsychiatry, I*(2), 300–307.

Pardeck, J. (2002a). A commentary on what social workers need to know about the Individuals with Disabilities Education Act and the Americans with Disabilities Act. *Journal of Social Work in Disability and Rehabilitation, 1*(2), 83–94.

Pardeck, J. (2002b). A critical analysis of the social work literature on disabilities. *Journal of Social Work in Disabilities and Rehabilitation, 1*(2), 1–5.

Parham, T. A., White, J. L. and Ajamu, A. (1999). *The Psychology of Blacks: An African Centered Perspective* (3rd Ed.) Englewood Cliffs, NJ: Prentice-Hall.

Park, J., Turnbull, A. P., & Turnbull, H. R., III. (2002). Impacts of poverty on quality of life in families of children with disabilities. *Exceptional Children, 68*(2), 151–170.

Parsons, T. (1951). *The social system.* New York: Free Press.

Patterson, J. (2002). Lesbian and gay parenthood. In M. H. Bornstein (Ed.), *Handbook of parenting: Vol. 3. Being and becoming a parent* (2nd ed., pp. 317–338). Mahwah, NJ: Erlbaum.

Patterson, J. B., McKenzie, J., & Jenkins, J. (1995). Creating accessible groups for individuals with disabilities. *Journal for Specialists in Group Work, 20*(2), 6–82.

Patterson, K. T. (2001, December). The effect of gender on a predictive model of violent behaviors in rural youth using a contextual framework. *Dissertation Abstracts International: Section B: The Sciences and Engineering, 62*(5-B), 2259.

Patti, R. (2000). The Landscape of Social welfare administration. In R. Patti (ed.), *The handbook of social welfare administration* (pp. 3–25). Thousand Oaks, CA: Sage.

Paul, J. P. (1996). Bisexuality: Exploring/exploding the boundaries. In R. C. Savin-Williams & K. M. Cohen (Eds.), *The lives of lesbians, gays and bisexuals* (pp. 426–455). Orlando, FL: Harcourt Brace.

Payne, M. (1996). *Modern social work theory* (2nd ed.). Chicago: Lyceum Books.

Peak, D. T. (1977). The elderly who face dying and death. In D. Baron (Ed.), *Dying and death: A clinical guide for caregivers* (pp. 210–221). Baltimore: Williams & Wilkins.

Pearlin, L. I. (1991). Life strains and psychological distress among adults. In A. Monat & R. Lazarus (Eds.), *Stress and coping: An anthology* (3rd ed.). New York: Columbia University Press.

Pearlman, L. A., & Saakvitne, K. W. (1995). *Trauma and the therapist: Countertransference and vicarious traumatization in psychotherapy with incest survivors.* New York: Norton.

Peck, S. S., & Manocherian, J. (1989). Divorce in the changing family life cycle. In B. Carter & M. McGoldrick, *The changing family life cycle: A framework for family therapy* (2nd ed.). Boston: Allyn & Bacon.

Pellebon, D. A., & Anderson, S. C. (1999). Understanding the life issues of spiritually-based clients. *Families in Society, 80*(3), 229–238.

Penn, P. (2001). Chronic illness: Trauma, language and writing: Breaking the silence. *Family Process, 40*(1), 33–52.

Perez-Foster, R. (1998). The clinician's cultural countertransference: The psychodynamics of culturally competent practice. *Clinical Social Work Journal, 26*(3), 253–270.

Perry, B. D. (1994). Neurobiological sequelae of childhood trauma: Post traumatic stress disorders in children. In M. Murberg (Ed.), *Catecholamine function in post-traumatic stress disorder: Emerging concepts* (pp. 233–255). Washington, DC: American Psychiatric Press.

Perry, B. D. (1997). Incubated in terror: Neurodevelopmental factors in the "cycle of violence." In J. D. Osofsky (Ed.), *Children in a violent society* (pp. 124–149). New York: Guilford Press.

Perry B. D. (2002a). Childhood experience and the expression of genetic potential: What childhood neglect tells us about nature and nurture. *Brain and Mind, 3,* 79–100.

Perry, B. D. (2002b). Neurodevelopmental impact of violence in childhood. In D. H. Schetky & E. P. Benedek (Eds.), *Principles and practice of childand adolescent forensic psychiatry* (pp. 191–203). Washington, DC: American Psychiatric Publishing.

Perry, M., Kannel, S., & Dulio, A. (2002). *Barriers to medicaid enrollment for low-income seniors: Focus group findings.* The Kaiser Commission on Medicare and the Uninsured. Retrieved July 5, 2005, from http://www.kff.org/medicaid/upload/141101.pdf

Persons, J. B., Davidson, J., & Tomkins, M. A. (2001). *Essential components of cognitive-behavioral therapy for depression.* Washington, DC: American Psychological Association.

Peterson, B. E., & Stewart, A. J. (1996). Antecedents and contexts of generativity motivation at midlife. *Psychology and Aging, 11*(1), 21–33.

Phan, L. T., Rivera, E. T., & Roberts-Wilbur, J. (2005, Summer). Understanding Vietnamese refugee women's identity development from a sociopolitical and historical perspective. *Journal of Counseling and Development, 88,* 305–383.

Phinney, J. S. (1989). Stages of ethnic identity development in minority group adolescents. *Journal of Early Adolescence, 9,* 34–49.

Phinney, J. S. (1992). The multigroup ethnic identity measure: A new scale for use with diverse groups. *Journal of Adolescent Research,* 7(2), 156–176.

Phinney, J. S. (1996). When we talk about American ethnic groups, what do we mean? *American Psychologist, 51,* 918–927.

Phinney, J. S., & Alipuria, L. L. (1990). Ethnic identity in college students from four ethnic groups. *Journal of Adolescence, 13,* 171–183.

Phoenix, A., & Owen, C. (1996). From miscegenation to hybridity: Mixed relationships and mixed-parentage in profile. In B. Bernstein & J. Brannen (Eds.), *Children, research and policy* (pp. 111–135). London: Taylor & Francis.

Piaget, J. (1932/1965). *The moral judgment of the child.* New York: Free Press.

Piaget, J. (1936/1952). *The origins of intelligence in children.* New York: International Universities Press.

Piaget, J. (1945/1951). *Play, dreams and imitation in childhood.* New York: Norton.

Piaget, J. (1951). *Judgment and reasoning in the child.* London: Routledge & Kegan Paul.

Piaget, J. (1952). *The origins of intelligence in children.* New York: International Universities Press.

Piaget, J. (1962). *Play, dreams, and imitation in childhood.* New York: Norton.

Piaget, J. (1963). *The language of intelligence.* New York: International Universities Press.

Piaget, J. (1969). The intellectual development of the adolescent. In A. Esman (Ed.), *Adolescent development* (pp. 104–109). New York: International Universities Press.

Piaget, J. (1972). *The principles of genetic epistemology.* New York: Basic Books.

Piaget, J., & Inhelder, B. (1969). *The psychology of the child.* New York: Basic Books.

Pianta, R. C. (1999). Early childhood. In W. K. Silverman & T. H. Ollendick (Eds.), *Developmental issues in the clinical treatment of children.* Boston: Allyn & Bacon.

Piastro, D. B. (1999). Coping with the transitions in our lives: From "afflicted" identity to personal empowerment and pride. *Reflections, 5*(4), 42–60.

Pincus, S. H., House, R., Christenson, J., and Adler, L. (n.d). *The emotional cycle of deployment: A military family perspective.* Retrieved October 19, 2006 from http://www.hooah4-health.com/deployment/familymatters/emotionalcycle.htm

Pinson-Milburn, N. M (1965). *Grandparents raising grandchildren: Health status needs and implications for policy.* Unpublished report, University of Maryland, College Park, Center of Human Services Development.

Piotrkowski, C. S., & Hughes, D. (1993). Dual-earner families in context: Managing family and work systems. In F. Walsh (Ed.), *Normal family processes* (2nd ed.). New York: Guilford Press.

Planning Institute of Jamaica. (2003). Kingston, Jamaica, W.I.

Pleck, J. H. (1990). Family-supportive employer policies: Are they relevant to men? In J. C. Hood (Ed.), *Men's work and family roles.* Newbury Park, CA: Sage.

Pliszka, S. R. (2003). *Neuroscience for the mental health clinician.* New York: Guilford Press.

Plomin, R., & DeFries, J. C. (1985). *Origins of individual differences in infancy: The Colorado adoption project.* New York: Academic Press.

Poggio, B. (2006). Editorial: Outline of a theory of gender practices. *Gender, Work and Organization, 13*(3), 225–233.

Pollack, O. (1960, March). A family diagnosis model. *Social Service Review, 34,* 1–50.

Ponse, B. (1978). *Identities in the lesbian world: The social construction of self.* London: Greenwood Press.

Popple, P. R., & Leighninger, L. (2001). *The policy-based profession* (2nd ed.). Boston: Allyn & Bacon.

Popple, P. R. (1995). The Social Work Profession: History. *In Encyclopedia of Social Work* (19th Ed.). *3,* 2282–2292.

Popple, P. R., & L. Leighninger. (1993). *Social work, social welfare, and American society* (2nd ed.). Boston: Allyn & Bacon.

Porter, R. (1997). The politics of bilingual education. *Society, 34*(6), 31–39.

Posada, G., Jacobs, A., Richmond, M. K., Carbonell, O. A., Alzate, G., Bustamante, M. R., & Quiceno, J.

(2002). Maternal caregiving and infant security in two cultures. *Developmental Psychology, 38,* 67–78.

Posner, M. I., & Rothbart, M. K. (2000). Developing mechanisms of self-regulation. *Development and Psychopathology, 12,* 427–441.

Poston, W. S. C. (1990). The biracial identity development model: A needed addition. *Journal of Counseling & Development, 69,* 152–155.

Powell, T. J. (1987). *Self-help organizations and professional practice.* Silver Spring, MD: National Association of Social Workers.

Powers, M. D. (Ed.). (2000). *Children with autism: A parent's guide* (2nd ed.). Rockville, MD: Woodbine House.

Price, P. (2004). *Neurotransmitters and neurons.* Retrieved August 25, 2004, from http://www.allaboutdepression.com/cau_02.html

Priest, D., & Hall, A. (February 21, 2007, p. A08). Swift action promised at Walter Reed, investigations urged as army moves to make repairs, improve staffing. *Washington Post,* p. A08. Retrieved from http://www/washingtonpost.com

Prohanska, T. R., Peters, K. E., & Warren, J. S. (2000). Health behavior: From research to community practice. In G. L. Albrecht, R. Fitzpatrick, & S. C. Scrimshaw (Eds.), *Handbook of social studies in health and medicine* (pp. 359–373). Thousand Oaks, CA: Sage.

Puchalski, C. M. (1999). FICA: A spiritual assessment. *Journal of Palliative Care.* Retrieved November 25, 2005, from AvailableServer\GcG\9464\Speaker&Syllabus\\9464SyllabusPuchaski.doc–10/19/ 99

Pugh, D. S., Hickson, D. J., & Hinings, C. R. (Eds.). (1985). *Writers on organizations.* Beverly Hills, CA: Sage.

Quadagno, J. (2002). *Aging and the life course: An introduction to social gerontology.* New York: McGraw-Hill.

Queener, J. E. & Martin, J. K. (2001). Providing culturally relevant mental health services; collaboration between psychology and the African American church. *Journal of Black Psychology, 27*(1), 112–122.

Quinn, J. B. (2001, June). Shame of the rich: Making themselves poor. *Washington Post,* financial section, p. H.02.

Quinn, N. (1991). The cultural basis of metaphor. In J. W. Fernandez (Ed.), *Beyond metaphor: The theory of tropes in anthropology* (p. 57). Stanford, CA: Stanford University Press.

Quintanta, S. M., & Lapsley, D. K. (1990). Rapprochement in late adolescence. *Journal of Adolescence, 13*(4), 371–385.

Rabin, B. J. (1980). *The sensuous wheeler: Sexual adjustment for the spinal cord-injured.* San Francisco: Multi Media Resource Center.

Radke-Yarrow, M., McCann, K., DeMulder, E., Belmont, B., Martinez, P., & Richardson, D. T. (1995). Attachment in the context of high-risk conditions. *Development & Psychopathology, 7,* 247–265.

Raj, R. (2002). Towards a transpositive therapeutic model: Developing clinical sensitivity and cultural competence in the effective support of transsexual and transgendered clients. *International Journal of Transgenderism, 6*(2), 1–45.

Raley, R. K. (1996). A shortage of marriageable men? A note on the role of cohabitation in black-white differences in marriage rates. *American Sociological Review, 61,* 973–983.

Rashkin, E. (1999). The haunted child: Social catastrophe, phantom transmissions, and the aftermath of collective trauma. *Psychoanalytic Review, 86*(3), 433–453.

Reid, O. G., Mims, S. & Higginbottom, L. (2005). *Post traumatic Slavery Disorder: Definition, diagnosis and treatment.* Charlotte, N.C.: Conquering Books.

Reinecke, M. A., Dattilio, F. M., & Freeman, A. (Eds.). (2003). *Cognitive therapy with children and adolescents: A casebook for clinical practice.* New York: Guilford Press.

Reisch, M., & Gambrill, E. (1997). *Social work in the 21st century.* Thousand Oaks, CA: Pine Forge Press.

Reiss, D. (1981). *The family's construction of reality.* Cambridge, MA: Harvard University Press, 1981.

Rennie, R., & Landreth, G. (2000). Effects of filial therapy on parent and child behaviours. *International Journal of Play Therapy, 99*(2), 19–37.

Reskin, B., & Padavic, I. (1994). *Women and men at work.* Thousand Oaks, CA: Pine Forge Press.

Resnick, M. D., Bearman, P. S., Blum, R. W., Bauman, K. E. H., Jones, J., Tabor, J., et al. (1997). Protecting adolescents from harm: Findings from the National Longitudinal Study on Adolescent Health. *Journal of the American Medical Association, 278*(10), 820–832.

Resse, D. J., & Raymer, M. (2004). Relationships between social work involvement and hospice outcomes: Results of the national hospice social work survey. *Social Work, 49*(3), 415–422.

Rethinking Schools Online. (2002). *Does bilingual ed work?* Retrieved October 18, 2005, from http://www.rethinkingschools.org/archive

Rhodes, S. (1977). A developmental approach to the life cycle of the family. *Social Casework, 58*(5), 301–311.

Richardson, C. (1992, October/November). Employee involvement: Employee empowerment, total quality management. *Labor Page*, 73.

Richman, J. M., Bowen, G. L., & Woolley, M. E. (2004). School failure: An eco-interactional-developmental perspective. In M. S. Frasier (Ed.), *Risk and resilience in childhood: An ecological perspective* (2nd ed., pp. 133–160). New York: Sage.

Richmond, M. (1917). *Social diagnosis*. New York: Russell Sage Foundation.

Ridenour, R. I. (1984) The military, service families and the therapist. In F. W. Kaslow and R. I. Ridenour (Eds.) *The military family Dynamics and Treatment* (pp. 1–17). New York: Guilford.

Right to die. (2005, July 11). *Time*, p. 29.

Riksen-Walraven, M. (2000). *Tud voor kwaliteit in de kinderopvang*. Amsterdam: Vossius.

Rizzuto, A. (1979). *The birth of the living god: A psychoanalytic study*. Chicago: University of Chicago Press.

Robbins, S. P., Chatterjee, P., & Canda, E. R. (1998). *Contemporary human behavior theory: A critical perspective for social work*. Needham Heights, MA: Allyn & Bacon.

Robinson, T. (1993). The intersections of gender, class, race, and culture: On seeing clients whole. *Journal of Multicultural Counseling & Development, 21*(1), 50–58.

Robinson, T. L. (1999). The Intersections of Dominant Discourses Across Race, Gender and Other Identities. *Journal of Counseling and Development, 77* (pp. 73–79).

Rodriguez, A. R. (1984). Special treatment needs of children of military families. In F. W. Kaslow & R. I. Ridenour (Eds.), *The military family: Dynamics and treatment* (pp. 46–72). New York: Guilford Press.

Rogler, L. H. (1994). International migrations: A framework for directing research. *American Psychologist. 49*(8), 701–707.

Rogoff, B., & Chavajay, P. (1995). What's become of research on the cultural basis of cognitive development? *American Psychologist, 50*, 859–877.

Rolland, J. S. (1988). A conceptual model of chronic and life threatening illness and its impact on families. In C. S. Chilman, E. W. Nunnaly, & F. M. Cox (Eds.), *Chronic illness and disability*. Newbury Park, CA: Sage.

Rolland, J. S. (1989). Chronic illness and the family life cycle. In E. A. Carter & M. McGoldrick (Eds.), *The changing life cycle: A framework for family therapy* (2d ed.). Needham Heights, MA: Allyn & Bacon.

Rolland, J. S. (1994). *Families, illness, and disability: An integrative treatment model*. New York: Basic Books.

Romney trims, signs budget. (2005, July 1). *The Republican*, p. A9.

Ronen, T. (2004). Cognitive-behavioral therapy with children and families. In R. A. Dorfman, P. Meyer, & M. L. Morgan (Eds.), *Paradigms of clinical social work: Vol. 3. Emphasis on diversity* (pp. 59–83). New York: Brunner-Routledge.

Rooney, R., & Chovanec, M. (2004). Involuntary groups. In C. D. Garvin, L. M. Gutierrez, & M. J. Galinsky, *Handbook of social work with groups* (pp. 212–227). New York: Guilford Press.

Roos, S. (2002). *Chronic sorrow: A living loss*. New York: Brunner-Routledge.

Root, M. P. P. (1990). Resolving "other" status: Identity development of biracial individuals. In L. Brown & M. P. P. Root (Eds.), *Diversity and complexity in feminist therapy* (pp. 575–593). New York: Harrington Park Press.

Root, M. P. P. (1994). Mixed-race women. In L. Comas-Diaz & B. Greene (Eds.), *Women of color integrating ethnic and gender identities in psychotherapy* (pp. 231–236). Lanham, MD: Rowman & Littlefield.

Root, M. P. P. (1999). The biracial baby boom: Understanding ecological constructions of racial identity in the 21st century. In R. H. Sheets & E. R. Hollins (Eds.), *Racial and ethnic identity in school practices* (pp. 67–87). Mahwah, NJ: Erlbaum.

Roots, C. R. (1998). *The sandwich generation: Adult children caring for aging parents*. New York: Garland.

Rosario, M., Schrimshaw, E. W., Hunter, J., & Braun, L. (2006). Sexual identity development among lesbian, gay, and bisexual youths: Consistency and change over time. *Journal of Sex Research, 43*(1), 46–58

Rose, V. K. (2005). What employment programs should health services invest in for people with a psychiatric disability? *Australian Health Review, 29*(2), 185–188.

Rosen, H. (1998). Meaning-making as a meta framework for clinical practice. In R. Dorfman (Ed.), *Paradigms of clinical social work* (Vol. 2, pp. 257–289). New York: Brunner/Mazel.

Rosenberg, E. B. (1992). *The adoption life cycle: The children and their families through the years*. New York: Free Press.

Rosenheck, R., & Koegel, P. (1993). Characteristics of veterans and nonveterans in three samples of homeless men. *Hospital and Community Psychiatry, 44*(9), 858–863.

Rothberg, B., & Weinstein, D. (1996). A primer on lesbian and gay families. *Journal of Gay and Lesbian Social Services, 4*(2), 55–68.

Rotheram-Borus, M. J., & Bradley, J. (1990). Evaluation of suicide risk. In M. J. Rotheram-Borus, J. Bradley, & N. Obolensky (Eds.), *Planning to live: Evaluating and treating suicidal teens in community settings* (pp. 109–136). Tulsa: University of Oklahoma, National Resource Center for Youth.

Rotheram-Borus, M. J., Hunter, J., & Rosario, M. (1994). Suicidal behavior and gay-related stress among gay and bisexual male adolescents. *Journal of Adolescent Research, 9*, 498–508.

Rotheram-Borus, M. J., Rosario, M., & Koopman, C. (1991). Minority youths at high risk: Gay males and runaways. In M. D. Colten & S. Gore (Eds.), *Adolescent stress: Causes and consequences* (pp. 181–200). New York: Aldine de Gruyter.

Rothman, J. C. (2003). *Social work practice across disability*. Boston: Allyn & Bacon.

Rounds, K. A. (2004). Preventing sexual transmitted infections among adolescents. In M. W. Fraser (Ed.), *Risk and resilience in childhood: An ecological perspective* (pp. 251–279). Silver Spring, MD: NASW Press.

Rowe, W., Bennett, S. K., & Atkinson, D. R. (1994). White racial identity models: A critique and alternative proposal. *Counseling Psychologist, 22*, 129–146.

Roy, A., Cooper, M., & Lesser, J. (2008). A comparative cross-cultural study of depression and help-seeing behavior among older Chinese adults in Boston and Guangzhou, China. *International Journal of the Humanities, 6*(7), 79–84.

Rubin, K. H., Burgess, K. B., Kennedy, A. E., & Stewart, S. L. (2003). Social withdrawal. In E. J. Mash, & R. J. Barkley (Eds.), *Child psychopathology* (2nd ed., pp. 330–371). New York: Guilford Press.

Rudd, M. D., Joiner, T., & Rajab, M. H. (2001). *Treating suicidal behavior*. New York: Guilford Press.

Russell, G. M. (1996). Internalized classism: The role of class in the development of self. *Women & Therapy, 18*(3/4), 59–71.

Rust, P. C. (1996). Finding a sexual identity and community: Therapeutic implications and cultural assumptions in scientific models of coming out. In E. D. Rothblum & L. A. Bond (Eds.), *Preventing heterosexism and homophobia* (pp. 87–124). New York: Sage.

Rutter, M. (1995). Maternal deprivation. In M. H. Bornstein (Ed.), *Handbook of parenting: Vol. 4. Applied and practical parenting* (pp. 3–31). Hillsdale, NJ: Erlbaum.

Rutter, M., Kreppner, J. M., & O'Connor, T. G. (2001). Specificity and heterogeneity in children's responses to profound institutional privation. *British Journal of Psychiatry, 179*, 97–103.

Rutter, M., & O'Connor, T. G. (1999). Implications of attachment theory for child care policies. In J. Cassidy, & P. R. Shaver (Eds.), *Handbook of attachment* (pp. 823–844). New York: Guilford Press.

Ryff, C. D., Lee, Y. H., Essex, M. J., & Schmutte, P. S. (1994). My children and me: Midlife evaluations of grown children and self. *Psychology and Aging, 9*, 195–205.

Rygh, J. L., & Sanderson, W. C. (2004). *Treating generalized anxiety disorder*. New York: Guilford Press.

Rylance, B. J. (1998). Predictors of post-high school employment for youth identified as severely emotionally disturbed. *Journal of Special Education, 32*, 184–192.

Saarni, C. (1993). Socialization of emotion. In M. Lewis & J. M. Haviland (Eds.), *Handbook of emotions* (pp. 435–446). New York: Guilford Press.

Saarni, C. (1999). *The development of emotional competence*. New York: Guilford Press.

Sabatelli, R. M., Meth, R. L., & Gavazzi, S. M. (1988). Factors mediating the adjustment to involuntary childlessness. *Family Relations, 37*, 388–343

Safran, J. D., & Muran, J. C. (2000). *Negotiating the therapeutic alliance: A relational treatment guide*. New York: Guilford Press.

Safran, J. D., & Reading, R. (2008). Mindfulness, metacommunication, and affect regulation in psychoanalytic treatment. In S. F. Hick & T. Bien (Eds.), *Mindfulness and the therapeutic relationship* (pp. 122–140). New York: Guilford Press.

Sagrestano, L., McCormick, S. H., Paikoff, R. L., & Holmbeck, G. N. (1999). Pubertal development and parent–child conflict in low-income African-American adolescents. *Journal of Research on Adolescence, 9*, 85–107.

Salamon, L. M. (1997). *Holding the center: America's nonprofit sector at a crossroad, a report for the Nathan Cummings Foundation*. New York: The Nathan Cummings Foundation.

Saleebey, D. (2006). A paradigm shift in development perspectives?: The self in context. In A. Lightburn & P. Sessions (Eds.), *Handbook of community-based clinical practice* (pp. 46–63). New York: Oxford University Press.

Samantrai, K. (2004). *Culturally competent public child welfare practice*. Pacific Grove, CA: Thomson Brooks/Cole.

Sandhu, D. S., & Aspy, C. B. (1997). *Counseling for prejudice prevention and reduction*. Alexandria, VA: American Counseling Association.

Sands, D. J., & Weymeyer, M. L. (1996). *Self determination across the life span: Independence and choice for people with disabilities*. Baltimore: Paul Brookes.

Sanson, A. V., & M. K. Rothbart. (1995). Child temperament and parenting. In M. Bornstein (Ed.), *Parenting*, Vol. 4 (pp. 299–321). Hillsdale, NJ: Jason Aronson.

Santrock, J. W. (1997). *Life span development* (7th ed.). New York: McGraw-Hill.

Satir, V. (1967). *Conjoint family therapy* (Rev. ed.). Palo Alto, CA: Science and Behavior Books.

Satir, V. (1972). *Peoplemaking*. Palo Alto, CA: Science and Behavior Books.

Saucier, M. G. (2004). Midlife and beyond: Issues for aging women. *Journal of Counseling and Development, 82*, 420–425.

Saulnier, C. F. (1996). *Feminist theories and social work: Approaches and applications*. Binghamton, NY: Haworth Press.

Saunders, E. A., & Arnold, F. (1991). Borderline personality disorder and childhood abuse: Revisions in clinical thinking and treatment approach. *Work in Progress* 51. Wellesley, MA: Stone Center Working Paper Series.

Saville, J. (2003). Historical memories of slavery in the aftermath of reconstruction. *Journal of American Ethnic History, 22*(4), 69–76.

Savin-Williams, R. C. (1990). *Gay and lesbian youth: Expressions of identity*. Washington, DC: Hemisphere.

Savin-Williams, R. C. (1995). Lesbian, gay male, and bisexual adolescents. In A. R. D'Augelli & C. J. Patterson (Eds.), *Lesbian, gay, and bisexual identities over the lifespan*. New York: Oxford University Press.

Savin-Williams, R. C. (1998). Lesbian, gay and bisexual youth's relationships with their parents. In C. J. Patterson & A. R. D'Augelli (Eds.), *Lesbian, gay and bisexual identities in families: Psychological perspectives* (pp. 75–98). New York: Oxford University Press.

Savin-Williams, R. C., & Berndt, T. J. (1990). Friendship and peer relations. In S. S. Feldman & G. R. Elliott (Eds.), *At the threshold: The developing adolescents*. Cambridge, MA: Harvard University Press.

Scanapieco, M., & Connell-Carrick, K. (2005). *Understanding child maltreatment: An ecological developmental perspective*. New York: Oxford University Press.

Scanzoni, J., & Marsiglio, W. (1991). Wider families as primary relationships. *Wider families*. Binghamton, New York: Haworth Press.

Scarr, S. (1969). Social introversion-extraversion as a heritable response. *Child Development, 40*, 823–832.

Schacter, D. L. (1996). *Searching for memory: The brain, the mind, and the past*. New York: Basic Books.

Schaefer, C. E., Jacobsen, H. E., & Ghahramanlou, M. (2000). Play group therapy for social skills deficits in children. In H. G. Kaduson & C. E. Schaefer (Eds.), *Short-term play therapy for children* (pp. 296–345). New York: Guilford Press.

Schaefer, C. E., & Reid, S. (2001). *Game play: Therapeutic use of childhood games*. New York: Wiley.

Schaie, K. W. (1977/1978). Toward a stage theory of adult cognitive development. *Journal of Aging and Human Development, 8*, 129–138.

Schaie, K. W. (1993). The Seattle longitudinal studies of adult intelligence. *Current Directions in Psychological Science, 2*, 171–175.

Schaie, K. W. (1994). The course of adult intellectual development. *American Psychologist, 49*, 304–313.

Schaie, K. W. (1996). *Intellectual development in adulthood: The Seattle longitudinal Study*. New York: Cambridge University Press.

Schaie, K. W., & Willis, S. L. (1993). Age difference patterns of psychometric intelligence in adulthood: Generalizability within and across ability domains. *Psychology and Aging, 8*, 44.

Schaie, K. W., Willis, S. L., Jay, G., & Chipuer, H. (1989). Structural invariance of cognitive abilities across the adult life span: A cross-sectional study. *Developmental Psychology, 25*, 652–662.

Schamess, G. (1996a). Ego psychology. In J. Berzoff, L. M. Flanagan, & P. Hertz (Eds.), *Inside out and outside in: Psychodynamic clinical theory and practice in contemporary multicultural contexts* (pp. 68–98). San Francisco: Jason Aronson.

Schamess, G. (1996b). Structural theory. In J. Berzoff, L. M. Flanagan, & P. Hertz (Eds.), *Inside out and outside in: Psychodynamic clinical theory and practice in contemporary multicultural contexts* (pp. 49–65). San Francisco: Jason Aronson.

Scheibel, A. B. (1992). Structural changes in the aging brain. In J. E. Birren, R. B. Sloane, & G. D. Cohen (Eds.), *Handbook of mental health and aging* (2nd ed.). San Diego, CA: Harcourt Press.

Schiller, I. Y. (1995). Stages of development in women's groups: A relational model. In R. Kurland & R. Salmon (Eds.), *Group work practice in a troubled society*. New York: Haworth Press.

Schlegel, A., & Barry, H. (1991). *Adolescence: An anthropological inquiry*. New York: Free Press.

Schneiders, S. (1993). Feminist spirituality. In M. Downey (Ed.), *The new dictionary of catholic spirituality* (pp. 394–406). Collegeville, MN: Liturgical Press.

Schope, R. D. (2002). The decision to tell: Factors influencing the disclosure of sexual orientation by gay men. *Journal of Gay and Lesbian Social Services, 14*,10–21.

Schopler, E., & Mesibov, G. B. (Eds.). (2001). *Understanding Asperger syndrome and high functioning autism*. New York: Kluwer Academic.

Schore, A. N. (2001). Effects of a secure attachment relationship on right brain development, affect regulation, and infant mental health. *Infant Mental Health Journal, 22*, 7–66.

Schorr, A. (1964). Slums and Social Insecurity. London: Thomas Nelson, Ltd.

Schorr, A. (1997) Passion and Public Policy. Cleveland: Davis Press.

Schover, L. R. (1998). Sexual dysfunction. In J. C. Holland (Ed.), *Psycho-Oncology* (pp. 494–499). New York: Oxford University Press.

Schram, S., & Soss, J. (2001). Success stories: Welfare reform, policy discourse, and the politics of research. *Annals of the American Academy of Political and Social Sciences, 577*, 49–65.

Schriver, J. M. (1995). *Human behavior and the social environment: Shifting paradigms in essential knowledge for social work practice*. Boston: Allyn & Bacon.

Schriver, J. M. (2001). *Human behavior and the social environment: Shifting paradigms in essential knowledge for social work practice* (3rd ed.). Needham Heights, MA: Allyn & Bacon.

Schriver, J. M. (2004). *Human behavior and the social environment: Shifting paradigms in essential knowledge for social work practice* (4th ed.). Boston: Allyn & Bacon.

Schulenberg, J., Maggs, J., Steinman, K., & Zucker, R. (2001). Development matters: Taking the long view on substance abuse etiology and intervention during adolescence. In P. Monti, S. Colby, & T. O'Leary (Eds.), *Adolescents, alcohol, and substance abuse: Reaching teens through brief interventions* (pp. 19–57). New York: Guilford Press.

Schulz, K. (2004, August 22). Did antidepressants depress Japan? *Sunday New York Times Magazine*, pp. 39–41.

Schwartz, R. C. (1995). *Internal Family Systems Therapy*. New York: Guilford Press.

Schwartz, W. (1961). The social worker in the group. In *The social welfare forum* (pp. 146–177). New York: Columbia University Press.

Schwartz, W. (1971a). On the use of groups in social work practice. In W. Schwartz & S. Zelba (Eds.), *The practice of group work* (pp. 3–24). New York: Columbia University Press.

Schwartz, W. (1971b). Social group work: Interactionist approaches. In R. Morris et al. (Eds.), *Encyclopedia of social work* (pp. 1252–1262). New York: National Association Press.

Schwartz, W. (1994). The social worker in society. In T. B. Rossi (Ed.), *Social work: The collected writings of William Schwartz* (pp. 109–119). Itasca, IL: F. E. Peacock.

Scott, C. E. (1977). Healing and dying. In D. Baron (Ed.), *Dying and death: A clinical guide for caregivers* (pp. 141–149). Baltimore: Williams & Wilkins.

Scott, J. (2002, February 7). Foreign born in U.S. at record high. *New York Times*, p. A18.

Search Institute. (2004a). *40 developmental assets of adolescence*. Retrieved October 12, 2005, from http.//www.searchinstitute.org/assets/40Assets.pdf

Search Institute. (2004b). *40 developmental assets for middle childhood. Building assets is elementary: Group activities for helping kids ages 8–12*. Retrieved from http://www.search-institute.org/assets/

See, L. A. (1998). Diversity in the workplace: Issues and concerns of Africans and Asians. In A. Daly (Ed.), *Diversity in the workplace*. Washington, DC: NASW Publication.

See, L. A., Bowles, D., & Darlington, M. (1998). Young African American grandmothers: A missed developmental stage. *Journal of Human Behavior in the Social Environment, 1*(2–3), 281–303.

Segal, Z. V., Williams, J. M., & Teasdale, J. D. (2002). *Mindfulness based cognitive therapy for depression: A new approach in preventing relapse*. New York: Guilford Press.

Seligman, M. E. (1975). *Helplessness: On depression, development and death*. San Francisco: Freeman.

Seltzer, M. M., Floyd, F. & Hong, J. (2004). Accommodative coping and well-being of midlife parents of children with mental health problems or developmental disabilities. *American Journal of Orthopsychiatry, 74*(2), 187–195.

Seltzer, M. M., & Heller, T. (1997). Families and care giving across the life course: Research advances on the influence of context. *Family Relations, 46*(4), 321–323.

Serbin, L. A., Powlishta, K. K., & Gulko, J. (1993). *The development of sex typing in middle childhood*. Monographs of the Society for Research in Child Development 58.

Sernau, S. (2001). *Worlds apart: Social inequalities in a new century*. Thousand Oaks, CA: Pine Forge Press.

Seruya, B. (1997). *Empathic brief psychotherapy*. Northvale, NJ: Jason Aronson.

Shafritz, J. M., & Ott, J. S. (1987). *Classics of organization theory* (2nd ed.). Chicago: The Dorsey Press.

Shapiro, F. (2001). *Eye movement desensitization and reprocessing (EMDR)* (2nd ed.). New York: Guilford Press.

Shaver, P. R., & Hazan, C. (1988). A biased overview of the study of love. *Journal of Social and Personal Relationships, 5*, 473–501.

Shaw, J. A. (2007). The acute traumatic moment—Psychic trauma in war: Psychoanalytic perspectives. *Journal of the American Academy of Psychoanalysis and Dynamic Psychiatry, 35*(1), 23–38.

Shay, K., & Burris, J. F. (2008). Setting the stage for a new strategic plan for geriatrics and extended care in the Veterans Health Administration: Summary of the 2008 VA of the art conference, "the changing faces of geriatrics and extended care: Meeting the needs of veterans in the next decade." *Journal of the American Geriatrics Society, 56*, 2330–2339.

Shaywitz, S. (1998). Current concepts: Dyslexia. *The New England Journal of Medicine, 338*(5), 307–312.

Shaywitz, S. (2003). *Overcoming dyslexia: A new and complete science-based program for reading problems at any level.* New York: Knopf.

Shea, C. (1998). *Psychiatric interviewing: The art of understanding*. Philadelphia: Saunders.

Sheafor, B. W., & Landon, P. S. (1987). Generalist perspective. In A. Minahan et al. (Eds.), *Encyclopedia of social work* (18th ed.). Silver Spring, MD: National Association of Social Workers.

Sheinberg, M., & Fraenkel, P. (2001). *The relational trauma of incest: A family-based approach to treatment.* New York: Guilford Press.

Sher, K. J., Walter, K. S., Wood, P. K., & Brent, E. E. (1991). Characteristics of children of alcoholics: Putative risk factors, substance use and abuse and psychopathology. *Journal of Abnormal Psychology, 100*, 427–448.

Sherrell, K., Buckwalter, K. C., & Morhardt, D. (2001). Negotiating family relationships: Dementia care as a midlife developmental task. *Families in Society, 82*(4), 383–392.

Sherwood, R. J., Shimel, H., Stolz, P., & Sherwood, D. (2004). The aging veteran: Re-emergence of trauma issues. *Journal of Gerontological Social Work, 40*(4), 73–86.

Sherwood, S., Ruchlin, H. S., Sherwood, C. C., & Morris, S. A. (1997). *Continuing-care retirement communities*. Baltimore: Johns Hopkins University Press.

Shidlo, A. (1994). Internalized homophobia: Conceptual and empirical issues in measurement. In B. Greene & G. Herek (Eds.), *Lesbian and gay psychology: Theory, research, and clinical applications* (pp. 176–205). Thousand Oaks, CA: Sage Publications.

Shirk, S. R. (1999). Development therapy. In W. K. Silverman & T. H. Ollendick (Eds.), *Developmental issues in the clinical treatment of children* (pp. 60–73). Boston: Allyn & Bacon.

Shonkoff, J. P., & Phillips, D. (Eds.). (2000). *From neurons to neighborhoods: The science of early childhood development.* Washington, DC: National Academy Press.

Siegel, A. (1996). *Heinz Kohut and the psychology of the self.* London: Routledge.

Siegel, D. J. (1999a). *The developing mind: How relationships and the brain interact to shape who we are.* New York: Guilford Press.

Siegel, D. J. (1999b). *The developing mind: Toward a neurobiology of interpersonal experience.* New York: Guilford Press.

Siegel, D.J. (2006). An interpersonal neurobiological approach to psychotherapy. NY: W. W. Norton.

Siegel, D. J. (2007). *The mindful brain: Reflection and attunement in the cultivation of well-being.* New York: Norton.

Siegler, R. S. (1996). *Emerging minds: The process of change in children's thinking.* New York: Oxford University Press.

Silverman, W. K., & Ginsburg, G. (1995). Specific phobias and generalized anxiety disorder. In J. S. March (Ed.), *Anxiety disorders in children and adolescents* (pp. 151–181). New York: Guilford Press.

Simpson, J. A. (1999). Attachment theory modern evolutionary perspective. In J. Cassidy & P. R. Shaver (Eds.), *Handbook of attachment: Theory, research, and clinical applications* (pp. 115–140). New York: Guilford Press.

Singer, M. S., Stacey, B. G., & Lange, C. (1993). The relative utility of expectancy-value theory and social-cognitive theory in predicting psychology student course goals and career aspirations. *Journal of Social Behavior and Personality, 8*, 703–714.

Skidmore, R. A. (1990) Social Work Administration (2nd ed.) Englewood Cliffs, NJ: Prentice Hall.

Slaby, R. G., & Frey, K. S. (1975). Development of gender constancy and selective attention to same sex models. *Child Development, 46*, 849–856.

Slavin, R. E., Madden, N. A., Karweit, N. L., Dolan, L., & Wasik, B. A. (1992). *Success for all: A relentless approach to prevention and early intervention in elementary schools.* Arlington, VA: Educational Research Service.

Slavin, R. E., Madden, N. A., Karweit, N. L., Dolan, L. J., & Wasik, B. A. (1994). "Wherever and whenever we choose . . . " The replication of Success for All. *Phi Delta Kappan, 75*(8), 639–647.

Sluzki, C.E. (1992). Disruption and reconstruction of networks following migration relocation. *Family Systems Medicine, 10*(4), 359–365.

Smedley, B. D., Stith, A. Y., & Nelson, A. R. (Eds.). (2002). *Unequal treatment: Confronting racial and ethnic disparities in health care*. Washington, DC: Academy Press.

Smelser N. J. (1980). Issues in the study of work and love in adulthood. In N. J. Smelser & E. H. Erikson (Eds.), *Themes of work and love in adulthood* (pp. 1–26). Cambridge, MA: Harvard University Press.

Smith, L. (1989). *Domestic violence: An overview of the literature*. London: Home Office Research and Planning Unit.

Smith, R. E. (1995). Settlements and neighborhood centers. In *Encyclopedia of Social Work.* (19th ed.). (vol. 3, pp. 2129–2135). Washington DC: NASW Press.

Snidman, N., Kagan, J., Riordan, L., & Shannon, D. C. (1995). Cardiac function and behavioral reactivity. *Psychophysiology, 32*, 199–207.

Snow, C. W., & McGaha, C. G. (2003). *Infant development* (3rd ed.). Upper Saddle River, NJ: Prentice Hall.

Solomon, B. B. (1976). *Black empowerment: Social work in minority communities*. New York: Columbia University Press.

Somers, M. D. (1993). A comparison of voluntarily childfree adults and parents. *Journal of Marriage and the Family, 55*, 643–650.

Sorenson, R. L. (2004). *Minding spirituality*. Hillsdale, NJ: Analytic Press.

Sparks, D. (2004). How to have conversations about race: An interview with Beverly Tatum. *National Staff Development Council, 25*(4), 48–52.

Spencer, R. (2000). A comparison of relational psychologies. *Work in Progress*, No. 5. Wellesley, MA: Stone Center Working Paper Series.

Spitz, R. (1965). *The first year of life: A psychoanalytic study of normal and deviant development of object relations*. New York: International Universities Press.

Sroufe, L. A. (1989). Relationships, self and individual adaptation. In A. J. Sameroff & R. N. Emde (Eds.), *Relationship disturbances in early childhood* (pp. 70–104). New York: Basic Books.

Sroufe, L. A. (1990). Considering normal and abnormal together: The essence of developmental psychopathology. *Development & Psychopathology, 2*, 335–347.

St. Clair, M. (2000). *Object relations and self psychology* (3rd ed.). Pacific Grove, CA: Brooks/Cole.

Stamm, B. H., Stamm, H. E., IV, Hudnall, A. C., & Higson-Smith, C. (2004, January–March). Considering a theory of cultural trauma and loss. *Journal of Loss and Trauma, 9*(1), 89–111.

Stams, G. J. M., Juffer, F., & van IJzendoorn, M. H. (2002). Maternal sensitivity, infant attachment, and temperament in early childhood predict adjustment in middle childhood: The case of adopted children and their biologically unrelated parents. *Developmental Psychology, 38*, 806–821.

Standford, P. E., Happersett, C. J., & Morton, D. J. (1991). Early retirement and functional impairment from a multi-ethnic perspective. *Research on Aging, 13*, 5–38.

Stanley, J. L. (2004). *Biracial lesbian and bisexual women: Understanding the unique aspects and multicultural processes of multiple minority identities*. Retrieved from http://www.haworthpress.com/store/product.asp?sku=J015

Statistics of Canada. (2003). *Divorces*. Retrieved January 10, 2006, from http://www.statcan.ca

Steers, R. M., & Porter, L. W. (1991). *Motivation and work behavior* (5th ed.). New York: McGraw-Hill.

Stein, J. O., & Stein, M. (1987). Psychotherapy, initiation and the midlife transition. In L. C. Mahdi, S. Foster, & M. Little (Eds.), *Betwixt and between: Patterns of masculine and feminine initiation* (pp. 287–303). La Salle, IL: Open Court.

Steinberg, D. (1997). *The mutual-aid approach to working with groups*. Northvale, NJ: Jason Aronson.

Steinberg, L. (1996). *Adolescence* (5th ed.). Boston: McGraw-Hill.

Sterlin, R. A. (2005). Where relational theory and attachment theory intersect: A real relationship and a real attachment. *Clinical Social Work Journal, 34*(2), 161–173.

Stern, D. N. (1977). *The first relationship: Mother and infant*. Cambridge, MA: Harvard University Press.

Stern, D. N. (1985). *The interpersonal world of the infant*. New York: Basic Books.

Sternberg, J., & Wagner, R. K. (1993). The ocentric view of intelligence and job performance is wrong. *Current Directions in Psychological Science, 2*, 1–5.

Sternberg, M., & Rosenbloom, M. (2000). "Lost childhood": Lessons from the Holocaust. *Child and Adolescent Social Work Journal, 17*(1), 5–17.

Sternberg, R. J. (1985). *Beyond IQ: A triarchic theory of human intelligence*. New York: Cambridge University Press.

Stiver, I. (1991). Beyond the Oedipus complex: Mothers and daughters. In J. Jordan, A. G. Kaplan, J. B. Miller, I. P. Stiver, & J. L. Surrey (Eds.), *Women's growth in connection: Writings from the Stone Center* (pp. 97–121). New York: Guilford Press.

Stohs, J. H. (1992). Intrinsic motivation and sustained art activity among male fine and applied artists. *Creativity Research Journal*, 245–252.

Stokes, K. (1990). Faith development in the adult life cycle. *Journal of Religious Gerontology, 7*(1 & 2), 167–184.

Stolorow, R. (1991). The intersubjective context of intrapsychic experience with special reference to therapeutic impasses. In R. C. Curtis (Ed.),. *The relational self: Theoretical convergences in psychoanalysis and social psychology* (pp. 17–33). New York: Guilford Press.

Stone, J. H. (ed.) (2005). Culture and disability: Providing culturally competent services. Thousand Oaks, CA: Sage.

Stone, R. (2008, March 25–27). *Partner or consumer? Family caregiving in geriatric care.* Paper presented at the 2008 VA State of the Art Conference, The Changing Faces of Geriatrics and Extended Care; Meeting the Needs of Veterans in the Next Decade, McLean, VA.

Straker, G. (2006). Signing with a scar: Understanding self-harm. *Psychoanalytic Dialogues, 16*(1), 93–112.

Strean, H. (1996). Psychoanalytic theory and social work treatment. In F. Turner (Ed.), *Social work treatment: Interlocking theoretical approaches* (4th ed., pp. 523–555). New York: Free Press.

Stroufe, L. A. (1997). Psychopathology as outcome of development. *Development & Psychopathology, 9*, 251–268.

Stryker, S. (1980). *Symbolic interactionism: A social structural view.* Menlo Park, CA: Benjamin/Cummings.

Stuart, O. W. (1992). Racism and disability: Just a double oppression. *Disability and Society,* 7(2), 177–188.

Sturgeon, J. (2006, September). Bullies in cyberspace. District Administration, 43–47. Retrieved November 13, 2008, from http:// www .districtadministration.com

Substance Abuse and Mental Health Services Administration. (2005). *The National Survey of Drug Use and Health (NSDUH) report: Substance abuse among older adults: 2002–2003 update.* Rockville, MD: Substance Abuse and Mental Health Services Administration, Office of Applied Studies. Retrieved January 1, 2009, from http://www.drugabuse.gov/whatsnew/meeting/ bbsr/bbpowerpoint/gfroerer.ppt

Sue, D. W. (2001). Multidimensional facets of cultural competence. *The Counseling Pschologist; 29;* November, pp. 790–821.

Sue, D. W., Carter, R. T., Casas, J. Manuel, Fouad, N. A., Ivey, A. E., Jensen, J., La Fromboise, T., Manese, J. E., Ponteretto, J. G., Vasquez-Nutall, E. (1998). *Multi-cultural counseling competencies: Individual and organizational development.* Thousand Oaks, CA: Sage.

Sue, D. W., Ivey, A. E., & Pedersen, P. B. (1996). *A theory of multicultural counseling and therapy*. Pacific Grove, CA: Brooks/Cole.

Sue, D. W., & Sue, D. (2003). *Counseling the culturally different: Theory and practice* (4th ed.). New York: Wiley.

Sullivan, G., & Reynolds, R. (2003). Homosexuality in midlife: Narrative and identity. *Journal of Gay and Lesbian Social Services, 15*(3–4), 153–170.

Sullivan, H. (1953). *The interpersonal theory of psychiatry.* New York: Norton.

Suomi, S. J. (1995). Attachment theory and nonhuman primates. In S. Goldberg, R. Muir, & J. Kerr (Eds.), *Attachment theory: Social, developmental, and clinical perspectives* (pp. 185–201). Hillsdale, NJ: Analytic Press.

Surrey, J. L. (1984). Eating patterns as a reflection of women's development. *Work in Progress* 9. Wellesley, MA: Stone Center Working Paper Series.

Surrey, J. L. (2005). Relational psychotherapy, relational mindfulness. In C. K. Germer, R. D. Siegel, & P. R. Fulton (Eds.), *Mindfulness and psychotherapy* (pp. 91–110). New York: Guilford Press.

Surrey, J. L., Kaplan, A. G., & Jordan, J. V. (1990). Empathy revisited. *Work in Progress* 40. Wellesley College, MA: Stone Center Working Paper Series.

Sviridoff, M., & Ryan, W. (1997). Community-centered family service. *Families in Society, 78*, 128–139.

Swanson, H. L., Harris, K. R., & Graham, S. (Eds.). (2003). *Handbook of learning disabilities*. New York: Guilford Press.

Swartz, S. (1995). Community and risk in social service work. *Journal of Progressive Human Services, 61*(1), 73–92.

Swenson, C. R. (1998). Clinical Social Work's Contribution to a Social Justice Perspective. *Social Work, 43*(6), November.

Szasz, T. (1970). *The manufacture of madness*. New York: Delta.

Szkrybalo, J., & Ruble, D. N. (1999). "God made me a girl": Sex category constancy judgments and explanations revisited. *Developmental Psychology, 35*, 393–402.

Szymanski, D. M., & Chung, Y. B. (2001). The lesbian internalized homophobia scale: A rational theoretical approach. *Journal of Homosexuality, 41*(2), 372.

Takahashi, K. (1990). Are the key assumptions of the "Strange Situation" procedure universal? A view from Japanese research. *Human Development, 33,* 23–30.

Takamura, J. (1999). Getting ready for the 21st century: The aging of America and the Older Americans Act. *Health and Social Work, 24*(3), 232–246.

Tan, R. S. (2001). Memory loss as reported symptom of andropause. *Archives of Andrology, 47*(3), 185–189.

Tangenberg, K. M. (2003). Linking feminist social work and feminist theology in light of faith-based service initiatives. *Affilia, 18*(4), 379–394.

Tanner, J. M. (1990). *Fetus into man* (2nd ed.). Cambridge, MA: Harvard University Press.

Tannock, R., & Brown, T. E. (2000). Attention-deficit disorders with learning disorders in children and adolescents. In T. E. Brown (Ed.), *Attention-deficit disorders and co-morbidities in children, adolescents and adults* (pp. 231–295). Washington, DC: American Psychiatric Press.

Tatum, B. D. (1993). Racial identity development and relational theory: The case of black women in white communities. *Working Paper Series, 63* (pp. 1–9). Wellesley, MA: Wellesley College: The Stone Center.

Tatum, B. D. (1997). *"Why are all the black kids sitting together in the cafeteria?" and other conversations about race*. New York: Harper/Collins.

Tenenbaum, H. R., & Leaper, C. (2002). Are parents: gender schemas related to their children's gender-related cognitions? A meta-analysis. *Developmental Psychology, 38,* 615–630.

Terkelsen, K. G. (1980). Toward a theory of the family life cycle. In E. A. Carter & M. McGoldrick, *The family life cycle: A framework for family therapy*. New York: Gardner.

Terr, L. (1988). What happens to early memories of trauma? *Journal of the American Academy of Child and Adolescent Psychiatry, 1,* 96–104.

Teti, D. M., Sakin, J., Kucera, E., Corns, K. M., & Das Eisen, R. (1996). And baby makes four: Predictors of attachment security among preschool-aged firstborns during the transition to siblinghood. *Child Development, 67,* 579–596.

Thomas, A., & Chess, S. (1977). *Temperament and development*. New York: Brunner/Mazel.

Thomas, A., & Chess, S. (1986). The New York longitudinal study: From infancy to early adult life. In R. Plomin & J. Dunn (Eds.), *The study of temperament: Changes, continuities, and challenges*. Hillsdale, NJ: Erlbaum.

Thomas, C. (1999). Narrative identity and the disabled self. In M. Corker & S. French (Eds.), *Disability discourse*. Buckingham, UK: Open University Press.

Thompson, A., Hollis, C., & Richards, D. (2003). Authoritarian parenting attitudes as a risk for conduct problems: Results of a British national cohort study. *European Child and Adolescent Psychiatry, 12*(2), 84–91.

Thompson, E. (2001). Empathy and consciousness. In E. Thompson (Ed.), *Between ourselves: Second person issues in the study of consciousness*. Thorverton, UK: Imprint Academic.

Thompson, J. D. (1967). *Organizations in action*. New York: McGraw-Hill.

Thompson, L., & Walker, A. J. (1989). Gender in families: Women and men in marriage, work and parenthood. *Journal of Marriage and the Family, 51,* 845–872.

Thompson, R. A. (1997). Sensitivity and security: New questions to ponder. *Child Development, 68,* 595–597.

Thompson, R. A. (1998). Early sociopersonality development. In W. Damon & N. Eisenberg (Eds.), *Handbook of child psychology: Vol. 3. Social, emotional, and personality development* (5th ed., pp. 15–104). New York: Wiley.

Thompson, W. E. (1992). Spirituality: Spiritual development and holiness. *Review for Religions, 51*(5), 646–658.

Thorn, B. (2004). *Cognitive therapy for chronic pain*. New York: Guilford Press.

TIAA-CREF Public Affairs. (2004a, Summer). *Balance: Quarterly news and tools from TIAA-CREF*. New York: Author.

TIAA-CREF Public Affairs. (2004b, Winter). *Balance: Quarterly news and tools from TIAA-CREF*. New York: Author.

TIAA-CREF Public Affairs. (2005, Spring). *Advance: Quarterly news and tools from TIAA-CREFF*. New York: Author.

Tick, E. (2005) *War the the soul: Healing our nation's veterans from post-traumatic stress disorder*. Wheaton, IL: Quest Books.

Timmer, D. F. (1998). Group support for teenagers with attention deficit hyperactivity disorders. *Social Work in Education, 17,* 194–198.

Timmins, C. L. (2002) The impact of language barriers on the healthcare of Latinos in the United States: a review of the literature and guidelines for practice. *Journal of Midwifery and Women's Health, 47*(2), 80–96.

Tizard, B., & Phoenix, A (1993). *Black, white or mixed race?* London: Routledge.

Torres-Gil, F. (1984). Retirement issues that affect minorities. In H. Dennis (Ed.), *Retirement preparation*, Lexington, MA: Lexington Books.

Toseland, R. W., & Rivas, R. F. (2001). *An introduction to group work practice* (4th ed.). Needham Heights, MA: Allyn & Bacon.

Toseland, R. W., & Rivas, R. F. (2004). *An introduction to group work practice* (5th ed.). Needham Heights, MA: Allyn & Bacon.

Tracy, E. M., & Whittaker, J. K. (1993). The social network map: Assessing social support in clinical practice. In J. B. Rauch (Ed.), *Assessment: A sourcebook for social work practice* (pp. 295–308). Milwaukee, WI: Families International.

Treasure, J., Schmidt, U., & van Furth, E. (Eds.). (2003). *Handbook of eating disorders*. Chichester, UK: Wiley.

Troiden, R. R. (1988). Homosexual identity development. *Journal of Adolescent Health Care, 9*(2), 105–113.

Troll, L. E. (1985). *Early and middle adulthood: The best is yet to come—maybe* (2nd ed.). Monterey, CA: Brooks/Cole.

Tronick, E. Z. (1989). Emotions and emotional communication in infants. *American Psychologist, 44*(2), 112–119.

Tronick, E. Z., & Gianino, A. (1986). Interactive mismatch and repair: Challenges to the coping infant. Zero to Three. *Bulletin of the Center for Clinical Infant Programs, 6*(3), 1–6.

Tronick, E. Z., & Weinberg, M. K. (1997). Depressed mothers and infants: Failure to form dyadic states of consciousness. In I. Murray & P. J. Cooper (Eds.), *Postpartum depression and child development* (pp. 54–81). New York: Guilford.

Tropman, J. E., Erlich, J. L., & Rothman, J. (2001). *Tactics and techniques of community intervention* (4th ed.). Itasca, IL: F. E. Peacock.

Tropman, J. E., Johnson, H. R., & Tropman, E. J. (1992). *Committee management in human services: Running effective meetings, committees, and boards* (2nd ed.). Chicago: Nelson-Hall.

Tseng, W. S., & Streltzer, J. (1997). *Culture and psychopathology: A guide to clinical assessment*. New York: Brunner/Mazel.

Tsoh, J., Chiu, H. F. K., Duberstein, P. R., Chan, S. S. M., Chi, I., Yip, P. S. F., & Conwell, Y. (2005). Attempted suicide in elderly Chinese persons: A multi-group controlled study. *American Journal of Geriatric Psychiatry, 13*, 562–571.

Tuckman, B. W. (1965). Developmental sequence in small groups. *Psychological Bulletin, 63*(6), 136–142.

Tuckman, B. W., & Jensen, M. A. C. (1977). Stages of small group development revisited. *Group & Organizational Studies, 2*(1), 419–27.

Turk, D. C., & Okifuji, A. (2001). Psychological factors in chronic pain: Evolution and revolution. *Journal of Clinical and Consulting Psychology, 70*, 678–690.

Turner, J. B. (1998). Foreword. In P. L. Ewalt, E. M. Freeman, & D. L. Poole (Eds.), *Community building: Renewal, well-being, and shared responsibility* (pp. ix–x). Washington, DC: National Association of Social Workers.

Turner, P. J., & Gervai, J. (1995). A multidimensional study of gender typing in preschool children and their parents: Personality, attitudes, preferences, behavior, and cultural differences. *Developmental Psychology, 31*, 759–772.

Turner, S. G., Kaplan, C. P. & Zayas, L. (2004). Suicide attempts by adolescent Latinas: An exploratory study of individual and family correlates. *Child and Adolescent Social Work, 19*(5), 357–374.

Twemlow, S. W., & Sacco, F. C. (2008). *Why school antibullying programs don't work*. New York: Jason Aronson.

Tyson, J. (2007). Compassion fatigue in the treatment of combat related trauma during wartime. *Clinical Social Work Journal, 35*, 183–192.

Uncapher, W. (1999). Electronic homesteading on the rural frontier: Big sky telegraph and its community. In M. A. Smith & P. Kollock (Eds.), *Communities in cyberspace* (pp. 264–289). London: Routledge.

UNICEF Innocenti Research Centre. (2000). A league table of child poverty in rich nations. *Innocenti Report Cards* (No. 1), 1–32. Florence, Italy: Author

United Nations. (2001). *World social situation*. New York: Author.

U.S. Bureau of the Census. (1976). Population profile of the United States, 1975. *Current Population Reports*, Ser. P. 20, No. 292. Washington DC: U.S. Government Printing Office.

U.S. Bureau of the Census. (1992). *Statistical abstracts of the United States: 1992* (112th ed.). Washington, DC: U.S. Government Printing Office.

U.S. Bureau of the Census. (1997). *Statistical abstract of the United States* (117th ed., p. 1975). Washington, DC: U.S. Government Printing Office.

U.S. Bureau of the Census. (2001). *Statistical abstract of the United States: 2001* (121st ed.). Washington, DC: Government Printing Office.

U.S. Census Bureau. (2000). *Money income in the United States; Current population reports since 1999*. Department of Commerce, Economics and Statistical

Division Publication No. P60–209. Washington, DC: Government Printing Office.

U.S. Census Bureau. (2003). *Statistical abstract of the United States* (123d ed.). Washington, DC: U.S. Government Printing Office.

U.S. Department of Education. (2002). *Digest of education statistics, 2001.* Washington, DC: Government Printing Office.

U.S. Department of Health and Human Services. (2003). *Definitions of child abuse and neglect.* 2003 Child Abuse and Neglect State Statute Series: Statutes-at-a-Glance. National Clearinghouse on Child Abuse and Neglect Information. Retrieved October 20, 2005, from http://www.nccanch.acf.hhs.gov/general/legal/statutes/define/cfm

U.S. Department of Health and Human Services. (2004). *Report: Nursing homes improved.* Retrieved December 22, 2004, from http://www.cnn.com/2004/HEALTH/12/22/nursing.homes.ap/index.html

U.S. Department of Labor, Women's Bureau (2002). Facts on Working Women. Available online: http://ww.dol.gov/wb/wb_pubs/hotjobs02.htm

U.S. Surgeon General. (2001). *Adults and mental health.* Retrieved October 20, 2005, from http://www.surgeongeneral.gov/library/mental health/chapter4/sec1/html;mental_health2001

Urban Institute. (2004). *Who graduates? Who doesn't? A statistical portrait of public high school graduation, 2001.* Washington DC: Author.

Urban Institute. (2005). *Juvenile drug courts and teen substance abuse.* Retrieved October 15, 2005, from http://www.urban.org/justice

Vaillant, G. E. (1983). *The natural history of alcoholism.* Cambridge, MA: Harvard University Press.

Vaillant, G. E. (1995). *The wisdom of the ego.* Cambridge, MA: Harvard University Press.

Valverde, L. A. (1998) Future strategies and Actions: Creating Multi-Cultural Higher Education Campuses. In L. A. Valverde and L. A. Catenell Jr. (Eds.). *The Multicultural Campus* (pp. 19–29). Walnut Creek CA: Altamira Press.

Van den Bergh, N. (Ed.). (1995). *Feminist practice in the 21st century.* Washington, DC: NASW Press.

Van Den Boom, D.C., & Hoeksma, J. B. (1994). The effect of infant irritability on mother–infant interaction: A growth-curve analysis. *Developmental Psychology, 30,* 581–590.

van der Kolk, B. A. (1994). The body keeps the score: Memory and the evolving psycho-biology of posttraumatic stress. *Harvard Review of Psychiatry, 1*(5), 253–265.

van der Kolk, B. A. (1996a). The body keeps the score: Approaches to the psychobiology of posttraumatic stress disorder. In B. van der Kolk, A. McFarlane, & L. Weisaeth (Eds.), *Traumatic stress: The effects of overwhelming experience on mind, body, and society* (pp. 214–242). New York: Guilford Press.

van der Kolk, B. A. (1996b). Trauma and memory. In B. van der Kolk, A. McFarlane, & L. Weisaeth (Eds.), *Traumatic stress: The effects of overwhelming experience on mind, body, and society* (pp. 279–303). New York: Guilford Press.

van der Kolk, B. A. (1998). Trauma, memory, and the integration of experience. Retrieved September 15, 2005, from http://www.his-online.de/veranst/vortrag/vanderkolk.htm

van der Kolk, B. A., & McFarlane, A. (1996). The black hole of trauma. In B. van der Kolk, A. McFarlane, & L. Weisaeth (Eds.), *Traumatic stress: The effects of overwhelming experience on mind, body, and society* (pp. 3–24). New York: Guilford Press.

van der Kolk, B. A., & Van der Hart, O. (1989). Pierre Janet and the breakdown of adaptation in psychological trauma. *American Journal of Psychiatry, 146,* 1530–1540.

van der Kolk, B. A., & Van der Hart, O. (1991). The intrusive past: The flexibility of memory and the engraving of trauma. *American Imago, 48*(4), 425–454.

VanFleet, R. (1994). *Filial therapy: Strengthening parent–child relationships through play. Practitioner's Resource Series.* Harrisburg, PA: Family Enhancement and Play Center; Sarasota, FL: Professional Resource.

VanFleet, R. (2000). *A parent's handbook of filial play therapy.* Boiling Springs, PA: Play Therapy.

Van IJzendoorn, M. H., & Sagia, A. (1999). Cross-cultural patterns of attachment: Universal and contextual dimensions. In J. Cassidy & P. R. Shaver (Eds.), *Handbook of attachment: Theory, research and clinical applications* (pp. 198–225). New York: Guilford Press.

Van Wormer, K., Wells, J., & Boes, M. (2000). *Social work with lesbians, gays, and bisexuals: A strengths perspective.* Needham Heights, MA: Allyn & Bacon.

Vaughan, F. (1991). Spiritual issues in psychotherapy. *Journal of Transpersonal Psychology, 23*(2), 105–119.

Vaughn, B. E., & Bost, K. K. (1999). Attachment and temperament: Redundant, independent, or interacting influences on interpersonal adaptation and personality development? In J. Cassidy & P. R. Shaver (Eds.), *Handbook of attachment:*

Theory, research, and clinical applications (pp. 198–225). New York: Guilford Press.

Vaughn, B. J. (2005). Positive behavior support as a family-centered endeavor. *Journal of Positive Behavior Interventions, 7*(1), 55–58.

Vecchiolla, F. J., Roy, A. W., Lesser, J. G., Wronka, J., Walsh-Burke, K., Gianesin, J., et al. (2001). Advanced generalist practice: A framework for social work practice in the twenty-first century. *Journal of Teaching in Social Work, 21*(3/4), 91–104.

Viswanath, K., Kosicki, G. M., Fredin, E. S., & Park, E. (2000). Local community ties, community-boundedness, and local public affairs knowledge gaps. *Communication Research, 27*(1), 27–50.

Voldmar, F. R. & Klin, A. (2007). Handbook of Pervasive Developmental Disorders. NY: John Wiley & Sons.

Vondra, J. I., Shaw, D. S., Swearingen, L., Cohen, M., & Volkmar, F. R. (Eds.). (2007). *Autism and pervasive developmental disorders* (2nd ed. Cambridge, MA: Cambridge University Press.

Vondracek, F. W., & Porfeli, E. J. (2002). Counseling psychologists and schools: Toward a sharper conceptual focus. *Counseling Psychologist, 30*(5), 749–756.

Vosler, N. R. (1996). *New approaches to family practice: Confronting economic stress.* Thousand Oaks, CA: Sage.

Vosler, N. R. (1999). Families. In E. Hutchison (Ed.), *Dimensions of human behavior: Person and environment.* Thousand Oaks, CA: Pine Forge Press.

Vygotsky, L. S. (1934/1986). *Thought and language* (A. Kozulin, Trans.). Cambridge, MA: MIT Press.

Vygotsky, L. S. (1978). *Mind in society: The development of higher mental processes.* Cambridge, MA: Harvard University Press. (Original works published in 1930, 1933, and 1935).

Wagenseller, J. P. (1998). Spiritual renewal at midlife. *Journal of Religion and Health, 37*(3), 265–272.

Wagner, R. K., & Sternberg, J. (1991). *Tacit knowledge inventory.* San Antonio, TX: The Psychological Corporation.

Wald, L. (1915). The House on Henry St. Newark: Henry Holt and Co.

Waldner, L. K., & Magruder, B. (1999). Coming out to parents: Perceptions of family relations, perceived resources, and identity expression as predictors of identity disclosure for gay and lesbian adolescents. *Journal of Homosexuality, 37*(2), 83–100.

Walker, A. (1983). *In search of our mothers' gardens.* New York: Harcourt Brace Jovanovich.

Walker, L. J. (1984). Sex differences in the development of moral reasoning: A critical review. *Child Development, 55*, 677–691.

Walker, S. (2005). Towards culturally competent practice in child and adolescent mental health. *International Social Work, 48*(1), 49–62.

Wallerstein, J. (1985). The overburdened child: Some long-term consequences of divorce. *Social Work, 30*(2), 116–123.

Walsh, J. (1997). Community building in theory and practice: Three case studies. *National Civic Review, 86*, 291–314.

Walsh, J. (2003). The psychological person: Cognition, emotion and self. In E. D. Hutchinson (Ed.), *Dimensions of human behavior: Person and environment* (2nd ed., pp. 151–184). Thousand Oaks, CA: Sage.

Walsh, M., Galassi, J., & Murphy, J. (2002). A conceptual framework for counseling psychologists in schools. *Counseling Psychologist, 30*(5), 682–704.

Walters, S. T., Ogle, R., & Martin, J. E. (2002). Perils and possibilities of group-based motivational interviewing. In W. R. Miller & S. Rollnick (Eds.), *Motivational interviewing: Preparing people for change* (2nd ed.). New York: Guilford Press.

Wapner S., & Demick, J. (1999). In Silverman, W. K., & Ollendick, T. H. (Eds.). *Developmental Issues in the Clinical Treatment of Children.* Boston, MA: Allyn and Bacon.

Wapner, S., & Demick, J. (1998). Developmental analysis: A holistic developmental, systems-oriented perspective. In R. M. Lerner (Ed.), *Theoretical models of human development. Handbook of child psychology* (5th ed., pp. 761–805). New York: Wiley.

Wapner, S., & Demick, J. (1999). Developmental and clinical practice: A holistic, developmental, systems-oriented approach. In W. K. Silverman & T. H. Ollendick (Eds.), *Developmental issues in the clinical treatment of children* (pp. 3–30). Boston: Allyn & Bacon.

Warfield, M. E. (2001). Employment, parenting, and well-being among mothers of children with disabilities. *Mental Retardation, 39*(4), 297–309.

Warren R. L. (1978). *The community in America.* Chicago: Rand McNally.

Waslick, B., & Greenhill, L. (2003). *Textbook of child and adolescent psychiatry* (2nd ed.). Washington, DC: American Academy of Child and Adolescent Psychiatry, American Psychiatric Press.

Waters, E., & Cummings, E. M. (2000). A secure base from which to explore close relationships. *Child Development, 71*, 164–172.

Waters, E., Vaughn, B. E., Posada, G., & Kondo-Ikemura, K. (Eds.). (1995). Caregiving, cultural, and cognitive perspectives on secure-base behavior and working models: New growing points of attachment theory and research. *Monographs of the Society for Research in Child Development,* 60(2–3, Serial No. 244).

Watson, M. (1998). African American siblings. In M. McGoldrick (Ed.), *Revisioning family therapy: Race, culture and gender in clinical practice.* New York: Guilford Press.

Watt, S. K., Robinson, T. L., & Lupton-Smith, H. (2002). Building ego and racial identity: Preliminary perspectives on counselor-in-training. *Journal of Counseling & Development, 43*(2), 184–194.

Webb, N. B. (1996). *Play therapy with children.* New York: Guilford Press.

Webb, N. B. (Ed.). (1999). *Play therapy with children in crisis: Individual, group, and family treatment* (2nd ed.). New York: Guilford Press.

Weber, G. K. (1976). Preparing social workers for practice in rural systems. *Journal of Education for Social Work, 12,* 108–115.

Weber, L. (1998). A conceptual framework for understanding race, class, gender and sexuality. *Psychology of Women Quarterly, 22,* 13–22.

Wechsler, H., Davenport, A., Dowdall, G., Moeykens, B., & Castillo, S. (1994). Health and behavioral consequences of binge drinking in college: A national survey of students at 140 campuses. *Journal of the American Medical Association, 272,* 1672–1677.

Wechsler, H., Dowdall, G. W., Davenport, A., & Rimm, E. B. (1995). A gender-specific measure of binge drinking among college students. *American Journal of Public Health, 85*(7), 982–985.

Wedenoja, M. (1999). Persons with psychiatric disabilities. In R. Mackelprang & R. Salsgiver (Eds.), *Disability: A diversity model approach in human service practice* (pp. 167–201). Pacific Grove, CA: Brooks/Cole.

Weingarten, K. (1997). From "cold care" to "warm care": Challenging the discourses of mothers and adolescents. In C. Smith & D. Nylund (Eds.), *Narrative therapies with children and adolescents* (pp. 307–338). New York: Guilford Press.

Weinrach, S. G. (2002). The counseling profession's relationship to Jews and the issues that concern them: More than a case of selective awareness. *Journal of Counseling and Development, 80,* 300–314.

Weisner, T. S., & Bernheimer, L. P. (1998). Children of the 1960s at midlife: Generational identity and the family adaptive project. In R. A. Shweder (Ed.), *Welcome to middle age (and other cultural fictions)* (pp. 211–257). Chicago: University of Chicago Press.

Weisner, T. S., & Wilson-Mitchell, J. E. (1990). Nonconventional family life-styles and sex typing in six-year-olds. *Child Development, 61,* 1915–1933.

Weiss, G., & Hechtman, L. T. (1993). *Hyperactive children grown up: ADHS in children, adolescents and adults* (2nd ed.). New York: Guilford Press.

Weiss, J., Sampson, J., & the Mount Zion Psychotherapy Research Group. (1986). *The psychoanalytic process: Theory, clinical observations, and empirical research.* New York: Guilford Press.

Weisz, J. R., Southam-Gerow, M. A., Gordis, E. B., & Connor-Smith, J. (2003). Primary and secondary control enhancement training for youth depression. In A. E. Kazdin & J. R. Weisz (Eds.), *Evidence based practice with children and adolescents* (pp. 165–183). New York: Guilford Press.

Weisz, J. R., & Weersing, V. R. (1999). Developmental outcome research. In W. K. Silverman & T. H. Ollendick (Eds.), *Developmental issues in the clinical treatment of children* (pp. 457–469). Boston: Allyn & Bacon.

Wellman, B. (1999). From little boxes to loosely bounded networks: The privatization and domestication of community. In J. L. Abu-Lughod (Ed.), *Sociology for the twenty-first century: Continuities and cutting edges* (pp. 94–114). Chicago: University of Chicago Press.

Wellman, B., & Gulia, M. (1999). Virtual communities as communities: Net surfers don't ride alone. In M. A. Smith & P. Kollock (Eds.), *Communities in cyberspace* (pp. 167–194). London: Routledge.

Wells, L. E., & Stryker, S. (1989). Stability and change in self over the life course. In P. B. Baltes, D. L. Featherman, & R. L. Lerner (Eds.), *Life-span development and behavior* (Vol. 8, pp. 191–229). Hillsdale, NJ: Erlbaum.

Wells, M. O., & Gamble, D. N. (1995). Community practice models. In R. L. Edwards (Ed.-in-chief), *Encyclopedia of social work* (Vol. 1, 19th ed., pp. 577–694). Silver Spring, MD: NASW Press.

Wendell, S. (2001). Unhealthy disabled: Treating chronic illnesses as disabilities. *Clinical Psychology,* 57(11), 1277–1288.

Werner, E. E. (2000). Protective factors and individual resilience. In J. P. Shonkoff & S. J. Meisels (Eds.), *Handbook of early childhood intervention* (2nd ed., pp. 115–132). Cambridge, UK: Cambridge University Press.

Werner, H. (1957). The concept of development from a comparative and organismic point of view. In D. Harris (Ed.), *The concept of development* (pp. 125–148). Minneapolis: University of Minnesota Press.

Wetle, T. T., & Fulmer, T. T. (1995). A medical perspective. In H. R. Moody (Ed.), *Aging: Concepts and controversies* (4th ed.). Thousands Oaks, CA: Pine Forge Press.

Wheeler, E. A., Ampadu, L. M., & Wangari, E. (2002, January). Lifespan development revisited:

African-centered spirituality throughout the life cycle. *Journal of Adult Development, 9*(1), 71–78.

White, D. (1999). *Too heavy a load*. New York: Norton.

White, R. F. (1959). Motivation reconsidered: The concept of competence. *Psychological Review, 66*, 297–333.

White, R. F. (1963). *Ego and reality in psychoanalytic theory. Psychological Issues* (Vol. 2). New York: International Universities Press.

White, R. W. (1971, September). The urge towards competence. *American Journal of Occupational Therapy, 25*, 271–274.

White, R. W. (1974). Strategies of adaptation: An attempt at systematic description. In G. V. Coelho, D. A. Hamburg, & J. E. Adams (Eds.), *Coping and adaptation* (pp. 47–68). New York: Basic Books.

Whitney, J. W. M., Burbank, V. K., & Ratner, M. S. (1986). The duration of maidenhood. In J. B. Lancaster & B. A. Hamburg (Eds.), *School age pregnancy and parenthood*. Hawthorne, NY: Aldine de Gruyter.

Whitney-Thomas, J., & Moloney, M. (2001). "Who I am and what I want?: Adolescents' self-definition and struggles. *Council for Exceptional Children, 67*(3), 375–389.

Wikipedia. (2009). *Acceptance and commitment therapy*. Retrieved July 26, 2009, from http://en.wikipedia.org/wiki/Acceptance_and_commitment_therapy

Wilensky, H., & Lebeaux, C. (1965). *Industrial society and social welfare*. New York: Free Press.

Williams, J. H., Ayers, C. D., Van Horn, R. A., & Arthur, M. W. (2004). Risk and protective factors in the development of delinquency and conduct disorder. In M.W. Fraser (Ed.), *Risk and resilience in childhood: An ecological perspective* (pp. 209–250). Washington DC: National Association of Social Workers Press.

Willis, S. L. (1989). Adult intelligence. In S. Hunter, & M. Sundell (Eds.), *Midlife myths: Issues, findings and practice implications*. Newbury Park, CA: Sage.

Willis, S. L., & Schaie, K. W. (1999). Intellectual functioning in midlife. In S. L. Willis, & J. D. Reid (Eds.), *Life in the middle* (pp. 105–146). San Diego, CA: Academic Press.

Wilson, G., & Ryland, G. (1949). *Social group work practice*. Boston: Houghton Mifflin.

Wilson, G. T. (1995). Behavior therapy. In R. J. Corsini & D. Wedding (Eds.), *Current psychotherapies* (5th ed., pp. 197–228). Itasca, IL: F. E. Peacock.

Wilson, J. P., & Lindy, J. D. (Eds.). (1994). *Countertransference in the treatment of PTSD*. New York: Guilford Press.

Wilson, W. J. (1996). *When work disappears: The world of the new urban poor*. New York: Knopf.

Winkler, R. C., Brown, D. W., van Kepper, M., & Blanchard, A. (1988). *Clinical practice in adoption*. New York: Pergamon Press.

Winnicott, D. W. (1965). *The maturational process and the facilitating environment*. New York: International Universities Press.

Winnicott, D. W. (1982). *Playing and reality*. New York: Routledge.

Winterowd, C., Beck, A. T., & Gruener, D. (2003). *Cognitive therapy with chronic pain patients*. New York: Springer.

Winters, K. C. (2001). Assessing adolescent substance use problems and other areas of functioning: State of the art. In P. Monti, S. Colby, & T. O'Leary (Eds.), *Adolescents, alcohol and substance abuse reaching teens through brief interventions* (pp. 80–109). New York: Guilford Press.

Wituk, S. A., Shepherd, M. D., Slavich, S., Warren, M., & Meissen, G. (2000). A topography of self-help groups: An empirical analysis. *Social Work, 45*(2), 157–165.

Wolf, E. S. (1988). *Treating the self: Elements of clinical self psychology*. New York: Guilford Press.

Wolfinger, N. H. (2000). Beyond the intergenerational transmission of divorce: Do people replicate the patterns of marital instability they grew up with? *Journal of Family Issues, 21*, 1061–1086.

Woodworth, R. (1994, September). *Grandparent-headed households and their grandchildren: A special report*. Washington, DC: AARP Grandparent Information Center.

Worell, J., & Remer, P. (1992). *Feminist perspectives in therapy: An empowerment model for women*. New York: Wiley.

World Health Organization. www.who.int. Retrieved January 16, 2006.

Wozniak, J., & Biederman, J. (1996, June). A pharmacological approach to the quagmire of co-morbidity in juvenile mania. *Journal of the American Academy of Child & Adolescent Psychiatry, 35*, 826–828.

Wozniak, J., Biederman, J., Kiely, K., Ablon, J. S., Faraone, S., Mundy, E., et al. (1995, December). A pilot family study of childhood-onset mania. *Journal of the American Academy of Child & Adolescent Psychiatry, 34*, 1577–1583.

Yale Developmental Disabilities Clinic. (2005). *Information about pervasive developmental disorders*. Retrieved September 12, 2005, from info.med.yale.edu/chld-stdy/autism/pddinfo.html

Yarrow, M. R., Scott, P. M., & Waxler, C. Z. (1973). Learning concern for others. *Developmental Psychology*, 240–260.

Yip, P. S. F., Chi, I., Chiu, H., Wai, K. C., Conwell, Y., & Caine, E. (2003). A prevalence study of suicide ideation among older adults in Hong Kong SAR. *International Journal of Geriatric Psychiatry, 18*(11), 1056–1062.

Yoshikawa, H. (1994). Prevention as cumulative protection: Effects of early family support and education on chronic delinquency and its risks. *Psychological Bulletin, 115*, 27–54.

Youngstrom, E. A., Findling, R. L., & Feeny, N. (2004). Assessment of bipolar spectrum disorders in children and adolescents. In S. L. Johnson & R. L. Leahy (Eds.), *Psychological treatment of bipolar disorders* (pp. 58–83). New York: Guilford Press.

Yust, K. M. (2003). Toddler spiritual formation and the faith community. *International Journal of Children's Spirituality, 8*(2), 133–149.

Zandy, J. (1996). Decloaking class: Class identity and consciousness count. *Race, Gender & Class, 4*, 723.

Zastrow, C., & Kirst-Ashman, K. K. (1997). *Understanding human behavior and the social environment* (4th ed.). Chicago: Nelson-Hall.

Zayas, L. H., Kaplan, C., Turner, S., Romano, K., & Gonzalez-Ramos, G. (2000). Understanding suicide attempts by adolescent Hispanic females. *Social Work, 45*(1), 53–60.

Zierler, S., & Krieger, N. (1997). Reframing women's risk: Social inequalities and HIV infection. *Annual Reviews of Public Health, 18*, 401–36.

Zigler, E., & Hall, N. W. (2000). *Child development and social policy: Theory and applications*. New York: McGraw-Hill.

Zigler, E., & Lang, M. (1991). *Child care choices: Balancing the needs of children, families and society*. New York: Free Press.

Zila, L. M. & Kiselica, M. S. (2001). Understanding and counseling self-mutilation in female adolescents and young adults. *Journal of Counseling and Development, 79*, 46–52.

Zill, N., & Nord, C. (1994). *Running in place*. Washington, DC: Child Trends.

Zimmerman, M. A. (1995). Psychological empowerment: Issues and illustrations. *American Journal of Community Psychology, 23*(5), 581–599.

Zuniga, X. (2003, January–February). Bridging differences through dialogue. *About Campus*, 8–16.

Author Index

Subject Index